The Gaelic Crisis in the Vernacular Community

A comprehensive sociolinguistic survey of Scottish Gaelic

The Gaelic Crisis in the Vernacular Community
A comprehensive sociolinguistic survey of Scottish Gaelic

Conchúr Ó Giollagáin
Gòrdan Camshron
Pàdruig Moireach
Brian Ó Curnáin
Iain Caimbeul
Brian MacDonald
Tamás Péterváry

ABERDEEN UNIVERSITY PRESS

Published by Aberdeen University Press
University of Aberdeen
Aberdeen,
Scotland,
UK AB24 3UG

A CIP record for this title is available upon request from the British Library

ISBN 978-1-85752-080-4

Cover, typeset and design by riverdesignbooks.com
Printed and bound by Gomer Press (www.gomerprinting.co.uk)

Cover image (Hemis / Alamy Stock Photo) of Bàgh a' Chaisteil, Barraigh / Castlebay, Barra

Airson nan daoine anns na h-eileanan a thug cuideachadh leis an obair rannsachaidh seo agus airson nan daoine a chuireas am fiosrachadh gu feum.

Table of contents

Acknowledgements

This book emerges from the work of Soillse's Islands Gaelic Research Project (IGRP), conducted between 2015 and 2017. This publication is in essence the report of this project. Soillse is a multi-institutional and interdisciplinary research collaboration between the University of the Highlands and Islands, including its constituent college Sabhal Mòr Ostaig, the National Centre for Gaelic Language and Culture; the University of Aberdeen; the University of Edinburgh; and the University of Glasgow. Soillse was established in 2009 to provide research opportunities and post-graduate training in various academic disciplines relevant to the maintenance and revitalisation of Gaelic language and culture.

The authors are grateful to the Soillse board members who approved the IGRP budget from Soillse's project fund, for the ongoing support of the board for our work from the representatives of the participating universities and the representatives of Bòrd na Gàidhlig, as well as the Scottish Funding Council and Highlands and Islands Enterprise on the Soillse board. Since the inception of Soillse, the IGRP is the most significant project expenditure by Soillse on an integrated research project and, in this sense, it represents the partnership's primary research undertaking.

The authors wish to thank Uilleam MacDhòmhnaill, Head of Education, and Becky MacLean, Early Years Service Manager, Comhairle nan Eilean Siar, for their assistance in implementing the Preschool Survey, as well as the staff of the preschool units who assisted across the IGRP Research Area. We acknowledge, too, the support of the parents associated with the Preschool Survey.

In relation to the Teenager Survey, we thank all participants. We gratefully acknowledge the patience and assistance afforded the project by Dr Frances Murray, and her staff, at Sgoil MhicNeacail, Stornoway, Isle of Lewis; Mrs Aileen MacSween, and her staff, at Sgoil Sir E. Scott, in Tarbert, Isle of Harris; Mrs Annag MacLean, former head teacher, and the staff, at Sgoil Bhàgh a' Chaisteil, Isle of Barra; Mrs Alice Parkin, Mr Millar Macdonald, former head teacher, and Mr Gordon Young, head teacher at Sgoil Lìonacleit, Isle of Benbecula.

The authors are especially indebted to the local advisors in the islands of Scalpay, Grimsay and Eriskay who freely offered their advice and guidance. We wish to thank all community members in these three islands who helped to publicise our survey work and subsequent public meetings. This aspect of the project received valuable fieldwork assistance from Dr Cassie Smith-Christmas, Dr Catrìona NicNèill, Peigi Townsend, Gordon Wells and Eairdsidh Caimbeul. The Islands Gaelic Research Project could not have been completed without the support of the people of Scalpay, Grimsay and Eriskay. For their patience and co-operation, the authors remain most appreciative. We are also grateful to the participants and those who helped organise the 13 public meetings in various island districts which we arranged in conjunction with this research project.

The authors gratefully acknowledge the valuable contributions of Gordon Wells and Dr Daniel Bourgeois, who facilitated discussions and provided important comment on earlier drafts of the manuscript. We are indebted to Dr Peadar Morgan, the Research and Corpus Planning Manager at Bòrd na Gàidhlig, who prepared the IGRP maps. We are grateful to two external readers who read an advanced draft of this study and who suggested clarifications of key points. Any errors that may remain are the sole responsibility of the authors.

The project team would like to thank Professor Boyd Robertson and Dr Gillian Munro, as well as all the staff at Sabhal Mòr Ostaig; and Professor Neil Simco, Vice-Principal for Research and Impact at the University of the Highlands and Islands for their encouragement and support of our work. We also wish to acknowledge the support offered to Soillse and the IGRP team by the late Professor Ian Bryden.

We would like to express our gratitude to John Storey in the Gaelic Books Council for his valuable advice and assistance with the publishing process. The authors are very grateful to Latte and Melanie Goldstein, at River Design, for their thoughtful, patient and skilled approach to the design of the book. Similarly, we thank the staff of Gomer Press for their dedication and professionalism in producing and printing the book. The authors would like to express their gratitude to Professor Cairns Craig, the Director of Aberdeen University Press, for agreeing to publish this book. We also thank Dr Sandra Hynes of Aberdeen University Press for her considerate and effective assistance with the publication.

Above all, however, we would like to express our appreciation to the people in the Western Isles, Staffin on the Isle of Skye and Tiree who took part in the various aspects of the research. We are indebted to them all for generously sharing their time and their perspectives with us.

Roles of the IGRP authors

CONCHÚR Ó GIOLLAGÁIN

Conchúr Ó Giollagáin directed the IGRP study and is the principal author of this book – the report of the IGRP. He devised the aims, modules and methodology of the project and led the research team in carrying out the fieldwork and organising the data for analysis. Along with Gòrdan Camshron, Pàdruig Moireach and Tamás Péterváry, he co-devised the survey questionnaires. He was involved in all aspects of the data analysis and co-authored the nine chapters with colleagues as indicated below. He also participated along with Iain Caimbeul, Gòrdan Camshron and Pàdruig Moireach in organising and conducting the community and teenager meetings/focus groups. All authors contributed insights to various drafts of the chapters.

Conchúr is the Director of the UHI Language Sciences Institute and the Director of the Soillse sociolinguistic research network. He is the Gaelic Research Professor in the University of the Highlands and Islands, Scotland.

GÒRDAN CAMSHRON

Gòrdan Camshron, along with Pàdruig Moireach, was an IGRP fieldworker. He participated in all the field research aspects of the study and, in particular, he gathered and reported the descriptive statistics in Chapter 5 (Community Sociolingustic Survey) and Chapter 6 (Speaker Typology Survey). Along with Pàdruig Moireach and Iain Caimbeul, he took responsibility for presenting and analysing the data in the Appendices.

Gòrdan is a doctoral student of the UHI Language Sciences Institute.

PÀDRUIG MOIREACH

Pàdruig Moireach also participated in all the field research aspects of the IGRP and, in particular, he gathered and reported the descriptive statistics in Chapter 3 (Preschool Survey) and Chapter 4 (Teenager Survey).

Pàdruig is on the research staff in the UHI Language Sciences Institute and a part-time Gaelic tutor in Sabhal Mòr Ostaig.

BRIAN Ó CURNÁIN

Brian Ó Curnáin also worked on the data analysis of the module findings and he contributed, in particular, to the analysis of cross-tabulations in and between modules (Chapters 2–6). He participated in the copy-editing on drafts of the nine chapters and co-authored Chapters 1 and 7. He contributed to the Gaelic nexus analysis in Chapter 2 and provided additional insights to the chapters.

Brian is an Associate Professor in the School of Celtic Studies, the Dublin Institute for Advanced Studies.

IAIN CAIMBEUL

Iain Caimbeul co-authored Chapters 8 and 9 with Conchúr Ó Giollagáin, and contributed amendments to other chapters. He is a co-author of the IGRP's appendices.

Iain Caimbeul is a Research Fellow in the UHI Language Sciences Institute.

BRIAN MACDONALD

Brian MacDonald managed the statistical data of the various modules and assisted the IGRP team in organising the datasets for presentation and analysis. He participated in the statistical analysis of the findings and prepared the data for display in the dataset tables and figures. He conducted the statistical tests on the correlations between variables and contributed valuable insights on their implications to the other authors. Along with Conchúr Ó Giollagáin and Gòrdan Camshron, he co-authored the descriptive demolinguistic statistics in Chapter 2.

Brian is an affiliate of the Lèirsinn research project based at Sabhal Mòr Ostaig.

TAMÁS PÉTERVÁRY

Tamás Péterváry assisted with various aspects of the data processing, especially the design of databases for recording the questionnaire responses. Tamás participated in the preparation of the graphs and their analysis.

Tamás is a former Soillse researcher and is now an archaeologist in Veszprém, Hungary, where he directs archaeological excavations and community research projects.

Abbreviations

CnaG	Comunn na Gàidhlig
CSS	Community Sociolinguistic Survey, Chapter 5
GLP	Gaelic Language Plan
GME	Gaelic-medium Education
IGRP	Islands Gaelic Research Project
L1	Refers to a language acquired as an individual's first language, or 'mother tongue'
L2	Refers to a language consciously acquired other than as an individual's first language, or 'mother tongue'
LPP	Language Planning and Policy
NGLP	National Gaelic Language Plan(s)
NRS	National Records of Scotland
RA	Research Area
RLS	Reversing Language Shift
SD(s)	Study District(s)
SIR(s)	Standardised Incidence Ratio(s)
STS	Speaker Typology Survey, Chapter 6
UHI	University of the Highlands and Islands

IGRP Weblink

Appendices comprising supplementary data to the IGRP chapters are available at www.uhi.ac.uk/vernacularcommunity

1 INTRODUCTION

1.1 CONTEXT

The primary aim of this book is to provide contemporary data and analysis of the societal and spatial extent of Gaelic speakers and Gaelic speaking in the remaining vernacular communities in Scotland. This study is a baseline sociolinguistic survey focusing chiefly on the extent of the use and transmission of Scottish Gaelic as a communal language and on Gaelic-speaking identity in the Western Isles, in Staffin in the Isle of Skye and in the Isle of Tiree in Argyll and Bute.[1] The urgent need for this analysis stems from the fragile nature of the remaining vernacular communities, which has been highlighted in recent research (e.g. MacKinnon 2010a; 2011c; 2012; and Munro *et al.* 2011). The inter-related research modules in the Islands Gaelic Research Project (IGRP) set out to define the sociolinguistic prevalence of Gaelic in the current bilingual context of life in the islands. The study as a whole will assess the prospects for Gaelic as a vernacular and as a lived identity and determine the context for language-policy interventions which might support the social continuity of Gaelic speaking in the islands. We have prepared this book as an academic report of the IGRP, but we hope it will be of interest to those who are concerned about the fate of threatened linguistic minorities in the contemporary world, and especially to Gaels who are interested in the current reality and future vitality of Gaelic.

Working within the tradition of mainstream sociolinguistic enquiry, this book is the most comprehensive multi-modular study comprising an integrated analysis of the vernacular communal context of Gaelic. Gaelic is now effectively both a minority and a minoritised language in its remaining vernacular communities, most notably communities in the Western Isles (or the Outer Hebrides), which, to a large extent, were intact multi-generational Gaelic-speaking communities until as late as the 1970s and 1980s (excluding the urban settlement of Stornoway in Lewis). Currently, however, only 52% of those in the Research Area report an ability in Gaelic. Excepting the 50+ age cohort, a majority in these islands do not report a competence in Gaelic in the 2011 Census, now rendering Gaelic a minority language in these former vernacular communities. Additionally, Gaelic represents a minoritised formal or institutionalised identity in these communities in that virtually all formal or

1 Residual vernacular networks are to be found in other areas in Scotland, mainly among elderly people in districts such as Wester Ross; the Oban area; Lochaber; parts of the Isle of Skye not studied in this project, in addition to the migrant communities in Glasgow, Edinburgh and other urban areas.

institutional activity accedes to the functional primacy of English, except for specific Gaelic-medium activity in education and broadcasting.

The research project combines a series of surveys and community consultations as the basis for forming a diagnosis and prognosis of future prospects for Gaelic in the islands. Two surveys were conducted as area-wide surveys: one investigating the preschool age group and the other focusing on the late-teenage cohort, conducted in the four secondary schools in the Western Isles. Two other surveys concentrated on gathering detailed data on three specific areas within the islands. Three small island communities (Scalpay, Grimsay and Eriskay) were selected in which particularly high levels of Gaelic competence were indicated by 2011 Census figures, in order to investigate the sociolinguistic profiles of the strongest remaining Gaelic communities in the islands. The chapters detailing the survey findings are preceded by an analysis of how the language questions in the National Census depict the levels of ability and practice of Gaelic. Kenneth MacKinnon (2011c: 207) has referred to 'the actuality gap' between the enumeration of Gaelic ability in census results and the actual social practice of Gaelic in society. Comparing the results from the 2011 Census with the those from the IGRP also reveals a 'presentational gap' of how the numbers of those who report Gaelic ability are indicative of the actual social practice of Gaelic in communities in Scotland.

The qualitative aspects of the study are presented in the reports of eight focus group meetings conducted in the four secondary schools in the Western Isles; and in a series of 13 public consultations in the Study Districts, including Tiree and Staffin. The three community surveys afforded participants the opportunity to write comments and observations in the questionnaire forms or to communicate directly with the fieldworkers and researchers of the IGRP on issues important to the participants. Triangulating the results from all of these modules and analyses produced the baseline evidence to illustrate Gaelic familial and community practice at a far more fine-grained level of detail than the National Census can provide.

The on-going rapid contraction of Gaelic-speaking in the islands evidenced in this report provides an opportunity to reappraise how official language policy corresponds to the realities of minority-language endangerment in Scotland and elsewhere. Given that Gaelic is an officially-recognised minority language and that it is the object of significant policy and planning interest at national and regional levels, the data, analysis and proposed model of policy engagement are obviously relevant to other minority-language policy contexts grappling with late-modernity. The results of this project pose fundamental questions with regard to the relevance and efficacy of much minority-language policy, planning and interventions. Of course, with or without (official) support, vernacular decline is common among non-dominant linguistic groups, historically and particularly in modernity (e.g. Batibo 2005; Crystal 2000; Eberhard *et al.* 2019; Harrison 2007; Krauss 1992; Nettle and

Romaine 2000; Ó Giollagáin *et al.* 2007a,b; Ó Giollagáin and Charlton 2015; Olthuis *et al.* 2013; Simpson 2007, 2008). The final chapter of the book proposes a new model of language policy and societal engagement to effectively address the trajectory of contraction among the speaker group.

1.2 SOCIAL PHILOSOPHY AND SOCIETAL CHALLENGES IN MINORITY SOCIOLINGUISTIC TRANSFORMATIONS

This research is informed by a social-identity perspective (cf. Jenkins 2008: 37–38). We take it that such social identity is embodied in the self-ascribing, established group. Richard Jenkins (2008: 46) writes: 'First, identity is a practical accomplishment, a process. Second, individual and collective identities can be understood using one model, of the dialectical interplay of processes of internal and external definition'. The continuing existence of a self-ascribing Gaelic group is evident in current socio-cultural activity, collective and institutional processes, independent of its portrayal in this project and in other research. The current vulnerable state of Gaelic group-identity can be assessed from the data presented in this book, especially in Chapter 4.

We set out below the social philosophy which has informed the IGRP's approach to our enquiry into vernacular Gaelic-speaking. Much discursive comment on minority-language sociolinguistics has concentrated on various aspects of the tensions between individual cultural opportunity for and expression in minority languages in (post-)modernising heterogeneity, on the one hand, and the implications of the detraditionalising aspects of (post-)modernity for non-dominant collective cultures, on the other.[2] A focus on individual reflexive agency in the non-normative minority culture can be contrasted with the diminishing fortunes of the minority-language collective under the detraditionalising conditions of late modernity (Giddens 1991: 32–34). The individualised postmodernist perspective views minority culture as a post-collective amalgam of individual interests, i.e. minority cultural practice as an individual option, and, thus, downplays the concerns of the non-dominant collective to protect itself as a self-sustaining and stable social group, with the capacity to transfer its social identity to subsequent generations. This contrast mirrors Giddens' (1990: 16–17) analysis of the detraditionalising aspects of modernity: 'the disembedding of social systems' inherent in the dynamism of (post-)modernity. Given that the dynamism of (post-)modernity influences the minority group through the power

---

2 We refer to postmodernity in this study as it is generally used in contemporary sociology, i.e. the ongoing effects of a modernising dynamic underpinning social relations which are increasingly disembedded from collective and inherited (or traditional) narratives and influenced by relativist and situationalist perspectives of social interaction.

relations of the dominant cultural group, we can assume that these detraditionalising processes impact in a relatively stronger manner on the minority group, often culminating in cultural and language shift.

Ulrich Beck and Elisabeth Beck-Gernsheim view the post-traditional dynamic as a process of 'individualization' carrying an 'own life culture or self-culture': '"Self-culture" thus denotes what was at first negatively addressed with the concept of a *post-traditional lifeworld*: that is, the compulsion and the pleasure of leading an insecure life of one's own and co-ordinating it with the distinctive lives of other people' (Beck and Beck-Gernsheim 2010: 42).[3] That is to say, according to their analysis, the move from traditional to post-traditional society encouraged individualised socio-cultural possibilities while promoting a disinclination for collective social affiliation and for related received narratives underpinning adherence to communal entities. For those possessing the cultural resources of minority-language groups, the added complication, of course, is the detrimental effects that individualising processes have on social adherence of minority members to marginal or low-status language groups. Post-traditional individualisation tends to be mediated through high-status languages. The negative feedback loop of the recessive trajectory in minority-language cultures weakens the social basis in those languages. This means that the 'self-cultures' of individualisation and their 'self-politics' (Beck and Beck-Gernsheim 2010: 45) are an integral part of modernisation in majority-language cultures to the detriment of the minority language.

The challenges of postmodernity for minority cultures increase with intensification of individualisation in late capitalism. Beck and Beck-Gernsheim's (2010: 14–15) theory of individualisation posits:

> As modern society develops further, it is becoming questionable to assume that collective units of meaning and action exist. System theories, which assume an existence and reproduction of the social independence of the actions and thoughts of individuals, are thereby losing reality content. … the content, goals, foundations and structures of the 'social' are having to be renegotiated, reinvented and reconstructed. … The scurrying of the individualized lifestyles, elaborated in the personal trial-and-error process …, is unamenable to the need for the standardization of bureaucratized political science and sociology.

---

3 Presumably, Beck and Beck-Gernsheim's abstracted take on postmodernity adopts an antagonistic or, at best, a neutral view of the beneficial communal aspects of traditional life, while adopting, at the same time, a 'positive' view of the 'insecure' possibilities of individualised postmodernity. This perceived liberation from the collective constraints of traditional society ironically 'emancipates' individuals to their insecurity. This is in essence the postmodern(ist) conundrum in that the communal disintegration of traditional society is of little consequence to a postmodernist worldview which is largely indifferent to or incapable of generating secure collective possibilities.

Establishing 'collective units of meaning' in fragile minority cultures is even more daunting, given that in the modern era they did not develop, or were prevented from developing, both concepts and structures of essentialist nationalism. While the purported processes of individualisation in late modernity undoubtedly challenge notions of systematised agency and their cogency, such individualisation does not negate the real presence, effect and power of a vast array of public policy initiatives, of international knowledge transfer and of flows of wealth, influence and globalising trends. Clearly, the 'do-it-yourself' dimension of individualised postmodernity does not preclude individuals from partaking in non-individual, public and collective systems, despite postmodernist assertions to the contrary. In fact, it is the ubiquity of nation states and their polities that allows for so much individualisation. Linguistic minorities tend to have had only meagre experience of agency and power backed by public policy, therefore, reflexive individualisation processes may represent a much less-developed component of the minority or non-normative culture. Majority culture is the main driving force for reflexivity and (post)modernity, so that minority members access much of postmodernity via the majority culture. What may be experienced as individualisation in the majority culture is likely to be more akin to atomisation or acculturation for the minority culture. Members of both minority and majority may be influenced by similar postmodern processes, but these processes render contrasting outcomes, since (post)modernity tends to produce the acculturation of minorities. Majority groups retain their collective functionality in (post)modernity while minorities globally are highly threatened.

This study offers detailed demolinguistic evidence of the Gaelic group as a case in point in late-modern acculturation. This book is primarily concerned with the societal trajectory which has brought the vernacular practice of Gaelic to its current predicament, and the research approach prioritises a 'big picture' focus on the fate of the collective. However, we also adopt a mixed-method approach which has yielded insights on individual reflexive perspectives, for example in the community meetings, the teenager focus groups, other insights communicated to us by preschool teachers and direct correspondence to the IGRP team.

The communal practice of Gaelic has undergone a transformation from a situation of minority-language regional dominance to a state of residual use in an unreciprocated bilingualism which can be traced through the second half of the 20th century up to the present. This study situates the Gaelic-speaking community of the Western Isles on an advanced point on the timeline of bilingual contact with monolingual English speakers in local and wider social networks in which English-language practice predominates. Common to the general minority-language condition in late modernity, the non-dominant residual use of Gaelic among the minority bilingual group corresponds to the contracting social space for the peripheral culture which modernisation imposes on the minority. Among the other obstacles, the 'traditional' society (i.e. the societal context supporting the social practice of Gaelic) has been unable to integrate socio-economic modernity with the social vitality of Gaelic. The peripheral rural minority-language group has been subsumed into the dominant group's socio-economic expanding market in the typical processes of modernity. This has occurred in tandem with the long-established out-migration by islanders seeking employment and social mobility mainly in urban markets in Scotland or further afield. From the perspective of the Gaelic-speaking islanders, modernisation and its purported socio-economic opportunities have been accompanied by:

- Market diversification of a previously agricultural, traditional rural economy
- The integration of the local leadership into the civic practices of a monolingual state apparatus
- The integration of new social players in familial and community networks whose preference or competence is restricted to higher-status English
- The detraditionalising dynamic which transforms the social role of Gaelic in these communities to an individual option alongside the *lingua franca* function of English, i.e. the sociolinguistic irony of the individualisation of Gaelic and the concomitant progressive collectivisation of English.

Since the onset of post-war modernisation, all traditional Gaelic-speaking communities have undergone a transformation in which Gaelic has become an optional extra to the normative dominance of English. The residual aspect of Gaelic competence in the islands — and the even more-circumscribed social practice of Gaelic — demonstrates a residual bilingualism in the older age cohorts and even weaker competence and practice among the young. This residual bilingualism is primarily found in the older and, to a lesser extent, middle-aged social networks, formed prior to the erosion of more traditional social networks. On the other hand, the very marginal practice of, or acquaintance with Gaelic among the young is predominantly dependent on school support. For the young, therefore, Gaelic is primarily associated with a school setting and subject, which is mostly unreinforced by practice (in social networks).

It is clear from the IGRP results that the socio-economic modernisation in the islands has progressed without cognisance of the policy measures needed to support the sustainability of Gaelic in the communities. The departure from traditional society in the islands, which has accelerated since the 1960s, brought a degree of socio-economic progress to these communities but at the expense of the resilience of their Gaelic vernacular. It must be acknowledged, however, that the problems prevalent in the traditional phase (pre-1960), e.g. the limited local market opportunities and the ongoing out-migration of members of the speaker group, posed equally troublesome social challenges to the Gaelic community. Implementing socio-economic modernisation in the islands posed the unpalatable sociolinguistic conundrum for Gaels of being 'damned if you do and damned if you don't'. Pierre Bourdieu (1991: 81–82) defines the notion of 'habitus' as the socioculturally acquired behaviour which is based on the acquisition and functioning of various forms of capital in the social 'market' of a community. From this perspective of 'linguistic habitus' (Bourdieu 1991: 37–38), the ongoing process of modernisation destabilises the social and linguistic markets which had traditionally supported the societal practice and habitus of the minority language. This process is common in modernity and is ongoing in the Western Isles.

We hypothesise, therefore, that the current elderly cohort of the last remaining Gaelic-speaking communities have traversed a sociolinguistic path from local ascendency in their youth to a sociolinguistically marginal position in their old age within an English-dominant community. The corollary of this is that the youngest cohorts who have gained an English-Gaelic bilingual competence are a minority in their communities and, additionally, they have acquired this competence in a non-normative sociolinguistic context for both the family and school contexts. Especially for the young and the young adult age cohorts, Gaelic has been disembedded from its communal function and replaced by English. This is, of course, a central feature of minority-language shift.

1.3 MAINSTREAM PRACTICE IN MINORITY-LANGUAGE SOCIOLINGUISTICS

Our approach in this study is consistent with the sociolinguistic mainstream which focuses on evidence-based analysis of the demo-geography of the minority speaker group and related issues of the prevalence of minority socio-cultural practices, in tandem with examining the relevance of formal and informal supports for the demolinguistic vitality of the speaker group. Summaries of the mainstream approach can be found in Fishman (1991); Simons and Fennig (2018); and UNESCO (2003). For instance, Simons and Fennig (2018: 1) state: 'The general scholarly consensus, however, is that the key factor in gauging the relative safety of an endangered language is the degree to which intergenerational transmission of the language remains intact'; and similarly UNESCO (2003): 'A language is in danger when its speakers cease to use it, use it in an increasingly reduced number of communicative domains, and cease to pass it on from one generation to the next' (pg. 2) … 'The most commonly used factor in evaluating the vitality of a language is whether or not it is being transmitted from one generation to the next [Fishman 1991]' (pg. 7).

UNESCO (2003) also lists a series of key factors or diagnostic indicators which can be used to assess language vitality or endangerment:

- The speaker population
- The ethnic population; the number of those who connect their ethnic identity with the language (whether or not they speak the language)
- The stability of and trends in that population size
- Residency and migration patterns of speakers
- The use of second languages
- The use of the language by others as a second language
- Language attitudes within the community
- The age range of the speakers
- The domains of use of the language
- Official recognition of languages within the nation or region
- Means of transmission (whether children are learning the language at home or being taught the language in schools)
- Non-linguistic factors such as economic opportunity or the lack thereof.

It is the 'recognizable patterns and trends' of these factors in society which determine 'the relative safety of an endangered language' (UNESCO 2003).

Several authors (Fishman 1991; Lewis and Simons 2016) have developed diagnostic scales to assist language groups in assessing their relative position according to various sets of vitality/fragility indicators. The aim of these scales is to encourage language groups to identify priorities, based on a realistic assessment of current circumstances, in order to counteract a deterioration towards a more fragile point on the scale. Similar to many threatened languages, the circumstances of Gaelic in Scotland correspond to Levels 7 and 8 of the language shift and moribund categorisations in Paul Lewis and Gary Simons' (2016: 80–81) Extended Graded Intergenerational Disruption Scale (EGIDS), as adapted from Fishman's GIDS (1991: 87–109; see section 8.2.2 below for further detail on EGIDS). Level 7 is defined as: 'The child-bearing generation can use the language among themselves, but it is not being transmitted to children' (EGIDS 7). Level 8 is defined as: 'The only remaining active users of the language are members of the grandparent generation and older' (EGIDS 8). Despite the fact that the societal evidence indicates a general context of familial and communal erosion (EGIDS 7–8), much of the public policy debate about Gaelic has been focused on EGIDS Levels 1 and 2 'national' and 'regional' language promotion and status of L2 learning initiatives. This is another instance of erroneous emphasis on high status contexts in language revitalisation. In short, people often tend to feel the need to save threatened languages not for the purpose of everyday communication, but for reasons of language aesthetics, literary riches, language creativity and ethnic and religious heritage. But, paradoxically, language is practically saved primarily through everyday communication. As Lewis and Simons (2016: 100) have pointed out:

A weak language placed in direct competition with a stronger language, in any domain of use, is very likely going to become weaker. Experience is teaching us that the way to rebuild a failing language is by strengthening the identity of its users and cementing its face-to-face use.

For this reason, it is of vital importance to protect and promote the spaces and contexts in which the monolingual use of the threatened language is fully functional, in particular in familial and everyday communal situations. The aim here, as set out in greater detail for Gaelic in Chapter 9, is to protect and promote the threatened linguistic culture while at the same time stimulating bilingual functionality. In the unidirectional bilingualism[4] prevalent in minority-language contexts, particularly in the power dynamics of the Scottish Gaelic situation, where the minority language does not function fully in society, it is extremely difficult to acquire a developed function in the minority language and a loyal language identity. Thus, a policy of monolingual practice of the threatened language needs to be fostered to counteract the subtractive impact of the powerful language. In short, the more opportunities there are to fully use a minority language, the greater the likelihood that people will attain full minority competence. A strategy of targeted exclusivity is essential in protecting that which is threatened with extinction.

1.3.1 DIVERGENT APPROACH TO MINORITY-LANGUAGE SOCIOLINGUISTICS

The issue of the Gaelic vernacular crisis highlights the contrast between mainstream and divergent approaches to Gaelic sociolinguistic academic issues. The assumptions inherent in the latter approach that efforts of suscitating minority-language non-normativity through related peripheral networks and peripheral self-contained discursivist fora are clearly over-optimistic, especially when juxtaposed with: (a) the challenging social reality of the Gaelic group; (b) the obvious formal limitations of official support mechanisms to intervene in society on their behalf; and (c) the constraints in the existing academic focus for informing feasible alternatives to counteract the trajectory of demise. However, a main feature of the postmodernist approach is its self-generating discursivism, rather than any significant engagement with various levels of society.

---

4 The term unidirectional bilingualism refers to a form of bilingualism typically found in minority-language contexts where minority speakers are bilingual in both the minority and majority language, in contrast with majority first-language speakers who generally remain monolingual in the majority language (Matras 2009: 59). Prolonged and pervasive societal unidirectional bilingualism typically leads to reduced minority-language functionality and language shift.

In tracing the geographic demolinguistics of the remaining Gaelic-speaking islands, this study is a timely academic intervention in current debates concerning the fragility of vernacular minority languages in late-modernity. This is especially true when actual vernacular erosion is contrasted with discourses on 'new-speaker' innovation or so called 'vitality' (e.g. O'Rourke and Ramallo 2011; O'Rourke and Walsh 2015; O'Rourke, Pujolar and Ramallo 2015; McLeod and O'Rourke 2015; Smith-Christmas *et al.* 2018). The IGRP provides sociolinguistic data about the contemporary (and historical) reality of decline in the communities who possess, or possessed until recently, Gaelic-speaking as a primary social reality and identity. This obvious social decline in autochthonous vitality is in stark contrast to the 'new-speaker' discursive aspirations which have been cultivated by certain academics. For such 'new-speaker' discursivity, Gaelic is presented as an additional or occasional competence or identity to be acquired in the near or more distant future; existing more in academic discourse or imagination than in actual demography. In fact, we argue that the 'new-speaker' discourse about Gaelic supports a view of Gaelic identity as non-primary minority and complementary cultural practice to the dominant and normative English-language culture in Scotland. In other words, 'new-speaker' discourses, in our view, actually normalise vernacular communal decline, while often ignoring or obfuscating the implications and realities of that same decline for a postvernacular Gaelic present and future.

Following the presentation of the data from the various modules in Chapters 2–6, we will discuss in greater depth the implications of the postmodernist perspective in contemporary Gaelic sociolinguistics in Chapter 8. In the meantime, the following quotes from publications on various aspects of Gaelic-related sociolinguistics indicate some of the discursivist themes of post-territoriality, post-ethnicity and post-traditional communities which have been proposed recently in the postmodernist approach:

> According to the 2011 census, only 24.3% of Gaelic speakers were living in parishes in which more than 50% of the population could speak Gaelic … Such marginalisation limits the opportunities for Gaelic use and the potential for Gaelic maintenance and transmission; it also intensifies the perception of Gaelic as a minority language in terms of the lived experience of individual speakers. This increased dispersal of the Gaelic population makes territorial conceptions of the language … less meaningful and less workable in terms of policy and provision. (McLeod 2019: 4)

> Traditionally, both academic and policy discussions regarding how to stimulate greater social use of regional or minority languages have placed considerable emphasis on the need to promote local, neighbourhood-based networks, with the focus often on targeting specific territorial communities. While this type of local community-based approach should

not be discounted completely, greater attention needs to be given to the need to develop robust language promotion strategies that are tailored to contemporary urban and mobile lifestyles. Everyday social practices are now being stretched across wider areas, thereby influencing where, when and how people interact with each other, and, by extension, where they use their languages. (Lewis *et al.* 2019)

This 'quasi-ethnic concept of the Gael' [Oliver 2004: 2] and bounded, essentialist sense of Gaelic as being embedded in (and confined to) a specific place and social context have weakened considerably in recent decades, however, as the language has declined in its last 'heartlands' and the social base of the language has expanded, in particular with the increasing presence of 'new speakers' of Gaelic who have learned the language in school or in adulthood, ... [Glaser 2007; Oliver 2004 (see Oliver 2005)]. (McLeod 2019: 6)

The contributions in this volume reveal how Gaelic speakers are negotiating novel ways to maintain and enact their bilingual identities in socio-spatially diverse contexts. In doing so, they challenge older understandings of the Gaelic community as a single collective identity. A central concern is to identify the functions crucial to continued use of the language and the social conditions necessary to reproduce a speech community in the likelihood of minority identities being more or less decoupled from place or traditional forms of use [cf. Romaine 2007]. (MacLeod and Smith-Christmas 2018: 9)

... the decline of Gaelic as a 'mother tongue' is not necessarily incompatible with Gaelic's maintenance as an additional language used by an expanding bilingual population in private and social domains. ... The first emergent theme is one of ambiguity: ambiguity over what it means to be a 'Gael' in modern Scotland; ... ambiguity over the policy and planning mechanisms best-suited to support the maintenance of a community of Gaelic bilinguals. The second and related unifying theme is one of new speakerhood, which connects with a burgeoning theoretical debate over the possibilities for first and second language acquisition of minority languages in so-called 'post-traditional' communities. A third and final recurring theme is one of capacity: capacity within institutions and organisations which are committed to Gaelic language planning through statutory language plans or through their role in providing Gaelic materials and services. (MacLeod and Smith-Christmas 2018: 173–74)

It seems the Gaelic-speaking public has not yet bought into the 'new sociolinguistic order' [cf. O'Rourke *et al.* 2015] that the language management initiatives seek to bring about. ... As the authors in this volume show, the challenges and opportunities for revitalising Gaelic in Scotland are variegated and complex, and their implications for the future of the Gaelic community are unclear. (MacLeod and Smith-Christmas 2018: 178–79)

As we shall discuss in greater detail in Chapter 8, in our view, a discursivism which is unrelated to the sociolinguistic reality of the speaker group is unfortunately tantamount to a postmodernist fiddler playing on while vernacular speech goes up in flames! This book is rooted in mainstream minority sociolinguistics and, therefore, represents an alternative to the acquiescence, evasions and diversions in much of discursivist sociolinguistics. The various research modules, which are reported in this book, identify the level of endangerment and crisis in vernacular Gaelic communities. A sociolinguistic focus which avoids this situation is unproductive for the Gael, for learners of Gaelic, and for Gaelic scholarship and minority-language planning. In Chapter 9, we set out a series of mainstream minority-language planning and protection priorities, recommended for consideration by those in the vernacular group who may wish to ameliorate their current situation, and for those who have responsibility for the targeted use of public resources in the most constructive and advantageous manner. Our recommendations entail initiatives related to family, education, community, state supports and ethnographic retrieval.

2 CENSUS ANALYSIS

2.1 INTRODUCTION

This chapter examines Gaelic language data in the Research Area (RA, i.e. Western Isles, Staffin in the Isle of Skye, and the Isle of Tiree) based on the Scottish Census, chiefly the most recent Census of 2011. We include analysis of intercensal trajectories of Gaelic abilities and use in the Research Area for the thirty-year period of 1981 to 2011. We also set out the various geographic units used in the IGRP study. Following a brief literature review of the study of Gaelic demolinguistics, including an appraisal of difficulties in the interpretation of minority-language data, we present a descriptive analysis of the Scottish Census demolinguistic data, mainly for the period 1981–2011, on reported Gaelic ability and Family Household Gaelic use. The Gaelic ability data are assessed further in a statistical analysis of Standardised Incidence Ratios (SIRs), as an aid to analysis of geographical distributions and comparative vitality.

This census chapter of the IGRP presents:

- Historical overview of Gaelic demolinguistics
- Evaluation of language data in the Study Districts (SDs)
- Gaelic speaking ability among various age cohorts
- Gaelic use in Family Households (data available for the 2011 Census only)
- Geographic distribution of vitality indicators (SIRs) for the period 1981–2011
- Examination of language trajectories from 1951 to 2011, as complementary analysis to the more detailed examination of the 1981 to 2011 demolinguistics
- Analysis of the contraction and decline of the speaker group and language shift in diachronic and synchronic dimensions
- Intersection of speaker ability data and household use data (including the implications of the nexus of 45% (ability) intersecting with 15% (Family Household), and projections of trends towards this nexus)
- Prognosis for vernacular Gaelic
- Maps of Gaelic ability data in the SDs and age cohorts.

Additional demolinguistic data and descriptive statistics from the Census are provided in **Appendix 2**.

2.1.1 GEOGRAPHIC UNITS IN THE IGRP

The main geographic unit of analysis in the IGRP is the Study District (SD). A Study District comprises a group of contiguous townships. These grouped townships or SDs make up the 25 Study Districts of the Research Area of the IGRP. These SDs are geographic units which are meaningful to local community identity. The geographic unit of SD allows for analysis at a spatial level below that of the civil parish. The civil parish has been the most common geographic unit of Gaelic demolinguistic analysis. Map 2.1 illustrates the 25 SDs which comprise the IGRP Research Area.

There are eight geographic levels or units of analysis in this study (from the largest to the smallest, which we discuss both at aggregated levels and as separate units):

All of Scotland > Scotland outside of the Research Area > Research Area (RA) > Western Isles > Pooled Study Districts > All Rural Areas > Study Districts (SDs) > three islands of the Community Survey Module (Scalpay, Grimsay and Eriskay).

The census analysis in this chapter contains the following geographic categories: (1) All of Scotland; (2) the rest of Scotland, i.e. outside the RA; (3) the RA; (4) the Western Isles; (5) the Pooled SDs; (6) the SDs. In section 2.4.1.2, the 25 SDs are aggregated into seven larger geographic entities which we term Pooled Study Districts. The census data for the thirty-year period 1981–2011 covers the 25 SDs of the whole IGRP Research Area, whereas the census data for the twenty-year period 1951–1971 covers the Western Isles (and thus excludes the two SDs of Staffin and Tiree). A list of the SDs together with the Pooled Study Districts, is provided in Table 2.1. For analysis of data at Pooled Study District level, see section 2.4.1.2 and **Appendix A2.3**.

The IGRP Research Area comprises geographic regions where a substantial proportion of the population is reported to have an ability in Gaelic. These regions include the Western Isles, townships in Staffin in the northern part of the Isle of Skye, and the Isle of Tiree, and comprise the remaining geographic extent of the Gaelic vernacular group. The Research Area comprised 25 Study Districts made up of clusters of townships that correspond to the regional perceptions on the geographic extent of local communities, with, for clarity, districts 1 to 15 inclusive on the island of Lewis. Most of the 25 SDs are rural communities with relatively low population densities. Only the three Stornoway SDs contain urban settlements. We distinguish All Rural Areas (22 SDs) from the Pooled SD of Stornoway & Suburbs (three SDs) in Section 4.11, Table 4.27. The Benbecula Study District contains Balivanich, where a military facility has operated for many years and where English served as a primary language of communication for often large numbers of military personnel who were stationed there, along with their families (see sections 2.4.1.1 and 5.4.2.2).

Pooled Study District	Study District
Lewis North & West	01. West Side of Lewis (central) 02. West Side of Lewis (south) 03. Uig District 04. West Side of Lewis (north) 05. Ness
Lewis East	06. Tolsta 07. Loch a Tuath 08. Tong 12. South Point 13. North Point 14. North Lochs 15. South Lochs
Stornoway & Suburbs	09. Stornoway, Barvas Road suburbs 10. Stornoway Town 11. Stornoway, Point Road suburbs
Harris	16. North Harris 17. South Harris
North Uist & Benbecula	18. North Uist (north & west) 19. North Uist (south & east) 20. Benbecula
South Uist, Barra & Vatersay	21. South Uist (north) 22. South Uist (south) 23. Barra & Vatersay
Staffin & Tiree	24. Staffin, Skye 25. Isle of Tiree

Table 2.1 List of all Study Districts (25) contained in larger Pooled Study Districts (7)

2.1.2 DIACHRONIC ANALYTICAL FRAMEWORK IN THE RESEARCH AREA

As a guide to the analysis, we set out in this section a framework of the diachronic demolinguistic contraction of vernacular Gaelic in the Research Area. The main finding of the demographic data is that the Gaelic-speaking group has gone through a severe decline in the numbers and social density of speakers in the islands during the 1981–2011 period. This trajectory of decline has undermined the ability of the Gaelic-speaking cohort to reproduce itself. The evidence indicates three sequential or diachronic stages of continuing contraction, i.e. critical, residual and non-viable:

1. There has been a critical loss of high social density in the Gaelic-speaking group in the decade following 1981 and this contraction has continued since then. This initial loss of high density we term the **critical contraction phase** of the societal vitality of Gaelic (all SDs).
2. Following this critical contraction from 1981, the remaining vernacular

Sgìre an t-Suirbhidh
Research Area

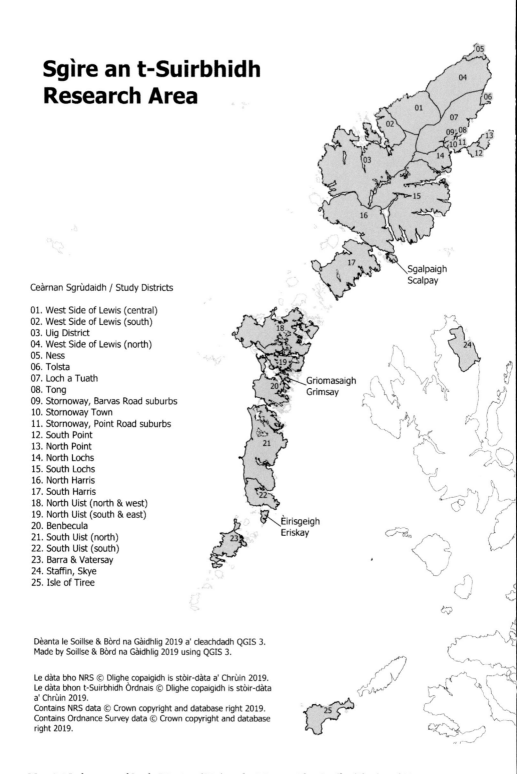

Ceàrnan Sgrùdaidh / Study Districts

01. West Side of Lewis (central)
02. West Side of Lewis (south)
03. Uig District
04. West Side of Lewis (north)
05. Ness
06. Tolsta
07. Loch a Tuath
08. Tong
09. Stornoway, Barvas Road suburbs
10. Stornoway Town
11. Stornoway, Point Road suburbs
12. South Point
13. North Point
14. North Lochs
15. South Lochs
16. North Harris
17. South Harris
18. North Uist (north & west)
19. North Uist (south & east)
20. Benbecula
21. South Uist (north)
22. South Uist (south)
23. Barra & Vatersay
24. Staffin, Skye
25. Isle of Tiree

Dèanta le Soillse & Bòrd na Gàidhlig 2019 a' cleachdadh QGIS 3.
Made by Soillse & Bòrd na Gàidhlig 2019 using QGIS 3.

Le dàta bho NRS © Dlighe copaigidh is stòir-dàta a' Chrùin 2019.
Le dàta bhon t-Suirbhidh Òrdnais © Dlighe copaigidh is stòir-dàta
a' Chrùin 2019.
Contains NRS data © Crown copyright and database right 2019.
Contains Ordnance Survey data © Crown copyright and database
right 2019.

Map 2.1 Index map of Study Districts (SDs) in the Western Isles, Staffin (Skye) and Tiree

social networks persisted in a **residual minoritised phase** up to the current period (2011 Census), while the societal dominance of the competing English-speaking networks grew[5] (all SDs).

3. The process of contraction continues in a given geographic unit (i.e. in a given SD or the RA) to a junction or nexus of 45% of inhabitants having an ability in Gaelic and 15% of Family Households using Gaelic in the home. This nexus is another critical point in the overall trajectory where the residual Gaelic networks contract even further to a **non-viable condition**. We term this stage the non-viable phase, i.e. 45% ability (or less) and 15% Family Household use (or less). This point is an important statistical prognostic result from our analysis of the census data (some SDs).

All SDs have gone through or are in phase 1 or 2 and some have moved into phase 3. Several other authors, in the fields of linguistics and sociolinguistics, have noted and described the ongoing geographical and generational process of contraction among the vernacular group. As far back as 1958, Kenneth Jackson predicted that: 'As things look at present Lewis seems likely to be the last refuge of the language, and those who wish to study it in the middle of the next century may still find there a few old people who can remember it' (Jackson 1958: 231–32). Carl Marstrander's previous prognostication was even more ominous: 'The Celtic family of languages is slowly but surely nearing its extinction. No national bombast nor Celtic Congresses can conceal this truth' (preface in Borgstrøm 1940). In the three decades from 1951 to 1981 (excepting the 1971 Census returns), there was a decline in the Gaelic-speaking proportion of the population in the Western Isles. Furthermore, the decade following the 1981 Census showed the contraction of the speaker-group below its high-density 80%+ proportion of the region's population.

We can cite two researchers, for instance, whose community-based fieldwork has demonstrated analyses similar to our three-phase framework. Will Lamb (2008 (with reference to MacKinnon 1994c: 126)) states: 'Examining the 1981 Census data, MacKinnon found there were still communities which had a proportion of under 25 year-olds reporting Gaelic usage levels as high or higher than individuals older than that'. From his own more recent research in Uist, Lamb concludes:

> At the risk of oversimplification it seems in Uist that there is a band of people generally over 65 years of age who are more Gaelic dominant. There

---

5 Needless to say, the Gaelic bilinguals are also inescapably assimilated into many English-dominant familial, friendship and institutional networks due to the *lingua franca* function of English, the presence of a large cohort of English monolinguals and English-favouring bilinguals in the communities. There are three dimensions to this assimilation: (a) the pragmatic function of communication; (b) affinity and the social pragmatic of 'getting along' with others and (c) the coercive and subordinating dimension, the naturalised expectation that the speakers of the minoritised and/or disfavoured language defer to the societal dominance of English and the favoured or higher-status of speaking English.

is another younger band who are equally comfortable in both languages. Speakers less than 45 years old may be functionally fluent in Gaelic but tend to be English dominant. In the crofting townships of North Uist, the generation born in the late 1960s is reckoned to be the last for whom Gaelic would have been the language of the playground. The last school in Uist with children who naturally spoke Gaelic to one another was Stoneybridge primary, in South Uist, where this continued until the 1980s at least. (Lamb 2008: 46)

Kirstie MacLeod (2017) draws a similar conclusion for Barra about the decline of Gaelic peer-group socialisation from the late 1970s:

Parents who took part in this study were born between the late 1970s and the early 1990s. Investigating the Gaelic language socialisation of young children in Barra highlights three important points. Firstly, today's young children are for the most part the second generation to be mainly socialised as English speakers and to have English as their peer language. Secondly, the intergenerational transmission of Gaelic is no longer feasible for the majority of parents of young children because they are not sufficiently proficient in Gaelic. Thirdly, the small number of today's parents who maintained Gaelic use with their own parents into adulthood are most likely to be those who use Gaelic with their children. (MacLeod 2017: 62)

2.2 METHODOLOGY AND ANALYSIS OF LANGUAGE QUESTIONS IN THE SCOTTISH CENSUS

The general approach in this chapter builds on the techniques and analysis used in similar demolinguistic studies of the census data of Gaelic and other minority-language populations (e.g. Mac an Tàilleir 2010, 2015; MacKinnon 1978, 1985, 1986, 1987, 1994a, 2006b, 2010a, 2011c; Norris 2004; Ó Giollagáin et al. 2007a, 2007b; Ó Giollagáin and Charlton 2015; O'Hanlon and Paterson 2015a, 2015b; and Ó Riagáin 1997).

We present geographic and age-cohort comparisons of the language question data in the four Scottish Censuses of 1981, 1991, 2001 and 2011.[6] The trajectory in the data is presented for the three decades from 1981 to 2011. In the case of the 2011 Census, analysis of the data on individual ability in Gaelic is compared with the data on Family Household use of Gaelic.

The 1981 (section 8) and the 1991 (section 12G) Censuses asked the following

---

6 For a discussion on the history of language questions in the Scottish Census see O'Hanlon and Paterson (2015a: 19) and MacKinnon (1978; 1985).

question: 'Can the person speak, read or write Scottish Gaelic?' Four possible responses were presented:

- Can speak Gaelic
- Can read Gaelic
- Can write Gaelic
- Does not know Gaelic.

In the 2001 Census (question 16), the option 'Understand spoken Gaelic' was added to the list. In our analysis, the categories of reported Gaelic ability and reported Gaelic speaker are based on a positive response to 'Can speak Gaelic'. We sometimes use the category (reported) Gaelic speaker as a convenient shorthand. But it is important to note that basing the category (reported) Gaelic speaker on a positive response to 'Can speak Gaelic' in reality does not represent actual active Gaelic speakerhood for some in that category, due to, for instance, the lack of household and communal use by a substantial proportion of those who have Gaelic ability (see, e.g. sections, 2.3.3, 2.4.3, 4.6.10). This constraint in categorisation, based on a positive response to 'Can speak Gaelic' in the Census, is of course problematic for a diagnosis and prognosis of Gaelic vitality, both for community members and language planners. The lack of active Gaelic speaking in the present, in contrast to higher levels of ability, is a huge constraint on the prospects for a communal future for vernacular Gaelic. This dichotomy is in fact a central aspect of our IGRP report. It is clear from this chapter, and the following chapters, that a positive response to 'Can speak Gaelic' cannot be readily equated with being an actual Gaelic speaker.

There is a low replacement rate in the population of the Western Isles, with a corresponding age bias towards older age groups in the population (2.3.4; Table 2.4; 2.4.1.1; Table 2.5). Based on Table 2.5, we can compare the RA percentage proportions to those for the rest of Scotland:

Research Area: 17% 3–17; 38% 18–49; 45% 50+;
Rest of Scotland: 17% 3–17; 45% 18–49; 38% 50+.

This older-age-skewed profile in the RA is detrimental to the vitality of a minority-language group, in particular given the other factors of out- and in-migration (e.g. MacKinnon 2010a, 2011a, 2014). This age profile skewed towards the older age groups has important implications for analysis of demolinguistic trends. In the context of the Western Isles, language shift is being led in particular by current middle-aged and younger speakers. As the proportion of younger speakers in the total population decreases, measuring language shift in the population as a whole fails to reveal actual trends among younger cohorts. Basically, a large group of older speakers can mask an emerging and increasing impact of smaller numbers of younger speakers, and can conceal critical sociolinguistic trends, including language shift. This contrast between analysis at the total-population level, not indicating rapid change, and age-structured analysis revealing rapid change among the younger cohorts is discussed in section 6.5.2.1, with regard to the aggregated age-skewed data for the three island communities examined in the Speaker Typology Survey (STS).

In the 2011 Census (questions 16 and 18), the same question was asked on English, Gaelic and Scots. An additional question asking whether the respondents used another language other than English at home was posed, with the following options:

- No, English only
- Yes, British Sign Language
- Yes, other – please write in.

Age cohorts are grouped in the following Aggregated Age Cohorts:

- 3 to 17 years
- 18 to 49 years
- 50+ years.[7]

Our analysis of Family Household use of Gaelic is based on data from Question 18 used for the first time in the 2011 Census (Do you use a language other than English at home? Tick all that apply. No, English only; Yes, British Sign Language; Yes, other — please write in).

We define a Family Household as a household which contains both adult(s) (age 18+) and child(ren) (age 3–17). Regarding the Family Household use of Gaelic, the National Records of Scotland provided the following household data (age 3+) for the 25 Study Districts:

- All households which contain both adults and children, i.e. Family Households
- Family Households where all adults are reported to use Gaelic (%)
- Family Households where all children are reported to use Gaelic (%)
- Family Households where all adults and all children are reported to use Gaelic (%).

---

7 Greater detail in the age-cohort breakdown was sought from the National Records of Scotland, i.e. into ten-year age cohorts as can be available for the higher geographic level of civil parishes. However, due to issues of disclosure in such small populations for many of the SDs, the data was provided in only three age cohorts. This is an obvious unavoidable drawback for our diachronic generational analysis.

2.3 LITERATURE REVIEW OF GAELIC DEMOLINGUISTICS

2.3.1 GAELIC SCOTLAND: HISTORICAL DEMOLINGUISTIC ANALYSES

Investigation of the historical demographic profile of Gaelic in Scotland has generally focused on the temporal and spatial changes of the speaker-group's territorial extent, and on processes and patterns of change in language use.

Spatial extent

Although contested in some quarters, it is generally accepted that Gaelic arrived in what we now call Scotland by around 500 AD, when the language began its expansion over much of Scotland. Around the beginning of the twelfth century a long decline began in terms of status, speaker numbers and usage, as well as a geographical contraction north and west (e.g. Withers 1988b: 136–38). Perceptions of division between 'Highland' and 'Lowland' emerged from around 1400 onwards (Withers 1988a: 4), whereby the Gael was seen as culturally distinct (Withers 1988a: 14–15). The earliest spatial extent for the 'Gàidhealtachd' has been calculated from the year 1698, based on a list of parishes for the planned distribution of Irish Gaelic Bibles (Withers 1984a: 33, 1982). Such a delineation, predicated on linguistic differentiation, created a notional Highland boundary which altered little in perception until the late nineteenth century (e.g. Selkirk 1806; Walker 1808; Murray 1873; Ravenstein 1879; and Thomson 1994: 109–14).

Historical speaker-group enumeration

As population data became both more comprehensive and reliable, a focus emerged on enumerating the dynamics of Gaelic decline. Alexander Webster's 1755 population survey of Scotland, (in Walker 1808 and see Kyd 1952) arguably offers the first measurable account of the Gaelic-speaking demography of Scotland giving a figure of 289,798, approximately 22.9% of Scotland's population (see, among others, Glaser 2007: 64; MacAulay 1992: 141).

Estimates of earlier Gaelic speaker numbers have been founded on whether Gaelic was used in worship or ordinarily in daily discourse but it is not generally possible to make any claim to historical accuracy about speaking, reading or writing ability in Gaelic (Withers 1986: 36–37). The paucity of hard data makes it difficult to accurately map the true areal and numerical extent of the Scottish Gaelic speaker population, at least until the advent of the UK-wide census in 1841. The phrasing of census questions from 1881 onwards allow assessment against a specific language question, when 6.2% of the Scottish population were enumerated as 'habitually Gaelic speaking'. Table 2.2 shows historical data for the Gaelic-speaking Scottish population.

Source	Population of Scotland	Gaelic-only speakers	Gaelic-only speakers as % of the total population	Gaelic and English speakers	Gaelic and English speakers as % of the total population
Walker, 1808[a]	1,265,380	289,798	22.9	No data	No data
Selkirk, 1806[b]	1,608,420	297,823	18.5	No data	No data
1881 Census	3,735,573	231,594	6.2	No data	No data
1891 Census	4,025,647	43,738	1.1	210,677	5.2
1901 Census	4,472,103	28,106	0.6	202,700	4.5
1911 Census	4,760,904	18,400	0.4	183,998	3.9
1921 Census	4,573,471	9,829	0.2	148,950	3.3
1931 Census	4,588,909	6,716	0.1	129,419	2.8
1951 Census	5,096,415	2,178	0.04	93,269	1.8
1961 Census	5,179,344	974	0.01	80,004	1.5
1971 Census	5,228,965	477	0.009	88,415	1.7
1981 Census	5,035,315	No data	No data	82,620	1.6

Table 2.2 *1755–1981 Number and percentage of Gaelic speakers; after Thomson (1994: 111).*
Note: 'a' = Webster's 1755 survey, in Walker (1808); 'b' = 1801 Census, in Selkirk (1806).

The lack of detail and frequent inaccuracy of census data have been noted by many demolinguists (e.g. Ethnologue, Eberhard *et al.* 2019; FitzGerald 1984). For instance, it is often impossible from census data to ascertain the true nature of the language ability, acquisition or use in a population as data for one census period are essentially static, capturing a particular temporal and spatial point, which might be (mis-) interpreted as stability. Indeed, Thomson bluntly refers to the census returns as 'notoriously inadequate' (see Withers 1984a: v).[8] However, single-period census data may offer insights into gender-differentiated and age-differentiated language ability and use. Past census returns can help construct a picture of out-migration to the Lowlands, and cities, of Scotland, and can indicate the relative strengths of Gaelic speaker populations both within and outwith the Gàidhealtachd.[9]

Kenneth MacKinnon and Charles Withers (see Thomson 1994: 109–14) stated that the earliest studies on Gaelic demographics could be no more specific than to

---

8 Wilson McLeod (2013: 2) points out that census returns are 'a rather crude instrument for measuring language skills and language use … due to the fact that there is no method for differentiating between fluent and non-fluent speakers of Gaelic, or to measure relative frequency of language use, or to validate the claims of those filling in the census. In other words, it is hard to know how accurately the figures reflect the reality on the ground'.

9 This point has contemporary relevance to interpreting community vibrancy among the primary (L1) and secondary acquirers (L2) of Gaelic.

note the presence of the language to a greater or lesser extent in specific areas, but in such a way that it would not be possible to accurately ascertain the exact spatial extent of the areas where Gaelic was spoken, or by how many people, or how frequently they spoke it. It was not possible to ascertain whether Gaelic speakers were solely monoglot Gaelic speakers, or whether they could speak English and whether they chose to use English or not if they were capable of it. Withers (1984a: viii) suggested that his research may in part have been inspired by the idea that previous studies of Scotland's Gaelic past had not succeeded in integrating the historical and socio-geographic perspectives. Withers (1981: 130) emphasised the need for a Gaelic voice, as it were, in academic attempts to describe the dynamics of the Gaelic minority condition. Withers (1988a: 110–12) states that the Gaelic Highlands have been subjected to an 'ideology of transformation' since the 1600s, of which anglicisation was a prerequisite for a broader assimilative project of the Scottish and British civil authorities which sought to transform religious, social and political life in the Highlands:

> The continued use of Gaelic acted, in the eyes of the Crown and Lowland civil authority, as a barrier to effective control over society in the Highlands. Anglicisation had to be a crucial first phase in the transformation of Highland Scotland: only after English had replaced Gaelic would the Highlands be civilised, loyal, and industrious. (Withers 1998a: 110)

In a broader context, the Celtic languages in general have all been subjected to thorough-going and long-established planned initiatives by the homogenising and centralising states which have sought to elaborate and formalise their internal and external power structures with which the non-dominant ethnolinguistic groups were induced or coerced to conform. In this sense, the current (highly-)threatened condition of the Celtic languages is the result of centuries of highly-effective majoritarian language planning.

Higher ability levels vs. lower practice levels
The gap between higher ability levels in Gaelic and lower levels of Gaelic use is, first and foremost, indicative of societal demise (in the community) preceding ability demise (among individuals), a typical scenario in language shift preceding death. It is also, secondarily, an indication of the weakness of the category of ability (in census returns) as a measure of actual language practice or use in social contexts. MacKinnon (2011c: 207) refers to this important minority-language social dichotomy as the 'actuality gap'. It is a central theme in various modules of the IGRP.

2.3.2 A BRIEF OVERVIEW OF CONTEMPORARY GAELIC CENSUS DATA ANALYSIS

In this section, we outline the approach taken by various authors to the analysis of contemporary Gaelic census data in Scotland. The main research we assess and critique is the 2015 report on the Gaelic language data of the 2011 Scotland Census for the National Records of Scotland (NRS). We also deal with the important findings in Iain Mac an Tàilleir (2010, 2015), MacKinnon (2011a, 2014) and McLeod (2005a). In recent times, the NRS have produced a specific decennial report which provides an analysis of the Gaelic language data recorded in the national census. A report on the Gaelic language data of the 2011 Census was commissioned by the NRS and produced by Fiona O'Hanlon and Lindsay Paterson (2015a,b). The analysis by age cohorts of the national data corroborates the findings of Lamb (2008), K. MacLeod (2017), MacKinnon (2010a, 2011c), Mac an Tàilleir (2010) and of the IGRP concerning the decline in Gaelic ability among the younger age cohorts, indicating the typical scenario of language shift:

> In 2011, the incidence of people [in Scotland] who were able to speak Gaelic was below the national average (1.1 per cent) up to age 7, and then remained above it (except at age 11) until age 15. The incidence of Gaelic speaking was below the national average at ages 16 and 17 and in all the age bands from 18 to 24 up to 45 to 54. It then rises above the national average again for people aged 55 and over. The peak incidence of Gaelic-speaking ability was at ages 75 and over (1.2 per cent), 65 to 74 (1.4 per cent) and at age 8 (1.3 per cent). (O'Hanlon and Paterson 2015b: 11)

In other words, Gaelic ability is commonest among those 55 years and over, and receives an apparent boost in the younger school-going cohort (presumably as a result of GME: 3.4.2–3.4.4; cp. 4.10.1.2; 4.10.2.1; 4.11.3). The O'Hanlon and Paterson NRS report comprises three levels of geographic analysis: (1) National (Scotland); (2) the 32 Council Areas in all of Scotland; and (3) the 871 Civil Parishes in all of Scotland (O'Hanlon and Paterson 2015a: 5). The report states that: 'Civil parish band was selected as the unit of analysis as census information has been analysed at this level of geography since 1891, and with the present boundaries since 1931, thus offering opportunities for historical comparison' (O'Hanlon and Paterson 2015a: 5).

The format of data depiction in O'Hanlon and Paterson's (2015a) report is primarily focused on civic national requirements of depicting national trends and speaker numbers in school-age cohorts, often attributable to Gaelic-medium education. This focus is for national stakeholders (2015a: 27; 2015b: 68). Addressing the national requirement, however, should not detract, in the case of minoritised languages, from a more in-depth scrutiny of comparisons and trajectories of speaker numbers, household usage and generational change in areas with higher or significant speaker densities, i.e. the linguistic geography of the existing community of speakers. From this point of view, there has been a gap in the NRS reports between national presentation and more local analysis on the communal and social salience of Gaelic.

In O'Hanlon and Paterson (2015a), seven custom-broken percentage bands are used. As shown in Table 2.3, each band is defined by its specific percentages of the population of a civil parish recorded as Gaelic speakers. Band A is the highest category and comprises 50% or more of the population. Band B comprises between 25% and less than 50% of the population. Band C comprises between 10% and less than 25%. Band D comprises between 5% and less than 10%; Band E 1.095% to less than 5%; Band F comprises more than 0% to less than 1.095%; with Band G representing civil parishes with 0% Gaelic speakers.

Civil Parish Bands	% Gaelic speakers
A	50%+
B	25% to less than 50%
C	10% to less than 25%
D	5% to less than 10%
E	1.095% to less than 5%
F	more than 0% to less than 1.095%
G	0%

Table 2.3 Civil parish bands and percentage Gaelic speakers in O'Hanlon and Paterson (2015a)

The custom bands in the report, however, do not provide the 'detailed picture' mentioned by the authors in the following quote:

> The lower threshold of band E (greater than 1.095 per cent) corresponds to civil parishes where the incidence of Gaelic-speaking ability across all people resident in the parish is greater than the incidence of Gaelic-speaking ability across all people resident in Scotland (1.095 per cent). The thresholds of the other civil parish band categories were determined by a wish to provide a detailed picture of the distribution of Gaelic speakers across a range of Gaelic linguistic communities, and to compare the social and economic characteristics of Gaelic speakers living in such different linguistic contexts. (O'Hanlon and Paterson 2015a: 5)

In fact, the approach of the 2015 NRS report of, for instance, banding all areas above 50% together, is problematic for two main reasons: band colouring on the maps and the lack of detail above 50% speaker densities. All civil parishes above 0% (Band G) are depicted by shades of blue on a map of Scotland. This shading misleadingly suggests, at first glance at least, that Gaelic is more prevalent nationally than in the actual reality of speaker densities, numbers or frequencies of use. Furthermore, some of the shading is indistinct, rendering it hard to distinguish between the bands. The data reveal that, in the decade to 2011, those bands with the highest proportion of residents who reported ability in Gaelic saw the largest proportional falls in speaker numbers; levels of distribution spread across the bands indicate a generalised fall in numbers, despite percentage increases in the younger age cohorts. In terms of age cohorts, significant percentage increases in numbers reporting Gaelic ability were recorded between 2001 and 2011 for the 0–2 age group (26.5%), 3–4 age group (30.0%) and 18–24 age group (12%). For over-25s, however, the trend was uniformly negative: 25–34 (-10.0%); 35–49 (-3.4%); 50–64 (-2.7%); 65 and over (-4.8%) (O'Hanlon and Paterson 2015a; 2015b). Of those people enumerated as having Gaelic ability 45% were aged 50 or over. The combination of the insufficiently-detailed banding with the large-scale level of geographical analysis (i.e. the civil parish; see 2.4.3), hampers analysis of speaker densities in the Gaelic communities. Gaelic ability at the civil parish level has dropped in the 2011 Census to below 65% or less and such low densities conflate areas with higher and lower densities of residents with Gaelic ability. According to the 2011 Census there are five civil parishes that have Gaelic ability levels at or above 60% of the population: Barvas (64%), Barra (62%), North Uist (62%), South Uist and Harris (both on 60%).

Other approaches to the analysis of Gaelic language census data, including those of Mac an Tàilleir (2006; 2010; 2015), have concentrated on demographic changes throughout the 20th century and likely future trajectories. For example, Mac an Tàilleir (2010) undertook an analysis of Gaelic language census data at the civil parish level. He also acquired disaggregated data at the township level, comparing those areas which in 1901 recorded levels of 75%+ (of Gaelic ability) to the percentage levels of the corresponding areas in 2001. In this way, he assessed the Gaelic language vitality of these townships and areas. Drawing on the yardsticks implemented in Ireland in the 1920s as a comparison to the areas now regarded as 'Gaelic-speaking' in Scotland, Mac an Tàilleir (2010: 20) says:

> Tha e inntinneach, nuair a chuireadh Saorstát Éireann air chois anns na 1920an, gur e 80% an t-slat-tomhais a chuirte gu feum ann a bhith a' buileachadh inbhe oifigeil Gaeltachta air àite sam bith. Aig an àm sin, thugadh Gaeltacht air còrr is 180 ceàrnaidh, ach chan eil ach an deicheamh cuid dhiubh sin air fhàgail a rèir rannsachadh Uí Mhurchadha (2001), agus gu math nas lugha na sin an Alba a rèir a' phàipeir seo.

> [It is interesting that when the Irish State was founded in the 1920s, 80% (ability in Irish) was the yardstick used for awarding official status as a Gaeltacht area. At that time, over 180 districts were designated as being Gaeltacht areas, but only 10% of those areas are left now according

to research by Ó Murchadha (2001) and far fewer than that in Scotland according to this paper.][10]

In a more recent study, Mac an Tàilleir (2015) utilises data for council areas and civil parishes to draw out broader trends from the 2011 Census (such as the fact that 48.5% of residents with Gaelic ability live in the Lowland council areas, in the so-called Galltachd), as well as more detailed comparable data for townships. In the analysis by Mac an Tàilleir (2015: 35–36) only two non-contiguous township areas (i.e. Island of Scalpay in North Harris; and Na Meadhanan in South Uist) were identified which had over 75% of residents recorded with Gaelic ability in 2011. This compares to three township areas with over 80% in 2001. Nevertheless, Mac an Tàilleir's analysis (*ibid.* 45–49) has also highlighted that some township areas have seen decadal increases in proportions with Gaelic ability of as much as 10% from 2001 to 2011. These township areas included Garryvaltos (Gearraidh Bhailteas/Milton)/Askernish (+10%), Shader/ Ballantrushal (+3%), Keose (+4%), Balivanich (+7%), and Vatersay (+3%).

Similar to Mac an Tàilleir's analysis of higher-percentage areas, MacKinnon (2011a) emphasised the critical importance of a high-density Gaelic speaker group within localities:

> The significance of these Gaelic-predominating areas is that local incidence needs to equal or exceed 70.711% for the chances of random encounters between local Gaelic speakers to exceed 50%. In the case of simple majority areas, this chance factor reduces to 25%+. By 2001 only Barvas in northern Lewis could be said to be Gaelic-predominating (with a 74.7% incidence of Gaelic speakers). (MacKinnon 2011a: 1)

Based on MacKinnon's analysis, therefore, predominance can be defined as a situation where 70%+ of the resident population report an ability in Gaelic.

MacKinnon's more recent work (e.g. 2011a; 2011b; 2011c, 2014) has suggested a shift in priority, from analysing the demolinguistic contraction of Gaelic in what used to be termed 'the Gaelic heartland' to assessing the context of Gaelic ability and practice outside those areas. Taking a wider perspective beyond sub-regional data analysis, McLeod (2005a: 182) speaks of perceptions of Gaelic in the latter decades of the 20th century becoming more 'national', and, therefore, he juxtaposes the albeit limited state and institutional provision for Gaelic on a Scotland-wide scale with the loss of the traditional 'heartland'. The emphasis on the national debate chimes with the increased provision for primarily urban Gaelic learners with marginal network engagement, the increased focus on the challenges of low speaker densities

---

10 Translations from Gaelic to English are provided by the IGRP authors unless otherwise indicated. The term Gaeltacht refers to officially designated Irish-speaking districts in parts of seven counties in the Irish Republic (according to 1956 and 2012 Acts).

(mainly in the Central Belt) and the challenging aspirations of creating functional Gaelic communities in the future in Scotland. There are clear contradictions in these aspirations.[11] For instance, in comparing vibrancy indicators (of relative strength of usage and ability), McLeod (2013) states:

> While the growth in younger speakers is a positive indicator, it would be a serious mistake to equate children who acquire the language in schools in urban areas, living in homes and communities where there are few opportunities to use Gaelic, with older, first-language speakers living in predominantly Gaelic-speaking areas where Gaelic is widely used in the community. The fact that only 52% of people in the Western Isles can now speak Gaelic is profoundly discouraging. (McLeod 2013: 2)

2.3.3 LEVELS OF BILINGUAL ACQUISITION AND COMPETENCE IN GAELIC

In this section we discuss the various levels of bilingual acquisition and competence in Gaelic found among the population of the Research Area (RA). It is common in language shift situations that minority-language acquisition is less than complete. Our interpretation of the census figures, in the context of this multi-modular research, is that there is a sliding scale of various levels of Gaelic ability and practice in the RA. A static reading of minority-language census data can, of course, mask contrasts in the normative targets associated with the asymmetrical bilingual dynamic of acquiring English as a dominant societal language, generally yielding full acquisition of English, and acquiring Gaelic to a level commensurate with its generational, institutional and/or minoritised function, generally yielding less than full acquisition of Gaelic in younger speakers. As a result of two inter-related aspects of the sociolinguistic make-up of the islands in the study, i.e. a) the *lingua franca* function of English and b) the bilingual dimension of Gaelic language functionality, we can assume that nearly all the RA inhabitants broadly correspond to a target of normative functional acquisition in English. In short, the vast majority are high-functioning English speakers and users. 48% of inhabitants in the RA have acquired or are acquiring a competence in English only, given that they report no competence in Gaelic. For the 52% of the population in the RA for whom Gaelic ability is reported in the 2011 Scottish Census, however, a similar normative profile of Gaelic acquisition (similar to high English competence) cannot be assumed. We cannot assume that all of the 52% are high-functioning Gaelic speakers and users (see section 8.4.4; as well as, for instance, data showing probable results of GME participation (Figure 2.7, 2.4.1.1)). In fact, Gaelic

---

11 There is a view in some policy circles that prioritising high status and Scotland-wide initiatives can compensate for vernacular loss (8.4.1.1).

ability in this subgroup of the population (52%) could be interpreted according to (at least) nine competence profiles:

- A full acquirer of native Gaelic
- An incomplete acquirer of native Gaelic
- A bilingual acquirer of Gaelic as an additional language to English in a bilingual English-Gaelic household
- A bilingual acquirer of Gaelic due to Gaelic inputs from extended familial or communal networks
- A school acquirer of Gaelic
- A partial acquirer of Gaelic from educational inputs
- A learner of Gaelic who has not acquired functional competence
- A person familiar with several Gaelic words and phrases
- A person with very low or no ability in Gaelic but reported as having an ability in Gaelic (for instance, out of a desire to express support for Gaelic).

The Gaelic-reporting proportion of the RA population could be sub-divided into those nine profiles of differing competences or social productivity in Gaelic, ranging between full Gaelic competence and non-fluent aspirational Gaelic ability (and identity). In contrast, as mentioned above, the sociolinguistic profile for the English-speaking networks corresponds to a more uniform profile of both normative competence and language practice, with the possible exception of the language practice of the relatively small population of immigrants from non-English-speaking cultures.

In a similar vein, the interpretation of Gaelic ability in households where all family members are reported as having a competence in Gaelic could refer, for instance, to the following 10 profiles:

- A household in which all members speak Gaelic as the primary means of communication, with the competence of the traditional acquisition of Gaelic
- A household in which all members speak Gaelic as the primary means of communication, but at an incomplete level of Gaelic acquisition among some of the household, most especially among the young
- A household in which the adults/parents/guardians speak Gaelic among themselves but not with the children
- A household in which the adult(s) speak(s) Gaelic among themselves (and with their own age cohort) and where the children have acquired their competence from school
- A household in which the adults have a competence in Gaelic and do not speak it in the home
- A household in which the children have a competence in Gaelic and do not speak it in the home

- A household in which the adults and the children have a competence in Gaelic and do not speak it in the home
- A household in which the adults do not have a competence in Gaelic but are reported as having a competence in Gaelic out of a desire to express support for Gaelic
- A household in which the children do not have a competence in Gaelic but are reported as having a competence in Gaelic out of a desire to express support for Gaelic
- A household in which the adults and the children do not have a competence in Gaelic but are reported as having a competence in Gaelic out of a desire to express support for Gaelic.

From this perspective of multiple sociolinguistic profiles or practices, the census figures necessarily represent a substantial oversimplification of actual sociolinguistic complexity, in particular the lacunae in the reporting of nonpractice and incomplete acquisition of Gaelic. And in this respect, the census data portray the most positive depiction of Gaelic ability and use which can be indicated in demolinguistic data. In juxtaposing the language data from the Census with the data and profile analysis in Chapters 3, 4, 5 and 6 of this IGRP report, we present a more realistic portrayal of Gaelic-language practices and competences (cp. fluency vs. conversational ability as a more accurate indicator of practice in section 4.5.4).

2.3.4 OTHER DEMOGRAPHIC AND SOCIO-ECONOMIC ASPECTS OF GAELIC DEMOLINGUISTIC FRAGILITY

The consultancy group Hall Aitken in conjunction with Ionad Nàiseanta na h-Imrich produced a report on behalf of Comhairle nan Eilean Siar, Western Isles Enterprise and Communities Scotland (2007) which indicated the challenging demographic and socio-economic issues faced by the Western Isles. The report showed a population decline of around 40% in the Western Isles between 1901 and 2001, alongside concerns about an ageing population and continuing out-migration of younger age cohorts for reasons of education, employment and housing. MacKinnon (2011a, 2014) provides analysis of migratory trends and challenges in Gaelic-speaking communities.

The employment opportunities available in the Western Isles were reported as not matching the expectations of those entering the labour market and/or were not suitable for the labour market qualifications of the local population. Consequently, there is an evident out-migration of the economically active population, particularly within the younger age cohorts, with the subsequent impact on school rolls at primary and secondary levels. The research findings also indicated that more females migrated out of the Western Isles than in the case of males, due to lack of suitable employment opportunities (sectors such as fishing, agriculture and construction being traditionally male-oriented). A view also emerged from interviews and focus groups that the 'economic and social expectations of women have changed more quickly over the past ten or so years than that amongst men' (Hall Aitken 2007: 23).

In addition to local-level analysis of population issues and challenges, the National Records of Scotland also produce population projections for Local Authority and sub-Authority localities. The 2012-based principal population projections by age cohorts for the Western Isles are set out in Table 2.4. The projections in the table confirm the demographic challenges (and related socio-economic effects) of significant contractions identified by the Hall Aitken report. For instance, the youth cohort in all rural localities is projected to fall by between 54% and 61%, with projected loss of 28% for all of the Western Isles. The only area showing predicted relatively stable population with 9% overall growth is the Stornoway district.

Area	Number of people			Percentage change	
Western Isles	**2012**	**2026**	**2037**	**2012–26**	**2012–37**
All Ages	27,560	26,115	24,615	-5%	-11%
0–17	5,225	4,378	3,772	-18%	-28%
18–49	10,002	7,843	6,658	-22%	-33%
50+	12,333	13,963	14,185	13%	15%
Lewis (excl. Stornoway) and Harris					
All Ages	8,417	7,331	6,295	-13%	-25%
0–17	1,389	893	635	-36%	-54%
18–49	2,741	1,708	1,087	-38%	-60%
50+	4,287	4,730	4,572	10%	7%
Stornoway (Stornoway-Point-Broadbay)					
All Ages	13,092	13,752	14,233	5%	9%
0–17	2,642	2,624	2,670	-1%	1%
18–49	5,142	4,977	4,920	-3%	-4%
50+	5,308	6,151	6,644	16%	25%
Uist and Barra					
All Ages	6,051	5,032	4,086	-17%	-32%
0–17	1,194	792	467	-34%	-61%
18–49	2,119	1,158	651	-45%	-69%
50+	2,738	3,082	2,968	13%	8%

Table 2.4 *Projections of population change for the Western Isles, as well as local breakdown; 2012–2026 and 2012–2037. Source: National Records of Scotland. Note: The reliability of projections decreases further into the future. Therefore, caution should be used particularly with the projections for 2037.*

2.4 GAELIC DEMOLINGUISTICS

2.4.1 ANALYSIS OF REPORTED ABILITY IN GAELIC

We provide the analysis of the census data in four main sections: (1) reported ability in Gaelic per Study District; (2) reported ability in Gaelic per Pooled Study District; (3) reported Gaelic use in Family Households; and (4) Standardised Incidence Ratios.

2.4.1.1 *STUDY DISTRICTS BY GAELIC ABILITY AND AGE COHORTS*

The following two tables provide a summary from the census returns on reported ability in Gaelic for the 2011 Census (Table 2.5) and comparative data from 1981, 1991, 2001 and 2011 (Table 2.6).[12] The tables indicate both the numbers and percentages of those with reported ability in Gaelic both in the entire population of the Research Area and according to Aggregated Age Cohorts in the Study Districts and in the rest of Scotland (see **Appendix A2.1** for additional data and comparisons).

As stated, Table 2.6 provides a comparative summary of reported ability in Gaelic in the 1981–2011 census periods for each of the Study Districts and for the rest of Scotland. The data are adapted from the following official resources: Table CT_0079a_2011 / Table CT_0079a_2001 / Table CT_0079a_1991 / Table CT_0079a_1981.

---

12 Crown copyright 2016. For further information on variables in the presented tables, see www.scotlandscensus.gov.uk/variables. In order to protect against disclosure of personal information, some records have been swapped between SDs so that some cell values will be affected, particularly those with small values.

2011	All people aged 3 and over			Aged 3 to 17			Aged 18 to 49			Aged 50+		
Study District	Total	Speaks Gaelic	Speaks Gaelic (%)	Total	Speaks Gaelic	Speaks Gaelic (%)	Total	Speaks Gaelic	Speaks Gaelic (%)	Total	Speaks Gaelic	Speaks Gaelic (%)
01. West Side of Lewis (central)	1,012	635	62.75	174	75	43.10	340	180	52.94	498	380	76.31
02. West Side of Lewis (south)	807	476	58.98	122	65	53.28	293	155	52.90	392	256	65.31
03. Uig District	760	397	52.24	112	42	37.50	241	104	43.15	407	251	61.67
04. West Side of Lewis (north)	933	614	65.81	129	79	61.24	349	199	57.02	455	336	73.85
05. Ness	1,228	788	64.17	207	121	58.45	412	231	56.07	609	436	71.59
06. Tolsta	491	277	56.42	105	37	35.24	156	62	39.74	230	178	77.39
07. Loch a Tuath	1,525	833	54.62	331	143	43.20	613	288	46.98	581	402	69.19
08. Tong	614	269	43.81	130	34	26.15	266	116	43.61	218	119	54.59
09. Stornoway, Barvas Road suburbs	1,606	671	41.78	365	100	27.40	728	254	34.89	513	317	61.79
10. Stornoway Town	4,861	1,906	39.21	711	188	26.44	2,001	573	28.64	2,149	1,145	53.28
11. Stornoway, Point Road suburbs	1,353	519	38.36	236	50	21.19	538	169	31.41	579	300	51.81
12. South Point	1,428	690	48.32	262	85	32.44	567	222	39.15	599	383	63.94
13. North Point	757	327	43.20	131	38	29.01	271	79	29.15	355	210	59.15
14. North Lochs	873	456	52.23	125	35	28.00	320	125	39.06	428	296	69.16
15. South Lochs	889	486	54.67	150	69	46.00	303	146	48.18	436	271	62.16
16. North Harris	955	618	64.71	124	79	63.71	319	174	54.55	512	365	71.29
17. South Harris	914	521	57.00	128	55	42.97	297	161	54.21	489	305	62.37
18. North Uist (north & west)	955	583	61.05	134	74	55.22	306	178	58.17	515	331	64.27
19. North Uist (south & east)	624	377	60.42	70	40	57.14	212	124	58.49	342	213	62.28
20. Benbecula	1,283	678	52.84	251	120	47.81	555	269	48.47	477	289	60.59
21. South Uist (north)	867	570	65.74	181	109	60.22	313	204	65.18	373	257	68.90
22. South Uist (south)	972	640	65.84	165	119	72.12	342	202	59.06	465	319	68.60
23. Barra and Vatersay	1,222	761	62.27	249	137	55.02	445	257	57.75	528	367	69.51
24. Staffin, Skye	469	233	49.68	67	48	71.64	165	69	41.82	237	116	48.95
25. Isle of Tiree	626	240	38.34	92	47	51.09	210	57	27.14	324	136	41.98
Total: Research Area	28,024	14,565	51.97	4,751	1,989	41.86	10,562	4,598	43.53	12,711	7,978	62.76
Rest of Scotland	5,090,199	43,037	0.85	860,666	7,167	0.83	2,308,670	17,739	0.77	1,920,863	18,131	0.94
Total: Scotland	5,118,223	57,602	1.13	865,417	9,156	1.06	2,319,232	22,337	0.96	1,933,574	26,109	1.35

Table 2.5 *Reported ability in Gaelic in the 2011 Scottish Census (Adapted from Table Ct_0079a_2011 Spoken Ability in Gaelic: Study Districts by Age with Percent)*[13]

With the exception of Benbecula and Stornoway, all the Study Districts are marked with descending sparklines (small line charts) indicating percentage decline in reported ability in Gaelic and a fall in the overall number of residents with Gaelic ability from the 1981 to the 2011 period. The aggregated category 'Rest of Scotland' shows a decrease for aggregated all ages but an increase for the 3–17 age cohort in reported ability in Gaelic from 0.51% in 1981 to 0.83% in 2011. In the national context (all of Scotland), census returns reveal a less extreme and more gradual recent trajectory of decline across Scotland, as the percentage of those aged three and older reported as having ability in Gaelic fell from 1.64% of the population in 1981 to 1.37% ten years later, to 1.20% in 2001, and to 1.13% in the 2011 Census.

13 The standard statistical outputs, issued by the NRS, on Gaelic ability for the 2011 Census indicate that 57,375 people in Scotland have an ability in spoken Gaelic. The figure of 57,375 entails combining categories of responses to the Gaelic language question to constitute the 'Speaks Gaelic' classification. The corresponding figure in the IGRP is 57,602. The higher value in the IGRP (higher by 227) can be explained by the inclusion of the 'Speaks and writes but does not read' Gaelic responses from the NRS category of 'Other combination of skills in Gaelic'.

TRENDS	ALL AGES (aged 3+)					AGED 3 to 17					AGED 18 to 49					AGED 50+				
1981 to 2011	Gaelic Speakers (%)				TREND	Gaelic Speakers (%)				TREND	Gaelic Speakers (%)				TREND	Gaelic Speakers (%)				TREND
Study Districts	1981	1991	2001	2011		1981	1991	2001	2011		1981	1991	2001	2011		1981	1991	2001	2011	
01. West Side of Lewis (central)	95.4	86.5	73.3	62.7		91.1	75.8	50.5	43.1		94.3	85.8	70.7	52.9		98.7	92.4	86.2	76.3	
02. West Side of Lewis (south)	90.3	79.8	70.4	59.0		84.7	68.7	70.3	53.3		85.3	71.9	62.0	52.9		96.5	90.7	78.3	65.3	
03. Uig District	89.3	79.9	68.6	52.2		85.9	68.1	62.4	37.5		83.9	73.4	55.6	43.2		94.5	87.1	80.7	61.7	
04. West Side of Lewis (north)	95.6	83.6	74.3	65.8		92.2	64.9	62.0	61.2		93.5	82.5	69.3	57.0		99.2	94.9	83.8	73.8	
05. Ness	94.6	88.9	76.2	64.2		91.6	82.1	67.2	58.5		93.3	86.5	69.4	56.1		97.0	94.1	83.5	71.6	
06. Tolsta	91.1	81.2	72.4	56.4		85.4	59.6	37.8	35.2		87.6	80.8	65.9	39.7		99.0	93.3	89.9	77.4	
07. Loch a Tuath	88.2	75.8	65.6	54.6		81.9	59.3	51.3	43.2		87.5	73.7	58.6	47.0		93.0	91.0	82.3	69.2	
08. Tong	79.6	64.9	55.2	43.8		65.8	38.0	37.0	26.2		85.7	62.9	45.7	43.6		84.5	87.8	76.6	54.6	
09. Stornoway, Barvas Road	69.6	53.3	49.0	41.8		47.0	24.9	31.5	27.4		68.6	46.4	39.3	34.9		88.6	82.4	73.9	61.8	
10. Stornoway Town	57.9	49.1	45.0	39.2		35.5	21.0	26.3	26.4		55.3	43.0	35.9	28.6		77.8	73.1	62.5	53.3	
11. Stornoway, Point Road	65.5	47.4	45.0	38.4		38.4	16.2	28.3	21.2		62.7	43.1	34.6	31.4		87.0	75.8	64.2	51.8	
12. South Point	86.0	68.7	59.3	48.3		70.5	46.7	39.7	32.4		85.8	64.6	53.7	39.2		95.5	88.1	76.2	63.9	
13. North Point	81.2	62.8	53.2	43.2		66.8	44.4	24.8	29.0		80.2	56.4	43.2	29.2		93.9	85.3	75.7	59.2	
14. North Lochs	89.8	78.1	61.9	52.2		83.3	59.8	33.6	28.0		87.1	75.3	53.9	39.1		96.0	90.2	78.4	69.2	
15. South Lochs	89.6	76.0	63.0	54.7		80.6	50.0	42.4	46.0		86.9	70.1	53.1	48.2		95.0	91.5	79.6	62.2	
16. North Harris	90.6	83.7	70.3	64.7		89.0	75.2	59.1	63.7		88.9	81.4	61.0	54.5		92.7	88.6	80.0	71.3	
17. South Harris	88.5	78.6	69.1	57.0		84.2	67.0	54.1	43.0		85.9	72.8	67.2	54.2		92.1	87.6	75.9	62.4	
18. North Uist (north & west)	87.8	76.9	67.6	61.0		86.2	62.1	59.7	55.2		82.0	72.5	64.4	58.2		94.7	89.6	74.2	64.3	
19. North Uist (south & east)	86.2	74.1	69.0	60.4		83.5	63.1	55.7	57.1		82.1	69.9	69.0	58.5		92.9	85.8	76.0	62.3	
20. Benbecula	52.4	52.7	58.1	52.8		46.1	41.3	50.6	47.8		46.0	49.2	53.4	48.5		86.3	79.4	71.0	60.6	
21. South Uist (north)	85.9	77.9	70.6	65.7		80.5	74.1	70.5	60.2		83.5	74.4	70.7	65.2		94.4	88.1	70.6	68.9	
22. South Uist (south)	91.3	81.6	75.3	65.8		89.3	72.4	59.9	72.1		89.6	77.7	71.3	59.1		95.9	92.1	86.2	68.6	
23. Barra and Vatersay	86.2	76.1	68.5	62.3		82.7	68.4	55.8	55.0		83.5	74.7	66.7	57.8		94.3	84.0	77.9	69.5	
24. Staffin, Skye	88.6	79.5	62.7	49.7		89.4	74.1	64.0	71.6		85.9	77.3	56.6	41.8		90.6	84.3	69.3	48.9	
25. Isle of Tiree	74.3	59.3	47.9	38.3		61.4	50.0	50.3	51.1		69.7	52.3	38.4	27.1		83.1	69.3	54.8	42.0	
Total: Research Area	79.8	68.9	60.6	52.0		69.1	51.0	46.8	41.9		76.0	63.8	53.0	43.5		91.2	85.2	74.5	62.8	
Rest of Scotland	1.1	1.0	0.9	0.8		0.5	0.5	0.7	0.8		1.1	0.9	0.8	0.8		1.7	1.3	1.1	0.9	
Total: Scotland	1.6	1.4	1.2	1.1		1.0	0.9	0.9	1.1		1.5	1.2	1.0	1.0		2.3	1.9	1.6	1.4	

Table 2.6 *Decadal percentage trends in Gaelic ability from the 1981 to the 2011 Scottish Censuses*

Figure 2.1 indicates changes in percentage distributions of reported ability in Gaelic in the four census periods in the 25 Study Districts. This chart is based on data under the heading 'ALL AGES (aged 3+)' in Table 2.6.

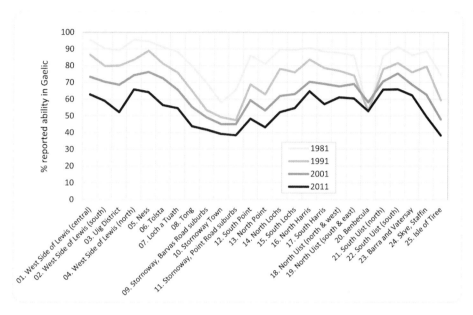

Figure 2.1 Percentage distributions of reported ability in Gaelic in the four census periods in the 25 Study Districts, 1981–2011

The chart indicates what has already been stated, a decline in reported ability in Gaelic from 1981 to 2011 in all Study Districts, except for Benbecula, which emerges as an outlier in the geographic distribution, being far lower in 1981 than surrounding SDs. This was due to its unique circumstances as a military base of predominantly English-speaking staff and families. When a decision was taken to change the base's status, a number of personnel moved out and, perhaps, Gaelic-competent families from other parts of Uist moved in, leading to a comparative rise in reported ability in Gaelic as the proportion of non-Gaelic speakers fell (see section 5.4.2.2).

Figures 2.2 to 2.5 illustrate the Study Districts ranked according to reported ability in Gaelic as recorded in the 2011, 2001, 1991 and 1981 census returns respectively. We also refer to these percentage figures as Crude Vitality Rate. (See **Appendix A2.2** for additional data and comparisons on the highest ranking SDs in the 2011 Census.)

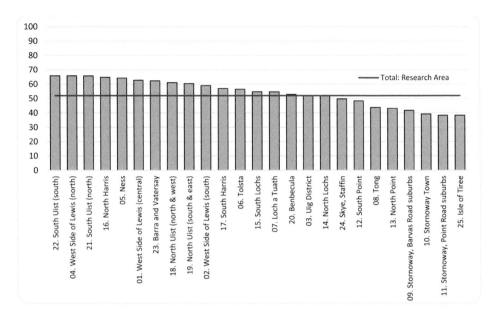

Figure 2.2 *Study Districts ranked by percentages according to reported ability in Gaelic for the 2011 Census*

Figure 2.2 shows that the average percentage ability for the ranked Study Districts in 2011 was 52%, and ranged from 66% in South Uist (south) to 38% in the Isle of Tiree, a spread of 28% points.

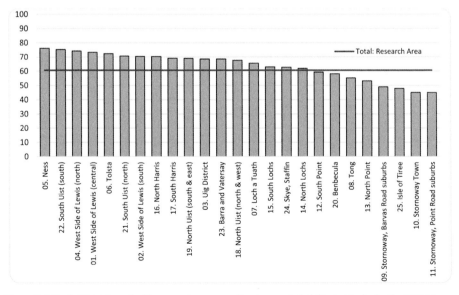

Figure 2.3 *Study Districts ranked by percentages according to reported ability in Gaelic for the 2001 Census*

Figure 2.3 shows that the average percentage ability for the ranked Study Districts in 2001 was 61%, and ranged from 76% in Ness to 45% in Stornoway (Point Road suburbs), a spread of 31% points.

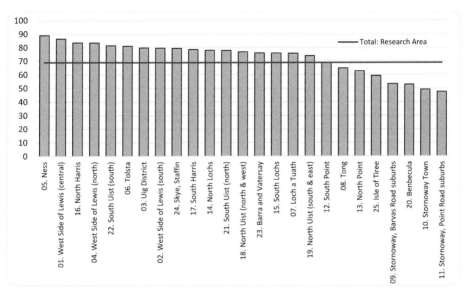

Figure 2.4 Study Districts ranked by percentages according to reported ability in Gaelic for the 1991 Census

Figure 2.4 shows that the average percentage ability for the ranked Study Districts in 1991 was 69%, and ranged from 89% in Ness to 47% in the Stornoway (Point Road suburbs), a spread of 42% points.

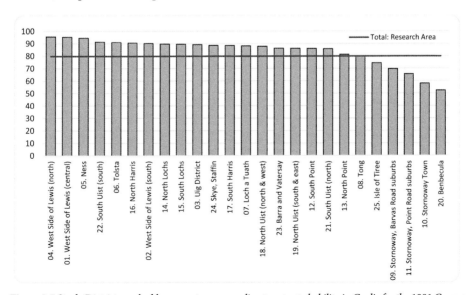

Figure 2.5 Study Districts ranked by percentages according to reported ability in Gaelic for the 1981 Census

Figure 2.5 shows that the average percentage ability indicated in the ranked Study Districts in 1981 was 80%, and ranged from 96% in the West Side of Lewis (north) to 52% in Benbecula, a spread of 44% points.

By combining the curves based on Figures 2.2–2.5, in Figure 2.6a we illustrate the Study Districts in independent descending order according to reported ability in Gaelic in the four census periods 1981–2011.[14] This figure corresponds to the data in the left-hand set of columns labelled 'ALL AGES' in Table 2.6. Besides indicating a general decrease, the graphs also indicate a change in the distribution pattern. The curve of the 1981 Census drops at the c. 85% value. This drop marks an important tipping point in the profile of the Research Area (section 2.4.1.5.1). A similar, though less pronounced, tipping point is distinguishable in the curve of the 1991 Census (at the c. 75% value), while it is not distinguishable in the curves of the 2001 and 2011 Censuses where the distribution flatlines

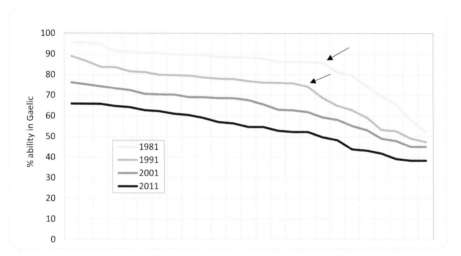

Figure 2.6a Percentage ability in Gaelic for all ages in Study Districts, in independent descending percentage order in the 1981–2011 census periods

In Figure 2.6b, we present the ability data of the Study Districts for the three separate age groups in independent descending order in the same four census periods. Therefore, Figure 2.6b contains three times as much detail as the related Figure 2.6a.[15] The data in this figure corresponds to the three sets of columns labelled 'AGED 3 to 17', 'AGED 18 to 49' and 'AGED 50+'.

14 Independent curves here refer to data lines where the point on the horizontal X-axis does not necessarily denote the same SD in the various lines.

15 Figure 2.6b, therefore, contains 75 data points (3 (age groups) x 25 SDs) per census year, whereas Figure 2.6a contains 25 data points per census year.

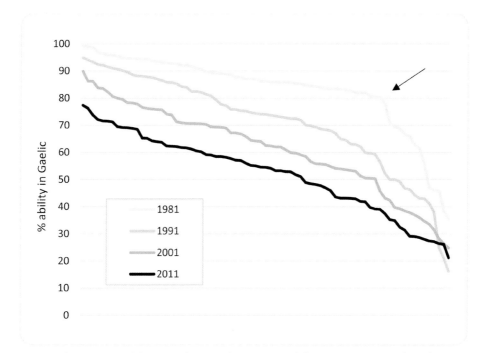

Figure 2.6b *Percentage ability in Gaelic in Study Districts and three age groups, in independent descending percentage order in the 1981–2011 census periods*

In Figure 2.6b, there are also easily discernible tipping points in the data curves for 1981 at 80%, for 1991 at 60% and for 2001 at 50%. As in the related Figure 2.6a, the most striking drops can be seen in the earlier censuses, in particular 1981.

Figure 2.7 shows reported ability in Gaelic for the SDs in the 2011 Census according to age cohorts and in descending order of values pertaining to the 'Aged 50+' age cohort. As is also evident in Table 2.6, the chart reveals that ability in Gaelic is considerably higher among the 'Aged 50+' cohort than in the younger cohorts. In three Study Districts — South Uist (south), Staffin (Skye), and the Isle of Tiree — the reported ability in Gaelic in the 'Aged 3 to 17' age cohort surpassed the reported ability in Gaelic in the 'Aged 50+' age cohort, presumably because of the provision of GME in these SDs. In the case of the two latter SDs (Staffin and Tiree), we find the greatest gap between those 50+ and the 3–17 cohort. The greater ability in the younger age cohort suggests the effect of GME on the Gaelic ability profile in these districts.

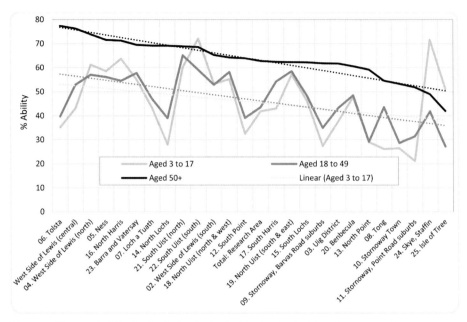

Figure 2.7 *Reported ability in Gaelic for the Study Districts in the 2011 Census according to age cohorts and in descending order of values pertaining to the 'Aged 50+' cohort*

Figure 2.8 illustrates the decline in the number of Gaelic speakers in the 50+ and 3 to 17 age groups in the RA from 1981–2011.

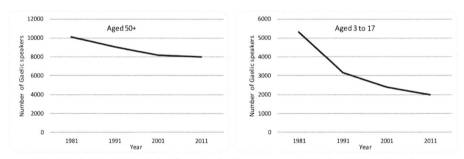

Figure 2.8 *Number of Gaelic speakers per decade illustrating rate of decline in the 50+ and 3 to 17 year-old age groups*

Figure 2.8 shows the faster rate of decline of those with Gaelic ability among the 3–17 age cohort in comparison to those aged 50+. Those with Gaelic ability among the 50+ age group fell from 10,116 to 7,978 in this thirty-year period, whereas the 3–17 age cohort fell from 5,329 to 1,989. Those with Gaelic ability aged 3–17 currently (in 2011) represent 7.1% of the RAs population while the comparable percentage of young Gaelic speakers was 17.6% of the RA population in 1981.

2.4.1.2 POOLED STUDY DISTRICTS

In this section, we analyse and illustrate the Gaelic ability data for larger geographical units. These larger units we term Pooled Study Districts, of which there are seven (Table 2.1). Figure 2.9 illustrates the percentage decrease of reported ability in Gaelic in the 1981–2011 census periods in the Pooled SDs. The greatest decrease occurred in the Staffin & Tiree Pooled SD (46%), while the smallest decrease occurred in the Pooled SD of North Uist & Benbecula (18%; see section 2.1.1). (See **Appendix A2.3** for additional data and comparisons.)

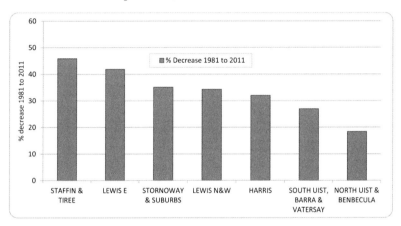

Figure 2.9 *Percentage decrease from 1981–2011 census periods in reported ability in Gaelic in the Pooled Study Districts in descending order*

Figure 2.10 provides a summary of reported ability in Gaelic of all ages (3+) in the 1981–2011 census periods in the Pooled Study Districts.

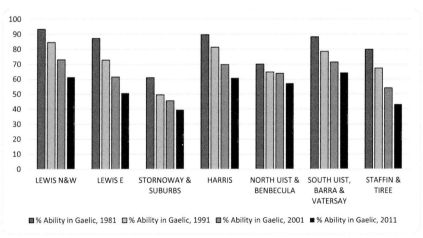

Figure 2.10 *Decadal percentage trends in reported ability in Gaelic in the 1981–2011 census periods in the Pooled Study Districts, in order from north to south of the RA*

Figure 2.10 shows a substantial and consistent decadal decline in all Pooled SDs, except for the less consistent or slower rates of decline in the two Pooled SDs which have relatively important rural-town settlements: Stornoway & Suburbs; and North Uist & Benbecula, both of which started from a lower base. Figure 2.10, therefore, adds decadal detail to the overall decline in Pooled SDs as displayed in Figure 2.9. The highest range in terms of ability in Gaelic is for the Pooled SD of Staffin & Tiree (79% in 1981 to 43% in 2011, a spread of 36% points). This is followed by Lewis East (87% in 1981, 51% in 2011, a spread of 36% points), Lewis North & West (93% in 1981, 61% in 2011, a spread of 32% points), Harris (90% in 1981, 61% in 2011, a spread of 29% points), South Uist, Barra & Vatersay (88% in 1981, 64% in 2011, a spread of 24% points), Stornoway & Suburbs (61% in 1981, 40% in 2011, a spread of 21% points) and North Uist & Benbecula (70% in 1981, 57% in 2011, a spread of 13% points).

2.4.1.3 *REPORTED GAELIC USE IN FAMILY HOUSEHOLDS*

In Table 2.7 we provide a summary of reported use of Gaelic in the 2011 Census for all households with children (aged 3–17 years), i.e. Family Households. The data is shown for the 25 SDs, the whole IGRP Research Area, as well as the rest of Scotland and all of Scotland. The number of Family Households in the RA varies from 41 (Staffin, Skye) to 441 (Stornoway Town) with an average of c. 110 per SD.

Census 2011	All Family Households	Family Households where all adults use Gaelic (%)	Family Households where all children use Gaelic (%)	Family Households where all adults and all children use Gaelic (%)
Study district	BASE (N)	Percentage of all family households which contain both adults and children		
01. West Side of Lewis (central)	97	35.1	30.9	24.7
02. West Side of Lewis (south)	68	38.2	33.8	29.4
03. Uig District	66	21.2	22.7	16.7
04. West Side of Lewis (north)	75	40.0	44.0	36.0
05. Ness	113	40.7	41.6	31.0
06. Tolsta	46	17.4	23.9	13.0
07. Loch a Tuath	182	27.5	28.0	24.2
08. Tong	74	23.0	14.9	12.2
09. Stornoway, Barvas Road suburbs	213	11.7	14.6	7.0
10. Stornoway Town	441	11.3	14.1	8.6
11. Stornoway, Point Road suburbs	144	16.0	16.7	11.8
12. South Point	153	24.2	23.5	17.0
13. North Point	81	14.8	19.8	11.1

Census 2011	All Family Households	Family House-holds where all adults use Gaelic (%)	Family House-holds where all children use Gaelic (%)	Family Households where all adults and all children use Gaelic (%)
Study district	BASE (N)	Percentage of all family households which contain both adults and children		
14. North Lochs	78	21.8	23.1	16.7
15. South Lochs	85	31.8	34.1	23.5
16. North Harris	65	40.0	38.5	26.2
17. South Harris	70	25.7	32.9	20.0
18. North Uist (north & west)	89	34.8	40.4	30.3
19. North Uist (south & east)	43	20.9	25.6	16.3
20. Benbecula	148	19.6	29.1	15.5
21. South Uist (north)	97	45.4	48.5	39.2
22. South Uist (south)	90	41.1	50.0	33.3
23. Barra & Vatersay	135	34.8	40.0	28.1
24. Staffin, Skye	41	39.0	53.7	39.0
25. Isle of Tiree	59	18.6	28.8	15.3
Total: Research Area	2753	24.8	27.6	19.4
Rest of Scotland	531400	0.2	0.3	0.2
Total: Scotland	534153	0.3	0.4	0.3

Table 2.7 *Reported Gaelic use in Family Households based on information in the 2011 Census for the 25 Study Districts, the Research Area, the rest of Scotland and all of Scotland*

Table 2.7 provides the data for the analysis illustrated in Figures 2.11–2.14. The percentages are strikingly low for the rest of Scotland, outside the Research Area, which illustrates the challenge to Gaelic vitality in a national sociogeographic context (see section 2.3.2). In the Research Area we can identify 533 Family Households in which all adults and all children are reported as using Gaelic or 19.4% of all Family Households in the RA. Figure 2.11 illustrates the percentage of Gaelic use in Family Households where all adults are reported to use Gaelic, based on information from the 2011 Census (i.e. the data in the third column from the left in Table 2.7). The highest percentage of these households is 45% in the South Uist (north) Study District and the lowest percentage is 11% in Stornoway Town, with an overall average of 25%.

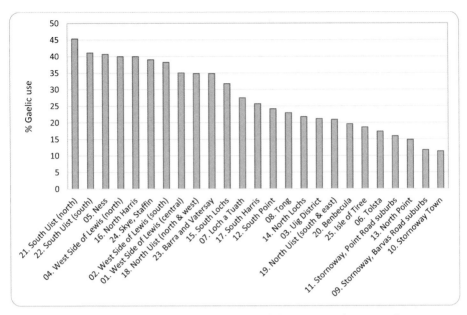

Figure 2.11 Percentage of Family Households where all adults are reported to use Gaelic, in descending order, based on information from the 2011 Census

Figure 2.12 illustrates the percentage of reported use of Gaelic in Family Households where all children are reported to use Gaelic (i.e. data in the second column from left in Table 2.7). The highest percentage of these households is 54% in the Staffin (Skye) Study District and the lowest percentage is 14% in Stornoway Town, with an overall average of 28% for these Family Households.

Figure 2.13 illustrates the percentage of Gaelic use in Family Households where all adults and all children are reported to use Gaelic (i.e. data in the right-hand column in Table 2.7). The highest percentage of these households is 39% in the South Uist (north) SD and the lowest percentage is 7% in Stornoway (Barvas Road suburbs), with an overall average of 19%.

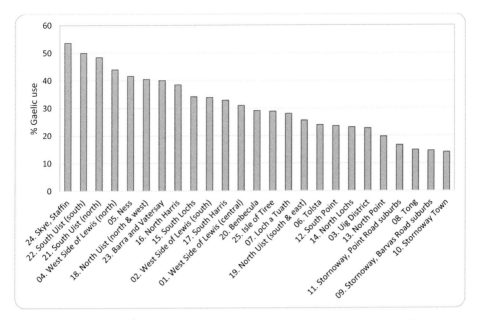

Figure 2.12 Percentage of Family Households where all children are reported to use Gaelic, in descending order, based on information from the 2011 Census

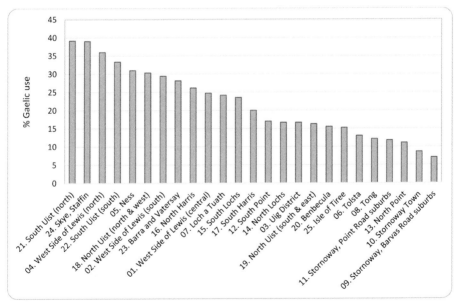

Figure 2.13 Percentage of Family Households where all adults and all children are reported to use Gaelic, in descending order, based on information from the 2011 Census

It is important to analyse the relation between adult use of Gaelic and children's use in Family Households. Adult language use in the family household is a primary driver of children's use. We can therefore ask, in a given household, for instance, what is the relation between the amount of adults who speak Gaelic, on the one hand, and the amount of children who speak Gaelic, on the other? In short, how much of a difference does it make for children's use of Gaelic, whether all adults or only some adults in the Family Household use Gaelic? In order to attempt to answer this question, based on the data in Table 2.7, as well as additional data for Family Households where some adults (i.e. not all) use Gaelic, we analysed only those Family Households where all children use Gaelic. This was to see how such positive outcomes for children's reported Gaelic use in Family Households are achieved. In the Family Households where all children use Gaelic, therefore, we compare in Figure 2.14, for each SD, the percentages of Family Households where all adults use Gaelic to the percentages of Family Households where only some adults (i.e. not all) use Gaelic.[16] For each of the 25 SDs, the dark-coloured data bar on the left indicates the percentage of these Family Households where all adults use Gaelic. The light-coloured data bar on the right for each SD indicates the percentage of these Family Households where some (i.e. not all) adults use Gaelic. It is clear from Figure 2.14 that having all adults using Gaelic in the Family Household has a substantially more positive relation with children's reported Gaelic use than having only some adults using Gaelic. For instance, in SD 06 Tolsta in East Lewis, 75% of Family Households where all adults use Gaelic have all children using Gaelic, in contrast with only 13% of Family Households where some adults use Gaelic having all children using Gaelic. The value of 75% of Tolsta Family Households where all adults use Gaelic in Figure 2.14 corresponds to the 13% of households in the fourth data column in Table 2.7 for Tolsta, which is a subset of the 17.4% of Family Households in the second data column of Table 2.7 for Tolsta. Furthermore, the gravity of this context for Gaelic vitality is underlined by the small subset of Family Households (right-hand column Table 2.7) where all adults and all children use Gaelic. That proportion is 13% for Tolsta SD and 19% of all the Family Households (left-hand data bars in Figure 2.14) in the RA as a whole. That is to say, the left-hand data bars in Figure 2.14 pertain to the data in the right-hand column in Table 2.7 which is a subset of the second data column in the same table.

---

16 In the Research Area, there are only a few Family Households where no adults use Gaelic and all children are reported to use Gaelic. This marginal category of Family Households is not included in Figure 2.14. The Staffin Study District contains 41 households with adults and children, as reported in the 2011 Census. The Census reports that there are 16 Family Households where all adults use Gaelic and, of them, 16 where all children also use Gaelic, corresponding to the 100% categorisation (left-hand data bar) for this profile in Staffin.

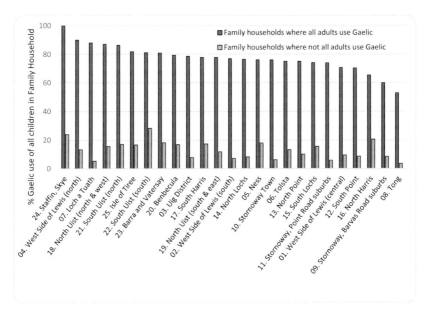

Figure 2.14 *Percentage of Family Households where all children use Gaelic, by Family Households where all adults use Gaelic, and by Family Households where not all adults use Gaelic, in descending order of all adults using Gaelic, based on information from the 2011 Census*

The contrast illustrated in Figure 2.14 is an indication of the importance of the concept of comprehensiveness in minority-language contexts, in particular in relation to language acquisition. The concept of minority-language comprehensiveness highlights the requirement for prioritising contexts where the minority language is dominant, often to the exclusion of the majority language (cf. Fishman's Xmen (1991: 92–105); Lewis and Simons 2016: 184). This concept is also relevant to the S-curve threshold, to the speaker density, and tipping-point phenomena in the minority-language group (see 2.4.1.5.1).

2.4.1.4 *VERNACULAR DEMOGRAPHY IN THE WESTERN ISLES: COMPARISON OF ABILITY WITH USE*

In this section, we compare data on Gaelic ability with its use at home in the Western Isles as reported in the 2011 Census. We restrict our discussion here to the Western Isles to aid comparison with previous datasets and reports going as far back as 1951 (see section 2.4.2). As shown in Table 2.8, in the 3–17 age group, 1,894 have ability in Gaelic and 1,357 (72% of them) use Gaelic at home. In the 18–49 age group, 4,472 have ability in Gaelic and 3,145 (70%) use it at home. In the 50+ age group, 7,726 have ability and 6,380 (83%) use it at home. These represent gaps between ability and use by age group of: 28% (3–17); 30% (18–49) and 17% (50+), with the greatest gaps in the parental and young age cohorts, indicating that the gap has worsened in comparison to the oldest generation in this census data (see section 2.5.1).

Age	Population	Ability in Gaelic		Use Gaelic at home		
		Number	% of age group	Number	% of speakers with Gaelic ability	% of age group
3–17	4,592	1,894	41.2	1,357	71.6	29.6
18–49	10,187	4,472	43.9	3,145	70.3	30.9
50+	12,150	7,726	63.6	6,380	82.6	52.5
Total	26,929	14,092	52.3	10,882	77.2	40.4

Table 2.8 Ability in Gaelic compared with use of Gaelic at home by age groups, Western Isles, 2011 Census

Based on the data in Table 2.8, we compare in Figure 2.15 ability in Gaelic with use of Gaelic at home in the three age cohorts for the Western Isles from the 2011 Census.

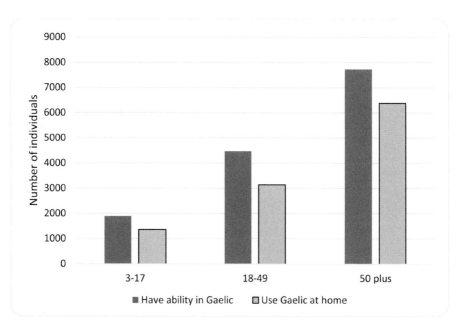

Figure 2.15 Comparison of ability in Gaelic with use of Gaelic at home by age cohorts, Western Isles, 2011 Census

Figure 2.15 reveals that ability in Gaelic is greater than use of Gaelic among all age groups, with the highest Gaelic ability and use in the oldest age group (50+) and the lowest in the youngest age group (3–17). As stated, ability and use decrease from the oldest to the youngest.

It is reasonable to assume that the upper limit of active Gaelic speakers in the Western Isles can be approximated to the number of those who are reported to use Gaelic at home in Census 2011, i.e. 10,882 speakers or 40% of the total population of the Western Isles (Table 2.8).[17] Given the evidence in Chapters 3 and 4 of the even lower level of home use, in comparison to the census data, in particular among the young, the figure of 10,882 is, as stated, an upper limit or the most positive view of vernacular practice. These 10,882 Gaelic speakers are comprised mainly of 50yrs+ (59%) who are dispersed over a large area. For the sake of comparison, the total Gaelic speaker population in the 2011 Census is 57,602 (Table 2.5).

2.4.1.5 *STANDARDISED INCIDENCE RATIO (SIR)*

In this section, we explain the concept of Standardised Incidence Ratio (SIR). SIR analysis gives a clearer understanding of the comparative Gaelic vitality of the 25 Study Districts. SIR values provide a method of comparing actual numbers of Gaelic-competent individuals in an SD, and the SD's three age groups, to the average for the RA, and the RA's three age groups. We then present a cluster analysis of speaker Gaelic abilities in the 25 Study Districts through the 1981–2011 census periods.

When analysing raw census data on Gaelic ability, crude percentage values may carry anomalies caused by different Gaelic ability levels across age groups. The Standardised Incidence Ratios (SIRs) enable comparison across the 25 Study Districts by negating any such anomalies. The Standardised Incidence Ratio values are calculated for each Study District based on the ratio between an 'expected' number and the actual 'observed' number of residents with Gaelic ability in each district. First, a ratio for each of the three age groups (3–17 years, 18–49 years and 50+) is calculated based on the number of those reported with Gaelic ability divided by the total population for each age group across all the districts. The 'expected' figure for each SD is derived from the sum of expected residents with Gaelic ability calculated for each age group in each SD from the overall age-group ratios.

The SIR is the ratio of observed and expected Gaelic speakers. Therefore a SIR value of 1 occurs when the expected number equals the observed number. The SIR analysis allows for a standardised comparison of the relative strength of an SD vis-à-vis other SDs. It also provides a method for categorising the SDs in similar sociolinguistic profiles across the geographic distribution in the Research Area.

Table 2.9 comprises Standardised Incidence Ratio of reported ability in Gaelic in the Study Districts in the 2011 Census. The tables for the SIRs from 1981–2001

---

17 In addition to this data for the Western Isles, the supplementary information on the whole Research Area in Table 2.5 indicates that Staffin (Skye) SD and the Isle of Tiree SD report 233 and 240 with Gaelic ability in their total populations (3yrs+) respectively, and 48 and 47 with Gaelic ability respectively in the 3–17 age cohort.

census periods are presented in **Appendix 2 (A2.4).** Based on these SIR tables and starting with the most recent census, Figures 2.18 to 2.21 illustrate the Standardised Incidence Ratios in the 2011–1981 periods, in descending order of values for the 25 SDs. The values, and therefore the descending order, for each census period are calculated independently. Thus, the order of SDs varies slightly from figure to figure.

2011		Aged 3-17				Aged 18-49				Aged 50+				All ages (3+)		
Study Districts	SIRi	P (pop)	S (speaks Gaelic)	Rate	Rate x Pop	P (Pop)	S (speaks Gaelic)	Rate	Rate x Pop	P (Pop)	S (speaks Gaelic)	Rate	Rate x Pop	P (pop)	E i	S (speaks Gaelic)
		S Pij	S Sij	Rj	Rj.Pij	S Pij	S Sij	Rj	Rj.Pij	S Pij	S Sij	Rj	Rj.Pij			
		4,751	1,989	0.4186		10,562	4,598	0.4353		12,711	7,978	0.6276				
01. West Side of Lewis (central)	1.190	174	75	0.4186	72.845	340	180	0.4353	148.014	498	380	0.6276	312.567	1,012	533.426	635
02. West Side of Lewis (south)	1.121	122	65	0.4186	51.075	293	155	0.4353	127.553	392	256	0.6276	246.037	807	424.665	476
03. Uig District	0.975	112	42	0.4186	46.889	241	104	0.4353	104.916	407	251	0.6276	255.452	760	407.256	397
04. West Side of Lewis (north)	1.249	129	79	0.4186	54.006	349	199	0.4353	151.932	455	336	0.6276	285.579	933	491.516	614
05. Ness	1.216	207	121	0.4186	86.660	412	231	0.4353	179.358	609	436	0.6276	382.236	1,228	648.254	788
06. Tolsta	1.081	105	37	0.4186	43.958	156	62	0.4353	67.912	230	178	0.6276	144.358	491	256.229	277
07. Loch a Tuath	1.082	331	143	0.4186	138.573	613	288	0.4353	266.860	581	402	0.6276	364.662	1,525	770.095	833
08. Tong	0.876	130	34	0.4186	54.424	266	116	0.4353	115.799	218	119	0.6276	136.827	614	307.050	269
09. Stornoway, Barvas Rd suburbs	0.848	365	100	0.4186	152.807	728	254	0.4353	316.923	513	317	0.6276	321.982	1,606	791.712	671
10. Stornoway Town	0.757	711	188	0.4186	297.659	2,001	573	0.4353	871.104	2,149	1,145	0.6276	1,348.810	4,861	2,517.573	1,906
11. Stornoway, Point Rd suburbs	0.745	236	50	0.4186	98.801	538	169	0.4353	234.210	579	300	0.6276	363.407	1,353	696.418	519
12. South Point	0.942	262	85	0.4186	109.686	567	222	0.4353	246.835	599	383	0.6276	375.960	1,428	732.480	690
13. North Point	0.827	131	38	0.4186	54.843	271	79	0.4353	117.976	355	210	0.6276	222.814	757	395.633	327
14. North Lochs	0.991	125	35	0.4186	52.331	320	125	0.4353	139.307	428	296	0.6276	268.632	873	460.270	456
15. South Lochs	1.038	150	69	0.4186	62.797	303	146	0.4353	131.906	436	271	0.6276	273.653	889	468.357	486
16. North Harris	1.207	124	79	0.4186	51.912	319	174	0.4353	138.872	512	365	0.6276	321.354	955	512.138	618
17. South Harris	1.064	128	55	0.4186	53.587	297	161	0.4353	129.294	489	305	0.6276	306.919	914	489.800	521
18. North Uist (north & west)	1.137	134	74	0.4186	56.099	306	178	0.4353	133.212	515	331	0.6276	323.237	955	512.549	583
19. North Uist (south & east)	1.121	70	40	0.4186	29.305	212	124	0.4353	92.291	342	213	0.6276	214.655	624	336.251	377
20. Benbecula	1.049	251	120	0.4186	105.081	555	269	0.4353	241.610	477	289	0.6276	299.387	1,283	646.078	678
21. South Uist (north)	1.278	181	109	0.4186	75.775	313	204	0.4353	136.260	373	257	0.6276	234.112	867	446.147	570
22. South Uist (south)	1.255	165	119	0.4186	69.077	342	202	0.4353	148.884	465	319	0.6276	291.855	972	509.816	640
23. Barra and Vatersay	1.209	249	137	0.4186	104.244	445	257	0.4353	193.724	528	367	0.6276	331.397	1,222	629.364	761
24. Skye, Staffin	0.937	67	48	0.4186	28.049	165	69	0.4353	71.830	237	116	0.6276	148.752	469	248.632	233
25. Isle of Tiree	0.720	92	47	0.4186	38.516	210	57	0.4353	91.420	324	136	0.6276	203.357	626	333.293	240

Table 2.9 Standardised Incidence Ratio of reported ability in Gaelic in the Study Districts in the 2011 Census

The formula for the calculation of the Standardised Incidence Ratio and the meanings of the relevant abbreviations are set out here.

$$SIRi = \frac{\Sigma\, Sij}{Ei} \qquad\qquad Ei = \Sigma\, Rj.Pij \qquad\qquad Rj = \frac{\Sigma\, Sij}{\Sigma\, Pij}$$

Figure 2.16 *Formulas used to calculate the SIRs for the 25 SDs*

SIR Formula : Definitions	
SIRi	Standardised Incidence Ratio for each Study District
Ei	Expected number of Gaelic speakers for each Study District
P	Population by age group in each Study District
S	Number of Gaelic speakers by age group in each Study District
Σ Pij	Sum of population within each age group
Σ Sij	Sum of Gaelic speakers within each age group
Rj	Rate of Gaelic speakers within each age group
Rj.Pij	Rate of Gaelic speakers within each age group X Population in each Study District and age group

Figure 2.17 *Guide to abbreviations in the SIR data formulas and tables (according to Gaelic ability in Census)*

As mentioned above, SIR values above 1 indicate Gaelic ability above average for the RA, whereas values below 1 indicate Gaelic ability below average for the RA. This is clear from the SIRi values in the second left-hand column in Table 2.9. The highest SIR value of the 25 SDs in Table 2.9 is 1.278 (SIRi) for South Uist (north). This calculation is a reflection of the relatively high ratio of Gaelic speakers (S) in this SD across the three age cohorts. The actual number of Gaelic speakers (570 (S Total)) is considerably higher than the expected number of Gaelic speakers of 446.1 (Ei) because South Uist (north) is far above the average for Gaelic ability in the population of the RA. On the other hand, the third lowest SIR value of the 25 SDs in Table 8 is 0.757 (SIRi) for Stornoway Town. The actual number of Gaelic speakers (1,906 (S Total)) is considerably lower than the expected number of Gaelic speakers of 2,517.6 (Ei) because Stornoway Town is far below the average. As we see from the formula calculations, the Rj is simply the rate of Gaelic speakers within each age-group across all the areas. This is a central component of the calculation of SIRs, in that it irons out any age-related anomalies which can be occluded in the portrayal of crude percentages of reported Gaelic ability in a given SD.

Figures 2.18–2.21 present a series of decadal charts for the Standardised Incidence Ratios of Gaelic speakers in the 25 Study Districts. These charts provide a profile of the range of Gaelic ability through space and time. The SIR analysis traces changes in these distributions for each decade from 2011 back to 1981. Clustering techniques are applied to the distribution of the SIRs to give an indication of natural groupings of districts. This identifies the geographic density of speakers. Figures 2.18–2.21 provide a K-means analysis of SIRs in the 25 SDs, presented in order from 2011 back to 1981.[18] A higher number of clusters are found in the most recent censuses. The increasing number of clusters indicates a statistical fragmentation in the Gaelic speaker-group as a whole. In Figure 2.21 for the 1981 Census, for instance, there are three clusters, whereas in Figure 2.18 for the 2011 Census there are five clusters. Figure 2.21 (1981) has a small lowest-scoring cluster comprising only two SDs, i.e. Benbecula and Stornoway Town (far right of Figure 2.21). The salience of the contrast between 1981 SIRs is similar to the greater differentiation seen in the census data curves of 1981, i.e. the 'tipping point' in the 1981 Census data of Figures 2.6a,b. The two English-dominant rural towns in these lowest-scoring SDs are of relevance for this low scoring. The next lowest-scoring cluster is a cluster of three SDs which also contains urbanising SDs, i.e. Stornoway (Barvas Road suburbs) and Stornoway (Point Road suburbs). In comparison, the more rural districts are found in the highest-scoring cluster in Figure 2.21, comprising 20 SDs. This 1981 cluster of higher-scoring SDs breaks down across the decades into three clusters. These three new clusters, added to the lower two, then make up a total of five clusters in the distribution of SIRs in the two most recent censuses: 2001 (Figure 2.19) and 2011 (Figure 2.18). This comparative analysis of SIRs over time (2011–1981) indicates that the earlier high social density of Gaelic speakers has been dissipated. It is clear over time that most SDs remain in a relatively similar position in relation to the position of other SDs on the SIR vitality scale.

2.4.1.5.1 *THRESHOLD IN S-CURVE OF IRISH VERNACULAR DEMOGRAPHY*

There are important parallels between the analysis of Scottish Gaelic and Irish census-based demolinguistics (and many other language-shift scenarios). These parallels entail the concepts of language vitality thresholds, tipping points, S-curve demolinguistics and comprehensiveness in minority-language practice. These quantitative concepts correlate with qualitative issues and results in minority-language protection (Péterváry *et al.* 2014). In this section, we draw a comparison

---

18 K-means analysis is a method of clustering related data in a distribution. K-means clustering partitions observations into K clusters in which each observation pertains to the cluster with the nearest mean. This mean serves as a prototype for the cluster. See **Appendix A2.4** for median percentages for the SIR fits for the various clusters.

with the Gaeltacht statistical analyses in Ireland and set out two inter-related central methodological issues and language-planning imperatives:

1. The comparative basis for the SIR methodology in the Irish Gaeltacht; and
2. The concept of the vitality threshold in the inverted S-curve of demolinguistic vernacular data.[19]

Recent studies in Ireland have concentrated on the late 20th century decline of the former high-density Irish-speaking areas of the officially-designated Gaeltacht. The language questions in the Irish Census are more indicative of minority-language social practice than those of the Scottish Census. In the Irish Census questions differentiate between ability in Irish and the daily speaking of Irish (within and outside the education system). In the Gaeltacht, there is a substantial gap between the portion of the population who report an ability in Irish and those who report the daily speaking of Irish. For instance, in the 2016 Irish Census, 66% of the 96,090 Gaeltacht population (3yrs+) report an ability in Irish as opposed to 21% who report speaking Irish daily (outside the education system).

In 2007, Ó Giollagáin *et al.* (2007a,b) published the most detailed demolinguistic description and sociolinguistic analysis of vernacular Irish: the *Comprehensive Linguistic Study of the Use of Irish in the Gaeltacht*. In 2015, based on the 2011 Census, Ó Giollagáin and Charlton published an update on the 2007 study. Both these studies are based on the smallest geographic census units, termed electoral divisions, i.e. small statistical units of grouped-townland census data which may be disclosed. SIR analysis formed an important part of both of these studies (2007a,b and 2015). SIRs are significant indicators of vernacular vitality or decline in the Gaeltacht because they are based on daily-speaking data and because some of the electoral divisions contained both relatively high numbers and relatively high densities of daily Irish speakers. Daily speaking can be equated to vernacular practice or use. In contrast with the Gaeltacht data, the lack of daily-speaking information, or some other comparative measure, is a constraint in the Scottish Census Gaelic data and analysis. The two Gaeltacht studies indicate that only c. 20% of the officially designated Gaeltacht retained substantial Irish vernacular use. Further, in these most (until recently) vibrant areas, vernacular use among the young is restricted to a minority of less than a quarter. The analogous SIR methodology in both these Gaeltacht studies indicates that a high density of active Irish speakers are required to sustain the use of Irish as

---

19 An S-curve is a sigmoid or logistic curve which has exponential growth over small ranges but is asymptotic in its overall range. A reversed S-curve refers to a distribution curve where high scores are divided from low scores by a steep fall in the middle range of the curve. In this publication, we use the term 'S-curve' to refer to both a normal S-curve and an inverted or reversed S-curve. Language-shift situations often involve two types of S-curves: the normal S-curve of the increasing language in a negative correlation to an inverted S-curve of the recessive language — these two typically combine to form an X-curve.

a community language in a given location. Areas where over 67% of the population speak Irish on a daily basis entail minority-language practice at or above a critical communal threshold. Communities above this threshold have a relative stability or a slower decrease in minority-language use. These areas with over 67% daily use are referred to as Category A districts (with weaker areas designated as Category B and weakest as Category C). These two Gaeltacht studies indicate a reversed S-curve in the distribution of the demolinguistic data in the Gaeltacht. This curve indicates two critical turning-points in the data and divides the distribution into three sections. The first (upper) section of the reversed S-curve, above 67%, corresponds to a more sustainable vernacular usage (above a phase of rapid decline). The second (middle) section falls below the 67% threshold and denotes the acceleration point indicating rapid decline in vernacular vitality. The third (lower) section lies past the deceleration point in the curve, indicating final residual or slower vernacular decline. Therefore, the critical point between the upper and middle sections of the curve indicates a threshold, which is termed 'the language vitality threshold' (Ó Giollagáin and Charlton 2015). The issue of comprehensiveness in language-practice policy and planning (2.4.1.3) is, therefore, a central aspect of maintaining a community's capacity to sustain language use above this critical threshold. Comprehensiveness, among other requirements, refers to social contexts where the primacy of the minority language is productive and normative (and where the majority language is not included). The concept of minority-language comprehensiveness is clearly in contrast with common official policy promotion and the practice of 'bilingualism' reinforced in some academic discourses.

With regard to the Scottish Gaelic context, there is clear evidence of S-curve and tipping-point phenomena. Section 6.5.2.1 (STS) provides evidence of the relatively gradual decline in fluency in Gaelic before the c. 70% threshold in the population of Western Isles origin, followed by rapid decline below the critical threshold after 1970 in the combined data for the three islands of Scalpay, Grimsay and Eriskay. Section 5.8.2.2, Figure 5.29, also shows a trajectory similar to an S-curve in the distribution of *Gaelic only* language practice in the Research Area. Figures 2.6a and 2.6b (2.4.1.1) show tipping points in the Gaelic ability curves in the profile of the 25 SDs. An S-curve of language shift is also produced by Daniel M. Abrams and Stephen H. Strogatz (2003: 900) with regard to, among others, Gaelic in Sutherland 1880–2000 based on census data from Withers (1984a: 213–234 [1881–1971 censuses]).

2.4.1.5.2 *SIRS AND K-CLUSTERS BASED ON THE FOUR CENSUSES 2011–1981*

In this section, we present the figures which summarise the SIR data and K-cluster analysis of the RA based on the four censuses from 2011–1981. Figure 2.18 shows the distribution of SIR values based on the 2011 Census.

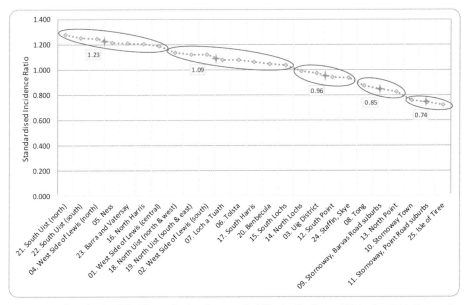

Figure 2.18 *Standardised Incidence Ratio of reported ability in Gaelic per SD in the 2011 Census, in descending order*

The SIR values range from 1.29 (highest-scoring SD: South Uist (north)) to 0.72 (lowest-scoring SD: Isle of Tiree) in the RA for the 2011 Census data. The score for each individual SD is indicated by a small diamond in the data line. As shown in Figure 2.18, the top three Study Districts were South Uist (north), South Uist (south) and West Side of Lewis (north). The lowest three were Stornoway Town, Stornoway (Point Road suburbs) and the Isle of Tiree. The K-means cluster analysis identified five clusters. Table 2.10 below presents the relevant values in the K-cluster analysis for the four census periods. The small cross in each cluster in the charts indicates the position of the mean value of the cluster (the SIR fit). The actual mean value or SIR fit for each cluster is given next to the cross. The K-cluster breakdown in Figure 2.18 for Census 2011 yields five groups. As shown in Table 2.10, the five cluster centres are: 1.23 (in a cluster containing seven SDs), 1.09 (eight SDs), 0.96 (four SDs), 0.85 (three SDs) and 0.74 (three SDs).

Figure 2.19 shows the distribution of SIR values based on the 2001 Census. The SIR values range from 1.24 to 0.74.

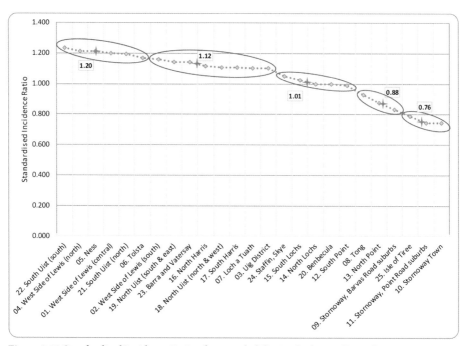

Figure 2.19 *Standardised Incidence Ratio of reported ability in Gaelic per SD in the 2001 Census, in descending order*

As shown in Figure 2.19, the top three Study Districts were South Uist (south), West Side of Lewis (north) and Ness; and the lowest three were Tiree, Stornoway (Point Road suburbs) and Stornoway Town. The K-cluster breakdown in Figure 2.19 for Census 2001 also yields five groups (Table 2.10).

Figure 2.20 shows the distribution of SIR values based on the 1991 Census. The SIR values range from 1.26 to 0.70. The top three SDs in Figure 2.20 are Ness, West Side of Lewis (central) and West Side of Lewis (north); and the lowest three are Stornoway (Barvas Road suburbs), Stornoway Town and Stornoway (Point Road suburbs). The K-cluster breakdown in Figure 2.20 for Census 1991 yields four groups, in contrast to the five clusters in Figures 2.18 and 2.19.

Figure 2.21 shows the distribution of SIR values based on the 1981 Census. The SIR values range from 1.18 to 0.70.

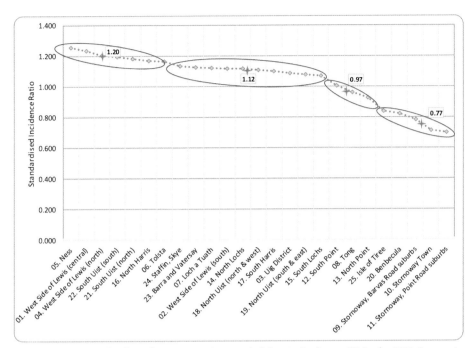

Figure 2.20 *Standardised Incidence Ratio of reported ability in Gaelic per SD in the 1991 Census, in descending order*

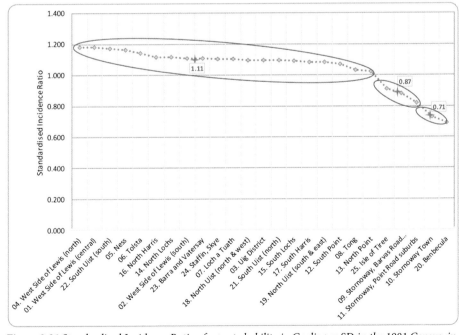

Figure 2.21 *Standardised Incidence Ratio of reported ability in Gaelic per SD in the 1981 Census, in descending order*

The top three SDs in Figure 2.21 are West Side of Lewis (north), West Side of Lewis (central) and South Uist (south); and the lowest three are Stornoway (Point Road suburbs), Stornoway Town and Benbecula. A large cluster of 20 SDs with higher SIR values is evident in the K-cluster breakdown in Figure 2.21 for Census 1981, with two further small groups with lower values.

2.4.1.5.3 *TRENDS IN SIRS FROM 1981 TO 2011*

Further evidence of the contraction of the Gaelic-speaking group from 1981 to 2011 can be gleaned from Table 2.10. Table 2.10 presents a comparison of the SIR fits (the mean of the SIR values corresponding to a given cluster) with the related median percentages for these fits, based on the K-means analysis of the Gaelic speaker percentages in the RA. The table presents these data in four columns (one for each census period from 2011 to 1981), each of which is subdivided into three columns containing SIR data.

K-Cluster	1981 Census			1991 Census			2001 Census			2011 Census		
	SIR fit	SDs per cluster	Corresponding % Gaelic speakers	SIR fit	SDs per cluster	Corresponding % Gaelic speakers	SIR fit	SDs per cluster	Corresponding % Gaelic speakers	SIR fit	SDs per cluster	Corresponding % Gaelic speakers
1	1.108	20	88.4	1.202	7	81.6	1.204	6	74.8	1.229	7	64.2
2	0.87	3	69.6	1.117	10	77.5	1.123	8	69.0	1.087	8	55.5
3	0.71	2	55.1	0.965	3	64.9	1.014	5	61.9	0.961	4	50.3
4				0.773	5	53.3	0.879	3	53.2	0.85	3	41.8
5							0.759	3	45.3	0.741	3	38.4

Table 2.10 *SIR means (i.e. SIR fits) and corresponding percentages in K-cluster analysis of spoken Gaelic in Censuses 2011–1981: population aged 3+*

The table illustrates a significant feature in the demolinguistic decline of how the median percentage of Gaelic speakers has fallen in all but one cluster comparison. For instance, the corresponding percentage values for the median points in the highest cluster in each census over the thirty-year period have fallen from 88.4% to 81.6% to 74.8% to 64.2%. The full range of the median percentages for the clusters narrows: 88.4% - 55.1% = 33.3pts (1981); 81.6% - 53.3% = 28.3pts (1991); 74.8% - 45.3% = 29.5pts (2001); and 64.2% - 38.4% = 25.8pts (2011). Furthermore, the increase from three to five clusters illustrates the statistical fragmentation of the vernacular group density over the three decades to 2011. In brief, the data fit analysis in Table 2.10 indicates that the sociolinguistic profile of the RA was stronger and more uniform in 1981 than in 2011 (see also section 2.5.4). The fragmentation occurs within a greater range of SIR values for 2011 but with a narrower Gaelic speaker percentage range.

2.4.2 RATE OF DECLINE IN GAELIC ABILITY NUMBERS, 1951–2011

In this section we discuss the rate of decline in the proportions and numbers of Gaelic-competent residents during the period 1951–2011 in the RA for 1981–2011 and in the Western Isles for 1951–1971. We use these two geographic units because our data for the thirty-year period 1981–2011 covers the IGRP Research Area, whereas our data for the earlier twenty-year period 1951–1971 covers the Western Isles (2.1.1). We discuss, in order: a) the proportional percentage decline in reported Gaelic ability; b) the absolute decline in Gaelic ability; and c) the decline in the range of percentage ability in Gaelic.

2.4.2.1 *THE PROPORTIONAL PERCENTAGE DECLINE IN GAELIC ABILITY, 1981–2011*

The main feature of the demolinguistic analysis from 1981 to 2011 in this chapter is the high rate of decline in reported Gaelic ability: a 35% decline over the thirty-year period. On average, the Research Area as a whole experienced a 13% proportional average loss in residents who reported Gaelic ability during each decade. The decadal decline indicates a remarkably consistent rate over the thirty-year period: 13.7% (1981–1991), 12.0% (1991–2001) and 14.3% (2001–2011).

The comparable contraction in the 3–17 year old age cohort is even greater than for the total population. This youngest cohort shows a 39% fall for the thirty-year period, corresponding to an average decadal fall of 15%. A particularly large contraction was evident in the decade from 1981 to 1991 in which this youngest cohort fell proportionately by 26%. The same period 1981–1991 represents the decade when Gaelic lost its high social density (80%) of speakers in the total population of the RA.

2.4.2.2 *ABSOLUTE DECLINE IN NUMBERS REPORTING GAELIC ABILITY, 1981–2011*

This same feature of contraction is also evidenced in the absolute numbers of those reporting Gaelic ability, as set out in Table 2.11. On average, the Research Area lost 3,220 residents with Gaelic ability each decade from 1981–2011, with a total loss of 9,661 over the thirty-year period (an absolute percentage decline of 39.9%).

In the decade from 1981–1991, the numbers with Gaelic ability in the Research Area dropped by 4,242, representing a 17.5% absolute fall from a base of 24,226 Gaelic speakers in 1981. The loss in terms of speaker numbers was smaller in the following decade to 2001, at 3,734 (18.7% loss). In the following ten-year period to 2011, the fall in numbers was less severe, with a loss of 1,685 (10.4% loss).

Census Year	Total population in RA	All Gaelic speakers	Percentage loss	Aged 3-17	Gaelic speakers Aged 3-17	Percentage loss Aged 3-17
	N	N	%	N	N	%
1981	30,359	24,226	-	7,711	5,329	-
1991	29,011	19,984	17.5	6,210	3,166	40.6
2001	26,794	16,250	18.7	5,117	2,395	24.4
2011	28,024	14,565	10.4	4,751	1,989	17.0

Table 2.11 *Total population, Gaelic speakers and percentage loss in Gaelic ability in RA, with 3–17 age cohort, 1981–2011*

Figure 2.22 illustrates the decadal absolute decline and percentage loss in Gaelic ability in the population of the Research Area (see also Table 2.11).

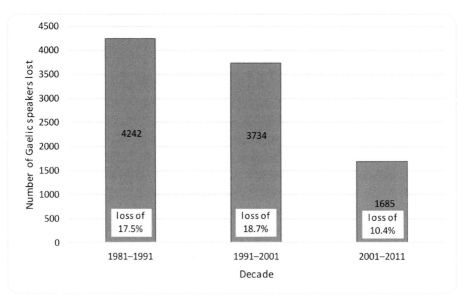

Figure 2.22 *Decline in absolute numbers and percentage loss of Gaelic speakers (i.e. Gaelic ability), RA, three decades 1981–2011*

Figure 2.22 shows the high absolute and percentage rate of decline in the two decades from 1981 to 2001. The absolute and percentage rate was lower for the decade from 2001 to 2011 (10.4%) as the Gaelic-competent group has contracted to 14,565 people, in contrast with 24,226 Gaelic speakers in 1981.

Figure 2.23 depicts the decline in numbers of Gaelic speakers in the 3–17 age group between 1981 and 2011 (see also three right-hand columns in Table 2.11).

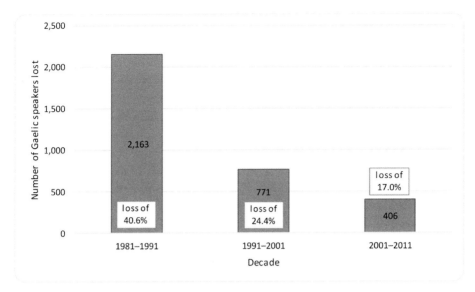

Figure 2.23 *Decline in absolute numbers and percentage loss of Gaelic-competent 3–17 year olds, RA, three decades 1981–2011*

The data in Figure 2.23 indicate that the decade from 1981 to 1991 marked a critical turning-point in the societal decline of Gaelic in the Research Area. Across the thirty-year period, the average decadal fall in the percentage of Gaelic-speaking children aged 3–17 was higher than for the population as a whole: the loss to the youngest cohort stood at an average of 27%, or 1,113 speakers each decade. The 1981 to 1991 decade witnessed a significant decline among the 3–17 age cohort from 5,329 to 3,166, a decadal absolute fall of 41%. Over the two more recent decades the percentage and number falls have decelerated but the cohort stood at fewer than 2,000 in 2011.

2.4.2.3   *ABSOLUTE DECLINE IN NUMBERS REPORTING GAELIC ABILITY, WESTERN ISLES, 1951–1991*

In order to chart the trend in Gaelic ability back to the 1951 Census, Figure 2.24 indicates the loss in numbers and proportional percentage decline of Gaelic speakers in the Western Isles between 1951 and 1991 (see section 2.4.2 for RA as geographic unit). Over this forty-year period the overall population remained relatively stable. In Figure 2.24, the four data bars indicate the decline in the numbers of Gaelic speakers for each ten-year period from 1951–1991. The bars correspond to the values on the Y-axis in the legend on the left-hand side of Figure 2.24. The trend line in the figure indicates the proportional percentage loss for each period. The percentage loss corresponds to the values on the right-hand Y-axis. The negative value for the 1971–1981 decade actually indicates an increase in those reporting Gaelic ability.

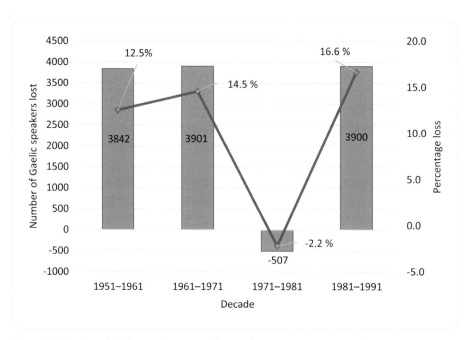

Figure 2.24 *Decline of Gaelic speakers in numbers and percentages, Western Isles 1951–1991*

Table 2.12 sets out the total population, numbers with Gaelic ability and percentage loss in Gaelic ability in the Western Isles in the thirty-year period from 1951 to 1991.

	Population in Western Isles	Gaelic speakers	Percentage loss
Census Year	N	N	%
1991	29,597	19,546	16.6
1981	30,716	23,446	-2.2
1971	31,001	22,939	14.5
1961	32,614	26,840	12.5
1951	35,596	30,682	

Table 2.12 *Western Isles population, number of Gaelic speakers and decadal percentage loss*

A trend of overall reduction in the numbers of Gaelic speakers was evident over the period from 1951 to 1991. There were 11,136 fewer reporting Gaelic ability in the Western Isles in 1991 than there were in 1951. This represents a contraction in the Gaelic-competent population of 36% over the four decades. The absolute number of Gaelic speakers in the Western Isles fell by 3,842 from 1951 to 1961, by 3,901 from 1961 to 1971 and by 3,900 from 1981 to 1991. Between 1971 and 1981 the number of Gaelic speakers increased by 507. MacKinnon (1991: 178–79) observes that this reversal in the trend can be attributed to the effect of bilingual educational provision on the increased reporting of Gaelic ability in the census (see the discussion in 6.5.2.1, Figure 6.15, relating to the influence of GME and section 5.8.2.2, Figure 5.28, relating to the effects of family language policy; and 3.3.4, Figure 3.9).

When the data are averaged over the whole period from 1951 to 1991 there was an average proportional percentage decline of 6% per decade; this includes the period 1971 to 1981 which showed an actual 2.2% rise. The overall contraction from 1951 to 1991 was 23%. In terms of absolute numbers, there has been an average loss of 2,784 Gaelic speakers per decade (or 11% absolute loss per decade) from 1951 to 1991. A fall of 12.5% in absolute numbers of Gaelic speakers occured in the decade following 1951, from a base of 30,682 Gaelic speakers in the Western Isles in 1951. As shown in Figure 2.24, the proportional percentage decline over each subsequent decade was 14.5% from 1961 to 1971, an increase of 2.2% from 1971 to 1981 and a decline of 16.6% from 1981 to 1991.

2.4.2.4 *PERCENTAGE GAELIC ABILITY RANGE IN THE RESEARCH AREA, 1981–2011*

The percentage ability in Gaelic for the population in the census data (3+ years) for the RA as a whole has contracted considerably from 80% in 1981 to 52% in 2011. This indicates a percentage-point decline of 28 in Gaelic ability in 30 years. The percentages for Gaelic ability in 1991 and 2001 are 69% and 61% respectively. It is worth noting that the range in percentage-point decline of Gaelic ability among the 3–17 age cohort for the 1981 to 1991 decade was 18 points (i.e. from 69% to 51%). This percentage-point decline in the youngest cohort in the earlier 1981–1991 decade corresponds to the percentage-point decline in the overall population of the RA in the later twenty-year period from 1991 to 2011, i.e. percentage-point decline of 17 (from 69% to 52%). There is a decline of 27 points in the 3–17 age cohort in the thirty-year period from 1981 (69%) to 2011 (42%). In the same thirty-year period, the 18–49 age group indicates a decrease of 33 points, from 76% in 1981 to 43% in 2011. The 50+ age group shows a decline of 28 points, from 91% in 1981 to 63% in 2011.

2.4.3 RESIDUAL, INTERSTITIAL AND MORIBUND NEXUS OF GAELIC ABILITY AND FAMILY HOUSEHOLD USE

In the 2011 Census returns, there is a significant gap between the level of reported Gaelic ability on the one hand and the considerably lower level of household practice of Gaelic on the other. In this section, we elaborate on the analytic and diagnostic importance of the mismatch between ability and practice. This phenomenon is emblematic of language shift scenarios worldwide. It may at times be avoided or evaded in public or academic discourses but it is critical to understanding the processes driving minority-language decline. In the RA, individuals with Gaelic ability comprise 52% of the population (3+yrs), but the Family Households, where all adults and all children are reported as speaking Gaelic, comprise only 19% of the total of Family Households (see section 2.4.1.3). In comparison with 19% fully-Gaelic speaking Family Households, 42% of the 3–17 age cohort report an ability in Gaelic in the 2011 Census. The lower rate of household practice of Gaelic, from the Family Household data, suggests that about one half of the young people do not practice Gaelic in a fully-Gaelic household and that they are, therefore, reliant on the educational system or on communal inputs not involving their parents (e.g. from grandparents) for the acquisition of their reported ability in Gaelic, see section 4.5.2, Figure 4.10 and Table 4.14.[20]

As would be expected, there is a strong correlation between household Gaelic use and Gaelic ability, in the various SDs. Figure 2.25 illustrates the very strong positive linear correlation ($R^2 = 0.785$; $p < 0.05$) between the percentage of Family Households where all children and all adults use Gaelic in each of the 25 SDs and the overall percentage of Gaelic speakers (i.e. reported Gaelic ability) in each of the 25 SDs.

---

20 We can compare 19% of Family Household use and the 42% ability in Gaelic (census data) with 21.1% mothers and fathers who use Gaelic with each other in the range of categories from Always to Mix, as reported in the Teenager Survey (4.6.6, Figure 4.31) and with 45.6% with ability in the categories of Fluent to Reasonable Gaelic (4.5.1, Table 4.11).

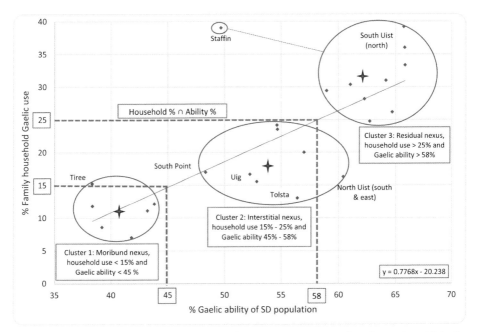

Figure 2.25 *Correlation, linear trend and nexus clustering in percentage of Gaelic speakers (ability) vs. percentage of Family Household use of Gaelic, 25 SDs, 2011 Census*

Figure 2.25 illustrates the linear trend of the correlation between the two variables of Gaelic ability and use. This correlation is based on the percentage of Gaelic ability as related to Family Household use of Gaelic. The Gaelic use data is calculated from Family Household use, based on households in which all adults and all children use Gaelic. For the purpose of this calculation, only Family Households in which all adults and all children use Gaelic are placed in the category of Gaelic Family Household. The vertical axis refers to the Family Household percentage of Gaelic use for the 25 SDs and the horizontal axis depicts the percentage of Gaelic ability in the same SDs. The trend line through the chart indicates the linear trend in how these two variables correlate with each other in relation to the 25 SDs of the RA as a whole. The top three diamonds in the upper right-hand corner are, therefore, the SDs with the highest levels of Gaelic ability and the highest levels of Family Household use of Gaelic. These top three diamonds represent the SDs, in descending order, of South Uist (north), West Side of Lewis (north), and South Uist (south). In the lower left-hand corner of the chart, the grouping of six diamonds represents the lowest levels of ability and Family Household use. They have below 45% Gaelic ability, and Family Household Gaelic use at or below 15%. These are the six lowest SDs: Tiree, Stornoway Town, Stornoway (Barvas Road suburbs), Stornoway (Point Road suburbs), North Point and Tong. Four of these SDs are in the environs of Stornoway. In general, based on the gradient of the line, a one-point increase in Gaelic ability yields a 0.78 increase in the level of Family Household use. From a visual inspection of Figure 2.25, it is clear that the percentage point gap (between ability and household use) in the trend line ranges between c. 25% at the bottom level and c. 35% at the top level, yielding an overall percentage gap of c. 30%. The projected continuation of the linear trend line intersects the X-axis at the value of 26.1% (Gaelic ability), which thereby corresponds to 0% Family Household use (on the Y-axis). That is to say, given the precise correlation in this household-ability nexus, when the proportion of those with Gaelic ability in a specific district falls to a quarter or less of the population, Family Household use ceases.

The relationship between Gaelic ability in a given SD and the Family Household use of Gaelic in the same SD provides a diagnostic indicator of Gaelic vitality. SDs evincing higher values in both variables have higher Gaelic vitality than SDs with lower values in either variable. For instance, the South Uist (north) SD records 66% of its population as having Gaelic ability, with Family Household Gaelic use of 39%; South Uist (north) evinces the best vitality score for this correlation (and is the highest right-most diamond in Figure 2.25). Comparatively, the mid-ranking SD, Uig District on the Isle of Lewis, records 52% of residents as having ability in Gaelic, but Family Household use is far lower, with just 17% of Family Household Gaelic use.

From a visual inspection of Figure 2.25, as pointed out above, we can distinguish two relatively compact groups at both extremes of the linear trend line, one in the bottom left of the chart containing the six SDs with the weakest Gaelic salience, the other in the top right containing the 10 strongest SDs. This leaves a third more diffuse mid-range group, containing nine SDs.[21] This is also reflected by the clustering calculation which identified three clusters, with cluster centres marked by a star and the encircled data points. From these groupings we can see that the weakest and strongest groups fall above and below two nexus intersections. We can designate these nexus groups using the shorthand 'Household%∩Ability%' (where ∩ stands for 'intersection'). The weakest six SDs fall below a nexus of 15% Family Household Gaelic use and 45% Gaelic ability, i.e. 15%∩45% (as indicated in the chart). The strongest 10 SDs are found above a nexus of 25% Family Household Gaelic use and 58% Gaelic ability, i.e. 25%∩58%. This means that the mid-range group falls between 15%∩45% and 25%∩58%, with the exception of North Uist (south & east) at 60.4% Gaelic ability and 16.3% Family Household use. For analytical purposes, it is useful to label these three groups, from the weakest to the strongest regarding the salience of Gaelic, as the Moribund nexus, the Interstitial (i.e. between two others) nexus and the Residual nexus. These three nexuses are demarcated and labelled in Figure 2.25.

---

21 Only eight of the nine diamonds representing the nine SDs in the Interstitial nexus are actually visible in Figure 2.25. This is because the values for two SDs are practically identical. These are Uig District and North Lochs (16.7%∩52.24%; 16.7%∩52.23% respectively).

Given all the evidence from the modules in the IGRP study, such as the reduction in the intergenerational transmission of Gaelic, the loss of competence among the young, as well as the decline in practice among the younger cohorts, and the general trajectory of demolinguistic contraction, it is clear that those SDs in the Moribund nexus have lost nearly all communal vitality and collective ability to transmit Gaelic to subsequent generations. The Moribund nexus entails a significant lower limit in the overall distribution of the Gaelic sociolinguistic data in the Research Area. The Interstitial nexus is the most diffuse grouping and is on a trajectory of decline below the Residual nexus and towards the Moribund nexus. The SDs in the Residual nexus are at a stronger vitality stage but are, under the current circumstances of English dominance among the young, moving along a trajectory of demolinguistic decline. Two SDs in the Interstitial nexus, which are worthy of comment, are labelled in Figure 2.25. These are Staffin (Skye) and South Point (Lewis). The distance of the diamond representing the Staffin SD in Figure 2.25 from the fit line indicates that Staffin is an outlier (but actually in the top-scoring cluster in the cluster analysis). The SD of South Point is geographically near to Stornoway town, and in Figure 2.25 South Point is the closest SD to the Moribund nexus, which is mainly centred on Stornoway.

Given the strong correlational and descriptive statistical relation between Family Household use and ability, it is clear that one side of the relation can be used with confidence to predict the other (by adding or subtracting c. 30% points to or from the relevant percentage). This is an important and powerful diagnostic feature of the analysis based on the Family Household and ability nexus. Therefore, when, for example, the Gaelic ability statistic is known for a given SD, we can predict the level of the Family Household use of Gaelic. For instance, any SD with a level of Gaelic ability at or below 45% has a level of Family Household use at or below 15%. Furthermore, in our analysis based on levels of Gaelic ability alone we can designate groupings or individual SDs as belonging to a Moribund set, an Interstitial set and a Residual set. We use the term 'set' in this indicative analysis to differentiate with the term 'nexus' based on levels of both Family Household use and Gaelic ability. An instance of analysis with indicative sets can be found in section 2.4.5. From the diachronic point of view, although the Family Household correlation may vary historically, in order to gain a deeper historical perspective, we can examine the levels of Gaelic ability in previous data sets, for instance in the 2001 Census, and categorise districts according to their membership in the relevant set. Accordingly, in the 2001 Census there were 19 SDs in the Residual set, four SDs in the Interstitial set and two SDs in the Moribund set. This contrasts with the 2011 Census which yields 10 SDs in the Residual nexus, nine SDs in the Interstitial nexus and six SDs in the Moribund nexus (Figure 2.25). In fact, in the earlier 1991 Census, according to the indicative diagnostic of percentage Gaelic ability, there were no SDs in the Moribund set, with four SDs in the Interstitial set and 21 SDs in (or above) the Residual set. And based on the 1981 Census, no SDs can be categorised in either the Moribund or Interstitial sets.

The geographic units of SDs are considerably smaller than civil parishes. The analysis at SD level indicates that there can be significant differences in the salience of Gaelic within the same civil parish (see section 2.3.2). For instance, the civil parish of Uig in west Lewis comprises the two SDs of the Uig District (mentioned above) and West Side of Lewis (south). However, these districts contrast both in relation to reported Gaelic ability and the Family Household use of Gaelic. 59% of the residents of the West Side of Lewis (south) are reported as having Gaelic ability, with 29% of Family Household Gaelic use, indicating stronger vitality than the neighbouring SD of Uig District. But, according to the banding in O'Hanlon and Paterson's (2015a), the civil parish of Uig is in Band A, ostensibly the strongest Gaelic category. Our analysis shows that the northern area of this civil parish, i.e. West Side of Lewis (south), has greater salience of Gaelic than the southern area, i.e. Uig District.[22]

The non-normative function of Gaelic and the asymmetric power relations in favour of English in these communities, combined with the considerable gap between household Gaelic use and individual Gaelic ability, clearly preclude a literal interpretation of the 45% ability data in Gaelic as equating with a 45% value in relation to the social productivity or salience of Gaelic in such communities.

Taking into consideration the overall evidence from previous studies and the IGRP study in particular, the diachronic trend in the data suggests that the Moribund nexus is comprised of (a) the vestigial language competences of the minority group, concentrated in the older age cohorts, following the displacement of Gaelic as a language of communal practice and, since 1985 and the beginning of GME, (b) Gaelic competences among the younger cohort acquired chiefly from institutional supports of the educational system. The Moribund nexus phase precedes the social loss of the language (Crystal 2000: 20; projected levels of 0%(Household)∩26.1%(Ability) mentioned above). Having lost the former societal salience of Gaelic, the emergence of a phase of institutionally supported secondary minority bilingualism is possible, primarily in schools (Ó Giollagáin 2014a: 24; Ó Giollagáin 2014b: 113, 121; Ó Giollagáin and Ó Curnáin 2016: 62; and Edwards 2017: 24).

---

22 This contrast between the greater level of demolinguistic detail available at the smaller geographic units of SDs and the comparative lack of analytic detail at the level of civil parishes, can, of course, be made in relation to many other aspects of the IGRP analysis. For instance, Maps 2.6–2.9 show differences between the five SDs in the two civil parishes of Uig and Ness.

2.4.4 DIACHRONY AND SYNCHRONY OF SOCIETAL DECLINE OF GAELIC AND SHIFT TO ENGLISH

In this section, we discuss the diachronic and synchronic dimensions of the societal decline of Gaelic and the shift to English based on our analysis of census data.[23] A central aspect of the diachronic dimension concerns the loss of a critical mass, or, in other words, the loss of a high social density of minority-language speakers, and the subsequent residual contraction that follows this critical point in decline. The critical loss of density in the census data occurred from the 1980s onwards in the overall RA. This contraction was a central turning-point in the communal decline of Gaelic social networks and the diachronic dimension of the social dynamic driving the process of language shift to English. The synchronic dimension relates in this case to an analysis of contemporary evidence of the speaker-group, for example in census data. The Gaelic speaker group is currently further along in the post-critical-mass residual-to-moribund phases of contraction. In the Residual and Interstitial nexus, the displacement of Gaelic from the familial, institutional and communal networks represents the post-critical-mass stages in the lifecycle of Gaelic in these communities. The Moribund nexus of the lowest SDs in Figure 2.25 represents the period which precedes the end result of language shift. The Moribund nexus denotes a milestone where Gaelic is largely restricted to marginal aspects of community life, institutional practice and to the elderly age cohorts, and beyond which the future social practice of Gaelic is rendered non-viable, without substantial and dynamic Gaelic revival efforts. In the contraction of the remaining Gaelic networks in the Moribund nexus, similar to other minoritised low-density speaker-groups, it becomes an insurmountable challenge to transfer the minority language and the related socio-cultural resources to any significant proportion of the following generations.

This survey identifies a significant demolinguistic turning-point in the Gaelic ability data of the islands after 1981. In the decade from 1981 to 1991, the islands lost the 80%+ social density of Gaelic speakers. Gaelic ability in the 3–17 age cohort contracted particularly severely in that decade. There was a fall of 41% of Gaelic speaker numbers among this young age cohort. The rate of Gaelic contraction from 1981 onwards indicates that English monolingualism was gaining in prominence.

---

23 Diachronic analysis considers data or features from different periods or change over time while synchronic analysis focuses on a specific time period, contemporary data, for instance. Understanding demolinguistic processes and trajectories, as well as their contemporary and future implications, requires a combination of diachronic and synchronic analysis. The absence of this analytical approach to demolinguistics is a common deficiency in certain discourses about majority and minority languages. This point is discussed further in Lenoach *et al.* (2012: 6–10).

The latest Gaelic ability and household data demonstrates the current dominance of English monolingualism. This has happened because of the power dynamics between majority monolingualism and minority bilingualism, typical in language shift. There is an asymmetric unreciprocated sociological dynamic between bilingual Gaels on the one hand and monolingual English speakers as well as English-favouring bilinguals on the other hand.

2.4.5 PROGNOSIS FOR GAELIC IN INTERCENSAL TRAJECTORIES

In this section, we present a prognostic analysis of projected future levels of Gaelic ability in the SDs and the RA, based on previous intercensal rates of decline. Table 2.13 presents, for each SD, a projection to 2021, based on applying the percentage mean rates of decline in Gaelic ability for the three intercensal decades 1981–1991, 1991–2001 and 2001–2011. This projected proportional percentage loss is calculated as follows: (% loss 1981 to 1991 + % loss 1991 to 2001 + % loss 2001 to 2011)/3; and given in the right-hand column of Table 2.13. Values of Gaelic ability below 45% are given in bold as are the corresponding names of the SDs. The 10 SDs with values below 45% can be categorised in the Moribund set, according to the analysis presented in section 2.4.3. The four SDs predicted to enter the Moribund set are given in bold italics in Table 2.13. These four SDs are: Uig District, South Point, North Lochs (all three in Lewis) and Staffin (in Skye). These four SDs are classified in the Interstitial nexus based on the 2011 Census data (Figure 2.25) so that a projected decline on the trajectory is to be expected.

Study District	Population (aged 3+) 2011	Gaelic ability % 2011	Projected % loss in Gaelic ability 2011 to 2021	Projected Gaelic ability % 2021
01. West Side of Lewis (central)	1,012	62.75	12.99	54.60
02. West Side of Lewis (south)	807	58.98	13.20	51.20
03. Uig District	760	52.24	16.17	*43.79*
04. West Side of Lewis (north)	933	65.81	11.70	58.11
05. Ness	1,228	64.17	12.02	56.46
06. Tolsta	491	56.42	14.61	48.17
07. Loch a Tuath	1,525	54.62	14.75	46.57
08. Tong	614	**43.81**	18.02	**35.92**
09. Stornoway, Barvas Road suburbs	1,606	**41.78**	15.40	**35.34**
10. Stornoway Town	4,861	**39.21**	12.15	**34.45**
11. Stornoway, Point Road suburbs	1,353	**38.36**	15.83	**32.29**
12. South Point	1,428	48.32	17.44	*39.89*
13. North Point	757	**43.20**	18.91	**35.03**
14. North Lochs	873	52.23	16.45	*43.64*
15. South Lochs	889	54.67	15.16	46.38
16. North Harris	955	64.71	10.53	57.90
17. South Harris	914	57.00	13.58	49.26
18. North Uist (north & west)	955	61.05	11.39	54.09
19. North Uist (south & east)	624	60.42	11.11	53.70
20. Benbecula	1,283	52.84	-0.61	53.17
21. South Uist (north)	867	65.74	8.52	60.14
22. South Uist (south)	972	65.84	10.30	59.06
23. Barra & Vatersay	1,222	62.27	10.27	55.88
24. Staffin	469	49.68	17.39	*41.04*
25. Tiree	626	**38.34**	19.80	**30.75**
Total for RA	28,024	51.97	13.31	**45.05**

Table 2.13 Actual number and percentage Gaelic ability in 2011 compared with projected percentage Gaelic ability in 2021

Six SDs were included in the Moribund set of below 45% for the analysis of the 2011 Census data. The number of SDs in this set is projected to increase to 10 in 2021. However, Table 2.13 and Figure 2.26 indicate that the RA, taken as a whole, will reach this Moribund set in 2021. With regard to the projected Interstitial set, which falls between Gaelic ability levels of 45% and 55%, it is projected to contain nine SDs in the data for 2021. The projected Residual set will be halved for 2021 and is predicted to contain only six SDs. These six SDs are: West Side of Lewis (north), Ness, North Harris, South Uist (north), South Uist (south), as well as Barra & Vatersay.

In Figure 2.26 we illustrate the corresponding data for the Western Isles, i.e. excluding the smaller SDs of Tiree and Staffin. Figure 2.26 presents the actual (data line) and projected (broken line) population (3+yrs) trend for the Western Isles. The data bars indicate the percentage of Gaelic ability (actual 1981–2011 and projected 2021). The left-hand Y-axis indicates the percentage values for Gaelic ability. The right-hand Y-axis indicates the population values.

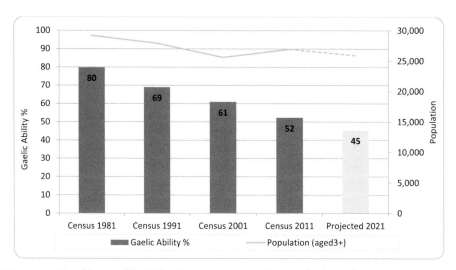

Figure 2.26 *Trend in actual (solid data line) and projected (broken line) population (3+yrs) and actual and projected (2021) percentage Gaelic ability, Western Isles*

It is clear from Figure 2.26 that the progressive reduction in Gaelic ability is substantial and that the proportion of the total number of Gaelic speakers (data bars) is declining. This brings the projected Gaelic speaker population of the Western Isles to the threshold of the Moribund set in 2021.

Figure 2.27 indicates the trends and projections in Gaelic ability for the 3–17 age cohort.

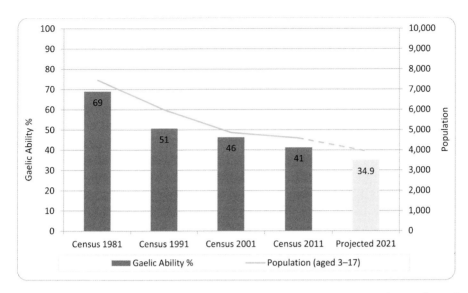

Figure 2.27 Trend in actual (solid data line) and projected (broken line) 3–17 yrs cohort and actual and projected (2021) percentage Gaelic ability, Western Isles

This indicates that the percentage Gaelic ability was just over 45% in the 2001 Census data (at 46%); it had fallen below 45% by 2011 and the projection for 2021 is that 35% of the projected 4,000 people in the youth cohort will have Gaelic ability.

2.5 SYNOPSIS AND CONCLUSIONS

The main findings of the statistical examination of the census data on Gaelic ability and use in this chapter are as follows:

1. The substantial rate of decadal decline (13% proportional decline, or loss of 3,220 speakers per decade) in Gaelic ability in the population as a whole and in the age cohorts (e.g. 15% proportional decline for the youth cohort).

2. The generational gaps in Gaelic ability between the older, adult and younger age cohorts (63%, 44% and 42% Gaelic ability respectively in 2011 Census). Furthermore: i) The reduction of ability among the young, as well as much other evidence, indicates that youth socialisation is dominated by monolingual use of English, to the exclusion of Gaelic. ii) The gap between the Gaelic ability data for the 50-yrs+ cohort (63%) and the data for the two other age cohorts, the 18–49 yrs cohorts (44%) and the 3–17 yrs cohorts (42%) in the 2011 Census, suggests that the two

cohorts born after 1960, i.e. under 50-yrs old, have had diminishing or limited experience of the social practice of Gaelic in high-density social networks. Most SDs of 80+% Gaelic ability were lost by 1991.

3. Actual use of Gaelic is far lower than Gaelic ability. This is seen in the substantial gap between the lower Family Household use of Gaelic (19% in 2011) and higher ability in Gaelic (52% in 2011).

4. Some SDs, Pooled SDs, and groups of SDs lead the way in the increasing salience and dominance of English, resulting in the growing Gaelic sociolinguistic fragmentation of the RA within a narrower percentage range.

5. Two important tipping points or thresholds appear in the diachronic analysis: i) The high social density of Gaelic ability at 80%+ of the population, and the precipitous decline below that rate, which has driven the process of language shift ever since; and ii) The lowest salience of Gaelic below the 15%∩45% nexus (point 6. below) where vernacular Gaelic is moribund and significantly marginalised.

6. Three main groups of fragility classes can be identified when Family Household Gaelic use is correlated with Gaelic ability data: a Residual nexus 20%∩55%; an Interstitial nexus (between both); and a Moribund nexus 15%∩45%.

7. The projected Gaelic ability data for 2021 indicates that the decline will continue and that the Interstitial and Moribund sets will grow, following the trend from social marginalisation to social erasure of Gaelic.

8. The levels of Gaelic use and competence among the two younger age cohorts, parental and young, are now too low to enable effective transfer of Gaelic to the emerging generation, resulting in projected further declines in Gaelic ability for 2021.

We discuss these points in turn below. We can, however, synopsise the historical decline of Gaelic evident in census data into five phases:

1. Up to the early 1980s. A high density phase in which slow contraction occurred but the percentage of the population with Gaelic ability remained over 80%.

2. Following the early 1980s. A phase of critical contraction below 80% of the population with Gaelic ability.

3. From the early 1980s to the present. A residual minoritised phase where the social salience of Gaelic continued to contract, with ability percentages at c. 65% and below.

4. From the early 2000s to the present, in an increasing number of SDs, a moribund minoritised phase where Gaelic is marginalised, and Gaelic ability falls to 45% or below.

5. A phase of societal erasure can be projected for Gaelic in its remaining historical habitat if current trends continue.

2.5.1 DEMOGRAPHIC DECLINE OF THE GAELIC GROUP

The Gaelic-speaking group has contracted at an average rate of decline of 13% for every ten-year period from 1981–2011. This equates to an absolute average loss of 3,220 Gaelic-competent residents per decade. The Gaelic-competent youth cohort (3–17 years) now stands at less than 2,000 people out of a total youth cohort of 4,592 in the Western Isles. A small minority-language group cannot survive this rate of societal contraction. The percentage ability in Gaelic for the population as a whole has contracted considerably from 80% in 1981 to 52% in 2011. This thirty-year period shows a percentage-point decline of 28 in Gaelic ability. The most optimistic estimation of the extent of the remaining vernacular group stands at about 11,000 people. This estimation of the upper numerical extent of the vernacular group is based on a comparison in section 2.4.1.4 of the Gaelic ability data in the RA (14,092 individuals in the 2011 Census) with those reporting using Gaelic at home (10,882 individuals). Another method of calculating the vernacular group size would be to multiply the Gaelic ability data (14,092) by the gradient of the linear correlation (0.78) between the ability and household use data. This correlation is discussed in section 2.4.3. This calculation yields a total of 10,991 individuals.

2.5.2 GAP IN GAELIC ABILITY BETWEEN THE OLDER, ADULT AND YOUNGER AGE COHORTS

A comparison of the young, adult and older age cohort Gaelic ability data indicates that the gap between the Gaelic data for the young and adult age cohort has decreased as the overall Gaelic ability data has contracted from 1981 to 2011. In 1981, 91% of the 50+ age cohort, 76% of the 18–49 age cohort and 69% of the 3–17 age cohort reported an ability in Gaelic (Table 2.6). In the 2011 Census, the respective cohort percentages are: 63% (50+); 44% (18–49 yrs) and 42% (3–17 yrs). In 1991 the age cohort comparison indicated a perceptible percentage difference: 85% (50+); 64% (18–49 yrs) and 51% (3–17 yrs). However, since the 2001 Census (75% (50+); 53% (18–49 yrs) and 47% (3–17 yrs)), the contrast has been increasingly noticeable between the higher rate for the 50+ year-old cohort and the rest (the two younger age cohorts coalescing to both having around half the cohort with Gaelic ability).

The data for the IGRP Research Area as a whole show a decline in Gaelic-speaking in the 3–17 age cohort of 27 points, from 69% in 1981 to 42% in 2011. The 18–49 age group in the IGRP area indicates a decrease of 33 points, from 76% in 1981 to 43% in 2011. The 50+ age group shows a decline of 28 points, from 91% in 1981 to 63% in 2011.

2.5.3 GAELIC FAMILY HOUSEHOLD USE AND GAELIC ABILITY; FRAGILITY NEXUS

52% of the 3+yrs population in the RA report an ability in Gaelic in the 2011 Census. This compares with 19% of the Family Households where all adults and all children are reported as speaking Gaelic. This indicates a significant gap between household practice of Gaelic and ability in Gaelic. Furthermore, for the sake of comparison, the value of 19% with Family Household Gaelic use is less than half of the 42% in the 3–17 age cohort who report Gaelic ability. Three main groups of fragility classes can be identified when Family Household Gaelic use is correlated with Gaelic ability data: a Residual nexus at or above 20%∩55%; Interstitial nexus (between both); and a Moribund nexus at or below 15%∩45%. The decline into the Moribund nexus indicates that the social use of Gaelic in those SDs has been reduced to the margins in its former vernacular sociogeographic contexts, amounting to cultural linguistic habitat loss.

2.5.4 GROWING GAELIC SOCIOLINGUISTIC FRAGMENTATION

The cluster analysis of the SIR values demonstrates that the distribution of these SD values becomes more fragmented as the average Gaelic ability has contracted from the 1981 to the 2011 Census. The data fit analysis of the K-clustering revealed that the 1981 Census data were distributed among three clusters. The strongest and largest cluster corresponded to almost all the rural districts of the RA (Lewis, Harris, Uist, Barra and Staffin). The middle weaker cluster is comprised of Tiree and two SDs surrounding Stornoway. The smallest and weakest cluster indicated the effect of the data of the rural town settlements of Stornoway and Benbecula.

In contrast, the K-clustering analysis of the 2011 Census data revealed that the SDs were distributed in five clusters. The strongest cluster, seven SDs, comprised SDs in the north west of Lewis, South Uist, Barra and North Harris. The lowest cluster comprised Stornoway and suburbs and the Isle of Tiree. The remaining SD data, with mid-range values, comprised two small clusters and a larger one.

The SDs with the reported highest percentage of Gaelic ability in the 2011 Census are South Uist (south), the West Side (north) and South Uist (north) at 66%, followed by North Harris (65%). The lowest percentage Gaelic ability is for the Isle of Tiree and Stornoway (Point Road suburbs) at 38%, followed by Stornoway Town (39%), and Stornoway (Barvas Road suburbs) at 42%.

The SDs indicating the most percentage-points decline in Gaelic ability in the 1981–2011 period are Staffin (39 points), followed by North Point, South Point, North Lochs (all at 38 points) and Uig (37 points). The districts evincing the least decline are Benbecula (growth of 0.5 point), Stornoway Town (19 points), South Uist (north) at 20 points, Barra & Vatersay (24 points) and South Uist (south) at 26 points.

When we compare the decline in Gaelic ability for all people (3+) in the 25 SDs in the thirty-year period from the 2011 Census to the 1981 Census (Tables 2.5 and 2.6), there is a range of 96% of Gaelic-competent residents in the highest SD to 52% in the lowest SD in 1981; yielding a spread of 44%. The corresponding range for 1991 is 89% to 47% (a spread of 42%). And for 2001 a range of 76% to 45% (a spread of 31%); and for 2011 a range of 66% to 38% (a spread of 28%). It is noticeable that, as the average level declines, the range in the levels of Gaelic ability contracts.

In all Pooled Study Districts, there is a decadal decline from 1981 to 2011. There are slower rates of decline in the two Pooled SDs containing rural-town settlements: Stornoway & Suburbs; and North Uist & Benbecula. The decreases ranged from 46% (Staffin & Tiree Pooled SD), to 18% (North Uist & Benbecula Pooled SD).

2.5.5 PROGNOSIS FOR GAELIC

The examination of census data suggests that the current trajectory of the remaining Gaelic-speaking networks in the islands is propelling the Gaelic group from the latter part of the residual minoritised phase into the penultimate phase of societal collapse. The projection for levels of Gaelic ability, based on an extrapolation of the current rates of decline, indicates that 10 of the 25 SDs in the islands will be in the Moribund set by 2021. Furthermore, the Research Area as a whole is also projected to be in this Moribund set by 2021. Therefore, unless there is a radical change in circumstances before the next census returns of 2021, the remaining Gaelic vernacular areas will move closer to, or pass, a point of societal collapse where Gaelic will be marginal in all generations. This clearly leaves little opportunity (at the time of writing in 2019) for serious language planning to engage productively with the remaining societal presence of vernacular Gaelic for feasible revitalisation efforts and results.

2.5.6 DEMOGRAPHIC AND SOCIO-ECONOMIC ASPECTS OF GAELIC DEMOLINGUISTIC FRAGILITY

The trajectory presented in this chapter portrays a challenging context of Gaelic demolinguistic fragility. Across what might be termed one generation covering the Census returns from 1981 to 2011, we are witnessing a grave threat to the societal existence of Gaelic in the islands. This depiction of threat to the sociogeographic viability of Gaelic must be considered along with the socio-economic challenges of living in such peripheral areas.

The census figures regarding Gaelic ability and use, together with the population and ability projections for 2021, clearly illustrate the scale of the challenge for future Gaelic revitalisation. There is no surviving multigenerational Gaelic-dominant vernacular community, nor can any remaining Gaelic community survive, given current circumstances and trends. Furthermore, for Gaelic to have a meaningful chance of revitalisation it is imperative to seriously address the socio-economic challenges, for instance the problem of stemming the population loss. These inter-related issues need to be addressed within the timeline of the next two National Gaelic Language Plans up to 2028 at both national and local levels, to attempt to secure a sustainable future for Gaelic in its last remaining vernacular communities.

2.6 DEMOGRAPHIC MAPS OF GAELIC VERNACULAR STUDY DISTRICTS, 1981–2011

In this section, we present two sets of progression maps of Gaelic ability data from the 1981–2011 Censuses for the 25 SDs (Tables 2.5 and 2.6). The Gaelic ability data for these census periods are mapped according to percentage custom breaks of 15 percentage points pertaining to the five Gaelic ability bands of 90%+, <90%, <75%, <60% and <45% of the population of each SD. The first set of maps (Maps 2.2–2.5) displays these bands for the whole 3+ year-old population and the second set (Maps 2.6–2.9) displays the corresponding distributions for the youngest cohort, 3–17-year olds. These maps illustrate the contraction and fragmentation of the geographic distributions of Gaelic ability; and that since 2011 the youth cohort has fallen below the 45% Gaelic ability level in almost half of the SDs, thus resembling the Moribund set (Map 2.9; cf. Table 2.4). The geographic changes are most apparent in Maps 2.6–2.9 of the youth data. From the point of view of the geographic spread of English social dominance, the small area comprising two SDs in Stornoway with <45% Gaelic ability in 1981 spreads in all directions to nine adjacent SDs in 2011 and further afield to South Harris SD (totalling 12 SDs <45%). Two SDs in Uist show some decadal increases over this period in the youth data: Benbecula and South Uist (south); presumably as a result of GME provision.

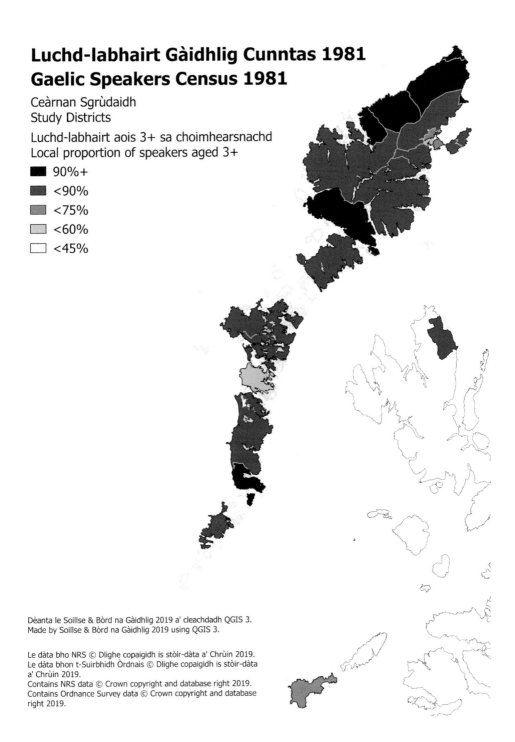

Luchd-labhairt Gàidhlig Cunntas 1981
Gaelic Speakers Census 1981

Ceàrnan Sgrùdaidh
Study Districts

Luchd-labhairt aois 3+ sa choimhearsnachd
Local proportion of speakers aged 3+

■ 90%+
■ <90%
■ <75%
□ <60%
□ <45%

Dèanta le Soillse & Bòrd na Gàidhlig 2019 a' cleachdadh QGIS 3.
Made by Soillse & Bòrd na Gàidhlig 2019 using QGIS 3.

Le dàta bho NRS © Dlighe copaigidh is stòir-dàta a' Chrùin 2019.
Le dàta bhon t-Suirbhidh Òrdnais © Dlighe copaigidh is stòir-dàta
a' Chrùin 2019.
Contains NRS data © Crown copyright and database right 2019.
Contains Ordnance Survey data © Crown copyright and database
right 2019.

Map 2.2 *Percentage custom breaks of residents with Gaelic ability in the Research Area, 1981 Census*

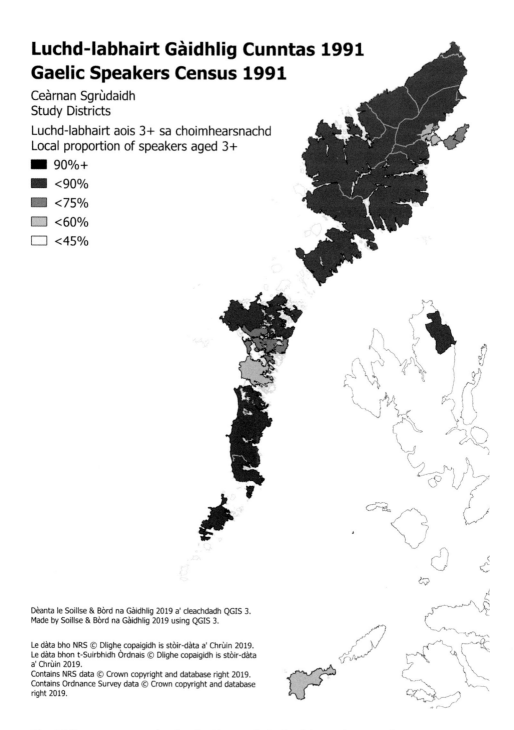

Luchd-labhairt Gàidhlig Cunntas 1991
Gaelic Speakers Census 1991

Ceàrnan Sgrùdaidh
Study Districts

Luchd-labhairt aois 3+ sa choimhearsnachd
Local proportion of speakers aged 3+

- ■ 90%+
- ■ <90%
- ■ <75%
- ■ <60%
- □ <45%

Dèanta le Soillse & Bòrd na Gàidhlig 2019 a' cleachdadh QGIS 3.
Made by Soillse & Bòrd na Gàidhlig 2019 using QGIS 3.

Le dàta bho NRS © Dlighe copaigidh is stòir-dàta a' Chrùin 2019.
Le dàta bhon t-Suirbhidh Òrdnais © Dlighe copaigidh is stòir-dàta
a' Chrùin 2019.
Contains NRS data © Crown copyright and database right 2019.
Contains Ordnance Survey data © Crown copyright and database
right 2019.

Map 2.3 *Percentage custom breaks of residents with Gaelic ability in the Research Area, 1991 Census*

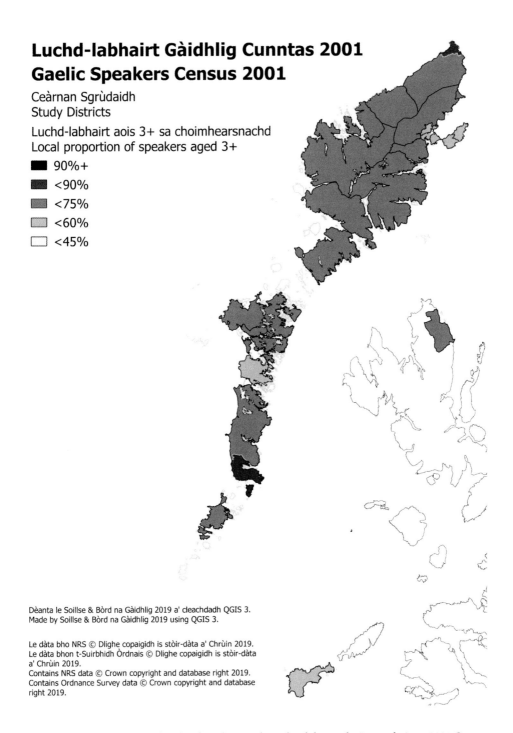

Luchd-labhairt Gàidhlig Cunntas 2001
Gaelic Speakers Census 2001

Ceàrnan Sgrùdaidh
Study Districts

Luchd-labhairt aois 3+ sa choimhearsnachd
Local proportion of speakers aged 3+

- 90%+
- <90%
- <75%
- <60%
- <45%

Dèanta le Soillse & Bòrd na Gàidhlig 2019 a' cleachdadh QGIS 3.
Made by Soillse & Bòrd na Gàidhlig 2019 using QGIS 3.

Le dàta bho NRS © Dlighe copaigidh is stòir-dàta a' Chrùin 2019.
Le dàta bhon t-Suirbhidh Òrdnais © Dlighe copaigidh is stòir-dàta
a' Chrùin 2019.
Contains NRS data © Crown copyright and database right 2019.
Contains Ordnance Survey data © Crown copyright and database
right 2019.

Map 2.4 Percentage custom breaks of residents with Gaelic ability in the Research Area, 2001 Census

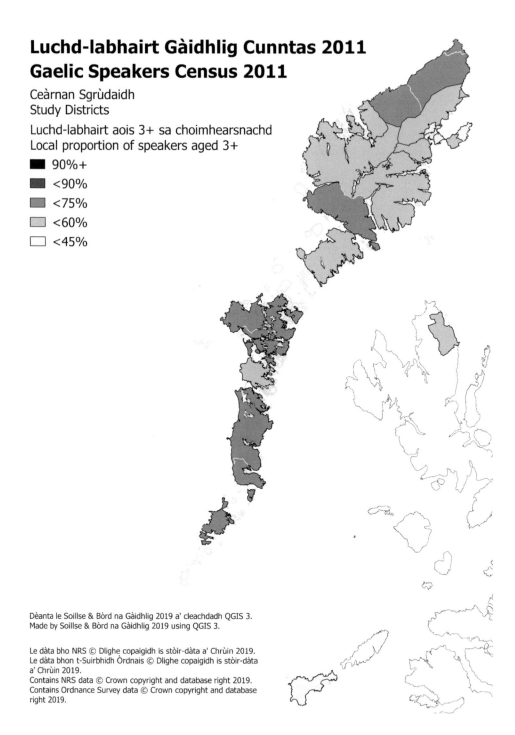

Luchd-labhairt Gàidhlig Cunntas 2011
Gaelic Speakers Census 2011

Ceàrnan Sgrùdaidh
Study Districts

Luchd-labhairt aois 3+ sa choimhearsnachd
Local proportion of speakers aged 3+

- ■ 90%+
- ■ <90%
- ■ <75%
- ☐ <60%
- ☐ <45%

Dèanta le Soillse & Bòrd na Gàidhlig 2019 a' cleachdadh QGIS 3.
Made by Soillse & Bòrd na Gàidhlig 2019 using QGIS 3.

Le dàta bho NRS © Dlighe copaigidh is stòir-dàta a' Chrùin 2019.
Le dàta bhon t-Suirbhidh Òrdnais © Dlighe copaigidh is stòir-dàta
a' Chrùin 2019.
Contains NRS data © Crown copyright and database right 2019.
Contains Ordnance Survey data © Crown copyright and database
right 2019.

Map 2.5 *Percentage custom breaks of residents with Gaelic ability in the Research Area, 2011 Census*

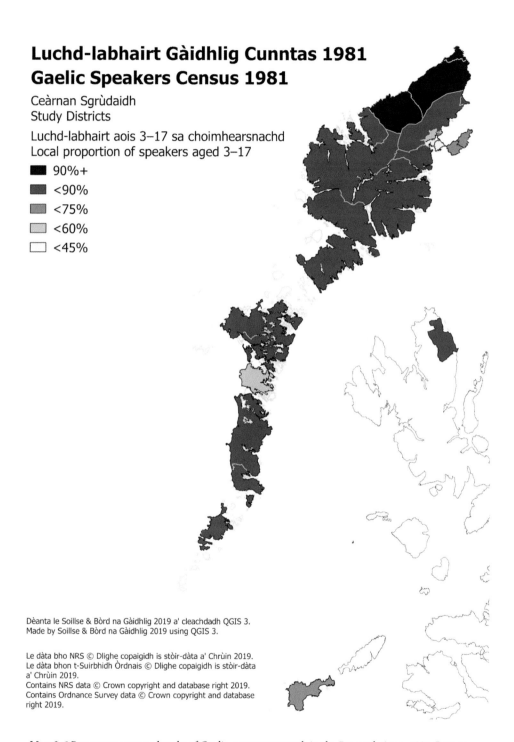

Luchd-labhairt Gàidhlig Cunntas 1981
Gaelic Speakers Census 1981

Ceàrnan Sgrùdaidh
Study Districts

Luchd-labhairt aois 3–17 sa choimhearsnachd
Local proportion of speakers aged 3–17

■ 90%+
■ <90%
■ <75%
■ <60%
□ <45%

Dèanta le Soillse & Bòrd na Gàidhlig 2019 a' cleachdadh QGIS 3.
Made by Soillse & Bòrd na Gàidhlig 2019 using QGIS 3.

Le dàta bho NRS © Dlighe copaigidh is stòir-dàta a' Chrùin 2019.
Le dàta bhon t-Suirbhidh Òrdnais © Dlighe copaigidh is stòir-dàta
a' Chrùin 2019.
Contains NRS data © Crown copyright and database right 2019.
Contains Ordnance Survey data © Crown copyright and database
right 2019.

Map 2.6 *Percentage custom breaks of Gaelic-competent youth in the Research Area, 1981 Census*

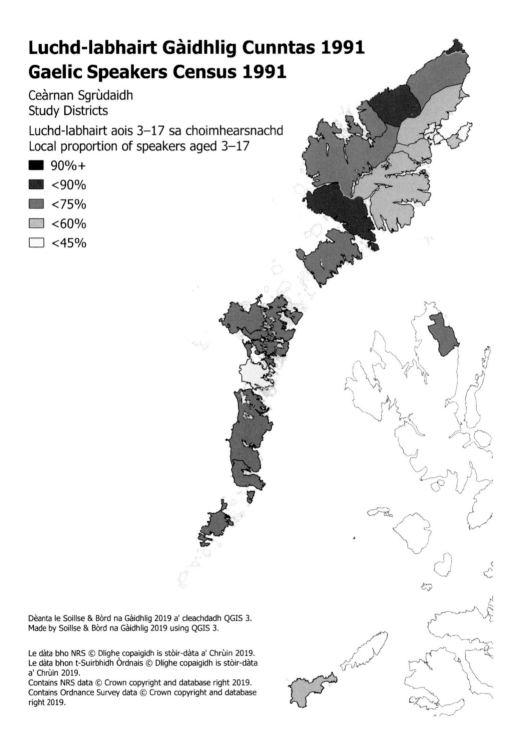

Luchd-labhairt Gàidhlig Cunntas 1991
Gaelic Speakers Census 1991

Ceàrnan Sgrùdaidh
Study Districts

Luchd-labhairt aois 3–17 sa choimhearsnachd
Local proportion of speakers aged 3–17

- ■ 90%+
- ■ <90%
- ▨ <75%
- ▨ <60%
- □ <45%

Dèanta le Soillse & Bòrd na Gàidhlig 2019 a' cleachdadh QGIS 3.
Made by Soillse & Bòrd na Gàidhlig 2019 using QGIS 3.

Le dàta bho NRS © Dlighe copaigidh is stòir-dàta a' Chrùin 2019.
Le dàta bhon t-Suirbhidh Òrdnais © Dlighe copaigidh is stòir-dàta
a' Chrùin 2019.
Contains NRS data © Crown copyright and database right 2019.
Contains Ordnance Survey data © Crown copyright and database
right 2019.

Map 2.7 *Percentage custom breaks of Gaelic-competent youth in the Research Area, 1991 Census*

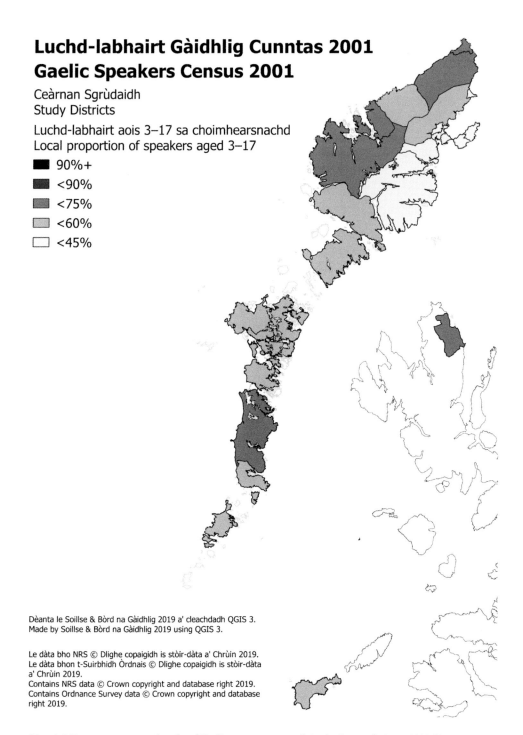

Luchd-labhairt Gàidhlig Cunntas 2001
Gaelic Speakers Census 2001

Ceàrnan Sgrùdaidh
Study Districts

Luchd-labhairt aois 3–17 sa choimhearsnachd
Local proportion of speakers aged 3–17

- 90%+
- <90%
- <75%
- <60%
- <45%

Dèanta le Soillse & Bòrd na Gàidhlig 2019 a' cleachdadh QGIS 3.
Made by Soillse & Bòrd na Gàidhlig 2019 using QGIS 3.

Le dàta bho NRS © Dlighe copaigidh is stòir-dàta a' Chrùin 2019.
Le dàta bhon t-Suirbhidh Òrdnais © Dlighe copaigidh is stòir-dàta
a' Chrùin 2019.
Contains NRS data © Crown copyright and database right 2019.
Contains Ordnance Survey data © Crown copyright and database
right 2019.

Map 2.8 *Percentage custom breaks of Gaelic-competent youth in the Research Area, 2001 Census*

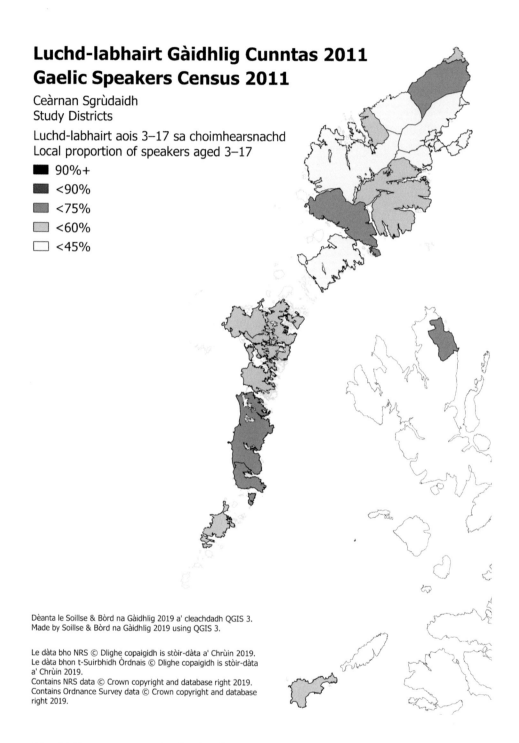

Luchd-labhairt Gàidhlig Cunntas 2011
Gaelic Speakers Census 2011

Ceàrnan Sgrùdaidh
Study Districts

Luchd-labhairt aois 3–17 sa choimhearsnachd
Local proportion of speakers aged 3–17

- ■ 90%+
- ■ <90%
- ■ <75%
- ■ <60%
- □ <45%

Dèanta le Soillse & Bòrd na Gàidhlig 2019 a' cleachdadh QGIS 3.
Made by Soillse & Bòrd na Gàidhlig 2019 using QGIS 3.

Le dàta bho NRS © Dlighe copaigidh is stòir-dàta a' Chrùin 2019.
Le dàta bhon t-Suirbhidh Òrdnais © Dlighe copaigidh is stòir-dàta
a' Chrùin 2019.
Contains NRS data © Crown copyright and database right 2019.
Contains Ordnance Survey data © Crown copyright and database
right 2019.

Map 2.9 Percentage custom breaks of Gaelic-competent youth in the Research Area, 2011 Census

3 SURVEY OF PRESCHOOL CHILDREN'S LANGUAGE ABILITY AND USE

3.1 INTRODUCTION

This chapter presents a descriptive statistical analysis of language use by preschool children and assesses the extent of social practice of Gaelic in the context of the family and preschools in the Research Area, i.e. the Western Isles, Staffin (Isle of Skye) and the Isle of Tiree. Census data, described in Chapter 2, offer a generalised depiction of Gaelic as a reported language competence (without any detailed data on actual degrees of individual competence or functionality). In contrast, the chief aim of this preschool module of the IGRP is to delineate the extent to which Gaelic survives as a language rooted in social practice and as a societal competence, as evinced in the familial transmission of native-spoken Gaelic. These indicators will allow a comparison of family transmission data with Gaelic ability data from the Census. This module, therefore, provides baseline familial and communal evidence on the current levels of competence and use of Gaelic as a family-transmitted language.

This module of the IGRP aimed to survey every preschool (in Gaelic: *sgoil-àraich,* plural *sgoiltean-àraich*) in the RA. Initially, all preschool units in the target area were identified (26 in all, 25 of which responded), and the numbers of pupils within those units for 2015–2016 were ascertained. The survey work was carried out in November and December 2015. A separate intake of children (according to birthdate and eligibility) entered the preschool environment from January 2016, but this later intake is not included in this survey. The aim of the survey was to cover the preschool cohort in the RA, and therefore all preschools were contacted and almost all were successfully surveyed, both English (six preschools) and Gaelic-medium (GM) (partly or wholly GM, 19 preschools; out of a total of 25 responding preschools; see section 3.3.1).

3.1.1 AIMS

The survey aimed to ascertain and differentiate the densities of family acquirers and preschool learners of Gaelic in the 3–5 age cohort. This preschool module is a study of Gaelic language ability and practice among children attending preschools. The survey was undertaken among preschool managers and teachers. Information on the Gaelic ability of the preschool children at the time of enrolment provides a gauge to assess the levels of Gaelic language practice in families. The survey also produces data which provide for an assessment of age-appropriate Gaelic competence, and assessment of the prevalence of Gaelic among this youngest peer-group. The survey also aimed to assess the perceived levels of Gaelic practice in the preschool catchment areas, thus further illuminating the receding social geography of Gaelic.

3.1.2 DEMOGRAPHICS

Data drawn from the 2011 Census indicate that 181 of 616 children aged 3–4 years in the RA speak Gaelic (i.e. 29.4% in Table 3.1). The 2011 Census indicated that the 3–4 age cohort, nationally, showed an increase of 30% in the numbers of individuals with Gaelic ability over the 10 years from 2001 to 2011 (613 to 797 in actual numbers), the largest of any age cohort. This represented an intercensal increase from 0.53% of the national age cohort to 0.70% of the national age cohort. However, the percentage of children in that cohort with *some* Gaelic skill fell during the same period, from 1048 (0.91%) in 2001 to 995 (0.86%) in 2011. Regarding the overall Gaelic speaker community in Scotland, 1% of the language's speakers were from the 3–4 cohort (O'Hanlon and Paterson 2015a: 10–13).[24] Seven civil parishes in Scotland (all in the Western Isles: Barra, South Uist, North Uist, Harris, Lochs, Uig, Barvas) were recorded as having over 50% of residents with Gaelic ability in 2011. In those civil parishes, 43.2% of the 3–4 age cohort could speak Gaelic, while 52% had some Gaelic skills. Stornoway was the only civil parish in the Western Isles which had less than 50% of residents with Gaelic ability in 2011. Table 3.1 shows that in the Western Isles as a whole, 29.5% of 3–4 year olds are reported to have Gaelic ability; and the RA has a corresponding 29.4%.

Analysis by Mac an Tàilleir (2015) on the 2011 Census yields similar numbers of children aged 3–4 years in the Western Isles who speak Gaelic. In the six areas comprising the Western Isles analysed by Mac an Tàilleir, he counted 29 children with Gaelic ability in Barra, 23 in South Uist, 9 in Benbecula, 8 in North Uist, 9 on the Isle of Harris, and 83 on the Isle of Lewis, totalling 161 children with Gaelic ability, as indicated in Table 3.1.

For Tiree, Coll and Mull combined, Mac an Tàilleir counted just two children or 6.5% of the 3–4 age cohort in those three islands who could speak Gaelic (and none who were enumerated as being able to understand only). For the Isle of Skye, Mac an Tàilleir identified, in the 3–4 age cohort, 44 (23% of the age cohort) who could speak Gaelic and an additional 12 children who could understand Gaelic.

---

24 Scotland's Census 2001 and 2011 — National Records of Scotland. Gaelic Report (part 1): Figure 3. Proportions drawn from tables: AT_003_2001 and AT_236_2011.

3–4 year olds	Source / Report	Total	Gaelic ability	% Gaelic ability
Western Isles	2011 Census	599	177	29.5%
Western Isles	Mac an Tàilleir (2015)	516	161	31.2%
Western Isles, Staffin, Tiree (RA)	2011 Census	616	181	29.4%

Table 3.1 Gaelic-speaking 3–4 year olds, Western Isles, RA, 2011 Census v. Mac an Tàilleir (2015)[25]

We can compare the numbers on Gaelic ability in this cohort to the enrolment numbers in early years GME, which are provided by Bòrd na Gàidhlig. The comparison of ability data with enrolment figures implies that over a third of GME preschoolers have no ability in Gaelic on enrolment. Bòrd na Gàidhlig's (2018b) Gaelic Education data for 2017/18 indicate 332 children in the Western Isles in 19 *sgoiltean-àraich*. This represents 66.3% of the age cohort in the Western Isles and 31% of the national total of children in *sgoiltean-àraich*. The 2017/18 data also show 54 *sgoiltean-àraich* nationally, with 1,078 children in attendance. The Bòrd's (2017a) Gaelic Education data for 2016/17 indicated 318 children in the Western Isles in 20 *sgoiltean-àraich*. This represents 63.5% of the age cohort in the Western Isles and 31% of the national total of children in *sgoiltean-àraich*. The 2016/17 data also showed 54 *sgoiltean-àraich* nationally, with 1,039 children in attendance.

3.1.3 HOUSEHOLD LINGUISTIC CONTEXT, CENSUS 2011

As mentioned above, the 2011 Census data indicate that 181 of 616 children aged 3–4 in the RA can speak Gaelic (i.e. 29.4% in Table 3.1). For the 3–4 age cohort nationally, of children reported as being able to speak Gaelic, 51% lived in households where all adults had some Gaelic language skills, 24% lived in households where some (but not all) adults had some Gaelic language skills and a further 25% lived in households where no adults had any Gaelic language skills (O'Hanlon and Paterson 2015a: 15–16). This suggests that, in Scotland as a whole, at least half of the children with Gaelic ability in the 3–4 age cohort have experienced familial transmission of Gaelic with the simultaneous presence of English spoken by other household members. Furthermore, it is clear from much other evidence that many adults with Gaelic ability are not actual Gaelic *speakers* in these family households. Nationally, 62.9% of those identified as having Gaelic ability in the 3–4 age cohort were reported as using Gaelic at home, suggesting a relatively high level of familial Gaelic use and experience for this 62.9% (O'Hanlon and Paterson 2015b: 60). This means that 37.1% do not speak Gaelic at home, implying that their level of Gaelic is probably quite low. It is reasonable to assume that most of the children in this 37.1% are in the process of

---

25 The difference between IGRP and Mac an Tàilleir's numbers may be due to issues related to standard outputs (2.4.1.1).

acquiring Gaelic at preschool. For the 3–4 age cohort, of those children reported as speaking Gaelic at home, 63% lived in households where all adults had some Gaelic language skills, 26% lived in households where some (but not all) adults had some Gaelic language skills and 10% lived in households where no adults had any Gaelic language skills (this entails that this 10% of children speak Gaelic among themselves at home or speak some Gaelic to non-Gaelic-speaking adults).

3.1.4 REVIEW OF LITERATURE ON EARLY-YEARS GME

There is a sizeable body of international literature on preschool minority-language contexts (e.g., for French in Canada, Fred Genesee *et al.* (1989) as well as, for Irish, Tina Hickey (1997, 1999) and Pádraig Ó Duibhir (2018)). Studies of minority-language early-years provision worldwide commonly report five main related points: i) the dominance of socialisation in the majority language; ii) a sub-optimal level of minority-language attainment, often termed immersionese (cf. 4.2.1.1); iii) the frequent link between limited language social salience and limited language acquisition; iv) (given these points) a common unrealistic expectation or optimism in outcomes of minority-language education; and v) the lack of financial, human and educational resources in the minority-language context. Many of these issues can have considerable negative impact, particularly with regard to their cumulative effects, on the quality of provision, language acquisition and preschool attainments.

Gaelic sociolinguistic studies relating to the preschool age cohort have focused to a large extent on the context and delivery of Gaelic-medium provision in educational and care facilities as components of policy interventions in support of Gaelic maintenance and regeneration. These studies have been national in their focus. Few studies have focused on the vernacular context of the Western Isles and in particular on Gaelic practice and acquisition among preschoolers and its relation to GME provision (cp. MacLeod *et al.* (2014) for primary school children in vernacular and non-vernacular geographic areas). Cassie Smith-Christmas (2012: 59) observes that:

> The conception of solely Gaelic, not bilingual, education is attributed to the formation of infant (aged 3–4 years old) playgroups. Inspired by the success of Welsh immersion education, parents concerned with the maintenance of Gaelic advocated the formation of playgroups where infants could be fully immersed in the language. They subsequently set up four 'cròileagan' (playgroups), and by 1981 there were playgroups operating in Oban, Edinburgh, Pitlochry, and Sleat, on Skye. In 1982, *Comhairle nan Sgoiltean-Àraich* (Council of Nursery Schools) was established to facilitate the provision of Gaelic playgroups through Scotland. In 1985, immersive Gaelic education extended to primary level, as parents, frustrated with the lack of Gaelic fluency pupils were attaining in the bilingual program, witnessed the comparative success of the immersive infant playgroups.

In general, the academic and public policy debates about the preschool age cohort concentrate on five concerns:

- Extending the provision and uptake of preschool Gaelic-medium education
- The minority sociolinguistic context of curricular implementation in this preschool sector, including the educational issues involved in providing GME among children with varying competences in Gaelic, often including no competence
- Professional development among preschool staff
- Provision of GME in a context where English is socially dominant
- GME preschool provision as a key component of Gaelic policy and revitalisation.

Bòrd na Gàidhlig's 2012–2017 National Gaelic Language Plan (2012) aimed for: 'An increase in the acquisition and use of Gaelic by young people in the home and increased numbers of children entering Gaelic-medium early years education' (2012: 8). The Bòrd further states:

> Early language learning produces an attachment and loyalty to a language and provides a basis for and expectation of continuity in Gaelic language learning. This development area will be prioritised and, through the delivery of effective early years support, activity and resources will be directed to initiatives that promote Gaelic in the home and early years. (Bòrd na Gàidhlig 2012: 18)

Turning to the context of this project's RA, and the Western Isles in particular, Comhairle nan Eilean Siar's Gaelic Language Plan 2013–2017 made only limited reference to preschool support. In 2016–17, there were 20 Gaelic-medium preschool units in the local authority area, with a further five private preschool providers. The Council's draft 2018–22 Gaelic Plan has early learning and childcare as one of its 10 priority areas, alongside its strategic objective of strengthening Gaelic in familial settings (Comhairle nan Eilean Siar 2017b: 10).

Aspirations in relation to GME preschool participation are pursued, of course, in their demolinguistic context. In this regard, MacKinnon (1999: 3) has argued that aspirations to acquire and revernacularise Gaelic through educational provision alone could not produce a feasible solution to the challenge of language revitalisation:

> The prospects of regeneration through Gaelic-medium playgroups and schooling are being rapidly overtaken by massive demographic loss of speakers … . Without adequate understanding of the problem, effective policies will not be capable of being applied in time, and a point of no return will be very shortly evident.

Serious minority-language revitalisation requires an integrated societal and educational approach. Preschools and schools alone are not enough.

3.1.4.1 *CHALLENGES IN GME PRESCHOOL SECTOR: IMMERSION AND RESOURCES*

Christine Stephen *et al.* (2010; 2011; 2012; 2013; 2016) have examined national Gaelic-medium preschool provision and highlighted related pedagogical challenges. Stephen *et al.'s* (2010) *Review of Gaelic-Medium Early Education and Childcare* for the Scottish Government comprises a survey of Gaelic preschool providers in Scotland (including childminders, playgroups, parent and toddler groups). They show (2010: 23) that most children (88%) enrolling in Gaelic preschools in Scotland come from English-only or mainly English-speaking backgrounds. For the majority of these children the preschool provides the predominant or only environment in which Gaelic is heard. Therefore, relatively low numbers of children have experienced Gaelic (cf. McPake and Stephen 2016: 107; Pollock 2010: 119‒20) prior to attending the preschool. This poses a challenge to the maintenance of a Gaelic environment for those attending GME provision for this age group (Stephen *et al.* 2010: 24). Indeed, Stephen *et al.* (2010: 24) found that only a third of providers surveyed adopted a 'full immersion' or Gaelic-only approach (in contrast to the current Education Scotland (2017) report which favours 'total immersion' in GME provision). The nature of the provision and the ubiquity of English outside the playrooms contributes to repeated 'shifts to English' inside the playrooms (Stephen *et al.* 2010: 26; cf. Stephen *et al.* 2012: 27). In general, the Gaelic-medium preschool system is primarily focused on assisting the development of some Gaelic competence in secondary bilinguals.

From the Stephen *et al.* (2010) report, we can summarise the major issues identified:

1. Children's learning and ensuring high-quality experiences for children
2. Effective approaches to support those children who are fluent as well as those learning Gaelic in the same environment
3. Ensuring practitioners are appropriately trained to deliver on the Curriculum for Excellence
4. Overcoming the lack of financial, human and educational resources for GME
5. Dealing with a range of parental expectations
6. Managing demand for GME provision and promoting its availability.

In the following discussion, we will review how these issues have been addressed in relevant reports. Stephen *et al.* (2016: 60-61) highlight the perceived importance of extending preschool uptake and provision as a part of the current revitalisation project:

> Establishing and extending the supply of GM preschool educational provision is an important part of the Gaelic language revitalisation policy, endorsed by the Scottish Government and implemented by Bòrd na Gàidhlig … translating language policy into effective pedagogy and practice is not straightforward.

On a practical level, the difficulties in resourcing Gaelic-medium preschools with educational aids were summarised by Stephen *et al.* (2012: 28) as follows:

> Identifying and acquiring appropriate resources was a major concern and source of frustration across providers. About two-thirds of the respondents to our survey included acquiring more Gaelic medium resources among their hopes for the future. The number and range of books published in Gaelic is limited and there is an even more restricted supply of other resources such as posters, DVDs, computer games … . Because many settings do not have access to the internet in the playroom they cannot take advantage of the resources emerging on Gaelic language websites.

3.1.4.2 *IMMERSION POLICIES AND PARENTAL VIEWS OF GME*

The report by Stephen *et al.* (2010) indicated that the levels to which Gaelic and English were actually used in bilingual or immersion preschool settings varied — often considerably — among providers. Their report raised the issue of expectations for Gaelic attainment in the context of varying levels of English and Gaelic inputs, especially given the limited number of contact hours per week, usually less than 20 hours (Stephen *et al.* 2010: 23). As stated, most children's exposure to Gaelic is solely through the preschool environment.

The current curricular guidance for preschools offering GME is that 'teachers will ensure that Gàidhlig [Gaelic] is the language of learning and communication, and that all areas of the curriculum are taught through the medium of Gàidhlig' (Learning and Teaching Scotland 2010: 2 and cited in O'Hanlon *et al.* 2012: iv). This policy formulation indicates greater clarity than previous iterations concerning best practice for Gaelic preschools. For instance, the following recommendation cannot be taken as best-practice immersion: 'a judicious blend of English and Gaelic which allows the children to express themselves freely' (Her Majesty's Inspectorate of Education 1994: 1). It is clear from a 2017 report of GME provision (Education Scotland 2017: 1) that preschool GME policy now favours a 'total immersion' approach. It is apparent, however, that 'total immersion' has not been attained in all GME preschools historically, as discussed above; and, from this module of the IGRP, it is evident that there is a high level of English use by children in these preschools.

Among earlier studies of GME preschool education, Alasdair Roberts' (1991) work on parental attitudes towards GME (cited in O'Hanlon 2012: 51-52) suggested that parents of preschool children in the Western Isles in the late 1980s were more inclined to support the idea of GME rather than actually ensuring their child participated in GME. These parental views reflected a competitive functional reality in which Gaelic was, or is, perceived as less advantageous in the long term (educationally and vocationally) than English. In addition to tensions between parental aspirations for GME and actual parental support for GME, we can cite the related problem pointed out by Joanna McPake and Christine Stephen (2016: 122) regarding the imbalance they observed in their pilot study conducted in two preschools in one (unspecified) local authority area, between the (parental and authority) expectations and what is linguistically and pedagogically achievable with a minority language which the children have not experienced in vernacular use:

> there has been insufficient attention in the literature on MLM (Minoritised Language Medium) early years education to the tension between the expectation, deriving from current thinking about effective preschool education, that playrooms are environments where children express their social and cognitive competence through language, and the expectation deriving from language revitalisation programmes, that children in MLM playrooms should make a strong start on the learning of what, for most, is a second language, not previously encountered.

In short, optimal acquisition in immersion contexts can be challenging even when the target-language is widely spoken in the children's environment, but acquisition of a language not heard outside the playroom is evidently more challenging.

3.1.4.3 STAFF DEVELOPMENT IN PRESCHOOL PROVISION

The report of Stephen *et al.* (2010: 20) indicated that the recruitment and retention of appropriately trained and skilled staff is challenging; many of the posts are part-time and salaries are generally low (2010: 11–12). The findings have been summarised in Stephen *et al.* (2012: 25):

> practitioners in Gaelic medium settings did not have good opportunities for training and professional development, wages were not high … the rate of staff turnover was considerable in some settings and not all practitioners

had non-contact time for planning and recording. These findings indicate that there is a need to improve the conditions in which practitioners work and develop their practice if children attending Gaelic medium provision are to be assured of high quality early years experiences.

Stephen *et al.* (2010: 24) further state that these employment-related conditions also contribute to the difficulty of maintaining a Gaelic-only preschool setting, noting that establishing such an environment 'is a challenge which few practitioners have been trained to meet'.

In the face of these operational, linguistic and social challenges, Stephen *et al.* (2010: 39-42) call for more staff development, increased funding for development of educational resources, sharing of knowledge and practices, and mechanisms to increase opportunities for home and informal use of Gaelic. Stephen *et al.* (2012: 32) emphasise the political dimension involved in addressing these issues:

> the provision of development workers or materials will not in itself ensure effective language learning and high-quality experiences … political support is necessary too to make the adjustments that will allow minority-language provision and bi-lingual preschool education to deliver all that is expected of it.

3.1.5 METHODOLOGY

The data on the preschool age cohort in the RA were obtained by means of a questionnaire distributed to preschools. A copy of the full questionnaire is provided in **Appendix 8**. A series of consultations were carried out at an early stage of the IGRP in 2015 with members of the Early Years Team from Comhairle nan Eilean Siar in Stornoway, Isle of Lewis, to confer with relevant stakeholders and to seek feedback on the appropriateness of the aims, design and content of the questionnaire. Comhairle nan Eilean Siar, the Highland Council, and Argyll and Bute Council granted approval for the preschool module of the project, including the questionnaire. Ethical approval for all research material and consent from the appropriate stakeholders was received before the survey was carried out. The IGRP team were particularly cognisant of the ethical issues involved in this survey, due to the age of the children and the onus put on school managers and staff to complete the questionnaire. In all cases, the respondents were free to ignore questions they found to be too sensitive or too burdensome to answer. Following agreement, the finalised questionnaires, information and consent forms, and parental opt-out documentation were forwarded by the IGRP team to Comhairle nan Eilean Siar's Early Years Team in November 2015. Gaelic and English versions of the questionnaire were available for completion by the preschool staff.

The Early Years Team distributed the materials to all preschool units in the Western Isles. Separate arrangements were made, with permission from the relevant councils, to distribute the documentation and surveys to the preschools in Tiree and Staffin, Isle of Skye.

The preschools received a separate questionnaire form for each child in order to obtain separate data on each individual child. These questionnaires were subsequently completed by preschool managers or teachers who assessed the Gaelic competences and language practices of each preschooler regarding two points in time: enrolment and time of survey. Completed questionnaires were then returned to the Early Years Team, Comhairle nan Eilean Siar. The Early Years Team then sent the completed questionnaires to the IGRP team. In the case of the Staffin preschool and Tiree preschool, materials were returned directly to the IGRP team.

The questionnaire contained one open-ended question and the rest were closed questions, which were constructed to be answered through:

- Categorical response
- Bounded continuous response, for most questions (the respondent is presented with a continuous scale, i.e. Likert scale).

Most of the questions, or statements functioning as queries, accommodated bounded continuous responses in Likert-type response items. The Likert-type response scale used in the IGRP questionnaires contained standard five-ordered response levels (with rare instances of three-, four- and six-ordered questions). This type of response scale was chosen for the following reasons:

- It is symmetric or 'balanced' as there are equal numbers of positive and negative positions
- It allows the respondents to express strength of agreement or disagreement
- It allows the responses to be represented in a binomial form by summing agree and disagree responses separately
- It allows for the depiction, at the item level, of a central tendency, which means that it allows the responses to be shown in a quasi-normal distribution. The last is especially important in visualising the collected data in histograms, affording visual comparisons of the data.

The preschool questionnaire consisted of 12 questions arranged in five sections:

- Background data (age and gender) (Question 1)
- Gaelic ability data (Questions 2–5)
- Language practice data (Questions 6–8)
- Perceived language practice in preschool catchment area (Supplementary Questions 1–4)
- Notes and comments.

The section of the survey on Gaelic ability also contained queries (Questions 4 and 5) about the degree to which the preschools contributed to the development of these abilities.

3.1.6 RESPONSE RATE

The Comhairle's co-operation helped ensure a high percentage response rate. In total, given a preschool population of 410 in the *sgoiltean-àraich*, 410 questionnaires were distributed to 26 preschool units (24 in the Western Isles), both English- and Gaelic-medium. 376 completed questionnaires were returned, along with 15 non-consent forms from parents giving a total of 391 responses. This equates to a 95.3% response rate. Three completed forms were returned in such a way that it was not possible to identify at which Western Isles preschool unit they had been completed, but they were included in the final results under a separate identifier code. One preschool unit declined to take part. This yields a completion rate of 91.7%, i.e. 376 in a total of 410. In 2011 the Census total population for 3–5 year-olds was 911 in the RA. This would imply that the figure of 376 completed responses in the IGRP total sample of 3–5 year-olds represents 41.3% of the relevant age cohort.[26] Bòrd na Gàidhlig's 'Dàta Foghlaim Ghàidhlig (Gaelic learning data)' for 2018–19 shows a total of 96,549 preschoolers aged 3–5 attending nurseries in Scotland; of this total, 1,078 preschoolers were enrolled in 56 GME *sgoiltean-àraich* throughout Scotland, representing 1.1% of preschool enrolments.[27] The survey obtained 376 completed questionnaires from 25 preschools, as shown in Table 3.2.

---

26 Table QS103SC Age by single Year in the 2011 Census indicates: 876 3–5 year olds in the Western Isles, 18 in Tiree and 17 in Kilmuir civil parish (Staffin), amounting to 911 in the Research Area.

27 http://www.gaidhlig.scot/wp-content/uploads/2019/07/D%C3%A0ta-Foghlaim-AM-FOLLAIS-2018-19-egn-2-PUBLIC-Education-Data-2.pdf.

Study District	N of completed questionnaires
01. West Side of Lewis (central)	15
02. West Side of Lewis (south)	2
03. Uig District	3
04. West Side of Lewis (north)	21
05. Ness	14
06. Tolsta	6
07. Loch a Tuath	15
08. Tong	11
09. Stornoway, Barvas Road suburbs	20
10. Stornoway Town	111
12. South Point	16
14. North Lochs	26
15. South Lochs	8
16. North Harris	17
17. South Harris	6
19. North Uist (south & east)	18
20. Benbecula	6
21. South Uist (north)	9
22. South Uist (south)	16
23. Barra & Vatersay	15
24. Staffin, Skye	4
25. Isle of Tiree	14
Origin not established	3
TOTAL	376

Table 3.2 *Numbers of completed questionnaires for preschool children by SD*

For the purposes of retaining anonymity of respondents, some of the Study Districts (e.g. Staffin and Tiree) were grouped together for reporting purposes. As stated, data are not reported at the level of individual preschools. As mentioned earlier, the questionnaires were offered both in Gaelic and in English. 13.6% of the questionnaires were completed in Gaelic and 86.4% were completed in English. This low rate of Gaelic administrative use is most likely an indicator of the levels of Gaelic literacy in one of the most Gaelic of current formal contexts.

3.2 RESPONSES TO IGRP PRESCHOOL SURVEY

3.2.1 GENDER AND AGE

There are 190 (51%) male and 181 (49%) female preschoolers in the survey response sample. Five responses did not specify gender. The average age of the children upon entering the preschool was 2 years 11 months and their average age at the time of the survey was 3 years seven months. There were two 2-year olds; 147 3-year olds, 183 4-year olds and 15 5-year olds; in the case of 29 preschoolers no indication was given as to their age. We decided to include the data of the two 2-year olds in the sample, despite indicating to the preschool directors that the survey was concerned with the 3–5 age cohort.

3.2.2 GAELIC ABILITY ON ENROLMENT

The first two of four questions in this section of the survey sought information on children's ability to speak and understand Gaelic, based on a five-point Likert scale, from fluent Gaelic to no Gaelic:

- *How would you describe the ability of the child in spoken Gaelic on arrival/ enrolment at the sgoil-àraich/preschool, considering their age?*
- *On enrolment at the sgoil-àraich/preschool, how would you describe the ability of the child to understand Gaelic?*

Table 3.3 shows the numbers and percentages of the reported ability data.

Ability in Gaelic at time of enrolment	Able to speak Gaelic		Able to understand Gaelic	
	N	%	N	%
Fluent native speaker ability	10	2.8	13	3.6
Good Gaelic	5	1.4	11	3.1
Reasonable Gaelic	14	3.9	26	7.2
A few words of Gaelic	72	20.1	82	22.8
No Gaelic	258	71.9	227	63.2
Total	**359**	**100.0**	**359**	**100.0**

Table 3.3. *Ability in speaking and understanding Gaelic at enrolment*

The responses to the two ability questions are also shown in Figure 3.1.

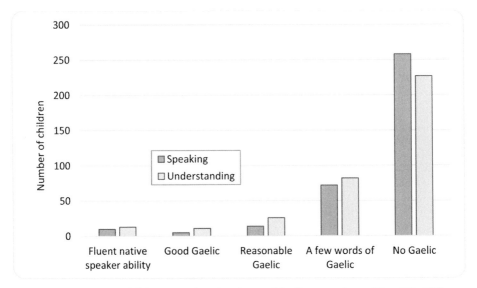

Figure 3.1 *Comparison of ability to speak and understand Gaelic on enrolment (Ns = 359, 359)*

Table 3.3 and Figure 3.1 demonstrate that the highest proportion of children had no ability in speaking or understanding Gaelic upon enrolment in preschool (71.9% and 63.2% respectively); followed by those who could speak and understand a few words of Gaelic on enrolment (20.1% and 22.8% respectively). Fewer than 4% of responses indicate either fluent native speaker levels of spoken Gaelic or understanding Gaelic on enrolment.

There is a major variance between the two relevant surveys on Gaelic ability among the preschool cohort, i.e. regarding the number of Gaelic-competent preschoolers: 161 (in Mac an Tàilleir (2015) for the Western Isles) vs. 15 (in the IGRP Preschool Survey) — a substantial difference between the two. The Mac an Tàilleir census study gives 161 (31%) with Gaelic ability for the 3–4 year olds, whereas the IGRP findings indicate 15 (4.2%) fluent or good speakers among the 3–5 year olds.[28]

---

28 As pointed out in the methodology section, this chapter does not present data particular to individual preschools, due to disclosure issues. However, **Appendix 3** presents some key ability and Gaelic practice data in the grouped format of Pooled Study Districts, to indicate spatial comparisons between the Study Districts.

3.2.3 ACTIVE AND PASSIVE ABILITY IN GAELIC AT THE TIME OF THE SURVEY

The questionnaire queried to what extent preschool participation contributed to the development of Gaelic language skills among the children. Given that the preschools provide the only context for Gaelic acquisition for the large majority of the children, these data predominantly represent the manager's assessment of second language acquisition attainment. Figure 3.2 displays the responses received to the two questions. The context implies a contrast between the child's ability in Gaelic on enrolment and at the time of the survey. The first question enquired about spoken ability (i.e. active ability) and the second about understanding (i.e. passive ability):

- *To what extent is the child's spoken ability in Gaelic due to the support of the sgoil-àraich/preschool?*
- *To what extent is the child's ability to understand in Gaelic due to the support of the sgoil-àraich/preschool?*[29]

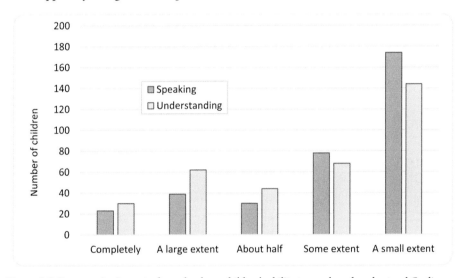

Figure 3.2 *Comparative impact of preschools on children's ability to speak and understand Gaelic (Ns = 344, 348)*

---

29 The need to keep the survey as brief as possible has resulted in there being two possible points of ambiguity in the two questions in this section: i) the questions do not differentiate between the small minority of children who have acquired Gaelic at home and the vast majority who have not acquired Gaelic at home; ii) the questions do not differentiate between the source (i.e. preschool for majority) and the extent of the ability. It is clear that the responses refer to the extent of the children's ability in Gaelic. For instance, in Table 3.4, the majority of responses indicate active Gaelic ability 'To a small extent' among 50.6% of preschoolers; and not that the preschool has contributed to a small extent. Overall, it seems that the responses to the two questions have indicated in general, therefore, the extent of Gaelic ability at the time of the survey. We can claim this because the results are consistent with other findings in the survey, particularly language use (see section 3.2.4.2).

This indicates that in the highest proportion of cases (50.6% (active) and 41.4% (passive)) the preschool contribution results in *A small extent* of Gaelic ability among the children. This chimes with the conclusions of Stephen *et al.* (2010), which illustrate the problems involved in developing Gaelic language skills solely in a preschool environment where most of the children have no ability in speaking or understanding Gaelic on enrolment, and without sufficient reinforcement of the language skills at home or in a wider societal setting.

Table 3.4 displays the responses to the two questions which indicate the children's active and passive Gaelic ability at the time of the survey (compare ability on enrolment in Table 3.3 in section 3.2.2).

Extent of Gaelic ability at time of survey	Active spoken ability in Gaelic		Passive understanding of Gaelic	
	N	%	N	%
Completely	23	6.7	30	8.6
To a large extent	39	11.3	62	17.8
About half	30	8.7	44	12.6
To some extent	78	22.7	68	19.5
To a small extent	174	50.6	144	41.4
Total	**344**	**100**	**348**	**100**

Table 3.4 Ability to speak (active) and understand (passive) Gaelic at time of survey

When we compare the competences on enrolment (Table 3.3) with competences at the time of the survey, we can have an overview of the extent of improvement in acquisition. This comparison indicates the positive contribution of the preschools.[30] Of the five corresponding levels, the biggest change in absolute numbers occurs in the weakest Gaelic ability categories. For instance in passive ability, 63.2% with no Gaelic on enrolment corresponds to 41.4% with a small extent of Gaelic at the time of the survey. At the other end of the ability scale, in relation to active ability, 2.8% fluent native speakers on enrolment corresponds to 6.7% highest on the scale (*Completely*) at the time of the survey. The strongest ability category on enrolment corresponds to a doubling of the percentage at the time of the survey, but these are represented by small absolute numbers and percentages.

---

30 This positive result is consistent with the survey data of Stephen *et al.* (2010: 23).

3.2.4 SPEAKING ENGLISH AND GAELIC

Three questions in the survey sought to establish which language was spoken by preschool children with three categories of people on a five point Likert scale. There was a sixth option of *Another language*. The first question enquired about language use on enrolment and the second about language use at the time of the survey. The third question asked about the child's language use in response to the Gaelic of the preschool staff. The questions were:

- *What language did the child speak to the following people at the time of enrolment at the sgoil-àraich/preschool?*
- *What language does the child speak to the following people now?*
- *When preschool staff speak to the child in Gaelic in which one of the following ways does the child respond?*

The categories of people were: 1) preschool teachers/practitioners; 2) other preschool staff (e.g. auxiliaries/support workers); and 3) other preschool children. Specifying language practice at the time of enrolment and at the time of the survey allowed for comparable evaluation over time. The results for these questions are given in the following sections: 3.2.4.1 to 3.2.4.4.

3.2.4.1 *CHILD'S LANGUAGE USE TO PRESCHOOL TEACHERS ON ENROLMENT AND TIME OF SURVEY*

Table 3.5 shows the numbers and percentages of responses regarding what language the child speaks to preschool teachers. It can be noted that there is a reduction in the number of responses in all the categories to these questions in relation to 'now' (at the time of the survey) in comparison to the higher level of responses in relation to 'on enrolment', in both Tables 3.5–3.7. Table 3.4 in section 3.2.3 gives a maximum of 348 for the time of survey responses. This implies that about 50 responses were not completed for 'now'.

Language spoken to preschool teachers	On enrolment		Now (at time of survey)	
	N	%	N	%
Gaelic only	7	1.9	5	1.7
Mainly Gaelic	3	0.8	13	4.5
Mix of Gaelic and English	18	4.9	45	15.5
Mainly English	36	9.8	76	26.1
English only	300	81.3	151	51.9
Another language	5	1.4	1	0.3
Total	**369**	**100.0**	**291**	**100.0**

Table 3.5 *Language spoken by children to preschool teachers, on enrolment and at time of survey*

Table 3.5 shows that 21.7% of children speak in Gaelic within the level of the top three Gaelic options at the time of the survey. The percentage data in Figure 3.3 indicate that the children mainly speak English to preschool teachers. Mean scores (from language use scale where 5 = English only and 1 = Gaelic only) indicate a marginal improvement in the use of Gaelic across all of the Study Districts: 4.7 on entry compared to 4.3 now.

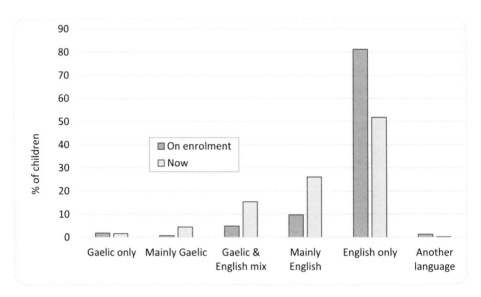

Figure 3.3 *Language spoken by children to preschool teachers, on enrolment and at time of survey, in percentages (Ns = 369, 291)*

Figure 3.3 shows that when compared to language use on enrolment in preschools, the percentage of children speaking *English only* now (i.e. at time of survey) to preschool teachers decreased (from 81.3% to 51.9%) while the percentage speaking *Mainly English* now has increased (from 9.8% to 26.1%), as have percentages for *Gaelic and English mix* and *Mainly Gaelic*. The percentages of children speaking *Gaelic only* to preschool teachers on enrolment and now are very low (1.9% on enrolment, 1.7% now). Overall, this shows a relatively small positive effect of preschool participation on increasing Gaelic speaking among the children. As highlighted previously in the discussion on Figure 3.1, many of the children's spoken Gaelic abilities are reported as limited at the time of the survey. This can be taken to correspond to the high proportion of children who continue to speak *Mainly English* or *English only* to preschool teachers and others (as indicated in the following sections), throughout their time at Gaelic-medium preschool. If we combine the two points of *Mainly English* and *English only* on enrolment and at the time of the survey, the resulting percentage comparisons are: 91.1% (on enrolment) vs. 78.0% (at time of survey), i.e. 13.1 percentage-point reduction, and a positive indicator for some degree of Gaelic speaking although there are c. 50 children less in the 'now' sample(s).

3.2.4.2 LANGUAGE SPOKEN BY CHILD TO OTHER PRESCHOOL STAFF

Table 3.6 shows the numbers and percentage responses regarding the language the children speak to other preschool staff. The main percentage change occurs in the *English only* responses: from 85.2% (on enrolment) to 59.4% (at time of survey), again showing a positive effect for some degree of Gaelic speaking.

Language spoken to other preschool staff	On enrolment		Now (at time of survey)	
	N	%	N	%
Gaelic only	6	1.7	4	1.4
Mainly Gaelic	2	0.6	9	3.1
Mix of Gaelic and English	9	2.5	23	8.0
Mainly English	31	8.7	80	27.8
English only	304	85.2	171	59.4
Another language	5	1.4	1	0.3
Total	**357**	**100.0**	**288**	**100.0**

Table 3.6 Language spoken by children to other preschool staff, on enrolment and at time of survey

Figure 3.4 illustrates the percentages of Gaelic and English spoken by the children to other preschool staff.

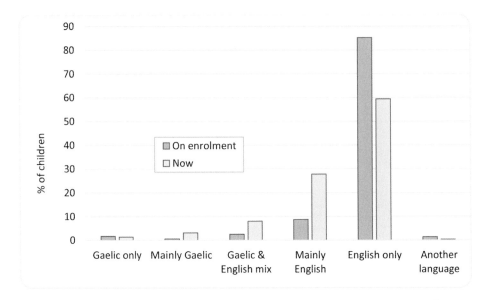

Figure 3.4 *Language spoken by children to other preschool staff, on enrolment and at time of survey, in percentages (Ns = 357, 288)*

Figure 3.4 indicates that English is the main language spoken to other preschool staff, on enrolment and at the time of the survey. This shows a high percentage of children speak *English only* or *Mainly English* to other preschool staff, both on enrolment (85.2%, 8.7%) and now (59.4%, 27.8%), with the percentage speaking *English only* decreasing through time and the percentage speaking *Mainly English, Gaelic and English mix* and *Mainly Gaelic* increasing. The percentage of those speaking *Gaelic only* to other preschool staff is low on enrolment and subsequently decreases (1.7% and 1.4% respectively).

3.2.4.3 *LANGUAGE SPOKEN BY CHILDREN TO OTHER PRESCHOOL CHILDREN*

The questionnaire asked what language each preschool child spoke to other preschool children. Table 3.7 shows the numbers and percentage responses regarding the children's language use to other preschool children. Similar to the other preschool language practice data in this chapter, the main change in percentages occurs in the weaker Gaelic practice data, with improvements between practice on enrolment and the time of the survey showing increased speaking of some Gaelic.

Language spoken to other preschool children	On enrolment		Now (at time of survey)	
	N	%	N	%
Gaelic only	2	0.6	1	0.3
Mainly Gaelic	2	0.6	2	0.7
Mix of Gaelic and English	7	2.0	17	5.9
Mainly English	26	7.3	48	16.8
English only	316	88.3	217	75.9
Another language	5	1.4	1	0.3
Total	**358**	**100.0**	**286**	**100.0**

Table 3.7 Language spoken by children to other preschool children, on enrolment and at time of survey

Figure 3.5 shows that the preschool children predominantly speak to each other in English.

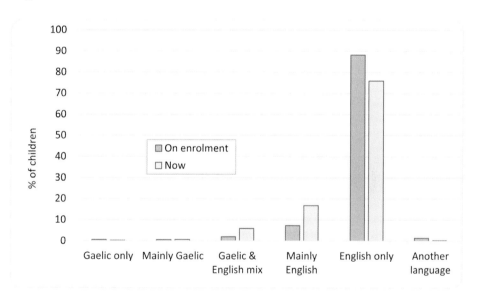

Figure 3.5 Language spoken by children to other preschool children, on enrolment and at time of survey, in percentages (Ns = 358, 286)

This two-period comparison of child language practice reveals that a high percentage of children speak *English only* or *Mainly English* to other preschool children, both on enrolment (88.3 + 7.3 = 95.6%) and at the time of the survey (75.9 + 16.8 = 92.7%). The use of *English only* decreases through time while the use of *Mainly English* and a *Gaelic and English mix* show increases. *Mainly Gaelic* and *Gaelic only* use represent very minor categories among the children both on enrolment and at the time of the survey. Slightly more children speak *Another language* to other children on enrolment (1.4%) than speak *Gaelic only* and *Mainly Gaelic* combined (1.2%).

3.2.4.4 *CHILD'S LANGUAGE OF RESPONSE TO PRESCHOOL STAFF*

The questionnaire asked what language is spoken by the children when responding to staff, when the staff speak to the children in Gaelic. The percentage results are shown in Figure 3.6. This indicates that the children usually respond in English when answering the Gaelic of preschool staff.

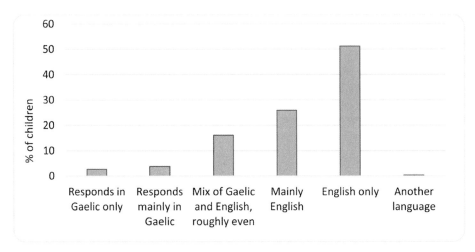

Figure 3.6 *Children's language of response to Gaelic of preschool staff (N = 367)*

The largest category pertains to the children who respond in *English only* (188, 51.2%), followed by *Mainly English* (95, 25.9%) and a *Mix of Gaelic and English* (59, 16.1%). The lowest percentages are for children responding *mainly in Gaelic* (14, 3.8%), in *Gaelic only* (10, 2.7%) or *Another language* (1, 0.3%).

3.2.4.5 *SUMMARY OF THE USE OF GAELIC AND ENGLISH*

The responses for language practice data taken together point to a situation where English is the main language spoken by children on enrolment, and that English continues to be used by the majority of them during their time there. We can conclude that English is overwhelmingly the home language for the majority of the children and that the use of English among infants predominates in the formal and informal activities of the preschools in the islands. In fact, preschoolers who speak *Another language* are as salient or as marginal as Gaelic-speaking preschoolers. This data on Gaelic speaking and on *Another language* in preschools shows that the use of these languages is clearly very marginal. Furthermore, this can be taken as an indication of very marginal familial use of languages other than English in the islands. Nevertheless, there is a consistent increase in the use of some Gaelic from the time of enrolment to the time of the survey, showing a positive effect of the preschools. Although the absolute numbers are small there is nonetheless a consistent decrease in the number of children who speak *Gaelic only*, indicating a slight change from *Gaelic only* to mixed use (cf. Hickey 2001). Tables 3.5–3.7 and the related figures show that the practice of *Mix of Gaelic and English* is more common than the combined categories of *Gaelic only* and *Mainly Gaelic*. In fact, the percentage values for *Mix* are in some situations about double (or more) the combined categories of *only* and *Mainly*. Furthermore, the percentage values in the category *Mix* increase more than those of *only* and *Mainly* from the time of enrolment to the time of the survey, at roughly a threefold increase.

3.3 SUPPLEMENTARY QUESTIONS

The questionnaire contained four supplementary questions, concerning the number and extent of Gaelic-medium preschools as well as the extent to which Gaelic was in daily use in the catchment area of each preschool. The choices of responses were given in four or five point Likert scales. The questions were:

- *What is the language policy of the sgoil-àraich/preschool?* (4 point Likert)
- *Over the last ten years, what percentage of children were already Gaelic speakers before they enrolled in the sgoil-àraich/preschool?* (a scale of five percentage ranges)
- *How would you describe the sgoil-àraich's/preschool's catchment area?* (5 point Likert relating to the local vitality of Gaelic)
- *In your opinion, to what extent do people in the following groups speak Gaelic on a day-to-day basis in your catchment area?* (5 point Likert; with six age cohorts)

As well as the question about the language policy in the preschools (3.3.1), the supplementary questions elicited information based on the perceptions of the preschool manager/teacher of the broader sociolinguistic context in which the preschools operated. For operational simplicity to avoid any possible loss of forms, it was decided to have only one questionnaire form. Therefore, the child-specific data required each form to be filled for each child. But the four supplementary questions needed only one reply for each preschool. This was indicated in the instruction at the beginning of the supplementary questions. A majority of respondents filled in only one form for their preschool, as instructed. A minority of respondents, however, filled in the supplementary data in each separate form.[31] This led to a discrepancy between some preschools yielding multiple responses and other preschools yielding only one response. In order to create comparable data, it was decided, for each preschool which had a single response format, to produce a total number of responses for that preschool based on the number of sampled children in the relevant preschool. For instance, if a hypothetical preschool with a single response format had five sampled preschoolers, that preschool would yield five identical responses. This combined method of calculation yielded a total of 339 responses for the supplementary questions.

The data from the supplementary responses can be given geographical precision. Given that we know which SD each preschool is in, and based on the responses to the supplementary questions, we can indicate the levels of perceived Gaelic ability and perceived Gaelic use in each SD or group of SDs or Pooled SDs. The results of these four supplementary questions are presented and analysed in the following sections.

3.3.1 LANGUAGE POLICY OF THE PRESCHOOL

19 out of 25 responding preschools (which included both English and Gaelic-medium preschools) identified themselves as wholly GME or partly GME (i.e. had a Gaelic-medium component as well as an English-medium component). These 19 preschools with whole or part GME had 225 children in attendance, representing 59.8% of sampled preschoolers (225 responses of N = 376). This leaves six preschools where the relevant data is deficient. Of these six, some preschools did not specify whether they were English or Gaelic-medium; whereas other preschools indicated they were both GME and English-medium preschools, but did not provide figures for children attending each stream. Therefore, given that there are six preschools (out of the total of 25) with deficient data, there is no sound basis in the analysis to differentiate between the data acquired from the various language-policy contexts. In other words, this analysis cannot differentiate the GME and non-GME groups, because it is not possible to discern the exact extent of the non-GME group, given the absence of some responses and the lack of numerical clarity in other responses. For instance, we cannot assess any possible correlations that might exist between the language-policy contexts of the preschools and any sociolinguistic outcomes or attainment. However, we do know that a majority of the preschools state that they are implementing a GME policy. Nevertheless, the lack of precision in the language-policy responses for some of the preschools does not impede the primary aim of the survey in assessing the levels of Gaelic competence and practice among the preschool cohort.

---

31 In fact, a number of the repeat responses varied from one form to the other, filled in for the same preschool. For this reason, all the responses were aggregated. And the data from the preschools with a single response was multiplied by the relevant number of children for each particular preschool.

3.3.2 PERCENTAGE OF GAELIC-SPEAKING CHILDREN ON ENROLMENT IN PRESCHOOLS, 2005–2015

In order to compare the data from the current group of children attending the preschools with previous intakes of children, the preschool managers/teachers were asked in this supplementary section of the questionnaire to provide their general perceptions of the proportion of Gaelic-speaking children on enrolment who had attended the preschool 'over the last ten years'. The respondents could indicate from one of five percentage ranges. These responses are presented in Figure 3.7, which illustrates that the respondents perceived that the majority of children had little or no Gaelic on enrolment over this ten-year period.

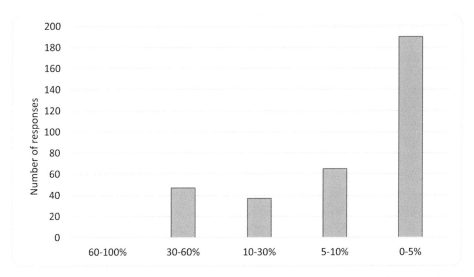

Figure 3.7 *Perception of percentage range of children speaking Gaelic on enrolment in preschool, 2005–2015, in descending order (N = 339)*

A majority of the responses received pertained to the 0–5% range of children entering preschool as Gaelic speakers. These perceptions of the ranges of preschooler competence in Gaelic over the 2005–2015 period in the preschool catchment areas demonstrate the marginal presence of Gaelic in island communities, and the limited extent of familial or intergenerational transfer of Gaelic. However, 44% of the responses perceive the extent of preschooler competence in Gaelic during the last 10 years to be more favourable than the information that emerges from the data on the current cohort, given that Table 3.3, with corresponding Figure 3.1, shows that 10 children (2.8%) had *Fluent native speaker ability* in Gaelic on enrolment and 13 (3.6%) had fluent native-level understanding. The actual numbers and percentages of responses and the perceived ranges of preschooler Gaelic competence on enrolment over the 2005–2015 time period are:

- 190 (56%) at 0–5%
- 65 (19.2%) at 5–10%
- 37 (10.9%) at 10–30%
- 47 (13.9%) at 30–60%
- 0 (0%) at 60–100%.

To summarise the respondents' perceptions, more than 75% (*N* 255/339) of the responses pertain to catchment areas in which 90% of those enrolling in the preschools over the last ten years had little or no Gaelic. These clearly English-dominant catchment areas correspond to 17 of the 25 SDs of the IGRP Research Area. The remaining eight SDs, corresponding to the preschool catchment areas, are listed in Table 3.8, with the 2011 Census percentage Gaelic ability data for the 3–17 age cohort of each SD for comparison. The preschool catchment areas in these eight SDs have Gaelic-speaking children at more than 10% (of preschoolers on enrolment over the previous ten-year period) in the perception of the preschool managers/teachers.

Perceived highest percentage ranges of Gaelic-speaking children	Non-disclosed Study District in Pooled SDs	2011 Percentage Gaelic ability 3–17 age cohort
30–60%	1 SD in Lewis N&W	43.1%
	1 SD in Lewis N&W	58.4%
	1 SD in South Uist, Barra & Vat.	60.2%
	1 SD in South Uist, Barra & Vat.	72.1%
10–30%	1 SD in Lewis N&W	53.2%
	1 SD in Lewis E	43.2%
	1 SD in Lewis E	32.4%
	1 SD in Harris	42.9%

Table 3.8 Eight non-disclosed Study Districts with highest perceived ranges of Gaelic-speaking preschoolers: 10%+ on enrolment in preschool, 2005–2015; and comparison with 2011 Census Percentage Gaelic ability for 3–17 age cohort

Four SDs fall within the 10–30% range, and the top four SDs fall within the 30–60% range — two in West Lewis and two in South Uist. Comparison with the 2011 Census data for the 3–17 age cohort shows that the perception responses and the census percentages correspond quite closely. As stated, however, the Gaelic passive ability data for the current preschool intake for the whole RA is considerably lower (than the top four SDs in Table 3.8) at 13.9% (i.e. *Fluent, Good,* and *Reasonable Understanding of Gaelic* in Table 3.3).

3.3.3 PERCEPTION OF EXTENT OF PARENTS' USE OF GAELIC WITH CHILDREN IN PRESCHOOL CATCHMENT AREA

Figure 3.8 displays the results of the question which asked the respondents how they would describe the preschool's catchment area by ticking the most apt description from the following five options:

- *An area in which most parents raise their children through the medium of Gaelic*
- *An area in which a substantial minority (less than 50%) of parents raise their children through the medium of Gaelic*
- *An area in which a small minority (less than 30%) of parents raise their children through the medium of Gaelic*
- *An area in which very few parents raise their children through the medium of Gaelic*
- *An area in which it is exceptional for parents to raise their children through the medium of Gaelic.*

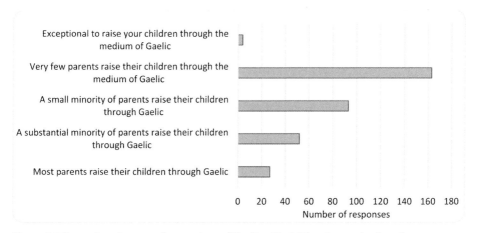

Figure 3.8 *Perception of extent of parents' use of Gaelic with children in preschool catchment area (N = 339)*

The results broadly indicate that raising children through Gaelic is perceived as pertaining to a minority of parents. The most commonly-held view (among preschool teachers) is that very few parents raise their children through the medium of Gaelic (163, 48.1%). This is followed by the view that a small minority of parents raise their children through Gaelic (93, 27.4%) and 52 of the responses (15.3%) claim that a substantial minority of parents raise their children through Gaelic. These results are also shown in Table 3.9.

Perceptions of proportions of children raised through Gaelic	Non-disclosed SDs in Pooled SDs
Most parents raise their children through Gaelic	2 SDs in South Uist, Barra & Vatersay
	1 SD in Lewis N&W
	1 SD in Staffin & Tiree
A substantial minority (less than 50%) of parents raise their children through Gaelic	2 SDs in Lewis N&W
	1 SD in Harris
A small minority (less than 30%) of parents raise their children through Gaelic	4 SDs in Lewis E
	4 SDs in Lewis E
	1 SD in Harris
	1 SD in Stornoway & Suburbs
	2 SDs in North Uist & Benbecula

Table 3.9 *Perceptions of proportion of children raised through Gaelic, by Pooled Study Districts*

This indicates that four SDs are reported here as areas where the majority of parents are perceived as raising their children through the medium of Gaelic. This view is not reflected in the reported Gaelic ability and practice findings of the cohort of children attending the preschools in these four SDs (3.2.2 Fig. 3.1 and 3.2.4 Figs. 3.3, 3.4, 3.5). The weight of evidence from the previous sections of the survey indicates that the perceptions of the parental use of Gaelic as shown in Figure 3.8 and Table 3.9 are over-optimistic, both for the RA as a whole, and for the specific SD. Finally, 10 SDs are perceived on average as having 'very few' or 'exceptional' parents raising children through Gaelic.

3.3.4 VIEWS ON GAELIC USE IN THE CATCHMENT AREAS BY AGE GROUPS

Respondents were asked to give their views on the extent to which Gaelic is used on a scale of one to five among six age groups in their catchment area. The question was:

- *In your opinion, to what extent do people in the following groups speak Gaelic on a day-to-day basis in your catchment area?*

The Likert scale options were from one to five, five representing the highest proportion of the relevant six age cohorts' daily use of Gaelic. A score value was attributed to each of the five levels of use: *Most of the time* 5; *Good amount of the time* 4; *Some of the time* 3; *Not much of the time* 2; *Not at all* 1. The mean-value results are shown in Figure 3.9 for each of the six age groups, from oldest to youngest. Thus, a high mean score indicates a higher proportion of use in the age group.

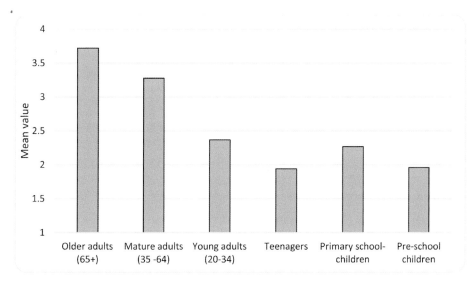

Figure 3.9 *Extent of perceived daily Gaelic use among different age groups in the preschool catchment areas, in descending order by age cohort (Ns = 326, 326, 326, 326, 340, 338)*

Respondents perceived that Gaelic is spoken more often among older and mature adults than among young adults, teenagers, primary-school children and preschool children. Respondents felt that primary-school children speak Gaelic more than teenagers or preschool children. None of the age groups receive a mean score of speaking Gaelic *Most of the time* or a *Good amount of time* (score of 4). Older adults (65+) and mature adults (35–64) are perceived (in a mean score) to speak Gaelic *Some of the time*, young adults (20–34) and primary-school children are perceived as speaking Gaelic *Not much of the time*, and the age cohorts of teenagers and preschool children are predominantly perceived as speaking Gaelic *Not at all*. The perceptions regarding the use of Gaelic in the various age groups may correspond more to the actual situation of Gaelic, and of the typical profile of a minority language undergoing shift by progressive decline of minority-language practice through the generations. There also appears a small positive effect for speaking Gaelic in educational initiatives of the primary cycle (cp. O'Hanlon *et al.* 2012: 38; sections 5.4.8–11, 5.8.2.2).

3.4 SUMMARY AND DISCUSSION

In this section we discuss the six main conclusions and implications which can be drawn from our survey of information provided by preschool staff concerning the Gaelic use and ability of preschool children and of Gaelic use in the preschool catchment areas:

1. The advanced state of decline in the societal use of Gaelic
2. The very marginal levels of familial transmission of Gaelic in all areas
3. The challenges of promoting the socialisation of Gaelic, now a minority language which has weak levels of societal reinforcement and very low densities of children with any Gaelic competence in the youngest age cohort
4. The organisational and pedagogical challenges associated with providing GME in the context of the high expectations for Gaelic attainment. The preschool language ability and practice data, however, indicate that age-appropriate levels of Gaelic attainment are not being met, which is actually to be expected given the overall societal weakness of Gaelic
5. Although some of the perception data does correspond to census results, there are, nevertheless, some over-optimistic perceptions among the preschool staff regarding the remaining geographic vitality of Gaelic, which is in contrast to the very marginal ability and practice of Gaelic among the preschoolers
6. The challenges for GME as a societal endeavour without sufficient societal presence.

Table 3.10 summarises the percentages of the highest attainment among the preschoolers in Gaelic fluency and practice.

	%	n	Total N
On Enrolment: *fluent native speaker, good,* or *reasonable Gaelic* ability	8.1	29	359
Gaelic attainment: *Completely, A large extent* or *About half*	26.7	92	344
On Enrolment: speaking *Gaelic only, Mainly* or *Mix of Gaelic and English* to preschool teachers	7.6	28	369
On Enrolment: speaking *Gaelic only, Mainly* or *Mix of Gaelic and English* to preschool children	3.2	11	358
Now: speaking *Gaelic only, Mainly* or *Mix of Gaelic and English* to preschool teachers	21.7	63	291
Now: speaking *Gaelic only, Mainly* or *Mix of Gaelic and English* to preschool children	6.9	20	286
Response to preschool staff in *Gaelic only, Mainly* or *Mix*	22.6	83	367

Table 3.10 *Key Gaelic positive data on fluency and use by preschool children*

Figure 3.10 shows results from the Preschool Survey which give an overview of the sociolinguistic contexts of the early-years cohort.

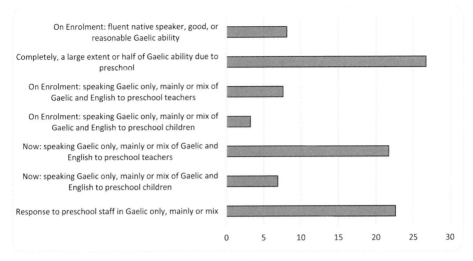

Figure 3.10 *Preschool key Gaelic positive percentages (Ns = 359, 344, 369, 358, 291, 286, 367)*

The data in Table 3.10 and Figure 3.10 indicate that 8.1% of children (29 children in total) enrolling in preschools have reasonable to fluent Gaelic. It is notable that although these 29 children were assessed as having reasonable to fluent Gaelic on enrolment, only 11 (3.2.%) spoke Gaelic to other preschool children at that time, indicating that most (i.e. 18 children) of those with a degree of Gaelic competence adapted to the peer-language function of English on enrolment. This is also reflected in the decrease over time in the use of *Gaelic only* by the children (e.g. in Tables 3.5, 3.6, 3.7 and Figures 3.3, 3.4 and 3.5).

The use of some Gaelic through time among the children themselves more than doubles (from 3.2% to 6.9). However, the number of preschool children who speak to other children in Gaelic remains small, at 20 children. Gaelic speaking to preschool teachers also increases (from 7.6% to 21.7%). This shows that 78.3% of children (228 of 291) continue to use English-only in Gaelic-medium preschools. Responses indicate that 26.7% of children attain relatively high levels of ability in Gaelic. Therefore, 73.3% of responses suggest preschoolers do not attain high levels of Gaelic competency.

3.4.1 SOCIETAL FRAGILITY OF THE GAELIC VERNACULAR OR POST-VERNACULAR

The survey responses in general, and the ability and practice data in particular, present an indication of the death of vernacular Gaelic in the context of the youngest age cohort. The Preschool Survey demonstrates that the current state of Gaelic peripheralisation can at best only provide for a cultural attachment to a socially-disembedded heritage or symbolic language. Under current circumstances, as Gaelic language management is currently formulated, this post-vernacular attachment to the heritage language is in fact the best-case scenario for Gaelic, even if significant proportions of the population can be persuaded to engage with the current institutional and policy provision for Gaelic.

The analysis of census data in Chapter 2 indicated a gap between the higher social densities of Gaelic speakers in the 50+ age cohort and the lower densities of the two younger age cohorts (3–17 and 18–49 years). Another significant gap was highlighted between the levels of Gaelic ability and the weaker levels of household use. The data presented here in Chapter 3 indicate that the societal condition of Gaelic is even weaker than evidenced in the census. MacKinnon (2011c: 207) has referred to this variance between official data on Gaelic and the social reality of actual levels of Gaelic practice in communities as the 'actuality gap'. The evidence in Chapter 3 indicates the highly marginal extent to which Gaelic is being transmitted to the youngest generation. In fact, attainment of competence in Gaelic prior to preschool enrolment, measured by actual Gaelic use on enrolment, is as marginal as the category of *Another language*, i.e non-English other languages, in the survey. Additionally, the data indicate that Gaelic has extremely limited social function among the preschool children and, by implication, among their parents' generation. The fact of the marginal social use by the parents' generation is corroborated by the responses of the preschool staff to the supplementary questions.

3.4.2 FAMILIAL TRANSMISSION OF GAELIC

The responses of the preschool staff to the questions in the survey about the Gaelic competences on enrolment of the preschool children are used here as indicators of the extent of familial transmission of Gaelic in these communities. We can conclude from this data that the home acquisition of Gaelic is now exceptional. The category of home acquirers of Gaelic is almost defunct. GME is now nearly the only context to assist the young in acquiring Gaelic. A large majority of children enrolling in preschools have no Gaelic ability. As noted above, Stephen *et al*.'s (2012: 22) analysis of the national preschool context stated: 'Practitioners are challenged to nurture and sustain the linguistic development of the small number of children who enter preschool having learned Gaelic at home and to help a much larger number of children who come from English-speaking homes to learn Gaelic'. The IGRP Preschool Survey indicates that this is now true for those communities in the islands, most of which were Gaelic dominant two generations ago, or prior to 1980.

The survey (3.2.2) indicates that 72% of preschool children are unable to speak any Gaelic on enrolment and 63% are reported as not being able to understand the language. Only 10 children (2.8%) are reported as having native speaker spoken ability for their age on enrolment in a preschool (seven males and three females). An additional five children (1.4%, three males and two females) are reported as having good spoken Gaelic on enrolment. When we combine the top three Gaelic ability classifications (*Fluent native speaker, Good,* and *Reasonable Gaelic*), we calculate that a little over 8% of the preschool group have had experience of the social practice of Gaelic prior to encountering it in the preschool (as discussed concerning Table 3.10).[32] Taking this data as an indicator of familial transmission of Gaelic, we conclude that only a very small proportion of parents (c. 10%) of the 3–5 age cohort in the Research Area are raising their children with any substantial amount of Gaelic.

3.4.3 LACK OF SOCIETAL REINFORCEMENT OF GAELIC AND LOW POSITIVE IMPACT OF GME

The development of Gaelic policy in the early-years sector, in the absence of the supportive context of familial and communal reinforcement, is replete with sociolinguistic difficulties. The small numbers of preschool children having a native-like or good understanding of Gaelic on enrolment, 24 children (6.7%) for the entire RA, means that these children by necessity conform to the peer *lingua franca* function of English which the majority establish in the preschools. Table 3.7 shows 88% of the preschoolers are reported as only speaking English to their fellow preschoolers on enrolment and this percentage reduces to 76% of the children at the time the survey was conducted (cf. Stephen *et al.* 2010: 23). Despite some increase in the use of Gaelic over time, English remains the only language of peer-group socialisation for a large majority of the children. This is a fundamental problem in any revernacularisation effort. The central importance of peer socialisation through the minority language in reinforcing home-based acquisition of the minority language has been demonstrated by, for instance, Péterváry *et al.* (2014: 199–200; 218–20) for Irish and Enlli Môn Thomas and Dylan Bryn Roberts (2011) for Welsh. This evidence indicates that the Gaelic-medium inputs from the preschool staff have a fairly low positive impact on Gaelic socialisation among the children. It is likely that the situation for Gaelic would be more acute without the GME presence and the efforts of the GME preschool teachers.

---

32 In their examination of the national context of preschool GME provision, Stephen *et al.* (2012: 28) indicate that 12% of the children attending the preschools had exposure to Gaelic at home (half of this 12% of children were considered to come from Gaelic-speaking families). The island data we present here are not directly comparable because our sample includes both GME and English-medium preschool provision for the islands.

3.4.4 GME PROVISION FOR PRESCHOOL CHILDREN

As stated in section 3.2.3, given that the preschools provide the only context for Gaelic acquisition for a large majority of the children, the active and passive ability data in section 3.2.3 predominantly represent the practitioners' assessment of attainments in second language acquisition. The preschool staff/managers' report that in the case of 50.6% of the children, the preschoolers are attaining spoken Gaelic abilities only to a small extent. Interpreting this data requires us to consider the overall context in which early-years GME is provided, namely, as discussed above, the weak levels of familial and communal acquisition of Gaelic and related issues concerning the weak reinforcement of Gaelic in socialisation processes among this age group; the limited time periods in which the children are exposed to a Gaelic environment in the preschools; resourcing issues; and elasticity in the continuum with English use in policy interpretation of what is entailed in early-years GME. In this overall context, and in the particular context of the mostly very limited or total lack of exposure that the children have to Gaelic in the out-of-school environment, actual official GME policies may be too ambitious in relation to acquisition of Gaelic as a second language from preschool. The data produced here are in line with McPake and Stephen's (2016: 122) contention that the sectoral expectations place a heavy burden on the preschool practitioners.

The data on the sociolinguistic dynamic between staff and children also raise challenging issues in relation to the minority-language dimension of GME. Figure 3.6 shows only 2.7% (10 children) of all children surveyed are reported to respond in *Gaelic only* when addressed in Gaelic by a staff member, with an additional 3.8% (14 children) responding mainly in Gaelic. Taken together, 24 children respond in *Gaelic only* or *Mainly Gaelic* when addressed in Gaelic by the preschool staff. O'Hanlon *et al.* (2012: 38) found the levels of Gaelic use in preschool curriculum delivery are lower in two contexts than in primary GME, i.e. Gaelic levels 'are high though not as high as in the immersion phase in the first three stages of primary school'; and in less formal school domains 'pupils in preschool tend to use less Gaelic than pupils at primary school'. The evidence in the Preschool Survey collected here shows that children's Gaelic use is not consistent with the level of Gaelic preschool practice reported in O'Hanlon *et al.* (2012: 38). The IGRP data indicate that both formal and informal use of Gaelic in the preschools is very low. For instance, 92.7% of the children are reported, at the time the survey was conducted (as opposed to on enrolment), as speaking only English or mainly English to other children in the preschools.

3.4.5 PERCEPTION OF GAELIC PRACTICE IN GEOGRAPHIC DIMENSION

As discussed in section 3.3.2, the preschool practitioners were asked to give their perceptions of the proportion of children who had spoken abilities in Gaelic on enrolment in preschool over the previous 10-year period. The majority of responses (56%) indicate that 0–5% of children had Gaelic-speaking ability. For parts of Lewis North & West and South Uist, Barra & Vatersay Pooled SDs, the percentage perceptions of Gaelic-speaking ability on enrolment was judged to range from 30–60%. It is noticeable that this 30–60% range for the 2005–2015 period is at variance with the current data in relation to the levels of spoken ability in these preschool areas. This variance could be an indicator of the recent rapid decrease in the proportion of home acquirers of Gaelic in these areas. Alternatively, it could indicate a gap between the perception of Gaelic's social presence over the last 10 years and the current sociolinguistic circumstances, or, of course, a combination of both possible explanations.

3.4.6 SOCIETAL DIMENSION OF GME IN THE ISLANDS

The main findings of this Preschool Survey highlight the societal weakness of Gaelic. In particular, the results indicate that the familial transmission of Gaelic in these communities is extremely marginal. Furthermore, despite the Gaelic-medium inputs from the GME preschool staff, English is the overwhelming medium of peer-group socialisation and also dominates communication by the children to GME staff. For the majority of the children surveyed here, the staff feel that GME participation is not contributing to a high proportion of children attaining sufficient Gaelic language competences. The dichotomy between the minority-language aspirations of GME on the one hand and the reliance by most of the children on the functional practice of English in the preschools on the other, highlights a basic fault line in attempting to implement GME provision in the absence of considerable efforts aimed at addressing the revitalisation of Gaelic in society. Put simply, the lack of communal Gaelic revitalisation has led to the current situation of an over-reliance on GME provision which cannot meet, or is not meeting, expectations for Gaelic regeneration. Preschool GME provision is being pursued without the significant corresponding family and societal revival efforts which are essential to a credible revitalisation. The familial and social efforts of reversing language shift have not been attempted to a level corresponding to the GME efforts.

From the joint perspective of the perceived insubstantial impact on Gaelic competence and the predominance of English speaking in the formal and informal interactions among the preschoolers, this survey portrays a context in which Gaelic is spoken to the children rather than with and by the children, despite the best efforts of the GME staff. The results of the IGRP Preschool Survey raise issues for Gaelic which are on one level both pedagogical and institutional but, on another more substantial level, clearly societal.

This chapter provides further evidence of the rapid recessive trajectory identified in Chapter 2. The overall implication of this chapter is that the parental generation in the island communities no longer speak Gaelic with their children to a sufficient degree to support the acquisition and social function of Gaelic. The current low levels of any practice of Gaelic in the intimate domains of family and neighbourhood, as indicated in the preschool data, are now too insubstantial to ensure the social reproduction of Gaelic anywhere.

4 SURVEY OF LANGUAGE USE AMONG TEENAGE PUPILS IN THE WESTERN ISLES

4.1 INTRODUCTION

This chapter provides data on Gaelic vitality or fragility issues relating to teenage high-school pupils in the Western Isles and these pupils' perception of and sociolinguistic participation in their families, schools and communities. This module of the Islands Gaelic Research Project (IGRP) sought to establish a comprehensive database on language background, geographic background, self-reported ability in Gaelic and English, including native-speaker ability in Gaelic, sources of Gaelic acquisition, family language practice and language dynamics among high-school students in their late teens. Complementary to the general portrayal of linguistic competence in the 2011 Census, analysed in Chapter 2, data in this chapter will illustrate the levels of Gaelic transmission in the home, and the prevailing attitudes towards Gaelic among teenage pupils.

The module is centred on a questionnaire-based self-report study of secondary school (i.e. high school) pupils in S5 and S6 aged between 16 and 18 in the Western Isles, the Comhairle nan Eilean Siar authority area. All four secondary schools in the Western Isles participated, these being Sgoil MhicNeacail / Nicolson Institute (Isle of Lewis), Sgoil Sir E. Scott (Isle of Harris), Sgoil Lìonacleit (Benbecula) and Sgoil Bhàgh a' Chaisteil / Castlebay Community School (Barra). The full Research Area was not included as Staffin does not have its own secondary school, and GME in the secondary school in Tiree is restricted to the teaching of Gaelic as a subject.

The need to understand how institutional provision articulates with this age group in relation to aspirations for Gaelic and communal practice of Gaelic is central to any Gaelic regeneration efforts. Given that members of this age group will form the basis for the emerging parental cohort, gathering reliable data on abilities, practices and attitudes serves to establish a clear trajectory of Gaelic vitality or fragility. The resultant analysis will be central to informing suitable Gaelic policy and planning for the use of Gaelic.

4.1.1 AIMS

This module administered a questionnaire-based survey among 16–18 year olds in all four secondary schools in the Western Isles. The survey sought to determine:

- The pupils' and parents' geographic background
- Their language acquisition and sources of Gaelic attainment
- Their self-reported abilities in Gaelic and to a lesser extent in English
- Their social and institutional practice of Gaelic and English
- Their attitudes and opinions about Gaelic in society and related institutional provision
- Self-ascription of identity and other identity issues
- Their opinions on the prospects for Gaelic
- The prospects of participation by them in possible initiatives to support and promote Gaelic.

4.2 OVERVIEW OF GAELIC-MEDIUM SECONDARY EDUCATION IN SCOTLAND

In order to give a general context to the survey of secondary pupils in Western Isles schools, this section provides an overview of the numbers of pupils attending Gaelic-medium education in Scotland as well as providing summary data on attainment levels in Gaelic subjects (i.e. secondary-level subjects taught through Gaelic-medium). We also review some of the available literature about reported attitudes of young people to the use of and support for Gaelic.

4.2.1 GAELIC-MEDIUM SECONDARY SCHOOL PUPILS IN SCOTLAND AND LEVELS OF ATTAINMENT

Education statistics are produced by Bòrd na Gàidhlig. The Bòrd provides a minimal definition of Gaelic-medium education at the secondary level as the provision by the school of Gaelic as a subject for fluent speakers (O'Hanlon *et al.* 2012: 3). Gaelic-medium secondary education, therefore, must provide as a minimal requirement the subject of Gaelic for fluent speakers. The provision of other subjects through the medium of Gaelic is optional within the bounds of Bòrd na Gàidhlig's definition. Secondary pupils can study (1) Gaelic for fluent speakers; (2) Gaelic for learners; and (3) other school subjects through the medium of Gaelic.[33] In 2017–18, there were 15 subjects available in Scottish secondary schools through the medium of Gaelic,

---

33 The 2011 Scottish Qualifications Authority's classification of Gaelic education entails more Gaelic provision than the single subject provision of Gaelic. According to this definition, any secondary school which provides at least one subject through the medium of Gaelic, in addition to Gàidhlig itself, is classified as providing Gaelic-medium secondary education. See: Scottish Qualifications Authority (2011b) Table 1.13, Pupils in Scotland, issued as a supplementary spreadsheet to Summary Statistics for Schools in Scotland.

including Gaelic as a subject.[34] However, a maximal provision of all subjects being taught through Gaelic is exceptional or non-existent.

Table 4.1 shows the number and percentage of schools offering GME in secondary schools over the period 2011 to 2018. The table also indicates the number of teachers, as well as the number of subjects offered as part of Gaelic-medium provision.

	2011/12	2012/13	2013/14	2014/15	2015/16	2016/17	2017/18
Subjects available through GME	15	13	13	14	17	15	15
Teachers of Gaelic as a subject	60	65	59	66	51	63	59
Teachers of other subjects *via* GME	38	40	35	40	38	38	44
Total Gaelic teachers	98	105	94	106	89	101	103
Total schools with GME subjects	35	33	33	32	30	31	31
Total schools in Scotland	364	364	363	361	360	358	359
GME schools as % of Total schools	10%	9%	9%	9%	8%	9%	9%

Table 4.1 Number of Secondary Schools offering Gaelic-medium Education (GME): 2011–2018. Source: Bòrd na Gàidhlig. Note: "Teachers of other subjects via GME" are teachers of subjects through the medium of Gaelic but not Gaelic as a subject. "Teachers of Gaelic as a subject" also teach other subjects through the medium of Gaelic.

During the school year 2017–18, Gaelic-medium education was offered at 31 secondary schools across 12 Local Authority areas in Scotland. As the data in Table 4.1 illustrate, there has been relatively little change in the number of subjects available since 2011. Similarly, the number of Gaelic teachers has remained relatively steady despite the additional resources that have been targeted at various kinds of Gaelic teacher training courses. Overall, secondary schools offering Gaelic-medium education account for 9% of all secondary schools in Scotland.

---

34 http://www.gaidhlig.scot/bord/research/education-data/.

Secondary schools	2011/12	2012/13	2013/14	2014/15	2015/16	2016/17	2017/18	% Change 2011–18
Total GME	1,104	1,104	1,181	1,204	1,193	1,272	1,251	13.3%
Total in Scotland	292,972	292,972	288,578	284,168	281,355	280,408	281,405	-4%
GME as % of Total	0.38%	0.38%	0.41%	0.42%	0.42%	0.45%	0.46%	n/a

Table 4.2 *Gaelic-medium and total pupils in secondary school education in Scotland, 2011–2018. Source: Bòrd na Gàidhlig*

The number of secondary pupils in GME across Scotland over the period 2011 to 2018 is shown in Table 4.2. The table shows that since the school year 2011–12 there has been a modest increase (147 pupils or 13.3%) in the number of secondary school pupils registered for Gaelic-medium education. The proportion of Gaelic-medium students within the total secondary school pupil cohort in Scotland has also increased slightly over this period. Nevertheless, it only accounts for 0.46% of the overall number of secondary school pupils in Scotland in the school year 2017–18.

Gaelic for:	2011	2012	2013	2014	2015	2016	2017	2018	% Change 2011–2018
Fluent Speakers	**NUMBER OF EXAM ENTRIES**								
National 5	n/a	n/a	n/a	175	167	158	151	183	+5%
Higher	116	95	117	122	135	132	126	123	+6%
Advanced Higher	18	34	19	26	38	31	28	30	+67%
	NUMBER OF EXAM ENTRIES								
Learners	2011	2012	2013	2014	2015	2016	2017	2018	
National 5	n/a	n/a	n/a	163	109	145	115	107	-34%
Higher	127	110	119	103	97	84	69	75	-41%
Advanced Higher	18	22	21	20	30	24	9	11	-39%

Table 4.3 *Number of exam entries, 2011–2018. Source: Scottish Qualifications Authority*

The number of entries for the three most advanced exams in Gaelic as a subject for fluent speakers and learners is shown in Table 4.3. In the Scottish Qualifications Authority's publication, the term fluent speaker comprises that of the native speaker. As Table 4.3 illustrates, only the entries taking the Gaelic Advanced Higher fluent speaker exam have seen any substantial increase since 2011. The other categories show no substantial change or a decrease in exam entries. The decrease is particularly noticeable in exam entries for Gaelic for learners. Both the Higher and Advanced Higher show substantial percentage falls in the number of learner pupils taking these exams.

This data support the statement made by Her Majesty's Inspectorate of Education (2011: 7) in their report that: 'Gaelic Medium Education in secondary schools is still at a very early stage of development', and that provision for GME at secondary level was not as developed as it was at primary level. Research reported in 2012 by O'Hanlon *et al.* (2012: ix) clearly indicated that, compared to primary school, at secondary school level there is a sharp fall in Gaelic-medium pupils' exposure to Gaelic in the curriculum. The O'Hanlon *et al.* (2012: ix) research also recorded that 14 secondary schools provided at least four subjects (including Gaelic as a subject for fluent speakers) through the medium of Gaelic in the first and second years of secondary school. This implies that about half of classified GME schools provided three or fewer subjects through the medium of Gaelic (including Gaelic as a subject). Only one secondary school offers all subjects through Gaelic (4.2.1.1).

School year	GME Primary	GME Secondary	Drop-off	Drop-off %
2014–15	2,818	1,204	1614	57%
2015–16	3,004	1,193	1811	60%
2016–17	3,145	1,272	1873	60%
2017–18	3,278	1,251	2027	62%

Table 4.4 *Numbers and percentage difference between GME primary and GME secondary education, 2014–18 (from Bòrd na Gàidhlig Education Data, 2018b)*

Table 4.4 shows the disparity in the numbers and percentages of pupils taking GME between primary and secondary schools. As O'Hanlon *et al.* (2012: 35) reported, the significant fall in the pupil numbers between primary school and secondary school and the fall in Gaelic curricular take-up also manifests itself in a sharp decline in Gaelic language use in most kinds of extra-curricular activity. The O'Hanlon *et al.* (2012) research also indicated that English remains the predominant language of communication between the secondary schools and parents of GME pupils. In summary, the research indicates decreases in three core aspects of GME between primary and secondary levels: 1) a drop-off by over half in pupil numbers; 2) a decrease in curricular take-up of subjects through Gaelic; and 3) a decline in extra-curricular Gaelic use. There are two other features of diminution within secondary GME: 4) decreases in the number of exam entries between 2011 and 2018, in particular entries for Gaelic for learners; and 5) the number of pupils opting for GME decreases between early and later years (discussed immediately below). Two areas of growth in secondary GME are: 1) a 13.3% increase in GME pupil numbers between 2011 and 2018; 2) a 67% increase in Advanced Higher Gaelic for fluent speakers between 2011 (18 pupils) and 2018 (30 pupils) (Table 4.3).

The Scottish Qualifications Authority (SQA) is the national body in Scotland responsible for the development, assessment, and certification of qualifications other than for degree level. SQA recognises its role as: 'Continuing development of secondary subject provision through the medium of Gaelic with a strategic plan for investment in future staff, including the retraining of existing Gaelic-speaking staff and opportunities for interested staff to learn Gaelic' (Curriculum for Excellence, Gaelic Working Group, SQA 2011a: 14). The SQA noted in its Gaelic Language Plan for 2015–20 that: 'in the five years since the publication of our previous Gaelic Language Plan there has been an increase in the number of children enrolling in Gaelic-medium primary education and more Gaelic Units opening, which is encouraging'. Although SQA recognises that 'it is important that this continues into secondary school, in particular into the Senior Phase, to enable progression and recognition' (2017: iv), the data in Table 4.3, and elsewhere, indicate that significant challenges will need to be addressed in relation to pupil numbers progressing and achieving positive outcomes in Gaelic qualifications and qualifications through Gaelic.

In spite of the recognition by SQA of the importance of continuity in educational provision and take-up among Gaelic pupils in secondary schools, there seems to be an absence of a supportive strategy at a national level to address these issues. The problem is exacerbated by the shortage of suitably-qualified teachers to deliver GME. With the current crisis in vernacular attainment and practice, availability of Gaelic-competent people to take up posts as teachers or educators and in other Gaelic-based employment and services, will clearly remain challenging or deteriorate further. Data shows that the number of pupils opting for GME continues to decrease considerably between early and later years in secondary schools. Bòrd na Gàidhlig (2017a) education data for 2016–17 indicate that whilst 283 secondary school pupils across Scotland took Gaelic as a subject for fluent speakers or for Gaelic learners level in S1 (i.e. 'Secondary 1', the first year of secondary school), this fell to 68 pupils in S6. This may be partially explained by the fact that all subject choices narrow in the senior cycle (i.e. in S5 and S6). A similar pattern is evident at the Gaelic secondary school in Glasgow, *Sgoil Ghàidhlig Ghlaschu* (termed the dedicated primary and secondary school for GME in Glasgow) where 51 pupils took Gaelic language as a subject in S1 but only 12 in S6 ('Dedicated' GME is defined as a school 'teaching and learning by means of the Gaelic language as spoken in Scotland', Statutory Guidance on Gaelic Education, Bòrd na Gàidhlig 2017b: 10).

4.2.1.1 *IMPLICATIONS OF THE NATIONAL EDUCATIONAL CONTEXT AND GAELIC COMPETENCES*

This brief analysis of the diminution of GME at secondary level in comparison to primary level, highlights that the current institutional approach to Gaelic revival, with GME at its core, is deficient in its own rather circumscribed terms, in the context of language revitalisation. The numbers and proportions are small in primary GME and even more marginal at secondary level and clearly do not amount to social revival. The decline in fluent Gaelic speakers and the loss of Gaelic-speaking communities is in no way being proportionally met by the reliance on a GME focus at a national level. The relatively small numbers gaining qualifications at the highest levels of achievement indicate the current constraints of this policy for a sustainable future for Gaelic.

The negative disparity in provision between primary and secondary levels as reported by O'Hanlon *et al.* (2012: ix) also acts as a brake on the development of Gaelic ability, as secondary GME is not provided in a consistent nor a coordinated manner across schools where GME is offered. Bòrd na Gàidhlig's 2016–17 educational data indicate that only the Glasgow Gaelic School (*Sgoil Ghàidhlig Ghlaschu*) reports offering 100% educational provision in Gaelic (at primary and secondary levels). Portree High School reports 32% (of subjects offered through Gaelic) with the three secondary schools in Harris, Benbecula and Tiree reporting 26% provision. The secondary school in the Western Isles with the highest number of secondary pupils, the Nicolson Institute in Stornoway, reports only 20% of subjects offered through Gaelic. Limitations in secondary provision put considerable constraints on the opportunities for pursuing educational completeness in the minority Gaelic context.

Additionally, there is evidence (e.g. Müller 2006 based on her doctoral research (Müller 2003)) that the Gaelic fluency of many GME pupils is not optimal and that pupils do not achieve a competence commensurate with the Gaelic of older, fluent, native speaker cohorts. The main aspiration inherent in GME is that the loss of vernacular speakers can be compensated for by GME efforts. Both from the perspective of the quantity of learners and the quality of their attainment, the research indicates that the primary GME aspiration is not being realised. The gap between some of the overly-optimistic GME aspirational assertions on the one hand and the reality of Gaelic attainment on the other is considerable. Native speakers are being 'replaced', for the want of a better word, by a far smaller number of those less functionally competent in Gaelic, and dominant in English, and who for the most part do not use Gaelic either outwith institutional contexts or to a meaningful extent after leaving school (Dunmore 2015; NicLeòid 2015).[35] Sìleas NicLeòid and Stiùbhart Dunmore (2018: 91) point out: 'Aig a' cheann eile, cha robh a' mhòr-chuid de na daoine a chaidh a thogail gun Ghàidhlig idir a-staigh a' cur an cuid Gàidhlig gu feum ach gu ìre glè bheag anns an latha an-diugh.' [On the other hand, the majority of those raised without Gaelic at home use very little Gaelic at present].

Second-language competence acquired through various types of immersion contexts, resulting in so-called immersionese, is problematic everywhere, even in Wales or Canada, for instance, with socially used Welsh or French available (3.4.3; Ó Riagáin 1997; Ó Duibhir 2018). In the context of immersion education in a language with relatively high social salience, vernacular-like second language competence is challenging. In the case of a language with limited or weak social salience combined with only partial and optional immersion provision, such as Gaelic in the Western Isles, the challenges of achieving competent acquisition are even greater. Vanessa Will (2012) also contends that the over-reliance on GME provision for acquisition can result in lack of competence in the social or out-of-school context:

> the kinds of linguistic and social input children receive when they experience the majority of their Gaelic language socialization in the GME classroom leave them without some of the semiotic tools that are necessary for interacting with older Gaelic-socialized speakers and for performing a range of social-linguistic tasks outside the context of the school.
>
> … after initially acquiring the formal elements of the Gaelic language, GM-educated children's skills in using the language for anything but a narrow set of academically-oriented functions remain stagnant. Indeed, by the time they progress to secondary education and are of an age at which they continue to expand their usage of English as new social domains open up to them thanks to their increased biological-social maturity, their shortcomings of the same skills in Gaelic become particularly obvious. Contrary to the typical trajectory of language socialization, which combines increasing social competence with growing numbers of opportunities to exercise that competence, the social-linguistic competence of most children enrolled in GME remains stagnant, or actually diminishes, in

---

35 For instance, NicLeòid (2015: 115) states that GME secondary pupils are not involved in Gaelic revitalisation outside of school: 'Cha do rinn gin de na sgoilearan iomradh air a' cheangal eadar ath-bheothachadh na Gàidhlig agus an dreuchd no a' phàirt a dh'fhaodadh a bhith aca fhèin san iomairt … cha robh coltas ann gun do thuig iad an ceangal eatarra, .i. ma tha FMG ann airson cur ri ath-bheothachadh na cànain, gum feum an siostam barrachd luchd-bruidhinn a 'chruthachadh' a bhios ga cumail a' dol, agus gu bheil 'ga cumail a' dol' a' ciallachadh — don luchd-bruidhinn sin — a bhith ga bruidhinn is ga cleachdadh, is chan ann a-mhàin san sgoil fhèin.' [None of the pupils mentioned the connection between Gaelic revitalisation and the effort or part they could play in this … it did not seem that they understood the connection between both, i.e. if the point of GME is to assist in revitalising the language, that the (education) system has to 'produce' more speakers to maintain it, and that 'maintaining it' means — for those speakers — to speak and practice it, and not only at school.]

130

relation to the expansion of their social-linguistic competence in English. (Will 2012: 15–17)[36]

4.2.2 ATTITUDES TOWARDS GAELIC AMONG YOUNG PEOPLE

In this section, we present an overview of the available literature regarding attitudes, ability and use of Gaelic amongst teenagers. One of the earliest studies of young adults' attitudes to Gaelic in the Western Isles was carried out by Barbara Bird (1993), over two research periods in 1989 and 1992. Eighteen-year olds in full-time education at Sgoil MhicNeacail, Sgoil Lìonacleit and Lews Castle College were interviewed, with the 83 respondents representing a broad cross-section of language abilities and home areas, as well as being split on relatively equal gender lines. Bird's results presented only limited data — not all of her research was included; for instance, opinions on language maintenance were omitted.

However, 80 of the 83 respondents indicated they would be unhappy to see Gaelic die out, 78 of 80 respondents wanted their own children to have the language and 69 of 80 wished to teach their children Gaelic themselves. Conversely, only 34 of 80 thought Gaelic would survive, reflecting a negative long-term outlook from a generation now likely to be the basis of the current parental cohort in the area. The survey revealed high levels of support for more Gaelic on television, for Gaelic being an optional subject in all Scottish secondary schools and for Gaelic being a requirement for jobs in the Western Isles. Bird (1993: 5) specifically noted: 'A clear response to a question concerning the desirability of Gaelic-medium education in secondary school was given by very few, and so this point has been omitted'. It was noted that respondents did show a clear wish to see Gaelic as a compulsory subject in the Western Isles.

Catherine Ann MacNeil's work (1995) is one of several studies specifically looking at young peoples' attitudes to Gaelic-medium broadcasting. Her work looked at just over 100 young people ranging between Primary 5 and Secondary 6 (i.e. S6), with 20% of the sample group in the 16–18-year old cohort, all of whom were from the Western Isles. When reporting young peoples' relationship with Gaelic identity, MacNeil states (1995: 26):

> They wanted to be able to identify Gaelic roots within such Gaelic programmes. However, they felt strongly that the contextual elements which provided this for programmes must be up-to-date, credible and associated with the fundamental enduring elements of Gaelic culture and life as they experience it, now.

Young people see the current and recent programme profile as not

---

36 For evidence of stagnation in acquisition among post-traditional native speakers of Irish, see Lenoach (2012: 66) and cp. Péterváry *et al.* (2014).

reflecting their experiences of life as young Gaelic speakers, but rooted more in an idealistic past, or that experienced by older speakers ... because of their identity as bilingual young people, living in bilingual communities, and preparing for what being an adult means in their world.

In a further research study, Morag MacNeil and Bob Stradling (2001: 37–38) interviewed 14–16 year olds in the Highlands and Islands who had been through GME. The authors suggested that:

We know, of course, that to some extent, these young people had a Gaelic-associated identity ascribed to them, in that they had all received their primary education through the medium of Gaelic. They would be known, to some extent, to be part of this grouping throughout their schooling, both within their peer-group and the broader adult community.

However, as they moved towards adulthood, and started to make more and more decisions for themselves, they appear to have held on to their language and cultural identifiers. For example, they indicated that *the ability to speak Gaelic* was very important to them. This has remained at the core of their sense of self — even though most of them by the age of 16 now received much, if not all, of their education through the medium of English rather than Gaelic.[37]

Of the young people surveyed by MacNeil and Stradling (2001), 90% indicated that Gaelic usage was integral to their self-perception, while heritage was regarded as being a vaguer, less straightforward cultural entity. There was, however, a much more pronounced association with place, with many respondents identifying their own locality, especially a 'Gaelic-speaking one' as being central to their self-identity. The authors regarded the English and Gaelic-speaking inputs, which the respondents saw as shaping their lives, as leading to a *bilingual* and *bicultural* identity for these young people. The young people were reported as displaying a high degree of language loyalty, even though Gaelic may not have been the most commonly used language.

Marion Morrison (2006: 150) looked at the lasting impacts of Gaelic-medium education on a sample of pupils in the Western Isles. She noted that 60% of the pupils never spoke to their friends and contemporaries in Gaelic, while a further 25% rarely did. This yields a total of 85% of no or very limited Gaelic peer usage. Morrison points out that 'very few pupils reported that they spoke to friends in Gaelic'.

A more recent attitudes survey was undertaken by Katarina Graffman *et al.* (2014) on behalf of the Soillse research partnership and MG ALBA regarding 'media behaviour among young Gaelic speakers'. The most relevant findings of the media behaviour survey for the purposes of the IGRP research are:

---

37 This is another illustration of the contraction of GME at secondary level (4.2.1).

1. A young person's media environment is not necessarily enlarged by increasing communication over digital networks as the communication takes place mainly within a limited circle of individuals. (2014: 4)
2. Young people have developed their own strategies for keeping themselves informed. Social media and peer-to-peer networks have great significance. It is often via their social networks that they obtain information, seeking further information on the basis of that. In Scotland, English is the main language when seeking information. (2014: 12)
3. There is an inherent feeling of uncoolness in relation to anything Gaelic. Gaelic media are for children and old people. Trying to create loyalty through children's programmes probably results in the opposite effect; something associated with childhood is as uncool as all things that parents and grandparents do. (2014: 15)

These conclusions of Graffman *et al.* (2014), based on actual youth practice and corresponding dominant youth identity, contrast with those of MacNeil (1995) and MacNeil and Stradling (2001), which reflect attitudinal youth identity, rather than actual enacted day-to-day vernacular. Graffman *et al.* also highlighted the relevance of the advent of social media and the use of new technology in the lives of young people. Graffman *et al.* (2014: 15) summarised their findings thus:

It is clear that Gaelic is something that exists in the schools and in the families (parents and grandparents) and is not used outside the school nor the home. In the wider context it is English that is the norm, especially in social friendship circles. Several of the informants emphasize the importance of Gaelic, but they do not use it in daily life outside the school environment. In this context, social media does not support Gaelic, rather the opposite, social media is a threat.

Stuart Dunmore's (2015) doctoral research was conducted in the Central Belt of Scotland and examined Gaelic immersion education outcomes, identities and language ideologies amongst L1 English speakers in English-speaking communities. The research was based on questionnaire responses from 112 individuals and included 46 supplementary interviews with Gaelic-medium educated adults in Scotland (Dunmore 2015: 96). The research found that the Gaelic use of respondents was limited (ten of the 46 supplementary interviewees using Gaelic on a daily basis, mainly at work) and it reported even more marginal use of Gaelic in the home context (see also Dunmore 2016). Regarding identity, Dunmore (2015: 1) contends that the respondents had 'negative perceptions of the traditionally defined, ethnolinguistic identity category 'Gael(s)' in their expression of language ideologies and identities'. Dunmore also asserts a perception among the respondents of linguistic 'snobbery' within the Gaelic community towards new speakers. Additionally, Dunmore (2015:

9) asserts that: 'The social currency of the term 'Gael' has been observed to decline as conceptions of Gaelic as a national resource have increased'. The majority of research participants did not self-identify as Gaels. Dunmore (2015: 12) states that:

> it nevertheless appears clear that if immersion students do not develop a strong sense of community belonging through their use of the target (Xish) language within the domains of school and home during childhood, they are unlikely to continue to use it extensively after school, or pass it on to their own children.

Dunmore's general contextual framework comprises the following problems or difficulties:

1. The importance of minority in-group identity self-ascription of the historical Gaelic group is overlooked;
2. Out-group problematising of Gaelic identity is left uncontested;
3. The newly-created civic Gaelic identity as an important aspect of contemporary Scottish national identity is unquestioningly accepted, despite the context of the ongoing demise of actual Gaelic communities in the Western Isles;
4. There is an absence of analysis as to what 'a strong sense of community belonging' should mean without a recognisable socialised and spatialised identity (see Fishman 1989: 193, 226, 265; 1991: 66–67, 378;[38] 2001a: 14–15; 2001b: 674–75), formerly ascribed as a 'Gael' by both the in-group and the out-group.

A crux of these problems is the confusion of the identity issues of a fragile in-group (with 'Gael' as a dominant actualised identity), on the one hand, with those of an out-group (with 'Gael' as secondary) on the other hand. And the in-group is further marginalised by the prioritisation of the aspirational perspective of the out-group. The intergenerational reduction in *prevalence* (i.e. self-ascription) and *realisation* (i.e. Gaelic speaking) of the identity as a Gael is evidenced for the Western Isles in sections 4.8.1.1 and 4.8.3–4. Nevertheless, identity as a Gael is shown to be of *relevance* in that there is a consistent statistically-significant positive correlation between self-ascription as a Gael and speaking Gaelic, as well as between self-ascription as a Gael and ability in Gaelic (e.g. 4.8.1.1, 4.8.1, 4.9.2). Therefore, there is a positive correlation in the Western Isles between the diminution of identity as a Gael and the increase in English-dominant practice and ability, and such a loss of identity is clearly problematic for any envisioned social continuity of Gaelic. According to IGRP data,

---

38 Fishman (1991: 67) synopsises this critical aspect of the competitive intercommunal dynamic as follows: '[t]he initial problem of RLS boils down to attaining a greater demographic concentration of the faithful, on the one hand, and judicious decisions as to which intercommunal boundary maintaining or reviving institutions to give priority to, on the other hand'.

weakening of identity as a Gael is correlated with loss of vernacular Gaelic, as such a loss of identity would be for many fragile minority-language groups, in particular when in-group identity can be actually more relevant in processes of minoritisation. The ironic cumulative effect of problems 1) to 3) above is common in inter-ethnic contacts and competition. In this instance, the historical Gael is effectively divested of collective identity formation while the historical ascriptive label and concept are appropriated by the contemporary civic Scottish identitarian discourse. This results in the lack of protection for the actual in-group social identity of the Gael while at the same time promoting a future notional identity for Gaelic. The contradiction in problem 4) above is that 'belonging' to historical Gaelic communities already has an ascription, and that ascription is being a Gael, the relevance of which is central to vernacular Gaelic vitality in those communities. These issues of in-group/out-group ascriptions and problems are discussed in more detail in other Celtic language contexts, for instance in Simon Brooks and Richard Glyn Roberts (2013); Lenoach *et al.* (2012: 5–6); Ó Giollagáin and Ó Curnáin (2016); Ó Giollagáin (2014b).

Fabienne Goalabré's doctoral research in the Western Isles (2011: 267–70) indicated (a) instances of intergenerational language shift whereby parents spoke Gaelic with their own parents (i.e. their children's grandparents) but not so much with their children and (b) it was also found that language use between adults and teenagers indicated a clear shift towards English: '[t]his shift shows the advance of English into the familial unit and this despite the occurrence of intergenerational language transmission' of Gaelic. In fact, 95% of respondents to one enquiry said that teenagers always answered them in English, with adults 'recognizing that the language to use with teenagers had become English'.

Focusing on the age cohort of GME-educated pupils aged 12 to 17 years from across the Highlands and Islands and those from urban backgrounds (Stornoway: 50 participants; Inverness: 21; Fort William: 26; Glasgow: 31), Melanie Burmeister (2008) found that the group of pupils surveyed in her research always used English for leisure activities and for speaking to friends; and that they used more English than Gaelic at home, in school and for speaking to older people. Of those pupils from the Western Isles, the research found that just over a third were more secure in themselves speaking English, and almost 43% had better ability in English than in Gaelic. Although Gaelic was rated as an essential marker of the teenage pupils' identity, Burmeister's (2008: 12) assessment of language practice of participants in the research was that: 'Gaelic is rarely used by the teenage respondents in everyday life'. Of particular interest was the research finding that teenagers from Glasgow self-reported greater confidence in their own abilities in Gaelic than teenagers from within the Western Isles. Burmeister's analysis (2008: 11): '[c]onsidered fluency according to region' and reported comparative Gaelic and English fluency as follows: 'Equally good, more secure in Gaelic' at 6.5% (N=2) in Glasgow; 0% in Highlands; 6.1% (N=3) in Western Isles.

Mòrag Stiùbhart's (2011) report *Cainnt nan Deugairean* was based on research conducted in 2006 for the Highland Council on the attitudes of teenagers towards the learning and subsequent use of Gaelic. The survey sample consisted of 101 pupils in the Highland Council area (in all secondary schools except two) who had completed GME at primary level, and 45 ex-GME pupils from the Highlands who had recently completed their secondary education. Stiùbhart's (2011: 276–77) research indicated that only 40% of teenage respondents studying Gaelic in secondary school would definitely consider raising their future children as Gaelic speakers, though 60% would definitely consider putting their future children through GME. On being asked for their views on the importance of Gaelic use in the home, for pastimes and in school, only 12% thought Gaelic was very important to them as a home language, 11% thought Gaelic was very important in social situations such as when involved in pastimes, and 62% of pupils thought it very important in a school setting.

When asked about future generations, 26% of Stiùbhart's 2006 sample thought Gaelic would be very important in a home setting, while 66% thought Gaelic education was very important. Out of the 26% that thought Gaelic would be very important in a home setting, three quarters of them came from homes where at least one parent spoke Gaelic. Out of the 74% that thought Gaelic would not be important in a home setting, 70% of this group came from a household where there was no Gaelic, indicating that because many teenage respondents had come to Gaelic from non-Gaelic speaking households, they themselves attached little importance to Gaelic being spoken at home. Their views of Gaelic use reflected their own experiences in that sense (cf. 4.7.1, 4.7.6, 4.8.1, 4.8.1.1, 4.8.4).

Stiùbhart pointed out that increasing numbers of children entering some form of Gaelic education in primary or secondary schools are coming from non-Gaelic speaking homes and she highlighted the negative consequences of this, in terms of Gaelic continuing as a mother tongue in the future. She also raised the question as to where teenagers are speaking Gaelic if they are not speaking it at home. Generally, Stiùbhart found that teenage respondents do not speak to their parents in Gaelic, use Gaelic very minimally in the wider neighbourhood and do not speak to their own age group in Gaelic, leaving the school as the main locus for use and engagement with the language. Some may speak Gaelic to their grandparents and older people as a mark of respect. Others may use Gaelic when speaking to their parents, when abroad or in situations where they do not want others to understand what they are saying. She pointed to the lack of available social situations such as youth and sports clubs where teenage respondents and younger children can socialise together and work to improve their Gaelic, due partly to a lack of suitably fluent and qualified young instructors.

A contradiction between positive attitudes towards a minority language or a notion of language identity on the one hand and the social and communal use of that language on the other is also a major language-policy problem outside of Scotland in many minority-language situations (e.g. Gerald Roche (forthcoming)). This has been shown, for instance, by the research of Ó Giollagáin *et al.* (2007a; 2007b) with young minority-language speakers in the Gaeltacht in Ireland. That research found that strong reported language ability and positive language attitudes were poor predictors of actual practice among the younger generation. Areas defined as Category A Gaeltacht have the highest densities of daily Irish speakers (2.4.1.5.1). In the Category A Gaeltacht areas an overwhelming number of young people were (strongly) in favour of Irish. However, only 24% of young people in Category A districts spoke Irish within their peer group, significantly lower than in their family or neighbourhood networks. Only 9% of the 15–18 age cohort spoke Irish within their peer group in the Gaeltacht as a whole (i.e. all districts in all Categories A, B, and C; Ó Giollagáin *et al.* 2007b Caibidil 4 [Chapter 4]).

4.3 METHODOLOGY

A questionnaire comprising 43 questions was administered in September and October 2016 by the research team in secondary schools in the Western Isles, the Comhairle nan Eilean Siar authority area. The questionnaire was made available in both English and Gaelic. Both versions were scrutinised to ensure that the import and meaning of the questions in both languages were the same. The survey is a self-report study delivered and completed on-site in secondary schools. Fieldworkers were present to distribute the questionnaires and oversee the process. A time period of 45 to 50 minutes was allotted for the completion of the survey. All pupils in the cohort in each school answered the questionnaire at the same time, so as to reduce the possibility of cross-contamination of data if groups were to respond at different times.

The survey questionnaire and research methodology were approved by the Board of Ethics of the University of the Highlands and Islands and Comhairle nan Eilean Siar's Gaelic Education Advisory Committee. All four secondary schools in the Western Isles were approached and agreed to participate. The IGRP staff involved in delivering this questionnaire had Protection of Vulnerable Groups clearance. All data collected were anonymised and treated in the strictest confidence, to ensure that it would not be possible to identify individual responses in the presented results.

Given that the survey was conducted in a school setting, consent issues and ethical considerations were observed. In order to achieve a high percentage response rate, the research team achieved school acceptance for the project by drafting questionnaire and support materials early in the project, and visiting the target schools no less than eight months in advance to inform stakeholders of plans. Comhairle nan Eilean Siar's Gaelic Education Advisory Committee and Department of Education and

Children's Services were kept informed of the development and implementation of the questionnaires. Given the sensitive and multifaceted nature of the questionnaire approach in this module, it was essential to ensure that the survey procedures were appropriate and that the questions were suitable.

The research method applied in the survey questionnaire was quantitative, although there were some qualitative questions where pupils had an opportunity to submit their views and opinions regarding the Gaelic language. While some questionnaire outputs were binary, the majority were based on continuous bounded responses as in Likert-type items. The survey questions were arranged under the following five sections:

- Section A: Background Data
- Section B: Ability in Gaelic and comparative English ability
- Section C: Language practice
- Section D: Opinions and attitudes
- Section E: Identity.

The IGRP team acquired details on the secondary schools in the relevant districts, including:

- Numbers of students in the relevant age group
- To what extent those still attending schools represented a significant proportion of the 16–18 age group in the districts (with the IGRP team being aware that the chosen methodology and survey mechanism necessarily precluded the participation of those in the target age group who had already left school)
- School language policy and practice
- Curricular approach to Gaelic.

It is important to note that the teenagers' survey had a community as well as an individual focus (rather than an institutional focus). Corresponding to the five sections A–E, there were self-report answers on five themes:

- Background
- Gaelic ability and comparative English ability
- Gaelic and English usage
- Attitudes to Gaelic
- Identity.

Although the work was carried out through the Western Isles' secondary schools, and school-based Gaelic speaking levels were queried, the principal emphasis was not on use and practice of Gaelic in the school or in institutional contexts among 16–18 years of age, and there was no focus on, or assessment of educational provision or attainment. The IGRP team asked teachers to permit participation by students who were between 16 and 18, and this mostly corresponded with S5 and S6 pupils. Because of the mix of ages in senior cycles, 46 15-year old pupils also completed the survey with their peers. Therefore, 46 15-year olds and 259 16–18 year old pupils (with only one 18-year old) make up the full sample of 305 (cf. Table 4.5). Nevertheless, we retain the label 16–18 year olds and we include the data from the 15-year olds in the analysis because it provides a greater sample and more robust findings. Examination of school rolls of 2014–15, and comparison with the school rolls for the academic year 2016–17, allowed the IGRP team to conclude that approximately 46% of the age cohort, based on school rolls, 16–18 years of age (represented by S5 and S6), in the Western Isles was included in the survey. On the day of the survey in their school some students were unavailable to participate, hence the participation rate of approximately 46%.

When the survey questionnaire was completed, two one-hour focus group sessions were held concurrently (one in English for non-Gaelic speakers, and one in Gaelic) in each of the four schools. These comprised six pupils from S5 or S6 in each focus group and were intended to give further information on sociolinguistic practice and attitudes. These focus groups were structured and the same questions were asked in each group.

4.3.1 PUPIL AND SCHOOL PERCENTAGES AND NUMBERS PARTICIPATING IN SURVEY

The questionnaires were offered both in Gaelic and in English. Of the 305 questionnaires returned, 257 (84.3%), were completed in English and 48 (15.7%) were completed in Gaelic. Some pupils surveyed did not respond to all the questions relevant to them, as is common in surveys of this length. Additionally, 12 questionnaires were commenced but were only partially completed, as far as a few initial questions. These available initial responses in these 12 surveys are nevertheless included in the data results. Table 4.5 indicates the schools and the numbers of pupils who participated in the study.

Secondary schools	Number of pupils	Percentage (of all pupils in survey)
1 Sgoil MhicNeacail	207	67.9
2 Sgoil Sir E. Scott	37	12.1
3 Sgoil Lìonacleit	34	11.2
4 Sgoil Bhàgh a' Chaisteil	15	4.9
5 Not completed	12	3.9
Total	305	100

Table 4.5 Number and percentage of participating pupils

4.3.2 HOME AREA: POOLED STUDY DISTRICTS AND STUDY DISTRICTS

In this section we report where the pupils are from in the Western Isles. Table 4.6 shows the numbers of pupils grouped by Pooled Study District, where such information was given.

Pupils' home area in Pooled Study District	Pupils	
	N	%
1 Lewis N&W	49	16.7
2 Lewis E	80	27.3
3 Stornoway & Suburbs	78	26.6
4 Harris	37	12.6
5 North Uist & Benbecula	19	6.5
6 South Uist, Barra & Vatersay	30	10.2
Total	293	100.0

Table 4.6 Number and percentage of participating pupils, by Pooled Study Districts

The smallest geographic unit for data reporting in the Teenager Survey is that of Pooled Study District. For the sake of completeness, Table 4.7 shows the numbers and percentages of pupils who participated, grouped by Study District (in the Western Isles), where such information was given.

Study Districts	N	%	Study Districts	N	%
1 West Side of Lewis (central)	15	5.1	13 North Point	5	1.7
2 West Side of Lewis (south)	7	2.4	14 North Lochs	10	3.4
3 Uig District	10	3.4	15 South Lochs	8	2.7
4 West Side of Lewis (north)	3	1.0	16 North Harris	22	7.5
5 Ness	14	4.8	17 South Harris	15	5.1
6 Tolsta	9	3.1	18 North Uist (north & west)	4	1.4
7 Loch a Tuath	21	7.2	19 North Uist (south & east)	0	0
8 Tong	13	4.4	20 Benbecula	15	5.1
9 Stornoway, Barvas Road suburbs	23	7.8	21 South Uist (north)	8	2.7
10 Stornoway Town	46	15.7	22 South Uist (south)	7	2.4
11 Stornoway, Point Road suburbs	9	3.1	23 Barra & Vatersay	15	5.1
12 South Point	14	4.8			

Table 4.7 Number and percentage of participating pupils, by Study District (N = 293)

We do not report on the Study District level because of the small numbers involved and because of issues of disclosure. In the following section we present the results of the survey of the 16–18 teenage cohort in the four Western Isles secondary schools.

4.4 BACKGROUND: GENDER, AGE AND SCHOOL YEAR; PLACE OF ORIGIN

Section A of the survey sought information relating to pupils' backgrounds. In this section we present the data relating to pupils' gender, age, school year, and their general place of origin in the Western Isles and the wider United Kingdom or further afield. The pupils' gender, age and school year are shown in Table 4.8.[39]

Gender	Male	Female	% Male	% Female
Number of pupils	162	139	54	46
Age	Age 15	Age 16	Age 17	Age 18
Number of pupils	46	181	73	1
School year	S4	S5	S6	
Number of pupils	1	190	104	

Table 4.8 *Gender (number and percentage), age and school year (N = 295)*

Figure 4.1 includes seven categories indicating where pupils came from originally and whether they had moved to the Western Isles.

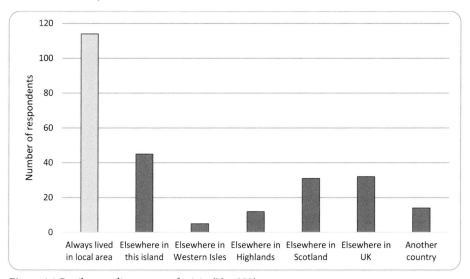

Figure 4.1 *Pupils according to area of origin (N = 253)*

---

39 Additional detailed breakdown of data from the Teenager Survey is presented in **Appendix 4**.

Figure 4.1 shows that 114 pupils (45.1%) had *Always lived in local area* (lighter grey column). Aggregating this with *Elsewhere in this island* and *Elsewhere in Western Isles* indicates that the majority of the pupils surveyed (164, 64.8%) had not lived anywhere other than the Western Isles. Those pupils whose origin was outside the Western Isles were equally divided between *Elsewhere in Scotland* (31, 12.3%) and *Elsewhere in the UK* (32, 12.7%), totalling 25% of students. In all, 35% of students originated from outside the Western Isles. Those pupils who had moved residence were asked to specify their age range when they moved. 27 pupils (10.7%) were aged between 0 and 4 when they moved to their current residence, 59 (23.3%) were aged between 5 and 11, and 20 (7.9%) were aged between 12 and 17.

4.4.1 PARENTAL ORIGIN AND PARENTAL ABILITY IN GAELIC

Figure 4.2 presents the area of origin of the pupils' parents.

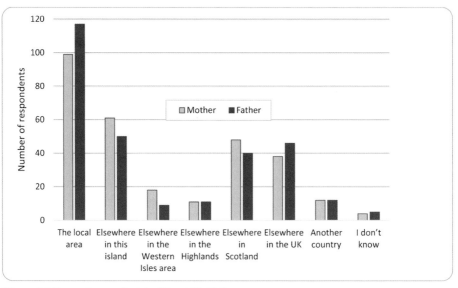

Figure 4.2 *Parental area of origin (Ns = 291, 290)*

The majority of parents, i.e. 354 (60.9% of parents), have a Western Isles origin. 218 parents (37.5%) come from outside the Western Isles, either from other areas in Scotland, the UK or another country. It was not indicated or known where nine parents were from. For 49 respondents (16.8% of pupils), both parents are from the local area. Figure 4.3 indicates reported parental ability in Gaelic.

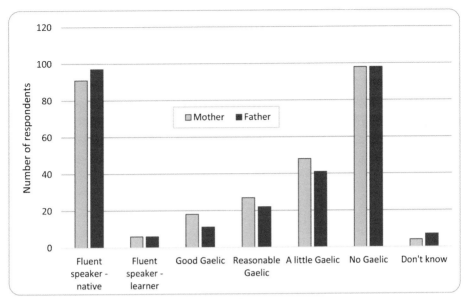

Figure 4.3 *Parental ability in Gaelic (Ns = 292, 282)*

The data depict the highest proportions of parents as having either *No Gaelic* or as *Fluent native speakers* of Gaelic, with little difference between mothers and fathers regarding language competences.

Table 4.9 presents the numbers and percentages of parents aggregated into three groups: *Fluent Gaelic* (native and learner), another group comprising parents with *Good Gaelic* or *Reasonable Gaelic* and a third group with *A little Gaelic* or *No Gaelic*.

Parental ability	Mother		Father	
	N	%	N	%
Fluent Gaelic	97	33.7	103	37.5
Good or reasonable Gaelic	45	15.6	33	12.0
Little or no Gaelic	146	50.7	139	50.5
Total	288	100.0	275	100.0

Table 4.9 *Number and percentage of aggregated parental ability in Gaelic (Ns = 288, 275)*

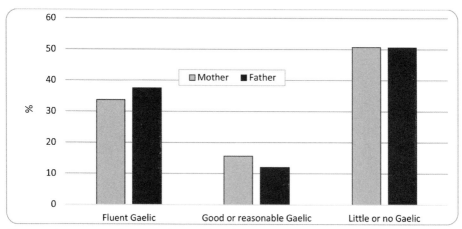

Figure 4.4 *Percentages of aggregated parental Gaelic ability (Ns = 288, 275)*

Figure 4.4 presents the aggregated percentage data from Table 4.9. The data indicate a high proportion of parents have *Little* or *no Gaelic*, followed in prevalence by parents with *Fluent Gaelic*. Although numerical and percentage differences are small, more fathers than mothers are fluent in Gaelic (two data bars on the left). Furthermore, more mothers have less than fluent Gaelic in comparison to fathers (two central data bars).

Aggregating further into two groups, the data show an even split in population, roughly half of parents with some Gaelic and half with little or no Gaelic. 142 mothers (49.3%) and 136 fathers (49.5%) have *Good* or *Reasonable* or *Fluent Gaelic*, compared to 146 mothers (50.7%) and 139 fathers (50.5%) who have *Little* or *No Gaelic*. We can also divide the data at the middle of the six-point Likert scale, with one group comprising *Fluent native* and *Fluent learner* and *Good Gaelic* on the one hand, and the other comprising *Reasonable* and *Little* and *No Gaelic* on the other hand. This yields two groups of greater and lesser competence in Gaelic. The group with the greater competence contains 229 parents (40.7% of parents: 115 mothers and 114 fathers). The group with less competence contains 334 parents (59.3%: 173 mothers and 161 fathers).

A detailed breakdown, by Pooled Study Districts, of parental origin, parental Gaelic ability, pupil Gaelic ability and pupil Gaelic usage is given in **Table A4.1** in **Appendix 4**.

4.4.2 PRIMARY SCHOOL LOCATION AND LANGUAGE(S) OF INSTRUCTION

Figure 4.5 shows the areas where the pupils attended primary school. The majority of pupils (281, 95.3%) attended primary school in their local area or elsewhere in the same island. Most pupils received their education in a Western Isles primary school. 230 pupils (78%) attended the local primary school, 51 (17.3%) attended a primary school *Elsewhere on same island* and five (1.7%) attended a primary school elsewhere in the Western Isles.

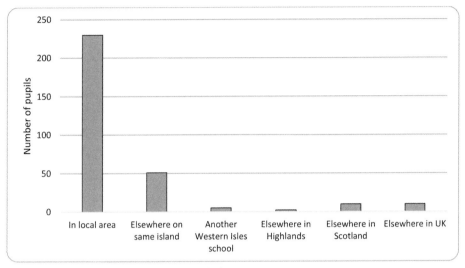

Figure 4.5 *Location of primary school attended (N = 295)*

Figure 4.6 shows the extent to which English or Gaelic were used as mediums of instruction in the pupils' primary schools. The data on the language medium of primary school instruction is taken from the teenager responses to the question on: *When you were in primary school, in what language were the subjects, other than Gaelic, taught?*

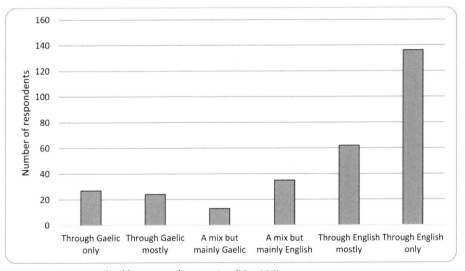

Figure 4.6 *Primary school language of instruction (N = 297)*

A higher proportion of pupils (198, 66.7%) attended mostly English or English-only primary schools. More than three-quarters (233, 78.5%) of pupils received their primary education in a mainly, mostly or English-only setting. 27 pupils (9.1%) received instruction in Gaelic-only in primary school and another 24 (8.1%) received their primary schooling mostly through the medium of Gaelic. There is an aggregated total of 64 pupils (21.6%) in the three Gaelic-dominant categories of *Through Gaelic only*, *Through Gaelic mostly* and *A mix but mainly Gaelic*. On the other hand, as stated above, the aggregated total when the responses *Through English only*, *Through English mostly* and *A mix but mainly English* are grouped is 233 (78.5%).

Table 4.10a and Figure 4.7 show aggregated numbers and percentages of language of instruction in three groups:

Gaelic mostly or only (*Through Gaelic mostly* or *Through Gaelic only*);

Mix (*A mix but mainly Gaelic* or *A mix but mainly English*);

English mostly or only (*Through English mostly* or *Through English only*).

In summary, the majority (66.7%) of pupils received their primary school education through English mostly or only.

	Pupils	Percent
Gaelic mostly or only	51	17.2
Gaelic and English mix	48	16.2
English mostly or only	198	66.7
Total	297	100.1

Table 4.10a Numbers and percentages of language of instruction in primary school

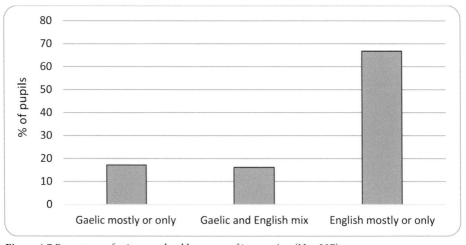

Figure 4.7 Percentage of primary school language of instruction (N = 297)

Table 4.10b shows a summary of the educational history of the pupils with regard to the medium of instruction and Gaelic as a subject.

Educational history	Pupils	
	Number	%
Primary schooling through GME	70	26.3
Primary schooling through English Medium	188	70.7
Primary school Gaelic as a subject	44	16.5
Secondary schooling through GME	29	10.9
Secondary schooling through English Medium	175	65.8
Secondary Gaelic as learner	88	31.1

Table 4.10b *Summary of pupils' educational history (N = 266)*

It is of interest to see what relationships might hold between the pupils who attended GME or non-GME primary school, on the one hand, and their sociolinguistic and linguistic experiences, practices and identities, on the other. As well as their attendance at GME or non-GME primary school, from this and other sections of the Teenager Survey, we know the following:

1. Language-medium of instruction at primary level (Figures 4.6 and 4.7);
2. Language practice of parents to the pupil (4.6.1);
3. Language practice of the pupil to her/his parents (4.6.2);
4. Pupil's fluency or ability in spoken Gaelic (4.5.1);
5. Pupil's conversational ability in Gaelic (4.5.4);
6. Pupil's self-ascribed identity as a Gael (4.8.1).

These six quantified variables are presented in cross-tabulated form in this order in Table 4.10c, in six or five-point Likert scales where relevant.

All six correlations in Table 4.10c are statistically significant. The first cross-tabulation shows the obvious relationship between the language medium of instruction at primary level and attendance at GME or non-GME primary school, i.e. attendance at GME correlates with greater amount of Gaelic language medium than non-GME. The second cross-tabulation shows the positive relationship between parents who speak some level of Gaelic to their children and their children attending GME primary school. Of those pupils attending GME, 17.9% of parents speak *Always* or *Mainly Gaelic* to their children, whereas among the non-GME pupils the corresponding percentage is 4.3%. On the other hand, children whose parents speak *Always* or *Mainly English* to their children, make up 64.2% of the GME pupils, while among the non-GME pupils the equivalent percentage is 94.2%. The correlations in Table 4.10c, in particular cross-tabulations 2 and 3, indicate that GME is primarily

1. Language of instruction*	Gaelic only (%)	Gaelic mostly (%)	Mix mainly Gaelic (%)	Mix mainly English (%)	English mostly (%)	English only (%)
GME	27 (40.3)	21 (31.3)	10 (14.9)	9 (13.4)	0	0
non-GME	0	1 (0.5)	2 (0.9)	23 (10.5)	61 (27.9)	132 (60.3)
2. Parent language input*	Always Gaelic	Mainly Gaelic	Mix Gaelic - English	Mainly English	Always English	
GME	4 (6)	8 (11.9)	12 (17.9)	28 (41.8)	15 (22.4)	
non-GME	2 (1)	7 (3.3)	5 (2.4)	73 (34.9)	122 (58.4)	
3. Child output to parent*	Always Gaelic	Mainly Gaelic	Mix Gaelic - English	Mainly English	Always English	
GME	5 (7.5)	4 (6)	15 (22.4)	26 (38.8)	17 (25.4)	
non-GME	1 (0.5)	5 (2.3)	6 (2.8)	45 (20.8)	159 (73.6)	
4. Child fluency*	Native	Fluent Learner	Good	Reasonable	Little	No Gaelic
GME	38 (56.7)	16 (23.9)	6 (9)	3 (4.5)	4 (6)	0
non-GME	4 (1.8)	1 (0.5)	26 (11.7)	37 (16.7)	83 (37.4)	71 (32)
5. Child conversational ability*	Comfortably	Relatively well	Reasonably	A few words	No ability	
GME	29 (43.3)	29 (43.3)	6 (9)	3 (4.5)	0	
non-GME	5 (2.3)	12 (5.5)	46 (21)	76 (34.7)	80 (36.5)	
6. Child identity as Gael*	Yes	No	Prefer not to say			
GME	51 (81)	6 (9.5)	6 (9.5)			
non-GME	38 (18.1)	145 (69)	27 (12.9)			

*Table 4.10c Numbers and percentages of primary school GME vs. non-GME, by 1. Language of instruction; 2. Parental language input spoken to child; 3. Child output spoken to parent; 4. Child fluency; 5. Child conversational ability; and 6. Child identity as Gael in binary choice. (All correlations are statistically significant, marked * = p. < 0.05.)*

serving English-practicing parents and pupils, but that GME also serves a substantial proportion of parents who speak Gaelic to their children. Of the 38 parents who speak some Gaelic (*Always, Mainly* or *Mix*) to their children, 24 (63.2%) send their children to GME, whereas 14 (36.8%) Gaelic-practicing parents send their children to non-GME. In the third cross-tabulation, on child output to parents, we see that 64.2% of GME pupils speak *Always* or *Mainly English* to their parents, whereas 94.4% of non-GME pupils speak *Always* or *Mainly English*. There are similar correlations between higher levels of Gaelic-positive features in attendance at GME primary school and the other variables. In cross-tabulation 4, 80.6% of GME pupils are either native speakers or fluent learners of Gaelic in comparison to an equivalent of 2.3% of non-GME pupils. We see a similarly large contrast in the conversational ability comparison in the fifth cross-tabulation. The sixth cross-tabulation on Gaelic identity shows a much stronger correspondence between GME attendance and self-ascription as a Gael (81% of GME pupils vs. 18.1% of non-GME pupils).

4.5 ABILITY IN GAELIC

Section B of the survey asked questions about the Gaelic abilities of the pupils and sought to establish levels of comparative competence in Gaelic and English for pronunciation, reading, writing, speaking, understanding and holding a conversation. This part of the survey covered the extent of Gaelic transmission and acquisition, and the students' ability to express a range of emotions in Gaelic and English.

4.5.1 ABILITY IN SPOKEN GAELIC

Table 4.11 presents the numbers and percentages of the spoken Gaelic ability of the respondents. There are 137 pupils who self-report within the range of *Fluent* to *Reasonable Gaelic*. This represents a percentage of 45.7% (rounded) of the cohort. This percentage of 45.7% can be compared to the 41.9% of 3–17-year olds with reported ability in Gaelic in the 2011 Census (2.4.1.1, 2.4.3).

Ability in spoken Gaelic	Pupils	Percentage
Fluent speaker – native	43	14.3
Fluent speaker – learner	18	6.0
Good Gaelic	34	11.3
Reasonable Gaelic	42	14.0
A little Gaelic	91	30.3
No Gaelic	72	24.0
Total	300	100

Table 4.11 Numbers and percentages of ability in spoken Gaelic

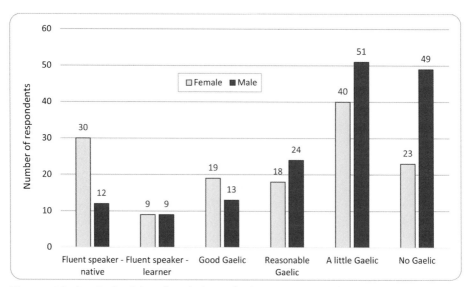

Figure 4.8 *Spoken Gaelic ability of pupils, by gender (N = 139, 158; Total N = 297)*

Figure 4.8 illustrates the spoken Gaelic ability of the respondents by gender. This figure illustrates that just over half of pupils have *A little Gaelic* or *No Gaelic*, i.e. 163 pupils (54.9% of 297 pupils; see also the discussion on the practice of Gaelic in Family Households in 2.4.3). At the Gaelic competence end of the spectrum, 92 pupils (30%) have good or fluent Gaelic (aggregated from *Good Gaelic* and *Fluent speaker – learner* and *Fluent speaker – native* respondents). 42 pupils (14.1%) are fluent in Gaelic (native speaker ability), and an additional 18 (6.1%) are fluent having learned the language. A comparison of this ability data shows more females than males in the higher Gaelic ability categories, and correspondingly, more males in the lower Gaelic ability categories.

Table 4.12 and Figure 4.9 show the numbers and percentages for Gaelic ability by Pooled Study Districts, presented in order of descending ability in Gaelic. Pupils are aggregated into two groups: those with fluent or good Gaelic together, in contrast with those who have reasonable, little or no Gaelic.

Pooled Study District	Fluent or Good Gaelic		Reasonable, Little or No Gaelic	
	N (Total = 95)	%	N (Total = 198)	%
1 Lewis N&W	23	46.9	26	53.1
2 Lewis E	28	35.0	52	65.0
3 Harris	13	35.1	24	64.9
4 North Uist & Benbecula	6	31.6	13	68.4
5 South Uist, Barra & Vatersay	9	30.0	21	70.0
6 Stornoway & Suburbs	16	20.5	62	79.4

Table 4.12 *Numbers and percentages of pupils' ability in Gaelic, by Pooled Study District (Ns = 49, 80, 37, 19, 30, 78)*

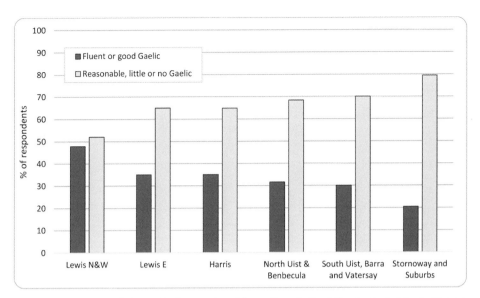

Figure 4.9 *Percentage ability in Gaelic in order of descending Gaelic ability, by Pooled Study Districts (Ns = 49, 80, 37, 19, 30, 78)*

The aggregated percentages of pupils with reasonable, little or no Gaelic are higher than 50% in each of the Pooled SDs.

4.5.2 GAELIC TRANSMISSION, SOURCE OF ACQUISITION AND ABILITY

The survey sought to determine from whom or in what context pupils primarily acquired their ability in Gaelic. The question was: *If you can speak Gaelic, from whom did you acquire your ability in Gaelic?* The nine multiple-choice responses offered to pupils were: *Both parents; Mother; Father; Grandmother; Grandfather; Other relatives; Preschool or school; Community; Other.* Figure 4.10 shows the pupils' responses.

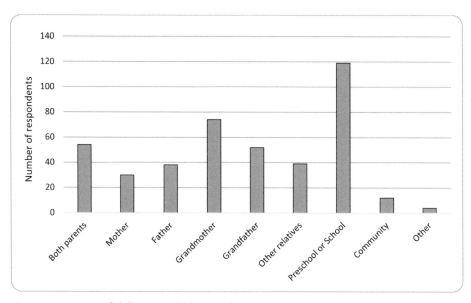

Figure 4.10 *Sources of ability in Gaelic (N = 213)*

The total number of respondents to this question was 213. This number corresponds quite closely to the number of 228 pupils who indicated their ability in Gaelic ranged between fluent and a little Gaelic, as aggregated from the data in Table 4.11. Given 213 respondents and 338 responses, the pupils identified an average of 1.6 options of sources for their Gaelic acquisition. The highest number of responses indicate that pupils acquired their Gaelic from *Preschool or school*, followed in prevalence by *Grandmother* and *Both parents*. Those acquiring their Gaelic from *Both parents* (54, or 25.3% of respondents) account for less than half the responses of those who acquire their Gaelic from *Preschool or school* (119, or 55.9% of respondents). Those acquiring their Gaelic from their *Father* (38, or 17.8% of respondents) account for close to half the number of responses of those acquiring their Gaelic from their *Grandmother* (74, 34.7%). Grandmothers and grandfathers combined (126, 59.2%), i.e. grandparents, are numerically higher than, although quite close to, the three combined categories of parents (122, or 57.3% of respondents); i.e. *Both parents* (54, 25.3%) plus *Mother* (30, 14.1%) plus *Father* (38, 17.8%). These two categories of all parents (57.3%) and all grandparents (59.2%) are actually close to the category of *Preschool or school* (55.6%). *Other relatives* (39, 18.3%) are similar in number to *Father* and greater in number than *Mother*. 12 responses (5.6% of respondents) indicated Gaelic ability was acquired from the wider community.

As demonstrated in section 4.5.1, the ability of these respondents has been self-reported by them. We can therefore analyse any possible correlations between a pupil's source or sources of Gaelic acquisition and the same pupil's Gaelic ability. For instance, we can analyse the level of Gaelic ability found in pupils who indicate that they have acquired their Gaelic from *Both parents*. Table 4.13 and Figure 4.11 show the six Gaelic ability categories, by number and percentage, of the 54 pupils who stated that they acquired their Gaelic from *Both parents*, based on the same pupils' reported ability in Figure 4.8 (4.5.1).

Ability in Gaelic	N	%
Fluent speaker — native	24	44.4
Fluent speaker — learner	3	5.6
Good Gaelic	13	24.1
Reasonable Gaelic	8	14.8
Little Gaelic	6	11.1
No Gaelic	0	0
Total	54	100

Table 4.13 *Numbers and percentages of ability in Gaelic, when Gaelic is acquired from both parents*

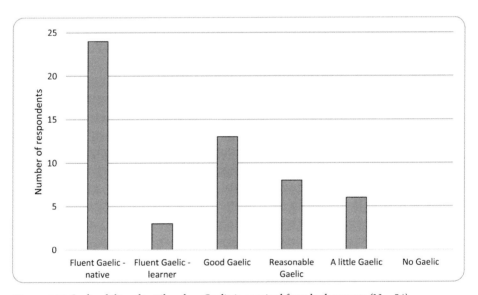

Figure 4.11 *Gaelic ability of pupils, when Gaelic is acquired from both parents (N = 54)*

Among the pupils indicating that they have acquired their Gaelic from *Both parents*, the aggregated majority (40, 71.4%) report *Fluent Gaelic* or *Good Gaelic*. 24 pupils (44.4%) have fluent native-speaker ability.

Of the 95 pupils, from data given in Table 4.11 and Figure 4.8, with fluent or good Gaelic, 40 of them (74.1% of this aggregated Gaelic ability category) indicated that *Both parents* (Figure 4.10) were the primary sources of their Gaelic ability. As discussed in section 4.5.4, the pupils' self-reported ability in conversation in Gaelic may be a more accurate measure of actual ability. To allow for a comparison between pupils' conversational ability in Gaelic and their source of acquisition of that ability, we applied a score to the five-point Likert scale as follows: *Comfortably* = 5, *Relatively well* = 4, *Reasonably* = 3, *A few words* = 2 and *No ability* = 1. This also allows for mean scores to be calculated and combined for further analysis. The closer the score is to 5 the higher the ability in conversational Gaelic of any individual or group. Table 4.14 shows the mean conversational ability score in Gaelic for 10 subgroups according to the source of Gaelic ability. Many of these subgroups are, of course, intersecting.

Source (parental input, grandparental input, (pre)school input)	Mean Conversational Ability Score	N
Parental ± ANY other	**3.57**	115
Grandparental ± ANY other	**3.34**	82
(Pre)school ± ANY other	**2.74**	119
Parental ONLY	**3.76**	45
Grandparental ONLY	**2.42**	12
(Pre)school ONLY	**2.25**	63
Parental and **grandparental** but not (pre)school	**3.69**	26
Parental and **(pre)school** but not grandparental	**2.92**	12
Grandparental and **(pre)school** but not parental	**3.17**	12
Parental and **grandparental** and **(pre)school**	**3.47**	32

Table 4.14 *Mean conversational ability score in Gaelic and source of Gaelic acquisition (parent (mother and/or father and/or both parents) grandparent, (pre)school or combination of sources)*

Figure 4.12 shows the same mean scores for conversational ability in Gaelic in descending order of the 10 subgroups.

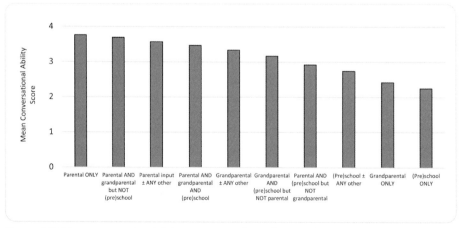

Figure 4.12 *Mean conversational ability score in Gaelic and source of Gaelic acquisition (parent, grandparent, (pre)school or combination of sources)*

Table 4.14 and Figure 4.12 show that the highest score is 3.76 in the category of *Parental input ONLY* and the lowest scoring is 2.25 in the *(Pre)school ONLY* category. The four groups with the highest mean scores are (in descending order): *Parental input ONLY, Parental AND grandparental input but NOT (pre)school, Parental input ± ANY other source, Parental AND grandparental AND (pre)school input.*[40] These four highest scoring subgroups all comprise categorical parental sources (i.e. these are the subgroups which necessarily comprise parents (only where *Parental* is indicated)). Whereas other subgroups such as *Grandparental ± ANY other* include grandparents categorically, and parents (where applicable) and other sources (where applicable). The only other categorical parental subgroup is the fourth lowest-scoring (2.92) subgroup of *Parental AND (pre)school but NOT grandparental* (N = 12), which is the smallest categorical parental subgroup. The three lowest-scoring subgroups are *(Pre) school ± ANY other, Grandparental ONLY, (Pre)school ONLY*. These three subgroups comprise the two categorical (pre)school subgroups, scoring similar to the small subgroup of *Grandparental ONLY* (N = 12).

In Table 4.15, we compare the conversational ability of pupils, in the five-point Likert scale, between two sets of sources, allowing for an analysis of grandparental input. In the four leftmost data columns in Table 4.15, we compare three sources of ability (with or without any grandparent involvement) from *Parental only ± grandparental, Parental and (pre)school ± grandparental*, and *(Pre)school only ± grandparental*. In the four rightmost columns, we compare three sources of ability from *Grandparental only, Grandparental and (pre)school*, and *(Pre)school only*. Four of these subgroups contain relatively robust numbers of pupils for comparison and statistical analysis.

	Parental only ± grandparental	Parental and (pre) school ± grand- parental	(Pre)school only ± grand- parental	Total	Grand- parental only	Grand- parental and (pre) school	(Pre) school only	Total
No ability	6	1	14	21	1	0	14	15
A few words	7	11	29	47	6	3	26	35
Reasonably	14	12	21	47	4	4	17	25
Relatively well	17	13	10	40	1	5	5	11
Comfortably	27	7	1	35	0	0	1	1
Total	71	44	75	190	12	12	63	87

Table 4.15 Comparison of conversational ability in Gaelic with six sources of ability (where 'only ±' stands for 'excluding all other inputs except ±') allowing for analysis of grandparental input

---

40 A case-study of a context corresponding to *Parental AND grandparental AND (pre)school* is presented in Smith-Christmas (2016). See also footnote 56.

Table 4.15 shows that the highest ability level of *Comfortably* (numbers in bold) is attained by 35 pupils and by 1 pupil in the two comparisons. Of the 35 pupils, 34 (97.1%) have categorical parental sources. After aggregating conversational ability into two subsets *Comfortably* vs. *Less than comfortably* (i.e. categories from *Relatively well* to *No ability* inclusive), we can test for significance of these two subsets against various input permutations.

When we test for significance between conversational ability and *Parental* source (i.e. *Parental only* ± *grandparental* and *Parental and (pre)school* ± *grandparental*) or *(Pre)school* source (i.e. *(Pre)school only* ± *grandparental*), using the Pearson Chi-square test, this yields a significant result ($X^2 = 32.921$, p. < 0.05). A similar comparison between *Grandparental* source (i.e. *Grandparental only* and *Grandparental and (pre)school*) and *(Pre)school only* source revealed that no significant difference exists between *Grandparental* input and *(Pre)school* input in terms of conversational ability output. The data and analysis in this section demonstrate the centrality of parents as sources of Gaelic ability. In comparison to parents, the other sources of Gaelic ability in grandparents and (pre)school correlate with far lower levels of ability.

4.5.3 COMPARISON OF COMPETENCES IN GAELIC AND ENGLISH

The data analysed in this section is based on the responses to the question: *How would you describe your ability in both Gaelic and English in relation to the following skills?* Pupils' comparative competences in both Gaelic and English in terms of understanding, speaking, reading, writing and pronunciation were self-assessed by respondents across a five-point Likert scale: *Very good, Good, Reasonable, Poor* and *Very poor*. The question was laid out in such a manner that the pupils gave their responses for Gaelic and then for English in the five competences which were queried sequentially. To allow for a comparison between pupils' ability in Gaelic and English, we applied a score to the five-point Likert scale as follows: *Very good* = 5, *Good* = 4, *Reasonable* = 3, *Poor* = 2 and *Very poor* = 1. This also allows for mean scores to be calculated and combined for further analysis.

Table 4.16 and Figure 4.13 show the average ability scores in Gaelic and English across the five queried competences.

Ability	Average Gaelic	Average English	N Gaelic	N English
Understanding	2.92	4.86	298	300
Speaking	2.64	4.81	293	300
Reading	2.64	4.74	295	298
Writing	2.41	4.66	294	296
Pronunciation	2.83	4.68	293	298

Table 4.16 *Average ability scores in Gaelic and English across five competences, in order of competences queried*

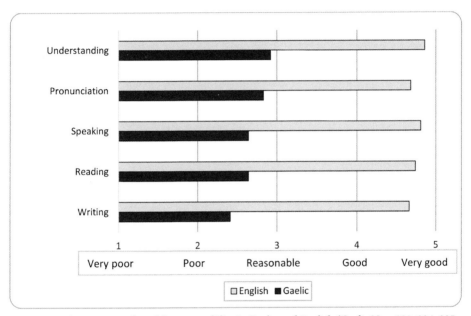

Figure 4.13 *Comparison of pupils' average ability in Gaelic and English (Gaelic Ns = 293, 294, 295, 293, 298; English Ns = 298, 296, 298, 300, 300)*

It is evident that Gaelic competences are all substantially lower than all English competences. This is to be expected, given that there are English monolinguals in this cohort (cf. 72 pupils (24%) have *No Gaelic* in Table 4.11, 4.5.1). The lowest average skill level is for writing in Gaelic, followed by reading in Gaelic and speaking in Gaelic. Receptive language skills are of course typically greater than productive skills. Furthermore, in bilingual speakers' abilities, a non-dominant language typically has lower competences, but also a greater range within those competences, than for a dominant language. The comparative competences of the teenage pupils conforms with these two characteristic patterns. The combination of these two patterns typically results in a greater gap between receptive and productive skills in the non-dominant language of bilinguals than in their dominant language (e.g. Dorian 1980; 1981). In the pupils' competence data, the gap or range between highest and lowest competence in Gaelic (Understanding 2.92 – Writing 2.41: range of 0.51) is greater than in English (Understanding 4.86 – Writing 4.66: a narrower range of 0.20). In short, as is typical in nondominant or secondary language competences, receptive Gaelic skills (understanding and reading) are more developed than productive Gaelic skills (speaking and writing), all of which are far less developed than in English.

Much further analysis and comparison of this and related data can be carried out. For instance, we can calculate the averages of all five skills for each language and compare these average competences. This can be done for each student separately and for the student group as a whole, as well as for any subgroups. The average of the responses for Gaelic skills among all students ranged between *Poor* and *Reasonable*, while the corresponding average for all English skills ranged between *Good* and *Very good*. This shows that, on average, ability in English is far superior to ability in Gaelic in all five skills.

We can furthermore compare the size of the groups of pupils who claim various levels of competences in both languages. Table 4.17 and Figure 4.14 show the comparative numbers and percentages of those who considered themselves *Very good* or *Good* in both Gaelic and English competences, i.e. the most competent and balanced bilinguals in the pupil cohort.

Competence	Gaelic		English	
	N	%	N	%
Understanding	110	36.9	293	97.7
Speaking	87	29.7	292	97.3
Reading	91	30.8	287	96.3
Writing	69	23.5	275	92.9
Pronunciation	96	32.7	282	94.6

Table 4.17 *Numbers and percentages of pupils with 'Very good' or 'Good ' competences in both Gaelic and English*

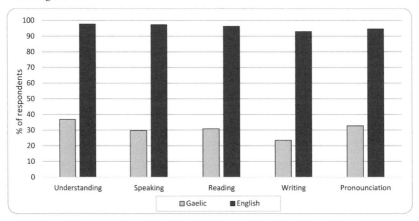

Figure 4.14 *Percentage comparison of pupils with 'Very good' or 'Good' competences in both Gaelic and English (Ns = 293, 292, 287, 275, 282)*

A similar pattern to the overall cohort's bilingual competences is evident in this cohort of the most competent bilingual pupils. There are clearly far fewer in the *Very good* or *Good* Gaelic subgroups than in the English equivalents. Basically, about a third of the pupils are in the *Very good* or *Good* Gaelic subgroups, while nearly all of the cohort are in the English subgroups. As a median percentage across all the competences, 30.8% of pupils consider themselves as *Very good* or *Good* in Gaelic, whereas 96.3% of pupils consider themselves as *Very good* or *Good* in English.

Similar to the larger gap or range in Gaelic competences than in English competences, discussed above (Table 4.17), there is a larger range in cohort size or averages in Table 4.17 within Gaelic competences (Understanding 36.9% – Writing 23.5%: a range of 12.4%) than within English competences (Understanding 97.7% – Writing 92.9%: a range of 4.8%).

4.5.4 ABILITY TO CONVERSE IN GAELIC

The questionnaire contained a question which asked the pupils about their ability to hold a conversation in Gaelic on a five-point Likert scale. The following question in the questionnaire queried about comparative conversational ability in Gaelic and English. In this section we present the Gaelic conversation ability data, and describe the comparative data in the following section below. Table 4.18 and Figure 4.15 show the responses to this question, i.e. the number and percentages of pupils according to their abilities to converse in Gaelic, by gender. The responses to this question are consistent with the six-point Likert-scale data on Gaelic ability shown in Figure 4.8.

Ability to converse in Gaelic Gender	Comfortably (N, %)	Relatively well (N, %)	Reasonably (N, %)	A few words (N, %)	No ability (N, %)	Total N
Female	20 (58.9)	29 (70.7)	29 (52.7)	35 (44.3)	26 (30.6)	139
Male	14 (41.1)	12 (29.3)	26 (47.3)	44 (55.7)	59 (69.4)	155
Total N	34 (100)	41 (100)	55 (100)	79 (100)	85 (100)	294
Percentage	11.6%	13.9%	18.7%	26.8%	28.9%	n/a

Table 4.18 Numbers and percentages of pupils' ability to converse in Gaelic, by gender

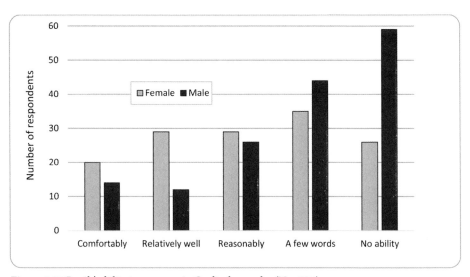

Figure 4.15 *Pupils' ability to converse in Gaelic, by gender (N = 294)*

34 pupils (20 females and 14 males) or 11.6% of the whole sample are able to converse *Comfortably* in Gaelic. When we compare these data to those in Table 4.11 and Figure 4.8, we see that in response to the earlier question, 61 pupils claim to have *Fluent* and 95 claim *Fluent* or *Good Gaelic*. This indicates that there are a higher number of pupils self-categorising in the higher general ability range (of Table 4.11 and Figure 4.8) than in the case of the more specific conversational ability range (of Table 4.18 and Figure 4.16 in this section). From this comparative perspective, it appears that not all *Fluent* or *Good Gaelic* can be cross-categorised in the data as corresponding to comfortable conversation. Ability to converse *Comfortably* in Gaelic yields the smallest number or subgroup of pupils with Gaelic ability. Self-reported conversational ability may well be the most precise indicator of actual Gaelic ability in the Teenager Survey (see the discussion pertaining to Tables 4.20 and 4.23, 4.6.2). In section 4.6.2, we discuss the combined parental input and combined child output with regard to language practice. When we check for correlations between the Combined Parental Input Score and pupils' ability, in the forms of conversational ability on one hand and fluency on the other, we find a near-significant correlation (p. = 0.085) between the Combined Parental Input Score and pupils' conversational ability. But the correlation between the Combined Parental Input Score and pupils' fluency is not significant (p. = 0.247). This is a further indication that self-reported conversational ability may be a more precise indicator of Gaelic competence than self-reported fluency.

When we combine the percentages within the range *Comfortably* to *Reasonably*, we find that 44.2% of pupils fall within this range. This value of 44.2% is similar to the 41.9% of 3–17-year olds with Gaelic ability in Census 2011 (2.4.1.1, 2.4.3; cp. 45.7% of ability in 4.5.1). This comparison indicates higher proportions of males than females having *A few words* or *No ability* in Gaelic. The obvious corollary of this higher number of males in the weaker Gaelic ability group is that there are more females in the stronger Gaelic ability group, as seen in the responses to this question. More females than males can converse *Comfortably* or *Relatively well* or *Reasonably* in Gaelic.

We are interested to discover if there is any correspondence between a pupil's area of origin and their conversational abilities. Figure 4.16 shows ability to converse in Gaelic as cross-referenced with the pupil's place of origin (based on the data in section 4.4) aggregated into two categories, i.e. whether the pupil has always lived in the Western Isles, or has lived somewhere else previously.

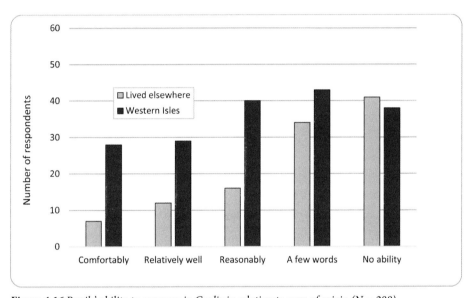

Figure 4.16 Pupils' ability to converse in Gaelic in relation to area of origin (N = 288)

This comparison shows that highest abilities in conversing in Gaelic, i.e. *Comfortably*, *Relatively well* or *Reasonably*, correlate with a Western Isles' origin. Those who have lived somewhere else previously are more likely to be limited to *A few words* or *No ability* in Gaelic. 28 (80%) of those who can converse *Comfortably* in Gaelic are from the Western Isles, as are 29 (70.7%) who can converse in Gaelic *Relatively well*. 40 (71.4%) of those who can hold a conversation *Reasonably* in Gaelic are from the Western Isles. 43 (55.8%) of those who have *A few words* are from the Western Isles, as are 38 (48.1%) of those with *No ability* to hold a conversation in Gaelic.

4.5.5 COMPARISON OF CONVERSATIONAL ABILITY IN GAELIC AND ENGLISH

In a related question, students were asked to *Please compare your ability to hold a conversation in Gaelic and English* with a response choice of three options as shown in Figure 4.17.

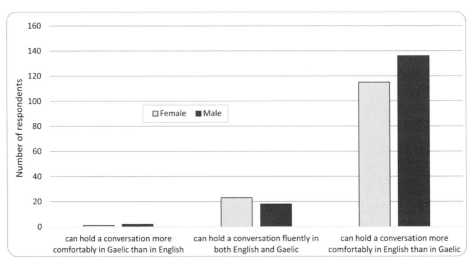

Figure 4.17 *Pupils' comparative ability to hold a conversation in Gaelic and English, by gender (N = 298)*

The responses are consistent with the rest of the ability data and demonstrate that a large majority of pupils are more comfortable in English than in Gaelic. Few reported themselves as balanced bilinguals in the context of having fluent conversational ability in both English and Gaelic (42 pupils, 14.1%), and fewer still are more comfortable in Gaelic than they are in English (3, 1%). Interestingly, the number of Gaelic-dominant and balanced-ability bilinguals in the comparative conversational data (i.e. 42 + 3 = 45) is closer to the number of pupils categorised as *Fluent speaker (native)* (43) in Table 4.11 and Figure 4.8, than to the number who report they can hold a conversation *Comfortably* in Gaelic (34) in Figure 4.15. This seems to indicate that comparative bilingual abilities are generally self-reported less accurately (i.e. more positively) than separate self-assessments of language skills when queried independently for each language. This is consistent with the finding in Figure 4.17 showing higher ability to converse comfortably in English rather than Gaelic. In this context, the comparative balanced bilingual abilities in Figure 4.17 were self-reported more positively (and possibly less accurately) than separate self-assessments of language skills when queried independently for each language, e.g. for Gaelic in Figure 4.15. When measured against objective language-proficiency tests, it is noted in Li Sheng *et al.* (2014: 366) that speakers evince less accurate self-assessment of balanced bilingualism in comparison to more accurate self-assessed language-dominance. Self-assessment of comparative language skills may be more complex than self-assessment of language skills of each language separately. Ethan Zell and Zlatan Krizan (2014: 118) show that the accuracy of self-evaluations of abilities is higher in tasks of low complexity. In comparative balanced bilingual self-assessment both the task of balanced bilingual performance and the task of self-assessment of that performance are clearly complex and difficult.

4.5.6 ABILITY IN GAELIC AND ENGLISH TO DISCUSS TOPICS AND EXPRESS EMOTIONS

Pupils were asked to rate their abilities to discuss six topics pertinent to teenage life: music, sport, computers and gaming, homework, social life and films. The question was: *Please indicate whether or not you have difficulty in the following situations.* Four options were offered for each topic: *No difficulty, Some difficulty, A lot of difficulty* and *I rarely discuss this topic.* The question was laid out in such a manner that the pupils gave their responses for Gaelic and then for English in the six topics which were queried sequentially. Students' ability in discussing these topics in Gaelic is presented in Figure 4.18. Although the fourth option of *I rarely discuss this topic* could possibly be interpreted ambiguously, it is clear from the English response data in **Appendix 4**, **Figure A4.1** that all these topics are relevant to most pupils in English. It is, therefore, reasonable to assume that many of the pupils who chose the fourth option (*I rarely discuss this topic* in Gaelic) did so for the purpose of indicating the option of most difficulty.

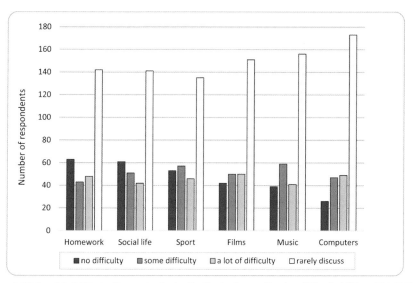

Figure 4.18 Pupils' ability to discuss topics in Gaelic, in descending 'no difficulty' (Ns = 296, 295, 291, 293, 295, 295)

As shown in Figure 4.18, of pupils claiming to have *no difficulty* discussing the topics in Gaelic, discussing *Homework* (63, 21.3%) and *Social life* (61, 20.7%) are the topics that are least difficult, followed by *Sport* (53, 18.2%), *Films* (42, 14.3%), *Music* (39, 13.2%) and *Computers* (26, 8.8%). We can compare, for instance, the similar number of 75 pupils (Table 4.18) who can converse *Comfortably* or *Relatively well* in Gaelic. The percentages of those choosing the *no difficulty* option range between 8.8% and 21.3%. The data indicate that a large percentage of pupils (an average of 50.9% over all topics) *rarely discuss* any of the topics in Gaelic, i.e. we can assume that they have the greatest difficulty in discussing these topics in Gaelic. The three least-discussed topics (i.e. *rarely discuss*) in Gaelic are *Computers and gaming* (173 pupils, 58.6%), *Music* (156 pupils, 52.9%) and *Films* (151 pupils, 51.5%). Of those who choose one of the first three options, i.e. that can discuss the six topics in Gaelic to some degree, a higher aggregated proportion report *some difficulty* or *a lot of difficulty* than report *no difficulty*.

Regarding respondents who stated that they have *a lot of difficulty* discussing the topics in Gaelic, discussing *Films* (50, 17.1%) and *Computers* (49 pupils, 16.6%) in Gaelic are the subjects that present most difficulty, followed by *Homework* (48, 16.2%) *Sport* (46, 15.8%), *Social life* (42, 14.2%) and *Music* (41, 13.9%).

The pupils' responses on their ability to discuss topics in English are shown in **Figures A4.1** and **A4.2** in **Appendix 4.** These demonstrate that a high proportion of pupils has *no difficulty* discussing all the topics in English. The responses of the survey cohort in relation to how they express emotions in Gaelic and English are shown in **Figures A4.3** and **A4.4** respectively in **Appendix 4.** As with the findings on topics, emotions are expressed better in English than in Gaelic. A high proportion of pupils (an average of 58.2% across all categorised emotions) have *a lot of difficulty* expressing emotions in Gaelic.

4.6 SPEAKING GAELIC AND ENGLISH IN FAMILY AND COMMUNITY

Section C of the survey contained questions about the practice of spoken Gaelic and English. It investigated the language practices of pupils and their families and language practices in community and school. The survey also sought to investigate whether there are any changes in language practice in families as children grow older. The questionnaire also sought pupils' views on the availability of services in Gaelic in their localities and how often they use Gaelic media.

4.6.1 LANGUAGE SPOKEN TO PUPILS BY FAMILY MEMBERS

The questionnaire asked what language their various family members speak to the pupils. The family members included were: mother, father, older siblings, younger siblings, others in house. The range of six options for each of those members in the questionnaire was: *Always Gaelic, Mainly Gaelic, Gaelic and English mix (roughly even), Mainly English, Always English* and *Another language*. Results are shown in Table 4.19 and Figure 4.19.

Language spoken by	Mother	Father	Older siblings	Younger siblings	Others in house
Always Gaelic	10 (3.4%)	6 (2.1%)	2 (0.8%)	2 (0.9%)	5 (2.6%)
Mainly Gaelic	12 (4.0%)	14 (4.9%)	4 (1.7%)	4 (1.8%)	10 (5.2%)
Gaelic and English mix, roughly even	30 (10.1%)	32 (11.1%)	11 (4.5%)	9 (4.0%)	11 (5.7%)
Mainly English	64 (21.5%)	56 (19.4%)	30 (12.4%)	33 (14.5%)	17 (8.8%)
Always English	174 (58.6%)	170 (59.0%)	188 (77.7%)	172 (75.8%)	139 (72.0%)
Another language	7 (2.4%)	10 (3.5%)	7 (2.9%)	7 (3.1%)	11 (5.7%)

Table 4.19 *Language spoken to pupils by family members and others in the house*

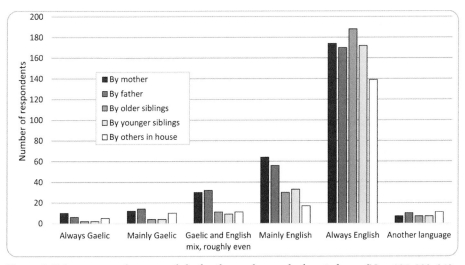

Figure 4.19 *Language spoken to pupils by family members and others in house (Ns = 297, 288, 242, 227, 193)*

English is overwhelmingly the language spoken by all members of the family to the pupils. Familial Gaelic, as manifested in the *Always Gaelic* and *Mainly Gaelic* categories is vestigial. Aggregating categories, pupils have 22 mothers (7.4%) and 20 fathers (7.0%) who speak *Always Gaelic* or *Mainly Gaelic* to them. In total, there are 52 teenagers who receive Gaelic input in any of the three categories of *Always Gaelic* or *Mainly Gaelic* or *Mix* from either their mother and/or from their father (cp. 4.6.2, Table 4.20). Twelve siblings, i.e. six older siblings (2.5%) and six younger siblings (2.7%) speak *Always Gaelic* or *Mainly Gaelic* to pupils.

The range of speaking *Another language* to pupils lies between 2.4% of mothers and 5.7% of other residents in the family home. The response option *Another Language* is independent of the five-point Likert options on a scale of Gaelic/English practice. Therefore, this category cannot be included in the specific analysis of Gaelic/English practice 'continuum', since the levels of use of *Another language* are not indicated. The category *Another language* refers to an additional or other language, such as the languages spoken by new residents in the islands from different parts of Eastern Europe. *Another language* is, therefore, of a different order to the other categories in the response options and consequently it is not directly comparable to the scaled responses for Gaelic and English. However, we can compare the actual numbers indicating language practice within the Gaelic/English scale to the numbers indicating practice of *Another language*. Because there are indications of productive use of *Another language* in the relevant households, in particular, among siblings, and noting practice of *Another language* among preschoolers (3.2.4.1, Table 3.5 and Figure 3.3), it is reasonable to assume that the level of use in many of these households, where *Another language* is practiced, is high enough to yield productive attainment and that the level of use can be usefully compared to the levels corresponding to *Always Gaelic* and *Mainly Gaelic*. As can be seen in Table 4.19, when the numbers speaking *Always Gaelic* (25) and *Mainly Gaelic* (44) to pupils are combined (i.e. 69), they are greater than the combined numbers speaking *Another language* (42) to pupils. On the other hand, slightly more respondents indicate they are spoken to in *Another language* by their older (7) and younger (7) siblings (i.e. 14) than are spoken to in *Always Gaelic* and *Mainly Gaelic* by their older (6) and younger (6) siblings (i.e. 12). There are more fathers who speak *Another language* (10 fathers) to the pupil respondents than there are who speak *Always Gaelic* (six fathers). There are more older and younger siblings who speak *Another language* to pupils than there are older (2) and younger (2) siblings who speak *Always Gaelic* to pupils. In short, for the sake of comparison, if we take *Always Gaelic* and *Mainly Gaelic* to stand for vernacular Gaelic, then *Another language* and vernacular Gaelic are comparably marginal in the language practice input of the total pupil cohort (cp. the discussion on Figures 4.18 and 4.19 with the analysis of conversational ability in section 4.5.4).

Figure 4.20 compares the percentages for people who speak *Always Gaelic* and *Always English* to pupils at home.

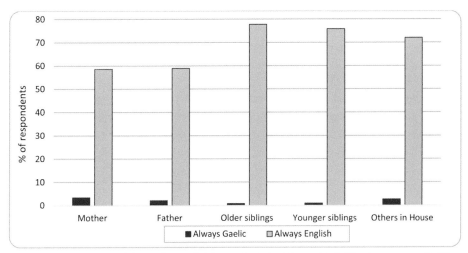

Figure 4.20 *Percentage of those who speak 'Always Gaelic' v. 'Always English' at home to pupils (N = 297, 288, 242, 227, 193)*

Table 4.19 and Figure 4.20 demonstrate that older (77.7%) and younger (75.8%) siblings most often speak *Always English* to pupils, followed by *Others in house* (72%), *Fathers* (59%) and *Mothers* (58.6%). The numbers and percentages of parents who always speak in Gaelic to their teenage children are very small (10 mothers, 3.4%, six fathers, 2.1%). The numbers and percentages of siblings in the Western Isles who always speak to the pupils in Gaelic are also very small. We see that the lower levels of Gaelic practice among siblings than the levels of parental Gaelic practice to pupils, as indicated in the responses to this question, are consistent with the lowering levels of inter-sibling practice of Gaelic as pupils grow older (4.6.2). This is an indication of the weakness of Gaelic transmission and socialisation.

We can interpret the category *Gaelic and English mix, roughly even* as indicating a high prevalence of codemixed or codeswitched speech in this category. It is reasonable to classify members of this category as codeswitchers. The numbers of these codeswitchers are generally greater than the numbers in the categories of *Always Gaelic* and *Mainly Gaelic* combined. On the other hand, with regard to English-dominant practice, i.e. *Always English* and *Mainly English*, there are in general three times more non-codeswitchers (i.e. *Always English*) than people in the *Mainly English* category. This follows a typical pattern in unidirectional bilingual communities, with common codeswitching in the subordinated language and normal monolingual mode in the dominating language (Matras 2009: 59; Péterváry *et al.* 2014: 22–23), and is further evidenced in other language-practice data in the IGRP survey (e.g. 5.4.10) and in other sociolinguistic descriptions of Gaelic (e.g. MacAulay 1982, 1986; Smith-Christmas 2012).

4.6.2 LANGUAGE PRACTICE THROUGH TIME WITHIN FAMILIES AND LANGUAGE TRANSMISSION

The question '*What language do you speak to the following people now and what language did you speak to them when you were younger?*' aimed to discover if there are differences in patterns of Gaelic use and of English use within families through time, i.e. if pupils speak more or less Gaelic with their families now (mothers, fathers, older siblings and younger siblings) than they did when they were younger. The language spoken by pupils with their mothers at four different age grades in their upbringing, from 5–8 years of age to the present, is displayed in Figure 4.21.

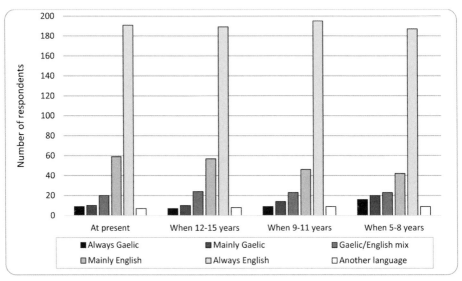

Figure 4.21 *Language spoken by pupils to their mother now and at three younger ages (Ns = 296, 295, 296, 297)*

As illustrated in Figure 4.21, English is the main language spoken by pupils to their mother across all the age cohorts in the Western Isles. Secondly, as well as being marginal from the earliest age grade, the rate of Gaelic use (i.e. *Always* and *Mainly*) decreases by about half as the pupils grow older. The percentage of *Always Gaelic* is halved from the youngest age group to the present. Those pupils speaking *Always Gaelic* or *Mainly Gaelic* to their mothers now are few in number (9 + 10 = 19 pupils, 6.4%). More pupils spoke *Always Gaelic* or *Mainly Gaelic* to their mothers when aged 5–8 (36, 12.1%) than do now (19, 6.4%). There is no marked difference in language practice by children with their mother from age 9–11 onwards. This greatest reduction in *Always* or *Mainly Gaelic* use occurs between 5–8 and 9–11 years. 187 pupils (63%) spoke *Always English* to their mothers when aged 5–8, while 191 (64.5%) speak *Always English* to their mothers now.

The language spoken by pupils to their fathers at four age grades in their upbringing, from 5–8 years old to the present, is displayed in Figure 4.22.

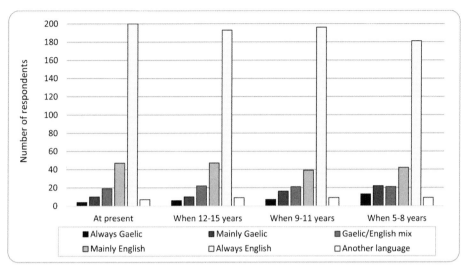

Figure 4.22 *Language spoken by pupils to father, now and at younger ages (Ns = 287, 287, 288, 288)*

Figure 4.22 indicates that English is the main language pupils speak to their fathers across all these age periods in the Western Isles (e.g. 247 pupils or 86.1% report using *Mainly English* or *Always English* to their fathers now). Four pupils (1.4%) speak *Always Gaelic* to their fathers now. Aggregating the two highest levels of Gaelic speaking, the amount of pupils who always or mainly spoke Gaelic to their fathers when aged 5–8 (35, 12.1%) is more than double the amount who do so at present (14, 4.9%). As with mothers, the most appreciable decline in Gaelic speaking to fathers occurs between age 5–8 and 9–11.

The language practice of both parents to their children can be compared with the practice of the children to both their parents. The language practice of parents can also be compared with their children's abilities. In short, how mothers and fathers speak to their children and how their children speak and can speak to them in turn. This will give us an indication of what the correspondences are between specific language-practice inputs from parents and language-practice and language-ability outcomes as measured by child outputs to parents and child abilities. More specifically, this will show which parental language practices, by mothers and fathers, result in optimum Gaelic language practice and ability in children. Out of the total teenager sample of 305, the subset of 52 teenagers (4.6.1, Figure 4.19) who have parental Gaelic input in the categories of *Always Gaelic* or *Mainly Gaelic* or *Gaelic and English Mix* is obviously small, and this needs to be borne in mind when attempting to derive any implications or conclusions from these patterns of practice and ability.

Since intergenerational vitality or fragility of Gaelic is our primary focus, we can first investigate to what extent there is intergenerational loss or gain in the separate language practice categories. For example, we can ask how the practice and ability of children whose parents speak a *Gaelic and English mix* compares to the practice and ability of children whose parents speak *Gaelic only*. Table 4.20 shows the cross-tabulated language practices of mothers and fathers to their children (data in Figure 4.20) and the language practices of children to mothers and fathers now (data in Figures 4.21 and 4.22).

Mother to child	Child to mother now					
	Always English	Mainly English	Mix Gaelic / English	Mainly Gaelic	Always Gaelic	Total
Always Gaelic	0	0	0	1	8	9
Mainly Gaelic	2	1	2	7	0	12
Mix of Gaelic and English	4	9	14	1	0	28
Mainly English	15	39	4	0	0	58
Always English	96	3	0	1	1	101
Total	117	52	20	10	9	208

Father to child	Child to father now					
	Always English	Mainly English	Mix Gaelic / English	Mainly Gaelic	Always Gaelic	Total
Always Gaelic	0	0	0	1	4	5
Mainly Gaelic	2	1	2	8	0	13
Mix of Gaelic and English	5	8	15	1	0	29
Mainly English	21	28	1	0	0	50
Always English	93	6	1	0	0	100
Total	121	43	19	10	4	197

Table 4.20 Cross-tabulated numbers of mother and father language-practice input and child output

In Table 4.20, those cells where parental and child practice are the same are outlined with a double border, cells containing a change in child practice towards higher Gaelic use are in bold (9 cells, totalling 19 pairs (parent and child)), and those cells containing a change in child practice towards higher English use are shaded in grey (14 cells, totalling 74 pairs). To identify the most favourable outcome for children's Gaelic, a series of Chi-square tests were undertaken on 2x2 groupings based on extent of Gaelic use for both mother and child and for father and child. They focused on the language practice of parents using *Always Gaelic, Mainly* or at least a *Mix of Gaelic and English* and discounted those who used *Mainly English* or *Always English*. It was clear from the cross-tabulations (presented in Table 4.20) that higher use of Gaelic from parents to their children generally leads to a reciprocal higher use of Gaelic from their children. The analysis led to the following findings:

- In descriptive terms, as noted below, of 10 cases where the mother speaks *Always Gaelic* to her teenage children, all but one of the teenagers speak *Always Gaelic* to their mother. In comparison, cases where the mother speaks *Mainly Gaelic* or a *Mix of Gaelic and English*, the teenagers also speak *Mainly Gaelic* or a *Mix of Gaelic and English*, never *Always Gaelic*.
- Chi-square analysis, comparing frequencies within the two variables (parent input vs. child output) across the '*Always*' compared with '*Mainly or Mix*' categories with mothers' inputs, proved to be significant ($X^2 = 28.160$, p. < 0.05).
- Similarly, with fathers. Of the five cases where the father speaks *Always Gaelic*, four of the teenagers always used Gaelic reciprocally. Again, comparing the frequencies across the two categorical variables proved to be significant ($X^2 = 23.881$, p. < 0.05).
- Regrouping into an '*Always* and *Mainly Gaelic*' vs. a '*Mix of Gaelic and English*' categories gave a similar pattern. Almost all teenagers (16 of 19 cases for mothers, and 13 of 15 for fathers) who were spoken to *Always* or *Mainly* in Gaelic, *Always* or *Mainly* speak back to their parents in Gaelic. This too was significant ($X^2 = 22.146$, p. < 0.05 for mothers and teenagers; and $X^2 = 20.216$, p. < 0.05 for fathers and teenagers).

Table 4.21 and Figure 4.23a show the numbers and percentages of decrease or increase within each category of language practice by comparing the mother's and father's input practices with the child's output practices.

Language spoken by	Mother to child	Child to mother	Father to child	Child to father	% child vs. mother	% child vs. father
Always Gaelic	10	9	6	4	-10.0	-33.3
Mainly Gaelic	12	10	14	10	-16.7	-28.6
Gaelic and English mix, roughly even	30	20	32	19	-33.3	-40.6
Mainly English	64	59	56	47	-7.8	-16.1
Always English	174	191	170	200	9.8	17.6
Another language	7	7	10	7	0.0	-30.0
Total	297	296	288	287		

Table 4.21 Numbers and percentages of language practice loss or gain, as measured by comparison of language spoken to child by mother and father, with language spoken by child to mother and father

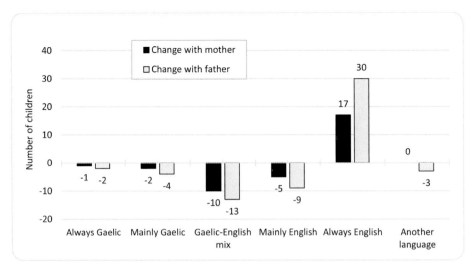

Figure 4.23a Number of children with change in language practice in comparison to language practice of mother and father to children (Ns = 247, 245, 247, 247)

Table 4.21 and Figure 4.23a show that, for instance, in the top row of Table 4.21, there are 10 mothers who speak *Always Gaelic* (as input) to the teenagers and that there are nine teenagers who speak *Always Gaelic* to their mother (as output); and that the corresponding numbers for fathers are six (input) and four (output). This shows that there is one child less (1 in the left-hand pair of data bars in Figure 4.23a) who speaks *Always Gaelic* to their mother than there are mothers who speak *Always Gaelic* to their child; and that there are two children less (2 in the left-hand pair of data bars in Figure 4.23a) who speak *Always Gaelic* in comparison to similar paternal input. We can take four main points from the comparisons in Table 4.21 and Figure 4.23a:

1. The category of *Always English* is the only one that increases, for both parental inputs (mothers 17, 9.8%; fathers 30, 17.6%), while all five other categories contract, for both parental inputs (except mothers' *Another language*, point (5) below);

2. The highest numeric and percentage loss for language practice is in the category of *Gaelic and English mix*, and this is the case in relation to input from both mothers (10, 33.3%) and fathers (13, 40.6%);

3. In the five contracting categories, the loss in language practice for fathers is consistently greater than for mothers, with concomitant greater increase in the *Always English* category in comparison to the input from fathers;

4. In the top three categories of Gaelic use (*Always, Mainly* and *mix*), the least numeric and percentage loss is found in the category of mothers who speak *Always Gaelic* to their child (1, 10%).

In the category of *Another language* there are two main points of interest:

5. Mothers show no loss (seven mothers);
6. The percentage loss for fathers speaking *Another language* is similar to that for fathers speaking Gaelic; but the percentage loss for fathers speaking *Another language* (30%) is less than for fathers speaking *Gaelic and English mix* (40.6%).

These tendencies are consistent with other evidence showing the marginality of vernacular Gaelic and the weakness of Gaelic transmission in the monolingualising social trajectory. If we take the lowest level of loss to indicate the highest level of child attainment of Gaelic practice, in the Teenager Survey, we find that mothers who speak *Always Gaelic* to their child get the most productive results, as measured by child output level to the mother (point (4) above).

There is comparable data relating to parental input and child output in the community survey module (CSS, Chapter 5: 5.4.10; 5.8.2.2). As outlined here with regard to teenagers' parental sources of acquisition, the contrast between parental input and less child Gaelic output is evidenced in the CSS. In fact, at the highest level of parental Gaelic input, the CSS input vs. output comparisons (5.4.10, Figure 5.19) indicate a higher rate of loss than the Teenager Survey input vs. output comparisons. In the CSS, a comparison can be made between *Gaelic only* ('raised in') input to child vs. *Gaelic only* ('speaks now') output to parent. This comparison is: 10 (parents) vs. 4 (children). This amounts to a greater rate of input–output loss in the CSS data (6, 60%) than any instance in the teenager data. This may probably be explained by the fact that the CSS data entails a diachronic element. The CSS compares parental input *when* the children were raised with what children speak *now* (at the time of the survey; 5.8.2.2, Figures 5.28–32). In contrast, the teenager comparisons (presented in Tables 4.20 and 4.21) are synchronic, entailing parental and child practice at the time of the survey. There is, of course, evidence, in section 4.6.2 above, of substantial loss of Gaelic practice through time by the teenagers, particularly between the ages of 5–8 and 9–11 years. Loss of higher-level Gaelic output by preschoolers is also seen in Chapter 3 (3.2.4.1, Tables 3.5–3.7). If analysed in the diachronic dimension, therefore, we can infer that the rates of loss would also be greater for the Teenager Survey than in the synchronic analysis presented in this section. We can also infer that there is a loss through time in parental Gaelic input to children. For instance, given that the synchronic proportions of *Always Gaelic* are 'mother : child' at 10 : 9, and 'father : child' at 6 : 4, we can infer from the earlier proportions of *Always Gaelic* at age 5–8 years being 'mother' : 16 and 'father' : 13, that the synchronic mother and father inputs are lower than they were at age 5–8 years. There is an implied rate of loss as follows: inferring that c. 16 mothers at 5–8 years reduces to 10 mothers 'now', and c. 13 fathers reduces to 6 fathers 'now'. This loss of familial minority-language practice is common in language shift (see footnote 56 for real-time Gaelic evidence). In mixed-language households, mothers, being more commonly the child's primary carer, have generally been shown to have greater influence on the child's language attainment, and there are indications of fathers being less productive in providing minority-language input. In comparison to Welsh-competent mothers, Welsh-competent fathers spoke less Welsh to their children who were in turn more likely to become monolingual English speakers, although the numbers in Jean Lyon's (1996: 193) sample were small. Gabrielle Varro (1998: 123) also found in France that second-generation Franco-American fathers spoke less English to their children than second-generation Franco-American mothers did. Similarly in Scandinavia, Sally Boyd (1998: 43–47) reports less minority-language input to children and less minority-language proficiency among children of minority-language-speaking fathers (where English is the minority language; Sirkku Latomaa (1998: 54) also reports less minority-language transmission from American fathers than American mothers in Finland). We can now turn to the examination of any possible correlations between parental Gaelic input and the child's ability in Gaelic. Table 4.22 gives the cross-tabulated data between the Gaelic-practice input of mothers and fathers and Gaelic-attainment outcome in the form of the children's ability in spoken as well as in conversational Gaelic.

Mother to child	Child's ability to converse in Gaelic					
	Fluent speaker – native	Fluent speaker – learner	Good Gaelic	Reasonable Gaelic	A little Gaelic	Total
Always Gaelic	8	0	0	0	1	9
Mainly Gaelic	6	2	2	2	0	12
Mix of Gaelic and English	12	3	5	4	4	28
Total	26	5	7	6	5	49

Mother to child	Child's ability to converse in Gaelic					
	Comfortably	Relatively well	Reasonably	A few words	No ability	Total
Always Gaelic	8	0	1	0	0	9
Mainly Gaelic	6	3	1	1	0	11
Mix of Gaelic and English	9	13	2	1	3	28
Total	23	16	4	2	3	48

Father to child	Child's ability in spoken Gaelic					
	Fluent speaker – native	Fluent speaker – learner	Good Gaelic	Reasonable Gaelic	A little Gaelic	Total
Always Gaelic	6	0	0	0	0	6
Mainly Gaelic	7	2	2	1	1	13
Mix of Gaelic and English	12	4	5	5	4	30
Total	25	6	7	6	5	49

Father to child	Child's ability to converse in Gaelic					
	Comfortably	Relatively well	Reasonably	A few words	No ability	Total
Always Gaelic	6	0	0	0	0	6
Mainly Gaelic	6	4	1	1	0	12
Mix of Gaelic and English	11	9	6	3	1	30
Total	23	13	7	4	1	48

Table 4.22 Mother's and father's Gaelic practice to child vs. child ability in spoken Gaelic and in conversational Gaelic

We can see from Table 4.22 that greater levels of Gaelic input from mothers and fathers correlate with greater levels of child ability, both in spoken and in conversational Gaelic. There is a noticeable contrast between child ability of those who receive *Always* or *Mainly Gaelic* input (with their Gaelic ability distributed to the left-hand columns in the table), on the one hand, and those who receive a *Mix of Gaelic and English* input (with their Gaelic ability distributed across all ability columns in the table), on the other hand. This contrast between *Always/Mainly* vs. *Mix* is most clearly seen in child conversational ability. In fact, when tested for significance with Pearson's Chi-square test, the relationship between Gaelic input and Gaelic spoken ability is not significant; whereas the relationship between Gaelic input and Gaelic conversational ability is significant. This can be interpreted as a corroboration that self-reported Gaelic conversational ability is closer to actual ability than self-reported Gaelic spoken ability (as noted in 4.5.4). More specifically, mother *Always Gaelic* and *Mainly/Mix* vs. child *Fluent/Good* and *Reasonable/Little* is not significant ($X^2 = 0.814$, p. > 0.05). And similarly, father *Always Gaelic* and *Mainly/Mix* vs. child *Fluent/Good* and *Reasonable/Little* is not significant ($X^2 = 1.979$, p. > 0.05). But conversational ability does yield statistical significance: eight out of the nine cases, where the mother speaks *Always Gaelic*, the teenagers can converse *Comfortably* in Gaelic. In comparison, of the 39 cases where mothers speak *Mainly Gaelic* or a *Mix of Gaelic and English* to their children, less than half (15) can converse *Comfortably* in Gaelic ($X^2 = 7.451$, p. < 0.05). All six cases, where the father speaks *Always Gaelic* to his child, correlate with the teenagers being able to converse *Comfortably* in Gaelic ($X^2 = 7.453$, p. < 0.05). And, as with mothers, less than half of cases where the father speaks *Mainly Gaelic* or a *Mix of Gaelic and English*, could the teenager converse *Comfortably* in Gaelic. There are indications that codemixing can have a detrimental effect on acquistion (Byers-Heinlein 2013; Varro 1998: 111, 115), as well as correlating with decreased ability in general (Ó Curnáin 2012: 349, 356, citing M. C. Jones (2005: 171), Toribio (2004: 170–72) and de Leeuw *et al.* (2010: 39)).

It is of interest to examine how the combined input of both parents might correlate with their child's output to both parents. To allow for a combination and comparison of these inputs and outputs, we applied a score to the five-point Likert scale as follows: *Always Gaelic* = 5, *Mainly Gaelic* = 4, *Gaelic and English mix* = 3, *Mainly English* = 2, *Always English* = 1. The combined input and output will increase the numbers in the cross-tabulated cells and, therefore, give a stronger basis for statistical analysis. We can combine both inputs, on the one hand, and both outputs, on the other. That is, we can combine the inputs of both parents to yield a Combined Parental Input Score. And we can combine the outputs of pupils to both parents to yield a Combined Child Output to Parents Score. Both these scores are, therefore, based on averages, between:

a) the practice of both parents to the pupil (i.e. (Mother + Father)/2); and

b) the practice of the pupil to both parents (i.e. (To Mother + To Father)/2).

For instance, with regard to the Combined Parental Input Score, given that *Always English* scores '1', if both parents speak *Always English* to the pupil, the Combined Parental Input Score for that pupil will be 1 (i.e. 1 + 1 = 2/2 = 1). By the same token, if both parents speak *Always Gaelic*, the Combined Parental Input Score will be 5 (i.e. 5 + 5 = 10/2 = 5). If, for instance, one parent speaks *Always English* and the other *Always Gaelic*, the Combined Parental Input Score will be 3 (i.e. 1 + 5 = 6/2 = 3). Similarly, if both parents speak *Gaelic and English mix* to the pupil, the Combined Parental Input Score will be 3 (i.e. 3 + 3 = 6/2 = 3). Therefore, there are obviously different combinations or permutations that yield the same average combined score, as instanced in two 'paths' to a combined score of 6/2 = 3 (correspondingly termed *Combined Gaelic and English mix*). In fact, there are three permutations for a combined score of 3 (1 + 5; 3 + 3; and 2 + 4), two permutations for scores of 2, 2.5, 3.5 and 4, and only one combination each for a score of 1, 1.5, 4.5 and 5. Any potential differentiated impact of these permutations will, of course, be subsumed under the combined scoring mechanism, but, as stated, the results of parental input combinations and pupil output combinations are of interest in themselves and increase the basis for statistical analysis. The Combined Child Output to Parents Score is calculated using the same scoring mechanism. For instance, if a pupil speaks *Gaelic and English mix* to her/his father and *Mainly Gaelic* to his/her mother, the Combined Child Output to Parents Score for that pupil will be 3.5 (i.e. 3 + 4 = 7/2 = 3.5).

These combined scores can be compared in a cross-tabulation to check for further possible correlations between parental input and pupil output. Table 4.23 presents the cross-tabulated Combined Parental Input Scores and Combined Child Output to Parents Scores for a total of 290 pupils.

		Combined Child Output to Parents Score									
		1	1.5	2	2.5	3	3.5	4	4.5	5	Total
Combined	5	0	0	0	0	0	0	1	0	5	6
Parental	4.5	1	0	0	0	1	0	0	1	0	3
Input	4	1	0	1	0	0	1	4	0	0	7
Score	3.5	1	0	0	0	2	2	0	0	0	5
	3	3	1	6	0	9	1	0	0	0	20
	2.5	2	0	3	8	2	0	1	0	0	16
	2	14	7	21	3	0	0	0	0	0	45
	1.5	17	20	5	1	0	0	0	0	0	43
	1	140	3	1	0	1	0	0	0	0	145
Total		179	31	37	12	15	4	6	1	5	290

Table 4.23 Cross-tabulated Combined Parental Input Score (5–1 left column) with Combined Child Output to Parents Score (1–5 second row)

As we did with the presentation of the data in Table 4.22 above, in Table 4.23 here we use shaded data cells to indicate a change towards higher English use in output in comparison to input, double-bordering to indicate no change between input and output, and numbers in bold font to indicate a change toward higher Gaelic use in output. We can summarise what Table 4.23 reveals, as follows:

1. A strong positive correlation exists between Combined Parental Input Scores and Combined Child Output to Parents Scores (r_s = 0.771, N = 290, p. < 0.01).

2. Of the 290 pupils, by far the dominant group have *Combined Always English* input and output, achieving 1 in both scores, i.e. 140 pupil outputs from 145 parental inputs.

3. It is clear from the numbers in the shaded boxes that the scores for a total of 62 pupils change towards higher English output, in comparison to parental input.

4. The numbers in bold show that the scores for a total of 18 pupils change towards higher Gaelic output, considerably less than the 62 pupils with increased English output.

5. As in Table 4.22, those input categories which show the greatest proportions of change, or Gaelic loss, towards higher English output in Table 4.23 are those which do *not* entail the highest Gaelic input, i.e. greater loss of Gaelic does *not* entail *Combined Always Gaelic* (total of six pupils scoring 5).

6. From the point of view of the transmission of Gaelic, the highest productive return of parental input is among those six pupils whose two parents speak to them always in Gaelic, since five of these six pupils speak *Combined Always Gaelic* to these parents.

7. All other categories which involve some Gaelic input (i.e. 1.5–4.5 Combined Parental Input Score) entail a proportional loss of about a half of the separate subgroups towards increased English output from pupils, despite the level of Gaelic input.

8. It is noteworthy that the degree of loss from combined Gaelic input to combined pupil output can be substantial. This is evident in the 22 pupils who speak *Combined Always English* to both parents, achieving a Combined Child Output to Parents Score of 1, despite Combined Parental Input Scores in the range of 2–4.5. Similarly, there are 17 pupils who speak *Combined Always English*, i.e. a Child Output Score of 1, in contrast to Combined Parental Input Score of 1.5.

9. Of the 18 pupils who indicate a change towards increased combined Gaelic output in comparison to combined input, nearly all of them (13) pertain to English-dominant input categories (i.e. 1–2 Combined Parental Input Score) and English-dominant output categories (i.e. 1.5–2.5 Combined Child Output to Parents Score), i.e. a basic increase

of 0.5 in the Combined Child Output to Parents Score. In other words, the increased Gaelic output is small, basically moving one cell to the right in Table 4.23, especially in contrast with the greater increase in English output, often moving more than one cell to the left (i.e. a change in Combined Child Output to Parents Score of ≥ 1).

Using Pearson's Chi-Square, we tested the categorical relationship between the quantified type of parental input and the quantified type of pupil output, based on the Combined Parental Input Scores and Combined Child Output to Parents Scores. As one would expect, there is a significant correlation between *Combined Always Gaelic* (5) input and *Combined Always English* (1) input on the one hand, and *Combined Always Gaelic* (5) output and *Combined Always English* (1) output on the other, with a p-value of < 0.01. In order to boost the numbers in the higher Gaelic categories, we tested for significance between parental input of *Combined Always Gaelic* and *Combined Mainly Gaelic* (3.5–5) on the one hand, versus *Combined Mix* (2.5–3; i.e. *Combined Gaelic and English mix*) on the other; and of pupil output of *Combined Always Gaelic* and *Combined Mainly Gaelic* (3.5–5) on the one hand, versus *Combined Mix* (2.5–3) on the other. This relationship is also statistically significant (p. < 0.01).

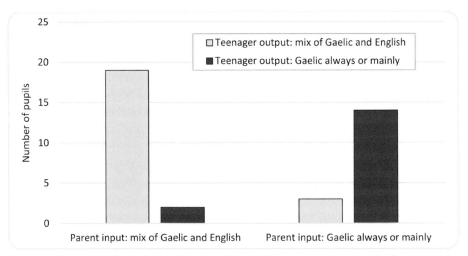

Figure 4.23b *Combined parental input and combined child output, speaking Gaelic always, mainly or a mix (N = 38)*

Figure 4.23b shows the numbers of combined parental input and combined pupil outputs in two categories: *Combined Gaelic and English mix* (2.5–3) vs. *Combined Always Gaelic – Combined Mainly Gaelic* (3.5–5 termed 'Gaelic always or mainly'). There is a clear correlation between parental input and pupil output. Of the 21 pupils whose parents speak to them in a *Combined Gaelic and English mix*, 19 speak to their parents in a *Combined Gaelic and English mix*, and only two of this subgroup of pupils speak to their parents in 'Gaelic always or mainly'. As is shown in Table 4.23, a further 15 pupils receive a *Combined Gaelic and English mix* input, but their output is even lower than 2.5–3 Combined Score and is therefore not indicated in Figure 4.23b. On the other hand, of the 17 pupils whose parents speak 'Gaelic always or mainly' to them, 14 pupils also speak 'Gaelic always or mainly' to their parents, with three of this subgroup of pupils speaking a *Combined Gaelic and English mix* to their parents. As also shown in Table 4.23, a further four pupils receive 'Gaelic always or mainly' from their parents, but the output of these pupils falls below 2.5 Combined Score and it is therefore not indicated in Figure 4.23b.

As discussed in section 4.5.4, we also checked for the relationship between the Combined Parental Input Score and pupils' ability, in the form of self-reported conversational ability and self-reported fluency. The relationship between the Combined Parental Input Score and pupils' conversational ability is almost significant (p. = 0.085), but the correlation with fluency is not (p. = 0.247).

The language spoken by pupils (in the same age grades) to their older siblings is displayed in Figure 4.24.

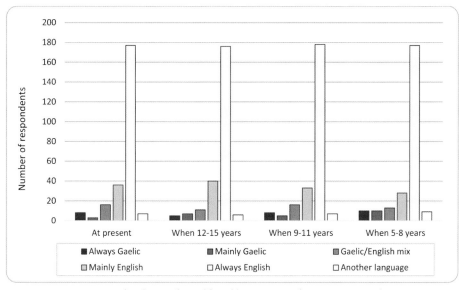

Figure 4.24 *Language spoken by pupils to older siblings, now and at younger ages (Ns = 247, 245, 247, 247)*

English is used by the majority of pupils in conversation with older siblings (177 responses or 71.7% using *Always English* now, 36 responses or 14.6% using *Mainly English* now, making a total of 213 or 86.3%). The categories of *Always Gaelic* now (8 pupils, 3.2%) or *Mainly Gaelic* now (3 pupils, 1.2%) to older siblings show the residual dimension of Gaelic in sibling interaction (a total of 11 pupils, 4.5%). There is a decline in Gaelic use with older siblings over time. In the 5–8 age group, a total of 20 (8.1%) pupils spoke *Always Gaelic* (10, 4%) or *Mainly Gaelic* (10, 4%) to their older siblings. As seen with practice to mothers and fathers, Gaelic-dominant practice to older siblings: 1) is roughly halved in number through the age grades: 11 (4.5%) now speak *Always Gaelic* or *Mainly Gaelic* with their older siblings; and 2) the main period of loss of Gaelic-dominant practice occurs at the age grade of 9–11 years of age.

The language spoken by pupils to their younger siblings is displayed in Figure 4.25. As with the findings for practice by the pupils to older siblings, Gaelic use declines over time. Although Gaelic-dominant practice is marginal, as in the other figures, practice by older siblings to younger siblings appears to be more stable through time (in comparison with Gaelic practice to older siblings and parents).

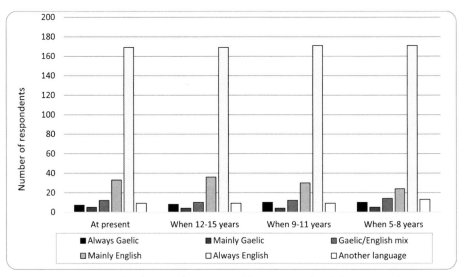

Figure 4.25 *Language spoken by pupils to younger siblings, now and at different ages when younger (Ns = 235, 236, 236, 237)*

English is the main language spoken by pupils to their younger siblings. 12 pupils (5.1%) reported that they speak *Always Gaelic* or *Mainly Gaelic* to their younger siblings now (*Always Gaelic* seven pupils, 3%; *Mainly Gaelic* five pupils, 2.1%). There is a slight decline in the Gaelic spoken by pupils to their younger siblings through time. *Always Gaelic* and *Mainly Gaelic* now comprises 12 pupils, and contrasts with 15 pupils at age 5–8.

4.6.3 LANGUAGE PRACTICE THROUGH TIME WITH FRIENDS AND NEIGHBOURS

The pupils were asked to indicate what language they speak to friends and neighbours and in other settings now and what language they spoke when they were younger. The same four age grades were covered as for household use within families (4.6.2). Figure 4.26 displays the results for the first question in the series, which asked the language spoken to friends.

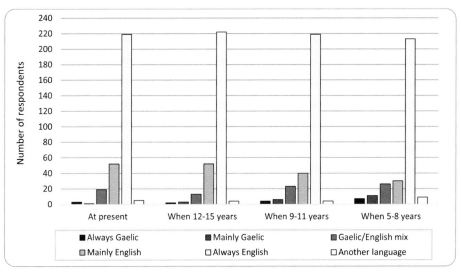

Figure 4.26 *Language used by pupils to their friends, at present and at three younger age grades (Ns = 299, 296, 296, 296)*

There is a relatively comparable profile of language practice, with the use of Gaelic decreasing at a similar rate as children grow older, in relation to the levels of Gaelic practice with parents, siblings and friends (Figures 4.21–4.24). A combined total of four pupils (1.3%) in the Western Isles speak *Always Gaelic* (three, 1%) or *Mainly Gaelic* (one, 0.3%) to their friends now, compared to a combined total of 18 (6.1%) who spoke *Always Gaelic* (seven, 2.4%) or *Mainly Gaelic* (11, 3.7%) to their friends when aged 5–8. A total of 271 pupils (90.6%) speak *Always English* (219, 73.2%) or *Mainly English* (52, 17.4%) to their friends now.

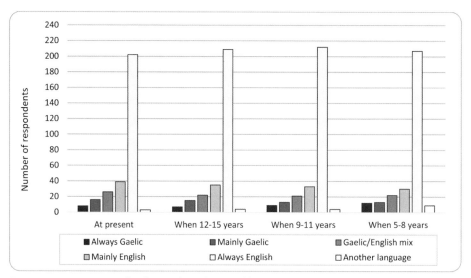

Figure 4.27 *Language spoken by pupils to their neighbours, at present and at three younger age grades (Ns = 294, 292, 292, 293)*

Figure 4.27 depicts the language spoken at four age grades by pupils to their neighbours. The data portray English as the dominant language, with a consistent profile for the pupils in their neighbourhoods through time. At present, 202 pupils (68.7%) always speak English and 39 (13.3%) mainly speak English to neighbours, making a combined total of 241 pupils (82%). There is no appreciable difference in the language spoken to neighbours for different age grades, if *Always Gaelic* and *Mainly Gaelic* numbers and percentages are aggregated for each age grade. Eight pupils (2.7%) speak *Always Gaelic* to their neighbours now and 16 (5.4%) speak *Mainly Gaelic* to their neighbours now. There are 12 pupils (4.1%) who spoke *Always Gaelic* to their neighbours aged 5–8 and 13 (4.4%) spoke *Mainly Gaelic* to their neighbours aged 5–8. When data from Figures 4.21–4.27 are compared, the predominance of English is evident across all age grade profiles, both as a household and neighbourhood language. Finally, we can note that the decline after the 5–8 age grade in practice of *Another language* in the contexts of friends (Figure 4.26) and neighbours (Figure 4.27) contrasts with the more stable numbers of respondents in the family context (Figures 4.24–4.25).

4.6.4 PUPILS' LANGUAGE PRACTICE IN VARIOUS CONTEXTS

The pupils were asked: *What language do you speak in the following situations?* The eight situations referred to were: *At school; With friends after school; At school sports; At other sports events; At social events* (e.g. ceilidhs, dances, clubs); *At friends' houses; In your own house; In a nearby town or village.* The question was intended to provide further information about Gaelic speaking in various situations and to assess where Gaelic is spoken by pupils. Figure 4.28 shows the results obtained.

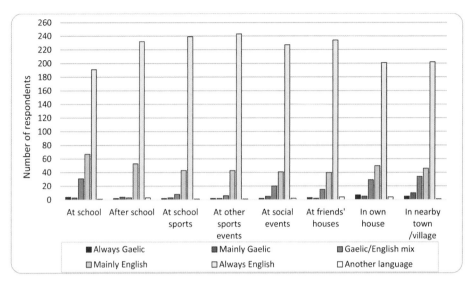

Figure 4.28 Language spoken by pupils in various situations (Ns = 297, 297, 296, 297, 297, 298, 296, 298)

English is the language most spoken in all situations and events by pupils (191 pupils or 64.3% always speak English and 67 or 22.6% mainly speak English). Gaelic use is very limited in all situations and events. The greatest number of pupils who speak *Always Gaelic* do so in their own home (seven pupils, 2.4%) or in a nearby town or village (five pupils, 1.7%). This is followed in order of prevalence by *At school* (four pupils, 1.3%) and *At friends' houses* (three pupils, 1%). *After school*, *At school sports*, *At other sports events* and *At social events* show two pupils (0.7%) for each category. The greatest number of pupils who speak *Mainly Gaelic* do so in *A nearby town or village* (10 pupils, 3.4%), followed in prevalence by in their own homes and *At social events* (five pupils for each category, 1.7%), *After school* (four pupils, 1.3%), *At school* and *At school sports* (three pupils for each category, 1%), and *At other sports events* and *At friends' houses* (two pupils for each category, 0.7%).

4.6.5 PUPILS' USE OF ENGLISH WITH GAELIC SPEAKERS

The gap in Gaelic ability versus use of Gaelic is shown both from census analysis (2.4.3) and the data in this survey (Figure 4.8, Figures 4.21–4.28, Figure 4.32). Figure 4.8 shows 61 pupils fluent, while Figure 4.19 indicates 42 mothers and fathers *Always* or *Mainly* speak Gaelic to pupils. Figures 4.21 and 4.22 show pupils speak *Always* or *Mainly* Gaelic to 19 mothers and 14 fathers. Ability in Gaelic is greater than home use of Gaelic. Figure 4.19 shows 69 responses indicating *Mainly* or *Always Gaelic* is spoken to pupils in the family home. However, from Table 4.19 we can calculate that 162 responses indicate Gaelic is spoken to pupils at home by family members and other residents (ranging from *Gaelic and English mix* to *Always Gaelic*). This is greater than the 95 pupils claiming *Fluent* or *Good Gaelic* in Table 4.11 (Figure 4.8), and somewhat greater than the 137 responses indicating pupil ability in the aggregated categories *Fluent* to *Reasonable Gaelic*.

Pupils with a *Fluent* or *Good Gaelic* competence were asked if they spoke English on a regular basis to anyone who spoke good or fluent Gaelic. According to the criterion of respondents having *Fluent* to *Good Gaelic*, one would expect about 95 respondents to answer this question (according to the responses in Table 4.12 and Figure 4.8). However, 246 pupils responded. Clearly, far more pupils have answered the question than was intended in the questionnaire. 172 pupils (69.9%) answered *Yes* (they do speak English to Gaelic speakers) and 74 (30.1%) replied *No*. If pupils answered *Yes*, they were then asked why they did this, with 169 pupils answering this query (which is fairly consistent with the number of 172 respondents who answered *Yes*). This means that the replies are not only from the specific cohort of competent Gaelic speakers intended in the questionnaire. A range of multiple options were offered to the respondents and they were asked to tick each statement that applied to them. Figure 4.29 shows the percentage of respondents who chose each option.

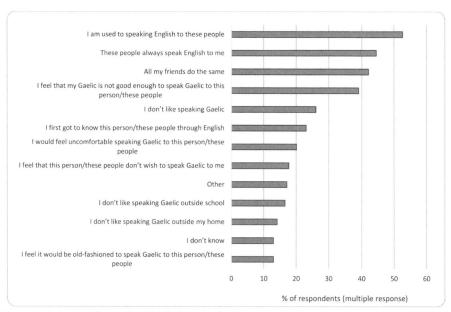

Figure 4.29 *Reasons for speaking English to people who have Gaelic, in percentages of respondents (N = 169)*

The reasons cited for speaking English are, in order of prevalence, *I am used to speaking English to these people* (89, 52.7%), followed by *These people always speak English to me* (75 pupils, 44.4%), *All my friends do the same* (71, 42%) and *I feel my Gaelic is not good enough to speak Gaelic to this person/these people* (66, 39.1%). These reasons are followed by *I don't like speaking Gaelic* (44, 26%), *I first got to know this person/these people through English* (39, 23.1%), *I would feel uncomfortable speaking Gaelic to this person/these people* (34, 20.1%) *I feel that this person/these people do not wish to speak Gaelic to me* (30, 17.8%) and *Other* (29, 17.2%). 28 (16.6%) responded *I don't like speaking Gaelic outside school* and 24 (14.2%) *I don't like speaking Gaelic outside my home.* 22 pupils (13%) responded *I feel it would be old-fashioned to speak Gaelic to this person/those people*, the least-cited reason.

A subsequent question asked how the Gaelic-competent pupils feel about speaking English to Gaelic speakers.[41] Four options were offered, and the results are shown in Figure 4.30.

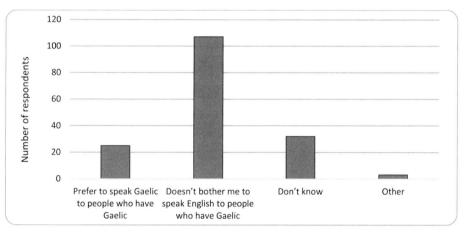

Figure 4.30 *Feelings about speaking English to people with Gaelic (N = 167)*

The greatest number of pupils (107, 64.1%) indicate that it does not 'bother' them to speak English to Gaelic speakers. 25 pupils (15%) *Prefer to speak Gaelic to people who have Gaelic*, but nevertheless speak English to them (presumably due to various contextual factors).

4.6.6 LANGUAGE SPOKEN IN FAMILY CIRCLE

A related question, the results of which are displayed in Figure 4.31, sought to elicit information on whether or not there is a difference between family language practice

---

41 The number of responses was 167, which is again higher than the relevant cohort. The same problem occurred in the data illustrated in Figure 4.31.

at home when parents are speaking to teenage respondents, the language practices of parents amongst themselves as well as the language spoken by parents with their *family/relatives* (i.e. their siblings, parents or relatives).

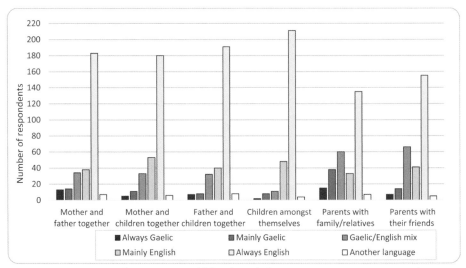

Figure 4.31 *Language spoken among pupils' family circle (N = 289, 288, 286, 284, 288, 288)*

As with the rest of the evidence in this survey, responses indicate that English is dominant in the family circle for the two youngest generations. Nevertheless, parents in the Western Isles speak more Gaelic with their own generation (and possibly older generations) than they do with their own children. This is, of course, typical in intergenerational language shift situations. There are 27 responses (9.3%) which indicate parents *Always* or *Mainly* speak Gaelic together. When we combine the categories of *Always*, *Mainly* and *Mix* for 'mother and father together', this yields a total of 61, or 21.1% of the responses. The percentage of 21.1% is comparable to the 19% of Family Households in the RA that practice Gaelic, based on the analysis of the 2011 Census in Chapter 2 (2.4.3). In fact, 16 mothers and their children (5.5%) *Always* or *Mainly* speak Gaelic together; while 15 responses show fathers and their children (5.2%) *Always* or *Mainly* speak Gaelic together. 10 children (3.5%) *Always* or *Mainly* speak Gaelic together. 53 parents (18.4%) *Always* or *Mainly* speak Gaelic with their family and relatives and 21 responses indicate parents (7.3%) *Always* or *Mainly* speak Gaelic with their friends. These numbers correspond quite closely with parental practice illustrated in Figures 4.21 and 4.22 (see also 2.4.3). With regard to sibling language practice (Figures 4.24 and 4.25), the proportions are also similar in Figure 4.31. The mixed language practice by *Parents with their friends* is three times more predominant than *Always* and *Mainly Gaelic*: seven parents *Always* speak Gaelic, 14

Mainly speak Gaelic and 66 have *Gaelic/English mix* with friends. A prevalence of language mixing is common in minoritised bilingualised communities, particularly in those undergoing language shift. In fact, the practice of the three highest levels of Gaelic speaking is a minority practice in this data. And practice of the two highest levels pertains to a minority within this minority, which is a common feature of much of the IGRP results. When we compare the left data column, i.e. *mother and father together*, with the data column for *parents with family/relatives*, we can see that the pupils' parents speak less Gaelic among themselves than with their own family/ relatives (i.e. sisters, brothers, and older relatives): *mother and father together* always speaking English (63.3%) and *parents with family/relatives* always speaking English (46.9%). A detailed breakdown of responses in relation to the data depicted in Figure 4.31 is given in **Tables A4.6** and **A4.7** in **Appendix 4**.

A further question in this series sought information on language practice in various day-to-day family situations. Figure 4.32 shows the results.

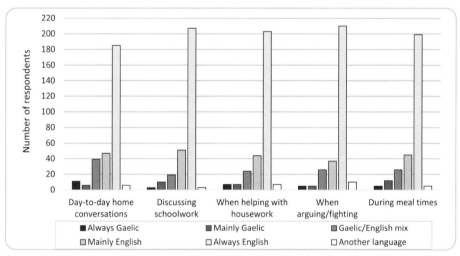

Figure 4.32 *Comparison of language used by pupils in day-to-day situations (Ns = 294, 293, 292, 293, 292)*

Figure 4.32 shows that the majority of pupils always speak English during all these family actitivies or occasions. Use of *Always Gaelic* for *Day-to-day home conversations* scores the highest Gaelic usage but is nonetheless very rare (11 pupils, 3.7%). The data in descending order for the number of pupils who speak *Always Gaelic* or *Mainly Gaelic* in these family situations is reported as follows: *Day-to-day home conversations* (17, 5.8% of responses) or *During mealtimes* (17, 5.8%), followed by *When helping with housework* (14, 4.8%), *Discussing schoolwork* (13, 4.4%) and *When arguing/fighting* (10, 3.4%).

Responses in relation to the pupils' frequency of access to and usage of Gaelic media and social media is given in **Figure A4.5** in **Appendix 4**. An average of 79.8% of pupils *Seldom or never* engage with Gaelic radio or TV, read Gaelic books or engage with social media through Gaelic. Those who do engage with Gaelic media or social media do so largely in a passive rather than active manner, i.e. watch and listen more than tweet or post (see the focus-group discussion in section 4.10.1.2 in which the presence of Gaelic on social media is perceived more positively).

4.6.7 OPINIONS AND LANGUAGE PRACTICE IN SCHOOL

Pupils in the survey group were asked whether they agreed or disagreed with a number of statements regarding their general views on the position of Gaelic within their respective secondary schools. The responses to the individual statements are given in **Figure A4.6** in **Appendix 4**. The main features are similar to the overall findings for use of English and Gaelic. Indifference (an average of 30.7%) and a marked preference for English rather than Gaelic textbooks in education (65.4% in favour) are the most prevalent responses.

A further question addressed the use of Gaelic and English in different situations at school, including the language the pupils speak to teachers and friends, in and out of class and after school. The responses illustrate the predominant use of English by the pupils in all these school-based situations. While there is slightly greater use of Gaelic to teachers in the classroom, overall the marginal practice of Gaelic in the pupils' school environment is clear. If a teacher is not present, no pupil reported (0%) always speaking Gaelic to friends at school, while six pupils (2%) speak mainly in Gaelic to friends at school. One pupil (0.3%) always speaks Gaelic at out-of-hours school events, while three (1%) speak *Mainly Gaelic*. Again, *Gaelic/English mix* is more prevalent than *Always* and *Mainly Gaelic*. A detailed breakdown of language practice in school situations is given in **Table A4.10** in **Appendix 4**.

4.6.8 LANGUAGE PRACTICE AMONG NEIGHBOURS AND IN THE COMMUNITY

The pupils were asked about language practice in their neighbourhood, with queries on the languages spoken by their neighbours with each other, with pupils' families and with pupils themselves, as shown in Figure 4.33.

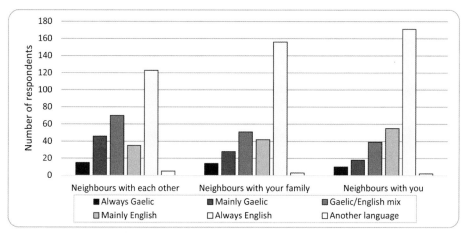

Figure 4.33 *Language spoken by neighbours with each other, with pupil's family and with pupil (Ns = 294, 294, 295)*

When we combine the data for *Always Gaelic* or *Mainly Gaelic*, we see that neighbours speak Gaelic twice as much among themselves than with teenage pupils and at an intermediate level when speaking with pupils' families. 61 pupils (20.8%) indicate their neighbours speak *Always Gaelic* or *Mainly Gaelic* among themselves, 42 (14.3%) indicate that neighbours speak *Always Gaelic* or *Mainly Gaelic* when with pupils' families, and 28 (9.5%) show that neighbours speak *Always Gaelic* or *Mainly Gaelic* with the pupils themselves. Similar to the family/relatives data (4.6.6), the mixed language mode is dominant among the three highest Gaelic-speaking categories. A detailed breakdown of responses to the categories shown in Figure 4.33 is included in **Table A4.11** in **Appendix 4**.

4.6.9 LANGUAGE PRACTICE IN LOCAL COMMUNITY

Pupils were asked in the survey if services were available in their local area in Gaelic, and if they would prefer to use a range of services in either Gaelic or English. The responses to both questions are in **Figures A4.7** and **A4.8** in **Appendix 4**. Where a language preference for local service provision is expressed, responses indicate pupils would slightly prefer English in such situations (an average of 28.9% across category responses), though a preference for mixed Gaelic and English service provision (an average of 28.1% across category responses) is also common. Gaelic-only provision of local services is the least popular choice, averaging 10.3% of responses across the categories. In relation to local service provision, *Preschool* (65.2% of category responses), *Church services* (59.2%) and *Community events* (51.9%) are most likely to be available in Gaelic. *Health services* (31.9%) and *Bank services* (24.7%) are the least likely to be offered in Gaelic.

Additionally, pupils were asked to specify the language they heard mostly being used by members of their local communities in different places such as preschool, church, local shops and community events in order to give an indication of the extent of Gaelic use in different situations in pupils' local areas. Pupils were asked to tick one of the four options in nine contexts. The results are shown in Figure 4.34.

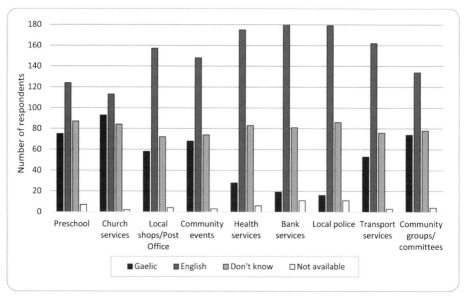

Figure 4.34 Language mostly heard by pupils at local services (Ns = 293, 292, 291, 293, 292, 293, 292, 294, 290)

English is the language mostly heard by pupils in local communities in all these situations or locations (an average of 52.2% for all situations). The high number of responses as *Don't know* can be explained perhaps by pupils not attending community events and/or a lack of such facilities as bank services and shops in their local areas (notwithstanding the option of *Not available* being relatively low).

Gaelic speaking in communities, according to the responses, is mostly (i.e. 20–32% of responses) heard in *Church services* (93 pupils, 31.9%), followed by *Preschool* (75, 25.6%), *Community groups* (74, 25.5%), *Community events* (68, 23.2%) and *Local shops/Post Office* (58, 19.9%). Use of Gaelic is heard less frequently (5–18%) in *Local police* services (16, 5.5%), followed by *Bank services* (19, 6.5%), *Health services* (28, 9.6%) and *Transport services* (53, 18%). A breakdown of individual response categories in Figure 4.34 is shown in **Table A4.14** in **Appendix 4**.

The pupils were asked to indicate one option of three concerning their language practice in the same nine contexts. Figure 4.35 indicates the language mainly used by pupils in different places and situations such as at preschool, church, local shops and community events.

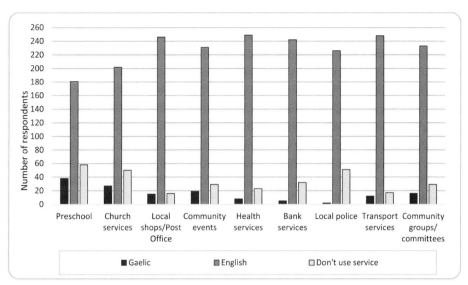

Figure 4.35 Language used by pupils at local services (Ns = 277, 279, 277, 279, 280, 279, 279, 277, 278)

This comparison of language practice in local settings by the teenagers demonstrates how marginal Gaelic-medium interaction among the young is with communal activities. English is used by the majority of pupils in all situations (an average of 82% of responses). The lowest use of Gaelic in local settings is for *Local police* (two pupils, 0.7%), *Bank services* (five, 1.8%) and *Health services* (eight, 2.9%), followed by *Transport services* (12, 4.3%) and *Local shops/Post Office* (15, 5.4%), followed by *Community events* (19, 6.8%) and *Community groups* (16, 5.8%). The most use of Gaelic by pupils in local settings is for *Preschool* (38 pupils, 13.7%) and *Church services* (27, 9.7%). Therefore, teenagers' own use of mainly Gaelic in the community ranges between 13.7% and 0.7%, in contrast with mostly Gaelic heard by pupils ranging from 31.9% to 5.5% in the community in general. A breakdown of individual response categories in Figure 4.35 is shown in **Table A4.15** in **Appendix 4**.

4.7 OPINIONS ON GAELIC AND ITS FUTURE

Section D of the survey entailed a series of questions about pupils' attitudes and opinions on the Gaelic language and its future. This section of the survey examined, among other issues, whether or not the pupils are supportive of Gaelic, of education and media in Gaelic and the reasons behind the pupils' responses. The questions asked what their feelings are about the strength of Gaelic in their local area, how they feel they themselves contribute towards supporting the language and how they see the future of Gaelic, both in general and in relation to their own situation.

4.7.1 FAVOURABILITY TOWARDS GAELIC

Pupils were asked to indicate on a five-point Likert scale how favourable they were towards Gaelic. The results are given in Figure 4.36.

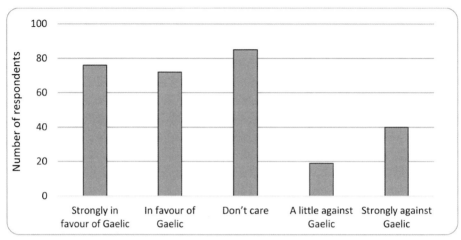

Figure 4.36 *Pupils' level of favourability towards Gaelic (N = 292)*

Roughly half of responses show favourability towards Gaelic and half are indifferent or against Gaelic. The most common single response indicated an indifference towards Gaelic, followed by being *Strongly in favour of Gaelic* and *In favour of Gaelic*. 76 pupils (26%) are *Strongly in favour of Gaelic*, with 72 (24.7%) *In favour of Gaelic*. 85 (29.1%) do not care. 19 (6.5%) are *A little against Gaelic* and 40 (13.7%) are *Strongly against Gaelic*. Grouped more broadly, 148 (50.7%) are *Strongly in favour of Gaelic* or *In favour of Gaelic*, with 59 (20.2%) being *A little against Gaelic* or *Strongly against Gaelic* and 85 (29.1%) indifferent. Setting aside the *Don't care* category, many more respondents are supportive of Gaelic than are against it.

As mentioned in the discussion of Table 4.18 (4.5.4), ability to converse *Comfortably* in Gaelic yields the smallest subgroup of pupils with Gaelic ability. Therefore, this indicator of ability to converse in Gaelic can serve as a basis of comparison with other variables. Figure 4.37 examines the relationship between Gaelic conversational ability and favourability towards Gaelic. This is a cross-tabulation of data pertaining to Figures 4.15 and 4.36.

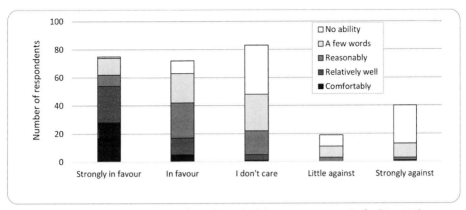

Figure 4.37 *Pupils' favourability towards Gaelic with ability to converse in Gaelic (N = 289)*

It is common for language ability and language loyalty or language identity to show positive correlations, and this tendency is discussed in sections 4.2.2, 4.7.10, 4.8.1, 4.8.1.1, 4.8.4, 4.9.3.1, 4.9.3.2. These cross-tabulated data in Figure 4.37 similarly illustrate a strong correspondence between Gaelic conversational ability and being in favour of Gaelic. Those who are more favourable towards Gaelic are more likely to have a higher level of conversational ability, while those with less conversational ability tend to be less favourable towards Gaelic or indifferent or more in opposition to the language. Of those *Strongly in favour* of Gaelic, 54 (72%) are pupils who can speak Gaelic *Comfortably* or *Relatively well*. Among those who are indifferent to Gaelic, we find one pupil (1.2% of the category) who can speak Gaelic *Comfortably*. No pupil who can speak Gaelic *Comfortably* is a *Little against* the language and one pupil (2.5%) who can speak Gaelic *Comfortably* is *Strongly against* the language. Conversely, 61 pupils with *A few words* or *No ability* in Gaelic (73.5% of the combined category) are indifferent to the language. 16 pupils (84.2%) with *A few words* or *No ability* in Gaelic are a *Little against* Gaelic and 37 pupils (92.5%) with *A few words* or *No ability* in Gaelic are *Strongly against* Gaelic. We can compare those who can converse *Comfortably*, *Relatively well* or *Reasonably*, on the one hand, with those who have *A few words* or *No ability* in conversation, on the other. This gives us two groups which we can term 'can converse' and 'cannot converse' in Gaelic. We can then compare these two groups in terms of their being in favour of Gaelic (*Strongly in favour*, *In favour*) or not in favour of Gaelic (*I don't care, Little against, Strongly against*). We find that, of those who can converse, 104 pupils are in favour and 28 are not in favour. Of those who cannot converse, 43 pupils are in favour and 114 are not. When we test for significance of the relationship between the ability and favourability variables, using the Pearson's Chi Square test, we find a p-value of < 0.05 ($X^2 = 75.802$). A breakdown of individual response categories in Figure 4.37 is shown in **Table A4.16** in **Appendix 4**.

4.7.2 REASONS FOR BEING IN FAVOUR OF OR AGAINST GAELIC

In a further question, pupils who were in favour of the Gaelic language were asked to indicate their reason(s) for being in favour of Gaelic from a choice of 11 multiple response options. Figure 4.38 shows the reasons pupils chose for being in favour of Gaelic.[42]

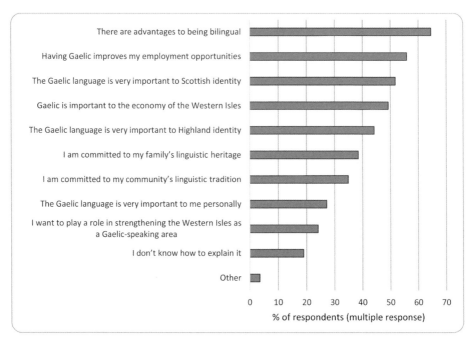

Figure 4.38 *Pupils' reasons for being in favour of Gaelic, in percentages (N = 195)*

The highest percentage returns regarding the pupils' reasons for having favourable perceptions of Gaelic are associated with the advantages of bilingualism (126 pupils, 64.6%) and the employment opportunities available through Gaelic (109, 55.9%), followed by the importance of Gaelic to Scottish identity (101, 51.8%) and to the economy of the Western Isles (96, 49.2%). The lowest percentage returns for being in favour of Gaelic (except for *Other* and *I don't know how to explain it*) are associated with maintaining the language in the Western Isles (47 pupils, 24.1%) and personal importance of Gaelic (53, 27.2%), followed by community linguistic tradition (68, 34.9%) and family linguistic heritage (75, 38.5%). The responses concerning these opinions indicate that the pupils see the most importance for Gaelic as a vehicle for

---

42 Note N = 195 here. This is greater than the total of 148 (= 76 + 72) in favour of Gaelic pertaining to Figure 4.36. It seems that some pupils, who did not indicate favourability towards Gaelic in the previous question, answered this question, leading to a higher than expected total N of 195 in Figure 4.38.

instrumental advantages and individual economic advantage as well as a similar level of importance for the economy of the Western Isles. The importance of Gaelic is rated higher for Scottish identity (51.8%) than for Highland identity (43.9%). Apart from *Other* and *I don't know how to explain it*, the two options most related to personal Gaelic identity (27.2%) and commitment to strengthening Gaelic in the Western Isles (24.1%) provide the two lowest percentages of respondents. This tendency for personal commitment to Gaelic to be lower than general levels of favourability towards Gaelic is a common feature in the IGRP results (4.7.5, 4.7.6) and is also present in the findings of the teenager survey in Ó Giollagáin *et al.* (2007b) with regards to Irish in the Gaeltacht. A breakdown of individual response categories in Figure 4.38 is shown in **Table A4.17** in **Appendix 4**.

Additionally, pupils were asked for their views on certain hypothetical situations: if Gaelic ceased to be an aspect of educational provision in the Western Isles and if Gaelic broadcasting were discontinued. A breakdown of the views presented by pupils is shown in **Figure A4.9** and **Table A4.19** in **Appendix 4**. 49.8% of responses indicated pupils would be *A little unhappy* or *Very unhappy* if GME was discontinued, while 49.2% would be *A little unhappy* or *Very unhappy* if Gaelic television broadcasting were to cease.

Pupils who had responded that they were not in favour of Gaelic were asked to indicate their reason(s) from a choice of nine multiple response options. The percentage results are shown in Figure 4.39.[43]

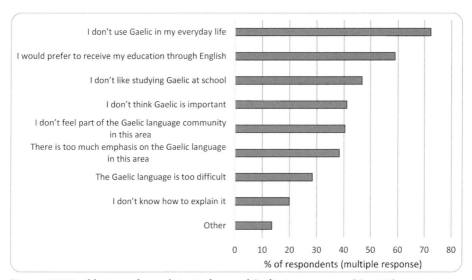

Figure 4.39 Pupils' reasons for not being in favour of Gaelic, in percentages (N = 140)

---

43 The number of pupils who answered this question (N = 140) is relatively consistent with the 144 who had actually indicated that they were not in favour of Gaelic (= 85 + 19 + 40, pertaining to Figure 4.36).

The three most common reasons given for not being in favour of Gaelic are that pupils do not use it in their everyday lives (102 pupils, 72.9%), that they would prefer their education in English (83, 59.3%) and almost half don't like studying Gaelic (66, 47.1%). The four least common reasons given for being not in favour of Gaelic (apart from *Other* and *I don't know how to explain it*) are that it is too difficult (40, 28.6%), followed by the statement that too much emphasis is placed on Gaelic (54, 38.6%), that pupils do not feel part of the local Gaelic community (57, 40.7%), and by the statement *I don't think Gaelic is important* (58, 41.4%). A breakdown of individual response categories in Figure 4.39 is shown in **Table A4.18** in **Appendix 4**.

4.7.3 PERCEPTIONS OF PEOPLE'S EFFECT ON GAELIC VITALITY AND FRAGILITY

A further question addressed the pupils' perceptions of which groups strengthen or weaken Gaelic in their area, on a five-point Likert scale. It sought information on how pupils view themselves, their friends, relatives and others in relation to strengthening or weakening the Gaelic language. Pupils were asked to rate this on a five-point numbered scale ranging from '+2' (strengthen Gaelic a lot) to '2' (weaken Gaelic a lot), with zero representing no effect on Gaelic. A summary of the results is given in Figure 4.40.

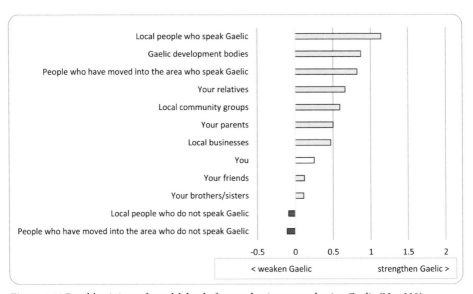

Figure 4.40 *Pupils' opinions of people's level of strengthening or weakening Gaelic (N = 289)*

The responses suggest that a high proportion of pupils believe that local Gaelic speakers strengthen Gaelic the most in their areas, followed by Gaelic bodies, people who move to the area and speak Gaelic, relatives and community groups, parents and businesses in the area. However, a high proportion of pupils rate people who have moved into the area and do not speak Gaelic among those who are least supportive of Gaelic, followed by local non-Gaelic speakers, and followed by their friends, their siblings, and the pupils themselves. It is striking that most groups' effects are indicated as positive (i.e. strengthen Gaelic), although none to a high degree (i.e. '+2'), with a narrow range of just over '1' (from 0.11 to 1.14). This means that even those who are seen as the most relevant with regard to strengthening Gaelic, are not perceived as strengthening Gaelic to a high degree. Scoring positive 0.25 is the category *You*, i.e. the pupils themselves, which we know from the data pertaining to Figure 4.26 comprises 90.6% who *Always* or *Mainly* speak English with each other (i.e. friends). This shows a substantial gap between the pupils' positive perception of the effect of their practice and their actual practice. The corollary of the highly positive perceptions is the non-prevalence of negative values, as evidenced by the absence of '2' and '1' on the scale in Figure 4.40. The overall impression gained from this is that it represents another instance of the gap between positive perceptions of Gaelic promotion and the reality of Gaelic fragility (e.g. sections 5.7.1; 4.7.4; 4.7.5, about half of respondents indicating non-negative prospects for Gaelic in Figure 4.45).

4.7.4 PERCEIVED STRENGTH OF GAELIC IN LOCAL AREA

The pupils were asked in a related question to describe, on a five-point Likert scale, the strength of Gaelic-speaking in the area where they live as a proportion of the local population. The results are shown in Figure 4.41.

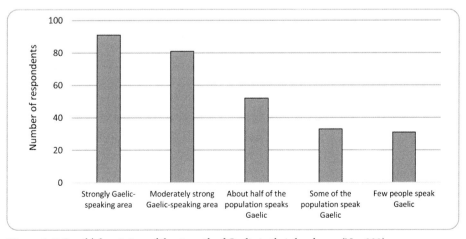

Figure 4.41 *Pupils' description of the strength of Gaelic in their local area (N = 288)*

The results show that over half of the respondents (172 pupils, 59.7%) describe where they live as a *Strongly* (91, 31.6%) or *Moderately strong* (81, 28.1%) Gaelic-speaking area. 52 pupils (18.1%) indicate that in their area *About half of the population speaks Gaelic*. Grouping the three highest categories together, i.e. *Strongly*, *Moderately strong* and *About half*, yields a subtotal of 224 pupils (77.8%) pertaining to these three most positive descriptions. Less positive are the 33 responses (11.5%) which indicate *Some of the population speak Gaelic*. And 31 (10.8%) indicate that *Few people speak Gaelic* in their area. Grouping the two lowest categories together, 64 pupils (22.2%) indicate that they live in an area where *Some* or *Few people speak Gaelic*.

The high proportions in the pupils' relatively positive descriptions of the strength of Gaelic in their areas does not correspond to their own depictions of their use of Gaelic or of its communal use or to much of the other data in the IGRP survey of the Western Isles or other sociodemographic analyses. However, their relatively upbeat depictions may be informed by a comparison with the practical absence of Gaelic speaking on the Scottish mainland. Furthermore, overly positive and overly optimistic depictions of minority-language vitality (as well as overly negative views) are common in minoritised communities in general, especially in more abstract terms, and in previously Gaelic-dominant contexts in particular. This is evidenced, for instance, in the IGRP survey here and in sections 3.3.3 (Table 3.9) and 4.7.3, as well as more realistic depictions such as that reported in section 3.3.4.

4.7.5 COMMITMENTS AND OPINIONS REGARDING GAELIC

Pupils were asked to agree or disagree, on a five-point Likert scale, with seven statements regarding the pupils' commitments, attitudes and opinions relevant to the future of Gaelic in the Western Isles. The percentages of the pupils' responses to each statement are given in Figure 4.42.

The most prevalent single response to each of the individual statements is one of indifference, although a majority response for indifference is not shown for any of the statements. Indifference is more commonly expressed for statements concerning: participation in Gaelic groups for young people (130 pupils, 44.8%); the statement that fluent Gaelic-speaking parents should raise their children in Gaelic (116, 40%); and regarding provision of Gaelic classes for anyone without Gaelic who lives in the Western Isles (115, 39.9%).

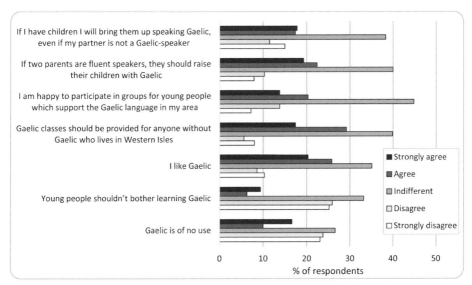

Figure 4.42 *Percentage levels of agreement by pupils to commitments to and relevance of Gaelic (Ns = 287, 290, 290, 288, 291, 286, 290)*

The highest agreement is evidenced in the *Strongly agree* responses to statements for liking Gaelic (59 pupils, 20.3%) and that fluent Gaelic speakers should raise their children in Gaelic (56, 19.3%), followed by pupils aspiring to raise children in Gaelic even if their partner is not Gaelic-speaking (51, 17.8%). With regard to the pupils who *Strongly agree* or *Agree* that they intend to raise their children in Gaelic, the subtotal of 101 pupils (35.2%) is more than the subtotal of 75 pupils who indicated that they can converse *Comfortably* or *Relatively well* in Gaelic (Table 4.18). But, if we add the category of reasonable conversational ability, yielding a subtotal of 130 pupils, the subtotal of 101 aspirant Gaelic-speaking parents can be calculated to be at least partly a subset of the 130. The highest disagreement is for the statements that *Young people shouldn't bother learning Gaelic* (72 pupils, 25.2% *Strongly Disagree*) and that *Gaelic is of no use* (67, 23.1%), followed by pupils aspiring to raise children in Gaelic even if their partner is not Gaelic speaking (43, 15%).

The responses to five of the seven statements show a majority indicating indifference or antipathy towards Gaelic. However, two of the statements show majorities in favour of Gaelic. These are in response to a negative statement about Gaelic, i.e. *Young people shouldn't bother learning Gaelic, Gaelic is of no use*. Of the three *I*-queries in this question, there is a reduction in agreement from *I like Gaelic* to *I will bring them up speaking Gaelic* to the least agreement in *I am happy to participate in groups*. We can interpret this as a decrease from an undemanding statement to a future aspiration and finally to a present commitment (see 4.7.2). A detailed breakdown of responses in Figure 4.42 is shown in **Table A4.20** in **Appendix 4**.

As is clear from Figure 4.42, the level of commitment demanded by speaking Gaelic is lower when greater personal effort is required. We can further analyse the relationship between having a favourable opinion towards Gaelic and a personal commitment towards speaking Gaelic; for instance, the personal effort of speaking Gaelic to friends. This would entail a very considerable personal and collective effort given the dominance of English practice and ability in the teenage cohort. In fact, speaking Gaelic to friends at all times entails the least percentage commitment from pupils (one of the options responded to in Figure 4.43), implying that it would be the most challenging undertaking for this cohort. In Figure 4.43 we compare data for favourability towards Gaelic (Figure 4.36) and a willingness to speak Gaelic to friends (Figure 4.46).[44] In Figure 4.43, the first two data bars in favour of Gaelic correspond to their equivalent data bars in Figure 4.36, whereas the third data bar in Figure 4.43 combines the three data bars of *Don't care, A little against Gaelic* and *Strongly against Gaelic* from Figure 4.36.

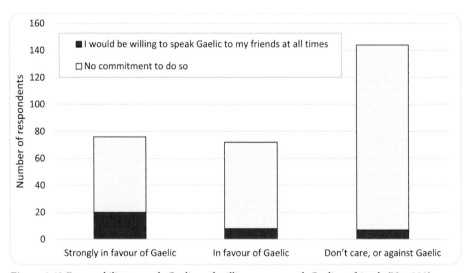

Figure 4.43 *Favourability towards Gaelic and willingness to speak Gaelic to friends (N = 292)*

Even among those who are in favour of Gaelic, few would make the commitment to speak Gaelic within their peer-group. As illustrated in Figure 4.36, of the 76 respondents who were *Strongly in favour of Gaelic*, 20 pupils, about one in four, indicated that they would be willing to speak Gaelic to their friends at all times. About half that amount, about one in eight, of those who were simply *In favour of Gaelic*, would be willing to speak Gaelic to their friends at all times. Seven pupils, or about one in twenty, of those who are not in favour of Gaelic would be willing

---

44 N = 292 for data pertaining to Figure 4.36; N = 208 for willingness to speak Gaelic to friends. We can take the latter to be a subset of the former.

to speak Gaelic to their friends at all times. We shall see that similar tendencies are evidenced in the subset of pupils who identify as a Gael, as well as those who have positive opinions of Gaelic (4.8.1).

4.7.6 FEELINGS REGARDING POSSIBLE USES OF GAELIC

The pupils were asked how strongly they agreed, on a five-point Likert scale, with 13 statements about possible or proposed Gaelic use and about their own future intentions for using Gaelic. The percentage responses for each of the 13 statements are shown in Figure 4.44. Of the 13 statements, one was negative towards Gaelic.

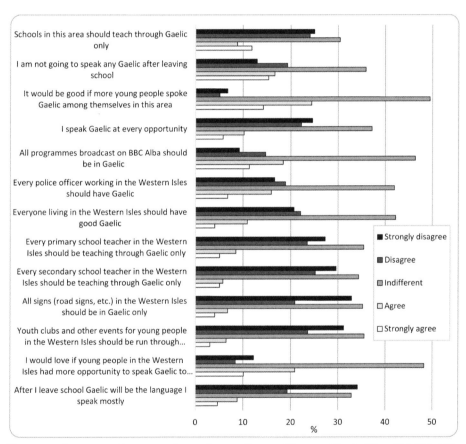

Figure 4.44 *Percentage of agreement by pupils regarding possible uses of Gaelic (Ns = 296, 295, 295, 293, 293, 296, 294, 293, 294, 292, 292, 296, 295)*

Figure 4.44 demonstrates that indifference is the most prevalent response to all the statements. The highest indifference is indicated for *I would love if young people in the Western Isles had more opportunity to speak Gaelic to one another* (143 pupils,

48.3%), at a similar level to *It would be good if more young people spoke Gaelic among themselves in this area* (146, 49.5%), followed by *All programmes broadcast on BBC ALBA should be in Gaelic* (136, 46.4%), *Everyone living in the Western Isles should have good Gaelic* (124, 42.2%) and *Every police officer working in the Western Isles should have Gaelic* (124, 41.9%).

The highest score for strong agreement is for the statement *I am not going to speak any Gaelic after leaving school* (45 pupils, 15.3%) which is detrimental for Gaelic. The next four highest scores for strong agreement are positive towards Gaelic: *It would be good if more young people spoke Gaelic among themselves in this area* (42, 14.2%), *Schools in this area should teach in Gaelic only* (35, 11.8%), *All programmes broadcast on BBC ALBA should be in Gaelic* (33, 11.3%) and *I would love if young people in the Western Isles had more opportunity to speak Gaelic to one another* (30, 10.1%). However, 16% of pupils indicate that they speak Gaelic at every opportunity, and 13.5% *Strongly agree* or *Agree* that *After I leave school Gaelic will be the language I speak mostly*.

The highest score for strong disagreement is for the statement *After I leave school Gaelic will be the language I will speak mostly* (101 pupils, 34.2%), followed by *All signs (road signs, etc.) in the Western Isles should be in Gaelic only* (96, 32.9%), *Youth clubs and other events for young people in the Western Isles should be run through Gaelic only* (91, 31.2%), *Every secondary school teacher in the Western Isles should be teaching through Gaelic only* (87, 29.6%) and *Every primary school teacher in the Western Isles should be teaching through Gaelic only* (80, 27.3%). That is, this strong disagreement to these five statements indicates a lack of support for Gaelic. As discussed in section 4.7.5 (Figure 4.42), these responses further indicate a tension between the pupils' aspirations for Gaelic (Figures 4.46 and 4.47) and their commitment to or support for the use of Gaelic in a range of social and institutional situations (e.g. in Figures 4.32, 4.33 and 4.35). A detailed breakdown of responses in Figure 4.44 is shown in **Table A4.21** in **Appendix 4**.

4.7.7 STRENGTH OR WEAKNESS OF GAELIC IN 20 YEARS' TIME

Pupils were asked to indicate their assessment, on a five-point Likert scale, of the relative strength or weakness of Gaelic in the future, as shown in Figure 4.45.

A higher proportion of pupils (145, 51.4%) feel that Gaelic will be in a weaker condition in 20 years' time: *Much weaker* (85 responses, 30.1%) or *A little weaker* (60 responses, 21.3%). 65 pupils (23%) believe Gaelic will be in a stronger condition: *A little stronger* (41, 14.5%) or *A lot stronger* (24, 8.5%). 72 pupils (25.5%) think Gaelic will be *Just the same*. There is a significantly positive correlation between Gaelic ability and future aspirations. Those who have *Fluent* or *Good Gaelic* (Figure 4.8, 4.5.1), were significantly ($p. < 0.01$) more likely to indicate that they felt that Gaelic would be stronger in 20 years' time (cp. discussion on Figure 4.40).

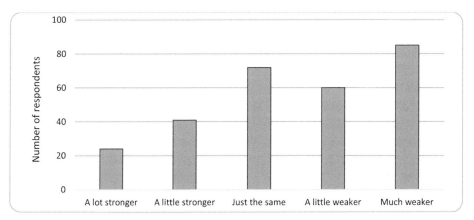

Figure 4.45 *Pupils' assessment of the relative strength or weakness of Gaelic in 20 years' time*
(N = 282)

4.7.8 WHAT WOULD PUPILS BE PERSONALLY WILLING TO DO FOR GAELIC IN THEIR AREA?

A related language-attitude question asked pupils what they personally would be willing to do to ensure that their area would remain Gaelic-speaking. A series of 12 statements beginning *I would …* or *I would be willing* (to …) were offered. Pupils ticked relevant boxes to indicate what they were willing to do. The response rate to this question is low, i.e. 208 pupils responded and 97 did not. It is likely that many of the non-responses indicate a lack of willingness or ability to engage in these Gaelic-speaking activities. If that is so, the percentages of willingness to use Gaelic would be even lower. For instance, those willing to speak Gaelic to everyone who has Gaelic would be reduced from 51% to 34.8% of the total sample.

The highest percentages show a willingness *to speak Gaelic to everyone who has Gaelic* (106, 51%), followed by *encourage those living locally to learn Gaelic* (96, 46.2%), *to stay living in the area and to be active in the community* (66, 31.7%) and *to always speak Gaelic to my parents* (63, 30.1%). The statements attracting the least percentage willingness among the pupils are: *other* (unspecified, 35, 16.8%), a willingness *to speak Gaelic to my friends at all times* (35, 16.8%), *to speak Gaelic to my boyfriend/ girlfriend at all times* (37, 17.8%) and *to write to local representatives demanding services through Gaelic in this area* (39, 18.8%). Respondents who identified as a Gael and those with conversational ability in Gaelic were significantly more likely to be willing to undertake almost all the activities in Figure 4.46 when compared with those with little or no conversational ability and who did not identify as a Gael. The only exception was in *willingness to stay living in the area and be active in the community* where there were no significant differences in terms of conversational ability nor Gaelic identity.

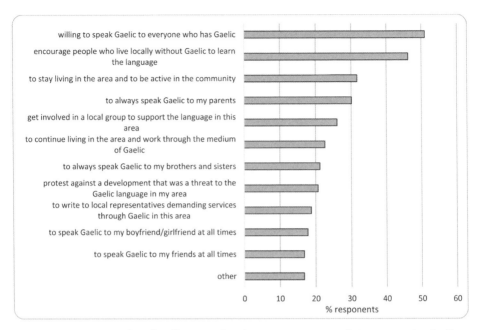

willing to speak Gaelic to everyone who has Gaelic

encourage people who live locally without Gaelic to learn the language

to stay living in the area and to be active in the community

to always speak Gaelic to my parents

get involved in a local group to support the language in this area

to continue living in the area and work through the medium of Gaelic

to always speak Gaelic to my brothers and sisters

protest against a development that was a threat to the Gaelic language in my area

to write to local representatives demanding services through Gaelic in this area

to speak Gaelic to my boyfriend/girlfriend at all times

to speak Gaelic to my friends at all times

other

0   10   20   30   40   50   60
% respondents

Figure 4.46 Percentage of pupils willing to undertake activities to ensure their area remains Gaelic-speaking, in descending percentage order (N = 208)

4.7.9 WILLINGNESS OF PUPILS TO RAISE THEIR CHILDREN IN GAELIC

In the responses to the question about the pupil's willingness to raise their children in Gaelic over half of the pupils (164, 58.8% of responses) indicate that they do not intend to raise their children through Gaelic. Whereas 115 (41.2%) indicate they intend to do so. Figure 4.47 shows the results of this future-oriented question in which pupils were asked if they intended to raise their children through Gaelic (*Yes/No*) in a cross-tabulation with the pupils' ability data (*Fluent* or *Good Gaelic* vs. less Gaelic (Figure 4.8, 4.5.1)). The results of the cross-tabulation of these questions are presented in Figure 4.47. Of those who are fluent, 85% (68 pupils) indicated that they would be willing to raise their children in Gaelic. This correlation is significant (X^2 = 91.693, p. < 0.05).

A comparison of the pupils' language intentions for rearing their own children with previous responses offered in the survey indicates a gap between, on the one hand, their aspirations for Gaelic, and their practice and competence in Gaelic on the other. Of the total of 305 pupils participating in the survey, these 115 pupils, representing 38% of the sample, indicate that they intend to raise their children through Gaelic. This 115 is more than double the amount of pupils (47, 16%) who currently speak Gaelic at every opportunity (see **Appendix A4.16, Table A4.21**), and more than double the 53 pupils (25.5% of 208) willing to always speak Gaelic to parents (Figure 4.46, 4.7.8), and considerably more than the 61 (20.3% of 300 pupils) who self-reported as fluent (Table 4.11, 4.5.1).

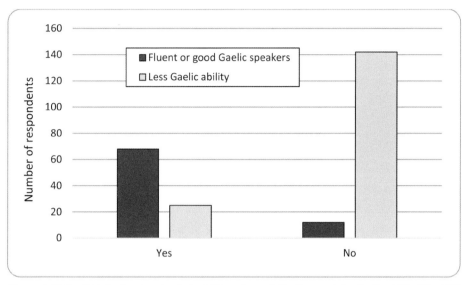

Figure 4.47 *Pupils' intention to raise their children through Gaelic or not, by Gaelic ability (N = 247)*

4.8 IDENTITY

The final section of the survey, Section E, investigated cultural and linguistic identity. The questions in this section enquired about identity ascription in binary and multiple formats and examined how language ability influenced issues of ascription.

4.8.1 ARE YOU A GAEL?

Pupils were asked if they considered themselves to be Gaels. They were given three possible options: *Yes*, *No* and *Prefer not to answer*, the results of which are shown in Figure 4.48. By giving only two main choices in this query, we sought to determine the largest possible extent of those in the cohort who would identify as Gaels. The responses to a further question on expanded identity self-ascriptions are analysed in sections 4.8.3 and 4.8.4, in which a smaller cohort self-ascribe as Gaels.

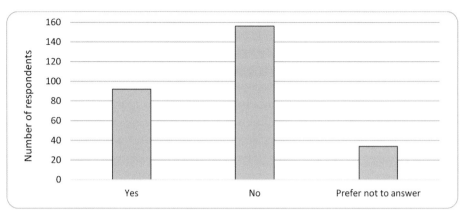

Figure 4.48 *Pupils' self-ascription as Gaels (N = 282)*

These responses reveal that the largest proportion of pupils (156 pupils, 55.3%) do not consider themselves to be Gaels. 92 pupils (32.6%) do consider themselves to be Gaels and 34 (12.1%) *Prefer not to answer.* A significantly high proportion (p. < 0.01) of those who are fluent speakers or have good Gaelic (Figure 4.8, 4.5.1) identified as Gaels. Figure 4.49 provides information on the correspondence between self-ascription as a Gael (Figure 4.48) and ability in spoken Gaelic.

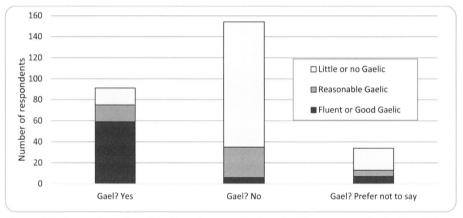

Figure 4.49 *Comparison of pupils' self-ascription as Gaels and ability in spoken Gaelic (N = 279)*

This demonstrates that those who identify themselves as Gaels are more likely to have a *Good* level of Gaelic ability. Those who do not identify as Gaels are more likely to have *Little or No Gaelic.* The category responses illustrated in Figure 4.49 are given in **Table A4.22** in **Appendix A4.17**.

We can also enquire what correspondence there might be between self-ascription of Gaelic identity and an ability to converse in Gaelic (cp. similar cross-tabulation in Figure 4.49). Figure 4.50 and Table 4.24 illustrate the relationship between identity as a Gael and ability to converse in Gaelic (on a scale from *no ability* to *comfortably* (from Figure 4.15, 4.5.4)).

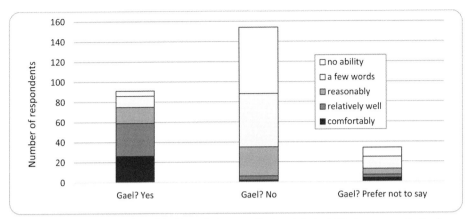

Figure 4.50 *Comparison of pupils' self-ascription as a Gael and their ability to converse in Gaelic (N = 279)*

This data comparison indicates that there is a strong positive correlation between pupils' ability to converse in Gaelic and their self-identification as Gaels. The pupils with a stronger conversational ability in Gaelic are more likely to identify themselves as Gaels. Conversely, those with a weaker conversational ability in Gaelic are less likely to identify as Gaels.

As shown in Table 4.24, 26 pupils (28.6% of the total of 91 pupils who self-identify as Gaels) can converse *Comfortably* in Gaelic. Two pupils (1.3% of the total of 154 pupils who identify themselves as non-Gaels) can converse *Comfortably* in Gaelic .

Ability to converse in Gaelic	Identify as a Gael	Not a Gael	Prefer not to say
Comfortably	26	2	4
Relatively well	33	4	3
Reasonably	16	29	6
In a few words	11	53	12
No ability	5	66	9
Total	91	154	34

Table 4.24 *Ability to converse in Gaelic and self-identification as a Gael*

As set out in section 4.7.1 (with regard to the positive correlation between conversational ability in Gaelic and favourability towards Gaelic), we can compare those who can converse in Gaelic (*Comfortably, Relatively well* or *Reasonably*) with those who cannot converse in Gaelic (*A few words* or *No ability*). We can then compare these two groups in terms of their identifying as a Gael (*Gael? Yes*) or not (*Gael? No*). We find that those who identify as a Gael, 75 pupils can converse in Gaelic and 16 cannot. On the other hand, of those who do not identify as a Gael, 35 can converse and 119 cannot. The relationship between conversational ability and Gaelic identity is significant ($X^2 = 83.105$, p. < 0.05).

4.8.1.1 *IDENTITY AS GAEL AND FAMILY LANGUAGE PRACTICE*

Figure 4.51 compares the results for self-ascription as a Gael with current family language practice. The family language practice data are discussed in section 4.6.1 (Figure 4.19). The family practice was indicated by the pupils in a five-point Likert scale (assigned here values from 5 to 1): *Always Gaelic* (5); *Mainly Gaelic* (4); *Mix of Gaelic and English* (3); *Mainly English* (2); *Always English* (1). As stated, family language practice is given on a scale of 5 (*Always Gaelic*) to 1 (*Always English*). This allows us to calculate mean scores for all the pupils taken as a group, for subgroups of pupils or for individual pupils. For instance, a mean score of 3 would indicate that practice lies half way between *Always English* (1) and *Always Gaelic* (5). Based on language practice with their mother, those identifying as a Gael score a mean of 2.25. This represents the highest subgroup mean, as indicated in Figure 4.51. In general, the pupils who identified as a Gael reported that they speak Gaelic in a family context more often than those who do not identify as a Gael (or preferred not to answer) (cp. the correlation of SIR and Gaelic identity data in Figure 7.4, in section 7.2.1). Mean family practice scores indicated English was the predominant language for all respondents.

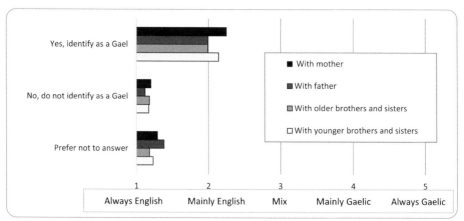

Figure 4.51 *Self-ascription as Gael and mean family language practice score with parents and siblings (N = 273)*

Those who do not identify as a Gael (or preferred not to answer) had mean family practice scores close to 1, indicating they almost always speak English. In contrast, those who identified as a Gael had mean family scores close to 2, indicating they mainly speak English but speak at least some Gaelic. The language practice mean scores with parents and siblings are similar. Three general points can be made with regard to self-ascription as a Gael for the teenage cohort:

    1. A smaller cohort self-ascribe as Gaels than older generations (5.5);

2. Within this cohort of self-ascribing Gaels actual Gaelic practice is marginal (cf. 4.2.2);
3. Self-ascription as a Gael correlates positively with Gaelic ability (both fluency and conversation) and practice in the family.

4.8.2 WHO IS A GAEL?

A multiple-choice question in this section of the questionnaire elicited views on perceived group identity. Figure 4.52 shows the percentages of the respondents who chose from the five options concerning who is a Gael.

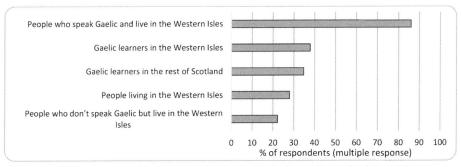

Figure 4.52 *Percentage views on those considered to be Gaels, descending order (N = 264)*

The results indicate a correspondence between speaking (and/or learning) Gaelic and ascription as a Gael. Some speaking of or ability in Gaelic is seen as being more important than place of residence in determining who pupils consider to be a Gael. Of the five categories offered, *People who speak Gaelic and live in the Western Isles* are most likely to be considered as Gaels (228 of 264 respondents, 86.4%). This is followed by *Gaelic learners in the Western Isles* (100, 37.9%) and *Gaelic learners in the rest of Scotland* (92, 34.8%). These two highest ascriptions clearly combine place and Gaelic-speaking. Next is *People living in the Western Isles* (74 pupils, 28%) followed by *People who don't speak Gaelic but live in the Western Isles* (59, 22.3%). The lowest category corresponds closest to the actual language practice of most of the pupils. This may explain why many of them do not self-ascribe as Gaels.

4.8.3 IDENTITY OR IDENTITIES AS GAEL, LOCAL, SCOTTISH OR BRITISH

The final question asked the pupils to indicate how they would describe their identity. Pupils were given six categories to choose from: *Gael*; *Local, e.g. Leòdhasach, Hearach, Siarach, Sgalpach*; *Scottish*; *British*; *Something else* and *Prefer not to answer*. They were asked to tick each category that applied to them, allowing for singular or multiple ascriptions. Results are shown in Figure 4.53, with a comparison to those identifying as a Gael in the binary choice question (pertaining to Figure 4.48).

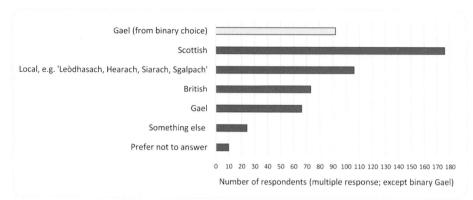

Figure 4.53 *Number of pupils in categories of pupils' description of their own identity, in descending order (Ns = 282, 283)*

Almost one in three of the respondents (30.7%, i.e. 87 of 283 respondents) choose more than one identity. A total of 76.7% of the pupils do not describe themselves as Gaels. *Scottish* is the most common identity category among the pupils (176, 62.2%), followed by *Local* (106, 37.5%), *British* (73, 25.8%) and *Gael* (66, 23.3%). In comparison to the data in Figure 4.48, where a binary choice was offered, and where 92 (32.6%) self-ascribe as Gaels, the responses to multiple-choice identity ascription yield less self-ascription as Gaels, i.e. 26 less. Of the 92 pupils who self-ascribe as Gaels in response to the binary choice question (Figure 4.48), their choices of multiple identities in descending order are: *Scottish* (66, 71.7% of the 92 binary choice Gaels), *Gael* (59, 64.1%), *Local* (53, 57.6%), *British* (23, 25%), *Something else* (2, 2.2%), *Prefer not to say* (0). In contrast with pupils' identity (32.6% *Gael* (binary) or 23.3% *Gael* (multiple response); *Local* (37.5%)), adults in the community surveys (section 5.5; **Appendices A5.5.5, A5.6.5, A5.7.5**), show much higher levels of self-identification as 'Gaels' (79% *Gael* (binary) or 70.6% *Gael* (multiple response)) and as *Local* (72.2%). This indicates a weakening of adherence to those self-ascribed identities among younger people. The strengthening of British ascription or identity and the weakening of identity as a Gael was, of course, a longstanding policy of the British state.

Gael?	Yes			No	
Identity	Number	Percent responses	Percent binary Gaels	Number	Percent binary non-Gaels
Scottish	66	32.5	71.7	86	54.4
Gael	59	29.1	64.1	4	2.5
Local	53	26.1	57.6	39	24.7
British	23	11.3	25.0	46	29.1
Something else	2	1.0	2.2	16	10.1
Prefer not to answer	0	0.0	0.0	5	3.2
Total responses	203	100.0		196	

Table 4.25 Multiple-choice identity, among those pupils who identify as a Gael (Gael? Yes) or not (Gael? No) in the binary choice (N = 92; 158)

The numbers of responses and the two related percentages (of total multiple responses and of 92 pupils who are binary-choice Gaels) are presented in Table 4.25. This shows that, when given multiple choices, of those who choose *Gael* in a binary choice, 71.7% choose *Scottish* and only 64.1% choose *Gael*. Or to put it another way, this means that 35.9% of 92 'binary Gaels' do not identify as a *Gael* given multiple options. Furthermore, more than one in two of the 'binary Gaels' (58.7%, i.e. 54 of 92) choose more than one identity. The breakdown between mono- vs. bi- vs. tri-identities etc., in the multiple choice option for 'binary Gaels' is: one identity x 36; two identities x 13; three identities x 23; four identities x 18 (five (or six) identities x 0; no identity x 2). This means that the 'binary-Gael' subset of the teenagers are more multi-identitarian than the group as a whole and clearly more multi-identitarian than 'binary non-Gaels'. In fact, slightly more identity options are chosen by the 92 'binary Gaels' (203 options) than are chosen by the 158 'binary non-Gaels' (196 options). The breakdown in the multiple choice option for 'binary non-Gaels' is: one identity x 130; two identities x 15; three identities x 6; four identities x 0; five identities x 0 (six identities x 3; no identity x 4). The group as a whole, and the 'binary non-Gaels' even more so, reflect more mono-identitarianism with dominant *Scottish* ascription (see points (1) and (3) below), corresponding to dominant monolingualism in English.

We have information on identity self-ascription from three groups in the Teenager Survey (**IV** the set of all Teenagers, **II** the subset of teenagers with binary identity as a Gael, and **VI** the subset of teenagers with binary identity as not a Gael or as a 'non-Gael'). And from the respondents in the Community Sociolinguistic Survey (CSS, sections 5.5, 5.5.1; N = 177, all of whom are adults) we have information on three further groups: **III** all CSS Adults; **I** the subset of CSS Adults with native Gaelic fluency; **V** the subset of CSS Adults with very little or no Gaelic (*A few words of*

Gaelic or No Gaelic). We can therefore compare the quantified proportional choices of multiple identities among these six groups in the following schema, in descending order of prevalence of identity as a Gael:[45]

I	Gaelic CSS Adults:	**Gael**	≥	LOCAL	≥	Scottish	>>	*British*
II	Gael Teenagers:	Scottish	≥	**Gael**	≥	Local	>>	*British*
III	CSS Adults:	Scottish	≥	Local	≥	**Gael**	>>	*British*
IV	Teenagers:	Scottish	>>	Local	>>	*British*	>>	**Gael**
V	Non-Gaelic CSS Adults:	Scottish	≥	*British*	>>	Local	>>	**Gael**
VI	Non-Gael Teenagers:	Scottish	>>	*British*	≥	Local	>>>	**Gael**

There are six main features of note in these comparisons:

1. Fluent **I** Gaelic-speaking CSS Adults have *Gael* as first choice; corresponding to **II** Gael Teenagers who are the group with *Gael* in next-highest position. All other groups, **II–VI**, choose *Scottish* as first choice. Speaking dynamically, the five other groups, **II–VI**, can be viewed as 'promoting' *Scottish* to primary position in their self-ascribed identities.

2. **I** Gaelic CSS Adults are the only group who choose *Local* more than *Scottish* (highlighted by capital letters, LOCAL, in the schema above).

3. The three groups who choose *Gael* more than *British* self-ascription (**I** Gaelic CSS Adults, **II** Gael Teenagers and **III** CSS Adults) choose three identities to fairly equal levels (which are highlighted by an outline in the schema), with *British* as fourth and substantially lowest option (in italics in schema). In short, one can describe the structure of these multiple identities as 'Other identities' >> *British* (for groups **I–III**).[46] This is in contrast with **IV** Teenagers, **V** Non-Gaelic CSS Adults and **VI** Non-Gael Teenagers who choose *British* more than *Gael* self-ascription: their identity choices are more quantitatively differentiated or less equally multi-identitarian. The structure of the multiple identities of the **IV** Teenagers and the **VI** Non-Gael Teenagers subset could be summarily described as *Scottish* >> 'Other identities'.

---

45 The symbols in the schema can be read as: ≥ 'slightly more than'; >> 'substantially more than'; >>> 'far more than'.

46 The average number of identities for four of these subsets are: **I** Gaelic CSS Adults 3.1 identity options; **II** Gael Teenagers 2.2 identity options; **V** Non-Gaelic CSS Adults 1.3 identity options; and **VI** Non-Gael Teenagers 1.2 identity options. The two non-Gael(ic) subsets (**V** and **VI**) are clearly less multi-identitatarian.

4. Apart from the position of *Gael*, the quantified order of the three other identities is stable for three groups (**II** Gael Teenagers, **III** CSS Adults, **IV** Teenagers), i.e. *Scottish > Local > British*. The 'promotion' of *British* and 'demotion' of *Gael* (in bold type in the schema above), or the swap in positions, is notable in the comparison of the **IV** Teenagers with the other two subgroups, **II–III**.

5. The subgroup of **VI** Non-Gael Teenagers are distinct from the other groups in that:
   a. they have the lowest overall rates of positive self-ascription (maximum 54.4% as shown in Table 4.25 above) perhaps indicating less identitarian engagement (with the choice of options provided in the questionnaire);
   b. one clearly dominant identity: *Scottish* (as underlined in the schema);
   c. only groups **V** and **VI** have *British* identity in second-highest position, above *Local*, the highest position for *British* identity of the six groups. For the **VI** Non-Gael Teenagers, all three other identities are far above marginal *Gael*.

6. Having chosen to display the groups in descending order of the position of identity as *Gael*, a summary of the comparative positions of the four identity categories can be set out, and interpreted dynamically, as follows:
   a. *Gael* is in first position in group **I** and fourth position in groups **IV–VI**;
   b. *Local* is in second position in group **I** and in third position in groups **II** and **V–VI**;
   c. *Scottish* is in third position in group **I** and in first position in groups **II–VI**;
   d. *British* is in fourth position in groups **I–III** and in second position in groups **V–VI**.

4.8.4 SYNOPSIS OF IDENTITY AND OTHER POSITIVE FACTORS CONCERNING GAELIC

In this section, we present a synopsis of the proportions of the pupils who indicate positive identity, attitudes and aspirations towards Gaelic. Figure 4.54 shows the percentage results of seven key attitudinal and language-practice variables which are supportive of Gaelic from the Teenager Survey data, discussed in the previous sections.

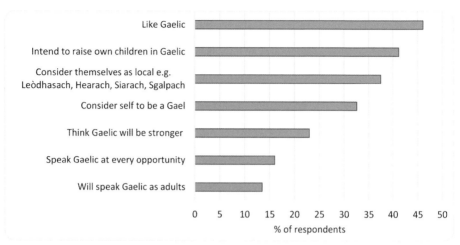

Figure 4.54 *Percentages of seven key factors concerning Gaelic (Ns = 291, 247, 283, 282, 282, 292, 296)*

An examination of the responses to this selection of key attitudinal and language-practice factors indicates that:

46.1% like Gaelic (Figure 4.42);

41.2% intend to raise their children through Gaelic (Figure 4.47);

37.5% ascribe to a local identity (Figure 4.53);

32.6% consider themselves to be Gaels (in the basically binary option in Figure 4.48);

23% believe Gaelic will be stronger in the future (i.e. *A lot* or *A little stronger* in Figure 4.45);

16% speak Gaelic at every opportunity (Figure 4.44); and

13.5% *Strongly agree* or *Agree* that *After I leave school Gaelic will be the language I speak mostly* (Figure 4.44).

The limited role Gaelic plays in the lives of the young people is depicted in this survey in general, and in the low percentages of pupils who indicate that they speak Gaelic at every opportunity (16%) or intend to speak Gaelic as adults (i.e. when they leave school: 13.5%). This actual marginality contrasts with a relatively substantial degree of affection towards Gaelic (46.1%) and with a moderate proportion of this cohort aspiring to raise their children in Gaelic (41.2%). Local identity (37.5% multiple response) is stronger than identity as a Gael (32.6% binary response; 23.3% multiple response).

Up to this point in the synopsis of positive attitudinal and practice data for Gaelic, all Study Districts in the Research Area have been included. We can, however, investigate the data at greater geographic detail. For instance, since the demolinguistic analysis in Chapter 2 (e.g. 2.4.1.1, 2.4.1.3) demonstrates that the three Study Districts of Stornoway are among the districts with the weakest Gaelic vitality, it may be instructive to analyse Stornoway and the rest of the RA separately, according to the key attitudinal and language practice factors. In Figure 4.55, therefore, we present the percentages of the seven key values in what we can term as 'rural areas' (i.e. the SDs outwith Stornoway).

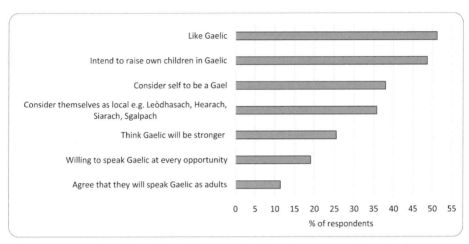

Figure 4.55 *Percentages of seven key factors concerning Gaelic in rural areas (i.e. outwith Stornoway) (Ns = 207, 199, 200, 215, 200, 209, 210)*

In Table 4.26 the comparative percentages are presented for the whole Research Area and for the rural areas (i.e. outwith Stornoway).

	Percentage of all RA	Percentage of rural areas
I like Gaelic	46.1	51.2
Intend to raise their children in Gaelic	41.2	48.7
Consider self to be a Gael	37.5	38.0
Consider themselves as local	32.6	35.8
Think Gaelic will be stronger	23.0	25.5
Speak Gaelic at every opportunity	16.0	19.1
Will speak Gaelic as adults (i.e. after leaving school)	13.5	17.6

Table 4.26 *Comparison of seven key factors for Gaelic: all Research Area vs. rural areas*

This comparison indicates that the divergence between aspiration for and the practice of Gaelic is similar in these two geographic contexts. However, pupils in rural areas yield higher favourable percentages than those in the RA as a whole.

Table 4.26 and Figures 4.54 and 4.55 show that the proportion of pupils who intend to speak Gaelic as adults (13.5% or 17.6%) is substantially less than those who intend to raise their children in Gaelic (41.2% or 48.7%). This represents a difference between the two categories of roughly three or four multiples. This seems to be an indication that there is a stronger association of Gaelic with the context of child-rearing than with the context of adulthood. Or, in other words, the strongest active context for Gaelic is seen as heritage transmission, dissociated for the most part from adult practice. There is, of course, an obvious internal contradiction between these two factors, in that, to put it simply, a parent cannot raise a child in Gaelic without being an adult speaker of Gaelic. A further contradiction is that, without an adult context for Gaelic, any heritage transmission efforts will have limited results (cf. the discussion in section 4.5.2 on the implications of the source of Gaelic ability for the attainment levels in Gaelic competence).

4.9 LEVELS OF ENGLISH USE AND OF GAELIC ABILITY ACCORDING TO SOCIOLINGUISTIC VARIABLES

In this section, we analyse the relationship of language practice and ability with the sociolinguistic basis of that practice and ability among the teenage cohort. We compare the level of English use and the level of Gaelic ability, on the one hand, with sociolinguistic variables on the other hand, such as the source of Gaelic acquisition, geographic origin of parents, parental Gaelic ability, etc. This will allow us to give an overview of the associations between the sociolinguistic drivers and the resulting practices and abilities. We introduce two new summary scores in this section, an English practice score and a Gaelic ability score with which we compare the sociolinguistic variables. These summary scores are calculated from the relevant results discussed in the previous sections of this Teenager Survey.

4.9.1 ENGLISH USE SCORE AND GAELIC ABILITY SCORE ACCORDING TO SOURCE OF GAELIC ACQUISITION

To summarise the extent of English and Gaelic use by the teenagers, an English use score was calculated for each individual based on their response to questions on language practice. We term this the English use score because English is the dominant language practiced among the teenagers.

The Use Score was based on the mean value of the 20 questions relating to the respondents' Gaelic use now with family (questions 17a, 17e, 17j, 17n), with friends and neighbours (18a and 18e), at events (19a to h) and at school (25a to f) all using the same value categories (1 = Always Gaelic, 2 = …) from section C.

This English use score is effectively the mean value from the responses to the 1 to 5 scale in questions in Section C (Using the Gaelic language) in the questionnaire where 1 equals *Always Gaelic*, 2 *Mainly Gaelic*, 3 *A mix of Gaelic and English*, 4 *Mainly English* and 5 *Always English* across a range of situations. English use scores closer to 1 represent greater use of Gaelic, while scores closer to 5 represent greater use of English. This allows us to calculate mean scores for individuals or for subgroups of pupils, or for all the pupils taken as a whole. Respondents with English use scores of up to 2.99 were categorised as 'Gaelic users'. English use scores from 3.00 to 3.99 were categorised as 'Use both languages'. Scores of 4.00 and over were categorised as 'English users'. Given that a higher level of English use indicates a lower level of Gaelic use, it is obvious that lower levels of the English use score indicate higher levels of productive Gaelic use.

First of all, we analyse the different levels of practice of English among the subgroup of pupils who have indicated how they have acquired Gaelic (section 4.5.2), according to whether they acquired it from parent(s) or from (pre)school. In Figure 4.56 we compare the mean English use scores of pupils who have acquired their Gaelic from their parent(s) with the mean English use scores of those who have acquired their Gaelic exclusively from (pre)school. The source of Gaelic for the 'from parents' category includes: parent(s) and any of all other sources but not (pre)school and the source of Gaelic for the 'from (pre)school' category includes: (pre)school and any of all other sources but not parent(s). Therefore, the 'Gaelic acquired from parents' group excludes any pupils who indicated that they had also acquired Gaelic from (pre)school. Likewise, the 'Gaelic acquired from (pre)school' group excludes those who had also indicated parental input to their Gaelic language acquisition.

Figure 4.56 *Mean English use score of two subgroups: Gaelic acquired from parent(s) vs. Gaelic acquired from (pre)school (N = 73, 74)*

In Figure 4.56 the mean English use score (3.89) for pupils who have acquired their Gaelic from one or both parents indicates a greater level of Gaelic practice, and a lower level of English practice than for the higher value (4.76) depicted for pupils whose source of Gaelic acquisition was the (pre)school. In short: 1) both subgroups score close to or over 4, the value of 4 and higher indicating 'English users'; 2) those who have acquired Gaelic in (pre)school have a mean score close to 5 on the English use score, i.e. they are overwhelmingly English dominant in practice. This figure shows the weakness of Gaelic language transfer, and in particular, the low sociolinguistic productivity of the (pre)school as a basis for Gaelic practice.

We can also analyse the relationship between the source of Gaelic acquisition and the resulting level of Gaelic ability. We can do this by calculating a Gaelic ability score. A Gaelic ability score of 5 to 0 was assigned to each teenager based on their response to Question 9 in Section B of the questionnaire, as shown in Figure 4.8 (4.5.1). A higher score represents a greater level of ability in Gaelic. A score of 5 indicates full Gaelic fluency, while a score of 0 indicates no ability in Gaelic. Figure 4.57 illustrates mean Gaelic ability scores for the same two subgroups (as in Figure 4.56 above) from those who indicated they have acquired Gaelic: those who acquired their Gaelic from their parent(s) or exclusively from a (pre)school context.

Figure 4.57 *Mean Gaelic ability score of two subgroups: Gaelic acquired from parent(s) vs. Gaelic acquired from (pre)school (N = 73, 75)*

Figure 4.57 illustrates clearly that mean Gaelic ability scores, ranging between 3.29 and 1.92, are substantially lower than the maximum ability of 5. Those who acquired their Gaelic from one or both parents have a higher mean Gaelic ability score than those who acquired their Gaelic in a (pre)school context only.

4.9.2 ENGLISH USE SCORES AND GAELIC ABILITY SCORES ACCORDING TO OTHER SOCIOLINGUISTIC FACTORS

In the previous section, we examined the association of practice and ability with a main source of that practice and ability, i.e. parent(s) or (pre)school. In this section we extend the application of the English use and Gaelic ability scores and widen the analysis of the relationship between language practice and Gaelic ability and other sociolinguistic and demographic factors discussed in previous sections. For this purpose, we calculated aggregated average English use scores and Gaelic ability scores for the following six categories:

- Pupils' supportiveness to Gaelic (based on the two positive responses to question 29 on their level of favourability towards Gaelic)
- Pupils' identity, Gael *Yes* vs. *No* or *Prefer not to say* (4.8.1), from question 40 on identity
- Pupils' place of upbringing, within or outwith the Western Isles (4.4), from question 4
- Parental origin, within or outwith the Western Isles (4.4.1), from question 5a and 5b
- Parental Gaelic ability, at least one fluent Gaelic-speaking parent (4.4.1), from question 6a and 6b
- Pupils' gender (4.4) from question 1.

Mean figures were compared between the paired subcategories and any significant differences identified, which we discuss in the following sections.

In the following two figures we illustrate the mean scores for (a) English use (Figure 4.58) and (b) Gaelic ability (Figure 4.59) according to the sociolinguistic and demographic variables in binary pairs. To test for significance, the non-parametric Mann-Whitney test was applied. In all cases, the differences between the paired subcategories were statistically significant with p. < 0.05.). See **Table A4.23** in **Appendix A4.18** for statistical values.

Aggregated English use scores are presented for each of the demographic and sociolinguistic pairs in Figure 4.58.

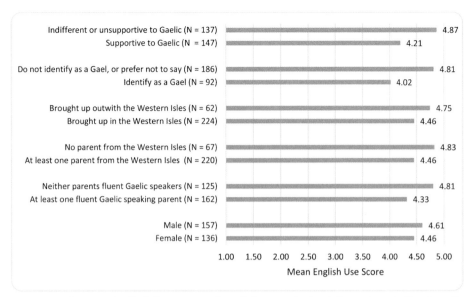

Figure 4.58 Comparative English use scores of pupils for six paired sociolinguistic variables of pupils and parents

Although the average English use scores across the subgroups come close to 5 (5 represents using always English), several subgroups had lower scores, closer to 4, indicating at least some use of Gaelic (1 represents using always Gaelic). As is to be expected, those with more positive values in Gaelic-related factors have lower English use scores. The Gaelic-positive members of the six paired variables range from 4.02 to 4.46. Whereas the Gaelic-negative members of the variables range from 4.61 to 4.87. As the values in Figure 4.58 illustrate, from the point of view of the Gaelic-positive member of each pair, we can place these six sociolinguistic factors in ascending order of mean English use. The value is lowest among those who:

identify as a Gael (4.02); followed by those who are
supportive to Gaelic (4.21); followed by those who have
at least one Gaelic-speaking parent (4.33);
with the remaining three factors scoring the same value (4.46); those
brought up in the Western Isles; and those who have
at least one parent from the Western Isles; and
females.

In effect, the ascending English use order presented here indicates the productive Gaelic use in descending order. As we shall see in relation to Figure 4.59, a similar pattern is evident for levels of Gaelic ability according to the same six sociolinguistic variables.

For the sake of comparison, from the point of view of the narrower range in the Gaelic-negative members of each pair, we can place these six sociolinguistic factors in ascending order of mean English use:

males (4.61); followed by those
brought up outwith the Western Isles (4.75); followed by those who do not identify as a Gael, or prefer not to say (4.81); and neither parent fluent Gaelic speaker (4.81); followed by those who have no parent from the Western Isles (4.83); followed by those who are indifferent or unsupportive to Gaelic (4.87).

In effect, this order presents the lowest to the highest users of English from these six sociolinguistic categories, with the highest category being one pertaining to a lack of favourability towards Gaelic: 'those who are indifferent or unsupportive of Gaelic'.

The Gaelic ability score is a 5 to 0 value assigned to each respondent based on their response to a question on Gaelic ability in the questionnaire. A score of 5 represents full Gaelic fluency, while a score of 0 represents no Gaelic ability. Averaged Gaelic ability scores are presented for each of the paired demographic and sociolinguistic variables in Figure 4.59.

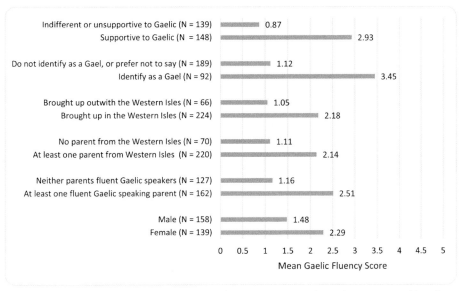

Figure 4.59 *Comparative Gaelic ability scores of pupils for six paired sociolinguistic variables of pupils and parents*

Again, as is to be expected, those with more positive values in Gaelic-related factors have higher Gaelic ability scores. The Gaelic-positive members of the six paired variables range from 2.14 to 3.45. Whereas the Gaelic-negative members of the variables range from 0.87 to 1.48, which is lower and narrower than the Gaelic-positive members' range. As the values in Figure 4.59 illustrate, from the point of view of the Gaelic-positive member of each pair, we can place these six factors in descending order of mean Gaelic ability, i.e. from the highest Gaelic ability to the lowest within the sociolinguistic factors. Highest Gaelic ability is found among those who:

identify as a Gael (3.45); followed by those who are

supportive to Gaelic (2.93); followed by those with

at least one Gaelic-speaking parent (2.51); followed by

females (2.29); followed by those

brought up in the Western Isles (2.18); followed by those who have

at least one parent from the Western Isles (2.14).

These values all have significantly higher mean Gaelic ability scores than their opposite paired category. Again for the sake of comparison, from the point of view of the narrower range in the Gaelic-negative members of each pair, we can place these six sociolinguistic factors in descending order of mean Gaelic ability. Those who have the highest Gaelic ability among this subgroup are:

males (1.48); followed by

neither parent fluent Gaelic speaker (1.16); followed by those who

do not identify as a Gael, or prefer not to say (1.12); followed by those who have

no parent from the Western Isles (1.11); followed by those

brought up outwith the Western Isles (1.05); followed by those

who are indifferent or unsupportive of Gaelic (0.87).

In brief, of the six sociolinguistic factors, identifying as a Gael correlates with the highest levels of Gaelic practice and Gaelic ability. On the other hand, not being favourable towards Gaelic, i.e. being 'indifferent or unsupportive to Gaelic', correlates with the highest levels of English practice and the lowest levels of Gaelic ability. Interestingly, although identifying as a Gael has the highest correlation for the Gaelic-positive members of the six paired factors, its opposite, i.e. not identifying as a Gael, or preferring not to say, falls in the mid-range correlations for Gaelic-negative members of the factors. Furthermore, it is remarkable that the three highest positive factors for Gaelic (in relation to the Gaelic-positive subgroups) are consistent in their position of relevance in both Gaelic practice and Gaelic ability:

identify as a Gael (4.02 English use score; 3.45 Gaelic ability score);

supportive to Gaelic (4.21 English use score; 2.93 Gaelic ability score);

at least one Gaelic-speaking parent (4.33 English use score; 2.51 Gaelic ability score).

In summary, those with more positive values in Gaelic-related factors have significantly lower English use scores and higher Gaelic ability scores. Gaelic vitality is substantially higher among those who have acquired their Gaelic from their parent(s) rather than from a (pre)school context. And, of the six sociolinguistic factors analysed, the three factors of pupil identity, pupil favourability towards Gaelic, as well as parental ability in Gaelic, evince the highest values of Gaelic vitality.

4.10 SECONDARY SCHOOL PUPILS: FOCUS GROUP DISCUSSIONS

This element of the IGRP consisted of a series of focus group discussions, held with S5 and S6 pupils aged between 15 and 18 in Western Isles' secondary schools, to gauge their views on the state of Gaelic in their areas and their views on the current situation of Gaelic in general. Eight 50-minute meetings were held with focus groups in the four Western Isles secondary schools (Sgoil MhicNeacail, Sgoil Sir E. Scott, Sgoil Lìonacleit and Sgoil Bhàgh a' Chaisteil) between 5 September 2016 and 5 October 2016. Four meetings were held with Gaelic-medium groups and four with English-medium groups, one for each language group in each school. There were six pupils in each of the groups (48 pupils in total), representing 15.7% of the 305 pupils who completed questionnaires. The two focus groups were run concurrently, but in separate rooms. Two IGRP team members were involved in each session, one to lead the discussion and ask questions, with the other to take notes. A teacher from each school was present at the initial phase of each focus group session in a supervisory and non-contributory capacity. In the following sections, we present a summary of the main points and recurring themes from these conversations.

4.10.1 GAELIC-MEDIUM FOCUS GROUPS

Participants in the Gaelic-medium focus groups were generally sympathetic towards efforts to develop the language and to improve its position as an integral component of the culture and heritage of the Western Isles. However, they also indicated that they felt disengaged from Gaelic agencies and their institutional policies, and that they had limited interaction with Gaelic organisations and support strategies.

4.10.1.1 *YOUTH PRACTICE AND ABILITY IN GAELIC LOCALLY*

In general, there was agreement among participants that Gaelic was in a weakened state and declining in use locally, and that many of the younger generation did not speak it. The reasons indicated by the young people for this situation included the following: insufficient numbers of children in Gaelic-medium education (GME);

a lack of continuity in GME for many secondary school subjects, leading to limitations in their own fluency in Gaelic; the increasing number of English-speaking monolinguals moving into formerly Gaelic-speaking areas; that their friends do not speak Gaelic, and an overall lack of confidence among the young in speaking Gaelic as they feel their spoken skills in Gaelic are not adequate as a basis for social interaction. They indicated that their ability to understand Gaelic was generally better than their spoken skills in the language. Some perceived their reading and writing skills to be more developed than their spoken skills, and that the older generations have better spoken skills than the pupils themselves. It was recognised that those who acquired Gaelic at home developed far greater fluency than those who learned Gaelic at school.

Many participants associated Gaelic use with traditional lifestyle practices such as crofting, rather than in youth networks. They acknowledged that the older generations had better Gaelic than younger generations, with grandparents having much better Gaelic than parents. They also claimed that Gaelic is much weaker in communities now than it was when their parents and grandparents were growing up, resulting in fewer opportunities to use the language in a range of social domains. They indicated that very few parents spoke Gaelic to children, even in circumstances when the parents had an adequate fluency in Gaelic. They claimed there is a general assumption among elderly members of the community that the young do not have adequate Gaelic to engage in social interaction with them through Gaelic.

Many of those indicating that they had an ability in Gaelic stated that they spoke the language at home, with their grandparents, at school (but only in the classroom), to older neighbours and older people. The pupils claimed they did not use Gaelic socially with each other outside the classroom. Some stated they spoke Gaelic every day, ranging from the odd word or phrase to more extended conversations in family settings. Many indicated that they did not speak any Gaelic outside an educational setting, with one participant stating it would be 'strange' to speak Gaelic outside the classroom. A significant majority of all those who attended these meetings pointed out that it is much 'easier' to speak English as most young people of their age do not have Gaelic.

4.10.1.2 *ATTITUDES TOWARDS GAELIC AND ITS FUTURE*

Participants in the Gaelic-medium focus groups felt that the young generation in general was not particularly supportive of Gaelic, especially if they did not take Gaelic as a subject in school. Whilst the participants indicated that they were sympathetic to the language and that Gaelic was important to many of them on a personal level, they were aware that more of an effort was required by young Gaelic speakers to use the language more frequently and to take pride in it, as they recognised that the onus was on the younger generation to maintain Gaelic in the future. Some stated that they had never spoken about Gaelic issues amongst themselves and that Gaelic was not something they had strong feelings about. Others indicated they were very proud that they could speak Gaelic.

In order to improve the standing of Gaelic, it was felt that more children should be encouraged to speak it by taking advantage of the existing opportunities to do so, such as Sradagan (Gaelic activity clubs) and to speak Gaelic as much as possible. It was proposed that those who lack confidence in their Gaelic ability should be encouraged and supported by providing more opportunities to use Gaelic outside of a school setting.

Their discussion on Gaelic in the school system focused mainly on the issue of enhancing Gaelic-medium education (GME) in the islands. GME provision was seen by them as a vital aspect in stemming or reversing the trend of decline for Gaelic as a community language, with some participants maintaining that Gaelic would be stronger in future as the number of GME pupils increased. Some participants claimed that younger children coming through GME provision in the future could have better developed Gaelic skills than themselves, i.e. the teenage focus group participants, if GME continued to expand. Others suggested that Gaelic in the islands would be in a much weaker position in 20 years' time as the number of Gaelic speakers would continue to decline, with one participant stating that Gaelic would be stronger in big cities in mainland Scotland, rather than in the islands.

The issue of the use of Gaelic in social media emerged in the discussion also. Several participants suggested that the older generations do not recognise how much Gaelic is used on social media amongst younger Gaelic speakers, leading to older people being over-pessimistic about the future of the language.

Looking to the future use of Gaelic, some pupils indicated a desire to raise their own children in Gaelic. In the case of those who felt that they had not acquired Gaelic skills at a sufficiently high level to do so, many participants claimed that they would enrol their children in GME to ensure that their children would have the opportunity to learn Gaelic.

4.10.1.3 *VIEWS ON GAELIC ORGANISATIONS*

Many of the pupils were not aware of the specific roles and remits of agencies working on Gaelic development and promotion. In the cases where participants did identify public bodies that contribute to positive initiatives in support of Gaelic, some mentioned the work of BBC ALBA and Radio nan Gàidheal in enhancing the visibility of the language in Scotland. Fèisean nan Gàidheal and Comunn na Gàidhlig were praised by some for their work with young people, and Stòrlann for the resources it provided for schools. Besides being in general agreement that public bodies should support Gaelic, the overall perception from the focus groups was that Gaelic development issues only articulated in a marginal way with the lives of the young. In this context of the lack of engagement with formal initiatives, the young placed more emphasis on the need to promote the use of the language in the local community.

The Scottish Government was seen as being supportive of the language. Many welcomed the increased job opportunities for Gaelic speakers provided by organisations such as BBC ALBA and Radio nan Gàidheal. Out of the four meetings, Bòrd na Gàidhlig was mentioned as having a role in the maintenance of Gaelic by only one participant. Similarly, the participants were unaware of the local authority's role in Gaelic development in their area.

4.10.2 ENGLISH-MEDIUM FOCUS GROUPS

The English-medium focus groups followed the same format as the Gaelic-medium sessions. In general, the participants in these groups indicated considerably weaker levels of Gaelic ability in comparison to the ability levels stated by the participants in the Gaelic sessions. However, their analysis of the societal presence and practice of Gaelic in the islands corresponded to that of the Gaelic-medium focus groups. In contrast with the Gaelic-medium focus group, attitudes regarding the language ranged from mild support to negative feelings, and in some cases hostility towards it. Overall, the attitude expressed towards the future of Gaelic was one of apathy, with many participants adopting a neutral position towards its current fragile state.

4.10.2.1 *YOUTH PRACTICE AND ABILITY IN GAELIC LOCALLY*

Similar to the Gaelic-medium focus groups, Gaelic was perceived to be much weaker now than in the past, and that its use in homes or in the wider community was in decline, although some stated they heard quite a lot of Gaelic around them on a daily basis. The older generations were considered to have better Gaelic than the younger age groups. Participants indicated that the younger generation lacked confidence in speaking the language, though some in the English-medium focus groups pointed out that they could understand Gaelic reasonably well and that they could read and write it to an extent. Most stated that they could not hold a conversation in Gaelic, beyond a few simple phrases. In general, participants in the English-medium focus groups emphasised language attitudes and future prospects for Gaelic, rather than discussing their own Gaelic-language ability and practice.

Among the reasons given for the current situation of Gaelic, many participants were of the opinion that Gaelic was not seen as appealing, interesting, useful or relevant to the majority of the younger generation, apart from the opportunities of Gaelic-medium jobs. It was stated that the young generation is not very supportive of Gaelic development in general, with many expressing the feeling that Gaelic development efforts were a waste of time, as competence in English is pervasive. Many contributions to discussions on the decline of Gaelic in the islands focused on the perceived lack of interest and ability in the language, the higher utility, the wider communicative function and 'easiness' of English, as against the limited utility of Gaelic and its weakness in the community. Gaelic was generally seen by participants as a school subject, rather than being of practical use to them. One attendee did not know anyone of her age group who spoke Gaelic regularly outside of school. GME was not, on its own, perceived as an adequate intervention to halt the decline of the language, though it was acknowledged as an important component in Gaelic development.

4.10.2.2 *ATTITUDES TOWARDS GAELIC AND ITS FUTURE*

Some participants were mildly positive about Gaelic, seeing it as a part of the Western Isles' tradition, culture and communal heritage, stating that more should be done to encourage people to learn Gaelic. Others said that they felt pressure from members of older generations to carry on the use of Gaelic and to speak more Gaelic. They suggested that encouragement and support for younger people to use Gaelic would be more effective than reliance primarily on institutional approaches associated with GME provision. However, the overall perception from the English-medium focus groups was that of indifference regarding the fragility of Gaelic.

Hearing older people speak Gaelic made some pupils wish they could speak it themselves, and some regretted not being able to speak it. The idea that being bilingual 'looks good on your CV' was also mentioned and some participants felt that Gaelic as a 'selling point' for the tourism industry and the economy in the islands was important. They indicated, however, that these positive feelings do not in themselves motivate them to learn or to use Gaelic. In their discussion of future prospects for Gaelic and their intentions for their own children, some indicated that they intended to enrol them in GME, but the majority did not intend to do so.

Some negative sentiments were expressed regarding what was seen as 'favouritism' or 'special treatment' for Gaelic-medium pupils, leading to complaints that GME pupils had access to privileges unavailable to non-GME pupils. Others felt that too much money was being spent on the language, at a time when aspects of island life and infrastructure were in need of modernisation. Mixed views were expressed on the future of the language: one participant indicated that he/she would be 'proud' if Gaelic was no longer spoken in the Western Isles in 20 years; another pupil said that the thought of no Gaelic being spoken in the future as 'very scary'. Participants also had mixed views on whether Gaelic would be in a weaker or stronger state in years to come. One participant expressed the view that Gaelic promotion would be more successful if the language was more 'useful' in everyday life. However, the general feeling across the English-medium focus groups was that of apathy towards Gaelic's future survival.

4.10.2.3 *VIEWS ON GAELIC ORGANISATIONS*

Similar to the discussion in the Gaelic-medium focus groups, the participants indicated that they were not particularly aware or informed about the Gaelic promotion activities of various public bodies. Bòrd na Gàidhlig, the Scottish Government, Highland Council, Comunn na Gàidhlig, BBC ALBA and Radio nan Gàidheal were mentioned unprompted in general terms as being supportive of Gaelic promotion, but the pupils did not indicate in specific terms how the activities of these public bodies impinged on the pupils' experience of Gaelic, besides GME-related issues. Comhairle nan Eilean Siar was mentioned in relation to the provision of GME. Some pupils were aware of Gaelic bodies having visited their schools on one or two occasions, but only to talk to the Gaelic-medium pupils.

4.10.3 CONCLUSIONS FROM FOCUS GROUP DISCUSSIONS

The fragility of vernacular Gaelic was addressed candidly by the pupils in the focus groups. Much of their contributions correspond to the other results of the IGRP survey. There was a greater general level of Gaelic ability and support for Gaelic and its heritage in the Gaelic-medium focus groups than in the English-speaking groups, with the former showing more sympathy and the latter more antipathy or indifference towards Gaelic. The main themes discussed in the teenage focus groups were the general decline in intergenerational transmission of Gaelic as few parents speak Gaelic to children; the pupils' own lack of ability in Gaelic, including a lack of conversational ability and confidence, in particular in comparison to older generations; the greater levels of Gaelic attainment among home-acquirers than among school-acquirers of Gaelic; the low levels of Gaelic-speaking by the young; the dominance of English ability and practice among the young, rendering Gaelic largely redundant in their social practice; their limited engagement with Gaelic language-awareness and support strategies, and with Gaelic organisations and bodies (with the relative exception of Gaelic television). Pupils felt support for Gaelic would need to provide more encouragement and opportunities for Gaelic-speaking among the young, greater uptake of and continuity in GME, greater effort by young people to support Gaelic, including their own commitment to bring up their children in Gaelic or enrol them in GME. The majority in the English-speaking focus groups indicated they did not intend to enrol their children in GME. The English-speaking groups also voiced concerns on the waste or unfair channelling of resources on Gaelic and Gaelic speakers. Some pupils recognised the socio-economic and cultural significance of

Gaelic, while others felt the importance of the level of Gaelic in social media was not appreciated by older people.

4.11 CONCLUSIONS

The conclusions, emerging from the data and information generated by the survey of language use amongst teenage pupils in the Western Isles, reflect the same general sociolinguistic issue raised by the perceptions among preschool staff of the Gaelic language use and linguistic ability of preschool children, i.e. the marginal societal practice of Gaelic in the islands. Table 4.27 provides an overview of the key summary data from the survey of the teenagers by Pooled Study Districts, as well as All Rural Areas (i.e. Study Districts outwith Stornoway; All Rural Areas = all Pooled SDs except the Pooled SD of Stornoway & Suburbs).

Pooled Study District	Mother from the islands (%)	Father from the islands (%)	Mother and father fluent in Gaelic (%)	Pupils reported fluent in Gaelic (%)	Always or mainly speak Gaelic to their parents (%)	Always or mainly speak Gaelic to their friends (%)	Always or mainly speak Gaelic to their neighbours (%)
Lewis N&W (N = 49)	58.4	58.4	40.8	32.7	12.6	4.3	12.5
Lewis E (N = 80)	61.5	65.8	17.5	18.8	5.1	1.3	13.1
Harris (N =37)	54.0	55.5	42.9	21.6	8.4	0.0	5.6
North Uist, Benbecula (N = 19)	55.5	83.4	27.8	26.4	5.3	0.0	5.3
South Uist, Barra & Vatersay (N = 30)	60.7	72.4	30.0	20.0	0.0	0.0	10.7
Stornoway & Suburbs (N = 78)	72.0	53.4	5.5	14.1	1.3	1.3	2.6
Research Area (Western Isles)	61.2	60.6	18.4	20.3	5.1	1.3	8.2
All Rural Areas (N = 215) Areas other than Stornoway	58.8	64.8	29.7	23.4	6.6	1.4	10.6

Table 4.27 *Percentages of parental origin, parental ability and pupils' Gaelic ability and practice, by Pooled Study Districts and All Rural Areas*

The data in the table clearly illustrate that Gaelic is not the main language of communication between teenagers and their parents. In one Pooled SD (South Uist, Barra & Vatersay), none of the teenagers providing a response to the survey reported that they either *Always* or *Mainly* spoke Gaelic to their respective parents. This is despite the finding that 30% of both parents were fluent in Gaelic and with 30% of teenagers self-reporting that they also were capable of speaking Gaelic. In three of the Pooled SDs (Harris; North Uist & Benbecula; and South Uist, Barra & Vatersay), the teenagers self-reported that they never spoke Gaelic *Always* or *Mainly* to their friends. Overall, in all areas outside Stornoway, slightly less than 7% of teenagers reported speaking Gaelic to their parents *Always* or *Mainly,* despite the finding that around 30% of parents were reported as being fluent in the language. No Pooled SD had more than 45% of both parents fluent in Gaelic. These findings broadly reflect data from the 2011 Scotland Census, in which 40% of the Western Isles age cohort of between 18 to 39 years reported that they could speak Gaelic (close to the 35.5% of parents in the Teenager Survey) and 41.9% of the age group of 3 to 17 years were reported as speaking Gaelic according to the Census returns (National Records of Scotland, table DC2120SC; the non-standard output in Table 2.5 (2.4.1.1) yields 41.3% for this age cohort in the Western Isles).

4.11.1 ABILITY, PRACTICE AND ATTITUDES TOWARDS GAELIC

The primary point to emerge from the analysis in this chapter is that the Gaelic language exists at the margins of the daily lives and personal interests of the majority of teenagers across the Western Isles. Chapter 4 provides the added dimension in the IGRP of self-reported data and complements the data in Chapter 3, in which informants reported on preschoolers attending their facility.

The evidence presented in this chapter brings to a sharper focus the findings concerning the decline in Gaelic from the census data in Chapter 2 and the marginality of Gaelic practice and ability amongst preschool children in Chapter 3. From the perspective of these three data sets, it appears indisputable that the islands now comprise English-language dominant communities, with Gaelic playing a supporting role as a historical linguistic inheritance associated with the oldest and previous generations. The evidence as reported by the teenagers participating in the survey indicates low levels of ability, practice and participation in Gaelic-speaking activities so that, for the most part, there is a disassociation of this age group from the traditional Gaelic linguistic and cultural heritage of their respective island communities. The evidence of the Teenager Survey points to:
- Low levels of ability in all dimensions of Gaelic competence
- Marginal levels of practice of the language across domains of usage
- Marginal presence of Gaelic in their experience of primary and secondary schooling
- Common indifference to the place of Gaelic in their lives
- A pessimistic perspective, but also somewhat contradictory opinions, on the future of Gaelic within families and communities in the islands.

A number of the survey questions (with results given in Figures 4.8, 4.13, 4.17 and 4.18) sought to ascertain the levels of Gaelic and English ability amongst the teenagers. The evidence clearly shows the small proportion of pupils indicating the highest ability in Gaelic, with only 14% (43 pupils) self-reporting that they considered themselves to have native speaker fluency in Gaelic. In contrast, 54% (164 pupils) indicated that they had little or no ability to speak Gaelic. Gaelic fluency attainment in the most competent categories is closely associated with a Western Isles' background, with some 80% of those who report being comfortable in conversational Gaelic being from the islands. However, a key finding (Figure 4.10) indicates that most respondents, i.e. 56% of pupils, acquire their ability in Gaelic from attendance at (pre)school. The next highest source of acquisition is from the pupils' grandmothers. This is in itself an indicator of the overall weakness of familial and/or communal transmission of Gaelic to the next generation. In relation to conversational and topic-based fluency in Gaelic, the findings given in Figure 4.17 show 3 pupils (1%) can hold a conversation more comfortably in Gaelic than in English. Figure 4.18 reveals the percentages of pupils claiming to have *No difficulty* in Gaelic when discussing topics relating to *Sport* (18.2%), *Films* (14.3%), *Music* (13.2%) and *Computers* (8.8%) are lower than the percentage of pupils who claim fluency in Gaelic (20.3%, Figure 4.8). In the results of the topic-based fluency data, the Gaelic-fluent pupils indicate that they have a higher level of function in English than for equivalent skills in Gaelic.

4.11.1.1 *HOUSEHOLD PRACTICE AND TRANSFER OF GAELIC*

The reported use of Gaelic in homes in the Western Isles for this young age cohort is low. Only 12 pupils (4.1%) indicate they speak *Always* or *Mainly* Gaelic at home (Figure 4.28), with four (1.3%) reporting that they *Always* or *Mainly* speak Gaelic to their friends (Figure 4.26). We can compare the levels of Gaelic use in households as reported in the Teenager Survey, on the one hand, with the percentage of Gaelic-speaking Family Households which was attained from the 2011 Census, on the other. In the teenage data, a percentage of c. 7% of parents speak *Always* or *Mainly* Gaelic to pupils (Figure 4.19), and 4.1% of pupils indicate they speak *Always* or *Mainly* Gaelic at home (Figure 4.28). Therefore, the percentages of Gaelic household use in the teenage data, i.e. between c. 7% and 4%, is substantially lower than the proportion of 19.4% Gaelic-speaking Family Households which was attained from the 2011 Census data (Table 2.7, section 2.4.1.3). In relation to the parents' use of Gaelic with pupils (Table 4.19 and Figure 4.20), it was reported that only six fathers (2.1%) and 10 mothers (3.4%) *Always* speak Gaelic to their children; with 22 mothers (7.4%) and 20 fathers (6.9%) speaking *Always* or *Mainly* Gaelic.

The Teenager Survey demonstrates that the transmission of Gaelic within families is at an extremely low level, with English being the predominant language spoken by pupils, both with their parents and their siblings (Figures 4.19–4.25). The questions relating to pupil interaction with other members of the community (Figures 4.26–4.28) indicate that English dominance continues with all age cohorts and in different social settings, including with friends and neighbours. The detail of the data findings concerning language use over time indicates that slightly more Gaelic was spoken by mothers, fathers and siblings to pupils up to age nine, after which less Gaelic was used to and by the pupils in their social interactions. A consistent pattern of increased English-language use was established after that age, suggesting that peer-group socialisation through English becomes a more dominant factor in establishing language use around that age, rather than familial language practice. In other words, the findings show more Gaelic familial use by respondents at ages 5–8 than at present (15–18 years old). Figure 4.21 shows 36 pupils *Always* or *Mainly* spoke Gaelic to their mothers when aged 5–8, as compared with 19 pupils presently, whilst Figure 4.22 indicates 35 pupils *Always* or *Mainly* spoke Gaelic to their fathers aged 5–8, compared with 14 at present. This represents a reduction in about half of the previously Gaelic-speaking younger cohort. This pattern of decreasing familial Gaelic use by pupils as they grow older is also noted in relation to language use with siblings and friends.

Clearly, the attainment of Gaelic ability in a familial or community setting is now an exceptional practice. This non-normative aspect of Gaelic is compounded by the evidence which suggests that whilst young people may acquire Gaelic in (pre)school, the level of ability and use will inevitably remain limited due to a lack of peer and community socialisation in Gaelic. About two thirds of the parents of this teenage cohort are from the Western Isles, with Figure 4.2 showing 354 parents (61%) of that origin. In addition, 103 fathers (37.5%) and 97 mothers (33.7%) are reported as being fluent in Gaelic, with 94% of the total of these Gaelic-fluent parents being native speakers. This actual Gaelic-fluent base of over a third of parents has transferred a marginal social practice of Gaelic to the subsequent generation, i.e. the teenagers surveyed here. The sizeable contraction in the minority-language active speaker-group from one generation to the next, e.g. 9.3% of parents with Gaelic-dominant language practice with each other, in contrast with 3.5% Gaelic-dominant teenagers with each other (Figure 4.31, section 4.6.6), can be compared to the threshold phenomena discussed in section 2.4.1.5.1.

As we saw in Table 4.9, 35.5% of parents are reported as being fluent in Gaelic. The difference in reported ability for those with fluent Gaelic between the parental generation and the pupil cohort surveyed is around 15 percentage points. Table 4.27 shows that 18.4% of pupils have two Gaelic-fluent parents. However, the data for the language spoken by mothers and fathers with their children such as in Figure 4.31 (language use among different family members, including between parents and children), which indicate that 16 mothers (5.5%) and 15 fathers (5.2%) *Always* or *Mainly* speak Gaelic with their children, highlight the disparity between ability in Gaelic and its familial use.

As for those pupils who report Gaelic acquisition, the survey responses in Figure 4.11 indicate that the young are more likely to have fluent or good Gaelic (74.1%)

if Gaelic is acquired from both parents. However, the familial (parental) transfer of Gaelic is now roughly as common as acquisition from (pre)school and from the grandparents (sources of ability in Gaelic, Figure 4.10). The findings clearly show that higher levels of proficiency in Gaelic are associated with home-based and wider familial acquisition.

In relation to ability, Figure 4.8 shows that 18 of the 61 survey respondents reporting as fluent speakers (29.5% of the total) indicate they acquired their fluency from (pre) school. This rapid decline in familial transmission has clear negative implications for practice and ability in Gaelic. This is illustrated in section 4.9.1 with less practice and ability in Gaelic among (pre)school-acquirers than among home-acquirers, and is pointed out by the pupils themselves (4.10.1.1, 4.10.3) and by Müller (2006). Figure 4.23a (4.6.2) shows that there is consistent intergenerational loss between parental practice taken as input and the pupils' practice to parents taken as output. In the top three categories of Gaelic use (*Always*, *Mainly* and *mix*), the least intergenerational loss is found for mothers who speak *Always Gaelic* to their children. In fact, mothers have greater success than fathers in setting higher levels of familial Gaelic practice. This greater maternal influence on language transfer is also found in the acquisition of *Another language* (4.6.2). A central element in Gaelic familial decline is that the younger age groups are less functional in Gaelic and they have low levels of practice and ability at present, and they are even less likely to speak Gaelic once they have left the education system.

The data supplied by the teenagers correspond to the data from other modules of the IGRP survey, and other sociolinguistic descriptions, in that a mixed language practice (*Gaelic and English mix*) is more common than practice of *Always* or *Mainly* Gaelic. There is a small increase through age grades in monolingual English practice (increased *Always English* with fathers in Figure 4.22, section 4.6.2; Figure 4.23a; but relatively stable numbers of *Always English* in Figure 4.27 with neighbours). Furthermore, the greatest intergenerational loss between parents and children is found between mixed-practice parents and their children, i.e. 'the highest percentage loss for language practice of both mothers and fathers is in the category of *Gaelic and English mix*' (4.6.2).

4.11.1.2 *LOSS OF COMMUNITY PRACTICE AND SOCIETAL REINFORCEMENT OF GAELIC*

The decline in Gaelic use in the family over time is also reflected in the findings concerning communal or social use of Gaelic. Only four secondary school pupils in the IGRP age cohort report they *Always* or *Mainly* speak Gaelic to their friends now, compared to 18 who *Always* or *Mainly* spoke Gaelic to their friends when aged five to eight (Figure 4.26). These findings contrast with the findings for Gaelic use with neighbours, which retain more stable levels of Gaelic use as pupils grow older (Figure 4.27).

Additionally, Gaelic use is very limited in wider social settings (Figure 4.28). The greatest number of pupils who *Always* speak Gaelic do so in their own home (seven pupils, 2.4%) or in the nearest village or town (five pupils, 1.7%). Other settings range from four to two pupils *Always* speaking Gaelic. The greatest number of pupils who speak *Mainly Gaelic* do so in a nearby town or village (ten pupils, 3.4%), with other settings ranging from five to two pupils speaking *Mainly Gaelic*.

The most common reason given by pupils for speaking English to Gaelic speakers was that they are used to speaking English to them (Figure 4.29). As regards their feelings on this issue, most pupils are indifferent to speaking English with people who are capable of speaking Gaelic. 25 pupils (15% of respondents to the question) indicate that they would prefer to speak Gaelic to those who have Gaelic.

The data presented in Chapter 4 clearly illustrate that the crucial combined dynamic of Gaelic socialisation within families and youth peer-group reinforcement is now almost non-existent, according to the reports by the teenagers in this Western Isles survey group. The current situation, as also indicated in Chapters 2 and 3, shows that the communal linguistic resilience of the Gaelic native speaker group has collapsed. The evidence from the Teenager Survey highlights that the language is no longer practiced or regarded by the young people currently resident in the islands as a normal language of community socialisation to any appreciable level. Given that the Western Isles represent the last-remaining spatial extent of Gaelic communal practice, the marginal practice of Gaelic among the young of these islands signals the assimilation of the last social habitats for Gaelic into English-speaking social norms, similar to the spatial and social context of the rest of Scotland. In short, the pupils' testimony indicates the final stages of the socio-geographic collapse of the Gaelic community.

4.11.1.3 *ATTITUDES, PERCEPTIONS TOWARDS GAELIC AND IDENTITY AS GAEL*

Whilst 50.7% of pupils are either in favour or strongly in favour of Gaelic, 49.3% are indifferent or against the language (Figure 4.36). There is a strong correspondence between higher levels of competence in Gaelic and being in favour of Gaelic (Figure 4.37, 4.7.1). The reasons for being in favour of Gaelic indicate instrumental or economic motives (the perceived advantages of bilingualism and the potential employment opportunities afforded by competence in Gaelic: Figure 4.39). Those pupils indicating that they are not in favour of Gaelic cite their lack of daily use of it and a preference for receiving education through English as the most common reasons (4.7.2). Nevertheless, there is inconsistency in some of the responses relating to the pupils' perception of Gaelic, their sense of cultural identity, and aspirations for the future use of Gaelic. For example, whilst pupils report positively on the strength of the language within their respective localities (Figure 4.41), this does not correlate with the pupils' own use of Gaelic or communal and social use of Gaelic (Figures 4.28, 4.32, 4.33, 4.35).

Furthermore, a small majority of responses indicate that pupils would be a little unhappy or very unhappy should no children be raised through Gaelic in the Western Isles (see **Figure A4.9** in **Appendix A4.15**), with 41.2% of responses (Figure 4.47) indicating that pupils intend to raise their own children in Gaelic. However, when this intention is compared with Gaelic ability (Figure 4.8, 20.3% fluent in Gaelic) and practice (Figure 4.26, 90.6% *Always* or *Mainly* speak English to their friends), the aspiration is not grounded in current reality.

Local people who speak Gaelic and Gaelic development bodies are felt to be more supportive of the language than the teenagers themselves (4.7.3). A related response indicates that the pupils consider themselves to be among the least supportive of Gaelic (Figure 4.40). In addition, 51.4% of pupils feel that Gaelic will be a little or a lot weaker in 20 years (Figure 4.45). When the attitudinal data are taken in conjunction with the tenor of the focus group discussions, we find that there is a widespread belief among the pupils that the language will have little relevance or limited value to them in the years ahead.

The findings on identity show 32.6% of the teenagers identify as Gaels (Figure 4.48) in the binary, and a lower percentage identify as Gaels than for Scottish, Local or British identity (Figure 4.53) in the multiple option question. There is a strong correlation between identity as a Gael, ability to converse in the language and a familial practice of Gaelic (Figure 4.51). The results from the survey portray a high level of disassociation from Gaelic identity (Figure 4.48 shows 55.3% of respondents not self-identifying as Gaels) and a high degree of indifference and some hostility in evidence towards the Gaelic language (e.g. Figures 4.36, 4.42 and 4.44). These findings indicate a significant difference of opinion from the research of MacNeil and Stradling (2001) in the Highlands and Islands, when 90% of respondents in that survey indicated that Gaelic usage was an integral element of their perception of themselves as individuals. Additionally, the diminishing bond of association and identity with Gaelic resonates very strongly with the Graffman *et al.* (2014) study where young people in Scotland clearly associated the language as a construct of the school setting and generally the language of older people.

4.11.2 INPUT-OUTPUT LOSS; ABILITY-PRACTICE DISPARITY

Where parents have a Western Isles' background and/or fluency in Gaelic, it is more likely that pupils will have some Gaelic ability themselves. Parental and familial competence in, and use of, Gaelic in the home is associated with greater levels of Gaelic ability in respondents. When we compare parental language input to pupil language output (4.6.2), we see that there is a strong tendency of increased English output from pupils to parents, and that parental input of Gaelic-English mix loses the greatest number and percentage of children to increased English output. The least percentage loss of Gaelic parental input is found for mothers who speak *Always Gaelic*. The greater apparent success of monolingual parental Gaelic input, as seen in child output, accords with other minority-language studies (Gathercole and Thomas 2009; O'Toole and Hickey 2017) of parental strategies for optimising minority-language input to acquisition. By the same token, the least apparent success of the mixed language mode of input for Gaelic acquisition in this cohort finds corroboration in its test for significance ($X^2 = 28.160$, p. < 0.05). Furthermore, Figure 4.26 shows social use of Gaelic among pupils' peer-groups is extremely weak (four pupils or 1.3% of the overall cohort always or mainly speaking Gaelic to their friends now), and much weaker than the relatively low reported ability levels for spoken Gaelic within the cohort as a whole (Figure 4.8, 61 fluent pupils, 20.3%). The contrast is therefore between 20.3% fluent pupils and 1.3% Gaelic practice.

4.11.3 FUTURE FOR VERNACULAR GAELIC; ABILITY–PRACTICE DISPARITY IN CENSUS AND PUBLIC POLICY

Only a relatively small proportion of the pupils are acquiring fluent ability in Gaelic (be that from parents, education, or older generations). As stated, all the IGRP evidence shows that the successful intergenerational transfer of Gaelic is now exceptional (4.5.2, 4.6.2). Teenage peer practice of Gaelic is very rare. In considering the future trajectory for the language, there are considerable public-policy challenges to be addressed if Gaelic is to have any chance of revival as the language of the community, not least of which is the demographic structure of the islands and the future projections indicating continuing depopulation (2.3.4).

The disparity between reported ability in Gaelic and actual social use clearly indicates that census ability data cannot be interpreted as a social reality. This highlights the dangers of focusing solely on selected ability data from the census as a basis to support revitalisation initiatives (2.2). Relying on a combination of insufficiently-detailed ability statistics and levels of GME provision as the main bases for revitalisation strategies cannot serve as reliable indicators of positive Gaelic practice and attainment of functioning ability. Whilst there was indeed a small percentage improvement in the 2011 Scotland Census for the number of young people reporting an ability in spoken Gaelic, the overwhelming counter-evidence from the Teenager Survey shows that vernacular Gaelic is in crisis (and beyond the communal vernacular residual phase (2.4.3) for among young people).

4.11.4 EDUCATIONAL PROBLEMS AND POSSIBLE YOUTH INTERVENTIONS TO REVERNACULARISE GAELIC

The evidence of both the communal decline of Gaelic and the low levels of Gaelic competence among the teenage cohort indicates that without a community-wide revival of Gaelic, the loss of vernacular Gaelic will continue. Without a societal revival, the education system alone cannot effectively revive vernacular Gaelic (clearly evidenced, for example, in Chapter 3; and sections 4.2.1; 4.9.1; 8.4; 8.4.2). A shift to sole dependence on the school system for creating the next generation of fluent Gaelic speakers who are capable of contributing to its communal practice is not credible, both as a public policy assumption and as a basis for allocation of resources. The extent of the challenge involved in addressing this situation is evidenced in the current state of Gaelic educational provision. The main secondary school in the Western Isles, the Nicolson Institute in Stornoway, has provision for only 20% of teaching through Gaelic (Bòrd na Gàidhlig, Education Data 2016–17). A combination of the general weakness in the provision of education through Gaelic with the English-dominant peer practice at preschool (3.2.4) and at secondary school (Figure 4.28, 4.6.4) does little to assist with the maintenance of vernacular Gaelic in island families and communities. In the present context, the main function of Gaelic for the youth of the Western Isles is the curricular practice of Gaelic and possible cultural, educational or heritage value (4.10). Our results concur with the O'Hanlon *et al.* (2012: 35) reported finding that the use of Gaelic among pupils declines in the transition from primary to secondary school. This is not surprising for two main reasons: (1) the secondary schooling curriculum of the Western Isles is English-language dominant; and (2) the almost total dominance of English in peer-group socialisation has already set the context for the social exclusion of Gaelic from the lives of the young, as illustrated in Chapter 3 for preschoolers. In this context of the social and educational dominance of English, while the older generations are more likely to be competent users of Gaelic's 'elaborated code', the younger speakers' competences are more likely to be constrained by their limited exposure to a 'restricted code'.[47]

The acceleration of decline in vernacular Gaelic is likely to continue unless some radical remedial policies and practices are agreed and implemented in an integrated manner across families, schools and communities. We set out possible revitalisation initiatives for vernacular Gaelic in Chapter 9. We can outline briefly here, however, some core themes based on the results from the Teenager Survey. In any Gaelic youth revernacularisation efforts in the Western Isles it would be necessary to:

- Maximise educational supports, including full Gaelic immersion

---

47 See Bernstein (1971) on 'restricted and elaborated codes' in his sociological analysis of variance in language codes, and how Hulstijn (2017) distinguishes 'Basic Language Cognition' from 'Higher Language Cognition' as a way of measuring language proficiency.

- Address intergenerational failings in Gaelic acquisition, attainment and practice
- Increase Gaelic-dominant familial practice
- Encourage Gaelic-competent parents to raise their children through Gaelic
- Maximise socialisation through Gaelic
- Increase Gaelic-dominant communal practice
- Increase Gaelic-dominant engagement of the young with competent Gaelic speakers, most of whom are older, both in educational and communal contexts
- Provide digitally available records of Gaelic cultural, ethnographic and linguistic resources and as extensive a repository as possible in Gaelic for future generations (as suggested in Ó Giollagáin and Ó Curnáin 2016: 66; see for example the recordings of the Stòras Beò nan Gàidheal/An Taisce Ghaelach project)[48]
- Promote a positive, productive Gaelic identity among young people.

As set out in greater detail in Chapter 9, a more ambitious set of public-policy interventions focused on the use of Gaelic within families and the general community would be required if Gaelic is to have a social future in the islands.

---

48 Recordings available at: http://www.soillse.ac.uk/en/storas-beo-nan-gaidheal-sample/.

5 COMMUNITY SOCIOLINGUISTIC SURVEY OF GAELIC USE AND ATTITUDES IN THREE ISLANDS

5.1 INTRODUCTION

Chapters 5 and 6 set out the findings of the Community Survey module of the IGRP which comprises two related surveys of three small island communities. This chapter presents the main descriptive statistics from the Community Sociolinguistic Survey (CSS) of Gaelic practice and attitudes to Gaelic in three islands in the Western Isles where Gaelic was until recently dominant: Scalpay (in North Harris SD), Grimsay (in North Uist (south & east) SD) and Eriskay (in South Uist (south) SD). Each of these small islands is now connected by causeway or bridge to a larger neighbouring island.

The data presented in this chapter comprises the first of two inter-related surveys conducted independently of each other. The first survey (CSS) takes a census-based approach with one respondent per household and aims to assess community-wide trends in Gaelic language use, practice and attitudes. The second survey of the Community Survey module is the Speaker Typology Survey (STS), which gathers data from one local advisor per island, as set out in Chapter 6. In addition to the findings of the CSS, this chapter also summarises the main points made in 13 community consultations in the Research Area on the situation of vernacular Gaelic in the respective communities (5.7).

This IGRP module comprises a detailed quantitative sociolinguistic survey of three indicative traditional Gaelic communities in the Western Isles, and establishes the language competences and practices, as well as the speaker types, aggregated according to age cohorts. The approach adopted in this module borrows, in part, from methodologies in Ó Giollagáin *et al.* (2007a; 2007b) for Irish Gaeltacht areas, and from the survey of Gillian Munro *et al.* (2011) of Shawbost in west Lewis. Community-based language support initiatives should be grounded in a comprehensive depiction and understanding of the actual dynamics in the bilingualised context of contemporary or historical Gaelic neighbourhoods. An understanding of these dynamics cannot be based on national census data alone, as discussed in section 5.2 (and 2.2; 4.11.3; 6.8).

By extending these methodologies, this module seeks to establish a comprehensive analysis of an as-wide-as-feasible geographic coverage, and among comparable communities within the upper ranges of Study District profiles for Gaelic ability identified in the 2011 Census for Scotland. Following the analysis of the SD data pertaining to section 2.4.3 (Figure 2.25), two of the SDs (i.e. North Harris SD, South Uist (south)), which contain the islands of Scalpay and Eriskay, are at the upper range of highest SD vitality category, which is the Residual nexus of Gaelic ability and Family Household use; and one SD (i.e. North Uist (south & east)), which contains the island of Grimsay, is in the mid-range vitality category, i.e. in the Interstitial nexus. Furthermore, it is likely that these three islands equalled or surpassed the average Gaelic vitality factors of the SDs of which they form a part.

5.1.1 AIMS OF COMMUNITY SURVEY MODULE

The Community Survey module of the IGRP, presented in Chapters 5 and 6, aimed to undertake a mixed-method census-based survey in three small island communities with greater Gaelic vitality than the mean in the Western Isles. The first part of this module, the CSS, gathered data seeking to determine:
- Socio-cultural background of the local population
- Reported abilities, practices and attitudes to Gaelic
- Views on the vitality or fragility of the social use of Gaelic.

The second part of the module, presented in Chapter 6, assesses:
- Demographic factors
- Linguistic background
- Prevalence of home-based transmission of Gaelic
- Prevalence of school-based acquisition and productive use of Gaelic
- Speaker typologies.

Given that Scalpay, Grimsay and Eriskay represent relatively strong Gaelic-language profiles, this module of the two inter-related community surveys offers potentially the most positive localised depiction of the current social condition of Gaelic. When assessed together with the research findings of the preschooler (Chapter 3) and the teenager (Chapter 4) IGRP modules, the Community Sociolinguistic Survey provides a detailed understanding of the sociolinguistic dynamics of Gaelic in the Western Isles.

5.2 LITERATURE REVIEW; DEMOLINGUISTICS (1881-2011) AND SOCIOLINGUISTIC APPROACHES

Table 5.1 is compiled from the data presented in Comhairle nan Eilean Siar (2019), Duwe (2003–2012), and Mac an Tàilleir (2006, 2015) and illustrates the Gaelic speaker population of each island, and their percentages where available, from 1881 to 2011.

Census Year	Number of Gaelic speakers (as % of **Scalpay** population)	Number of Gaelic speakers (as % of **Grimsay** population)	Number of Gaelic speakers (as % of **Eriskay** population)
1881	498 (92%)	286 (98%)	464 (99%)
1891	496 (93%)	262 (92%)	424 (93%)
1901	553 (92%)	270 (93%)	440 (92%)
1911	589	362	453
1921	624	315	427
1931	636	259	420
1951	541	236	330
1961	470	239	231
1971	483	193	219
1981	438 (94%)	181 (92%)	182 (94%)
1991	349 (96%)	173 (85%)	135 (80%)
2001	270 (84%)	143 (71%)	104 (78%)
2011	220 (76%)	102 (61%)	102 (74%)

Table 5.1 *Numbers and percentages of Gaelic speakers, by island, 1881–2011*

Scottish Census data (Table 5.1) show that Gaelic speaker densities remained high and relatively constant, above 92% in all three islands surveyed, until 1981, with subsequent contractions in speaker numbers from decade to decade, except for Scalpay. This decline, according to the census data, began later in Scalpay, which retained a Gaelic speaker density of 96% in 1991. Across the three islands, the pattern of decline in Gaelic speakers as a percentage of the population between 1981 and 2011 is similar: in Scalpay (falling from 94% to 76%) and Eriskay (falling from 94% to 74%), but more pronounced in Grimsay (falling from 92% to 61%). However, as will be shown in sections 5.4.2, 5.4.8 and 5.4.9, the gap highlighted in this chapter between Gaelic ability (62.9% of respondents were *Fluent*) and the social practice of the language (29.6% of children were reported to have fluency in Gaelic, whereas 5.9% were reported as speaking only in Gaelic to respondents) is an illustration of the descriptive weakness of census fluency data which cannot be used as an indicator of the societal prevalence of a minority language (see, for example, 4.11.3 and 6.8). This point is also made by Withers in his work (e.g. 1984a; 1988a) on the demography of Gaelic in Scotland which focuses on geo-historical trajectories, at country-wide, regional and sub-regional level, and provides a framework for contemporary demographic studies. Withers draws attention to the limitations of attempting to understand patterns of language use or language change based on speaker-group numbers without considering wider political and social influences (cp. 2.2; 4.11.3).

Studies of Gaelic and its communities, in the Western Isles in particular, have often been focused on ethnography and anthropology. John Lorne Campbell (1950) examined Gaelic in a sociological context and provided recommendations for its maintenance and revitalisation. Donald F. Campbell and Raymond A. MacLean (1974) studied the situation of Gaelic in Nova Scotia, Canada. Frank Vallee (1954) researched the social condition of Gaelic in Barra in the early post-WW II years, noting that Gaelic then acted as a key representation of (self-)identity for the community.

Among a number of valuable works founded on anthropological or ethnographic perspectives, Sharon Macdonald (1997; 1999), observing ideological fissures in the Gaelic revitalisation movement of the 1980s, noted that identity construction is fluid, and predicated on social relationships mediated by contestation and diversity. Consequently, feelings about Gaelic-oriented initiatives were likely to be guided by cultural value judgments rooted in the functionality of Gaelic in social networks. Over three decades had elapsed between Susan Parman's ethnographic fieldwork on the Isle of Lewis in the early 1970s and the second edition of her work which drew attention to the rapid change which has transformed a Western Isles community by a combination of internal and external influences, acknowledging, as she does, that while numbers and percentages of Gaelic speakers have both declined, Gaelic has — drawing on Macdonald's work (mentioned above) — "undergone a remarkable 'renaissance'", predicated heavily on institutional efforts (Parman 2005: 13). Fraser MacDonald (2005: 160) draws out Parman's 'particular concern' regarding how meaning is constructed within the social and linguistic processes of the crofting community, and how terminology including 'Celt', 'Gael', 'crofter' and 'Highlander' comes to be imbued with levels of meaning nationally and sub-nationally, with contemporary resonance in debates about Gaelic and cultural identity, following the Gaelic Language Act.

Jack Coleman's work (1976) in Carloway, Isle of Lewis, traces the general decline of Gaelic use along with an increasing rate of Gaelic-English bilingualism and the latter's influence on the social contexts of Gaelic language practice in the community, especially on socialisation processes among children. Emily McEwan-Fujita (2010), who carried out research in South Uist and Benbecula in 2003, provides a useful general overview of sociolinguistic fieldwork in Gaelic communities. Her work focuses on the ideological tensions associated with promoting revivalist aims in an ongoing language shift situation. More recently, Munro et al. (2011) carried out an extensive micro-study of the Shawbost community on the Isle of Lewis, looking at self-reported language ability, language practice and issues of identity. Nancy Dorian's hugely influential output (e.g. 1978; 1981) spanning a half-century of study, with a strong emphasis on the Gaelic of East Sutherland, has placed the Gaelic condition in the wider internationalised context of language endangerment. Her work highlights the influence of societal marginalisation on the processes of minority-language change and obsolescence. Dorian has developed the influential concepts of 'linguistic lag' and linguistic 'tip', as well as the concept of the 'semi-speaker' (see 6.2).

5.2.1 LANGUAGE LOYALTY AND ATTITUDES TOWARDS GAELIC

MacKinnon's considerable contribution to the field of Gaelic sociolinguistic research has been particularly valuable in providing an overview of the demolinguistics of Gaelic in Scotland. His work in the Isle of Harris between 1972 and 1974 was arguably the first of its kind providing an extensive sociolinguistic study of Gaelic and its speakers (1977: 4). MacKinnon (1977) depicted Gaelic as a minority language which maintained a communal function in certain social domains independently of networked-institutional supports or civic reinforcement. This study explored the social patterns of language usage and attitudes towards Gaelic, among primary school and secondary school pupils, as well as adults. MacKinnon found that Gaelic predominated over English for more than half of respondents in 35 of 55 language situations such as speaking to parents, praying, buying petrol or quarrelling, in which they were asked whether they would use Gaelic primarily. This study 'involved a questionnaire survey of a systematic sample of the adult population', with MacKinnon (1977: 167) concluding that: 'the significance of Gaelic within community life is seen essentially as being bound up with everyday behaviour patterns. Language maintenance is not perceived as being in any way connected with political institutions'.

MacKinnon and MacDonald's study of language attitudes on the islands of Harris and Barra (1980) included an attempt to relate the strongest language-loyal Gaelic speakers to their various social roles in their communities, as well as examining reading, writing and speaking ability, and levels of language and cultural transmission. MacKinnon carried out similar research in Cape Breton Island (1983), while further examining Gaelic maintenance and Gaelic community vitality in the Isle of Skye and in the Western Isles simultaneously during the mid- to late-1980s (e.g. MacKinnon 1987; 1994c). The common feature in these community studies was the contracting social domain for Gaelic.

In the context of employment on the Isle of Lewis in the late 1970s, Iain Prattis (1990) found, to his surprise, that oil industrialisation did not accelerate the decay of the Gaelic language. Rather, a 'labour force drawn from an expatriate pool … overwhelmingly committed to the Gaelic speech community' saw Gaelic spoken at home by high percentages from sample groups outside Stornoway, and among repatriated oil workers in Stornoway and its industrial catchment villages. Among non-oil workers in Stornoway, Gaelic speech at home was lower, and Prattis acknowledged that future phases of oil development may have different impacts on the speech group. Previously, Judith Ennew (1978; 1980) indicated the contrasts in the use of Gaelic in Lewis in differing social settings and domains.

MacKinnon carried out a small-scale pilot study of attitudes towards Gaelic in Perth in 1980, expanded to three districts of the Isle of Skye later that year, and then further developed into a national survey on attitudes towards Gaelic (MacKinnon 1981) which encompassed a quota sampling of 1 in 5,000 people aged 15 or over in the 'lowlands'; this in itself took in 10 locations in all major urban areas and in each major regional area, before looking at the picture in the Highland region, in Argyll and Bute, in Skye and Lochalsh, and in the Western Isles. MacKinnon (1981: 4) demonstrated: 'an almost consistent strengthening of responses in support of Gaelic in relation to increasing incidence of Gaelic speakers in the population'. This is, of course, consistent with IGRP findings (4.7.1; 4.9.2). Recent attitudinal research has demonstrated that the concept of an ability in Gaelic contributes to a sense of Scottish national identity for a proportion of the Scottish population, both in the Lowlands and Highlands. Catriona West and Alastair Graham (2011: 35–36) note: 'Those with any understanding of Gaelic were more likely to feel that it contributed to a sense of national identity (67% compared to 36% amongst those with no understanding). Amongst those with fluent Gaelic, almost all (92%) stated that Gaelic was important to their national identity. This was in turn linked to location, with 54% of those in the Highlands and Islands stating that Gaelic was important to their national identity (24% very important), increasing to 63% amongst those in the West Highlands and Islands'. Paterson, O'Hanlon, Ormston and Reid (2014) indicate that while 76% of their respondents feel Gaelic is either very or fairly important to Scottish heritage, 14% feel that speaking Gaelic is either very or fairly important in relation to being Scottish.

5.3 METHODOLOGY OF COMMUNITY SOCIOLINGUISTIC SURVEY

The Community Sociolinguistic Survey took a census-type approach based on a structured questionnaire, administered by six IGRP fieldworkers (five native Gaelic speakers and one fluent learner) with two fieldworkers per surveyed island. The survey also afforded respondents the opportunity to provide qualitative input. The survey was demographically comprehensive and involved a co-ordinated strategy of visiting all ordinarily-occupied households in each community. In the months before the fieldwork, lists of these households were drawn up by IGRP fieldworkers working with local community advisors who had in-group knowledge. It is important to acknowledge that data gathering was generally conducted during office working hours and this is likely to be a contributing factor in the age profile of respondents, depicted in 5.4.2, as those who were at home and able to respond to the survey tended to be in older age groups. The preferred method of completing the surveys was through interviews, using one completed questionnaire per household. The interviewer read out the questions to the respondent and marked the answers herself or himself on the questionnaire form. Respondents who found this method to be inconvenient were given a choice to complete the questionnaire by themselves, and the fieldworker either waited or returned after an agreed period of time to collect the completed questionnaire. Fieldwork was generally carried out through the medium of Gaelic with Gaelic-speaking respondents, but the answers of some Gaelic-speaking respondents were recorded on English-language questionnaires, and vice-versa. In all cases, respondents were given the freedom, due to ethical considerations, to ignore questions they found to be too sensitive or too burdensome to answer. It must be pointed out that it was not possible for the fieldworkers to administer questionnaires to all of the households in their designated island due to, among other reasons, potential respondents' ill health or absence from home, refusal to participate in the survey, and so on. Sociolinguistic information (not found in the CSS) on these households was, however, included in the local advisor's data provided to the Speaker Typology Survey (Chapter 6).

There was a total of 180 respondents in the three small islands, corresponding to a total of 180 households surveyed. These respondents were generally mature members of the households. The *respondents* answered a single questionnaire per household, and this generated information on a total survey cohort of 484 individuals or *reported residents*. The total population of the three islands, according to Census 2011, is 595. In this chapter, therefore, where questions or data pertain to all members of a community these individuals will be referred to as *reported residents* (i.e. all 484 individuals). Table 5.2 shows numbers and percentages of respondents per island as well as the total number of households and population in each island according to the 2011 Census.

Island	Respondents	% Respondents	Households	Population
Scalpay	70	38.9	138	289
Grimsay	59	32.8	80	167
Eriskay	51	28.3	73	139
All three islands	180	100.0	291	595

Table 5.2 Numbers and percentages of CSS questionnaire respondents, by island (Information for all households from: Scotland's Census 2011 — National Records of Scotland, Table QS402SC)

The questionnaire consisted of 25 questions. One of these was an open-ended question and the rest were closed questions, which were constructed to be answered through:

- Binary response (respondent has two options to choose from, e.g. *Yes* or *No*)
- Nominal-polytomous response (respondent has more than two unordered options, e.g. multiple responses)
- Bounded continuous response, for most questions (respondent is presented with a continuous scale, i.e. Likert scale).

The questions were arranged under the following five sections:

- Section A: Background
- Section B: Language ability
- Section C: Language practice
- Section D: Identity
- Section E: Opinions on Gaelic and its future.

As stated, the questionnaires were offered both in Gaelic and in English. 38.3% of the questionnaires were completed in Gaelic and 61.7% were completed in English. The comparative and aggregated findings for the three islands are presented in the following sections of this chapter; and data for specific islands are presented in a few instances, along with the corresponding aggregated discussion. For the unaggregated, i.e. island-specific, findings for Scalpay, Grimsay and Eriskay from the CSS, see **Appendix 5**.

5.4 AGE, GEOGRAPHIC BACKGROUND, LANGUAGE ABILITY AND HOUSEHOLD PRACTICE OF RESPONDENT, SPOUSE/PARTNER AND CHILDREN

This section presents the findings for all three islands, in comparative and aggregated format, on gender, age profile, place of origin, language ability, language background and language practice for respondents and their spouse/partner,[49] as well as for children in their household. This affords an overall picture of the demolinguistics of the three islands, as well as providing a baseline for comparison of variations or trends arising in, or between, the islands. Further aggregated data relating to respondents is available in **Appendix 5**. For comparative purposes, Gaelic ability (5.4.2.1) and age profiles (5.4.2.2) are also presented for *reported residents* (from STS, Chapter 6).

---

49 For the sake of brevity, where appropriate, we use the term spouse to refer to either spouse or partner.

5.4.1 RESPONDENT'S GENDER, AGE COHORT AND PLACE OF ORIGIN

In the first section of the CSS survey questionnaire, information was elicited on the gender and age cohort of the respondents. Of those whose gender was recorded, 84 (46.9%) were male and 94 (52.5%) were female. Figure 5.1 details the respondents' age profiles across all survey districts and for each of the three islands surveyed.

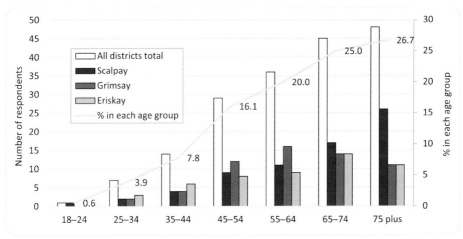

Figure 5.1 *Respondents' age cohort, by island and all districts (N = 180)*

The age profile of the respondents shows that the older age groups are more strongly represented. As the survey was largely conducted during office hours, the age bias among respondents is perhaps unsurprising: 71.7% of the respondents were 55 years old or over, and 83.2 % of the households did not contain school-age children. The median age of the total respondents was found to be in the 55–64 age cohort. 4.4% (eight individuals) of respondents were aged 18 to 34 (combining 18–24 (1) and 25–34 (7)), and 16.1% (29) were aged between 45 and 54. For a more detailed description and analysis of respondents' age profiles, see **Appendix 5**. Although it clearly should be kept in mind that the age profile of the respondents is biased towards the older age cohorts, the relevant age cohorts are illustrated in the analysis of the category of Gaelic ability; and the data on children's household language practice provides important details on the younger cohort (71 children in total, 5.4.4; 5.4.7; 5.4.9; 5.4.10; 5.8.2.2; and see extensive data on children's ability and practice in Chapter 6). The findings in Chapter 6 are closer to a full and representative sample.

Figure 5.2 displays the percentages of respondents' place of origin across the three islands and all islands together, according to six geographic categories.

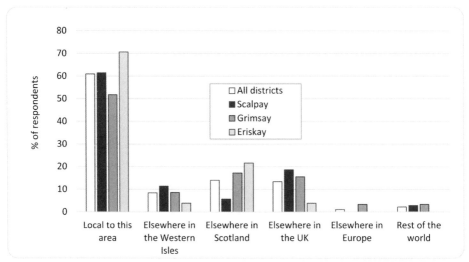

Figure 5.2 *Percentage of respondents' place of origin, by island and all districts (Ns = 179; 70, 58, 51)*

The majority of respondents indicated that they were *Local to this area*, with 60.9% stating that they were from one of the three islands surveyed, with a further 8.4% from *Elsewhere in the Western Isles*. 14% of the respondents came from *Elsewhere in Scotland* and another 13.4% came from *Elsewhere in the United Kingdom*, with 3.3% from outside the United Kingdom. Eriskay records the greatest percentages of respondents who are *Local to this area* (70.6%), and from *Elsewhere in Scotland* (21.6%). Scalpay records the greatest percentages of respondents from *Elsewhere in the Western Isles* (11.4%) and *Elsewhere in the UK* (18.6%).

5.4.2 RESPONDENT'S ABILITY IN SPOKEN GAELIC, BY AREA; BINARY ABILITY BY AGE

Figure 5.3 shows the percentages of respondents' ability in spoken Gaelic according to a six-point Likert scale.

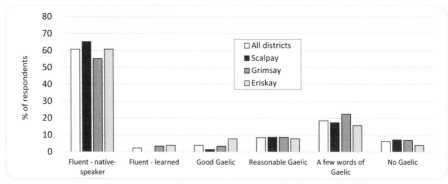

Figure 5.3 *Percentage of respondents' ability in spoken Gaelic, by island and all districts (N = 178)*

Figure 5.3 shows that 62.9% of respondents pertain to the two fluent categories (*Fluent – native speaker* and *Fluent – learned in school or later in life*). Scalpay exhibited the highest percentage of fluent native speaker ability among survey respondents with no-one claiming to have learned the language at a later point. Grimsay respondents recorded the lowest percentage of native speaker abilities. Approximately 25% of all respondents indicated they could speak *A few words* or *No Gaelic*.

For the sake of comparison, from the six-point Likert scale ability range, respondents were categorised into two ability groups: *Fluent* (comprising *native speaker* and *learned*) vs. *Not fluent* (comprising from *Good Gaelic* to *No Gaelic* inclusive). In Figure 5.4, we display the respondents' binary ability in spoken Gaelic according to age.

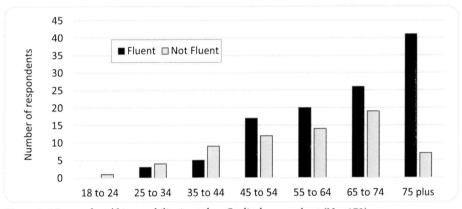

Figure 5.4 *Respondents' binary ability in spoken Gaelic, by age cohort (N = 178)*

Of the 178 respondents, there are 112 *Fluent* (62.9%) and 66 *Not fluent* (37.1%). Native speakers of Gaelic are proportionately dominant in the four age cohorts over 45 years of age. 85.4% of the 75+ age cohort have native-like Gaelic, and fluency varies little in the 45–74 age range (57.8%, 58.8%, 58.6% of the 65–74, 55–64 and 45–54 age cohorts, respectively). This suggests that a generational difference exists between the oldest respondents in which Gaelic fluency predominates, those born before c. 1970, and the younger respondents, born after c. 1970 among whom English fluency predominates (6.5.2.1). For the 35–44 age cohort, the proportion of fluent Gaelic speakers is 35.7%, and 42.8% in the smaller 25–34 age group.

5.4.2.1 COMPARISON WITH GAELIC ABILITY OF REPORTED RESIDENTS (STS)

For comparison with the group of 178 respondents, whose ability profile is displayed in Figure 5.4 above, we can examine Figure 5.5 which illustrates the ability in Gaelic of 483 *reported residents* in the three surveyed islands (as outlined in full in Chapter 6, section 6.5).

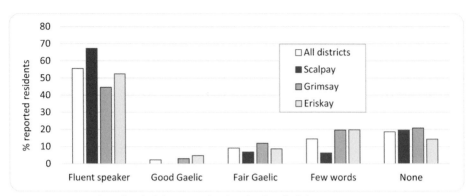

Figure 5.5 *Reported residents' ability in Gaelic, by island and all districts, STS (Ns = 483; 189, 168, 126)*

The assessment of Gaelic ability among *reported residents* indicated that 55.5% have fluent, native-speaker-like ability. 11.4% were reported as having either *Good Gaelic* or *Fair Gaelic* and 33.1% as having a *Few words of Gaelic* or *None*. Scalpay reported almost two-thirds of individuals (67.2%) as having fluent ability — the highest percentage recorded across any of the categorisations for all districts. Further information is given in Table 5.3.

Reported residents' ability in spoken Gaelic	All districts (%)	Scalpay (%)	Grimsay (%)	Eriskay (%)
Fluent speaker	268 (55.5%)	127 (67.2%)	75 (44.6%)	66 (52.4%)
Good Gaelic	11 (2.3%)	0	5 (3%)	6 (4.8%)
Fair Gaelic	44 (9.1%)	13 (6.9%)	20 (11.9%)	11 (8.7%)
Few words	70 (14.5%)	12 (6.3%)	33 (19.6%)	25 (19.8%)
None	90 (18.6%)	37 (19.6%)	35 (20.8%)	18 (14.3%)

Table 5.3 *Numbers and percentages of reported residents' ability in spoken Gaelic, by island and all districts (STS)*

5.4.2.2 *RESPONDENT'S BINARY ABILITY IN SPOKEN GAELIC, BY ISLAND*

Numbers and percentages of respondents' binary ability in spoken Gaelic are in given Table 5.4 for each island separately and for all three islands combined.

Age cohort	Scalpay (N = 69)		Grimsay (N = 58)		Eriskay (N = 51)		All districts (N = 178)	
	Fluent in Gaelic (%)	Not fluent in Gaelic (%)	Fluent in Gaelic (%)	Not fluent in Gaelic (%)	Fluent in Gaelic (%)	Not fluent in Gaelic (%)	Fluent in Gaelic (%)	Not fluent in Gaelic (%)
18–24	0 (0%)	1 (1.4%)	0 (0%)	0 (0%)	0 (0%)	0 (0%)	0 (0%)	1 (0.6%)
25–34	1 (1.4%)	1 (1.4%)	1 (1.7%)	1 (1.7%)	1 (2%)	2 (3.9%)	3 (1.7%)	4 (2.2%)
35–44	1 (1.4%)	3 (4.3%)	3 (5.2%)	1 (1.7%)	1 (2%)	5 (9.8%)	5 (2.8%)	9 (5%)
45–54	6 (8.7%)	3 (4.3%)	7 (12.1%)	5 (8.6%)	5 (9.8%)	3 (5.9%)	17 (9.6%)	12 (6.7%)
55–64	6 (8.7%)	4 (5.8%)	7 (12.1%)	8 (13.8%)	7 (13.7%)	2 (3.9%)	20 (11.2%)	14 (7.9%)
65–74	10 (14.5%)	7 (10.1%)	5 (8.6%)	9 (15.5%)	11 (21.6%)	3 (5.9%)	26 (14.6%)	19 (10.7%)
75+	22 (31.9%)	4 (5.8%)	11 (19%)	0 (0%)	8 (15.7%)	3 (5.9%)	41 (23%)	7 (3.9%)
Total (% of island)	46 (66.7%)	23 (33.3%)	34 (58.6%)	24 (41.4%)	33 (64.8%)	18 (35.2%)	n/a	n/a
Total (% of all districts)	46 (25.8%)	23 (12.9%)	34 (19.1%)	24 (13.5%)	33 (18.5%)	18 (10.1%)	112 (62.9%)	66 (37.1%)

Table 5.4 *Respondents' binary ability in spoken Gaelic, by age cohort and by island and all districts*

In the age cohorts under 45 for the three islands combined, respondents who are not fluent in Gaelic outnumber respondents who are. This situation is reversed in older cohorts, with clear dominance of Gaelic fluency only in the 75+ age cohort.

In the following three figures, based on the data in Table 5.4, we present the binary ability profile for each island separately. Figure 5.6 depicts respondents' binary ability in spoken Gaelic by age cohort in Scalpay.

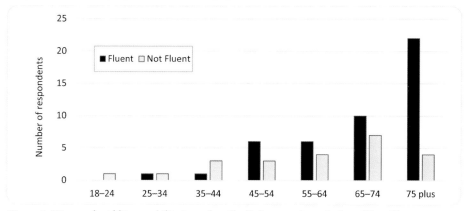

Figure 5.6 *Respondents' binary ability in spoken Gaelic by age cohort, Scalpay (N = 69)*

Figure 5.7 depicts respondents' binary ability in spoken Gaelic by age cohort in Grimsay.

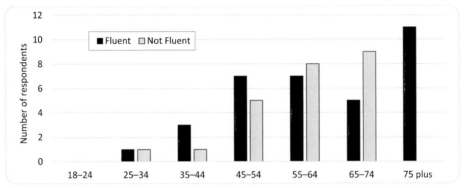

Figure 5.7 *Respondents' binary ability in spoken Gaelic by age cohort, Grimsay (N = 58)*

Figure 5.8 depicts respondents' binary ability in spoken Gaelic in Eriskay.

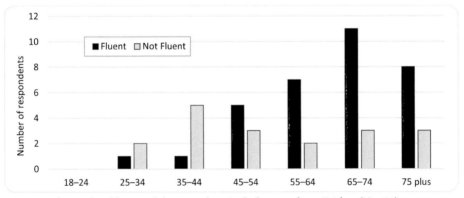

Figure 5.8 *Respondents' binary ability in spoken Gaelic by age cohort, Eriskay (N = 51)*

In examining the three depictions from the respective islands, we find that Eriskay and Scalpay more closely mirror the general situation across all three islands combined, but Grimsay has higher Gaelic fluency as opposed to non-fluency in the 35–44 and 45–54 age cohorts and greater numbers of non-fluent respondents in the 55–64 and 65–74 cohorts. The higher proportion of older non-fluent respondents in Grimsay may be related to an influx of people from outside the Western Isles and employment at a nearby military facility in Balivanich (see section 2.4.1.1).

5.4.3 RESPONDENT'S (BINARY) ABILITY IN SPOKEN GAELIC AND GEOGRAPHIC BACKGROUND

The results of a comparison between respondents' binary ability in Gaelic and respondents' background (5.4.1), or place of origin, are displayed in Figure 5.9.

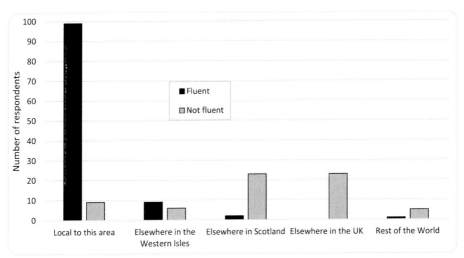

Figure 5.9 *Respondents' background and Gaelic fluency, all districts (N = 177)*

The results from this comparison show that most respondents (87.8%) from the Western Isles have fluent-speaker ability in Gaelic. Just 5.5% of those from elsewhere report a *Fluent* ability in Gaelic. Figure 5.10 displays the ability in spoken Gaelic of only those respondents who are local to the three islands (*Local to this area* in 5.4.1), for each island separately and aggregated across all three islands.

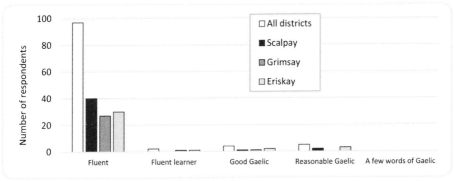

Figure 5.10 *Ability in spoken Gaelic of respondents 'Local to this area', by island all districts (Ns = 108; 43, 29, 36)*

There is a very high correspondence between being *Local to the area* and Gaelic fluency: across all survey areas, 89.8% of respondents local to the area have fluent, native-speaker abilities. 1.9% of people have fluent Gaelic learned later in life or in a school setting, 3.7% have *Good Gaelic*, and a further 4.6% have *Reasonable Gaelic*. No local respondent reported that they had language ability less than *Reasonable Gaelic*. These percentage results are broadly reflected across the three surveyed islands. For native-like fluency, Grimsay (93.1%) and Scalpay (93%) have the highest, while Eriskay has 83.3%.

5.4.4 RESPONDENT'S FIRST LANGUAGE(S)

To provide a comparison of language of upbringing and earlier language practice and change in practice, respondents were asked through which language they were raised. The percentage results are given in Figure 5.11.

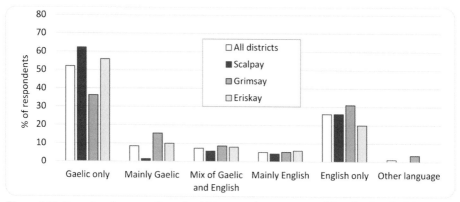

Figure 5.11 *Percentage language through which respondents were raised, by island and all districts (Ns = 177; 69, 58, 50)*

Figure 5.11 evinces a largely binomial distribution at both ends of the Gaelic–English language continuum: 52% of the aggregated respondents were raised through *Gaelic only* and 26% of the respondents were raised through *English only*. In only one instance did any of the other categories (*Mainly Gaelic; Mix of Gaelic and English, roughly even* and *Mainly English*) exceed 10% of the respondents, i.e. 15.5% *Mainly Gaelic* reported for Grimsay.

As for the separate islands, in Scalpay, 62.3% of respondents were raised through *Gaelic only*, with 26.1% of respondents raised exclusively through English. The remaining respondents were raised through some form of mixed language input (*Mainly* or *Mix*). The picture was similar in Eriskay, where 56% were raised through *Gaelic only*, and 20% raised through *English only*. The other respondents (24%) were spread across categories of some mixed input. Grimsay evinced a clearer language shift scenario, with fewer respondents raised only through Gaelic (36.2%) than in the other two islands, and more through *English only* (31%). Those raised through *Mainly Gaelic* totalled 15.5% in Grimsay, as stated above, considerably higher than in the other two islands for this category.

5.4.5 GEOGRAPHIC BACKGROUND AND GAELIC ABILITY OF RESPONDENT'S SPOUSE

Where relevant, respondents were asked to indicate the geographic background of their spouse, with the results given in Figure 5.12.

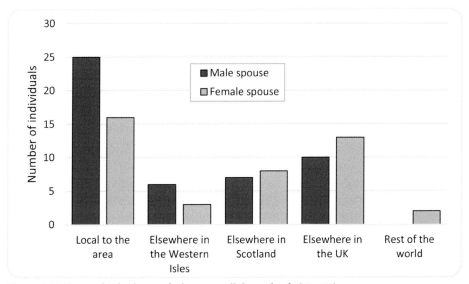

Figure 5.12 *Geographic background of spouses, all three islands (N = 92)*

Figure 5.12 shows that 41 spouses (44.5%) were local to the survey district, with a further nine (9.8%) from another part of the Western Isles. 15 (16.3%) spouses were from *Elsewhere in Scotland*, while 23 (25%) were from *Elsewhere in the UK* and two spouses (2.2%) were from outside the UK (*Rest of the world*).

The Gaelic ability data of the respondents' spouses, according to the same six-point Likert scale (5.4.2; with the *Fluent – learned* category with no returns), are given in Figure 5.13.

Figure 5.13 indicates that male spouses have a higher ability in spoken Gaelic than female spouses. 52.9% of the male and 40% of the female spouses have *Fluent native-speaker* ability, while 37.2% of the male spouses and 48.9% of the female spouses have *A few words of Gaelic* or *No Gaelic*. The higher rate of male spouse fluency in Gaelic (52.9%) corresponds with the higher proportion of male spouses raised through *Gaelic only* (42%), as reported in the discussion of Figure 5.14. Of the 45 female spouses, 18 (40%) are fluent and 35.6% were raised through *Gaelic only* (cf. Figure 5.14). No respondents claim that they have a spouse who has learned Gaelic to fluency. Overall, therefore, male spouses tend to be raised through Gaelic, tend to be of local origin, and to be fluent in Gaelic to a greater degree than female spouses. This can be related to the greater tendency of in-marriage of females rather than males. Regarding his research on the Isle of Harris in the 1970s, MacKinnon (1977: 87) says: 'It may also be significant to note that whereas in 1957–8 there was only one case of an English mother-tongue child of whose parents the father alone spoke Gaelic, fifteen years later there were eleven such cases, indicating a much greater propensity for a local father to bring an outsider or non-Gaelic-speaking wife into his home'. He further points out (1977: 134) that 'a selective 'creaming off' of the brightest children', particularly girls rather than boys, distorts that population structure and leads to a 'relative scarcity of younger women of marriageable and childbearing age.' Ó Giollagáin's (2002: 52) research in the Ráth Chairn Gaeltacht in Co. Meath, Ireland, found a much stronger propensity for the mother to transmit Irish to her children in cases where her partner was an English speaker than for an Irish-speaking father (with an English-speaking partner) to do so. Indeed, no instance of a father in these mixed sociolinguistic circumstances was identified in Ráth Chairn as a home transmitter of Irish. Given the small population profile in the Ráth Chairn, marrying in/partnership into the area is very common. This research project identified three marriage/partnership sociolinguistic profiles: a) Ráth Chairn locals in partnership with a person from another Gaeltacht region in which Irish transmission was more likely; b) male Ráth Chairn natives marrying or in partnership with an English speaker from the Co. Meath hinterland with no transmission of Irish; and c) female Ráth Chairn natives marrying or in partnership with an incoming English speaker with partial home transmission of Irish (2002: 47–48).

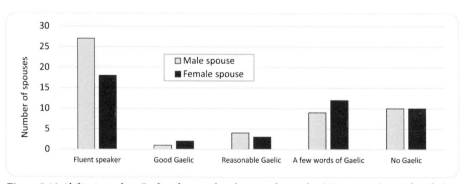

Figure 5.13 *Ability in spoken Gaelic of respondents' spouse, by gender (Ns = 51 males, 45 females)*

5.4.6 SPOUSE'S FIRST LANGUAGE

For those who have spouses, respondents were also asked to indicate whether their spouse had been raised through *Gaelic only, English only* or some mix of the two languages during their childhood, as shown in Figure 5.14 on a five-point Likert scale. Here, the 2.2% of spouses from outside the UK (*Rest of the world* in Figure 5.12) are excluded from Figure 5.14.

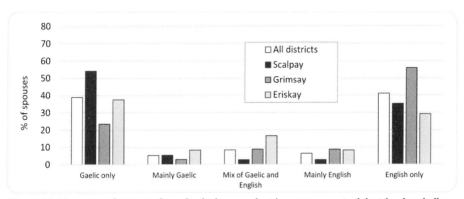

Figure 5.14 *Percentage language through which respondents' spouse was raised, by island and all districts (N = 95)*

In Figure 5.14, the geographical reference is to the respondents' location (for instance, 54.1% of the respondents in Scalpay indicate that their spouse was raised through *Gaelic only*). The data reveal a largely binomial distribution (with both *Gaelic only* and *English only* close to 40% each). Further analysis indicates a slight variance by gender. Of the 50 male spouses, 42% were raised through *Gaelic only* with 34% raised in *English only*; while, of the 45 female spouses, 35.6% were raised through *Gaelic only* and 48.9% were raised through *English only*. A mixed-language input for spouses was a less common scenario, standing at 20% for the combined categories of *Mainly Gaelic, Mix of Gaelic and English*, and *Mainly English*. In all three islands combined, marginally more spouses were raised through *English only* (41.1%) than *Gaelic only* (38.9%). Some form of mixed input accounted for 20% of spouses. If we compare the category of *Gaelic only* at 38.9% with all other categories at 61.1% and compare that with other data such as the high proportion of fluent speakers in the 75+ age cohort in Figure 5.4 (5.4.2), the shift away from the high social density of Gaelic speakers in these communities becomes apparent. Again, Grimsay was arguably the outlier in results, as 55.9% of respondents' spouses were raised through *English only* (compared to 35.1% on Scalpay and 29.2% on Eriskay in the same category). On Scalpay, as stated above, 54.1% of spouses were raised through *Gaelic only*, more than double the 23.5% on Grimsay; the same category accounted for 37.5% on Eriskay.

5.4.7 LANGUAGE SPOUSE SPEAKS TO RESPONDENT IN THE HOUSEHOLD

The language practice of the respondent's spouse to the respondent indicates the proportional dominance of *English only* practice in this context, as shown in Figure 5.15.

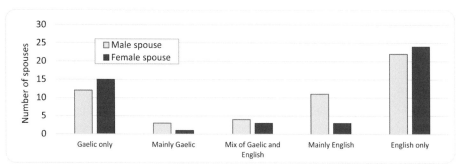

Figure 5.15 *Language spouse speaks to respondent in the household, by gender (Ns = 52 males, 46 females)*

Figure 5.15 reveals a largely binomial distribution with a slight gender imbalance. Male spouses are more inclined to use mid-categories (34.7%), i.e. *Mainly Gaelic* and *Mix of Gaelic and English* as well as *Mainly English*, than female spouses (15.2%). Of the 52 male spouses, 42.3% speak *English only* as opposed to 23.1% who speak *Gaelic only*. Of the 46 female spouses, 52.2% speak *English only* as opposed to 32.6% who speak *Gaelic only*. Overall, the data show that substantially more spouses speak in *English only* and *Mainly English* than speak in the equivalent Gaelic categories, again indicative of an ongoing shift to English practice, in contrast to older generations. Combining the genders, 31.6% of respondents report that their spouses speak only or mainly Gaelic to them, while 46.9% report that their spouses speak *English only* to them.

A cross-comparison is presented in Table 5.5 to assess the language spoken by spouses in households to fluent Gaelic respondents.

Language spouse speaks	Male spouse	Female spouse	Total (%)
Gaelic only	10	14	24 (53.3%)
Mainly Gaelic	2	1	3 (6.7%)
Mix of Gaelic and English, roughly even	3	0	3 (6.7%)
Mainly English	2	2	4 (8.9%)
English only	4	7	11 (24.4%)
Total	21	24	45 (100%)

Table 5.5 *Language spoken by spouse in the household to respondent with fluent, native-speaker Gaelic*

47.6% of the male spouses and 58.3% of the female spouses spoke *Gaelic only* with the fluent native-speaker Gaelic respondents. We can delve deeper into the relationship between spousal language practice and spousal language upbringing and language ability. Table 5.6 cross-tabulates the language upbringing of respondents and their spouses.

Language of upbringing of respondent	Language of upbringing of spouse			
	Gaelic only or mainly	Mix of Gaelic and English	English only or mainly	Total
Gaelic only or mainly	35	3	17	55
Mix of Gaelic and English	1	5	1	7
English only or mainly	5	0	26	31

Table 5.6 Cross-tabulation of language of upbringing for respondents and spouses (N = 93)

When we examine Table 5.6, we can see that there are 35 couples in which both individuals were raised only or mainly in Gaelic, there are three couples where the respondent was raised only or mainly in Gaelic but the spouse was brought up through a mix of Gaelic and English, and there are 17 couples where the respondent was raised only or mainly through Gaelic but the spouse was raised only or mainly through English.

Table 5.7 cross-tabulates the Gaelic ability of the respondents and their spouses in two aggregated categories: Fluent (*Fluent native* and *Fluent learner*) and Non-fluent (from *Reasonable* to *No Gaelic*). This yields three types of couples: couples where both are fluent Gaelic speakers; mixed-ability couples where one partner is fluent and the other is not; and couples where both are non-fluent. For these three types of couples, the table compares the language practice of the couples (discussed above) and the language their first child is raised in (5.4.9) with the corresponding average Gaelic ability score for the child or children in the families of those same first children. The Gaelic ability score was calculated based on the ability scale from *Fluent* to *No Gaelic* (5.4.8) scoring 5 to 0 and averaged for the various cohorts of children. There are in total 91 couples (for whom the relevant data is available), i.e. 182 individuals. Of these 91 couples, 31 have children aged between 2 and 17. In our discussion, we take the language spoken by the spouse to the respondent as a general indicator of the language spoken by the couple.

Couples' Gaelic ability	Both Fluent	Mixed ability Fluent + Non-fluent	Both Non-fluent	Total
Number of couples	34	26	31	91
Language spoken by spouse to respondent:				
Gaelic Always or Mainly	26 (total 31)	1	0	27
Mix	3	0	2	5
English Always or Mainly	2	25	29	56
Subset of couples with young children (Child(ren)'s average Gaelic ability)	**8 (3.7)**	**12 (1.9)**	**11 (1.4)**	**31 (2.1)**
Child 1 raised in:				
Gaelic Always or Mainly	5 (4.4)	0	0	5 (4.4)
Mix	2 (2.5)	7 (1.9)	3 (2.1)	12 (2)
English Always or Mainly	1 (1.5)	5 (1.8)	8 (1.2)	14 (1.4)

Table 5.7 *Cross-tabulation of couples' spoken Gaelic ability and language practice of couple and practice with first child where applicable (as well as child(ren)'s average Gaelic ability score)*

This cross-tabulation for ability shows that there are 34 couples where both partners are fluent Gaelic speakers, and 26 couples where a fluent partner is in a household with a partner who is not fluent and, finally, 31 couples where both are non-fluent. This indicates a slight tendency for couples to share households with partners of similar language ability. Out of the 91 couples, a majority, 57 (62.6%) couples, are in partnerships where English will tend to be the *lingua franca* (i.e. 26 + 31). In fact, Table 5.7 indicates that 54 (59.3%) of these couples use *Always* or *Mainly English* (i.e. 25 + 29). This means that 25 of the 26 fluent Gaelic speakers in mixed-ability couples use little or no Gaelic with their partners. There are 94 (51.6%) fluent Gaelic speakers among the 182 individuals in these partnerships, but only 68 (37.4%) are in partnerships where the option to use dominant Gaelic is available, representing a loss of potential Gaelic use of 14.2 percentage points. We have the relevant data for 31 fluent couples and 26 mixed-ability couples. This yields a total of 88 (31 + 31 + 26) fluent individuals. Of these 88 fluent individuals, 53 (60.2%) speak *Always* or *Mainly* Gaelic with their partners. This represents a loss of 35 individuals or 39.8% of the Gaelic-practice potential in the cohort of fluent individuals. (Cp. the gap between Gaelic Family Household use and Gaelic ability in the nexus discussion of the census data in section 2.4.3.)

Table 5.7 also shows that there are 31 (34.1%) couples who have young children.[50] Eight of these 31 children (Child 1 of 31 couples) live in households where both

50 As will be shown in Table 5.9, there are 39 first children in the total sample for the three islands. We have the relevant cross-tabulation data for the subset of 31 children in Table 5.7.

parents are fluent Gaelic speakers. Of these eight children, five are raised in *Always* or *Mainly Gaelic*. Mixed-ability couples indicate a higher use of Gaelic with their child than with each other. There are no instances of mixed Gaelic practice in these mixed-ability couples in Table 5.7 but seven instances of the first child being raised in mixed Gaelic practice by the mixed-ability couples. This corresponds to the discussion of parents' efforts to increase Gaelic input to children (5.8.2.2; 6.5.2.1). The data in Table 5.7 show that of the 12 children who receive mixed input, seven (58.3%) of them are raised by mixed-ability couples. This indicates that mixed-ability couples are a substantial source of mixed input to children and such mixed input is a substantial proportion of the increased Gaelic input to children (as discussed in 5.8.2.2). It is also clear from Table 5.7 that all five (16.1%) children who receive *Always* or *Mainly* Gaelic input are raised by fluent couples. The other input cohorts are larger: *Mix* with 12 (38.7%) children and *Always* or *Mainly* English with 14 (45.2%). Finally, with regard to average Gaelic ability scores: 1) the five children receiving *Always* or *Mainly* Gaelic input score more than double the other categories (4.4 vs. 2 vs. 1.4); 2) the total of 12 children receiving mixed input do score more than the 14 children receiving *Always* or *Mainly* English input (2 vs. 1.4) but the main cohort of children receiving mixed input, the seven children of mixed-ability couples, score similar to the five children in the same couples category who receive *Always* or *Mainly* English input (1.9 ≈ 1.8). (Cp. Table 4.20 in 4.6.2.)

5.4.8 CHILDREN'S ABILITY IN SPOKEN GAELIC, BY BIRTH ORDER IN FAMILY

Respondents gave language ability and practice data on 71 children, aged 2–17, in a total of 39 family households.[51] Respondents indicated the ability in spoken Gaelic of children in the household aged between 2 and 17, on a six-point Likert scale. This ability is displayed in Table 5.8, and categorised according to the birth order of children in the family, or household. Figure 5.16 displays the same data but according to the number of children in the family household.

Language ability	Child 1	Child 2	Child 3 and Child 4	Total
Fluent – native speaker	9 (12.7%)	6 (8.5%)	4 (5.6%)	19 (26.8%)
Fluent – learned in school	1 (1.4%)	1 (1.4%)	0	2 (2.8%)
Good Gaelic	3 (4.2%)	2 (2.8%)	0	5 (7%)
Reasonable Gaelic	8 (11.3%)	5 (7%)	2 (2.8%)	15 (21.1%)
A few words of Gaelic	14 (19.7%)	7 (9.9%)	1 (1.4%)	22 (31%)
No Gaelic	4 (5.6%)	1 (1.4%)	3 (4.2%)	8 (11.3%)
Total	39 (54.9%)	22 (31%)	10 (14.1%)	71 (100%)

Table 5.8 *Ability of children in spoken Gaelic, by birth order in family (N = 71)*

---

51 The households contained a total of 92 children; this includes some who were aged 18 or older.

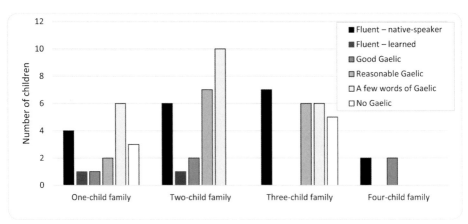

Figure 5.16 *Children's ability in spoken Gaelic by number of children in the family household (N = 71)*

The largely bimodal distribution of language ability in this cohort of children is evident. 19 (26.8%) children are reported to be *Fluent native speakers* and two children are reported to be *Fluent – learned in school* (when we combine these two categories we see that 29.6% of children are *Fluent*). 42.3% of the children had either *No Gaelic* or *A few words of Gaelic*. Compared with age-group fluency and acquisition data (see 5.4.2 for the respondents; 5.4.5 for the respondents' spouses; and 5.4.2.1 for the adult age profiles), the data for these children suggest that a trajectory of decline in the familial transmission of Gaelic has been established, and that those families with Gaelic-speaking children find themselves in communities with a growing prevalence of English and language mixing (5.8.2.2).

5.4.9 LANGUAGE(S) THROUGH WHICH CHILDREN WERE RAISED AND CHILDREN'S LANGUAGE PRACTICE

Where relevant, the respondents answered the following question regarding children in the household aged 17 or under: *Through what language were the following people in the household raised?* Table 5.9 summarises the responses for the total of 71 children (see also the discussion of Table 5.7).

Language raised through	Child 1	Child 2	Child 3 and Child 4	Total	%
Gaelic only	6	3	1	10	14.1
Mainly Gaelic	1	0	0	1	1.4
Mix of Gaelic and English, roughly even	14	9	3	26	36.6
Mainly English	10	6	4	20	28.2
English only	8	4	2	14	19.7
Total	**39**	**22**	**10**	**71**	**100.0**

Table 5.9 Language through which children in the respondent's household were raised, in children's birth order (N = 71)

The results in Table 5.9 are indicative of the increased prevalence of English-language input in childhood. Fewer first children were raised through *Gaelic only* than were raised through *English only*. The category of *Mix of Gaelic and English* is the largest single category. As many first children (35.9%) were raised through such a mixed-language input as there were in *Gaelic only* and *English only* combined. 90.8% of the 71 children were local to the three islands of the CSS. The totals from Table 5.9 are displayed in Figure 5.17.

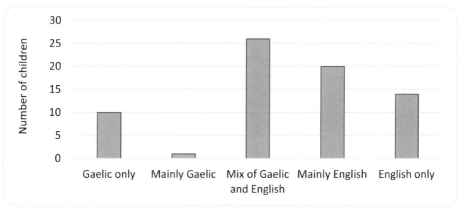

Figure 5.17 Language through which children in the respondent's household were raised (N = 71)

When we combine the categories of *Mainly English* or *English only* we see that almost half, i.e. 47.9%, of children have English-dominant input. Of the total number of children, 15.5% were raised through *Gaelic only* or *Mainly Gaelic*, with 36.6% having a *Mix of Gaelic and English*. Compared to the language the respondents were raised in (Figure 5.11), it is clear that familial transmission of Gaelic is becoming far less prevalent.

A further question examined intergenerational use of language, specifically what language children speak to the respondent in the household, with results displayed in Table 5.10 and Figure 5.18.

Language children speak to respondent	Child 1	Child 2	Child 3 and Child 4	Total	% of Total
Gaelic only	2	1	1	4	5.9%
Mainly Gaelic				0	
Mix of Gaelic and English, roughly even	10	5		15	22.1%
Mainly English	7	3	2	12	17.6%
English only	18	13	6	37	54.4%
Total	37	22	9	68	100%

Table 5.10 *Language children speak to respondent in the household, by birth order*

A majority of children (54.4%) speak *English only* to respondents, with a combined percentage of 72% speaking *English only* or *Mainly English*. Looking only at the first child in each family, 48.6% speak *English only* to the respondent, while just 5.4% speak *Gaelic only* to the respondent. In total only four (5.9%) children speak *Gaelic only* (or *Mainly Gaelic*) to the respondent. A mixed Gaelic–English mode at 22.1% is nearly four times more prevalent than a *Gaelic only* mode at 5.9%. A total of 19 (28%) children speak Gaelic to any appreciable extent to the respondents (from *Gaelic only* to *Mix of Gaelic and English*).

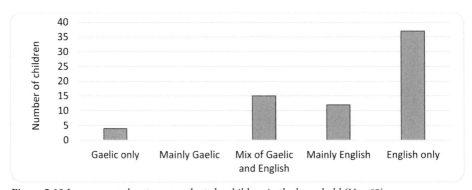

Figure 5.18 *Language spoken to respondents by children in the household (N = 68)*

5.4.10 CHILDREN'S LANGUAGE UPBRINGING, ABILITY AND PRACTICE

It is clear that the levels of children's ability in Gaelic are greater than the children's practice of Gaelic (29.6% are fluent, either native speakers or learners, Table 5.8, versus 5.9% using Gaelic only or mainly to respondents, Table 5.10). The disparity of 23.7 percentage points between ability and practice of Gaelic among the children can be compared to the language upbringing of the children, in order to see if there is a reduction between earlier input to children (as a major source of ability) and current practice by children to respondents. Figure 5.19 shows this rough input–output contrast (i.e. data from Tables 5.9 and 5.10 compared) by comparing the language children were/are raised through in the household with the language children speak to the respondent (as in Figure 5.18).

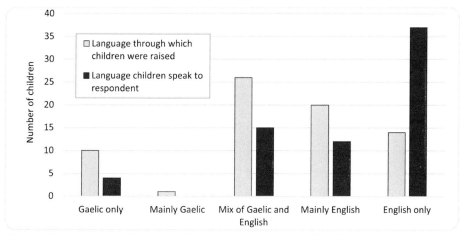

Figure 5.19 *Comparison of language children were/are raised through and language children speak to the respondent at time of survey (Ns = 71, 68)*

The comparison shows that the proportion of Gaelic inputs to children is greater than Gaelic outputs of children. In the categories of *Gaelic only*, *Mix of Gaelic and English* and *Mainly English* there is a loss of between a half and a third from input to output. Children's language practice shows a clear shift towards the use of English, with *English only* roughly doubling in Figure 5.19. We find a similar loss from parental input to teenagers' output of Gaelic in section 4.6.2.

Figure 5.20 depicts a cross-comparison of the Gaelic ability of the children (Table 5.8) with the language the children speak to the respondent in the household (Table 5.10).

We see that *English only* is the most prominent practice (65% of total of children). This *English only* practice category is comprised of 25 (41.7% of total) children who have no or a few words of Gaelic and 11 children who have *Good* or *Reasonable Gaelic*, and three children who have fluent Gaelic. The right-hand set of data bars shows that 14 children (23.3% of total) with fluent, good or reasonable Gaelic speak *English only*, thus evincing a lower rate of Gaelic output (speaking to respondents) than Gaelic ability. A further seven fluent speakers mix Gaelic and English. The six fluent Gaelic-speaking children who speak *Gaelic only* to the respondents in the household comprise 10% of the total number of children.

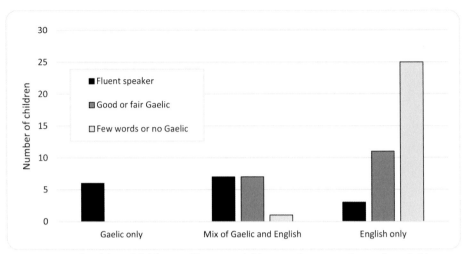

Figure 5.20 *Gaelic ability of children and language children speak to respondent in household (N = 60)*

5.4.11 LANGUAGE RESPONDENTS SPEAK TO PEOPLE IN DIFFERENT AGE COHORTS

Respondents were asked to indicate which language they speak to people in different age cohorts, according to the five-point Likert scale from *Gaelic only* to *English only*. Figure 5.21 displays the language practice of the respondents with the five age cohorts comprising the oldest (65+) to the youngest (primary school children).

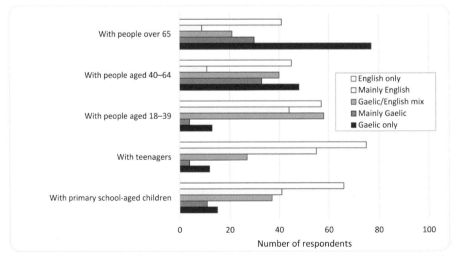

Figure 5.21 *Language spoken by respondents to people in a range of age cohorts (Ns = 178, 177, 176, 173, 170)*

Figure 5.21 provides a snapshot of language shift through three generations in the language practice of the respondents. Speaking:

- Gaelic (only and mainly) to older age cohorts, which is replaced by
- increased mixing to the 40–64 cohort, which is replaced by
- the prevalence of mixed Gaelic/English to the 18–39 cohort, which is in turn replaced by
- the dominance of English (only and mainly) spoken to the two youngest age cohorts.

With 43.3% of respondents stating that they speak *Gaelic only* to over-65s, the use of Gaelic is clearly biased towards those in that older age cohort. Noticeable, too, is the prevalence of the mixed practice spoken to the young adult cohort (18–39). The young adult cohort (18–39) is positioned between the Gaelic-dominant practice of the older generations and the English-dominant practice of the younger generations. The intermediary aspect in the three-generational language shift trajectory, therefore, of the young adult cohort is also intermediate in the respondents' actual language practice with them, evidencing the most mixed language practice of the age cohorts. Mixed language practice is, of course, common in intermediary generation(s) in language shift (Lenoach 2012; Matras 2009). This intermediate generation in a sense represents the sociolinguistic actualisation of the shift. From the intergenerational and language-shift point of view, the prevalence of mixing over other modes is short-lived, in this case c. 20 years in apparent time, and entails the penultimate stage before English dominance. More people claimed to speak *English only* to teenagers (43.4% of respondents) than claimed to speak *Gaelic only* to any other age cohort, suggesting the future position of Gaelic in the communities is likely to be weakened. One positive note is that more people claimed to speak *Gaelic only* (8.8%) or *Mainly Gaelic* (6.5%) to primary school-aged children than to teenagers for whom the percentages stand at 6.9% and 2.3% respectively. A slightly higher level of Gaelic is spoken to children of primary school age than with post-primary or young adult cohorts. This could be linked to a growing awareness of the institutional acquisition of Gaelic through Gaelic-medium education with primary children, as well as the shift through time towards English dominance seen among teenagers (4.6.3).

5.5 IDENTITY

This section of the questionnaire contained queries about the respondents' identity. The first question in this section was a binary question: *Do you consider yourself to be a Gael?* The responses indicate a strong affiliation with identity as a Gael. Of the 174 respondents to this question, 79% answered in the affirmative, while 18% did not and 3% indicated that this question did not apply to them (*N/A*). The second question about identity self-ascription was a multi-choice question: *How do you describe your identity?* It provided the following four options: *Local* (e.g. Leòdhasach, Niseach, Siarach; Hearach; Uibhisteach (Tuathach); Uibhisteach (Deasach); …);[52] *Gael; Scottish; British*. Respondents were free to choose as few or as many options as they felt were applicable.

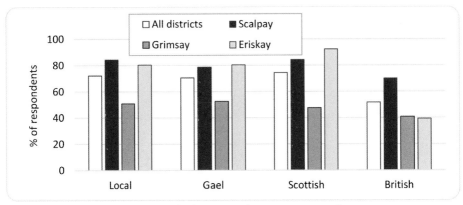

Figure 5.22 *Respondents' identity, multiple response (Ns = 177; 70, 58, 51)*

The binary choice question yields 79% of respondents identifying as a *Gael* in comparison to 70.6% identifying as a *Gael* in the multiple response question. All three identities of, in descending percentage order, *Scottish* (74.4%), *Local* (72.2%) and *Gael* (70.6%) are at a similar percentage. A lower percentage of 51.7% identified as *British*. Percentages for identity self-ascription from Grimsay are at lower levels than the other two islands, whereas Grimsay and Scalpay have a narrower range than Eriskay: Grimsay 52.5%–40.7%; Scalpay 84.3%–70%; Eriskay 92.2%–39.2%.

5.5.1 GAELIC IDENTITY AND ABILITY

A comparison was made between two of the responses to two related questions, namely whether respondents self-identified as a Gael (or not) and respondents' self-reported language ability in Gaelic, with the results displayed in Figure 5.23.

---

52 i.e. 'person from Lewis' etc.

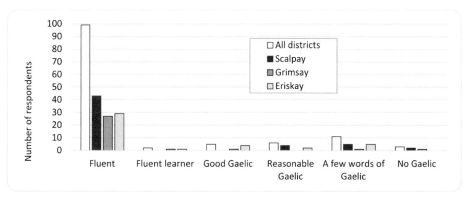

Figure 5.23 *Ability in spoken Gaelic of those who consider themselves to be a Gael (Ns = 126; 54, 31, 41)*

The data indicate a close correspondence between those who feel they hold the identity of a *Gael* and fluent ability in Gaelic. Across all districts, the vast majority (80%) of *Gaels* claim fluent, native-speaker-like ability in Gaelic, including those who had learned Gaelic later in life. Only 11% of respondents who self-identified as Gaels had only *A few words of Gaelic*, or *No Gaelic*. Indeed, no respondent in Eriskay who self-identified as a Gael claimed to have *No Gaelic*.

Figure 5.24 below presents a comparison of ability in spoken Gaelic (from *Fluent* to *No Gaelic*) across all districts for the four multiple choice identities.

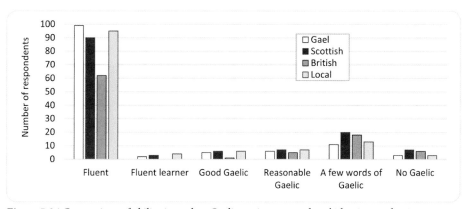

Figure 5.24 *Comparison of ability in spoken Gaelic against respondents' identity or identities (Ns = 126, 133, 92, 128)*

As stated above, respondents were asked to specify which identity, or which combination of identities, they possessed from a range of options: *Gael, Scottish, British, Local*. It is clear from the left-hand set of data bars that fluent native-speakers self-identify, in descending order, as: a *Gael* (99; 78.6% of 126 who identify as Gaels) and then a *Local* identity (95; 74.2% of 128 who identify as *Local*) more than a

Scottish identity (90; 67.7% of 133 who identify as *Scottish*), and clearly more than a *British* identity (62; 67.4% of 92 who identify as *British*). Of the 111 respondents who indicated that they are fluent in Gaelic and responded to the binary question on identity, all of them self-ascribe as Gaels, except in the case of one of the four fluent learners of Gaelic (5.4.2).

We can see how two sets of data bars on the right (lack of fluency) in Figure 5.24 contrast with those to the left (fluency in Gaelic). Thus, in contrast to fluent speakers, *Scottish* identity, followed by *British* identity followed by a *Local* identity were all felt more prominently than identity as a *Gael* among those who spoke *No Gaelic* or claimed to be able to speak only *A few words*, which again closely links identity as a *Gael* with fluency in Gaelic.

Perhaps the most interesting outcome from this question is that while 133 respondents identified as *Scottish* and 128 identified as *Local*, slightly fewer (126) identified as being a *Gael*. There are 92 respondents who claimed a *British* identity. However, of those who are fluent in Gaelic (native and learned, totalling 112 (Figure 5.4)), higher percentages identified as a *Gael* (80.2%) and as a *Local* (77.3%) than identified as *Scottish* (69.9%) or *British* (67.4%). Those who self-ascribed as a *Gael* in the binary identity question chose on average 3.1 multiple identities. Whereas those who did not self-ascribe as a *Gael* in the binary identity question chose on average 1.3 multiple identities. Self-ascribed Gaels are, therefore, more multi-identitarian than non-Gaels, as seen in the findings of the teenager identities (4.8.3). We can see that identity formation correlates with language competence acquisition. To put it simply, the minority generally undergoes unidirectional bilingualism and unidirectional multiple identity formation. Therefore, Gaels are multilingual and multi-identitarian. In contrast, the majority generally experiences monolingualism and singular identity formation. The non-Gaels are generally monolingual and mono-identitarian in the CSS findings. The self-ascription as a Gael seen here among these adult respondents is considerably higher than seen among the teenagers in sections 4.8.1 and 4.8.3.

5.5.2 PEOPLE RESPONDENTS CONSIDERED TO BE GAELS

Respondents were asked *Do you consider the following people to be Gaels?* and were invited to indicate which categories they chose from a list of options, as shown in Figure 5.25.

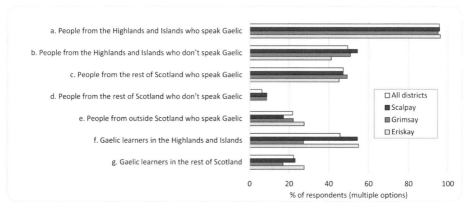

Figure 5.25 *People considered as Gaels by district (multiple response), by island and all districts (Ns = 179; 70, 58, 51)*

The data gathered for all respondents indicated that the category *People from the Highlands and Islands who speak Gaelic* was most closely associated with being a *Gael* (95.6%). However, by contrast, the second most common answer with which respondents agreed (49.4%) indicated that *People from the Highlands and Islands who don't speak Gaelic* were also associated with being a *Gael*. The lowest percentage of respondents (6.1%) to the question felt that *People from the rest of Scotland who don't speak Gaelic* were *Gaels*. By implication, there is a clear connection between geographic location and language ability when it comes to defining someone as a *Gael*. The separate islands demonstrate a very similar distribution of percentage choices, except for Grimsay in the option *Gaelic learners in the Highlands and Islands*, and to a lesser extent *Gaelic learners in the rest of Scotland*, in that the percentages chosen by the Grimsay respondents are notably lower than the other two islands.

5.5.3 WHAT IS A GAELIC COMMUNITY?

Respondents were asked *Would you consider the following to be Gaelic communities?* Figure 5.26 displays the percentages of respondents who chose each option from the list of descriptions of areas. Respondents could choose and tick any or all options they considered appropriate. The options listed in this question are necessarily hypothetical, but some respondents may have interpreted these options as referring to their own local experience and community.

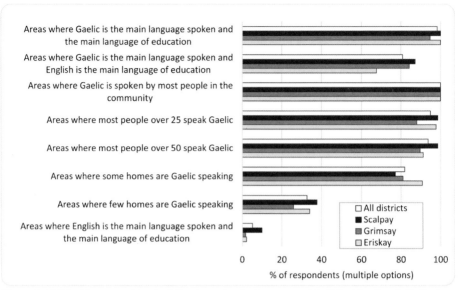

Figure 5.26 *'Would you consider the following to be Gaelic communities?', by island and all districts (Ns = 177–171)*

Most of the options were considered to be Gaelic communities by the majority (>80%) of the respondents. *Areas where Gaelic is spoken by most people in the community* received the highest support (100%). This indicates a majoritarian view of a Gaelic community comprising 'most people' speaking Gaelic, in contrast to the more abstract wording of 'main language' in other (slightly) lower-rated options. A similar percentage choice was indicated for *Areas where most people over 25 speak Gaelic* (94.8%) and *Areas where most people over 50 speak Gaelic* (93.6%). In terms of the difference between the statements *Areas where Gaelic is the main language spoken and the main language of education* (98.3%) and *Areas where Gaelic is the main language spoken and English is the main language of education* (80.9%), there was a difference of almost 20 percentage points. The second-least chosen option was *Areas where few homes are Gaelic speaking* (32.7%). *Areas where English is the main language spoken and the main language of education* was by far the least chosen (5.2%). In short, areas where most or some people speak Gaelic are considered as Gaelic communities. But areas with few people speaking Gaelic are rated low (32.7%) as Gaelic communities. Two options seem to concur most with the current situation: *Areas where most people over 50 speak Gaelic* and *Areas where some homes are Gaelic speaking* (81.9%). Of course, *some homes* being Gaelic speaking (81.9%) and English being *the main language spoken* (5.2%) are not mutually exclusive. The actual reality for most of the youngest age cohort, as evidenced in the IGRP, resembles the category which is not considered by the respondents to be a Gaelic community, i.e. *Areas where English is the main language spoken and the main language of education* (5.2%).

5.6 ADDITIONAL COMMENTS FROM SURVEY RESPONDENTS

The final section of the community questionnaire allowed for respondents to provide qualitative data by offering any further comments or observations in their own words. Broadly, the additional comments related to the perceived lower levels of ability in Gaelic among younger cohorts (as found in the IGRP in 4.10.1.1; cp. 4.5.3; 5.4.10; and ability data in Chapter 3), and the need for both support and classes for those who wished to learn Gaelic or improve their Gaelic skills. A general sense of disengagement with official Gaelic agencies, and their activities, was also expressed in many of the comments. Recurrent subjects also included the demographic problems affecting the communities of the Western Isles. A generalised belief was expressed that GME is beneficial for younger age groups in supporting their linguistic development. Notably, all of the principal themes arose across each of the three island communities. However, these themes should be interpreted in context, given the profile of the respondents.

5.7 COMMUNITY CONSULTATIONS ON GAELIC

This part of the research project consisted of a series of meetings held in the Western Isles, Staffin on the Isle of Skye, and in Tiree. The purpose of the meetings was to gauge the views of each community on the state of Gaelic and to gain an understanding of the main issues considered to impact on the language in their respective areas.

Thirteen meetings were held between 13 March 2017 and 16 May 2017, with the aim of giving further scope to the research by drawing on local opinion in Scalpay, Eriskay, Grimsay, South Uist, Benbecula, Barra, North Uist, Harris, Lewis (Stornoway, Ness, Uig), Staffin (Skye) and Tiree. The meetings were widely advertised in the communities beforehand. Nevertheless, only 75 people in total attended, 55 females and 20 males. Three people e-mailed comments afterwards, one of whom had not been able to attend a meeting in person. Eleven meetings were held in Gaelic and two were held in a Gaelic/English mix, as some participants were not fluent in Gaelic. Notes of meetings were made by IGRP fieldworkers in either Gaelic or English, depending on the writer's preference, and are given as written, with translations from Gaelic where necessary. The meetings were structured as follows: a brief (c. ten-minute) presentation and overview of census statistics, outlining the historical and contemporary position of Gaelic in Scotland and the Western Isles. The attendees were then asked to rate the strength of its usage in their local area on a scale of 1 to 10, 10 being optimal. The received scores from seven meetings ranged from 3 to 8, with the average being 6.5, which can be taken as indicative of attendees' perception of Gaelic's current situation as less than optimal.

The semi-structured meetings covered general attitudes, practice and policies, and community actions, new initiatives and the future. The initial section was followed by an open discussion (ranging from one hour to one-and-a-half hours in length) on the current situation of Gaelic in the local area, the level of community awareness of Gaelic policies, and what actions the attendees felt could be undertaken in the community to develop the language locally. In sections 5.7.1 to 5.7.3, we present the general themes that emerged from the structured questions posed to those attending, and in section 5.7.4 we present a synopsis of the discussions. The presentation includes verbatim quotes as well as paraphrasing of comments.

5.7.1 THE CURRENT SITUATION AND PRACTICE OF GAELIC

The overall perception by attendees is that Gaelic in the Western Isles is weak socially and communally, spoken by the older age cohorts and by some involved in educational and institutional activities. Concerning the networked practice of Gaelic, it was indicated that Gaelic is mainly confined to older native fluent speaker networks and to those involved with a traditional socio-economic island lifestyle, such as crofting. Many contributors to the discussions commented that marriages of English monolinguals and Gaelic speakers, coupled with increasing numbers of English-speaking monolinguals serve to dilute the social presence of Gaelic in the community. The same sociological processes contributing to the decline of Gaelic are felt to be in evidence in all areas.

The most common explanations offered for the decline of Gaelic in the islands are:

1. Generational gap in ability and practice
2. Demographic and social problems
3. Socioeconomic problems
4. Attitudinal and language practice problems
5. Public policy and planning problems.

These five factors are set out in detail below, along with indicative comments.

1. Participants felt that there is a generational gap in relation to ability and use of the language between the young and the older age groups, and in relation to the household use of Gaelic. It was also indicated that the levels of individual ability in Gaelic were not reflected in the family use of the language. Many commented that Gaelic is not as strong socially as it used to be, with a feeling that the language has declined among the younger age cohorts and that intergenerational language transmission mechanisms have weakened. It was felt that this linguistic and

cultural breakdown started one or two generations ago. The general depiction of Gaelic in the community is as follows: local older people (50+) in rural island communities tend to be fluent, while many young parents have not attained a similar capacity in Gaelic, and school-age children were considered much less fluent or often lacking Gaelic entirely. Attendees acknowledged that it is difficult to motivate the younger generation to speak Gaelic. A selection of related views from across the meetings are shown in the following comments:

Tha teaghlaichean ann, far a bheil na pàrantan fileanta sa Ghàidhlig ach 's e a' Bheurla a bhios aca anns an dachaigh. Tha a' Ghàidhlig air a dhol sìos gu mòr [*There are families where the parents are fluent in Gaelic but they speak English at home. Gaelic has declined a lot*]. (Scalpay)

Chan eil clann san sgìre cho fileanta 's a tha na ginealaich as sine … tha a' Ghàidhlig fhathast làidir am measg seann daoine [*Children in the area are not as fluent as previous generations were. Gaelic is still strong among older people*]. (Uig)

If Gaelic is not heard outside the school gates, what is the point? Gaelic at home is more important than Gaelic in school. (Uig)

Children in the primary school here get more French than Gaelic, which is pathetic. Gaelic is only taught in primary school for half an hour a week. (Uig)

Chan eil a' chlann a' bruidhinn Gàidhlig eadar iad fhèin san sgoil [*The children don't speak Gaelic among themselves in school*]. (Harris)

Chan eil e a' tighinn thuca gu nàdarra … a' Ghàidhlig a bhruidhinn taobh a-muigh na sgoile [*It doesn't come naturally to them … to speak Gaelic outside* school]. (North Uist)

Mur eil iad [a' chlann] ga cluinntinn aig an taigh, cha bhruidhinn iad i [*If they (children) don't hear it at home, they won't speak it*]. (South Uist)

Gaelic is fragile amongst the under-50s. It's questionable whether GME is making a difference, if families don't speak it. (Eriskay)

There is a missing generation of Gaelic speakers. (Grimsay)

Sometimes Gaelic is not seen by younger people as 'cool'. (Grimsay)

When the older generation dies out, Gaelic will die with them. The outlook for the under-30s is grim. (Ness)

Chanainnsa … chan eil daoine òga air an teagasg mun chultar is an dualchas aca fhèin. Chan eil guth air eachdraidh nan eilean … chan eil fhios againne cò sinne, cò às a thàinig sinn. Chan eil sian san fhoghlam a tha a' cur moit air an dualchas. Chan eil moit sa chultar no sa chànan [*I would say … young people are not taught about their own culture and heritage. There is no mention of the history of the islands … we don't know who we are, where we came from. There is nothing in the education (system) that places pride on heritage (issues). There is no pride in the culture or the language].* (South Uist)

2. Lifestyle and demographic changes were also cited, which coupled with a lack of confidence at individual and community levels to speak Gaelic have also contributed to the decline in Gaelic at a local level. The decline in crofting and township-based occupations were mentioned as contributing to Gaelic's decline: many people work nine to five and commute to their workplaces, and many are too busy with their work and family lives to take part in village activities. People do not interact with each other now as they did when the societies were based on more traditional ways of life associated with crofting communities. In relation to the islands' demography, the ageing population and lack of younger people are felt to be a factors in the lack of community vitality in many areas. The changing nature of the population was mentioned frequently, with many more monolingual English-speakers living in these communities now than was the case a decade or two ago. This is considered to have had a detrimental effect on the sociolinguistic dynamic of these communities. It was felt that the decline in the parental use of Gaelic has contributed to a considerable contraction in the cross-generational practice of Gaelic. In addition to the weak familial reinforcement of the language among the young, the generally negative effect of English-language television and social media was also mentioned. The lack of affordable housing in rural areas was highlighted as a problem, leading to young families leaving for towns such as Stornoway and cities on the mainland, further weakening the social and communal presence of Gaelic.

3. A weak economy, a lack of jobs and a shortage of educational opportunities to retain young people and families were commonly given as reasons for the decline in population and hence the decline in the language — a strong connection between the state of Gaelic and the state of the economy was mentioned at several meetings. The economic situation was described by one attendee in Grimsay as *'disastrous'*. Other comments included:

    Nam biodh obraichean ann, bhiodh teaghlaichean leis a' Ghàidhlig ann
    [*If there were jobs, there would be families with Gaelic].* (South Uist)

The outflow of the youth population seeking socio-economic opportunity elsewhere, combined with the in-migration of English-speaking monolinguals, has left the Gaelic-speaking group *'feeling very small'* (Tiree); *'Youth clubs are more fragile now, with smaller numbers'* (Eriskay).

4. Attitudinal issues associated with speaking Gaelic were raised on a number of occasions, with many people feeling that Gaelic is still viewed negatively by some or as holding people back from full linguistic attainment in English. Older generations often assume younger people do not have Gaelic and will address them in English, even when replied to in Gaelic. It was felt that more support and encouragement at community level by official Gaelic bodies could help to change things in this respect, by raising the profile and emphasising the value of the language. There is a feeling that Gaels are too polite and too ready to switch to English if one member in a group conversation does not speak Gaelic.

5. It was felt that current national policy and provision is not addressing the state of the language as a significant element of the islands' social and cultural identity. The official census figures were considered by some to give too optimistic a picture of both linguistic competence and the social reality of Gaelic. Some participants sought to draw attention to a perceived gap between official aspiration and the social reality of Gaelic, pointing to language agencies and public bodies having a general lack of engagement with community concerns. It was contended that the situation of Gaelic in these areas represented a marginal issue for Gaelic public agencies, despite official claims to the contrary. This view is reinforced by the assertions at the meetings that Gaelic agencies had never held gatherings in the areas to discuss such issues with the communities, as exemplified by the following:

> Chan eil daoine a' faicinn nam buidhnean (Gàidhlig) an seo [*People don't see the Gaelic groups here*]. (Scalpay)
> Cò an fheadhainn a tha a' bruidhinn [mu dheidhinn na Gàidhlig]? Chan eil fhios againn! [*Who are the people speaking (about Gaelic)? We don't know!*] (Barra)

It was pointed out that culture and language are felt to be strongly linked in the social dynamic of Gaelic in the islands. Several participants portrayed Gaelic's socio-cultural context as an anchor for the language, and contended that there would be little impetus for language development efforts if the Gaelic communities in traditional areas ceased to exist. As one participant in Grimsay observed, the language is 'more than just a collection of words'. Others commented:

> Air cùl a' chànain, tha an cultar [*Behind the language, there's the culture*]. (South Uist)
> Monoglots don't understand the value of a second language because

they don't own it. Language is about history, culture and identity, not about words. (Barra)

Mura bi Gàidhlig sna h-eileanan, bidh i leis a' ghaoith, dè math dha na buidhnean Gàidhlig cumail a' dol? [*If there is no Gaelic in the islands, it'll be finished, why bother continuing with the Gaelic groups?*] (Ness)

Chan eil Bòrd na Gàidhlig a' ceangal a' chultair ris a' chànan — tha an cànan air a sgaradh bhon chultar anns a bheil i. Chan eil seo na chuideachadh air sgàth 's gu bheil an dà chuid cho ceangailte [*Bòrd na Gàidhlig do not connect culture with the language — language is dissociated from the culture of which it is a part. This is not helpful as the two are so connected*]. (Uig)

There were some positive comments made during and in communications following the meetings:

Gaelic is not strong in Point, but since the shop opened, this has provided a focal point for Gaelic speakers. (Ness)

In general, Comhairle nan Eilean are very supportive of Gaelic and GME, and wish to see it expand. (Harris)

The Mòd helps motivate children, as does supportive teachers … the children who have gone through GME are very proud of having done so … (Harris)[53]

People are very proud of their Gaelic heritage … Gaelic is coming back … it's good that young children are attending preschools and immersed in Gaelic. (Scalpay)

Those that do have the language, however, place Gaelic very highly in their sense of identity, the language being not only important as a sense of distinctiveness, but also the means by which they maintain their rootedness to the community around them — in other words, I sense that Gaelic is at the top of the list, above what job you have, your accent, your taste in music, as a factor of cultural pride to those that speak Gaelic (as it should be). (emailed comment after Grimsay meeting)

As you know there has been initiatives seeking to reverse the trend and on the face of it perhaps having some success. (different emailed comment after Grimsay meeting, see 5.7.3)

There is a lot of support for the language, and a lot of people are working for the good of the language and doing a great job. (Stornoway)

There are lots of projects happening at a local level. (Staffin)

---

53 On the other hand, many cultural events such as Fèisean (Gaelic music festivals for the young) were thought by some to be held largely in English, though these events receive funding from Gaelic bodies.

Overall, the general feeling from the meetings is that as things stand and given the current social context, there will be very little Gaelic spoken in the communities in 20 years' time, unless measures are taken urgently to revitalise the language in the islands:

> If we don't do something about it now … there'll be a little spoken, but nothing like there is now. (Staffin)
>
> There is a need for severe remedial help. (Tiree)
>
> Nan tigeadh rudeigin a bha na thogail don Ghàidhlig, bhiodh sin na thogail do dhaoine [*If something came which gave Gaelic a lift, that would encourage people*]. (Benbecula)
>
> Feumaidh taic mhaireannach a bhith ann [*Continuous support must be given*]. (Harris)

5.7.2 CURRENT GAELIC POLICIES

The attendees seemed to view local GME and cultural activities (such as Mòd competitions) separately from national Gaelic policies and agencies which are perceived to be remote and dissociated from the communities, leading to a degree of disengagement and alienation from official bodies in the islands (8.3). This has led to a measure of cynicism in communities regarding the aims and objectives of policy-making bodies. Suggestions were made that Gaelic agencies should be based in island areas where Gaelic is still spoken, rather than on the mainland. It is generally felt that there is too much of a focus by official bodies on increasing learner numbers in urban and mainland areas rather than supporting the indigenous Gaelic language communities of the islands, as indicated by the following comments:

> Tha e math a bhith a' searmonachadh do dhaoine ann an Glaschu is Dùn Èideann, tha e furasta oir tha daoine 'romantic' mu dheidhinn [na Gàidhlig]. Tha còir aca a bhith air barrachd a dhèanamh an-seo [*It's all very good to be sermonising to people in Glasgow and Edinburgh, it's easy because people are romantic about it (Gaelic). They should have done more here*]. (Scalpay)
>
> Bu toil leam barrachd fios a bhith agam … dè fios a tha acasan a tha aig a' Bhòrd? […] Tha poileasaidhean aig a' Chomhairle ach chan eil fios againn gu bheil iad ann [*I would like to have more information … what do those at the Bòrd know? […] The Council have policies but we don't know that they exist*]. (Scalpay)
>
> Tha na *policies* fad air falbh bho na coimhearsnachdan. Tha beàrn ann eadar *policies* agus na daoine [*The policies are far away from the communities. There is a gap between policies and the people*]. (North Uist)

An fheadhainn aig a bheil ùidh … chan eil iad a' coimhead air a' *bigger picture*. Bidh a' Ghàidhlig ann, ach gu dè an ìre? [*Those who are interested … they aren't looking at the bigger picture. Gaelic will exist, but to what extent?*] (North Uist)

Tha iad gan cur [*policies*] air pàipear is an uair sin gan cur ann an drathair. Tha feum againn an siostam uile gu lèir a sgrùdadh. Tha sinn aig *tipping point* [*They put them (policies) on paper and then put them in a drawer. We need to examine the whole system. We are at a tipping point*]. (South Uist)

Feumaidh *balance* a chumail ceart eadar luchd-ionnsachaidh agus muinntir san dualchas [*There must be a proper balance kept between learners and those who live in the culture*]. (South Uist)

What good do they do if there's nobody to implement them? (Eriskay)

Tha a' Ghàidhlig … 's e gnìomhachas a tha ann. Chan eil thu airson a bhith a' bruidhinn a-mach is an siostam uile gu lèir a thoirt sìos [*Gaelic is … it's a business. You don't want to speak out and bring the whole system down*]. (Barra)

Tha mi air a bhith a' cur às mo chorp agus ag obair gu saor thoileach bho chionn fhada, a' cur air adhart tachartasan sa Ghàidhlig ach tha mi a-nis air leigeil roimhe … [*I have been fulminating/busting a gut and working voluntarily for a long time, putting on Gaelic events, but now I have given up …*]. (emailed comment after Stornoway meeting)

Dè seòrsa coimhearsnachdan mì-nàdarrach a thèid a chruthachadh sna bailtean mòra? Ma tha cànan agus cultar gu bhith ann còmhla, feumaidh *positive discrimination* a bhith ann. Tha na h-eileanan air am fàgail gu aon taobh [a thaobh phoileasaidhean] … feumaidh Bòrd na Gàidhlig a bhith an sàs sna coimhearsnachdan son dèiligeadh ri na gnothaichean sin. Chan eil ùidh aig Bòrd na Gàidhlig sna coimhearsnachdan an-dràsta [*What sort of artificial communities will be created in the big cities? If language and culture are to exist together, then there needs to be positive discrimination. The islands are left behind (in policy-making terms) … Bòrd na Gàidhlig must go into the communities to get involved with these issues. Bòrd na Gàidhlig is not interested in communities just now*]. (Ness)[54]

---

54 A related comment from a community activist in Ness, Lewis, was reported by the BBC on 1/8/18: 'Living in the Gaelic heartland, where the highest concentration of speakers is found, how does she feel about new learners with no link to the language? "I spent my life teaching Gaelic to people from every place under the sun but the day we lose the natural communities where Gaelic is spoken I think Gaelic is going to become like Latin", she says. "It'll be a dead language". She sees it as a priority for public funding to support the language in the areas where it is still spoken — and where there are a wealth of dialects with their own idioms and sayings'. http://www.bbc.com/capital/story/20180731-can-27m-a-year-bring-a-language-back-from-near-death.

Chan eil poileasaidhean Gàidhlig a' buntainn ri muinntir Ùig idir [*Gaelic policies have nothing at all to do with the people of Uig*]. (Uig)

Concerns were expressed that within the Western Isles, too much Gaelic-related work is Stornoway-based, with very few jobs for native speakers in more rural areas. In addition, it was stated that many Gaelic-related jobs are in mainland urban areas. This combined with the lack of affordable housing, it was felt, contributes to a drift away from rural areas. All these elements have the effect of promoting a counterproductive skills drain.

Too many policies are felt to have a symbolic orientation rather than being focused on substantive initiatives and outcomes. Participants acknowledged that they were not particularly aware of the aims and remits of the Gaelic bodies and how their activities impacted on Gaelic development. Official Gaelic plans were felt not to have any appreciable impact on language use within local communities. Attendees felt that the current policies articulate ineffectively with their concerns and do not address underlying issues in their communities. It was suggested that locally-developed plans, with all interested agencies co-operating with local community members in their development are seen as potentially more effective mechanisms for language revitalisation. Several participants stated that Gaelic bodies and local authorities do not receive sufficient funding for what they are trying to achieve, though others felt a more targeted use of resources in community development efforts would be more fruitful.

Mixed views were expressed in relation to Gaelic-medium education (GME). It was generally viewed as a welcome development in that it offered a setting for the young to learn and speak Gaelic. Without GME it was felt that the use of Gaelic among the young would be virtually non-existent: it provided a context for Gaelic acquisition as an institutional alternative to the now very much contracted familial and communal transmission. However, there were calls for more extracurricular activities through the medium of Gaelic and more advice and support for parents. The opposite view was also expressed, in that the support offered to parents to bring their children up in Gaelic was sufficient. Mixed-ability and composite classes at preschool and primary levels (where fluent children and learners are taught together) were seen as being detrimental to the Gaelic development of more fluent children. A lack of suitably-qualified Gaelic-speaking support staff for children with additional or special needs was also highlighted.

Several participants at the meetings commented on what they felt were limitations in Gaelic linguistic proficiency of some of the children and some of the teachers in GME. The lack of preschool teachers was seen as an area of concern. Some contributors stated that more emphasis should be placed on the spoken word than on reading and writing in order to enhance Gaelic attainment in schools. At one public meeting attention was drawn to what was considered a contradictory aspect of GME provision in the islands: that GME pupils have less exposure to Gaelic as they advance through the GME system because there is not sufficient subject provision in the language as they progress through the secondary level. Provision at secondary level was perceived as conforming mainly with English-medium education with some provision for Gaelic educational inputs, rather than the whole system being recognisably Gaelic in its institutional orientation.

The advisability of official bodies emphasising the numbers involved in Gaelic-medium education as a meaningful sociolinguistic indicator was questioned by some attendees. They suggested that the extent of its productive social use and the quality of Gaelic being spoken and Gaelic use in the home would be more realistic indicators of the salience of Gaelic. One attendee stated that it was 'shameful' that there is no full GME secondary provision in the Western Isles. This compared disfavourably to the GME provision in Glasgow, for instance. It was felt that planning for Gaelic in education, and Gaelic policy-making in general at local authority level, was not supported by adequate strategic attention.

The following selection of comments indicate the tenor of the discussion on educational matters:

Chan eil mòran Gàidhlig san àrd-sgoil, fiù 's dhan fheadhainn ann am foghlam tro mheadhan na Gàidhlig. Mar as fhaide a thèid iad air adhart san t-siostam, 's ann as lugha Gàidhlig a bhios iad a' faighinn agus 's ann as motha Beurla, mar sin 's e suidheachadh Beurla a th' ann le beagan Gàidhlig [*There is not much Gaelic in secondary school, even for those in GME. The further they proceed in the system, the less Gaelic they get and the more English, therefore it is an English environment with a bit of Gaelic*]. (Stornoway)

Chan eil taic gu leòr ann sa Ghàidhlig dhan fheadhainn le feumalachdan sònraichte, faisg air mar a tha ann am foghlam sa Bheurla. Mura bheil sin ann, bidh pàrantan a' taghadh foghlam sa Bheurla [*Support for pupils with special needs is not as good in GME as it is for English-medium provision. If the learning support is not there for GME, parents choose English-medium provision*]. (Stornoway)

Tha e rudeigin coimheach an toirt tro fhoghlam Gàidhlig ach nuair a thig e gu cànan nas 'specialised', chan urrainn dhaibh. Tha e eagalach. Tha farsaingeachd chainnt a dhìth [*It's a bit strange taking them through Gaelic education, but when it comes to more specialised language, they can't. It's terrible. Ability in a range of speech is needed*]. (Benbecula)

Tha e glè mhath a bhith a' gealltainn foghlam tro mheadhan na Gàidhlig air feadh na dùthcha, ach chan eil tidsearan ann [*It's all very well to promise GME throughout the country, but there aren't any teachers*]. (Benbecula)

Many participants at the meetings emphasised the need to encourage the use of Gaelic and suggested that the school system should not be viewed as a panacea for the social decline of Gaelic. The weak social presence of Gaelic outside the school system contributed to the perception among the young that Gaelic is viewed as a 'school language' and not relevant to life outside the classroom. In relation to the media, programming policy in BBC ALBA was criticised by some participants. They felt that some Gaelic broadcasting could be characterised as poor imitations of English-language programmes. Radio nan Gàidheal was praised for its local content and relevance to island communities.

Academic engagement with Gaelic concerns also attracted adverse comments. It was mentioned that there were signs of 'research fatigue' in the Gaelic communities with some attendees feeling that a great deal of research has been conducted on Gaelic and its culture to little practical effect or benefit for native-speaking communities.

5.7.3 ENVISIONED COMMUNITY ACTIONS, NEW INITIATIVES AND THE FUTURE

The perceived lack of official leadership and a lack of direction in public policy in relation to Gaelic development in the community was a recurrent theme at the meetings. Assertions by attendees to the effect that communities feel themselves to be disempowered and disengaged from Gaelic agencies received strong backing at the meetings. Given that these meetings were held in areas which represent the highest densities of Gaelic speakers, this lack of engagement poses significant challenges for the efficacy of Gaelic language policy. It was suggested that efforts to make Gaelic language policy operate more effectively are hindered by an inability in public bodies to understand this feeling of detachment among the public from official priorities. Several people stated that the island communities felt remote from centres of influence and possessed a very limited number of mechanisms by which their collective voices could be heard within existing political or institutional structures. The lack of focused policy on traditional or vernacular communities prevents a proactive and productive engagement with the issues faced by the remaining social networks of Gaelic speakers.

It was repeatedly stated that Gaelic speakers should be much prouder of the language and take every opportunity to speak it more in their communities. More activities providing opportunities for Gaelic speakers (fluent and learners) to gather together informally would be welcomed. The Comainn Eachdraidh (local historical societies) are seen as mechanisms for providing focal points for such activities, and for instilling a sense of community pride in the language and culture, possibly leading to further Gaelic-related developments. It is accepted that communities need to do more themselves to develop Gaelic-focused initiatives in their own areas. In order to avoid a sense of communal unease about the social decline of the language, the substantive aspects of this difficult issue remain unaddressed. It was pointed out that there is a degree of mutual culpability in how both the community and officialdom avert their gaze from the unpleasant reality of the ongoing societal demise of Gaelic. However, many contended that communities felt constrained by an inability to influence change. Attendees also contended that communities lack the confidence to address the decline of vernacular Gaelic without being given the support of formal structures. The current system of short-term project funding for two or three years is not seen as an effective mechanism for long-term Gaelic development in the islands, it was asserted.

The following comments suggest a series of approaches to current issues:

> Surely there are examples of good 'practice' (not exactly the right word in this context) of where Gaelic is flourishing which could then be replicated in other realms of life? (emailed comment after Grimsay meeting)
> I am distressed by the number of families in the islands who still send their children into English-medium education, rather than Gaelic — even more distressing is the fact that many locals, and Gaelic speaking families, will do as such. This is a mind-set which is decades old, and every effort should be made to change this. ... People should be encouraged to take pride in their identity, in their local cultural identity, and language should be promoted as integral to culture, to help people see it as fundamental to their culture, and hence, to who they are themselves. ... Those that do have the language, however, place Gaelic very highly in their sense of identity, the language being not only important as a sense of distinctiveness, but also the means by which they maintain their rootedness to the community around them. ... Academic work on the language is vital, but unless people on the ground, in communities, create opportunities for using, normalising and changing the devalued Gaelic mind-set, it will never improve. (different emailed comment after Grimsay meeting, see 5.7.1)

The difficulties involved in Gaelic community development efforts were highlighted in comments made by one attendee:

> Thòisich sinn ... bho chionn faisg air deich bliadhna a' cur air adhart dealbhan-cluiche dha clubaichean daoine a tha thairis air 60 ... Nuair a thòisich sinn bha ochd buidhnean ann ... bho chionn trì bliadhna cha robh ann ach trì buidhnean a ghabhadh sinn. Bha na còig eile ag ràdh 'Tha Goill againn nar cois a-nis, agus an dèan sibh rud sa Bheurla?' 'Cha dèan'. Bhithinn a' dèanamh clasaichean Gàidhlig sa choimhearsnachd agus cha robh taic bho na buidhnean Gàidhlig, neo a' cholaiste, neo a' chomhairle, a dh'aindeoin gach *strategy* agus plana a bhith a' co-obrachadh son adhartas

a thoirt air a' chànan. Tha mi an dòchas nach eil mi ro dhubhach ach tha mi a' dèanamh luaidh air an t-suidheachadh mar a tha mise ga fhaicinn anns na h-eileanan [*We started … nearly ten years ago to put on plays for clubs for over-60s … When we started there were eight groups … three years ago there were only three groups that would take us. The other five said that 'We have Goill (Lowlanders or non-Gaelic speakers) amongst us now and will you do something in English? No'. I had been running classes in the community and I did not receive any support / funding from the Gaelic groups or the college or the council, in spite of every strategy and plan to co-operate to develop the language. I hope that I'm not being too pessimistic but I am commenting on the situation as I see it in the islands*]. (emailed comment after Stornoway meeting)

Participants were concerned that Gaelic identity and culture were being devalued in the community. To counter this, suggestions were made at several meetings that some form of incentivisation and positive discrimination is required, such as the Gaelic apprenticeship schemes offered in Lewis. It was felt that there is a need to harness community development to link language, culture and the environment together in a sustainable manner and to reawaken a sense of Gaelic identity amongst the younger generations.

5.7.4 SUMMARY

The opinions and viewpoints expressed at the public meetings indicate a perceived need for more support and resources to maintain Gaelic in the Western Isles, Skye and Tiree. Given the general awareness of its current marginal social presence (even in what were the strongest remaining Gaelic-speaking locales), it was felt a change of direction and a reprioritisation in public policy is required if the language is to be revitalised as a vernacular. The discussions in community consultations reflect the depiction of the situation presented in other chapters in this report, indicating that the attendees are broadly aware of the social process unfolding around them. This can be seen in many of the observations about the social position of Gaelic in the Western Isles (and Tiree and Staffin):

- The generational gap in Gaelic competence and use
- The divergence between reported ability in Gaelic (in the census) and its much lower familial practice
- The contraction in the societal salience of Gaelic
- The related erosion of Gaelic culture as a marker of island identity
- The relatively minor level of importance accorded to Gaelic concerns in socio-economic development and in support agencies at local and national levels

- The limitations, given current priorities, in the capacity of public bodies to engage with the societal absence of Gaelic or reinforce the presence of Gaelic in the islands
- Limitations in the educational sphere.

Many of the issues highlighted in the meetings and the calls for greater support and strategic co-operation to intervene proactively in support of the Gaelic networks in island communities are not new, and have been set out in a number of papers and publications by various authors (e.g. MacKinnon (2011c), Munro *et al.* on Shawbost (2011) and the 'Cor na Gàidhlig' report (1982)). Several of the concerns in relation to Gaelic-medium education and social use of Gaelic among younger generations have been noted previously, in papers such as Dunmore (2015), Morrison (2006), Müller (2006), NicAoidh (2010) and Stiùbhart (2011).

Those in attendance at the meetings demonstrated a great deal of goodwill and concern for the future prospects of Gaelic in the islands; many attendees are involved in community development and language support initiatives in a professional or voluntary capacity. Many of the contributions to the meetings revolved around the theme of the importance of the social continuity of Gaelic in the islands as an integral component of the sustainability of Gaelic culture and identity in general. The promotion of Gaelic independent of its vernacular context in the island communities was regarded by many as a synthetic construct rather than an organic endeavour. It was felt that a synthetic construct would be even more difficult to sustain. The point was made on a number of occasions that the rationale to continue with language development efforts nationally would be severely compromised if the trajectory of demise of spoken Gaelic continued in the islands. In an associated observation, many participants contended that the concerns of the Gaelic vernacular speakers in the islands were not afforded adequate strategic attention in the broader national focus on language planning and policy. Several attendees voiced their concerns about the perceived remoteness from the centres of influence, and a lack of consultation, as well as a lack of opportunity to influence policy decisions and implementation. It was claimed that Gaelic-related concerns were hindered by a lack of effective leadership, and that the communities' views in public debates on Gaelic issues in general are rarely articulated and therefore do not inform current language development policies and practices at local or national levels. In turn, this lack of leadership means that Gaelic concerns are often considered a non-issue in relation to socio-economic and other developmental aims, even when focused on the remaining spatial extent of vernacular Gaelic.

It was pointed out that Gaelic speakers generally defer to the social dominance of English in all public forums and service provision even in the strongest remaining Gaelic areas. Some contributors spoke about the common concern that efforts to be more assertive in relation to the practice and promotion of Gaelic locally could lead to dissension and possible disharmony within the community, both from monolingual English speakers' points of view and from some Gaelic speakers' perspectives. This dilemma, it was pointed out, often led to local Gaelic revitalisation efforts taking the line of least resistance, resulting in an acquiescence with the social pre-eminence of English rather than offering the possibility of a dynamic outcome for the Gaels. It was felt that this in turn is a contributory factor in the perceived low levels of overt community interest and enthusiasm for participating in language planning efforts (5.8.1.1). In this regard, the communities themselves could be perceived as being equally evasive, as in the case of the official bodies. In short, the perceived communal and official aversion to facing up to the difficulties of addressing the reality of the decline of vernacular Gaelic was remarked upon.

5.8 MAJOR FINDINGS FROM THE COMMUNITY SOCIOLINGUISTIC SURVEY

5.8.1 MAIN FINDINGS FROM APPENDIX 5

This chapter, in the main, has presented the aggregated findings of the CSS. The main aim of **Appendix 5** is to present the data concerning Scalpay, Grimsay and Eriskay for each island separately, i.e. in unaggregated form. There is additionally some presentation of aggregated data in **Appendix 5**. The unaggregated data for the three islands indicates similar sociolinguistic patterns to the aggregated data. The weakest comparable profile is found for Grimsay and the strongest for Scalpay, in relation to the other islands. Some important aspects of the findings presented in the Appendix, but absent from the main body of data presented in the Chapter, are summarised here.

5.8.1.1 *ATTITUDES TOWARDS GAELIC, SUPPORT FOR GAELIC AND EQUIVOCAL ENGAGEMENT WITH GAELIC ISSUES*

The CSS findings confirm that a strong support for Gaelic is claimed, even among non-Gaelic-speaking respondents. It is in the survey question enquiring about what people would be willing to do to support the language in their own area that we see more of a reluctance to engage with official bodies. In the case of the suggested initiatives in support of Gaelic which require relatively little in the way of personal investment, such as using the language with those who can speak it, the willingness to participate or agree with the statement was almost 50 percentage points higher (but still very far from actual practice). MacKinnon (1977: 124), writing on the position in the Isle of Harris in the mid-1970s, suggested that similar views have existed in the longer-term: 'Agitation as an aspect of behaviour regarding language is absent in the Gaelic context. [...] Reluctance to initiate activism and agitation within a small community is common and understandable'. The divergence in the acceptability of the various statements is consistent with the prioritisation of the informal practice of Gaelic in minoritised and bilingualised neighbour and familial networks, over communal, societal, politicised or status-building measures in larger networks and more formal domains and interactions.

The responses in the survey indicate a divergence between language practice and many of the suggested actions respondents claimed they would take to mitigate the erosion of Gaelic in the community (**Figures A5.10** and **A5.21**). For example, 52.1% of children raised by respondents were raised with some Gaelic input (from *Gaelic only* to *Mix*; 5.4.9), yet 77.2% of respondents reported that they would support Gaelic in the area by speaking the language to all who have Gaelic. 30.7% of respondents in all districts report that they speak *Gaelic only* to their friends now (**A5.5.4**; **A5.6.4**; **A5.7.4**), but 80.6% claim they would speak Gaelic to their friends and neighbours. Notwithstanding these indications of commitment to speak Gaelic, 58.5% of respondents felt that the language would be weaker by 2036 (**Figure A5.9**), which is consistent with the finding that slightly more respondents speak *English only* to teenagers (43.4%) than speak *Gaelic only* at present to any age cohort (43.3% of respondents speak *Gaelic only* to the over-65 age cohort, representing the highest proportion of *Gaelic only* usage, although 46.2% of respondents reported speaking *Gaelic only to friends when younger*; see **A5.4.1.1** and **A5.4.2**). The CSS highlights a gap between the language attitudes and aspirations of the respondents and especially how they use Gaelic with the young. 88.8% of respondents claim to be *Very unhappy* with English only being spoken in the future (**Figure A5.7**) but 38.8% speak *English only* to children (**Figure A5.3**). The Teenager Survey results also show that only a small proportion of those parents and teenage children who have an ability in Gaelic actually converse with each other in Gaelic (4.6.1). The high proportion (88%) of survey respondents who felt that fluent Gaelic-speaking parents should raise their children in Gaelic (although 'parents' in the query can be interpreted as referring to one or two Gaelic-speaking parents), contrasts with the relatively-low proportions of all respondents who reported using *Gaelic only* with primary-school-aged children (8.8%), and *Gaelic only* with teenagers (6.9%); 52.1% of respondents raise children in their household with some Gaelic input (from *Gaelic only* to *Mix*).

On the other hand, these language attitudes are consistent with their future aspirations for Gaelic in the context of GME provision. 93.9% of respondents would be unhappy to see GME cease in the Western Isles, while 78.9% expressed themselves as being very unhappy at the thought that no children would be brought up in Gaelic in the future. However, the current levels of practice of Gaelic in the community are inconsistent with hopes for its future use. In the context of maintaining positive aspirations for Gaelic in the face of its societal demise, placing the communities' hopes for Gaelic in the GME basket is understandable.

5.8.2 MAIN FINDINGS

This chapter comprised a census-like survey of reported abilities in, and practices of, Gaelic, as well as attitudes to the language, in two of the islands currently exhibiting some of the strongest Gaelic-language profiles and one with a mid-range Gaelic profile. The survey also examined the participants' views on identity, and the vitality or fragility of Gaelic in its remaining social context.

The principal negative finding of this module was the increasing divergence between the high instance of fluent, native-speaker Gaelic ability among older respondents who claim a local or Western Isles background, the lower levels of fluency evinced in younger age cohorts and the concurrent demise of Gaelic socialisation in these younger cohorts as well as in many other social domains. This generational contrast suggests that Gaelic has become more marginal to communal life in the three islands. The language-practice data (5.4.7; 5.4.9; 5.4.10; **A5.4.2**) indicate that Gaelic is spoken largely by those in middle age and older age groups, while Gaelic is a peripheral aspect of the lives of the majority of those in the younger age cohort (outside GME).

5.8.2.1 *THE DEMOLINGUISTICS OF THE COMMUNITIES AND FAMILIES*

Indications in this chapter of the steep decline of intergenerational transmission and familial use of Gaelic among the younger cohorts mirror the findings in the surveys of the preschools (3.2.4) and the teenagers (4.11). The majority of respondents aged under 45 are not fluent in Gaelic (63.6%, 14 respondents out of a total of 22), with the fluent Gaelic speakers in the minority of under-45s (36.4%, 8 respondents). This corroborates the evidence in Chapter 6 which indicates a considerable contraction in the proportion of Gaelic speakers among those born in the 1970s (6.5). The more detailed evidence of Chapters 5 and 6 indicates that the 1970s was a major turning point in the contraction of Gaelic transmission (in contrast to the census data which shows a contraction from the 1980s onwards). The recurring theme of the gap between higher ability levels in Gaelic and lower levels of Gaelic use is also apparent in the sociolinguistic findings of the CSS.

In terms of age cohorts, 72% of respondents aged over 65 reported themselves as fluent in Gaelic, while 85.4% of those respondents aged over 75 indicated a similar level, with majorities (around 58%) fluent in each ten-year cohort over the age of

45. While 62.9% of all respondents are fluent in Gaelic, this percentage stands at 87.8% of those from the Western Isles (including local to one of the three islands). At a smaller geographical level, of those respondents who come from the three island communities, the proportion of fluent native-speaker ability in Gaelic across all age cohorts is 89.8%, with a further 1.9% of local respondents claiming to have learned Gaelic to fluency. By contrast, 36.4% of the local island respondents under 45 have fluency in Gaelic.

Regarding family household practice of Gaelic, 31.6% of respondents report that their spouses speak only or mainly Gaelic to them, while 46.9% report that their spouses speak *English only* to them (5.4.7). Nationally, according to the 2011 Census, c. 25,000 people (0.49% of the Scottish population) reported using Gaelic at home, which equates to 40% of all Gaelic speakers in Scotland. However, 15.5% of all respondents' children were raised in households only or mainly through Gaelic, while 47.9% of children were raised through *Mainly English* or *English only* (5.4.9). However, 54.4% of children were reported to speak *English only* to respondents at present, indicative of a further erosion of Gaelic's position as a household language (5.4.10).

5.8.2.2 *LANGUAGE PRACTICE IN BIOGRAPHICAL AND APPARENT TIME*

In this section, we draw various strands of information together from this and other chapters regarding the trajectories through time of the use of Gaelic and/or English. The responses to the Likert-scale queries on language practice in the several IGRP modules indicate the proportions of various language practices found among various age cohorts: from the monolingual mode in either Gaelic or English to more mixed-mode Gaelic–English practices. Through the generational practices sampled in the IGRP, we can see a development from a higher proportion of monolingual Gaelic practice to a prevalence of a mixed bilingual mode to monolingual English-dominant mode. This can be seen in considerable detail through (a) the separate communities, as well as through (b) the specific age cohorts and (c) through the individual's life span, as well as (d) individuals' differentiated practices with older, middle-aged, and younger cohorts. In the language-related information in this chapter, the varying proportions of bilingual modes are evident in the change from *Gaelic only* prevalent both in respondents' upbringing and in their practice with the oldest age cohort, and then a mixed mode in the respondents' speech to the 18–39 year-olds and finally to a dominant English-only mode spoken to the teenager cohort (5.4.11, Figure 5.21). Similarly, in Table 5.10 (5.4.9), a mixed Gaelic–English mode spoken by children at 22.1% is nearly four times more prevalent than a *Gaelic only* mode at 5.9%.

We present six figures to illustrate the developments, a synoptic version first in Figure 5.27 which shows four of the age-ranked categories which evince the (near) highest proportions of *Gaelic only*, *Mix* and *English only*. From a representative sample of the data (presented in separate detail in Chapters 3–5), Figures 5.27 and 5.28 illustrate the intergenerational developments in language practice, as percentages of individuals per cohort who practice these modes. First, Figure 5.27 shows the percentage language practice (from *Gaelic only* to *English only*) of four cohorts with maximal percentages (from the oldest (in apparent time) to the youngest (in apparent time)).

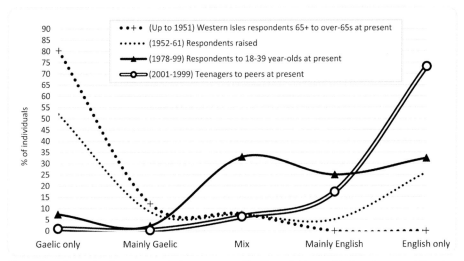

Figure 5.27 *Synopsis of percentages in language practice through biographical and apparent time in four sample categories*

The four categories of Figure 5.27 are included in Figure 5.28 which shows the percentage language practice of eight representative biographical and apparent-time cohorts, from the oldest to the youngest (see footnote 55). The synoptic presentation with the reduced number of categories in Figure 5.27 helps illustrate:

1. the mirror-image contrast between the *Gaelic only* dominant oldest ((*Up to 1951*) *Western Isles*) and *English only* dominant youngest ((*2001–1999*) *Teenagers*) categories, neither of which entail substantial percentages in the middle language-practice categories of *Mainly Gaelic*, *Mix* and *Mainly English* (practices which, when combined, are termed 'broader mixed mode' in this section);

2. the *Mix* dominant practice among the middle-ranked ((*1978–99*) *Respondent to 18–39*) age category.

As stated, Figure 5.28 displays a greater sample of these cohorts.

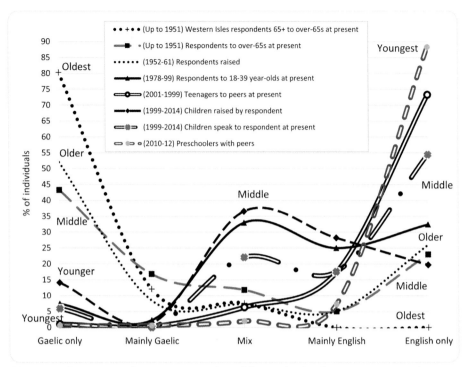

Figure 5.28 *Percentages in language practice through biographical and apparent time in eight sample categories*

In Figures 5.27 and 5.28, we give in parentheses the range of the birth periods of the relevant cohorts in order to give a general idea of the developments through the generations. The cohorts comprise the following:

(Up to 1951) Western Isles respondents, aged 65+, to over-65s at present (termed apparent time; cp. 5.4.11); with the year 1951 as the latest birth year calculated for those over 65 years in 2016 (year of CSS), taking the age cohort of the addressees and speakers as the comparator. Basically, this category represents the language practice of older Western Isles respondents with their age peers (over-65s, born pre-1952). (N = 66)

(Up to 1951) Respondents to over-65s at present (termed apparent time; 5.4.11); with the year 1951 as the latest birth year calculated for those over 65 years in 2016, taking the age cohort of the addressees as the comparator (the speakers comprise all age cohorts among the respondents and all geographic backgrounds).

(1952–61) Respondents raised (termed biographical time; 5.4.4); calculated on the birth range of the average age cohort of the respondents 55–64 in 2016 (5.4.1, *Another language* not shown in figure).

(1978–99) Respondents to 18–39 year-olds at present (termed apparent time;

5.4.11); with the years 1978–99 as the birth range for the 18–39 year-olds in 2016, taking the age cohort of the addressees as the comparator.

(2001–1999) Teenagers to peers at present (termed apparent time; 4.6.3, Figure 4.26, *Another language* not shown in figure); calculated on the birth range for 15–17 year-olds in 2016 (year of IGRP Teenager Survey).

(1999–2014) Children raised by respondent (termed biographical time; 5.4.9); calculated on the birth range for 2–17 year-olds in 2016, taking the age cohort of the addressees as the comparator.

(1999–2014) Children speak to respondent at present (termed apparent time; 5.4.10).

(2010–12) Preschoolers with peers (termed apparent time; 3.2.4.3, *Another language* not shown in figure); calculated on the birth range for 3–5 year-olds in 2015 (year of IGRP Preschool Survey).[55]

With regard to geographic origin, these categories can be differentiated broadly into two types: those of Western Isles background, and those from elsewhere. All the comparisons are therefore not comprehensively equivalent but they nevertheless reflect the actual communal dynamics of how the various (sub)groups affect the overall picture. Furthermore, the following groups are broadly speaking of a Western Isles background, and they span the full biographical or apparent-time range: *Western Isles respondents, aged 65+*; *Children raised by respondent*; *Children speak to respondent*; *Preschoolers with peers* (as well as *Western Isles respondents, aged 55+* in Figures 5.29–5.32). From a brief inspection of Figures 5.27 and 5.28, it is apparent that *Gaelic only* is found in higher proportions among the three oldest age categories of the eight displayed, that *Mix* of Gaelic and English is highest among

---

55 Apparent time refers to interpreting a speaker's age as an indicator and measure of language change through time, e.g. that the way older speakers speak is representative of older ways of speaking in comparison to younger speakers' speech which contains new developments and advanced changes. Biographical time refers to interpreting how speakers remember past linguistic use and experience, and in particular contrasts earlier experience with later and current language use. The conceptions of time in the composition of Figures 5.27–5.32 are complex, with some categories overlapping in their perspective of time. But we use them here to contribute to an overview of the intergenerational sociolinguistic dynamics and trajectory, with the maximal time span available in the IGRP data. Three categories entail apparent time (of the speakers): *(2001–1999) Teenagers to peers at present*; *(1999–2014) Children speak to respondent at present*; *(2010–12) Preschoolers with peers*. Two categories entail apparent time of the addressee (*(Up to 1951) Respondents to over-65s at present*; *(1978–99) Respondents to 18–39 year-olds at present*); and another category entails addressee apparent time modified by speaker apparent time (*(Up to 1951) Western Isles respondents 65+ to over-65s at present*; with a further analogous category in Figure 5.29: *(Up to 1951) Western Isles respondents, aged 55+, to over-65s at present*). Two categories entail biographical time: one, the biographical time of the respondents with regard to how they were raised (*(1952–61) Respondents raised*), and the other, the biographical time of the children addressees with regard to how they were raised by the respondents (*(1999–2014) Children raised by respondent*). Clearly the category of 'addressee apparent time', based on respondents' use to these cohorts, is only used as a vague pointer to the language practice common to these apparent-time age cohorts. This category is discussed further with reference to Figure 5.29 as well as in footnotes 56 and 58.

the three categories comprising speech to children and speech to young adults and children's speech, and that the highest proportions of *English only* are found among preschoolers, teenagers and children.

The data was displayed in Figures 5.27 and 5.28 with the development of language practices on the x-axis. We can also arrange the development with biographic and apparent time on the x-axis to visualise the time dimension more clearly. In Figure 5.29, a sample of similar basic data is shown through biographical and apparent time, illustrating how the three percentage curves of language modes *Gaelic only*, *Mix* and *English only* decrease and increase, according to the proportions of those practicing these modes.

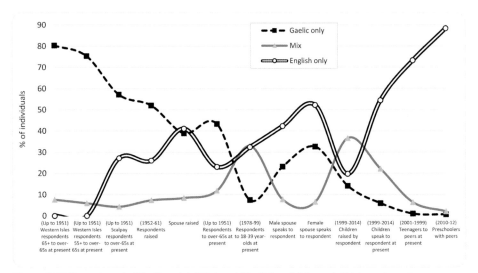

Figure 5.29 *Percentages in 'Gaelic only', 'Mix' and 'English only' through thirteen stages in sociobiographical and apparent time*

As an instance of how the time model is to be interpreted in Figures 5.29–5.32, the language practice of those placed further to the left on the x-axis, e.g. *(Up to 1951) Western Isles respondents, aged 65+, to over-65s at present*, can be taken to represent an earlier practice than those placed further to the right on the timeline, e.g. *(2001–1999) Teenagers to peers at present*, which represent a later practice. Figure 5.29 provides an additional apparent-time category in the age-ranked language practice data:

> *(Up to 1951) Western Isles respondents, aged 55+, to over-65s at present* (termed apparent time; cp. 5.4.11); with the year 1951 as the latest birth year calculated for those addressees aged over 65 years in 2016 (year of CSS), with the speakers including those born before 1962. (N = 85)

This age category, added in Figure 5.29, shows the reduction in use of *Gaelic only* by the cohort born before 1962 (which includes all of those born before 1952) in comparison to the older cohort born before 1952, even though the addressees are the same 'over 65s'. As would be expected, both the age of the addressee and of the age of the speaker are of relevance for language practice. This is an instance of the evidence behind the rationale for the age categorisations and analysis in biographical and apparent time (addressee, speaker) of these data. In this context, it should be noted that the age category of *(1999–2014) Children raised by respondent* coming on the x-axis before *(2001–1999) Teenagers to peers at present* is not in strict apparent-time order in Figures 5.29–5.32, given that the *Teenagers* have an earlier average year of birth than the *Children*. For the purpose of the consistency of the data curves, however, the order of these two categories are reversed, while noting that: 1) there is evidence in the IGRP that the social use of Gaelic decreases in the teenage age group (so that the teenagers are more 'advanced' along the trajectory than younger children, justifying their being placed after *Children* on the x-axis; cf. 5.4.8); 2) adolescents are commonly more advanced than younger children in apparent time in ongoing language change (e.g. Denis, Hunt Gardner, Brook and Tagliamonte 2019); cp. footnote 58); 3) in fact, if the data curves were to be portrayed with a consistent fall or rise, the category of *(1999–2014) Children raised by respondent* would come before *(1978–99) Respondent to 18–39 year-olds at present* on the x-axis, which indicates that respondents' practice speaking to the young adult cohort is more 'advanced' along the trajectory than when speaking to *Children*; and 4) the two *Children* age categories are, however, positioned next to each other on the x-axis to enable visual comparison and to avoid any more breaching of the apparent-time order. For the sake of comparison, three other categories are placed on the x-axis in more approximate positions without dates. These relate to spouse language background and practice: *Spouse raised*; *Male spouse speaks to respondent*; *Female spouse speaks to respondent*. We use the cover-term sociobiographical to refer to categories which do not fall within the apparent-time models.

The data curves in Figure 5.29 show an undulated curve of *Mix* and two curves of falling *Gaelic only* and rising *English only*. In fact, the curve of *Gaelic only* resembles an S-curve (reversed S-curve, to be precise: 2.4.1.5.1; 6.5.2.1). However, *Gaelic only* and *English only* show an upward and downward protuberance, respectively, at the apparent-time category of *(1999–2014) Children raised by respondent* (5.4.9). This reflects the greater practice of *Gaelic only* (at 14.1%; in contrast with <10% of nearest age-ranked cohorts) and less practice of *English only* (at 19.7%; in contrast with <40%–<60% of nearest age-ranked cohorts), spoken by respondents to young children, than anticipated, given the language shift trajectory (5.4.8–11). This effect of the rise of *Gaelic only* and the fall of *English only* is accompanied by the continued gradual increase of *Mix* to its actual highest point of 36.6% in this category of speech addressed by the respondents to children in the household (with the peak in the category of *Broader mixed mode* at 66.2% even more evident in Figure 5.30 below).

Clearly, when one mode decreases, this leaves the potential for other modes to increase. In this instance, the decrease in *English only* mode is accompanied by an increase in both *Gaelic only* mode and *Mix* mode. In fact, the percentage differences between the age categories on the three curves show the dimensions of the 'pinch' in *Gaelic only* and *English only* curves (at the category of *(1999–2014) Children raised by respondent*): the decreasing *English only* value is in the c. 10%–30% range, which can be viewed as contributing fairly equally to the increase in the *Gaelic only* category by c. 5% and to the increase in *Mix* in the range of c. 4%–14%. The equivalent full language practice percentages in Figure 5.30 are: 14.1% *Gaelic only*, 66.2% *Broader mixed mode*, 19.7% *English only*. One can interpret this increase in the practice of Gaelic (increased *Gaelic only* and *Mix* or *Broader mixed mode*; with the concomitant decrease in English), visualised in the 'pinch' in the data curves (in Figures 5.29–31), as a reflection of parental effort or family language policy of practicing more Gaelic in order to contribute to the familial transmission of Gaelic, against the social trajectory of decline in Gaelic use.[56]

It is important to recall that, for the sake of visual and initial analytic simplicity, *Mainly Gaelic* and *Mainly English* are excluded from Figure 5.29 (with the result that the percentages do not total to 100%) but their respective curves are, of course, of relevance, and evince a mirror-image pattern: *Mainly Gaelic* is higher than *Mix* for the four categories furthest to the left on the x-axis; whereas *Mainly English* is higher than *Mix* for the two categories furthest to the right on the x-axis; and *Mix* is higher than either *Mainly Gaelic* or *Mainly English* in the three remaining central categories: *(1978–99), (1999–2014), (1999–2014)*. This mirror-image pattern of the two *Mainly* categories can be seen in an inspection of Figures 5.27 and 5.28. Figures 5.30 and 5.31 below illustrate the full gamut of language practice by adding *Mainly Gaelic* and *Mainly English* into the aggregated category of *Broader mixed mode* in Figure 5.30; and by adding *Mainly Gaelic* and *Mainly English* into the categories of *Predominant*

---

56 Smith-Christmas (2016) describes the RLS efforts by members of the grandparental and parental generations in one family on the Isle of Skye. The RLS efforts of these family members, particularly by the grandmother and mother, sought to achieve the transmission of Gaelic to the third generation of the family born between 2002 and 2010. The third generation, however, are at best passive Gaelic acquirers at home (basically not speaking Gaelic at home), although they do use Gaelic in a GME context. Many of the themes in Smith-Christmas (2016) are also evidenced in the IGRP study: 1) the lack of productive or constructive evidence-based family language-planning advice for (grand)parents from any RLS agency or any public body; 2) the reduced ability and practice of Gaelic in the parental generation (born since 1970); 3) (grand)parental Gaelic input is less than child Gaelic output; 4) Gaelic ability in the three generations is greater than Gaelic practice among the three generations; 5) decrease or loss of practice of Gaelic after the early-primary school age; 6) the diachronic reduction in the use of Gaelic through the three generations and decrease in the speakers' productive use of Gaelic through time (2016: 34–35, i.e. real-time data with reduction in Gaelic between 2009 and 2014); 7) the most common language modes are monolingual English and codemixed Gaelic; 8) the negative impact of English peer-socialisation in GME settings; 9) the positive impact of GME in providing the primary productive context for the use of Gaelic (with GME staff); and 10) the general lack of Gaelic comprehensiveness in familial, communal, educational and regional contexts (see 2.4.1.5.1).

Gaelic and *Predominant English*, respectively, in Figure 5.31.

Taken together, Figures 5.27–5.32 present dynamic visualisations of the intergenerational shift from dominant monolingual practice of Gaelic, via a short period containing considerable mixed use, and currently proceeding towards English monolingualisation. They illustrate how the sociolinguistic wave of mixed use (the centre of the figures) is attendant on the wave of English use. In the overall trajectory from Gaelic dominance to English dominance, this mixed phase can be interpreted as a core aspect of the penultimate phase of shift with regard to language practice.

In fact, a certain degree of mixing is entailed in the three categories of language practice at the middle of the Likert continuum: *Mainly Gaelic*; *Mix of Gaelic and English* and *Mainly English*, which, when combined, can be termed the 'broader mixed mode'. Some sample percentages of this more broadly defined mixed mode are given here, showing also the trajectory of change through increased broader mixing (= *Mainly Gaelic + Mix of Gaelic and English + Mainly English*):

> *Respondents raised through* 20.9% broader mixing (5.4.4);
> *Respondents speak to over-65 year-olds* 33.7% broader mixing (5.4.11);
> *Respondents speak to 18–39 year-olds* 60.2% broader mixing (5.4.11);
> *Children raised through* 66.2% broader mixing (5.4.9);

followed by examples in which *English only* has become dominant in subsequent age cohorts and where both *Gaelic only* and the broader mixed mode are reduced and become marginal; as seen in the percentages of the broader mixed mode:

> *Children speak to respondents* 39.7% broader mixing (5.4.9);
> *Teenagers to peers* 24.1% broader mixing (4.6.3);
> *Preschoolers with peers* 9.9% broader mixing (3.2.4.3).

A further indication of the prevalence of mixing, and the proportions of other language practice modes, can be seen in STS data on language practice in the three-point Likert scale (*Gaelic only*, *Mix of Gaelic and English*, *English only*) with *Mix* in:

> households with young children at 35.3% *Mix* (6.6.2, Table 6.3).

When viewed in this category of broader mixed mode, the lifecycle of this mixing can be displayed in apparent time in Figure 5.30.

The total percentage of language practice is included in Figure 5.30, with none of the language-practice data excluded for ease of initial analysis or perspective. It is clear in Figure 5.30 that the *Broader mixed mode* waxes and then wanes as it crosses the *English only* curve at c. 45% and when *English only* becomes more prevalent at 54.4% *English only* and 39.7% *Broader mixed mode* among the age category of *(1999–2014) Children speak to respondent* at present.

As stated, the language practice category of the 'broader mixed mode' combines *Mainly Gaelic*, *Mix of Gaelic and English* and *Mainly English*; and thus aggregates the five-point language practice scale into three categories: *Gaelic only*, broader mixed mode, and *English only*. We also explicated above how the two language practice categories termed *Mainly*, i.e. *Mainly Gaelic* and *Mainly English*, decrease and increase respectively through to younger generations similar to how *Gaelic only* decreases and *English only* increases, except at the extreme ends of the apparent-time axis, where *Mainly Gaelic* and *Mainly English* are lower or higher than their nearest age group.[57] One can get an idea of the overall impact of the categories *Mainly Gaelic* and *Mainly English* on the apparent-time change by combining them with the values of *Gaelic only* and *English only* respectively to produce the categories *Predominant Gaelic* and *Predominant English*. The five-point language practice scale is thereby aggregated into three different categories: *Predominant Gaelic* (= *Gaelic only* + *Mainly Gaelic*), *Mix*, and *Predominant English* (= *English only* + *Mainly English*). The total language practice can, therefore, be analysed in this simplified trimodal perspective (in percentage terms, each apparent-time cohort adds up to 100%). Figure 5.31 shows this trimodal view-point of the language practice scale and its developments through the same sample of apparent time.

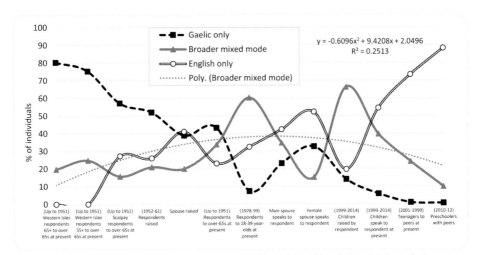

Figure 5.30 *Percentages in 'Gaelic only', 'Broader mixed mode' and 'English only' through thirteen stages in sociobiographical and apparent time (including polynomial linear trend line (Poly.))*

---

57 In Figure 5.28, *Mainly Gaelic* is slightly higher for the younger apparent-time category *(Up to 1951) Respondents to over-65s at present* than for the immediately older apparent-time category *(Up to 1951) Western Isles respondents, aged 65+, to over-65s at present*. Similarly, *Mainly English* is slightly lower for younger apparent-time category *(2010–12) Preschoolers with peers* than for the immediately older *(2001–1999) Teenagers to peers at present*.

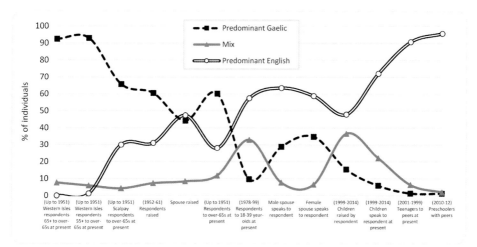

Figure 5.31 *Percentages in 'Predominant Gaelic', 'Mix' and 'Predominant English' through thirteen stages in sociobiographical and apparent time*

In Figure 5.31, we now have a fuller picture of the developments, in that, *grosso modo*, this trimodal analysis of language practices can be interpreted as being a more accurate depiction of the sociolinguistic situation than that of Figure 5.30 (with the *Broader mix mode*). The bilingualised language-practice patterns in the Western Isles resemble those of many minoritised language groups, in that they commonly show three prevalent language-practice modes: 1) code-mixed minority language; 2) majority language with some minority-language borrowings or low-level code-mixing; 3) code-switching (between codemixed minority language and the majority language). It is possible that the trimodal analysis in Figure 5.31 resembles this pattern: 1) *Predominant Gaelic* similar to code-mixed Gaelic; 2) *Predominant English* similar to English with some minority-language borrowings or low-level code-mixing; 3) *Mix* similar to code-switching between (code-mixed) Gaelic and English.

The overall pattern in Figure 5.31 is similar to Figures 5.29 and 5.30 above, including the kink in the curves at the age category of *(1999–2014) Children raised by respondent*, in this instance evinced by increased *Predominant Gaelic* (at 15.5%; in contrast to 9.7% and 5.9% of nearest age-ranked cohorts) and decreased *Predominant English* (at 47.9%; in contrast with 57.4% and 72.0% of nearest age-ranked cohorts). The most noticeable difference between Figure 5.31 and Figure 5.29 is that the *Mix* curve remains below *Predominant English* in Figure 5.31. In Figure 5.31 the *Mix* curve is initially slightly higher than the *Predominant English* curve, but the *Mix* curve rises at a slower rate than *Predominant English*, then *Mix* rises at a similar rate as *Predominant English*, but the *Mix* curve peaks and then falls, while *Predominant English* continues its rise towards the maximum of 95.6% among *(2010–*

12) Preschoolers with peers. The *Mix* mode, as it were, follows the rise of *Predominant English* for a period before decreasing to 2%.

Finally, in order to gain a very simplified overview of the general distribution of Gaelic and English through apparent-time language practice, we can aggregate language practice modes into a bimodal display, by dividing the percentages of *Mix* mode equally between *Predominant Gaelic* and *Predominant English* yielding two modes: *Total Gaelic* (= *Predominant Gaelic* + ½ *Mix*) and *Total English* (= *Predominant English* + ½ *Mix*). We can further simplify the display by excluding the age category of *(1999–2014) Children raised by respondent*, given that the curves fall and rise more consistently without it; in fact, similar to an age-grade effect in apparent time (of the addressee).[58] Figure 5.31 shows this bimodal analysis of *Total Gaelic* and *Total English* practice through sociobiographical and apparent time.

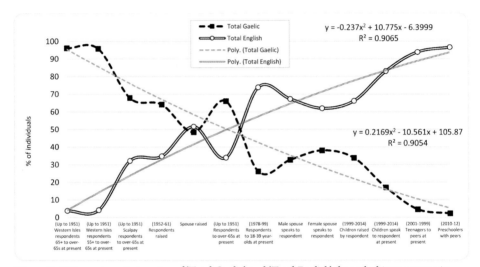

Figure 5.32 *Percentages in practice of 'Total Gaelic' and 'Total English' through thirteen stages in sociobiographical and apparent time (including polynomial linear trend lines (Poly.))*

With the data (curve) of *Mix* mode now equally divided between the two remaining modes, Figure 5.32 shows how the data curves and polynomial trend lines form an X-curve of fall of *Total Gaelic* and rise of *Total English*. The series of charts in Figures 5.27–5.32 shows:

- The rapidity of the almost-completed language shift, through the changing proportions of language modes in biographical and apparent time, spanning c. 60 years;

---

58 Recall that respondents speak more English *To teenagers* than *To primary school aged children* (5.4.11, Figure 5.21). Thus respondents follow the language practice of the 'adolescent peak' in apparent time of the addressee (as mentioned in discussion of Figure 5.29).

- The transience of mixed modes (in considerable proportions at >10%), spanning c. 20–30 years of apparent time;
- The *Mix* mode can be seen as a central feature of the overall process of shift — with *Mix* mode, when it increases, growing in tandem with *Predominant English*, while *Predominant Gaelic* contracts (being 'squeezed out' by the other two modes), and later *Mix* mode contracting in tandem with the contraction of *Predominant Gaelic* towards monolingualisation (Figure 5.31);[59]
- The lack of stability evident in the trajectories of the bilingualised practice;
- The efforts of some parents to contribute to the familial transmission of Gaelic, evident in higher Gaelic and mixed modes with concomitant reduction in English modes.

5.8.2.3 *GAELIC IDENTITY AND LOOKING TO THE FUTURE*

A large majority of respondents attest to the ascription of Gael (5.5). 79% of respondents answered that they saw themselves as Gaels, and a cross-comparison of questions on identity with questions of fluency resulted in 80% of 'Gaels' being fluent in Gaelic. 'Gael' is a primarily geolinguistic identity category. Identity ascription is clearly differentiated between the adult respondents in the CSS and the teenagers in the secondary schools survey (Chapter 4). The variance between the two surveys may well represent a generation gap in how identity is perceived in that a majority of the teenagers (55.3%) do not view themselves as Gaels (4.8.1). A cross-comparison of the teenage responses identifying as a Gael with familial use of Gaelic among teenagers indicates that greater familial use corresponds more closely with identity ascription as a Gael among the teenagers. However, with more teenagers ascribing a Scottish, local or British identity to themselves than identifying as a Gael, the significant erosion of Gaelic identity as a marker of community ascription in the Western Isles is brought into focus. Areas where some or most people speak Gaelic are considered to be Gaelic communities, but areas where English is the main language spoken and the main language of education are not considered to be Gaelic communities (5.5.3).

Across all three islands discussed in this chapter, 34.1% of all respondents believe that Gaelic will be a lot weaker in 20 years' time; in Scalpay, which has the greatest Gaelic speaker density, concentrated in the older age groups, 58% of respondents foresee Gaelic being a lot weaker (**A5.4.7**). The acute challenges facing Gaelic in the communities indicate that language planning initiatives, devised independently of the wider social and economic context of island life, will be insufficient to provide

---

59 Similarly, in their research in Na Meadhanan, South Uist, Rothach *et al.* (2016: 86–87) note the prevalence of the mixed mode in parent's input to child and the contraction of the mixed mode in favour of the use of English in the children's output to parents.

public policy supports for Gaelic speaker communities. In relation to the community-survey respondents, 83% of households did not contain school-aged children, while 72% of respondents were aged 55 or over. Comhairle nan Eilean Siar (2016a; 2016b) has publicly acknowledged troubling demographic projections for the next 25 years in its council area. The results of the islands survey in this chapter (in tandem with the Speaker Typology Survey) also highlight the extent of this challenge from a sociolinguistic perspective. In brief, the general population is ageing and Gaelic competence and practice is far less prominent among the proportionally decreasing younger age groups (6.9).

In the context of how public agencies engage with the demographic and socio-economic challenges in the Western Isles, the Gaelic communities appear to be an empty category. Across all areas, responses to several of the questions on support initiatives for Gaelic show that community members feel in general dissociated from relevant public bodies (5.7.4). The perceptions of future prospects for Gaelic among the respondents demonstrate a realistic societal understanding in relation to Gaelic's demolinguistic trajectory. In general, the interventions and policies of external agencies are viewed as offering very little practical benefit to Gaelic-speaking communities. MacKinnon (1977: 167) found that Gaelic maintenance was not perceived as a concern of political institutions, and the CSS found that Gaelic agencies and public bodies were perceived to offer limited positive support for the language in its *in situ* context.

In summary, when we consider that the Gaelic-language profiles in the communities of Scalpay, Grimsay and Eriskay are among the strongest still in existence, we can conclude from the islands survey that:

- Gaelic-speaking communities are in an advanced stage of language shift
- The familial and communal transmission of Gaelic is now marginal
- Only the older people have any appreciable experience of socialisation in Gaelic-language communal practice
- Gaelic is therefore marginal to the lives of the young.

The hopes invested in GME to counteract this fragile sociolinguistic condition of Gaelic and to bolster the numbers of Gaelic speakers in the future as a basis for linguistic regeneration in these communities, are evident in the findings discussed in **A5.3.6**.

6 ABILITY, HOUSEHOLD PRACTICE AND SPEAKER TYPOLOGY SURVEY IN THREE ISLANDS

6.1 INTRODUCTION

This chapter presents the findings from the Speaker Typology Survey (STS) which examines the bilingual Gaelic–English and the monolingual English abilities and types of speakers in the small islands of Scalpay, Grimsay and Eriskay, and how these ability profiles and typologies correlate with the household practice of Gaelic, including family households and related parental and child abilities. The STS findings allow us to present a comprehensive advisor-assisted assessment of language ability and practice of the entire populations and households of the three sampled small islands. This methodology can supplement the more subjective reported ability-data in census returns (2.3.3).[60] On the basis of these speaker ability categorisations, we were able to take a further step with the local advisors' assistance and produce an entire speaker-type profile of the populations. Furthermore, the age profiles of speakers according to their Gaelic ability and their geographic backgrounds allow us to pinpoint the dynamics of language shift (in apparent time) to a greater level of detail than in any other demolinguistic study of the Western Isles. This part of the multi-modular IGRP survey is the first ever multi-district study of its type in Scotland, investigating the bilingual synchronic and diachronic dynamics of the entire subpopulations and their households.

In this study, speaker typology entails the categorisation of individuals in the population according to their language abilities and the associated sources of language acquisition. In the STS we identify six speaker types on a continuum of Gaelic ability: *Native speaker of Gaelic*; *Neo-native speaker of Gaelic*; *Semi-speaker of Gaelic*; *Co-speaker of Gaelic*; *Learner of Gaelic*; *Speaker of English only*. The Speaker Typology Survey was conducted in Scalpay, Grimsay and Eriskay, areas identified as having relatively strong Gaelic profiles in the 2011 Census data for Scotland (as in the Community Sociolinguistic Survey (CSS) in Chapter 5). Unlike the related CSS in Chapter 5, which was based on data from each participating *respondent* (a total of 180 individuals reporting on their household), the STS is based on mediated assessments

---

60 It is accepted that definitions of language ability may be flexible, in that individuals may assess their own ability and that of others differently at various times. However, the confidence in the reliability of the information received under the guidance of our local advisors, as an accurate depiction of the contemporary distributions of Gaelic abilities in the surveyed islands, is bolstered by its general conformity with the profiles and trajectories of the data in the previous chapters (6.8).

provided by one well-informed *local advisor* for each island. These three local advisors provided the information about all *reported residents* (total of 484) living on a full-time or permanent basis in the three small island communities. Therefore, the STS in Chapter 6 supplements the findings of the CSS in Chapter 5. This STS methodology borrows from research carried out in Ireland (in three Irish Gaeltacht districts: Ráth Chairn, Co. Meath, and Ceathrú Thaidhg, Co. Mayo as well as Ros Muc, Co. Galway; Ó Giollagáin 2002; 2004a; 2004b; 2005; 2011), which gathered sociolinguistic data on speaker-type profiles of the entire sampled populations, constituting the bilingual dynamics of the districts. The speaker-type profiles in the three Irish Gaeltacht districts indicated greater minority-language vitality than in the three islands of the STS. The STS gathered data on the prevalence of Gaelic and English in the key domains of familial and household language practice. As discussed in section 5.1, Scalpay and Eriskay are classified among the strongest remaining Gaelic-speaking communities, with mid-range vitality indications for the North Uist (south & east) SD containing Grimsay. An indication of the fragility of, or level of threat to, vernacular Gaelic can be obtained from the combination in the STS of detailed profiling of speaker abilities and typologies across age cohorts and geographic backgrounds, as well as the key domain of the practice of Gaelic in family households with children.

6.2 LITERATURE REVIEW OF MINORITY-LANGUAGE SPEAKER TYPOLOGY

As stated, the STS research borrows from aspects of the Irish Gaeltacht surveys in Co. Meath, Co. Mayo and Co. Galway (Ó Giollagáin 2002; 2004a; 2004b; 2005; 2011). Ó Giollagáin's research demonstrated the relevance within communities of examining speaker typologies defined primarily by the sources of speakers' abilities. The major findings from that research were that: 1) in a given community, intergenerational transmission of Irish declines as the number of native Irish speakers declines; and 2) school acquirers of Irish represent a weak source for intergenerational transmission. In short, Ó Giollagáin pinpointed the importance of productive speakers, i.e. those who are successful intergenerational transmitters of Irish, and that the most productive speakers are native speakers. The relevance of categorisation of speaker abilities is central to demogeographic linguistics and to sociolinguistics globally, particularly in the minority sociolinguistics context of this study. Speaker categorisation is the cornerstone of reality-based minority sociolinguistics. Without categorisation and quantification, scientific population-wide investigation of the minority speaker group is impossible. Establishing an accurate analysis of the demogeographic quantity and quality of the existing speaker group is evidently crucial for minority-language protection and promotion. Coherent language planning, as practiced in mainstream sociolinguistics, is based on realistic assessments of population quantities and typologies (e.g. Batibo 2005; Bourhis and Landry 2008; Dorian 1980, 1981; Eberhard *et al*. 2019; Fishman 1991, 2001b; Lewis and Simons 2016; Moseley 2010). Of course, categories or speaker types should not be defined over-categorically and we should obviously allow for exceptions and continua of acquisition, attainment, competences and practices (e.g. Davies (2001: 517) and Mesthrie (2001b: 495)).

In the minority-language context and in the framing and implementation of language planning and policies in support of the maintenance and revival of (minority) languages, it is clearly of relevance to assess the roles of both native-speakers and non-native-speakers. The revisionist critique of speaker-categorisation, nevertheless, reproduces a binary perspective (section 1.3.1) on two key aspects of minority-language planning and policy:

> (a) language planning relevant to the vernacular speaker group, and (b) language planning relevant to the non-vernacular speaker group (in other words: (a) native speaker and (b) learner). The speaker-typology research in the STS eschews this binary perspective by rooting its analysis in the primary sociolinguistic feature affecting the vernacular Gaelic group: the proportion of productive speakers (i.e. those involved in successful intergenerational transmission of Gaelic) in the relevant community.

As already stated, classification of speaker abilities is clearly central to analysis of demolinguistics and crucial to minority-language sociolinguistics. Nevertheless, a postmodernist overcomplexification of recognised categories such as learner and native speaker in fact oversimplifies our understanding of speaker typologies. Oversimplification in this sense means a loss of important categorisations, a deliberate muddying of the waters leading to a form of sociolinguistic obscurantism. Most individual language competences can be clustered in sociologically and linguistically important distinguishable categories. As stated, this quantitative and qualitative categorisation of the ability continuum of language populations is central to mainstream sociolinguistics and is still widely applied and applicable to language acquirers and learners throughout the world. A good example of the superficial critique of categorisational mainstream sociolinguistics can be seen in O'Rourke and Ramallo's (2013: 297) discussion of Galician, where they claim there is 'a clear reification of the traditional native speaker'. This, of course, cannot deny the fact of reality that some Galician speakers have far greater competence in Galician than others and that the majority of those with greater competence can be categorised as native speakers in the accepted definition. This superior functionality of native speakers is, of course, true in countless other linguistic contexts, notwithstanding the (generally atypical) instances to the contrary. Suzanne Gessner *et al.* (2014: 11), for instance, define a native speaker, in relation to Canadian aboriginal languages, as 'someone who speaks and understands the language to the degree that she or he self-identifies or is identified by fellow community members as having the ability to converse and understand the language with no use of English' before further explaining that this normally means the first language learned in childhood, while also recognising that fluency in the aboriginal languages can be acquired by first-language speakers of English.

Furthermore, Gessner *et al.* refer to semi-speakers as being generally from a younger generation and with less language ability, but that large numbers of semi-speakers can be a resource for the language group and for language regeneration. In her work on East Sutherland Gaelic, Dorian (1981: 107) defined semi-speakers as speakers who are less competent in Gaelic than those she termed Gaelic-dominant bilinguals, as discerned through the quality of the speaker's linguistic performance. Dorian (1980: 89) has also suggested that 'the commonest figure in the linguistic socialization of the semi-speaker … is the grandmother', which is interesting in light of the sources of Gaelic acquisition for teenagers in the Teenager Survey module of the IGRP (4.5.2). The concept of young people's speech is ubiquitous in linguistic analysis of aboriginal languages in Australia. An early example of the centrality of the concepts of native speaker and semi-speaker can be found in Annette Schmidt's (1985) viewpoint that semi-speakers understand but do not speak a language in its normative form, within the continuum of the abilities among semi-speakers (i.e. of those approaching full competence to those with low functionality). Fishman (1991) used slightly different definitions, with his *semi-speakers* having partial functionality in a language, approaching the level of competence of the category of co-speaker (CO) employed in the IGRP Speaker Typology Survey (6.3.2). A further instance of the use of the term semi-speaker can be found in a publication by Michael Hornsby (2015a) who describes as semi-speakers of Yiddish people who spoke Yiddish as children but were unable to speak it fluently in adulthood. Definitions of native speaker and semi-speaker can emphasise sociological aspects of these concepts to various degrees. For instance, Maria Polinsky's (2011: 2–3) more sociologically inclined presentation of the issues is based on how the linguistic competence of the semi-speaker is perceived according to the normative criteria of the speaker group: 'Semi-speakers show many of the features attributed to heritage speakers'. Since instances of heritage language speech can be perceived as being lacking in completeness or being marked by some linguistic deficit, such semi-speaker speech may be perceived negatively by more functional speakers (see also Benmamoun *et al.* 2013).

To return to the context of young people's Gaelic, it is clear that full native speaker ability is rare and that those young people who self-report as fluent Gaelic speakers are often English-dominant bilinguals (8.4.4). Given the contraction in Gaelic-speaking networks and in Gaelic socialisation, evidenced in the IGRP survey and elsewhere, there simply is not enough Gaelic vernacular transmission to attain full competence in Gaelic for the average young person in the community so that most young speakers could be categorised along a continuum of abilities below that of older generations of Gaelic-dominant native speakers (4.5.4; 4.10.1.1; cf. Dorian 2014). Because there is more socialisation and transmission, both in communal and institutional practice, in the Irish Gaeltacht, there is a greater range and greater density of what might be termed Young People's Irish than in the Scottish Gaelic context (Péterváry *et al.* 2014; Lenoach 2012; Ó Curnáin 2007: 59–60; 2009; 2012; 2016; Ó Murchadha 2012; 2018).

Ó Giollagáin (2002; 2004a; 2004b; 2005) employed the term neo-native speaker to refer to the sociolinguistic categorisation of children of competent 2nd language acquirers of lrish living in Irish-speaking Gaeltacht districts (mostly as newcomers to these districts). He found that the neo-native speakers did not form a significant part of any age cohort in the Gaeltacht districts except in the case of the child and teenager cohorts in the Ráth Chairn Gaeltacht in Co. Meath (Ó Giollagáin 2002: 40–41). Dave Sayers (2012) quotes McLeod's (2008) discussion of Manx and Cornish and addresses the familial transmission of Cornish as a learned language which is not rooted in communal normative practice. In the case of Cornish learners who have maintained an ability in Cornish into adulthood and have transmitted the language to their children, he refers to this subsequent generation as neo-native speakers of Cornish.

In an Irish context, the term neo-native speaker has been used to refer to learners or 2nd language acquirers. Muiris Ó Laoire (2008: 260) refers to a shift in emphasis 'from the native speaker as the last bastion of the language to the significance of the pivotal part to be played in the survival of Irish in the future by the neo-native speaker who acquires Irish in school', while also acknowledging the difficulties in producing competent speakers in an institutional setting. Although Ó Laoire's depiction of the discursive 'eclipsis' of the native speaker is to some extent accurate, given the collapse in native speaker numbers in the Gaeltacht, his caveat regarding the typically higher functionality of the native speakers in contrast to learners, demonstrates that the use of the term (neo)native to describe learners only serves to obscure the sociolinguistic category distinctions and to weaken the analysis in particular concerning productive transmission of Irish. A similar effort at discursive repositioning can be seen in the 'new-speakerist' perspectives within minority-language promotion and protection initiatives.[61]

---

61 Alexandra Jaffe (2015: 23) emphasises the positive perceptions associated with the term 'new speaker', in contrast with 'semi-speaker'. O'Rourke and Walsh's (2015: 64) assertion is that the new speaker has gained competence in a language outside the home (in a school setting, for example), or as an adult, and as being one who uses that language with 'fluency, regularity and commitment'; i.e. what in mainstream linguistics has been understood as a high-functioning active L2 learner (although this is not stated by O'Rourke and Walsh (2015)). For further discussion and sociological critique of 'new-speakerism' in the context of minority-language planning, see Ó Giollagáin and Ó Curnáin (forthcoming).

An academic focus for some scholars has been to challenge how, or if, functional competence in a language maps onto fluent or native speaker categorisations, further extending debates over minority-language identity and in- and out-group speaker authority. Some scholars have sought to deconstruct concepts such as native speaker and in- and out-group authority from a postmodernist perspective, often indicating a preference for problematising by means of the trope of complexity, but without clarification (see Ó Giollagáin *et al.* (2012: 5) for a critique of complexitarianism). An instance of rather inconsequential complexitarianism can be seen in O'Rourke and Pujolar (2013: 61) who say that: 'problematizing nativeness and the native speaker concept in the context of language revitalization and minority-language research helps understand the ways in which specific social groups and linguistic forms acquire legitimacy'.

While Charles Ferguson (1983) is among the first to challenge the legitimacy of the native speaker concept, Alan Davies (2013: 18) points out that criticisms of native speaker concepts linked to English do not necessarily hold true for minority languages 'which tend, to a large extent, towards cultural identity within a confined land mass'. The social and linguistic tensions between native and non-native speakers of languages in revitalisation contexts has been widely discussed in the literature. Neriko Doerr (2009: 36) contemplates the "belief in the automatic and complete competence of 'native speakers' in their 'native languages'", while Jaffe (2015) positions the 'new speaker' against the 'native speaker' concept, and raises questions as to the legitimacy of the latter category as an appropriate model in revitalisation discourses. Susan Frekko (2009) and James Costa (2015) point to situations where 'native speakers' begin to feel disenfranchised from what have come to be regarded as standard speech varieties of Catalan and Occitan respectively. McLeod and O'Rourke (2015: 155) examine the 'terminological difficulty' that arises from the lack of a Gaelic-language equivalent of 'native speaker', and refer to the 'increasingly opaque' term *Gàidheal* or Gael. They relate this to James Oliver's (2005: 21) contention that it is not clear who or what a Gael is. See the alternative view discussed in section 4.2.2.

6.3 METHODOLOGY

As stated in the Introduction (6.1), the IGRP team consulted well-informed local advisors who had a long-term understanding of their communities' linguistic practice. The advisors were asked to assess the Gaelic ability of all those resident in their communities in order to build up a picture of the speaker population typology. These assessments were based on criteria discussed in detail with the advisors before the exercise. The survey thereby established common ground between the IGRP research focus and how local advisors viewed various speaker types. The three local advisors identified in total 484 reported residents in the three survey islands. Data-recording forms (see **Appendix 8**) were drawn up for the advisor-led speaker typology in the three island communities. An identifier number was generated for each household. The district and township in which each household was situated was then recorded. Forms could record data on up to 16 individuals and a variety of familial compositions in any one household. Each form had four separate data sections: Background data; Household language practice; Gaelic competence; and Speaker category.

6.3.1 BACKGROUND DATA; HOUSEHOLD LANGUAGE PRACTICE; GAELIC COMPETENCE; SPEAKER TYPES

As stated, the first three sections of the STS data-recording form contained questions on: Background data; Household language practice; and Gaelic competence. In the Background section, age, gender, and place of origin were recorded for each individual. The recording of age entailed approximating the individual member of the community within incremental ranges of 10 years; the advisors were so knowledgeable of their own communities that they were almost always confident of each individual's age category. In the Household language practice section, each household's most common daily language practice was assessed as: *Gaelic only*, an *Equal mix of Gaelic and English*, *English only*, or *Other language*. It was borne in mind that household practice might not necessarily reflect the levels of Gaelic competence of household members. In the section on Gaelic competence, each individual's Gaelic abilities were assessed by the local advisors and assigned to one of five categories — *Fluent Gaelic speaker*; *Good Gaelic*; *Fair Gaelic*; a *Few words of Gaelic*; *No Gaelic*. The advisors' experience of their communities meant that it was relatively straightforward for them to assign individuals to categories indicating little or no Gaelic competence.

6.3.2 SPEAKER TYPES

Each individual was categorised by the local advisor according to one of the following speaker types:
- Native speaker of Gaelic
- Neo-native speaker of Gaelic
- Semi-speaker of Gaelic
- Co-speaker of Gaelic
- Learner of Gaelic
- Speaker of English only

These six categories (following Ó Giollagáin (2011), and as set out in Ó Giollagáin (2002; 2004a; 2004b; 2005)), based on a combination of an individual's ability and language-acquisition experience, can be adapted to the context of Scottish Gaelic as follows:

Native speaker of Gaelic
The term *Native speaker* is defined here as being a competent speaker of Gaelic, likely to have acquired the language after being socialised in Gaelic in a familial and/or communal setting.

Neo-native speaker of Gaelic
The term *Neo-native speaker* is defined here as someone who acquired Gaelic in a familial or communal situation but as a child of non-native-speaking parents or guardians who learned the language themselves later in life (for example, in an educational or institutional setting) and who speak Gaelic as their household language. The existence of the speaker type *Neo-native speaker* would be a strong indicator of actualised and successful language revitalisation — being one of the major minority-language planning and policy objectives.

Semi-speaker of Gaelic
The term *Semi-speaker* refers here to an individual who has come from an environment with a mixed linguistic input, typically in that one parent or guardian is a *Native speaker* of Gaelic, while the other parent or guardian is a (monolingual) speaker of English. Gaelic will have been one of the household languages, typically used by a *Native speaker* parent, and the *Semi-speaker* will have attained some functional linguistic capability in Gaelic, rather than having attained a similar capacity via an educational setting. This ability in some cases may even approach that of a *Native speaker* for the relevant age cohort.

Co-speaker of Gaelic
The term *Co-speaker* is defined here as an individual who has attained a degree of social functionality in Gaelic through formal instruction, i.e. in a school setting. This means that their ability in Gaelic is not attained in a familial or communal context. A *Co-speaker* has greater ability in social interaction through Gaelic than a *Learner*. As with the *Neo-native speakers* and *Semi-speakers*, the *Co-speaker* category was one which was acknowledged as being likely to be less well-represented in the STS than in the Irish Gaeltacht context.

Learner of Gaelic

A *Learner* is defined here as an individual who is actively learning Gaelic in a (largely) post-statutory educational context, either through night classes, community classes, or informally in wider community interactions, etc. This classification may reflect a relatively wide spectrum of attainment, from people who may have recently started learning or who have made limited progress, to those with more highly-developed abilities in Gaelic but who do not possess the fluency of the *Co-speakers*.

Speaker of English only

Here, a *Speaker of English only* is defined as a person who has either no or (very) limited functional ability in Gaelic, so that a meaningful conversation in Gaelic is impossible. It does not necessarily follow that those classified as such are attitudinally negative towards Gaelic. In this category, we also include first-language speakers of languages other than Gaelic and English, due to the fact that English operates as the *lingua franca* for those speakers in the Western Isles. The STS research team was mindful that in-migration of L1 speakers of other languages has become more commonplace in the Western Isles in recent years.

Given that Gaelic-medium education did not begin until 1986 in the Western Isles (the first unit opened in Breasclete in that year), it is acknowledged that the variety of speaker types is unlikely to be as broad as in the Irish context, in that, prior to the introduction of GME, the linguistic profile of the Western Isles communities was made up of a clearer binary distinction between home acquirers of Gaelic with a bilingual competence in English, and monolingual speakers of English with awareness of Gaelic as a community language around them. GME would produce a context for the emergence of *Learners*, *Co-speakers* and, in the following generation, *Neo-native speakers*. Given the sparsity of these three categories in the STS, the social productivity of GME in the Western Isles has been lower than in the Irish (Gaeltacht) context. In particular, an absence to date of *Neo-native speakers* indicates a lack of success in Gaelic revitalisation in a social intergenerational context.

6.4 BACKGROUND AND AGE IN THREE ISLANDS

Here we discuss the combined findings for all three islands surveyed in the STS. Disaggregated data for the separate islands can be found in **Appendix 6**.

6.4.1 REPORTED RESIDENTS AND GENDER

Figure 6.1 displays numbers and percentages of reported residents by island, and across all three islands.

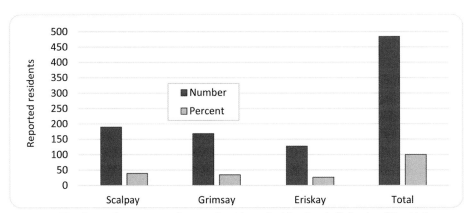

Figure 6.1 *Number and percentage of reported residents, by island and all districts (N = 484)*

In total, data from 484 people were assessed. Across all three islands, the greatest percentage of reported residents in the STS was recorded in Scalpay (39.1%, 189 reported residents), just over a third in Grimsay (34.7%, 168 reported residents), and just over a quarter in Eriskay (26.2%, 127 reported residents).

Across the three island communities, the gender balance for reported residents was 50.4% female and 49.6% male. Island-specific details are given in Table 6.1.

	Female	Male
All districts	50.4%	49.6%
Scalpay	50.8%	49.2%
Grimsay	46.4%	53.6%
Eriskay	55.3%	44.7%

Table 6.1 *Gender of reported residents, by island and all districts (N = 480)*

6.4.2 PLACE OF ORIGIN AND AGE COHORTS

Figure 6.2 displays the place of origin for the reported residents by percentage.

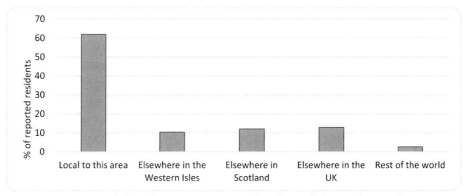

Figure 6.2 *Percentage of place of origin among reported residents, all districts (N = 481)*

What is clear across all the survey districts is the prevalence of reported residents who have a *Local* origin, at 62%, with a further 10% identified as being from *Elsewhere in the Western Isles*. Marginally more are identified as being from *Elsewhere in the UK* (12.9%) than from *Elsewhere in Scotland* (12.1%). Fewer than 3% are from outside the UK (*Rest of the world*).

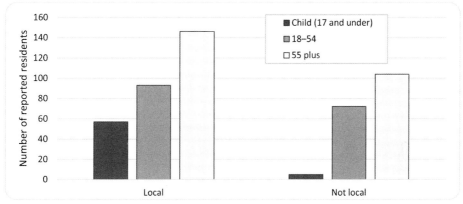

Figure 6.3 *Comparison of age group and place of origin, all districts (N = 477)*

In Figure 6.3, age and place of origin are compared. The cohort of reported residents identified as being *Local* is biased towards the older age groups: 49.3% of those who are *Local* are aged over 55. For the 18–54 age group, the percentage is 31.4%, while 19.3% of the *Local* cohort are children. Among those reported residents who are *Not local*, there is an even more obvious bias towards the older age groups: 57.5% are aged 55 or over, while 39.8% are aged 18–54; and 2.7% are children.

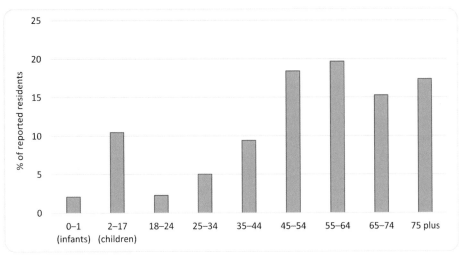

Figure 6.4 *Age profile by age cohort of reported residents, all districts (N = 478)*

Figure 6.4 details the age profile of reported residents, by percentage for each age cohort. Unlike the CSS findings in Chapter 5 (Figure 5.1), we see a bimodal distribution in Figure 6.4, but with a bias towards the older age cohorts. Here, all reported residents include younger residents. The majority in the Speaker Typology Survey were over the age of 55 (52.4%). The largest age cohort in percentage terms was the 55–64 group, at 19.7%. The low proportion of reported residents within the 25–44 age range (14.4%), coupled with the low percentages in the younger cohorts, provide clear evidence of the demographic challenges to reproducing the existing levels of population, let alone reproducing the Gaelic-speaking group (2.3.4). The proportion of the population under the age of 35 is low in all three islands (15.9% in Scalpay, 19% in Grimsay and 27% in Eriskay). The value of 10.5% of those in the 2–17 age cohort is lower than the 17% proportion for the total RA of the 3–17 age cohort (4,751/28,024; section 2.4.1.1, Table 2.5; also 17% (3–17) in the rest of Scotland, section 2.2).

6.5 GAELIC ABILITY DECLINE AND S-CURVE IN SHIFT TO ENGLISH

In this section, we discuss the assessed abilities of reported residents on a five-point Likert scale, and analyse their ability by their age cohorts and geographic backgrounds. Figure 6.5 portrays the percentage of Gaelic ability among the reported residents.

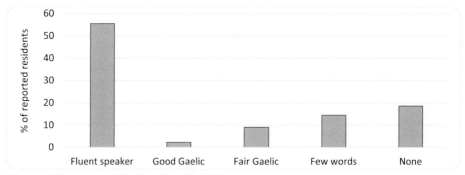

Figure 6.5 *Percentage of Gaelic ability (N = 483)*

Over half (268, 55.5%) of those individuals assessed are *Fluent Gaelic speakers*. Almost one-fifth (90, 18.6%) have no Gaelic competence and 70 (14.5%) have *A few words*. Together, these two categories (*A few words* and *None*) represent almost one-third of reported residents. Smaller percentages are reported for *Good Gaelic* (11 residents, 2.3%) and *Fair Gaelic* (44, 9.1%).

6.5.1 GAELIC ABILITY BY AGE GROUP

Figure 6.6 illustrates Gaelic ability by age group among reported residents in all three islands.

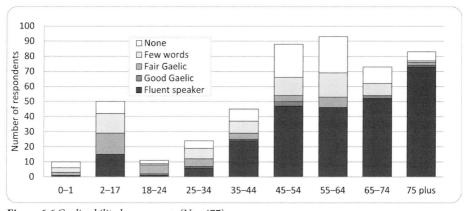

Figure 6.6 *Gaelic ability by age group (N = 477)*

Fluent speakers represent a small minority in younger cohorts. The incidence of higher densities of stronger Gaelic competences in the adult and older age groups indicates that fluency is heavily biased towards the older cohorts, highlighting the demolinguistic fragility of the speaker group and the extent of the challenge involved in its social reproduction.

The overwhelming majority of those aged 65 and over are fluent; in fact, of those over 75 years of age, 73 (88%) of the 83 reported residents are fluent speakers. Of the total of 88 reported residents in the 45–54 cohort, 47 (53%) are fluent. In the 35–44 age cohort, the percentage of fluent speakers was identical at 53%, but with fewer individuals in the cohort in comparison to the older age groups. Of the three remaining cohorts, 30% of reported residents aged 2–17, 9% of those aged 18–24, and 25% of those aged 25–34, are categorised as fluent speakers of Gaelic, but again these cohorts are comparatively small.

While it is obvious that infants in the 0–1 age group and in the early childhood years are in the earliest stages of language acquisition, we have chosen to include their data here in order to incorporate the full demographic range of the reported residents.[62]

6.5.1.1 *GAELIC ABILITY OF COHORTS UNDER-45 AND 45-AND-OVER*

In this subsection, we analyse in greater detail the correspondence of age and ability. We start with those aged under 45 years. As we shall see in the discussion of ability by background (6.5.2.1), it is among those under 45 that the language shift can be discerned in people of a local background. Figure 6.7 shows Gaelic competence by age group, for reported residents aged under 45.

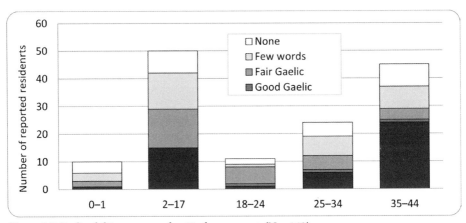

Figure 6.7 *Gaelic ability among under-45s, by age group (N = 140)*

---

62 Equally, the appraisal of language practice and competence of infants up to preschool age in comparative terms is not entirely apposite, as they are at a very early stage in the social and cognitive processes of acquisition. With this proviso that language practice and competence are age-appropriate, we asked our local advisors to envisage the likely future Gaelic ability of those children under four or five years, according to the various categories, based on their knowledge of Gaelic-language practice of those children's families and/or siblings.

For those under the age of 45 in the three islands surveyed, we can see from the data bars that Gaelic is losing prominence. A small majority (53.3%) in the 35–44 age cohort have *Fluent* Gaelic, but over a third (35.6%) have *A few words of Gaelic* or *No Gaelic*. The percentage contrast between the older 35–44 cohort (born in the 1970s) and the next youngest 25–34 age cohort (born in the 1980s) is from 53.3% *Fluent* Gaelic speakers to 25% in their age cohort. The percentage contraction by one half of the proportion with *Fluent* Gaelic in the 25–34 age cohort, falling to 25%, in comparison with the next older 35–44 cohort, indicates, in the apparent-time model, the ongoing impact of substantial demolinguistic and socio-cultural change since the 1970s and on into the 1980s. That 50% of the 25–34 age cohort have only *A few words* or *No Gaelic* indicates again a reduction of the possibility for the social use of Gaelic.

The two youngest cohorts reveal a gap in the ability spectrum: *Good Gaelic* is missing. None of those aged 17 years and under were assessed as having *Good Gaelic*. In fact, the category *Good Gaelic* is very marginal overall (e.g. 2% for all *Local* reported residents, 6.5.2.1), and far less prevalent than the equivalent category on the other end of the ability spectrum: *A few words of Gaelic*. The category *Good Gaelic* appears in the case of 2.1% of those under the age of 45. We can compare the similar percentage of 1.8% of those aged 45 and over for the category of *Good Gaelic*. We can compare the sparsity of the category *Good Gaelic* with the similar sparsity of the comparative speaker-type of *Semi-speaker* in section 6.7. In the 2–17 age cohort, 30% were recorded as fluent which may reflect both the impact of Gaelic-medium education as well as the residual effects of familial and household Gaelic transmission.

Turning our attention to those aged 45 and over, we can compare in Figure 6.8 the Gaelic ability of those in the 45-and-over cohorts.

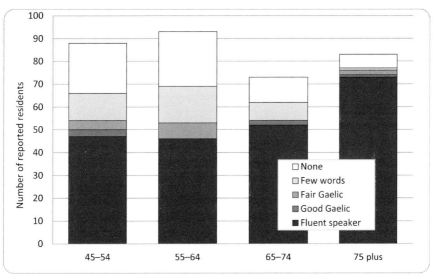

Figure 6.8 *Gaelic ability among those 45-and-over, by age group (N = 337)*

There are more than double the number of reported residents (337) aged 45 and over than there are in the 44 and under age groups (140). The two oldest age cohorts entail both the strongest numbers and proportions of *Fluent* and *Good Gaelic* speakers than the equivalent abilities for the two age cohorts in the 45–64 age ranges. 64.7% of those aged 45 or over have *Fluent* Gaelic. Only 1.8% of those aged 45 and over have *Good Gaelic*.

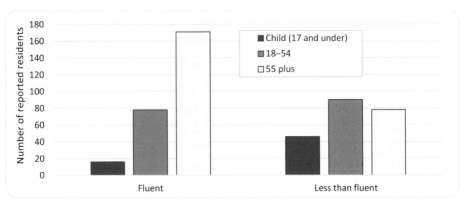

Figure 6.9 *Fluent and less than fluent, by three aggregated age groups (N = 479)*

Figure 6.9 compares those who are *Fluent*, on the one hand, with all other abilities, i.e. from *Good Gaelic* to *None*, on the other, by three aggregated age groups. As seen in the other figures above, fluency is biased towards the older age group. 64.5% of those who are identified as *Fluent* are aged 55 or over, with the percentages at 29.4% of those aged 18–54 and 6% of children aged 17 or under. Among those who are identified as not being fluent, there is a less defined difference between the three combined age groups.

In the percentage values in Figure 6.10, both ends of the ability spectrum are combined, i.e. *Fluent* and *Good Gaelic* on one side, with *Few words* and *None* on the other, and with *Fair Gaelic* in the middle of the spectrum. Age groups are aggregated into Older (over-45s), Young (less than 45) and All. There are two points of note in this distribution: 1) its bimodal nature with abilities mostly at both ends of the spectrum; and 2) the age category with the highest percentage (22.1%) of *Fair Gaelic* is those in the *Young <45s*.

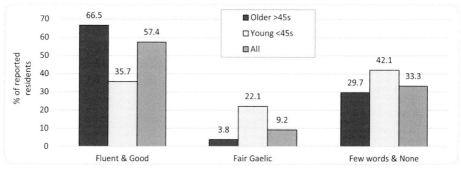

Figure 6.10 *Percentage of reported residents in three Gaelic ability categories, by two age groups and all ages (N = 477)*

6.5.2 GAELIC ABILITY BY BACKGROUND AND THE DIACHRONY OF LANGUAGE SHIFT IN THE WESTERN ISLES

Given the prevalence of in-migration to the Western Isles and the predominant use of English as the *lingua franca* by in-migrants, it is of central importance to any sociolinguistic assessment to investigate the geographic background of those living in the three island communities. Figure 6.11 examines Gaelic ability in relation to the geographic origin of reported residents.

Figure 6.11 *Gaelic ability by geographic origin (N = 480)*

The data indicate a clear link between a *Local* geographic origin and being a *Fluent speaker* of Gaelic. 77% of those identified as *Local* were identified as being in the *Fluent speaker* category. 2% of those who were *Local* had *Good Gaelic*, while 9% had *Fair Gaelic*. 12% had only *A few words* (23, 7.7%) of Gaelic, or *None* (13, 4.4%). Just 6% of those surveyed whose backgrounds were from outside the Western Isles were fluent. The profiles of *Local* (N = 298) and *Elsewhere in the Western Isles* (N = 49) are very similar — in descending order of Gaelic ability for *Elsewhere in the Western Isles* (*Fluent* to *None*): 34, 69.4%; 1, 2.0%; 3, 6.1%; 5, 10.2%; and 6, 12.2%. Thus, in comparison to those who are *Local* to the three islands, those from *Elsewhere in the Western Isles* have roughly 10% more at each end of the ability continuum, with similar percentages in the intervening categories. Fluency falls among those who are aged under 35. In the following section, the profiles of the *Local* and *Elsewhere in the Western Isles* categories are analysed in greater apparent-time detail (i.e. age cohorts).

6.5.2.1 GAELIC ABILITY BY AGE GROUP FOR THOSE OF LOCAL ORIGIN AND WESTERN ISLES ORIGIN

In this section, we analyse the Gaelic ability profiles of the two geographically and sociolinguistically most similar groups in the STS (6.5.2). These two groups are the most Gaelic-proficient groups of the STS. First, we analyse those from the *Local* category alone. Then we analyse the Gaelic ability profiles of members of the *Local* category combined with the category of *Elsewhere in the Western Isles*. Gaelic ability by age group is presented in Figure 6.12 for all of the 294 reported residents for whom a *Local* origin was indicated, i.e. those born in one of the three islands.[63] This is a 61.6% subset of the 477 reported residents for whom the geographic origin has been indicated (Figure 6.6).

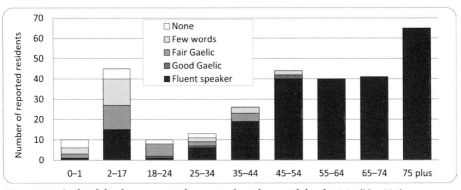

Figure 6.12 *Gaelic ability by age group, for reported residents with local origin (N = 294)*

The trajectory in Figure 6.12 also illustrates the clear detrimental demolinguistic turning-point away from high social densities of fluent Gaelic speakers which began in those born in the 1960s (45–54-year olds) and gained momentum during the 1970s (35–44-year olds), and even further in the 1980s (25–34-year olds) with *Fluent*

---

63 In section 6.5.2, it was indicated that 298 reported residents were identified as having a local origin. In the cross-tabulation between ability by age group of those with a local origin we have data on 294 individuals. This means that there are four individuals for whom age group data could not be ascertained in this cross-tabulation.

speaker density falling to less than half of the cohort (i.e. six out of a total of 13 in this small cohort). Among those aged 45 and over, a competence in Gaelic is almost universal. 97.9% of locals in the combined age groups over 45 were assessed as having fluent Gaelic; and no-one in this age range is reported as having no Gaelic.

Of the 35–44 age cohort, 19 (73%) are described as being *Fluent* in Gaelic; four (15%) had *Fair Gaelic* and three (12%) had *A few words*. The 25–34 age group contains 13 individuals. This is exactly half the size of the 35–44 cohort, and fewer than half of these 25–34-year-olds are *Fluent*. Two (15%) have *No Gaelic*, two (15%) have *A few words* of Gaelic, and two (15%) have *Fair Gaelic* with one (8%) having *Good Gaelic*. Overall, between those two age cohorts in the 25–44 age range, those *Fluent* in Gaelic decline from 73% of the 35–44-year-olds to 46% of the 25–34-year-olds.

The fact that the proportion of Gaelic-fluent speakers is higher among younger speakers aged 2–17, than among the two immediately older age cohorts, may be attributable to either the effects of Gaelic-medium education, and/or to efforts of Gaelic-speaking by family members.[64] For this young group, 15 (33%) were regarded as being *Fluent*, with 12 (27%) having *Fair Gaelic*. However, 18 (40%) of this cohort have only *A few words*, or *No Gaelic*.

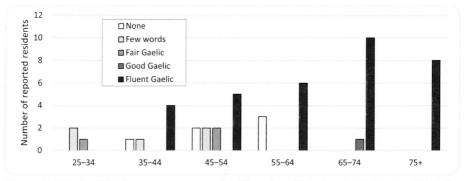

Figure 6.13 *Gaelic ability by age group, reported residents from 'Elsewhere in the Western Isles' only (N = 48)*

As shown in Figure 6.13 and discussed above (6.5.2), people born in the three islands and those born in the rest of the Western Isles are linguistically very similar. We can therefore combine the two groups to get a clearer view of Gaelic ability among those native to the Western Isles (in these three islands). In Figure 6.14, therefore, we combine these two geographic categories and illustrate the Gaelic ability by age cohort of those reported residents who have a geographic origin in the Western Isles.

---

64 An increase of practice of Gaelic in (pre)school years can affect the linguistic categorisation of this (pre)school cohort. This effect is found, for instance, in the Scottish Census data in 2.4.1.1 and in Irish Census returns (Ó Giollagáin and Charlton 2015: 124; cp. Mac Donnacha *et al.* 2005: 41–43) as well as in Welsh surveys (e.g. H. Jones 2012: 64). Cp. point (2) in discussion of Figure 6.15, as well as footnote 56.

This combined group comprises 342 individuals, i.e. 71.7% of the total 477 reported residents for whom the geographic origin has been indicated.

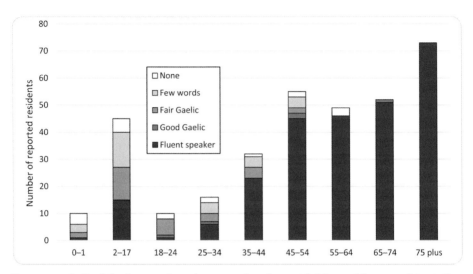

Figure 6.14 *Gaelic ability by age cohort, for reported residents with Western Isles origin (N = 342)*

Fluency in Gaelic is by far the most prevalent category among those reported residents aged 45 and over. In fact, 93% of those aged 45 and over are *Fluent*, with only 2% having no Gaelic. Among younger cohorts, aged 44 or less, 40.7% are *Fluent* although the *Fluent* proportion (among the under-45s) is raised by the high proportion of *Fluent speakers* among 35–44 age group.

In order to analyse the relationship between geographic origin and fluency in Gaelic according to the separate age profiles, Table 6.2 and Figures 6.15–6.16 show the numbers and percentages of Gaelic fluency in binary categorisation as *Fluent* vs. *Non-fluent* (from *Good Gaelic* to *None*) according to the geographic origin of the reported residents, based on the four categories of *Local, Other Western Isles, Local + Other Western Isles*, and *Elsewhere* (all origins outside the Western Isles), and nine age groups (from 75+ year-olds to infants) with the approximate corresponding decade of birth or birth year(s) for each age group in order to give an idea of change through apparent time.[65] This age-structured data, therefore, represents an apparent-time span of approximately 80 or 90 years (from the fluency of the youngest to the oldest in the population).

---

65 The apparent-time model is complicated here by in- and out-migration. For instance, a given individual born in the 1950s may not actually have been resident in the surveyed islands in the 1950s, particularly given the presence of in-migrant retirees in the Western Isles. Nevertheless, the Western Isles subset, at least, in the language shift data pertaining to Table 6.2 and Figures 6.15 and 6.16, reflect what was happening in the Western Isles in general over the apparent-time decades. The category of infants (i.e. 0–1 year-olds) are all taken as *Locals* (i.e. 10 infants in total).

Age group	Origin: Local			Other Western Isles			Local + Other Western Isles			Elsewhere			All		
(apparent time)	Total	Fluent	%	Total	Fluent	%	Total	Fluent	%	Total	Fluent	%	Total	Fluent	%
75+ (-1930s)	65	65	100	8	8	100	73	73	100	10	0	0	83	73	88
65 to 74 (1940s)	41	41	100	11	10	90.9	52	51	98.1	21	1	4.8	73	52	71.2
55 to 64 (1950s)	40	40	100	9	6	66.7	49	46	93.9	44	0	0	93	46	49.5
45 to 54 (1960s)	44	40	90.9	11	5	45.5	55	45	81.8	31	2	6.5	86	47	54.7
35 to 44 (1970s)	26	19	73.1	6	4	66.7	32	23	71.9	13	1	7.7	45	24	53.3
25 to 34 (1980s)	13	6	46.2	3	0	0	16	6	37.5	7	0	0	23	6	26.1
18 to 24 (1990s)	10	1	10	1	0	0	11	1	9.1	0	0	0	11	1	9.1
2 to 17 (2000s-)	45	15	33.3	5	0	0	50	15	30	0	0	0	50	15	30
0 to 1 (2015-)	10	1	10	0	0	0	10	1	10	0	0	0	10	1	10
Total	294	228	77.6	54	33	61.1	348	261	75.0	126	4	3.2	474	265	55.9

Table 6.2 Gaelic fluency of reported residents according to age group and geographic origin

In Table 6.2 the percentage value columns are shaded. These show the percentages of those who are fluent in Gaelic in each of the nine age groups in the five geographic categories. The low proportion of the 2–17 age cohort in comparison to the 3–17 age cohort in the Research Area (RA) in general is also evident in Table 6.2: 10.8% (50/464)[66] vs. 17% in RA (6.4.2). The contrast between the geographic categories, and the change through the age groups can be demonstrated in Figure 6.15.

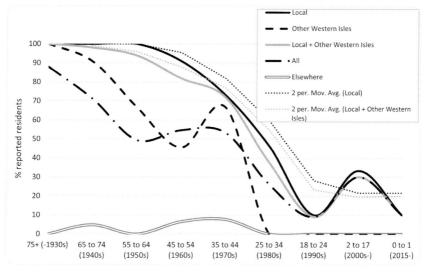

Figure 6.15 Percentage of Gaelic fluency among reported residents according to age group and geographic origin (including 2-period moving average trend lines)

---

66 464 (= 474 – 10). The 10 infants in the 0–1 age cohort are not included in this calculation, for comparison with the census language data, which does not include 0–2 age cohort.

Figure 6.15 and Table 6.2 show the shift in percentage Gaelic fluency through apparent time, as accurately as can be portrayed based on the synchronic data in the STS. Nine points can be made:

1. We can note the undulated data curve in the display of the category of the *Other Western Isles*, but the percentages in this category are based on very small numbers, so that the fall and rise in the age groups 45–54 and 35–44 are of no real consequence for the overall trajectory.

2. The rise in the three relevant data curves at the 2–17 age category is against the overall trend and indicates an increase in Gaelic fluency in apparent time. This increase can be interpreted as at least partly due to the influence of GME and extra parental effort of Gaelic input on this age group (5.8.2.2; 5.4.7–11; 3.3.4). Without this increase to 33.3%–30% (*Local*; *Local and Western Isles* and *All*) at the 2–17 age category, the data curves would flatten to c. 10%. Figure 6.16 below shows the data curves without infants (0–1), who are pre-linguistic, and (pre)school-goers (2–17), some of whom are in GME.

3. The proportional numbers of those from *Elsewhere* (i.e. *Outside the Western Isles*) are considerable, about a quarter (in total 126/474 = 26.6%) of the population, and their percentage Gaelic ability is very low and stands at 3.2% of the total for all age groups in the *Elsewhere* geographic category; the percentage is actually zero in three of the six relevant age groups. The percentage proportion in each age cohort who are from *Elsewhere* and are non-fluent is shown in Figure 6.16 below. Their highest proportion reaches 47.3% in the *55–64 (1950s)* cohort and their lowest proportions are 0% in the young *18–24 (1990s)* and 12% in the oldest *75+ (1930s)*. The proportion for the five age cohorts covering the age range 25–74 is 35.4%, i.e. about a third of that age range comprises people from *Elsewhere* with non-fluent Gaelic. This group from outwith the Western Isles has a substantial negative effect on the proportion of fluent Gaelic speakers in each of the six oldest age groups. The data curve of *Elsewhere* is the major contributor to the gap between the *All* data curve and the data curve for *Local + Other Western Isles*. This is most striking at the *55–64 (1950s)* cohort where the total of 47 non-fluent individuals (50.5% of the age cohort) is comprised of three individuals from *Other Western Isles* and 44 from *Elsewhere*. This is visualised in Figure 6.16 where the curve for the percentage *Elsewhere non-fluent* rises when the curve for percentage fluency among *All* falls, and *vice versa*. The mirror-image pattern of these two curves is particularly well-defined in the three oldest cohorts. In a way, the Western Isles cohorts (*Local*, as

well as *Local + Other Western Isles*) follow, with a gap of about one generation, the lead of the *Elsewhere*-affected total population cohort *All* (cf. (9) below).

4. The effect of the category of *Other Western Isles* on the combined category of *Local + Other Western Isles* can be seen by comparing the gap between the higher data curve for *Local* and the lower curve for *Other Western Isles*. The greatest gap between the curves can be seen for the age groups of *55–64 (1950s)* and *45–54 (1960s)*. It appears that in-migrants from *Other Western Isles* geographic origin had a lower proportion (of fluent Gaelic speakers) than the *Local* category in the relevant age groups, indicating earlier loss of high fluent speaker densities in those areas outside the three more sociolinguistically conservative islands of the STS.

5. Importantly, the curve of decrease in the percentage fluency of the combined Western Isles cohort (i.e. *Local + Other Western Isles*) shows a noticeable increased slope at the *35–44 (1970s)* age category. The curve falls gradually from 98.1% in the *65–74 (1940s)* to 71.9% in the *35–44 (1970s)* age cohort, a percentage-point change of c. 30 over a thirty-year period of apparent time (c. 10 percentage-point change per decade). In the decade between the *35–44 (1970s)* and the *25–34 (1980s)* age cohorts, the percentages fall more rapidly, from 71.9% to 37.5%, a percentage-point change of 33.4, representing a threefold acceleration. In this critical ten-year period, therefore, the proportions of *Fluent* vs. *Non-fluent* speakers are roughly reversed.[67]

6. The rapid rate of decline continues between the *25–34 (1980s)* and *18–24 (1990s)* age cohorts: from 37.5% to 9.1% in the *Local + Other Western Isles* category, representing a percentage-point change of 28.4.

7. Therefore, the percentage collapse from 71.9% to 9.1%, in the two decades of apparent time from 1970 to 1990 in the *Local + Other Western Isles* category, represents a percentage-point change of 62.8. This time span is clearly the period when Gaelic fluency declines the most and the fastest, towards erasure of its societal presence in

---

67 The decadal analysis of language shift here is comparable to the decadal analysis by FitzGerald (1984) of all Irish baronies in age-structured birth decades from 1771 to 1861. In the nine decadal comparisons for the 244 baronies of Ireland in that period (i.e. a total of 244 x 9 = 2196), rates of decadal decline of 30+ percentage points are very rare. There are in fact only 15 instances of 30+ percentage losses, amounting to 0.68% of the total number of decadal comparisons, ranging in value from 30 to 48 with a median of 32 (Ó Curnáin forthcoming). Similarly, there are 103 instances of 20+ losses in the Irish data, amounting to 4.7% of all decadal comparisons, with a range of 20–48 and median of 23. Furthermore, over three quarters of the instances of 30+, and just over half of the instances of 20+ are found in the two final decadal comparisons of the period, covering 1841 to 1861. This puts into perspective the rapidity of the ongoing language shift in the STS findings.

apparent time in these three islands. No other twenty-year period evinces such a steep slope. We can therefore identify the 1970s as the decade when those from the Western Isles in the three islands crossed the demolinguistic threshold into rapid decline (2.4.1.5.1).

8. The steepest slopes in the data curves represent the greatest decadal percentage-point losses. The highest, the second- and third-highest percentage-point losses, as well as the 1970–1990 twenty-year loss in the four relevant geographic categories, are:

Local:	36.2 *(1990s)*, 26.9 *(1980s)*, 17.8 *(1970s)*;
Other Western Isles:	66.7 *(1980s)*, 24.2 *(1950s)*, 21.2 *(1960s)*;
Local + Other Western Isles:	34.4 *(1980s)*, 28.4 *(1990s)*, 12.1 *(1960s)*;
All:	27.2 *(1980s)*, 21.7 *(1950s)*, 16.8 *(1940s)*;
1970–1990: 31.5 *Local*;	33.4 *Other Western Isles*; 31.4 *Local + Other Western Isles*; 22.1 *All*.

9. From the *35–44 (1970s)* on, the linguistic gap between those of Western Isles origin (*Local*, as well as *Local + Other Western Isles*) and the total population (*All*) becomes less pronounced, with loss of fluency trending towards assimilative language shift. Cf. (3) above.

For the sake of comparison with the separate age cohorts, we can include the total population in apparent time, as displayed in Figure 6.16, which retains the indicative data curves of the previous figure as well as: 1) the additional data of percentage fluency of the total apparent-time population; 2) the percentage in each age cohort who are from *Elsewhere* and non-fluent (as are the vast majority of this category; discussed in (3) above); and 3) excluding infants (0–1), and (pre)school-goers (2–17), in particular in order to portray the data of those outside the educational system.

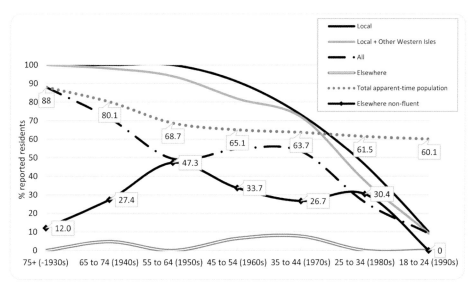

Figure 6.16 *Percentage Gaelic fluency by age group and geographic origin, including apparent-time population (excluding (pre)education cohorts), and percentage of those non-fluent from 'Elsewhere', by age group*

The concept of total apparent-time population is based on the fact that each age cohort added to all previous age cohorts are representative of the fluency percentages of that population. Total apparent-time fluent population is calculated, for instance, for the *75+ (1930s)* age cohort as the percentage of the number of fluent speakers of the total population, i.e. 73/83 = 88%. The total apparent-time fluent population, for the *35–44 (1970s)* age cohort is calculated based on the combination of that cohort and all previous cohorts, i.e. 242 *Fluent* speakers (= 73 + 52 + 46 + 47 + 24) in a total population of 380 (i.e. 83 + 73 + 93 + 86 + 45), yielding 242/380 = 63.7%. The main point arising from the comparison is that the age-cohort fluency trajectories fall at a far greater rate than the total apparent-time population fluency trajectory. The latter evinces a gradual fall from 68.7% for the *55–64 (1950s)* age cohort to 55.9% for the infant age cohort (not shown in Figure 6.16, calculated from the data producing Figure 6.15), a percentage-point change of 12.8 for c. 65 years of apparent time. The highest percentage-point loss in the total apparent-time population fluency occurs between the *65–74 (1940s)* and the *55–64 (1950s)* age cohorts, with a loss of 11.5 percentage points. The rate of descent in the slope of the total apparent-time population fluency curve actually decreases as the slopes of the *Local* and *Local + Other Western Isles* curve falls over the c. 70% threshold. The discrepancy between the age-cohort fluency trajectories, which are more indicative of intergenerational change, and the total apparent-time population fluency trajectory, can be attributed to two factors: 1) the small proportions of under-45s in the overall population (quite acute in the three islands (6.4.2)); and 2) the high proportion of fluent Gaelic speakers in the over-44s. This shows that analyses based on total population in these demographically and sociolinguistically changing communities may fail to reveal substantial intergenerational sociolinguistic transformation (2.2; 2.3.4; 2.4.1.4).

6.6 HOUSEHOLD LANGUAGE PRACTICE

The local advisors provided information on household language practice, according to four categorisations: *Gaelic only*, an *Equal mix of Gaelic and English, English only*, or *Other language*. We have this language practice information regarding 247 of the 270 households participating in the survey. In this section, we portray the aggregated data on household language practice in the three islands. One important caveat about this categorisation is that those living alone (sometimes having lived alone for many years) who are reported as being fluent speakers of Gaelic are assumed to have that language as their language of household practice. Given the gap between higher ability and lower practice of Gaelic evidenced in the Western Isles, the proportion of Gaelic practice in single occupancy households may overestimate Gaelic practice in these households. Obviously, living in this type of household does not provide the social context for the same sort of interpersonal interactions as in the case of multiple occupancy households. However, we assume a language of household practice in these cases because those living alone may participate in wider social networks in their communities. Furthermore, we can analyse separately single occupancy, multiple occupancy and family occupancy with young children where appropriate. In fact, the main focus of this household practice section of the STS is to investigate the prevalence of Gaelic practice in households with young children. We have two ways of analysing the household categories. We differentiate between single and multiple household occupancy and within multiple-occupant households the local advisors have provided the relevant detail of household composition, including family language practice (6.6.2), which is highly pertinent for Gaelic vitality or fragility. Figure 6.17 presents percentages of reported residents by category of language practice in the three islands.

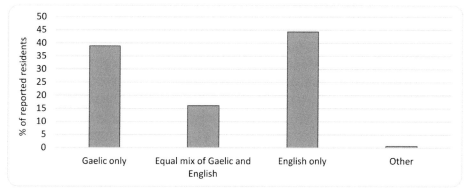

Figure 6.17 Percentage household language practice of reported residents (N = 483)

It is clear from Figure 6.17 that in percentage terms, there are now more individuals assessed as engaging in a practice of *English only* (44.3%) in the household than those engaged in *Gaelic only* practice (38.9%). Fewer people live in a household which has an *Equal mix of Gaelic and English* (16.1%).

6.6.1 SINGLE OR MULTIPLE OCCUPANCY, BY GAELIC FLUENCY AND SPEAKER TYPE

In this subsection, we present data on household types, i.e. single or multiple occupancy, and Gaelic fluency and speaker type. Figure 6.18 compares levels of Gaelic fluency with the household variable indicating single or multiple occupancy (without any recourse to language practice). The fluency data (as assessed by the project's local advisors) is cross-compared with the occupancy variable (independent of the advisors' assessment of household language practice).

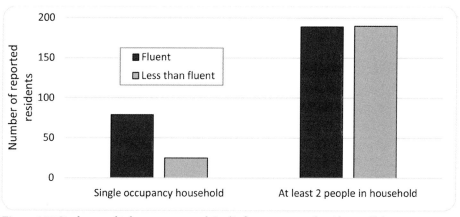

Figure 6.18 Single or multiple occupancy and Gaelic fluency, reported residents, all districts *(N = 483)*

The results indicate that in households where two or more people are resident we find a roughly equal number of reported residents who are fluent Gaelic speakers as who are not. However, in single occupancy households fluent Gaelic speakers predominate (76%), since many of the single households are comprised of older Gaelic speakers living alone.

Figure 6.19 compares speaker type (6.7), in a binary split of *Native Gaelic speaker* versus *Other*, with the household variable indicating single or multiple occupancy.

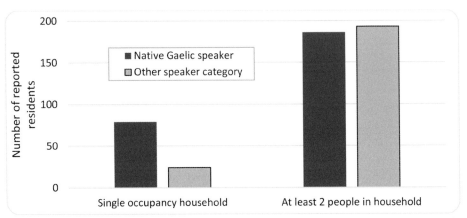

Figure 6.19 Single or multiple occupancy and speaker type or category, reported residents (N = 482)

For all reported residents, native Gaelic speakers are more than three times as likely to live alone in comparison to other speaker types. In multiple-occupant households, native speakers of Gaelic are as common as other speaker types.

6.6.2 HOUSEHOLD OCCUPANCY, COMPOSITION, ABILITY AND LANGUAGE PRACTICE

In this section, we present the key findings concerning household language practice, and in particular the proportion of Gaelic practice in family households, a primary determining factor of which is that both parents have Gaelic fluency. Figure 6.20 compares the number of reported residents who live in single- or multiple-occupant households with household language practice (divided into *Gaelic only* versus the combined categories of *English only*, *Equal mix* and *Other language*).

Those in a single occupancy are more likely to use Gaelic in the household (see remark on single occupancy households in section 6.6). In the cases of multiple occupancy households, the use of *English only*, *Equal mix* or *Other language* is twice as prevalent as the use of *Gaelic only*. For further analysis, see Figure 6.21.

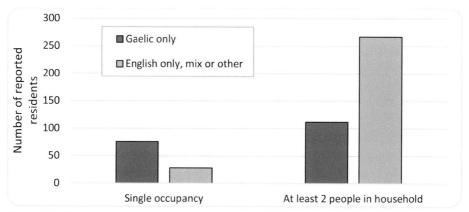

Figure 6.20 *Number of reported residents in single or multiple occupancy, by household language practice (N = 483)*

Figures 6.21–6.24 compare household occupancy and composition with language practice. We classify the households into three categories: single occupancy household; household with adults and no children; family household with children (aged 2–17) living at home. Table 6.3 and Figure 6.21 show the numbers and percentages of households in each of the three categories according to their household language practice. Table 6.3 contains in the right-hand column the household category 'Multiple occupancy (± children)' which combines the categories of 'Adults with children' and 'Adults without children'.

	Adults with children (%)	Adults without children (%)	Single occupancy (%)	Multiple occupancy (± children)
Gaelic only	5 (14.7%)	41 (36.9%)	76 (74.5%)	46 (31.7%)
Mix of Gaelic and English	12 (35.3%)	16 (14.4%)	4 (3.9%)	28 (19.3%)
English only	17 (50%)	54 (48.6%)	22 (21.6%)	71 (49%)
Total	34 (13.8% of total)	111 (44.9% of total)	102 (41.3% of total)	145 (58.7% of total)

Table 6.3 *Numbers and percentages of language practice, by household occupancy and composition (N = 247)*

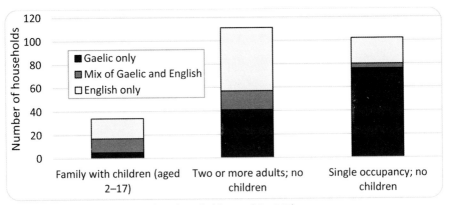

Figure 6.21 *Language practice in three household types (N = 247)*

Table 6.3 and Figure 6.21 highlight the demographic problems for these three surveyed islands and the Western Isles in general (2.3.4) and for intergenerational vernacular Gaelic — with only 34 family households with children (13.8% of all households), across the three islands. When we look at these 34 households (left-hand data column in Table 6.3; and left-hand data bar in Figure 6.21), we see that *English only* is the most common practice (50%). The next most prevalent practice is a *Mix of Gaelic and English* at 35.3% of these family households. The least common practice is *Gaelic only* (14.7%). As stated, these findings, in particular the small numbers and minoritised practice of *Gaelic only*, indicate the crisis in intergenerational transmission of Gaelic in the three islands.

We can now look at the 111 households where two or more adults live together without young children. This comprises the second-largest household composition category at 44.9% of all households. In these 111 households, *English only* practice is almost equally as prevalent as the combined categories of *Gaelic only* and *Mix of Gaelic and English* (57 households; 51.3%). The next occupancy category comprises 102 single occupancy households. Of these households, the majority are *Gaelic only*, representing the highest proportion of *Gaelic only* in the household classifications. One fifth practice *English only* and few practice a *Mix of Gaelic and English*. When we look at the 145 'Multiple occupancy (± children)' households, in the right-hand column in Table 6.3, we can see that this occupancy classification is the largest household category (58.7% of all households). In this category also, *English only* practice is almost equally as prevalent as the two categories of *Gaelic only* and *Mix of Gaelic and English* combined.

Figures 6.22–6.24 indicate that in the households where all or most residents have a Gaelic ability (*Fluent, Good* and *Reasonable*), Gaelic is the predominant language spoken in these homes. However, in the case of the households where a significant mix of abilities is found the use of English in these household dominates, almost to an exclusive extent. Figure 6.22 compares Gaelic ability and practice for the number of households with two or more occupants (i.e. the 145 multiple-occupant households, with and without children).

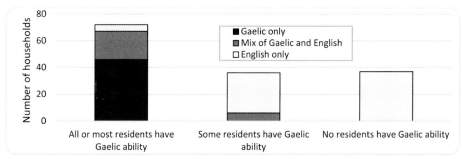

Figure 6.22 *Language ability of household residents, by household language practice (N = 145)*

Where all or most household occupants have an ability in Gaelic (72 or 49.7% of multiple-occupant households), *Gaelic only* (46, 63.9% of multiple households with majority Gaelic ability) or a Gaelic/English mix (21, 29.2%) predominates in the household (with *English only* in five households (6.9%)). But little Gaelic is spoken in other types of households where Gaelic competence is in the minority or is absent.

In the context of vernacular Gaelic fragility, having illustrated all multiple-occupant households with and without children, we present in Figure 6.23 the Gaelic ability and household practice for a key subset of multiple-occupant households, i.e. those comprising parents and children.

Figure 6.23 *Number of family households with language ability of household residents, by family household language practice (N = 34)*

Among the 34 family households with children, there are 17 family households where all or most of the residents have Gaelic ability (*Fluent, Good, Reasonable*) but of these 17, *Gaelic only* practice is found in five, with a *Mix of Gaelic and English* in nine and *English only* in three. In other words, the Gaelic profile for the young families is weaker than in the case of the general profile of multiple-occupant households.

Figure 6.24 compares parents' language ability with the language practice in the 34 family households with children.

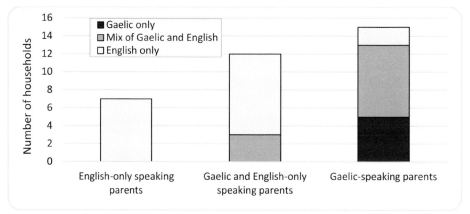

Figure 6.24 *Number of family households with language ability of parents, by family household language practice (N = 34)*

Of the 34 young families, the parents' competences are: seven households with two *English only* parents; 12 with one of parents *English only*; 15 with two Gaelic-competent parents. Figure 6.24 shows that the influence of the parent with an *English-only* ability is the strongest factor in determining the language practice of the household. In the case of the households with mixed parental ability (middle data bar), i.e. one *English-only* parent and one parent with some Gaelic ability, these households are overwhelmingly *English-only* family households. However, in the 15 households where both parents have Gaelic ability (*Fluent*, *Good* and *Reasonable*; the data bar on the right) the mixed use of Gaelic and English is more prevalent (eight households) than *Gaelic only* use (five households); and two (of the 15) households are *English only*. As is common in language shift scenarios, the need for a 'high return' of minority-language speaking children from minority-speaking parents would be a core aspect of revitalisation, but this is often absent, with this absence being a driving factor of the language shift, and this is clearly evidenced in Figure 6.24. There are 18 *English only* family households in contrast to five *Gaelic only* households, as against a potential of 15 *Gaelic only* (not to mention a possible five *Gaelic only* in the mixed parental category). This is, as stated, indicative of the level of the intergenerational vernacular crisis for Gaelic.

6.6.3 ABILITY, BACKGROUND AND HOUSEHOLD GAELIC PRACTICE

Percentage Gaelic-only household language usage is compared in Figure 6.25 with percentage of local background (6.4.2) of the reported residents, and percentage of Native Gaelic speakers (speaker type, 6.7), as well as percentage of Fluent Gaelic speakers (6.5), across all three survey islands.

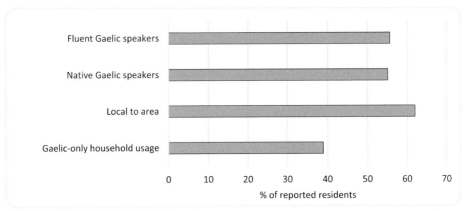

Figure 6.25 *Percentage fluent speakers, native speakers, local origin and Gaelic-only household usage (Ns = 268; 265; 298; 188, total 483)*

The comparison indicates that there is a gap between the percentage of reported residents who are fluent native speakers of Gaelic and who have a background local to the survey areas, and the percentage who use only Gaelic in their household (39%).

6.7 SPEAKER TYPES

The final assessment made during this survey entailed the breakdown of speaker types among reported residents, according to the six categorisations of the speaker typology (6.3.2). The percentages of reported residents in each speaker type are shown in Figure 6.26.

The most striking aspect of Figure 6.26 is the higher proportions of native speakers of Gaelic and English-only speakers in comparison with the other types, i.e. a bimodal distribution of bilingual native Gaelic speakers, on the one hand, and monolingual English speakers, on the other. This bimodal distribution of speaker types is typical in unidirectional bilingualism and language shift scenarios. The majority of speakers are *Native speakers of Gaelic* (55%). The next most prominent category is *Speakers of English only* (26.3%). (As noted in section 6.3.2, this category also includes speakers of languages other than English.) Those classified as active *Learners* of Gaelic come to 9.8%. There were fewer *Semi-speakers* (5.2%) and *Co-speakers* (3.7%). The small

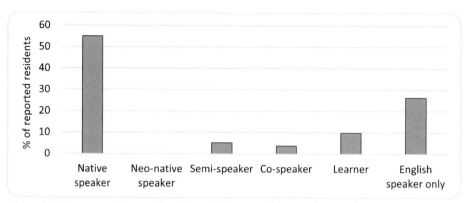

Figure 6.26 Percentage of reported residents in the six speaker types (N = 482)

proportions of the speaker types *Semi-speaker* and *Co-speaker* can be related to the small proportions of the corresponding ability category of *Good Gaelic* discussed in 6.5.1.1. The absence in any of the three islands of any *Neo-native speakers* of Gaelic (6.3.2) may be indicative of the slow trajectory of Gaelic-medium education in the Comhairle nan Eilean Siar authority area, and that there is as yet no significant trend emerging where parents, who have learned Gaelic in an institutional setting, have transmitted or are transmitting Gaelic to their children.

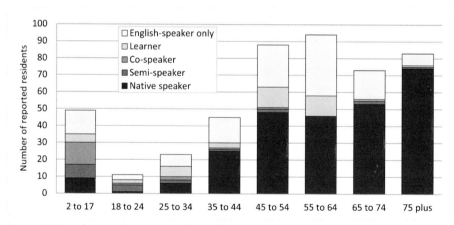

Figure 6.27 Speaker type by age group (N = 466)

Figure 6.27 examines the speaker typology by age group among those aged 2 years and older. Among those over the age of 35, *Native speaker* is the majority speaker type. As indicated many times above in the context of fluent Gaelic speakers, the speaker type *Native speaker* predominates particularly in the two oldest age groups: 89.2% of those aged 75 and over, for example. The *Native speaker* proportion becomes smaller in the younger age groups, and speaker typology becomes more diffuse with a greater number in the types *Learner*, *Co-speaker* and *Semi-speaker*.

6.8 COMPARISON OF STS WITH CENSUS

Nationally, (according to census figures) in the years from 1981 to 2011, the 3–17 age cohort has displayed a gradual upward trend in reported ability in Gaelic with the percentage in that age range rising from 0.51% in 1981 to 0.83% in 2011. Although the reporting category was very slightly different regarding age range (2–17 years), the STS found that the percentage of fluent speakers among reported residents in this cohort is higher, at 30%, than for the 18–24 (9%) or 25–34 age groups (25%). The higher proportion among this 2–17 year-old cohort seems to indicate that a proportion of this cohort is acquiring Gaelic ability from the educational system as opposed to home-based inputs. In the Scottish national context, older age cohorts show percentage declines: the 18–49 age cohort falls from 1.09% to 0.77% in the same thirty-year period, but with no change from 2001 to 2011, while the 50+ age group fell from 1.69% to 0.94% from 1981 to 2011.

Based on his examination of the 2001 Census data, MacKinnon (2010b: 64) pointed out that in over a quarter of all households in Scotland where all adults were Gaelic speakers, those adults had 'abandoned Gaelic as the language of upbringing'. He further noted that a fifth of Western Isles' households with all adults reported as Gaelic speakers had similarly not brought up their children with Gaelic as the household language. His observation closely mirrors the divergence, noted above (6.6.2, Figure 6.24), between Gaelic ability and family household practice, where, of 15 family households where both parents can speak Gaelic the breakdown is as follows: *Gaelic only* use (five households); mixed use of Gaelic and English (eight households); *English only* (two households). Where both parents have an ability in Gaelic, there is a strong tendency for the household use of a mix of Gaelic and English or to a lesser extent *Gaelic only* in homes with young families but English predominates in the households where only one of the parents has an ability in Gaelic. This practice of the majority language in households containing majority-language monolinguals is typical in minority-language situations and is evidenced in the mixed-ability couples in Table 5.7, 5.4.7 (CSS). It was also found, for instance, in Ráth Chairn, Co. Meath and in Ros Muc, Co. Galway in the Irish-speaking Gaeltacht (Ó Giollagáin 2002; 2005) and has been highlighted in Wales by Hywel Jones' (2012: 60) analysis of the Welsh language census data.

In Table 6.4 the summary Gaelic ability findings of the STS for the three separate islands and associated age cohorts can be compared to the census Gaelic ability data of the three Study Districts where those islands are located: Scalpay in North Harris SD; Grimsay in North Uist (south & east) SD; and Eriskay in South Uist (south) SD.

Age-group	North Harris SD	Scalpay STS		
	Speaks Gaelic %	Fluent %	Fluent–Fair %	Fluent–Few words %
3–17 yrs*	63.7	21.4	42.9	57.1
18–44 yrs	54.6	45.8	66.7	75.0
45+ yrs	71.3	75.8	77.9	83.2
Age-group	North Uist (south & east) SD	Grimsay STS		
	Speaks Gaelic %	Fluent %	Fluent–Fair %	Fluent–Few words %
3–17 yrs*	57.1	9.1	63.6	90.9
18–44 yrs	58.5	40.5	62.2	83.8
45+ yrs	62.3	50.5	58.7	76.1
Age-group	South Uist (south) SD	Eriskay STS		
	Speaks Gaelic %	Fluent %	Fluent–Fair %	Fluent–Few words %
3–17 yrs*	72.1	44.0	64.0	96.0
18–44 yrs	59.1	26.3	52.6	84.2
45+ yrs	68.6	63.3	72.2	84.8

Table 6.4 Comparison of summary Gaelic ability for three islands in STS with Gaelic ability from Census 2011, by associated age cohorts. *2–17 years for SD column.

It is clear from the comparison of the Gaelic ability data in the STS and the Census that the correspondence between the two older age cohorts is closer than between the youngest age cohort in the STS and in the Census. The two older age cohorts correspond fairly closely to the Fluent–Fair STS category. The youngest cohort in the Census corresponds closer to a wider range of ability categories in the STS. In Scalpay in particular the youngest cohort Fluent–Few words category at 57.1% is closest to the Census SD percentage of 63.7%. In other words, some of those in the youngest cohort who are categorised in the STS by the local advisors as having a *Few words of Gaelic* seem to be classified in the Census among those reported as having Gaelic ability.

6.9 CONCLUSIONS

The Speaker Typology Survey (STS), following the same geographic format as the Community Sociolinguistic Survey, encompassed all reported residents living on a permanent basis in the three islands of Scalpay, Grimsay and Eriskay. The STS examined community demographics, the linguistic background of reported residents, and speaker-type diversity in the context of three of the strongest remaining Gaelic-majority speaker communities in the Western Isles, in order to portray the contemporary language dynamics underpinning the ongoing replacement of Gaelic by English.

The major finding from the STS is the dynamic of intergenerational language shift observable among the population of Western Isles background, resident in the three surveyed islands, over the period of 40 years from c. 1960 to c. 2000 (6.5.2); with a small drop in Gaelic speakers in the cohort born in the 1950s, with an accelerating decline in each decade thereafter (in apparent time). Obviously, in-migrants from outwith the Western Isles are, in general, not Gaelic speakers, and the S-curve of language shift is most readily identifiable in the less irregular distributions among those of a Western Isles background. In the context of this rapid ongoing language shift, there is a stark contrast between older and younger cohorts of those of Western Isles background. 97.9% of *Local* reported residents aged over 45, born before c. 1970, were identified as being fluent Gaelic speakers, with a decline noted in the 35–44 age group (73%; Figure 6.12). The ability level among *Local* reported residents in the 25–34 age cohort, born in the 1980s, falls to 25%. However, the three profiles indicate that this 25–34 age cohort represents a small proportion of the populations. Examining all reported residents in the STS, regardless of origin, 64.7% of those aged 45 and over were fluent speakers. In contrast, 33.7% of those under 45 were *Fluent*. Although only nine reported residents were assessed as having *Good Gaelic*, the mid-scale Gaelic categories of *Good*, *Fair*, or *A few words* accounted for 16.6% of over-45s but almost half of under-45s (47.1%). These statistics indicate that fluency patterns are more fragmented for those born in the years after 1970.

It may be generally assumed that the parental generation is likely to be that of those aged 20–45. In the Teenager Survey, respondents in the Research Area reported that 33.7% of their mothers and 37.5% of fathers (section 4.4.1, Figure 4.4) have fluent Gaelic. These percentages correspond closely to the *Fluent* category assessed in the STS. Of those respondents to the community survey who were aged 44 or under, 36.4% reported fluency in Gaelic. For the 35–44 age cohort (who are reasonably likely to comprise much of the parental generation of children in senior years in high school), the fluency in Gaelic for the CSS reported 35.7% of this age group.

The contraction of the population in the under-35 age groups (with the exception of the 2–17 age cohort in Eriskay), combined with the proportional decline in Gaelic speakers, corroborates the analysis of the census data in Chapter 2 that significant demographic loss and accelerating demolinguistic shift occurred during the 1980s in the islands (see section 2.4.2.2). The combined effect of these two processes, i.e. depopulation and loss of intergenerational transmission, has produced a smaller cohort of Gaelic speakers, requiring a smaller cohort of English speakers to drive language shift to English; possibly leading to a more rapid and comprehensive erosion of intergenerational transmission and communal Gaelic socialisation.

There is a divergence between levels of ability in Gaelic, and the prevalence of Gaelic-only household practice across all three islands (Figure 6.25). For the three areas, fewer than 40% of reported residents use *Gaelic only* at home, whereas 55% are fluent and/or native speakers.

Sociolinguistic composition of the communities becomes less uniform in the younger age ranges compared especially to the older cohorts. The contrast is even greater when we compare younger and older age ranges with a Western Isles background exclusively. Generally, the findings on speaker numbers, and Gaelic speaker numbers and proportions, densities and age profiles are consistent with those of Munro *et al.* (2011: 7) who noted that 66% of the residents of Shawbost on the Isle of Lewis were fluent in Gaelic at the time of their survey, but that '... Gaelic fluency is concentrated amongst those aged 50 and older'.

In the national context, census returns reveal a less extreme and more gradual recent trajectory of decline across Scotland, as the percentage of those reported as having ability in Gaelic (outside the IGRP Research Area) fell from 1.14% of the population in 1981 to 0.96% 10 years later and to 0.87% in 2001, and to 0.85% in the 2011 Census.[68]

Of the three island surveys, Gaelic appears to be more prevalent in Scalpay and Eriskay, the two island communities with a greater proportion of reported residents having a *Local* origin. Figure 6.12 demonstrates that among those aged 35 and over, and who are local to the area, fluency in Gaelic is prevalent, while Figure 6.27 (speaker typology by age) depicts a position of native-speaker prevalence across all three islands for the 35 years and over age range.

Despite the current sociolinguistic crisis, Gaelic is still the language of the household for many in these islands, even for a small majority in Scalpay (52.9%). However, the broad picture indicates that English-only households (44.3%) are more common than Gaelic-only households (38.9%), with mixed-language households less prevalent. Gaelic practice in family households with children under 18 years is marginal (6.6.2). In Table 6.3 and Figure 6.21, for example, we find that of those households which contain children aged 2–17 (13.8% of all households), 14.7% have *Gaelic only* as their household language, while 50% use English at home, with the remaining households using both languages.

When speaker typology is cross-tabulated with household occupancy, it shows that 29.8% of native speakers live alone, and make up 76.7% of all single occupancy households. In the context of language practice and household make-up (Table 6.3), single occupancy households (41.3% of all households) represent the highest proportion of *Gaelic only* practice in households, at 74.5%. In close to half of multiple occupancy households (both as a whole, including young children; as well as without children) the language practiced is *English only*.

The distribution of speaker types mirrors the distribution of speaker abilities. Both are bimodal with an ageing bilingual native Gaelic speaker group (55% of residents), on the one hand, and an increasing and younger monolingual English group (26.3%),

---

68 From Scottish Census: Table CT_0079a_2011; Table CT_0079a_2001; Table CT_0079a_1991; Table CT_0079a_1981.

on the other (6.7). The absence of any *Neo-native speakers* of Gaelic in the speaker typology analysis shows an absence of transmission of Gaelic by parents who have learned Gaelic from (pre)school or from another formal setting.

We can say that Gaelic was overwhelmingly the communal language until about forty years ago in the three surveyed islands, and that it remains the primary daily language of interaction for many. However, Gaelic is in a marginalised position today among those under 45 years of age. As the two island communities of Scalpay and Eriskay rank amongst the highest anywhere for Gaelic ability and practice, and Grimsay ranks in the mid-range of Gaelic ability and practice, the results in this chapter illustrate a sample of the strongest Gaelic-speaking profiles to be found in the world today.

7 LINKING THE FINDINGS AND DRAWING CONCLUSIONS: TRACKING A TRAJECTORY OF DECLINE

The aims of this chapter are threefold: (1) to summarise the most important findings of the surveys (7.1); (2) to examine comparable data across the surveys to test for correlation in key variables (7.2; 7.2.1); and (3) to present the demolinguistic trajectory of the decline of the Gaelic vernacular group, according to their spatial distribution (7.2). In testing for correlation across module data, we took the key variables from the census data, the Teenager Survey and the Preschool Survey which were compatible according to Study District level analysis. We chose variables from these three survey modules due to their importance as indicators of the sociolinguistic vitality/fragility in the Research Area. This chapter draws together key findings from the various modules as inter-related evidence on the current condition of the Gaels.

7.1 MAIN FINDINGS

The principal aim of this study was to provide baseline data to indicate the contemporary societal condition of the remaining Gaelic vernacular communities in the islands of the Inner and (primarily) Outer Hebrides. Census data for the rest of Scotland indicate that weaker densities of Gaelic competence are found outside this IGRP survey area. Therefore, this study focuses upon and analyses those areas where Gaelic is more prevalent than anywhere else. In short, this is as good as it gets for the social prevalence of Gaelic. This study triangulated a series of modular surveys: the survey of preschoolers' Gaelic competence and practice, taken as an indicator of intergenerational transmission of Gaelic; the Teenager Survey; and two sets of community-based surveys, conducted in three separate districts. This subsection summarises the most important findings from the survey chapters. The summary follows the sequence of themes covered in the previous chapters:

- Demolinguistics of the vernacular group
- Intergenerational transmission
- Teenagers' social experience of Gaelic
- Profiles of communities
- Speaker typology of the profiled communities.

7.1.1 DEMOLINGUISTICS OF GAELIC'S VERNACULAR GROUP IN THE ISLANDS

We confine our summary here to the Gaelic-speaking group of the study. The main feature of Gaelic demolinguistic data from the Scottish Census is the demonstrable thirty-year trajectory of decline of Gaelic in the islands since 1981. For every ten-year period since 1981, there has been a 13% proportional average loss in Gaelic speakers. In absolute numbers, this represents an average loss of 3,220 Gaelic speakers each decade from 1981 to 2011. The proportional contraction over the thirty-year period is 35%, a net loss of 9,660 speakers. The contraction of the Gaelic-speaking group during the ten-year period of 1981–1991 was particularly critical to the social viability of Gaelic. It was during this decade that Gaelic speakers in the Western Isles fell below the high social density of 80%. In the decade from 1981–1991, the number of Gaelic speakers dropped by 4,242, representing an 18% absolute fall, taken from a base of 24,226 Gaelic speakers in 1981. However, the contraction for the 3–17 age cohort, many of whom were born in the 1970s, during this decade underwent an even more precipitous decline, from 5,329 to 3,166 speakers, representing a decadal absolute fall in speakers of 41%. The youth cohort reporting an ability in Gaelic in the 2011 Census stands at less than 2,000 speakers. While data from the 2011 Census indicate that 52% of the 3-yrs+ population report an ability in Gaelic, a comparison of the individual Gaelic ability data with the household use of Gaelic (19% of the total relevant households with adults and children) suggests that the current size of the Gaelic vernacular speaker-group extends to around 11,000 people (see sections 2.4.1.4 and 2.5.1). These are mainly 50yrs+ speakers, residing in this dispersed archipelago of islands.

The 25 Study Districts show an important divide at the intersection of 45% of inhabitants having an ability in Gaelic with 15% of households reporting the home use of Gaelic (2.4.3). The 19 Study Districts in the higher range of the spatial distribution retain some social salience of Gaelic; whereas the six Study Districts in the lower range represent a level which corresponds to societal loss. In these six moribund Study Districts, Gaelic is largely confined to elderly social networks, atypical familial practice and institutional provision.

Based on the current trajectory, we indicate that by 2021, 40% of the Study Districts will pertain to this moribund profile, at or below the 45%/15% sociolinguistic nexus. Based on the same extrapolation, the remaining 15 districts will have percentage levels of Gaelic competence in a range of 45–60%, as they edge closer to the nexus point of low viability. Under current conditions and trends, therefore, the prospects for Gaelic's vernacular habitat are clearly that of continued, rapid societal loss.

7.1.2   INTERGENERATIONAL TRANSMISSION AND COMMUNAL CONTINUITY OF GAELIC

The Preschool Survey in Chapter 3 was primarily designed as a social survey, rather than a pedagogical study. We ascertained information on the extent of Gaelic competences and practice among this age group as indicators of Gaelic intergenerational transmission. The survey was conducted in preschools in the Research Area irrespective of their GME policy (though 76% of the preschools provided some form of GME). The chief finding of the Preschool Survey corroborates the conclusion of the demolinguistic analysis of Chapter 2 and provides additional evidence of the advanced state of sociolinguistic collapse of the remaining Gaelic vernacular communities. The marginal levels of familial transmission of Gaelic in all the preschool catchment areas are indicated in the responses of preschool managers or teachers. A small proportion of preschoolers were judged to have *Fluent*, *Good* or *Reasonable* Gaelic on enrolment in the preschools: 8% of the 359 preschoolers. It is clear from this statistic alone that the home transmission of Gaelic has contracted to such an extent that it is now at the point of total loss. There is a considerable divergence between, on the one hand, the very low home practice of Gaelic among the preschoolers' young families in our survey and, on the other hand, the considerably higher level of household use of Gaelic indicated in the census. Therefore, the census presents a far more favourable portrayal of the prevalence of Gaelic. This survey provides additional evidence for the principal contention of the demolinguistic analysis in Chapter 2, that since the 1980s the island communities are no longer self-regenerating as Gaelic communities. Given how marginal the home transmission of Gaelic is, the remaining Gaelic networks are becoming confined to the elderly and some institutional practice.

The survey indicated that a small number of preschool children (24 children, i.e. 6.7% of the total) had a *Native-like* or *Good* understanding of Gaelic on enrolment. This implies that these children by necessity conform to the majority peer language of English. 88% of the preschoolers use only English with their fellow preschoolers on enrolment, with a small reduction in this percentage to 76% of the children as time passes. Despite some increase in the use of Gaelic over time, English remains the language of peer-group socialisation for a large majority of the preschoolers, indicating that the Gaelic-medium inputs from the preschool staff have a marginal impact on peer-group language socialisation.

The main implication of Chapter 3 is that the parental generation no longer speaks Gaelic to a sufficiently productive extent to support the social practice of Gaelic in the islands. Children therefore associate Gaelic more with GME provision than societal communication, and this in turn contributes to the dichotomy between the aspirations of GME for Gaelic use and the actual practice of English by the children in the preschools. This contradiction is evident in the invidious position of GME preschool providers who have to contend with the tension between attempting to implement GME aspirations and the absence of a transformative societal programme for the reversal of language shift, as well as the absence of adequate public policy provision for the language-in-society revival.

7.1.3 TEENAGERS' SOCIAL EXPERIENCE OF GAELIC

The chief conclusion in Chapter 4 from the survey of teenager Gaelic ability, use and attitudes, is that Gaelic impinges only marginally on the lives of these teenagers. The findings mirror the sociolinguistic pattern found in the survey of preschool children. A majority of the teenagers surveyed (54%, 163 pupils) indicate that they had little or no ability in spoken Gaelic. 61 pupils (20% of pupils) self-report in the survey as fluent in Gaelic, with 43 of these (14%) identifying as fluent native speakers and 18 (6%) as fluent learners. An additional 76 (25%) indicate that they had good or reasonable Gaelic. 56% of those pupils reporting an ability in Gaelic indicate that this was acquired from preschool or primary school.

The various questions on language use indicate that the social practice of Gaelic among teenagers is extremely weak. Only 12 pupils (4%) indicate that they speak mainly or only Gaelic at home, with four teenagers (1.3%) reporting that they always or mainly speak Gaelic to their friends. In relation to the parental use of Gaelic, it was reported that only six fathers (2.1%) and 10 mothers (3.4%) always speak Gaelic to their children. However, when we combine the responses of those teenagers who indicate that their parents speak *Mainly Gaelic* or *Always Gaelic* to them, the numbers increase to 22 mothers (7.4%) and 20 fathers (7%). When the bigger category of *Gaelic and English mix* is added to these, the numbers are 52 mothers (17.5%) and 52 fathers (18.1%).

The more positive data in the survey on attitudes to Gaelic demonstrate a noticeable gap between low levels of Gaelic language use and more favourable attitudes to Gaelic. 51% of the teenagers indicate that they are either in favour or strongly in favour of Gaelic. However, almost 30% of those surveyed report a level of indifference to Gaelic. Self-ascription of a Gaelic identity is strongly associated with the teenager's competence in Gaelic and family use of Gaelic. 55% of respondents did not self-ascribe as Gaels when asked this specifically. Although a significant proportion indicated multiple identity ascriptions, those indicating Scottish identity (62%) amounted to nearly twice the percentage of those identifying as Gaels (Figure 4.48 in section 4.8.1 indicating 32.6% as self-ascribing Gaelic identity). Self-ascription as a Gael was also lower than British self-ascription.

41.2% of the pupils indicate that they intend to raise their own children in Gaelic. However, this relatively strong aspiration for future Gaelic practice does not concur with their current practice of Gaelic, with ability in Gaelic (20.3% are fluent) and Gaelic use (90.6% mainly or always speak English to their friends). It represents an aspiration for Gaelic that is not grounded in their current sociolinguistic reality, and thus entails a commitment to the future that will first require the establishment of a social practice, i.e. using Gaelic for social interaction. This social practice has been absent during the foundational socialisation processes of their youth.

Only a relatively small proportion of the pupils are acquiring fluent ability in Gaelic either from their parents, from existing educational provision at preschool, primary and secondary levels, or from older generations. There are clear indications that parental input with the highest levels of Gaelic result in greater child attainment in Gaelic as evidenced by teenager Gaelic output and teenager Gaelic (conversational) ability. This is particularly true in the case of *Always Gaelic* input from mothers yielding high teenager Gaelic output. The more common parental input of *Gaelic and English mix* is far less successful in producing teenager Gaelic output and conversational ability. The intergenerational transmission of Gaelic and youth peer-group socialisation of Gaelic are now exceptional socio-cultural practices. These findings concur with the weak levels of familial transmission of Gaelic depicted in Chapter 3. The combined evidence presented in Chapters 3 and 4 shows that the communal practice of Gaelic does not extend beyond fragile and marginal social networks. The social continuity of Gaelic in the Western Isles has been lost. Prospects for a revival of any substantial social continuity for Gaelic will clearly need substantial efforts (see the discussion and recommendations in Chapter 9).

7.1.4 PROFILES OF GAELIC COMMUNITIES FROM COMMUNITY MODULE

Chapter 5 presents the findings from census-like surveys conducted in communities with some of the strongest Gaelic-speaking language profiles: Scalpay, Grimsay and Eriskay. The survey questionnaires were completed by 180 individual respondents who also reported data on other members of their household. The most noticeable feature from these surveys is the age-differentiated Gaelic fluency pattern, with older cohorts having a much greater level of fluency than younger age groups. Combining all survey areas, 85.4% of the cohort aged over 75 have fluency in Gaelic, while for the three ten-year age cohorts between 45 and 74 years, the percentage falls consistently to around 58%. A smaller percentage, 36.4%, of those under 45 years of local origin, have fluency in Gaelic. The weakening of the social densities of Gaelic fluency through the generations is mirrored in the contraction of the familial transmission of Gaelic, particularly within the last 40 years since the 1980s. This corresponds to the conclusions in Chapters 2–4. The use of *Gaelic only* or *Mainly Gaelic* with spouse/partner (i.e. an indicator of household use) was reported for 31.6% of respondents, while 46.9% use *English only*. However, only 15.5% of all children were raised in households practicing *Gaelic only* or *Mainly Gaelic*, and more than double that percentage, i.e. 36.6%, were raised in households practicing a *Mix of Gaelic and English*, while 47.9% were raised mainly or only through English.

Similar to the Teenager Survey in Chapter 4, positive attitudes towards Gaelic and aspirations for its future use contrasted with findings about the actual use of Gaelic, especially regarding crucial cross-generational use. 88% of respondents agreed with the statement that fluent Gaelic-speaking parents should raise their children in Gaelic. This contrasts with the low proportions of all respondents who reported using *Gaelic only* with children of primary-school age (8.8%), and *Gaelic only* with teenagers (6.9%).

The dynamics of the language shift and changing proportions of bilingual modes were demonstrated through biographic and apparent time. This demonstrates the rapidity of the shift spanning c. 60 years, the relative transience of the mixed mode of codemixed Gaelic, and the trajectory towards monolingual English mode, despite the efforts of some parents (against the trend) to contribute to familial transmission of Gaelic. In short, these three communities each demonstrate a similar recessive minority-language profile.

7.1.5 SPEAKER TYPOLOGY SURVEY

Chapter 6 presents the results of the Speaker Typology Survey, carried out also in Scalpay, Grimsay and Eriskay. The typology survey was conducted as an advisor-guided exercise, and provides an age-differentiated Gaelic profile of all but one of the 484 reported residents (similar to the Gaelic-ability information on 180 respondents in the related community module in Chapter 5).

The demolinguistic contraction can also be discerned in the Speaker Typology Survey: for residents of local origin, 98% aged over 45 years are fluent Gaelic speakers, with a noticeable decline to 73% in the 35–44 age cohort, and 46% of those aged 25–34 years. Regardless of origin, 64.7% of residents aged 45 years and over are fluent Gaelic speakers, while 33.7% of those aged under 45 are fluent. Despite the significant numbers of competent Gaelic speakers, the age-cohort comparisons clearly provide another indication of the assimilation of Gaelic bilinguals into English-language monolingual norms. These age-cohort comparisons were analysed as indicators of change through apparent time indicating the decadal dynamics within the populations based on their age and geographic background. The apparent-time analysis with differentiated geographic background shows how the rapid monolingualising trajectory proceeded through the decades. Those local to the three islands and elsewhere in the Western Isles and born in the two critical decades from 1970 to 1990 show a 62.8 percentage point loss in Gaelic ability. This represents a major demolinguistic tipping point. The correlates of this dynamic are also seen in the fragmentation of ability profiles of those born in the years after 1970 with almost half of them scoring in the mid-scale Gaelic categories of *Good*, *Fair* and *A few words*. Aggregating the distribution of the speaker typologies for the three areas, we see that 55% are bilingual native speakers of Gaelic; 26.3% are English-speaking monolinguals; 9.8% are *Learners* of Gaelic; 5.2% are *Semi-speakers* while 3.7% are *Co-speakers*. The speaker types therefore conform to two main profiles:

- Bilingual native speakers of Gaelic, with early-acquired English-language fluency, who acquired their Gaelic from older competent speakers in a household setting
- Monolingual native speakers of English.

7.2 INTER-MODULE ANALYSIS AND DATA CORRELATIONS

This section tests for correlations among key variables chosen from the IGRP analysis module of census data and one of the IGRP survey modules. Its primary aim is to develop a statistical analysis of key inter-module findings: the language data from the census and the Teenager Survey. It was decided to exclude the Preschool Survey from this inter-module analysis because the distribution of the preschools in the islands did not fit well with the geographic demarcation of the Study Districts; besides which several of the SDs had no preschool in them. This analysis, therefore, comprises tests for correlation between key variables in the IGRP census data analysis and the Teenager Survey and between variables within these modules. The correlations examine the level of correspondence between module variables which are indicative of the societal salience of Gaelic in:

Census Data Variables:
- Standardised Incidence Ratios (SIRs) of Gaelic use in the census data
- Decadal change expressed as a proportional percentage over the three decades in the proportion of Gaelic speakers in the SDs
- Household use of Gaelic.

Teenager Survey Variables:
- Parental competence in Gaelic
- Teenager's Gaelic Vibrancy Score (combined fluency and use scores)
- Teenager's identity ascription.

The distribution of the census data pertaining to the 25 Study Districts allows for correlation tests between census analysis data. However, the teenager data pertain to only 22 of the Study Districts. Three SDs were excluded in the analysis of correlations with Teenager Survey variables: Tiree and Staffin, being outwith the Western Isles, were not included in the Teenager Survey, and no questionnaires were returned from teenagers resident in Study District 19 North Uist (south & east). In the case of correlations between census data and the Teenager Survey, the comparisons are therefore limited to 22 Study Districts. Table 7.1, section 7.2.4, indicates which data was available for these comparisons.

Correlation tests were undertaken to measure the strength of the linear association between these variables from the two modules. As data for most variables were not normally distributed, the non-parametric Spearman's correlation coefficient (r_s) was used. This value, along with the significance (p), are attached to the label of each correlation figure below. Higher parental fluency, higher Standardised Incidence Ratios (SIRs, see section 2.4.1.5), and greater levels of Gaelic use in the household were associated with more use and higher ability in Gaelic within the teenage age cohort. The seven strongest and most statistically significant correlations (with p-value < 0.05) which were found are outlined in the following subsections (four correlations in Correlation Set I in section 7.2.1 and three correlations in Correlation Set II in section 7.2.2). Correlation Set I depicts how SIRs (based on the census module) significantly correlate with four variables: two from the census module and two from the Teenager Survey. Correlation Set II introduces a new variable based on the combined scoring of teenager Gaelic ability and use, which is termed Vibrancy Scores (see 7.2.2). The Vibrancy Scores show significant correlations with one variable from the census and two variables from the Teenager Survey. While the level of correspondence is reassuring for the analysis, it must be acknowledged that the strength of the correlations may arise from the fact that they are partly measuring related vitality variables.

7.2.1 CORRELATION SET I: STANDARDISED INCIDENCE RATIO (SIR) WITH PARENTAL GAELIC, HOUSEHOLD USE, RATE OF DECADAL DECLINE, GAELIC IDENTITY

Across the 22 SDs, a strong positive correlation exists between the Standardised Incidence Ratios (calculated from the percentage of Gaelic speakers in each of the Study Districts) and the percentage of teenagers both of whose parents are fluent in Gaelic. Figure 7.1 indicates that in areas where a higher percentage of the population had ability in Gaelic (SIR), fluency in Gaelic among both parents of teenagers was also higher. Three indicative SDs are labelled to show a low, medium and high-scoring Study District (see **Appendix 7** for data on the correlations).

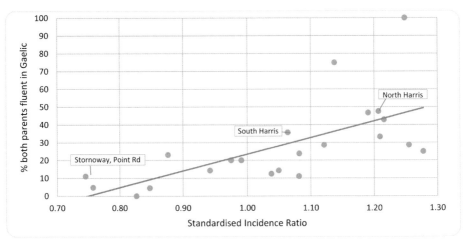

Figure 7.1 *Standardised Incidence Ratio and percentage of teenagers with both parents fluent in Gaelic; 22 SDs ($r_s = 0.724$, p. < 0.01)*

Across the 25 SDs, Figure 7.2 shows a strong positive correlation between the Standardised Incidence Ratios and the percentage of households where both adults and children speak Gaelic, i.e. Gaelic-speaking households. Figure 7.2 indicates that in SDs where a higher percentage of the population had ability in Gaelic (SIR), speaking of Gaelic by both adults and children in the household was also higher. Three indicative SDs are labelled to show a low, medium and high-scoring Study District.

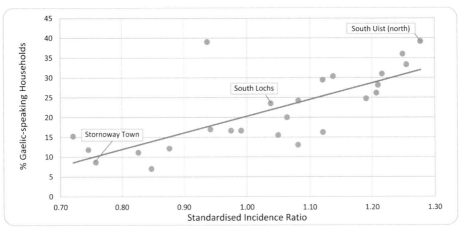

Figure 7.2 *Standardised Incidence Ratio and percentage of households where all adults and all children use Gaelic; 25 SDs ($r_s = 0.788$, p. < 0.01)*

Higher Standardised Incidence Ratios correlated with lower rates of decadal decline, as depicted in Figure 7.3. Study Districts with high Standardised Incidence Ratios of Gaelic speakers in 2011 had lower percentage decadal rates of decrease in Gaelic speakers over the three decades from 1981 to 2011. Conversely, Study Districts with the largest percentage decadal decreases in Gaelic speakers had the lowest SIR ratios. Decadal decline here is the overall proportional percentage fall over the three decades from 1981 to 2011.

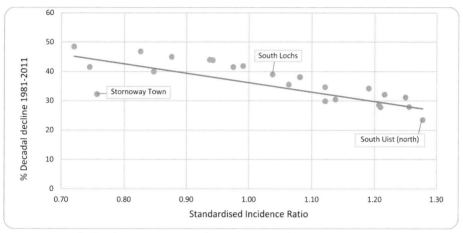

Figure 7.3 *Standardised Incidence Ratio and percentage rate of decadal Decline; 24 SDs ($r_s = -0.788$, p. < 0.01)*[69]

Figure 7.4 shows that areas with higher Standardised Incidence Ratios correlate positively with SDs that had higher percentages of teenagers who identified as Gaels.

Interestingly, the correlation between the SIR and the percentage of teenagers who state that they are supportive of Gaelic produces a weaker correlation (r_s = 0.378, p. < 0.05). Since SIR is an indicator of the use of Gaelic in the SDs, there are clearly strong correlations between SIR and other positive Gaelic variables. The lower correlation between SIR and support for Gaelic may possibly indicate that a considerable proportion of those who are supportive of Gaelic are not fluent speakers or users of Gaelic.

---

69 The SD of Benbecula records a decadal increase of 1% and is therefore not in the Figure. There are two SDs (Tolsta and Loch a Tuath) with the same SIR of 1.08 and the same percentage decline of 38% resulting in both SDs appearing in the same position in the Figure.

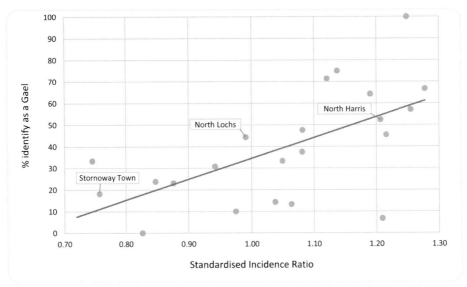

Figure 7.4 *Standardised Incidence Ratio and percentage of teenagers who identify as a Gael; 22 SDs* ($r_s = 0.584, p. < 0.01$)

7.2.2 CORRELATION SET II: VIBRANCY SCORES WITH SIR, HOUSEHOLD USE AND PARENTAL ABILITY

In this Correlation Set II, a new variable of "vibrancy" is used to summarise both Gaelic use and ability of teenagers for each of the 22 Study Districts. Vibrancy scores calculated for the high school survey respondents (based on their Gaelic ability and use) nearer to 1 indicate relatively higher levels of teenage Gaelic language ability and use in the SD; higher values nearer 5 indicate an SD where English is more prevalent. The strongest Gaelic vibrancy score was recorded at just over 3 for two neighbouring SDs in west Lewis, i.e. West Side (central (3.17) and north (3.23)).

As depicted in Figure 7.5, teenager vibrancy scores show a clear linear relationship with SIR, indicating that higher levels of Gaelic ability in the wider community relate to higher use and ability in Gaelic among the pupils.

Similarly, teenager vibrancy scores correlate with household Gaelic use from the census module, as shown in Figure 7.6.

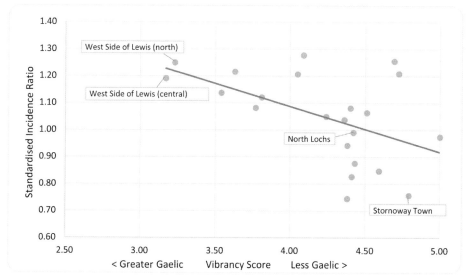

Figure 7.5 *Vibrancy score and Standardised Incidence Ratio; 22 SDs (r$_s$ = -0.470, p. < 0.05)*

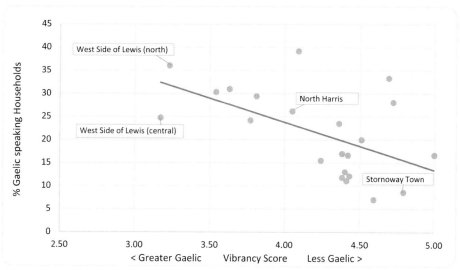

Figure 7.6 *Vibrancy score and percentage of households where all adults and all children use Gaelic; 22 SDs (r$_s$ = -0.528, p. < 0.05)*

A strong correlation is apparent between teenager vibrancy and the percentage of teenagers both of whose parents are fluent in Gaelic. Both of these variables are derived from the Teenager Survey. Communities with higher percentages of parental fluency corresponded to greater teenager Gaelic vibrancy. This is similar to the correlation between the Standardised Incidence Ratio and parental fluency in Gaelic (Figure 7.1).

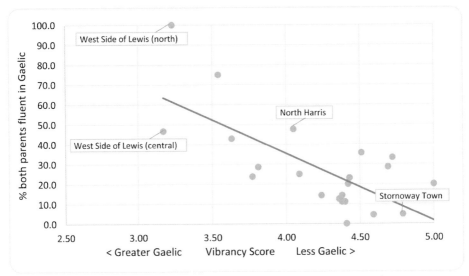

Figure 7.7 *Vibrancy score and percentage of both parents fluent in Gaelic; 22 SDs (r_s = -0.531, p. < 0.05)*

7.2.3 DATA CROSS-TABULATIONS

To summarise Correlation Set I: Study Districts with higher SIR scores were significantly (p. < 0.01) more likely to have:

- Higher levels of parental fluency and Family Household use.

And in Correlation Set II, Study Districts with higher levels of teenager Gaelic vibrancy were significantly (p. < 0.05) more likely to have:

- Higher Standardised Incidence Ratios
- Higher levels of parental fluency and Family Household use.

To examine possible relationships between key measurements across the surveys, cross-tabulations were applied and significance assessed using the non-parametric Pearson's Chi-square test. The 22 Western Isles Study Districts were classified into either a 'higher' or a 'medium-to-low' category based on the distributed magnitude of values for each of the following four variables:

- Teenager Gaelic vibrancy: 8 higher : 14 medium-to-low
- Household Gaelic use: 12 higher : 13 medium-to-low
- Parental Gaelic ability: 9 higher : 13 medium-to-low
- Standardised Incidence Ratios: 12 higher : 13 medium-to-low.

Significant (p. < 0.05) relationships were apparent in the five cross-tabulations (see **Appendix 7** for data on Cross-tabulations 1–5). These are summarised here and discussed further below.

Study Districts with high Standardised Incidence Ratios are significantly more likely to have a:
- Higher teenager Gaelic vibrancy (Cross-tabulation 3)
- Higher level of parental fluency in Gaelic (Cross-tabulation 4)
- Higher level of household use of Gaelic (Cross-tabulation 5).

Conversely, Study Districts with medium-to-low Standardised Incidence Ratios are significantly more likely to have a:
- Medium-to-low teenager Gaelic vibrancy (Cross-tabulation 3)
- Medium-to-low level of parental fluency in Gaelic (Cross-tabulation 4)
- Medium-to-low household use of Gaelic (Cross-tabulation 5).

Study Districts with higher teenager Gaelic vibrancy are significantly more likely to have a:
- Higher level of parental fluency in Gaelic (Cross-tabulation 2)
- Higher level of household use of Gaelic (Cross-tabulation 1).

Conversely, Study Districts with medium-to-low teenager Gaelic vibrancy are also significantly more likely to have medium-to-low levels of parental fluency in Gaelic and a medium-to-low household use of Gaelic.

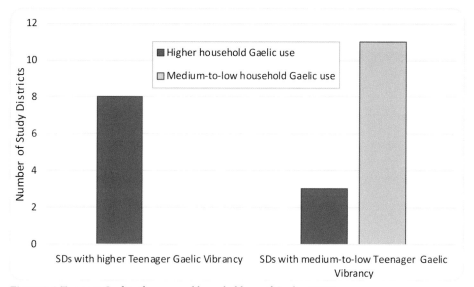

Figure 7.8 *Teenager Gaelic vibrancy and household use of Gaelic, 22 SDs*

Study Districts in which teenagers display higher levels of Gaelic vibrancy correlate with districts where household Gaelic use is at its strongest, pointing to a greater degree of parent-child interaction through the medium of Gaelic. Figure 7.8 demonstrates that, when measuring the vibrancy of teenagers' engagement with Gaelic against the household use of Gaelic, eight discrete Study Districts which evinced a higher level of Gaelic vibrancy corresponded with areas in which household use was higher. Medium-to-low levels of Gaelic vibrancy were identified in the remaining 14 Study Districts, of which three had higher reported levels of household Gaelic use.

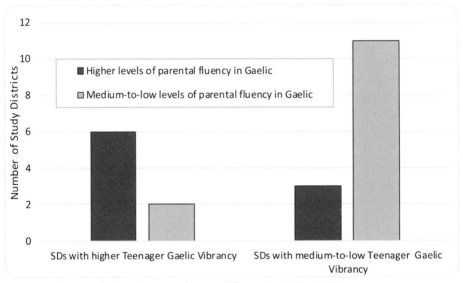

Figure 7.9 *Teenager Gaelic vibrancy and parental fluency in Gaelic, 22 SDs*

Figure 7.9 shows levels of teenager Gaelic vibrancy measured against parental fluency in Gaelic. Those SDs with higher scores for reported parental fluency in Gaelic also have generally higher Gaelic vibrancy for teenagers. Half of the study districts examined evinced medium-to-low levels of teenager Gaelic vibrancy where parental ability in Gaelic is similarly medium-to-low. The distinction is not as sharply defined in comparison to household Gaelic use (Figure 7.8). This may be an indication that household Gaelic use is more relevant for teenager Gaelic vibrancy, given that parental fluency is often not manifested in actual use with children.

Figure 7.10 shows the Standardised Incidence Ratio of Gaelic against teenager Gaelic vibrancy. Higher Standardised Incidence Ratios clearly pattern with higher teenager Gaelic vibrancy. There is no Study District which has both a medium-to-low Standardised Incidence Ratio and a higher teenager Gaelic vibrancy.

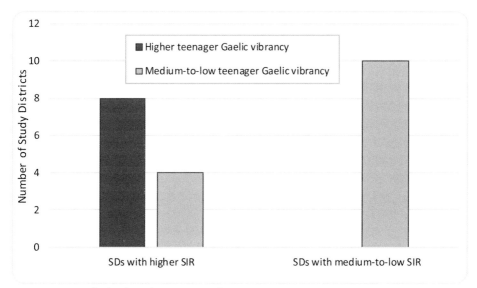

Figure 7.10 *Standardised Incidence Ratio and teenager Gaelic vibrancy, 22 SDs*

In Figure 7.11, we examine a cross-tabulation between the Standardised Incidence Ratios of Gaelic and reported levels of parental ability in Gaelic. Study Districts with higher SIRs of Gaelic also display higher levels of parental fluency in Gaelic. Conversely, districts with medium-to-low SIRs generally display medium-to-low levels of parental fluency in Gaelic. No districts with higher levels of parental Gaelic fluency have medium-to-low SIR scores.

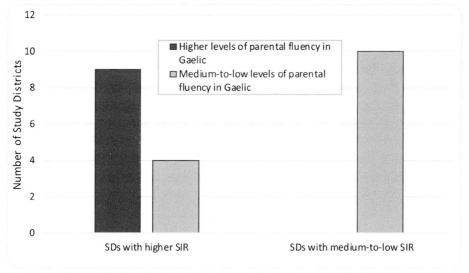

Figure 7.11 *Standardised Incidence Ratio and parental fluency in Gaelic, 22 SDs*

Figure 7.12 compares Standardised Incidence Ratios with household use of Gaelic, both analysed from 2011 Census data which is available for the 25 Study Districts. Figure 7.12 shows that most Study Districts which have a higher Standardised Incidence Ratio also have higher levels of Gaelic use in the household. Conversely, most Study Districts with medium-to-low Standardised Incidence Ratios also have medium-to-low levels of household use.

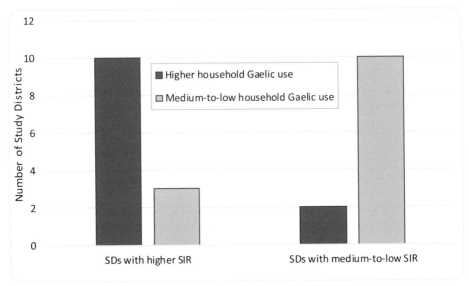

Figure 7.12 Standardised Incidence Ratio and household use of Gaelic, 25 SDs

7.2.4 CONCLUSION TO INTER-MODULE ANALYSIS

Both analytical approaches, i.e. the correlational analysis (7.2.1–2) and cross-tabulations (7.2.3), arrive at similar findings. The extent of use of Gaelic among teenagers and their level of ability in any particular area is undoubtedly determined by many factors. In this analysis, the contextual variables that appear to have the most positive impact on teenager Gaelic vibrancy are parental Gaelic fluency, household Gaelic use and SIR. All three combine to produce demolinguistic density, from the familial to the communal level. As shown in Table 7.1, the highest levels of teenager Gaelic use and teenager Gaelic fluency are typically found in:
- SDs where at least 25% of both pupils' parents are fluent in Gaelic (from Teenager Survey)
- SDs with at least 29% of households, containing adults and children, speak Gaelic within the Family Household (from census)
- SDs with SIR values of over 1.10 corresponding to c. 60%(+) Gaelic ability (from census)

- SDs with teenager Gaelic vibrancy scores below 4.10 (from Teenager Survey)
- SDs showing a proportional decline in Gaelic speakers of less than 35% across the three decades from 1981 to 2011 (from census)
- SDs where at least 45% of teenagers identify as Gaels (from Teenager Survey, cp. the discussion on how self-ascription as Gael and family language practice correspond to each other in section 4.8.1.1).

Table 7.1 presents the values of these key variables for the 25 Study Districts. For comparison, in particular with the SIR values, the corresponding Gaelic ability SD percentages from the 2011 Census are given in column 5. We can categorise the 10 SDs which reach the SIR threshold of 1.10 as:

- Five SDs, indicated by an asterisk in Table 7.1, which reach or exceed all higher level values: South Uist (north); West Side of Lewis (north); Ness, North Uist (north & west); and West Side of Lewis (south)
- Two SDs which meet all the higher criteria except in the case of teenager Gaelic vibrancy scores: South Uist (south) and Barra & Vatersay
- Three SDs which fall below the 29% threshold of households speaking Gaelic: North Harris; West Side of Lewis (central); and North Uist (south & east).

Study Districts	Standardised Incidence Ratios	% households where all children and all adults use Gaelic	% both mother and father fluent in Gaelic	% Gaelic-speakers	Teenager Gaelic Vibrancy Score (1 to 5 scale)	% identify as Gael	% decadal decrease 1981-2011
21. South Uist (north)*	1.28	39.18	25.0	65.74	4.09	66.7	23.5
22. South Uist (south)	1.26	33.33	28.6	65.84	4.69	57.1	27.9
04. West Side of Lewis (north)*	1.25	36.00	100.0	65.81	3.23	100	31.2
05. Ness*	1.22	30.97	42.9	64.17	3.63	45.5	32.1
23. Barra & Vatersay	1.21	28.15	33.3	62.27	4.72	6.7	27.8
16. North Harris	1.21	26.15	47.6	64.71	4.05	52.4	28.6
01. West Side of Lewis (central)	1.19	24.74	46.7	62.75	3.17	64.3	34.2
18. North Uist (north & west)*	1.14	30.34	75.0	61.05	3.54	75.0	30.5
19. North Uist (south & east)	1.12	16.28		60.42			29.9
02. West Side of Lewis (south)*	1.12	29.41	28.6	58.98	3.81	71.4	34.7
07. Loch a Tuath	1.08	24.18	23.8	54.62	3.77	47.6	38.1
06. Tolsta	1.08	13.04	11.1	56.42	4.40	37.5	38.1

Study Districts	Standardised Incidence Ratios	% households where all children and all adults use Gaelic	% both mother and father fluent in Gaelic	% Gaelic-speakers	Teenager Gaelic Vibrancy Score (1 to 5 scale)	% identify as Gael	% decadal decrease 1981-2011
17. South Harris	1.06	20.00	*35.7*	57.00	4.51	13.3	35.6
20. Benbecula	1.05	15.54	14.3	52.84	4.24	33.3	*-0.9*
15. South Lochs	1.04	23.53	12.5	54.67	4.36	14.3	39.0
14. North Lochs	0.99	16.67	20.0	52.23	4.42	44.4	41.8
03. Uig District	0.97	16.67	20.0	52.24	5.0	10.0	41.5
12. South Point	0.94	16.99	14.3	48.32	4.38	30.8	43.8
24. Skye, Staffin	0.94	*39.02*		49.68			43.9
08. Tong	0.88	12.16	23.1	43.81	4.43	23.1	45.0
09. Stornoway, Barvas Road suburbs	0.85	7.04	4.5	41.78	4.59	23.8	40.0
13. North Point	0.83	11.11	0.0	43.20	4.41	0	46.8
10. Stornoway Town	0.76	8.62	4.8	39.21	4.79	18.2	32.3
11. Stornoway, Point Road suburbs	0.75	11.81	11.1	38.36	4.38	33.3	41.5
25. Isle of Tiree	0.72	15.25		38.34			48.4

Table 7.1 *Scores and values for key demolinguistic density measures, 25 Study Districts in descending order of SIR*[70]

7.3 SUMMARY OF MAJOR FINDINGS OF IGRP

We can summarise the findings of the IGRP as follows:
1. The societal weakness of the Gaelic-speaking group in its remaining autochthony
2. The ongoing demographic crisis with a diminishing social density of Gaelic speakers
3. The marginal levels of societal and familial transmission of Gaelic
4. Peripheralisation of the Gaelic-speaking networks
5. Weak cross-generational practice of vernacular Gaelic
6. Low levels of youth socialisation through Gaelic
7. Weak articulation of Gaelic public policy supports and Gaelic bodies with the vernacular crisis.

---

70 In Table 7.1, SDs and values reaching or exceeding the higher demolinguistic criteria are given in bold, i.e. SIR over 1.10, as the defining criterion in column 2; 29% of households in column 3; 25% of both parents in column 4. Similarly, from a comparison of SIR values with the corresponding values in column 5 it is clear that the criterion correlates with a percentage of 60% or more, and these are, therefore, given in bold. Three outlier higher values, in three SDs (South Harris, Benbecula and Skye, Staffin), are given in bold italics. As discussed in section 7.2, there are 25 SDs from the census data and 22 from the Teenager Survey. Hence the three gaps in columns 4, 6 and 7.

In a nutshell, the IGRP has shown the progressive monolingualisation, from Gaelic-English bilingualism to English monolingualism, of all Study Districts. The Gaelic-speaking communities in the islands lost the capacity to renew themselves as a sustainable minority-speaking group in the 1980s, with less severe contraction in the 1970s. Under prevailing social conditions, the Gaelic group does not have the demographic or societal resources to sustain a communal presence in the islands beyond the next 10 years, except for isolated atypical networks of elderly speakers. As we set out in Chapter 9, a recognition of this reality by the speaker group and the relevant authorities will be crucial in any balanced discussions of a revival and an alternative policy process. An acceptance of this reality will be a first step by the community and authorities to indicate that the vernacular crisis will be taken seriously.

8 CONTEMPORARY SOCIOLINGUISTIC PROFILE OF GAELIC IN LANGUAGE PLANNING AND POLICY CONTEXT: RELEVANCE OF MANAGEMENT MODELS

8.1 INTRODUCTION

This study primarily offers a diagnosis of the crisis of vernacular Gaelic in the Western Isles, and Staffin (Skye) and Tiree. It offers, in addition, a general framework for engaging with this diagnosis to initially develop a new agenda to seek to address this challenge. In Chapter 9, we set out the initial framework. The present chapter examines how models of language planning or management relate to the current Gaelic-speaking group. This discussion offers a critique of the relevance of planning models to highly-threatened minority languages and sets out the context for a new model of engagement with the vernacular group. The new model is presented in greater detail in Chapter 9.

As this research has demonstrated, Gaelic has been supplanted as the primary language of family and community practice in the Western Isles, the last remaining vernacular context for the language. The picture emerging from this research is that the threat to the Gaelic vernacular is so severe that under current circumstances even marginal vestiges of Gaelic's communal presence will be soon lost. The pending loss of the Gaelic-practicing elderly social networks from these communities will mark the final stage. In essence, the various IGRP modules show that there is almost no cross-generational communal practice of Gaelic within the younger generations in the remaining indigenous community. MacKinnon (2011c) has referred to the trajectory that has given rise to this situation as 'runaway language shift'. If the Gaelic language is to survive at some level of communal practice within the next generation of speakers, then addressing the forces driving the current trajectory of decline is an obvious starting point. The critical issue to the sustainability of Gaelic centres on efforts to place intergenerational mother tongue transmission at the heart of any agreed agenda to reverse the decline (see discussion of EGIDS in section 8.2.2).

In the broader context of Gaelic public policy in Scotland, it is important to recognise the different requirements of the two main Gaelic constituencies, i.e. the indigenous Gaelic community on the one hand, and other networks outside the Western Isles on the other. The marginal demolinguistic aspect of Gaelic's social reality everywhere in Scotland suggests that both constituencies require each other to survive or prosper. Without a viable indigenous Gaelic community, which is the well-spring of Gaelic cultural and linguistic heritage, the learner groups may not only struggle to acquire Gaelic, but may also lose their ethnolinguistic *raison d'être*, finding themselves in a linguistic and cultural vacuum. As analysed in Chapter 2, the ongoing economic and demographic challenges in the Western Isles and other island groups exacerbate matters. The retention of young people and young families willing to contribute to community vitality will be central to any credible strategy of revitalisation.

8.1.1 HISTORICAL SOCIO-ECONOMIC DISADVANTAGE

Dorian (1981) examines Gaelic-speaking and its association with socio-economic disadvantage, resulting in the marginalisation of the group both locally and nationally. Gaelic became 'a stigmatized and stigmatizing language in the national setting' (1981: 67). With regards to East Sutherland, she found:

> … as the Highlanders stood to English-speaking Britain (including the Lowlands of Scotland), so the fisherfolk stood to the non-fishing population of East Sutherland. In each case, an entire subpopulation was stigmatized, paying severe social and economic penalties. Distinctive linguistic behaviour was a feature of the stigmatization in each case. It is not too much to say that both were cases of culture conflict. (Dorian 1981: 9)

The stigmatising discourse is evidenced in the use of derogatory terms such as 'maw' (Lewis), 'nattie' or 'slicer' (Benbecula) to refer to Gaelic speakers, or to those who live outwith the settlements of Stornoway in Lewis and outwith Balivanich in Benbecula. More broadly, Dorian depicts the Highlands as having many of the characteristics of an internal colony as depicted by Hechter (1975: 30–34):

> Certainly many of the characteristics of the internal colony … are true of the Highlands in general … recruitment of commercial and financial managers from the core rather than locally within the periphery; exploitation of, and discrimination against, a peripheral population distinguished by language or religion or other cultural markers. (Dorian 1981: 19–20)

The current advanced state of acculturation in the islands has presumably reduced a sense of stigmatisation among those undergoing acculturation. On the other hand, the Gaelic-loyal group is demographically more isolated and weaker than ever before. The difficult unremitting choice and challenge left to the remaining Gaelic-loyal group is to acquiesce with English dominance or struggle against it (cf. 5.7.4).

It has been noted that, in the face of majority-language assimilative pressures, minoritised language cultures tend to rely on language policies which are focused on an institutionalisation of minority-language practice, rather than on communal

8 CONTEMPORARY SOCIOLINGUISTIC PROFILE OF GAELIC IN LANGUAGE PLANNING
AND POLICY CONTEXT: RELEVANCE OF MANAGEMENT MODELS

363

and networked activity (e.g. Crystal 2000; Fishman 1991; and in the Irish context Ó Giollagáin 2002). The three island communities surveyed in the CSS, STS, and much of the RA, however, possess little of the institutional apparatus to engage in this form of resistance to language shift: no local schools, small church congregations, and few employers or workplaces, Gaelic-dominant or otherwise. Broadly, there is inconsistent and limited institutional provision to counter the weakened societal transmission of Gaelic and the associated difficulties discernible in the educational sector.

8.2 AN OVERVIEW OF THEORETICAL APPROACHES TO LANGUAGE PLANNING

8.2.1 INTRODUCTION

Language planning as a reflexively recognised intellectual category has gone through many phases of development since the initial efforts by Einar Haugen (1959) to set out the academic parameters of language planning within the discipline of linguistics, although it should be remembered that language planning and 'linguicide' were pursued long before these terms were coined, including much successful anti-Gaelic planning, e.g. the Education (Scotland) Act, 1872 (cf. Pollock 2007: 40–41). In framing the concept of language planning primarily within a linguistic framework, Haugen aligned the discipline's focus on language planning with the scrutiny and elaboration of the corpus planning requirements for target languages. From this linguistic perspective, scholars tended to view language planning as a linguistic problem or challenge, rather than as a social process. Critiques of this classical planning model revised the notion of the individual subject to prioritise the notion of the speaker(s) rather than focusing on speech, literacy, language and language acts. For example, Joan Rubin (1986) argued that not just authoritative actors, but rather the greatest possible number of concerned parties, including the 'target population', should contribute to the design and articulation of language planning targets for specific geographies and settings. This shift from an emphasis on language to an emphasis on language planning within a social system was a precursor to the ecological approach in language planning. The ecological approach was articulated by Robert B. Kaplan and Richard B. Baldauf (1997: xi) as: 'a body of ideas, laws, regulations, rules and practices intended to achieve the planned language change in the societies, group or system'.

Similarly, Robert Cooper's (1989) critique of previous models of language planning focused on the conceptual limitations in proposing a satisfactory theory of social change. His chief contention centred on the need for an integrated language planning model, premised on an adequate theory of social change, which has the capacity to contend with complex and multiple societal variables of language. In emphasising the importance of 'acquisition planning', as the third dimension of language planning (in addition to corpus and status planning), Cooper's expanded conceptualisation of language planning became influential: 'language planning refers to deliberate efforts to influence the behaviour of others with respect to the acquisition, structure, or functional allocation of their language codes' (Cooper 1989: 45). A central aspect of Cooper's and others' critique (cf. in particular Williams (1992) and Tollefson (1991)) was that the classical approach to language planning rested on an overly idealistic or a naïve articulation with real world problems. Rooting language-policy concerns in a specific theory of social change necessitates a high degree of political analysis prior to prescribing interventions in support of a language group. In this regard, the applied aspects of language policy and planning are realised through societal engagement which is backed by some form of political intervention.

The re-focusing of policy direction, which we propose in Chapter 9, reflects a fundamental change in approaches to language planning and policy based on the concept of agency, as set out, for instance, by Thomas Ricento (2000: 206): 'the key variable which separates the older, positivistic/technicist approaches from the newer critical/postmodern ones is agency, that is, the role(s) of individuals and collectives in the processes of language use, attitudes and ultimately policies'. A number of authors (cf. Ricento 2006; Hornberger 2006; Cooper 1989) consider that agency is now seen as a significant variable alongside, *inter alia*, ideology and ecology, in approaches appropriate for contemporary language planning, with the grassroots role of individuals vital in influencing localised language interventions.

8.2.2 EGIDS IN RLS, ADAPTED FROM FISHMAN'S GIDS

Fishman's Reversing-Language-Shift (RLS) model (Fishman 1991; 2001b) with its focus on the home-family-community nexus receives much attention in language policy. In his Graded Intergenerational Disruption Scale (GIDS), Fishman sets out a series of vitality levels which hinge on the notion of intergenerational transmission of the minority language from parents to their children. Fishman emphasised the centrality of the internal familial process of intergenerational transmission, and its prevalence in society, as critical aspects in determining the continuity of a language. Intended to be read accumulatively from the bottom up, the progressive attainment of the various grades indicates more vitality. More recently, an Extended Graded Intergenerational Disruption Scale (EGIDS) has been developed by Lewis and Simons (2016) as an improved diagnostic tool in RLS initiatives.

8 CONTEMPORARY SOCIOLINGUISTIC PROFILE OF GAELIC IN LANGUAGE PLANNING
AND POLICY CONTEXT: RELEVANCE OF MANAGEMENT MODELS

365

In Table 8.1, we present a version of this scale (Ó Giollagáin and Ó Curnáin, forthcoming).[71]

Level	EGIDS Label	Descriptive Diagnosis	UNESCO	Prescriptive Prognosis
0a	Global	The language is dominant in international and global contexts, including cultural, technical and new-media innovation, resulting in the assimilatory Anglosphere. Hypercentral English (de Swaan 2010)	Safe	Not applicable.
0b	International	The language is widely used between nations in trade, knowledge exchange, and international policy. Supercentral (de Swaan 2010)	Safe	Maintenance.
1	National	The language is used in education, work, mass media, and government at the national level. Central (de Swaan 2010)	Safe	Maintenance of national functions.
2	Provincial	The language is used in education, work, mass media, and government within major administrative subdivisions of a nation.	Safe	Maintenance of provincial functions. Expansion to national functions.
3	Wider Communication	The language is used in work and mass media without official status to transcend language differences across a region.	Safe	Maintenance of wider communication functions. Expansion to provincial functions.
4	Educational	The language is in vigorous use, with standardisation and literature being sustained through a widespread system of institutionally supported education.	Safe	a. Minority-language medium education under minority-language leadership. b. Minority-language medium education under majority-language direction.

71 The extensions to GIDS comprise the addition of internationally-vibrant languages to the scale, i.e. new EGIDS Level 0. Furthermore, we have distinguished two levels at the 'International' point (0) on EGIDS, incorporating the contrast between globalising English (0a) at the top of the hierarchy, with other international languages below (0b). Communal vitality and the penultimate stage of language shift, i.e. GIDS 6 and 8, are expanded to EGIDS 6a (communally robust), 6b (community losing speakers), and EGIDS 8a (grandparental active), 8b (grandparental passive).

Level	EGIDS Label	Descriptive Diagnosis	UNESCO	Prescriptive Prognosis
5	Developing	The language is in vigorous use, with literature in a standardised form being used by some though this is not yet widespread or sustainable.	Safe	Minority-language heritage education and minority-language literacy programmes.
6a	Vigorous	The language is used for face-to-face communication by all generations and the situation is sustainable.	Safe	Maintenance of high-density, intergenerational language transmission.
6b	Threatened	The language is used for face-to-face communication within all generations, but it is losing users.	Vulnerable	Reconstituting demographically concentrated home–family–neighbourhood initiatives.
7	Shifting	The child-bearing generation can use the language among themselves, but it is not being transmitted to children.	Endangered	Promotion of intergenerational transmission parental and family-support mechanisms and early-years initiatives.
8a	Moribund	The only remaining active users of the language are members of the grandparent generation and older.	Endangered	Promotion of transmission from the grandparent generation.
8b	Nearly Extinct	The only remaining users of the language are members of the grandparent generation or older who have little opportunity to use the language.	Endangered	Promotion of use and transmission from the grandparent generation.
9	Dormant	The language serves as a reminder of heritage identity for an ethnic community, but no one has more than symbolic proficiency.	Extinct	Acquisitional promotion, including home–family–neighbourhood initiatives.
10	Extinct	The language is no longer used and no one retains a sense of ethnic identity associated with the language.	Extinct	Retrieval, documentation and reconstruction of minority language for acquisition as L2.

Table 8.1 EGIDS: *Expanded Graded Intergenerational Disruption Scale (Lewis and Simons 2010) as adapted from Lewis and Simons (2016; 2017); UNESCO Language Endangerment Scale, and prescriptive prognosis adapted from Fishman (1991 and 2001b); from Ó Giollagáin and Ó Curnáin (forthcoming).*

8 CONTEMPORARY SOCIOLINGUISTIC PROFILE OF GAELIC IN LANGUAGE PLANNING
AND POLICY CONTEXT: RELEVANCE OF MANAGEMENT MODELS

367

Table 8.1 illustrates that EGIDS focuses on a number of discrete levels or domains of language function, i.e. a language which functions in institutional or official domains (Levels 1 to 3); its function in literacy (Level 4 and 5); and its practice in intergenerational transmission (Levels 6 to 8). Disruption at points 5 and 6 in the scale indicate the preconditions for language loss. In the case of officially-backed minority languages, such as Gaelic in Scotland, speakers may benefit from policy initiatives at the level of the institutional stages, EGIDS 1–4, while at the same time experiencing significant set-backs in the communal levels, EGIDS 5–7. This seemingly contradictory but well-known dynamic can give rise to competing assertions about minority-language vitality. For the witnesses and beneficiaries of minority-language institutional provision the language can be alive and revitalising and modernising in formal or sectoral practice, but for participants in contracting vernacular social networks the awareness of imminent language death is experienced as the implication of the *process* of erosion. In other words, language death for one participant can be experienced as language revitalisation for another (or for individuals, or for the same individual(s)).

However, the pivotal aspect of language death is the cessation in intergenerational transmission which occurs through a socio-political process of a dominant group displacing a minority's social practice (EGIDS 5–7). Often the in-group displaces itself through cooperation and assimilation with the dominant beach-head of the invasive culture. In the absence of adequate social and formal or state-supported mechanisms to maintain the minority's communal continuity, language shift is in fact the result of an 'undemocratic' dynamic in that it occurs through:

 a. A coercive process by which the minority has to contend with the socio-political power of the competing majority culture, often driven by the co-option of powerfully-positioned in-group members

 b. A combination of coercive and acquiescent processes, through which the normative power of the majority and the functional necessity of acquiring the majority socio-economic and cultural capital is foisted on and naturalised among the minority-language group

 c. Tipping-point dynamics driven by an (out-group) minority of majority-language monolinguals.

In short, the process involves a majority-language monolingual minority producing a minority bilingual group who in the following generation(s) become majority-language monolinguals. It is in this sense, of an initial minority (of majority speakers) pushing the autochthonous original majority over the precipice of geo- and demolinguistic tipping point, that language shift is so often 'undemocratic'.

8.2.3 ATTEMPTS AT POSTMODERNIST CRITIQUE OF GIDS MODEL

Whilst the GIDS model and its focus on intergenerational transmission has been influential in minority-language discourse, policy and practice, it has also been subjected to a critique which has sought to highlight its purported limitations in dealing with issues associated with societal transformations and its purported non-conflictual articulation with power mechanisms. Glyn Williams (1992) exemplifies the postmodernist and unconvincing problematising of mainstream minority-language sociolinguistics, while at the same time this postmodernist critique fails to offer a coherent alternative apart from its own postmodernist discursivism. In the following passage, Williams uses the term 'language contact', not in its usual sociolinguistic meaning, but to refer to language group interactions, conflict and replacement. His assertions could easily be contradicted by quotes from Fishman's extensive work, but we shall let Williams' citation speak for itself:

> The main orientations in the study of language contact have tended to involve typologies and perspectives which set great limitations upon what can be said about the inherent conflict between language groups that is a feature of language contact.
>
> The work of Ferguson and Fishman, in the form of the concepts of domain and diglossia, have become axiomatic in the sociology of language, when, in my view, they tend to be more of a hindrance than a help in analysing language contact. They both express an evolutionary continuum which depends upon highly questionable assumptions about the nature of modernity, tradition and progress. Within this expression about the nature and direction of social change there is a highly conservative orientation which is embedded in the various concepts. This has the consequence of marginalising the minority languages while also making it virtually impossible to express the anger and frustration experienced by members of minority-language groups confronted by the process of language shift. The main reason for this is that the perspective adopted by most writers on this issue is inherently consensual in nature and plays down conflict while ignoring power. (Williams 1992: 121–22)

Furthermore Williams posits:

> The heightened individualism and the loss of state hegemony, authority and power in confronting crises undermine citizenship, and its relationship to culture and language. The globalisation process seems to be driving a need to simplify economic activity by focusing on particular *lingue franche*. At the same time, the role of language and linguistic diversity in the reflexive process can make a profound contribution to the knowledge economy.

8 CONTEMPORARY SOCIOLINGUISTIC PROFILE OF GAELIC IN LANGUAGE PLANNING
AND POLICY CONTEXT: RELEVANCE OF MANAGEMENT MODELS

369

Yet, many languages and cultures remain locked in 'tradition', waiting to be reinterpreted. This reinterpretation will involve a concern with discourse and meaning, thereby allowing freedom from categorisation based on form. (Williams 2010: 228–29)

Williams attempts to argue that this reflexive reinterpretation of diversity in the globalised knowledge economy can be reconciled through a shift 'to a multiculturalism that is based on sharing and mutual comprehension' (Williams 2010: 229). There is obviously a large unsubstantiated assumption at the heart of this cosmopolitan aspiration about the assumed capacity of small demographic groups to participate in, let alone influence or change, the discourses on and trajectories of globalisation. In this regard, Ulrich Beck and Elizabeth Beck-Gernsheim's (2010) assessment of globalised intercultural contact, especially when combined with the overwhelming evidence of ethnolinguistic erosion, seems closer to the mark:

> People are expected to live their lives with the most diverse and contradictory transnational and personal identities and risks. Individualization in this sense means detraditionalization, but also the opposite: a life lived in conflict between different cultures, the invention of hybrid traditions. … Living your own life therefore can mean living under the conditions for radicalized democracy, for which many concepts and formulae of the first modernity have become inadequate. No one knows how the conflicting transnational identities can be politically integrated. (Beck and Beck-Gernsheim 2010: 26–27)

The societal depletion of small languages during the cultural contact of the 'first modernity' (19th century) has been and continues to be substantial. This does not provide an encouraging precedent, let alone a solid social basis, for minority cultures to influence the political integration which could be supportive of their part in the multiculturalist aspirations of postmodernity or postmodernism. An assumption that these minority groups can have a sustainable role in cosmopolitan identity formation veers more towards creative thinking or imaginative musings than social analysis and critique, and is yet another instance of the postmodernist prioritisation of the discursive over the real. Such an assumption of sustainability cannot be made from a realistic demolinguistic perspective.

8.2.4 'CATHERINE WHEEL' MODEL

Miquel Strubell's (2001a: 279–80) 'Catherine Wheel' model is complementary to Fishman's GIDS model in that it attempts to address some of the perceived limitations of Fishman's scalar progression through levels of language vitality. The Catherine

Wheel model emphasises a circular dynamic in language status change. Its point of reference is the individual participant in the minority-language group as a consumer of societal assets. It differs from Fishman's ethnolinguistic approach in that it stresses the conditions which are conducive to the consumption of the minority culture, and that it is dependent on the complementary interaction of the following constituent elements: (1) the language competence of individuals; (2) the social use of language; (3) the existence of products and services in this language and the demand for them; and (4) the motivation to learn and use this language. The underlying principles of the circular dynamic in Strubell's model may be summarised as follows: increased language learning or acquisition creates more demand for goods and services mediated through the language, leading to an increased supply of services in the language, and ultimately stimulating more consumption of the language. This aim of increased consumption, it is assumed, engenders a more positive perception of the utility of the language and encourages greater motivation to learn it, which allows for access to multiple personal, social and career advantages.

While the Catherine Wheel metaphor evokes a dynamic self-perpetuating process, it is unclear how the envisaged circular dynamic marks a significant advance on the 'linearity' of the GIDS model. The Catherine Wheel approach rests on assumptions which do not appear immediately relevant for highly marginalised languages and, in this sense, the application of the Catherine Wheel approach (cf. Walsh and McLeod 2008, discussed in section 8.3 below) represents an overly-optimistic view, or perhaps a naïve mismatch, of policy ambition with actual social capacity. From this perspective, it is difficult to see how the model's underlying assumptions could be applied to very small and fragmented minority languages, such as Scottish Gaelic, particularly in relation to three specific elements: a) Gaelic is not spoken in communities of speakers residing in appreciable social densities; b) there are low levels of demand for goods and services through the medium of Gaelic; and c) the expectation that the 'circular' dynamic of the model will generate 'more supply and consumption of goods and services' in Gaelic is not based on a realistic appraisal of the present day level of vitality of *in situ* Gaelic communities or emerging learner networks. In keeping with the model's metaphor, the Gaelic group simply does not possess the societal energy to drive the rotation of the wheel.

The models as developed by Fishman and Strubell are useful in many respects, and yield insights into certain dynamic elements that are relevant to addressing language shift and in prescribing revitalisation processes. However, it can be argued that the applicability of the Strubell model to the present situation of the Scottish Gaelic vernacular community is crucially limited. The issue for Scottish Gaelic in the implementation of various versions of such models, including more general endangered-language formulations suggested by Grenoble and Whaley (1998), is that

8 CONTEMPORARY SOCIOLINGUISTIC PROFILE OF GAELIC IN LANGUAGE PLANNING
AND POLICY CONTEXT: RELEVANCE OF MANAGEMENT MODELS

371

they either approach matters from a primarily linguistic perspective and/or that they propose mechanisms appropriate to larger languages, rather than highly minoritised languages such as Scottish Gaelic.

8.2.5 REGENERATIVE MODELS

The more 'community-systems' focused work of Irish and North American researchers provide alternative frameworks and mechanisms for planning and delivering minority-language revitalisation interventions (Bourhis and Landry 2008; Bourhis *et al.* 1997; 2010; Bourgeois and Bourgeois 2012; Lewis and Simons 2016; Ó Giollagáin and Ó Curnáin 2016). The interventionist frameworks suggested by these researchers are primarily based on two complementary approaches: the 'cultural autonomy' model proposed by Richard Y. Bourhis and Rodrigue Landry (2008) and the 'institutional completeness' framework as discussed by Raymond Breton (1964); Sheldon Goldenberg and Valerie Haines (1992); and Daniel Bourgeois and Yves Bourgeois (2012).

Ó Giollagáin and Ó Curnáin (2016: 62–67) emphasise four strategic requirements to address the recessive trajectory in highly-threatened linguistic minorities in general, and the Irish-speaking minority in particular. *Beartas Úr na nGael* [A new Deal for the Gael] recommends the establishment of new social structures and organisations, based on democratic agreements and organised along co-operative lines:

1. **Tearmann na nGael** [Irish linguistic zone(s)] to provide for the geographic protection of the remaining Gaeltacht speaker base, if and as sanctioned by the following organisations;
2. **Iontaobhas na nGael** [Community Trust for Gaels] to manage the resources of group members and to administer the benefits of membership;
3. **Dáil na nGael** [Assembly for Gaels] to provide political empowerment and leadership to enable practical actions;
4. **Acadamh na nGael** [Academy for Gaels] to undertake research and disseminate knowledge.[72]

The Bourhis and Landry (2008) formulation proposes an intervention model that links Fishman's RLS model within a group vitality framework. This 'cultural autonomy' model is often strategically linked with the 'institutional completeness' concept suggested by Breton (1964) to frame and analyse ethnic relations and conflicts within institutional dynamics in which the minority perspective is afforded opportunities for civic elaboration. In the Bourhis and Landry (2008: 186) approach, there are three

---

72 See also: 'Irish language needs communal not symbolic use', *The Irish Times*, 27 April 2016. http://www. irishtimes.com/opinion/comment-the-gaeltacht-must-be-broken-and-remade-to-save-irish-1.2625367.

dimensions of socio-structural variables that have a profound influence on the vitality of an L1 language community in inter-language-group situations: 'demography; institutional support and control; and status'. They also state that, 'within democracies, demographic factors constitute a fundamental asset for language groups as "strength in numbers" can be used as a legitimising tool to grant language communities with the institutional control they need to ensure their intergenerational continuity within multilingual societies'. (Bourhis and Landry 2008: 187, quoting Bourhis, El-Geledi and Sachdev (2007))

From the perspective of this research, the theoretical paradigm within which Bourhis and Landry's cultural autonomy concept is framed warrants serious consideration among the Gaelic group. The defining component of this model focuses on the degree of control a language community has within cultural and social institutions related to its linguistic and cultural vitality. Similar to the Fishmanian emphasis on the home-family-community nexus, Bourhis and Landry's theoretical paradigm rests on the key element of 'social proximity' in so far as: 'it provides the primary socialization in the minority group language (L1) essential for intergenerational language and cultural transmission as well as language group identity development'. (Bourhis and Landry 2008: 194)

Given the weak social densities of Gaelic speakers, the appropriate application of the model in the Scottish Gaelic context is challenging. The efficacy of the cultural autonomy approach to the Gaelic context would be predicated on a considerable collective effort to resist the established demolinguistic trend. Here lies the language-policy conundrum for fragmented vernacular groups: cultural autonomy can only emerge from a collective mandate; intergroup language dynamics between a subordinated linguistic minority and a dominant group are disruptive of minority collective organisation; and a minority communal identity can only exist if a group of speakers give practical expression to its cultural and linguistic resources in a social and spatial context. In other words, degrees of cultural autonomy require, first of all, that the collective has the capacity to protect its social proximity before it can consider its collective organisation. Therefore, in the absence of any meaningful collective organisation of a receding language group, its trajectory is toward societal erosion.

The related concept of 'institutional completeness', as a dimension of social proximity, is examined by Bourgeois and Bourgeois (2012: 293–304) in their analysis of its applicability to the Acadian community of Greater Moncton, New Brunswick, Canada. They conclude that: 'institutional completeness is a good theoretical and practical concept to describe, explain, and possibly predict conflicts between minorities and majorities' (2012: 303). They indicate that the extension of French-medium multi-sectoral institutional provision envisaged by the framework is warranted by the sizeable proportion of Francophones in the area.

8 CONTEMPORARY SOCIOLINGUISTIC PROFILE OF GAELIC IN LANGUAGE PLANNING
AND POLICY CONTEXT: RELEVANCE OF MANAGEMENT MODELS

373

8.2.6 VERNACULAR GAELIC IN REVITALISATION MODELS

The organisational resources of the Gaelic vernacular community and the extent to which they can provide necessary services in Gaelic, are far below the 'institutional completeness' of Acadian French. In fact, the marginal position of Gaelic vernacular concerns in the language planning and policy approach in Scotland forms part of the context of the sociolinguistic disadvantage of the Gaelic vernacular community. In order to have some degree of institutional completeness, and in particular agency for the Gaels, a degree of practical local democracy and institutional power would need to be devolved to them first. This important point forms part of our proposal for a new approach, as discussed in more detail in Chapter 9.

Therefore, our discussion of these language-policy frameworks has highlighted the disparity between the high level of aspiration for minority-language policy, and in certain academic discourses on the one hand, and the severity of the disruption to Gaelic social practice on the other. This combines with the almost non-existent support for the autochthonous group and the absence of independent agency of the Gaelic speaker group. These three challenges, i.e. the lack of policy and discursive relevance, the weak societal presence and the absence of group agency are addressed in our proposal for a new approach in Chapter 9.

Important analytical contributions have been made by François Grin (1990; 2003a; 2003b; 2016) and François Grin and François Vaillancourt (1999) in relation to the 'economics of language'. Grin's (2003b) sociolinguistic analysis is centred on the concept of the linguistic minority having access to a supportive market (in the widest socioeconomic sense of the term, e.g. in cultural goods). Sociolinguistic fragility is thus the result of disruption to markets and supports which had previously sustained the speaker group, and from this perspective, language shift manifests an ongoing process of market failure in the language group. According to Grin (2003a; 2003b; 2016), a market failure occurs when the price mechanism fails to allocate scarce resources efficiently, or when the operation of market forces leads to a net social welfare loss. In the context of minority languages, linguistic diversity is viewed in many public policy discourses as a desirable aspect of society and is thus seen as a public good. As Grin and Vaillancourt (1999: 100) contend, the maintenance of minority languages is an issue of promoting the public good. They state that the revitalisation of a minority language is, inevitably, a collective endeavour, and therefore in democratic states any decisions about the acceptability or excessiveness of resources expended for language maintenance and revitalisation should only be made in the context of democratic political entities. In this regard, the Gaelic Language (Scotland) Act 2005 can be viewed as a milestone for the Gaelic language, in that it emerged from a process of public consultation, political debate and legislative scrutiny.[73] In general, debates on Gaelic public policy are based in this public-good discourse. If Gaelic public policy can continue to rely on this type of moral support, the terms of reference for future debate will have to contend with issues of:

- The weak relevance of current strategic initiatives for the vernacular group
- The weak effectiveness or lack of equity in resource allocation
- The capacity of public bodies to deliver policy outcomes
- The negative social effect on the speaker group of the weak relevance of the policy.

In conjunction with the moral support and related civic symbolism, minority-language groups, such as the Gaels, need to be adequately equipped to tackle the enormity of the socio-political and ethnolinguistic challenge confronting them. Relevant approaches should be based on the ethnolinguistic agency of the group as set out in our proposal in Chapter 9.

8.3 PREVIOUS CONSULTATION ON GAELIC LANGUAGE PROMOTION

Pro-Gaelic language planning in Scotland was almost non-existent until the Highlands and Islands Development Board commissioned a report to assess the state of the language. The seminal report *Cor na Gàidhlig* ('The Condition of Gaelic') was authored by Màrtainn MacDonald in 1982. The report's recommendations set the foundations for much of the present institutional and operational support mechanisms for the revitalisation of Gaelic in Scotland. Following the publication of the MacDonald Report, Comunn na Gàidhlig (CnaG) was founded in 1984 by the then Scottish Office. CnaG's role was to co-ordinate new developments in Gaelic language policy, and in particular, policies in relation to an expansion of Gaelic-medium education and Gaelic language broadcasting. From the publication of the MacDonald report to essentially the mid-2000s, Gaelic development efforts were also focused on a campaign to establish a degree of formal legal protection for Gaelic.

CnaG campaigned effectively and developed a set of proposals for *Secure Status for Gaelic*, published in 1997. This was followed by Comunn na Gàidhlig's *Draft Brief for a Gaelic Language Act* published in 1999. In 2000, the Taskforce on Public Funding of Gaelic (commonly known as the MacPherson Task Force) issued a report which was commissioned by the Scottish Ministers of the newly-established devolved parliament. The report recommended that a Gaelic development agency be established to elaborate and deliver policy aimed at enhancing the status of Gaelic in Scotland and supporting its use in a range of social and formal settings.

---

73 The Gaelic Language (Scotland) Act 2005 was enacted on 1 June 2005, and commenced on 13 February 2006. It is the first piece of legislation which accords formal recognition to the Scottish Gaelic language.

8 CONTEMPORARY SOCIOLINGUISTIC PROFILE OF GAELIC IN LANGUAGE PLANNING
AND POLICY CONTEXT: RELEVANCE OF MANAGEMENT MODELS

375

The MacPherson Report led to the establishment of the Ministerial Advisory Group on Gaelic, chaired by Professor Donald Meek. In 2002, the Meek Group published their report *A Fresh Start for Gaelic* (Ministerial Advisory Group on Gaelic (2002)), which presented the case for a Gaelic Language Act. Subsequently, the commitment for such an Act was confirmed in the 2003 governmental programme, *Partnership for Government*, which promised the following high-level commitments relating to Gaelic:

- 'We will legislate to provide secure status for Gaelic through a Gaelic Language Bill
- We will continue to invest in Gaelic-medium education, including the provision of more teacher training places'.

Following public debate and parliamentary scrutiny, the Scottish Parliament passed the Gaelic Language Bill in April 2005; the Gaelic Language (Scotland) Act 2005 was signed into law in June 2005 and was commenced in February 2006.

The Gaelic Language (Scotland) Act 2005 established the statutory language planning agency, Bòrd na Gàidhlig, and the provisions of the Act set out the framework for the creation of Gaelic language plans in Scottish public bodies. The primary instruments of the Act were modelled to a considerable extent on the 1993 Welsh Language Act (Dunbar 2006: 17) which in turn borrowed from the 1988 Canadian Language Act (cp. Irish Language Act 2003). Bòrd na Gàidhlig operated in accordance with comparable functions to those of the Welsh Language Board, and it devised a similar system of language plans that were to be managed across the public sector.

The preamble to the Act provided an overview of the primary powers given to the Bòrd:

- 'functions exercisable with a view to securing the status of the Gaelic language as an official language of Scotland commanding equal respect to the English language, including:
- the functions of preparing a national Gaelic language plan; and
- of requiring certain public authorities to prepare and publish Gaelic language plans … in connection with the exercise of their functions and to maintain and implement such plans, and of issuing guidance in relation to Gaelic education'.

In the first National Plan for Gaelic for the period 2007–2012, language policy sought to emphasise the profile of the language:

We want Gaelic speakers to form a more positive image of their language as relevant to all aspects of their lives, and as one that is valued by the society in which they live. Greater status and usage is likely to create employment opportunities for those who have Gaelic language skills, and this will increase the desire to acquire Gaelic. Parents will have a greater incentive to pass it on in the home, for their children to acquire Gaelic in the school, and adult learners will perceive added benefits in seeking to acquire the language. (Bòrd na Gàidhlig 2007a: 29; similarly, Bòrd na Gàidhlig 2007b: 8)

The primary instrument of the 2005 Act was the requirement for Scottish public bodies to prepare and implement Gaelic language plans. The purpose of such plans was and is to expand the profile, acquisition and use of Gaelic across the public sector in Scotland. By providing for the use of Gaelic in the delivery of public services, as well as in the internal operations of public bodies, Gaelic Language Plans were to be formal policy instruments to increase the profile and visibility of the language, with the expectation that this would help raise the status of Gaelic in the public domain.

This approach to configuring the Bòrd's language-policy obligations under the 2005 Gaelic Act is redolent of Miquel Strubell's (1999; 2001a) rationale for his Catherine Wheel model of language planning. In fact, in a discussion of the Catherine Wheel planning model in relation to both the 2003 Irish Official Languages Act and the 2005 Gaelic Language (Scotland) Act, Walsh and McLeod (2008) are in general agreement as to the applicability of the Catherine Wheel model to Gaelic circumstances, except for certain implementational and sociolinguistic constraints. The authors state that:

> Drawing on Strubell's 'Catherine Wheel' language planning model (1996; 1998; 1999; 2001a; 2001b), this article examines the measures public bodies are expected to implement in order to increase their bilingual service provision and considers their implications for language revitalisation. Based on the limited previous experience of delivering public services in Irish and Gaelic, it identifies possible blockages which may impede the successful turning of the Catherine Wheel and suggests interventions to overcome them (pg. 22). … In the Scottish case, it remains too early to tell whether the Act will be implemented in such a way as to promote increased language use in accordance with the Catherine Wheel model. Much will depend on the successful implementation of the National Plan for Gaelic and of well-designed language plans on the part of public bodies. … As in Ireland, although ensuring an adequate supply of Gaelic-medium services will give rise to a range of significant difficulties, the real challenge will lie in seeking to ensure that Gaelic speakers are able and willing to use the language in relation to public services. (Walsh and McLeod 2008: 42)

As stated in section 8.2.4 above, it is doubtful that the requisite social and institutional components, that underpin the Strubell model, have been or are in place in order to actualise, as feasible societal endeavours, the objectives of the National Gaelic Plan or the Gaelic Language Plans (GLPs) of public bodies. The existing public policy

8 CONTEMPORARY SOCIOLINGUISTIC PROFILE OF GAELIC IN LANGUAGE PLANNING
AND POLICY CONTEXT: RELEVANCE OF MANAGEMENT MODELS

377

model for Gaelic, derived largely from the Strubell paradigm and framed within language act structures, assumes a relatively stable demographic speaker base and the existence of relevant interconnected power mechanisms to bring dynamism to the policy process. These key assumptions do not hold for what remains of the Gaelic communities of the Western Isles, or for other island or rural localities.

Both the reliance on frameworks from other jurisdictions, and disproportionate deference to Strubell's thinking, exhibit a failure to critique and take account of the need to localise the planning and policy approach to the specific demographic and policy constraints of a highly marginalised minority language, such as Scottish Gaelic. Since the current Gaelic policy model was not designed primarily to redress the low social densities of Gaelic speakers in the Western Isles, it is not surprising that the basic assumption underpinning the model — that the increased provision of Gaelic services will in the long run generate greater demand for Gaelic language acquisition — has failed to gain sufficient traction in the vernacular context. Indeed, echoing the problem of prioritising high-level EGIDS initiatives, which has been highlighted so many times in this IGRP report, MacKinnon (2012: 8) cautions that Gaelic language policy might be akin to an 'empty raincoat', in that 'we may be constructing a resplendent new Gaelic world of media, education system, and language plans but these fine vestments when opened up contain no person inside actually speaking and using the language'.

To date, no research evidence or comprehensive evaluation of the effectiveness of the Strubell-derived model in the Scottish context has been presented for public scrutiny. Recent research conducted by Ingeborg Birnie (2016) in the Western Isles concluded that a public body having a Gaelic language plan did not make a significant improvement to the use of Gaelic in the daily interactions of the community with the public body. Positive Gaelic language choice in those cases was based more on whether those involved were acquainted and whether they had a common interest or ability in Gaelic. Therefore, the National Plans for Gaelic, with their primary focus on status planning, meet a symbolic need to assert the civic presence of Gaelic in Scotland without creating the official capacity or mechanisms to influence behavioural change at the vernacular level. The major limitation of the current Gaelic language-policy approach can be seen in its focus on a nebulous civic totality (from the minority-language viewpoint), at the expense of a targeted approach to the societal realities in a defined locale such as the Western Isles.

8.3.1 ASSESSMENT OF NATIONAL SCOTTISH GAELIC PLANNING AS A POLICY-TO-IMPACT APPROACH

In this section, we assess national Scottish Gaelic planning based on Grin's (2003b) language-policy assessment model. The language planning framework for Gaelic in

Scotland generally follows a policy-to-outcome pathway as shown in Figure 8.1. The analytics in Figure 8.1 are adapted from Grin's (2003b) language-policy assessment model. It indicates realms of activity and interconnected developmental levels by which outcomes of official policy may be assessed.

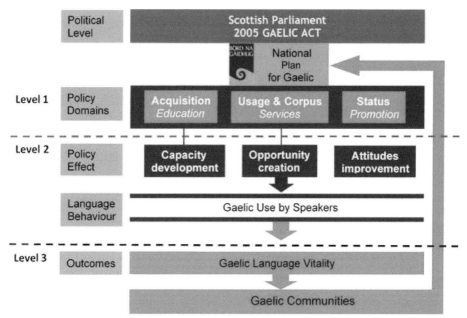

Figure 8.1 *A pathway-to-impact model for Gaelic language development (adapted from Grin (2003b))*

Figure 8.1 is a simplified overview of the links between the different levels of national policy as set out in the National Plan for Gaelic, and subsequent expected outcomes in relation to language use and vitality at the community level. The National Plan for Gaelic is renewed every five years, and provides the foundational basis for Gaelic language policy and planning in Scotland. The desired linkages are best understood by reading the figure's flow chart from '**Level 3**' upwards, in that the use of Gaelic in communities, the end of the causal impact chain, is the declared aim of Gaelic policy.

The levels of practice and decline of Gaelic in the community has been described in significant contemporary research: MacKinnon (e.g. 1994b; 1994c; 1998; 2006a; 2011c), Will (2012) and the Shawbost district research, undertaken by Munro *et al.* (2011). However, the overall impact on language use of successive National Gaelic Language Plans (NGLPs) implemented since 2007 has not been researched. The Bòrd is embarking on the third cycle of its 5-year National Gaelic Plans, and

8 CONTEMPORARY SOCIOLINGUISTIC PROFILE OF GAELIC IN LANGUAGE PLANNING
AND POLICY CONTEXT: RELEVANCE OF MANAGEMENT MODELS

379

previous plans have not adequately addressed, nor tackled at the appropriate level of intervention, the challenges associated with the social demise of the speaker group.

Nevertheless, there have been recent consultancy publications evaluating the effectiveness of national plan implementation, e.g. Jones *et al.* (2016). In summarising their evaluation of the impact of the 2007–12 National Plan for Gaelic, Jones *et al.* (2016) highlighted the following issues:

- The absence of clear benchmarks in the NGLP makes it more difficult to draw unambiguous conclusions with regard to the success (or lack) of implementation.
- A perceived lack of connection between the use of Gaelic in the home, early years and communities and in formal education was identified as a shortcoming in the current NGLP.
- Stakeholders' general perceptions of the NGLP tended to reflect their widespread sense that it was useful as a tool to demonstrate language-policy priorities to civil servants and politicians, and to some extent public bodies preparing their own GLPs. However, there was also a perception that the Plan was often of little use or no relevance to the wider Gaelic community.
- Widely held concerns that GME is currently prioritised over language maintenance in the Gaelic community may, in part, be assuaged by adopting a more inclusive and wide-ranging conception of education as a strategy for language development which makes greater use of the traditional communities. These should articulate more clearly goals for the strengthening of such communities, including the development of greater opportunities within them for social use of Gaelic in an expanding number of settings.

These four main points are central to the IGRP concerns.

In relation to Figure 8.1, Gaelic language planning and policy is focused primarily on **Level 1** of the model, with engagement in this policy domain being essentially focused on status factors and issues of the related public visibility of the language. The Gaelic language plans of public bodies, required under Sections 3 and 7 of the 2005 Gaelic Language (Scotland) Act, do not entail a strong direct operational linkage to the vernacular Gaelic speaker community. In short, the required feedback loop and monitoring of desired outcomes at **Level 3** are absent. Establishing clear evidence of an effective transition from **Level 2** to **Level 3** of the assessment model would represent significant progress for Gaelic-language vitality efforts in that they would indicate improvements in everyday domains, as envisaged in the Fishmanian (1991: 87–119) GIDS model and the emphasis it places on the home-family-community nexus (see section 1.3).

Similarly, Rob Dunbar (2000) highlights the disjointedness of policy application between **Levels 1**, **2** and **3** of this model and the lack of mutual engagement between **Levels 1** and **3**:

> the reality is that government support for this linguistic community is very limited, and … such support as does exist is insecure. More fundamentally, the Gaelic community itself has very little, if any control over any of the levers of power in the crucial areas of its day-to-day existence. (Dunbar 2000: 69)

Dunbar also notes that:

> unelected Scottish Executive bureaucrats cannot claim to represent the interests of the Gaelic community. Thus … we have decisions of fundamental importance to the future of the Gaelic community made by people who cannot in any meaningful sense be representative of or be held directly accountable to that community. (Dunbar 2000: 74)

Dunbar's observations are important. In essence, he is implying that very little has changed since the publication of the *Cor na Gàidhlig* report (MacDonald 1982) which highlighted the absence of positive official engagement with the Gaelic community. In other words, despite the discursive energy, legislative effort and the financial allocation through institutional provision for Gaelic, few practical **Level 3** outcomes for the Gaels have emerged. Therefore, the current policy-in-practice situation is similar in the receding speaker communities to the non-policy period prior to the 1980s. Similar to many formal RLS initiatives, the implementation of institutional initiatives often coincides ironically with the social decline of the language (Fishman 1991).

The prioritisation of **Level 2** initiatives falls into the conceptual trap highlighted by Fishman's GIDS model (see section 1.3). For instance, Dunbar (2011: 63) echoes Fishman's (1991: 380) caution that Gaelic policy is overly reliant on 'higher order props' which have little impact on Gaelic vernacular use. Additionally, Dunbar (2011: 65) highlights the gulf between the official rhetoric of support for the language and the day-to-day reality of limited levels of supply (**Level 2**) and demand (**Level 3**) for this support. This is consistent with his reservations (Dunbar 2011: 65) about the potential of legal instruments (**Level 1**) to influence day-to-day linguistic practice, especially at the level of communal interactions (**Level 3**). In this he warns against seeing language acts (such as the Gaelic Language (Scotland) Act) as 'silver bullets' with the capacity to change or influence the social dynamics of language use (Dunbar 2001: 57). In short, the provisions of these plans remain marginal to the language-in-society dimension of more vital minority policy concerns. Furthermore, due to the relatively late elaboration of official Gaelic policies in Scotland, as well as the lack of competence in Gaelic among many public service staff, most Gaelic speakers have grown accustomed to dealing with officialdom through English (Birnie 2016).

8 CONTEMPORARY SOCIOLINGUISTIC PROFILE OF GAELIC IN LANGUAGE PLANNING
AND POLICY CONTEXT: RELEVANCE OF MANAGEMENT MODELS

381

The implementational gap between **Levels 1** and **3** is also highlighted by McLeod's (2014: 12) analysis that Gaelic policy is framed in an over-optimistic view of language planning measures. He cautions that: 'There is a danger that language planning strategies may place excessive emphasis on formal policies and institutional provision by public authorities and fail to tackle the central problems of language acquisition and use in families and communities'. In highlighting the gap between language-policy aims and the actuality of the Gaelic condition, McLeod (2011) points out the vague and unspecific nature of some of the commitments given in a number of local authority and other public sector language plans, which makes assessments of progress and comparisons between them difficult. He suggests that there may be some degree of tokenism, institutional inertia and disingenuousness with respect to language plan processes (cf. the problem termed 'Irelandization' by Fishman (1991: 143)). Similarly, models of local development interventions, such as the Outer Hebrides Community Planning Partnership (cf. OHCPP Gaelic Policy 2018), tend to be structured and implemented by giving primacy to corporate administrative functions.

In summary, our discussion in this section points to weak links and a lack of monitoring between the status-building focus of the current approach to implement Gaelic language-policy objectives, and possible initiatives which could enhance the language-in-society dimension of promoting Gaelic. For a credible and meaningful minority-language policy in Scotland, the most urgent concern has to be the demolinguistic decline among the Gaelic group. In order to mitigate the legacy of the historical linguicidal intent towards Gaelic and to address the shortcomings of the current policy dispensation, a new strategy is required. Attempts to stabilise the present critical situation, and re-orientate revitalisation efforts towards a more sustainable pathway for future generations of speakers in the islands and elsewhere in Scotland require Gaelic policy to be centred on the communities and social networks who are committed to reviving vernacular Gaelic. A framework for this new approach is set out in Chapter 9.

8.4 WEAK RELEVANCE OF CONTEMPORARY PUBLIC POLICY TO GAELIC VERNACULAR CRISIS

In this section we discuss and critique how public policy and much postmodernist academic discourse deal with Gaelic in the vernacular and national context. We seek to demonstrate the limitations of the public policy and postmodernist approaches and we shall present our own framework based on mainstream sociolinguistics.

The evidence assembled in this study on Gaelic demolinguistics (Chapter 2) and the community surveys (Chapters 5 and 6) indicates that the older members of the Gaelic-speaker group have acquired the minority language as a language of primary socialisation and have experienced its vernacular function in communal-geographic contexts, and that they have related identity formation linked to historical continuity. For them, Gaelic identity and practice align with linear and contemporaneous processes of identity formation. Speaker-group membership in this context is reinforced by a normative cultural function in high demographic densities. This *in situ* social primacy was constrained, however, by the minority-language group's socio-political irrelevance to the majority monolingual English language group in the broader context of the Scottish and UK polity. This meant that English-language dominance beyond the Gaelic spatial context could impact strongly on Gaelic social densities, and that the Gaelic group itself had little power and influence beyond their own context.

During the 20th century, in addition to the sociolinguistic features of language shift (such as, the effects of in- and out-migration, acculturation, unidirectional bilingual dynamics, demographic vitality thresholds, bilingual minority-language sub-optimal acquisition), the process of language shift in the Western Isles, and in the wider Scottish context, has had seven broadly socio-political features:

1. The demographic contraction of the group practicing Gaelic as a language of primary socialisation.
2. The related loss of local social primacy of the Gaelic-speaking group as the social function of English encroaches and crowds out the functional social need for Gaelic in these communities.
3. The continued assimilation and acculturation of the Gaelic ethnos as a subordinated ethnicity within the Scottish and British identity. This process of expansive Scottish and British identity corresponds to Kaufmann's observation, adapted from Barth (1969), on the 'dynamic of dominant ethnicisation': 'If dominant ethnicity remains expansive, the preferred method for maintaining its boundaries is through assimilation rather than exclusion (Barth 1969)' (Kaufmann 2004: 1, 8). There has been only limited socio-political counteraction among the Gaelic group against subordinating assimilation.
4. The ineffectual policy response of Gaelic-oriented public bodies, particularly in the context of the linguicidal intent of the 1872 Education Act, the legacy of which was still felt up to the 1970s.
5. The legacy of official neutrality or insouciance of political structures (regional, parliamentary) regarding the implications of this trajectory of vernacular decline.
6. The longstanding lack of engagement in the university sector with the challenging societal reality of Gaelic in its traditional localities (Dunbar 2010b: 144, 146; NicAoidh 2010: 50; MacKinnon 1994b:

8 CONTEMPORARY SOCIOLINGUISTIC PROFILE OF GAELIC IN LANGUAGE PLANNING
AND POLICY CONTEXT: RELEVANCE OF MANAGEMENT MODELS

383

114, 2000: 148; McLeod 2001: 23[74]). Apart from some exceptions, especially in education language policy (cf. 8.4.2), the social sciences in Britain have not engaged with this issue. The focus of Celtic Studies has been on philology, linguistics, literary and cultural inheritances, as well as descriptive socio-demographics and sociolinguistics. More recently, a post-structural interest has emerged in Gaelic's contribution to cultural diversity. What has been lacking is mainstream applied minority-language sociolinguistics. In fact, as far back as 1982, the *Cor na Gàidhlig* (MacDonald 1982) highlighted many socio-political structural challenges which are still current and have not been addressed to any significant degree, either in policy or discourse.

7. In public policy, Gaelic has been prioritised as a secondary socio-cultural practice. This policy has emerged as an alternative and sanctioned compensation for the erosion of the Gaelic community.

The process of the erosion and contraction of vernacular Gaelic social densities has culminated in the final stage of language shift among the younger generations. The younger age cohorts, and especially the current youth cohort, increasingly socialise in the majoritarian English functional monolingualism. A very small minority are also socialised in the optional practice of Gaelic as a language of secondary functions. More of them mainly experience Gaelic within educational or performed domains. In this context, the multi-generational practice of Gaelic is experienced as a marginal societal reality for the younger age cohorts.

Combined with the lack of targeted scrutiny of the contraction of the Gaelic-speaking collective (see point 5 above), an ideological vacuum was filled by the civic symbolic promotion of Gaelic which conforms with an individualist ethic and continues to confine Gaelic to a secondary optional identity, additional to the normative role of English in society (see point 7 above). In fact, promoting high-status symbolic interventions can dissipate resources and energy from targeted community support efforts and is quite common in threatened language scenarios, as Fishman (1991: 380) states:

---

74 McLeod (2001: 23) states: 'Remarkably little sociolinguistic research — language use surveys, language attitude surveys and so on — has been conducted by the various Gaelic organizations or by government bodies … More generally, policy discussion of language policy matters, both within the Gaelic world and in Scottish public life more generally, is often conducted at a very superficial level'. In addition to the perceived low volume of research, McLeod is subsequently critical of its focus being limited to traditional Gaelic localities: 'Almost all research on Gaelic language use has been limited in its scope to traditional island communities, and there is very little data available on the extent to which speakers in other parts of Scotland make use of Gaelic in their social lives' (McLeod 2009: 26). McLeod's (2009) research suggestion has been at least partly addressed by Dunmore (2015) which, as we discuss in section 4.2.2, has shown that the social presence of Gaelic in urban settings is minimal.

The resulting mismatch of priorities can be not only disappointing (as in the case of Irish) but devastating as well (as in the case of Scottish Gaelic, with only some 80,000 speakers[75] and a well nigh complete reliance on the school and other higher order 'props'). What is sauce for the goose is by no means necessarily sauce for the gander. ... Probably only very fortunate RLS movements will succeed in 'putting it all together'. ... [I]t will be the shrewd pursuit of appropriate priorities that will differentiate between 'also rans' and those who have a real chance of coming out ahead.

The evidence from the Irish-speaking Gaeltacht (Ó Giollagáin *et al.* 2007a,b and Ó Giollagáin and Charlton 2015) indicates that the considerably more ambitious and longstanding LPP efforts failed to 'put it all together' for the Irish-speaking group. In the context of the Gaelic vernacular community in Scotland, it is unsurprising that vaguely-targeted and relatively recent language initiatives have failed to thrive. It is this contradictory dynamic between, on the one hand, the neglect of the contraction of communal acquisition and use of Gaelic and, on the other hand, the symbolic promotion of Gaelic as a constituent element of contemporary Scottish civic culture, which has opened up the space for the institutional discourses concerning individual efforts to acquire Gaelic. Rather than concerning themselves with the existing speaker collective, the university-led discourse is increasingly articulating a self-sustaining ideology based on individualised interest in the minority language. To this extent, it aligns with the neo-liberal zeitgeist and it is tantamount to an officially-sanctioned language policy allowing for minority-language assertions about Gaelic's role in promoting the polity's cultural diversity, while also being self-serving for university-based language professionals. The neo-liberal approach, therefore, adopts a *laissez-faire* or neutral stance in relation to the minority group's decline.

There is a dichotomy in how diversity is understood from the sociological perspective in contrast with the postmodernist point of view. From the sociological perspective, diversity is seen as comprising the societal interactions of groups who possess and convey the cultural and linguistic resources which make up the diversity. From the postmodernist perspective, diversity is seen as comprising the aspirations and assertions of individuals in relation to a peripheral practice of a marginal culture. Sociological diversity is a process by which groups produce diversity, whereas postmodernist diversity is an end product, celebrated as individualised cosmopolitanism. Individualised cosmopolitanism offers no credible basis for minority-language policies and supports. It is difficult to see what postmodernist sociolinguistic theory has to offer in order to ameliorate, or even engage with, the marginal and fragile reality of vernacular Gaelic. Given the emphasis to date on

---

75 See the analysis in section 2.5.1 indicating that the Gaelic vernacular group now comprises around 11,000 people.

8 CONTEMPORARY SOCIOLINGUISTIC PROFILE OF GAELIC IN LANGUAGE PLANNING
AND POLICY CONTEXT: RELEVANCE OF MANAGEMENT MODELS

385

symbolic and individualised approaches, it is little wonder that structures to support the Gaelic group in their traditional localities have failed to emerge during the period from the 1980s to the present.

8.4.1 POSTMODERNIST THEMES IN MINORITY-LANGUAGE SOCIOLINGUISTICS

We will present some instances of what are, in our opinion, some of the weaker postmodernist tropes common in minority-language sociolinguistics (Lenoach 2012: 74–92; 103–4). These include: creativity, the so-called multilingual turn, asocial language rights, apolitical third wave sociolinguistic analysis, false binary contrasts such as the contrast between 'authenticity and artifice', and individualised self-constructionism. As Coupland (2016) observes, sociolinguists need to be aware of their own role in producing discourses which (a) convey more about the scholars' lived life experience than they reveal about the focus of their study, and (b) supporting official dominant discourses:

> sociolinguistic theory needs to include theorising of the positionality of sociolinguistic professionals in relation to the issues and contexts that they address. ... when academics anticipate social and ideological changes that have not infused the whole (or even most) of the populations to whom they apply. ... How can sociolinguists intervene to challenge this institutional norm that involves the bracketing off of social context? (Coupland 2016: 24–26)

The new theoretical configurations of 'multilingual creativity' (Pietikäinen *et al.* 2016: 25) appear to be grasping at straws in the face of 'peripherality with minoritisation' (Pietikäinen *et al.* 2016: 27).[76] This new discursive framework offers little beyond 'recontextualisation in particular kinds of playfulness, creativity and contestation' (Pietikäinen *et al.* 2016: 4) to the minority-language group facing the recessive trend.

In the following citation, Ó hIfearnáin (2018: 152) displays several postmodernist tropes: the evasiveness of the 'multilingual turn'; a concern for discursive positioning; a stance of academicist complexity (of individualist concerns) against a strawman of simplicity (in relation to social processes); trite iconoclasm of language planning and policy, i.e. a thin deconstruction of language shift reversal; erroneous rhetoric equating traditional speaker competence with new-speaker self-constructionist

---

76 In the case of the Western Isles, a substantial proportion of the population have been bilingual for generations, and thus have had a long history of negotiating multilingual creativity. This creativity, however, has not protected them from increasing contemporary English monolingualisation and English dominance. Notwithstanding appeals to playfulness, the demolinguistics and power relations between the majority and minority-language group remain the most salient dynamic determining the minority multilingual condition.

possibilities; presentist evasion of previous social speaker-group reality and identity through unnecessary abstractionism:

> One of the themes that permeates all these papers [on new-speakerism, see Smith-Christmas *et al.* 2018] is what we might call the multi-lingual turn in minority-language sociolinguistics, where language shift is no longer seen as a simplistic process of linguistic displacement and the subject of efforts by individuals, communities, and authorities to reverse it, but one in which 'traditional' speakers may become multi-lingual. Rather than simply lose one language, in gaining another, just as new speakers, not necessarily even from the same ethnolinguistic background, may adopt minoritised languages as their own and take them on new journeys, rather than returning to a hypothesised abstract 'state of being' before the language shift took place. (Ó hIfearnáin 2018: 152)

The long-recognised dialectic features of additive and subtractive bilingualism are a core theme in the passage. But it is being presented as a postmodernist innovative insight by emphasising the additive side of bilingualism for both traditional minority-language speakers (who are often learners of majority languages, i.e. 'new speakers' of majority languages) and learners of minority languages (who are often 'traditional speakers' of majority languages). Therefore, the multilingual assumption is attempting to emphasise the additive aspect of minority multilingualism, i.e. the 'traditional' minority speaker gains the majority language and the 'new speaker' (i.e. the 'traditional' majority speaker) gains the minority language, and thus Ó hIfearnáin evades the realities of coercion, necessity, unidirectionality and loss from the minority perspective.

Such rhetoric can only obfuscate understanding and thus hinder sensible discussions and initiatives for both threatened 'traditional' communities, as well as 'new-speaker' language acquisition. An inconsequential 'new-speakerist' conceptualisation enables an escapist evasion of a troubling societal process of social erosion. Given these pseudo-sophisticated discursive tropes, the 'new-speakerist' approach is akin to minority-language professionals colluding among themselves to evade the social process of language death. In keeping with its genesis, this postmodernist approach is superficially complicated. Its superficiality comes from its disregard of the fundamentally social processes of language vitality and shift. It is the postmodernist sociolinguistic professionals who are complicating the understanding of the process, by the banal tropes of creativity and complexity for instance, as if either creativity or complexity are news to sociology.

Mainstream minority sociolinguistics has for many years emphasised the centrality of social processes involved in language maintenance and shift. For instance, Daniel Nettle and Suzanne Romaine (2000: 90) observe that: '[a] language dies out because

8 CONTEMPORARY SOCIOLINGUISTIC PROFILE OF GAELIC IN LANGUAGE PLANNING
AND POLICY CONTEXT: RELEVANCE OF MANAGEMENT MODELS

387

an enduring social network to which people sought to belong somehow ceases to be'. Similarly, David Harrison (2007: 5–8) and Claude Hagège (2009: 76–83) view the social erosion of a language as the result of a disruptive dynamic to 'a collective phenomenon' (Hagège 2009: 77).

The social process of language shift is often preceded by individual and social bilingualism. This has typically been the case of the demise of the modern Celtic-speaking language communities. For instance, the 'multi-lingual turn' is now a historical feature of the post-language-shift communities of the officially-designated Irish Gaeltacht districts of Erris in County Mayo,[77] East County Galway's Achréidh district and the Iveragh peninsula of County Kerry; of Scottish coastal districts of Lochaber, Easter Ross and many of the Argyll islands; of the youngest cohorts elsewhere in the Western Isles; of Wales' formerly Welsh-dominant districts of Penmaenmawr in Gwynedd, Llangynog in Carmarthenshire and Llanwrtyd in Powys; as well as most of Brittany's rural districts (cf. Hindley 1990; Hechter 1975; Tanner 2004; Durkacz 1982). References to the same so-called 'multi-lingual turn' in the process of monolingualisation of minority-language communities globally could be augmented to the hundreds, if not thousands (cf. Crystal 2000; Hagège 2009; Harrison 2007, 2010; Kulick 1992; Nettle and Romaine 2000).

In failing to differentiate the individual speakers' experience of minority languages from the destabilising sociological processes in the group, Ó hIfearnáin's use of the 'multi-lingual' trope attends to the possible individual consumption or experimental take-up of a minority language while evading the social trajectory of majority-language monolingualisation in the receding minority-language community. The related new-speakerist trope selects for asocietal individual minority-language assertions of optional cultural agency and deselects for indicators of minority-language social salience. In this way, the 'new speakers' can contend that a language lives through avowed assertions rather than collective practice. This precarious discursive step can lead to a sociolinguistics without society, which is a contradiction in terms. In such dubious sociolinguistics, language is characterised by language professionals rather than by a community of speakers. Language from such a perspective is what certain academics or policy-officials say it is, rather than a lived and meaningful socio-cultural experience and practice. In such an extremely asocial sociolinguistics, postmodernist musings correspond to the linguism of the most asocial versions of philologism. Forms of (socio)linguism, philologism and socially-dissociated academicism can be detrimental to positive minority-language initiatives and supports by deflecting attention and resources from more positive engagements on behalf of the threatened group.

---

77 With the possible exceptions of the Eachléim and Ceathrú Thaidhg districts of Erris, Co. Mayo, given higher densities of Irish-speaking networks (cf. Ó Giollagáin *et al.* 2007b: 150).

From the perspective of the recessive vernacular minority, the focus on individualistic consumption of the minority linguistic and cultural resources promulgated by postmodernist sociolinguistics has fostered a public policy and academic discourse on minority cultural diversity, without developing a societal diagnosis of minority-language loss or a prognosis of possible revitalisation.[78] Edwards (2012) has questioned the relevance of certain postmodernist tropes and associated 'jargon' to minority sociolinguistics:

> The illusion of progress is worse than stasis, but the pressures within today's social-science community — allied with the seductions of vacuous elements of postmodernity — encourage work of this sort that I have criticized here. Thus, particularly, in its insecure and weaker divisions, the academy often produces material of (at best) incestuous interest. (Edwards 2012: 37–38)

The trope of progress in Gaelic affairs can be particularly insidious if it is used as an evasion of the issue of societal loss. Additionally, assertions of progress in certain sectors (education, arts, and media) can also deflect attention from a widely held anxiety that the communal decline of Gaelic is not a priority for many public bodies. Some of these bodies benefit institutionally from adhering to vague aspirations for Gaelic, while accessing Gaelic-focused funding. In this regard, the prioritisation and perpetuation of institutional sectors can become a main aim of Language Planning and Policy (LPP) to the detriment of community-focused supports. This parallels the discursivist and academicist self-perpetuation, as discussed by Edwards (2012), and Steve Hewitt's observation on 'a whole industry of publications, meetings etc. on "new speakers"' (2017: 152). The absence of a communal focus and the implicit emphasis on institutional continuance can explain the lack of 'Gaelic personality' in 'Gaelic' LPP in that this LPP is primarily oriented towards civic Gaelic for Scotland rather than Gaelic for the Gaels or their community. The institutionalised approach can lead to the protection and promotion of LPP rather than the protection and promotion of Gaelic and its speakers.

A related concern, which contributes to this evasion of societal diagnosis, touches on aspects of the postmodernist theorising of the new economy. Glyn Williams (2010: 2) has traced the move in the social sciences away from formal structure and from the concept of collective agency, and Williams suggests instead a focus on the perspective of cultural diversity in the knowledge economy. This move from collective structure to individualisation is mirrored in a similar trajectory in sociolinguistics from 'first wave' studies to the current focus of the 'third wave' on stylistic use and

---

78 Grin (2018), Pavlenko (2018) and Edwards (2012: 34–35), among others, discuss the limitations of several postmodernist tropes, e.g. "superdiversity" and "translanguaging", and their possible constraining effect on the applied implications of this form of sociolinguistic enquiry for language policy.

8 CONTEMPORARY SOCIOLINGUISTIC PROFILE OF GAELIC IN LANGUAGE PLANNING
AND POLICY CONTEXT: RELEVANCE OF MANAGEMENT MODELS

389

semiotic meaning (Eckert 2012: 98; Ó Murchadha and Migge 2017; Smith-Christmas 2016). The development of sociolinguistics has been divided into three interlocking historical developments: a so-called first wave sociolinguistics concentrated on survey type investigations; a second wave focused on ethnographic analysis; and a third wave has concentrated on styles and repertoires and their semiotic meaning as well as identity construction. Third wave sociolinguistics, therefore, investigates how variation in linguistic styles and repertoires 'is a very broad-spectrum component of a broader semiotic system' (Eckert 2012: 97). Practitioners contend that third wave sociolinguistics imbues linguistic style with ideological import which contributes to 'ongoing and lifelong projects of self-construction and differentiation' (Eckert 2012: 98). In asserting a reversal of the concept of structure in the system of language production, however, some third wave approaches contend that linguistic styles are productive systems of social differentiation in themselves. However, 'third wave' minority sociolinguistics may help to evade a broader social focus by concentrating on instances of code-switching, on individual identity marking and on pragmatic stance. The third wave focus in relation to receding minority cultures can serve as an apolitical tool for assessing cultural content (taken out of minority social context), but avoids providing a critical apparatus for the minority's overall socio-cultural context, especially in interpreting how minorities articulate with existing power relations.

In a similar vein, the in-vogue binary contrast between 'authenticity and artifice' in the postmodernist view of minority linguistic diversity is more likely to be resolved by societal erasure rather than by any emancipatory assertion emanating from the 'globalised new economy':

> There may well be more continuity than rupture than we have thought in the globalized new economy. Nonetheless, we seem to be nearing the limits of linguistic national … regimes to organise our lives, finding systems breaking up into institutional reproduction and the boundary between authenticity and artifice breaking down. (Heller and Duchêne 2012: 19)

There is little of actual sociolinguistic substance for mainstream minority-language sociolinguistics in such postmodernist iconoclastic rhetoric.

In the case of a recessive minority language, the postmodernist assertions and evasions regarding social continuity are empty, beyond an ephemeralisation and possible commodification of its cultural resources. The social reality of decline among the minorities has undermined the critical mass of speakers in which late-modern 'hybridicist' cultural practice can be embedded (Ó Giollagáin and Ó Curnáin, forthcoming). There is a contradiction between the actual social reality of the minority-language group and the fabricated postmodernist discourse, a discourse which has created the context for the inconsequential 'metacultural discourses' involving 'performed re-creations of traditional genres and modes of production, once again raising complex questions of authenticity, ownership, entitlement and access' (Pietikäinen *et al.* 2016: 30). These discursivist themes form the mainstay of the questionable 'new-speaker' tropes (see also Ó Murchadha *et al.* 2018: 5). To this extent, postmodernist minority-language ideology avoids confronting its own 'illusions' and evades scientific scrutiny or proof:

> But its [i.e. postmodernist ideology's] cultural relativism and moral conventionalism, its scepticism, pragmatism and localism, its distaste for ideas of solidarity and disciplined organisation, its lack of any adequate theory of political agency: all these would tell heavily against it. (Eagleton 1996: 134)

8.4.1.1 *LANGUAGE RIGHTS AND 2005 GAELIC LANGUAGE ACT*

The irony of postmodernist sociolinguistics is that it contributes to a further marginalisation of the minority group and fails to address the group's historical and contemporary marginal position in the monolingual meta-narrative of the modern era. The postmodernist discourse has achieved some symbolic and institutional leeway for the Gaelic minority and encouraged further interest in the culture's aesthetic resources, but issues of societal empowerment remain challenging and elusive from the perspective of the adherents to the threatened speaker group. These challenges are instanced in the minority-language rights agenda in Scotland. The 2005 Act has created a focus on minority linguistic rights, which receives backing from the university sector. There is, however, a selective dimension to Gaelic language rights in the postmodernist perspective of minority sociolinguistics in that language rights are focused on individual provision and optional take-up or practice, rather than a focus on existing and actual community dynamics. This is a further instance of the postmodernist prioritisation of an aspirational perspective over social reality. In fact, the institutional provision for Gaelic, emerging from the minority rights agenda, has granted agency to an intermediary class who determine the content of Gaelic language politics, often determined by sectoral institutional requirements. The relationship between these institutional players and the generally monolingual out-group power class, i.e. (predominantly monolingual) English speakers, constitutes the primary political relationship and the guiding discourse for engaging with Gaelic issues. A correlate of this political relationship with the intermediary class is the limited proactive engagement with the rank and file of the Gaelic speaker group.

There is a contrast in public perception between the lack of recognition of ethnolinguistic issues and crisis in the Gaelic group on the one hand (cf. Bruce Granville Miller 2003: 219), and the affording of official minority status on the other. Rather than being the beneficiaries of enlightened capacity-building measures

8 CONTEMPORARY SOCIOLINGUISTIC PROFILE OF GAELIC IN LANGUAGE PLANNING
AND POLICY CONTEXT: RELEVANCE OF MANAGEMENT MODELS

391

to support the Gaelic group, symbolic status is dissociated from lived in-group experience and their social cohesion. This is a common ethnolinguistic conundrum for declining language minorities who are the recipients of degrees of official status. This form of recognition may contribute to the minority group's socialisation within broader identity-formation processes in the state, and enhance the visibility of the minority in civil structures, while at the same time being ineffectual as a mechanism of in-group agency. It is this contradictory dynamic that correlates with the Gaelic group being Scotland's indigenous minority and at the same time being destabilised in their autochthony. In short, the external dynamic of socio-political powerlessness combined with the internal dynamic of *in situ* instability pose a significant challenge to formalised language policy in Scotland; and a challenge to the credibility of language planning and policy in general where ethnolinguistic issues are dissociated from symbolic status concerns.

The results presented in this volume indicate that the provision to date has failed to address the critical contraction of the speaker group. This failure has arisen in part from policy being directed in favour of institutional provisions rather than societal outcomes. This has occurred in the context of a statist prerogative of determining a marginal policy issue within the limitations of a relatively small budget outlay. This public-authority orientation is not surprising given that much of the academic discourse has focused on increasing the civic status of Gaelic. In this respect, the approach focuses more on the policy providers rather than the recipients of the policies, i.e. supply-side sociolinguistics rather than demand-side sociolinguistics. This is one aspect of prioritising the symbolic over the social approach, as critiqued by Fishman (1991). Despite the lack of efficacy of this policy in countering the drivers of language shift, it is not surprising that governmental organisations have acquiesced with this orientation. The predominance of dependence on direct governmental financial assistance fosters a noncritical acceptance of this inadequacy. Points to this effect were made during the public consultations of the teenager and community surveys (sections 4.10.1.3 and 5.7.2). Gaelic policy debates are often perceived by native autochthony as 'in-house' debates rather than as a sincere engagement with an enthused public.

This individualisation of Gaelic has developed into a mutually-reinforcing dynamic with the sectoral focus on Gaelic-medium broadcasting, on the promotion of Gaelic performance and the arts, and scholarship on Gaelic heritage and culture. This sectoral focus promotes the civic appeal of the cultural assets of the declining Gaelic group without protecting the group's viability. From a broader social perspective and beyond sectoral concerns, the official policy efforts in support of Gaelic have concentrated primarily on two spheres:

    a. A civic engagement through the provisions of the Gaelic Language (Scotland) Act 2005

b. Gaelic-medium educational initiatives in some unitary council areas (GME primary provision in 14 of the 32 unitary council areas, and GME secondary provision in 12 unitary council areas).[79]

We discuss Gaelic in education policy in the following section.

8.4.2 GAELIC IN EDUCATION POLICY

Besides the Gaelic Language Act's general aspiration to promote the civic appeal and symbolism of Gaelic in Scottish public life and to boost the public visibility of Gaelic in official administration (cf. Dunbar 2011),[80] the Act suggests no executive instrument beyond Bòrd na Gàidhlig's powers to request public agencies to prepare language plans in support of Gaelic promotional initiatives. Around 60 of these language plans have been agreed, or are under development, in various public bodies in Scotland. The primary public instrument, therefore, to support the social presence of Gaelic in Scotland is the local authorities' educational policy to support Gaelic-medium or Gaelic streams in the schooling system in which Bòrd na Gàidhlig has a consultative role.[81]

In addition to the evidence indicating the long-standing demographic pressures on the Gaelic group and the political processes of marginalisation experienced by the minority, it is necessary to consider the related impact of the assimilative socio-cultural forces on the group. Several authors have examined the effects of English-medium education policy on the Gaelic-speaking group in the Highlands and Islands (see also the discussion on assimilation in section 2.3.1). Scottish educational policies acting, by design or by consequence, as a vehicle for both the overt and covert promotion of English at the expense of Gaelic in the historical context have been examined by J. L. Campbell (1950), M. MacLeod (1963), MacKinnon (1972a) and M. K. MacLeod (1981), for example, while a recent overview (O'Hanlon and Paterson 2015c) of the situation since the Education (Scotland) Act 1872 has provided much-needed context around the perceived 20th-century philosophical shift from social mobility to child-centred education. MacKinnon (1972b: 385) noted that the education of pupils from rural Highland and Island settings was 'essentially for export', resulting in a draining away of Gaelic-speaking potential community leaders as there was little,

---

79 2017–18 data from Bòrd na Gàidhlig (2018b).

80 'Chan eil teagamh sam bith nach àrdaich achd Pàrlamaide ìomhaigh agus inbhe cuspair na h-achda ann an dòigh air choireigin. A bharrachd air sin, a rèir na h-achda, is è 'cànan oifigeil na h-Alba' a tha anns a' Ghàidhlig, cànan a tha a' dleasadh spèis co-ionann ris a' Bheurla. Le sin, tha na faclan seo, an deas-chainnt seo, cuideachail.' (Dunbar 2011: 69) [Undoubtedly, the Act of Parliament will raise the profile and status of the aims of the act in some way. In addition to that, according to the act, Gaelic is an official language of Scotland, a language which warrants equal respect to that of English. In that respect, these words, this eloquence, is helpful].

81 Education (Scotland) Act 2016, part 2: http://www.legislation.gov.uk/asp/2016/8/part/2.

8 CONTEMPORARY SOCIOLINGUISTIC PROFILE OF GAELIC IN LANGUAGE PLANNING
AND POLICY CONTEXT: RELEVANCE OF MANAGEMENT MODELS

393

if any, consideration for how education could offer relevant preparation for life in pupils' own locales. Pollock's doctoral research on literacy in the Gaelic-medium primary setting (2007: 40–41) noted Gaelic's long-marginalised status in the context of largely assimilationist educational policies. MacKay (1996: 14) outlined the disconnect between the generalised educational experience of pupils in the Western Isles examined in the context of community-led education programmes:

> Schooling in the past was not concerned primarily with validating the experience of youngsters in their own community or with validating the use of their own language; rather, education has tended to be geared to preparing young people to cope with life away from the islands. … Young people in the Western Isles are socialised so as to feel that their own community is rather repressive and static, and that decline rather than development is the norm. It is not surprising that so many of them regard the relative anonymity and freedom of city life as a means through which they may be able to lead fuller and more fruitful lives.

Peter Mewett (1982) also elaborated on this theme, suggesting: 'Education, geared to the needs of the wider society, provides a channel of mobility to the more desirable jobs, and this also means migration. … "Success", therefore, as evaluated in mainstream culture, can often involve migration to secure a job equivalent to the person's educational attainments' (Mewett 1982: 232). Policies constructed around Gaelic's position in education, certainly until the post-WW II years, implicitly aligned with the prospect of social mobility; apparent policy concessions on teaching in Gaelic had, broadly, not been exploited; and Gaelic was taught as a subject, and often through English, rather than used as a medium in and of itself. Anderson (2013: 245) bluntly pointed out: 'that official policy made only minor concessions to the language; but there was nothing new in this, for Highland educational initiatives had always insisted on the primacy of English. It was not until after 1945 that serious efforts were made to promote bilingualism'.

The late Seonaidh Ailig Mac a' Phearsain (2011: 23–24), was an astute observer of island life having attended an island school in the late 1940s; he reinforces this appraisal from an in-group perspective:

> Bha ar ciad chànan air a casg, ge b' ann gun fhiosta no le rùn, le siostam foghlaim a bha nàimhdeil air a' char bu mhiosa no coma-co-dhiù air a' char a b' fheàrr, dhan choimhearsnachd agus dhan chànan. Anns a' bhun-sgoil bha thu faighinn foghlam ann an cànan choimheach. Anns an àrd-sgoil bha thu faighinn foghlam a bha gad ullachadh airson do chasan a thoirt leat agus an saoghal a thoirt fod cheann. Gus faighinn air adhart dh'fheumadh tu faighinn air falbh. Bha siostam foghlaim na h-Alba air a stèidheachadh air reachd agus air cleachdadh a dhèanadh cinnteach

nach ruigeadh tu àirde do chomais tro chànan na dachaigh agus na coimhearsnachd.

[Our first language was proscribed, whether by accident or design, by an education system that was at worst hostile, or at best indifferent, to the community and the language. In primary school you received education in a foreign tongue. In high school you received education that prepared you for going away from home and making your way in the world. To get ahead you had to leave. The Scottish education system was founded on statute and conventions which ensured that you couldn't develop your ability to its fullest through the language of the home and the community.]

One of the clear effects of this English-medium education was that the Gael was educated out of his/her own vernacular context and that recipients of this schooling were being prepared for participation in an English-medium-orientated socio-economic market. Given this protracted legacy of 'educating out' the Gaels, the resetting of education policy in the Western Isles following the establishment of Comhairle nan Eilean Siar (Western Isles Council) in 1975 in favour of optional bilingual streams in the existing system was a case of 'too little, too late' if successful revitalisation was expected. Seeking communal and educational traction for such a minoritising policy was going to be challenging, given its deference to the social primacy of English even among the Gaelic minority. The new parallel bilingual policy did not address the legacy of the ideological disadvantages of the Gaels, and there was scant recognition given to any sense of collective voices from among the Gaels. In other words, the normativity of English remained the primary unchallenged theme in how Gaelic education policy was perceived and enacted. The Gaels were also not afforded the backing of confident civic bodies nor the reinforcement of institutional coherence. The foundations of the 1975 Bilingual Education Project (discussed in Murray and Morrison 1985) were not assured enough to mount a serious sectoral challenge to the prevalence of the naturalised dominant ideology, which viewed the societal requirements of Gaelic's vernacular group as subordinate to those of English in all civic contexts, i.e. the ongoing socio-political legacy of the Education (Scotland) Act 1872, among all other forms of Anglicisation.

The initial bilingual reform also failed to grasp the policy opportunity to attempt to establish a vernacular orientation in schooling in communities where Gaelic was still practiced in relatively strong social densities. In the light of the demographic decline of the Gaelic-speaker group, the bilingual policy of the Western Isles Council appears to have been more successful as an optional Gaelic policy for Gaelic-English bilinguals and for (initially monolingual) English speakers rather than as a bilingual educational policy supporting a Gaelic community. The policy sought to adhere to the emerging child-centred philosophy in that it offered possibilities for individual

8 CONTEMPORARY SOCIOLINGUISTIC PROFILE OF GAELIC IN LANGUAGE PLANNING
AND POLICY CONTEXT: RELEVANCE OF MANAGEMENT MODELS

395

engagement with Gaelic heritage and culture. But this approach was at the expense of a broader educational focus on the challenges of providing child-centred education which would have been more socio-culturally relevant to the Gaelic context. It was well-meaning with regard to the individual pupil, but dissociated from the socio-cultural challenges of the minority group, although how much more Gaelic orientation would have been supported by the community is a moot point.

Faced now with the ongoing loss of what were until recently Gaelic communities, the aims of the current educational policy should be reconfigured. In a nutshell, what societal role can minority-language educational provision mean for (a) those children who know the minority language increasingly only in a postvernacular, or postsocial, context; and (b) for the older parent and grandparent generations whose vernacular or socialised Gaelic is being lost? In detail, the following questions should be addressed:

- How does bilingual policy in schools articulate with the challenges of societal decline in the minority-language group (as compared to its limited institutional practice)?
- How can minority bilingual policy be societally meaningful to young minority-language learners/speakers who have little or no experience of Gaelic in communal or vernacular contexts?
- What communal aim can minority bilingual educational policy serve (as compared with an individual cognitive rationale) when it is promoted independently of the social crisis of the speaker group?
- How can bilingual education policy be espoused as a compelling civic endeavour if it does not demonstrate an empathetic concern for the existing group of minority bilinguals as opposed to a policy aspiration for future bilinguals?
- In addition, under current conditions, following the likely future loss of the native-speaking group, what purpose will heritage bilingual education serve?

In the broader context of reassessing the efficacy of Gaelic language policy in general, and Gaelic education in particular, an assessment is overdue of how policy has engaged with the social context of the speakers and their communities. The current policy configuration emerged as a localisation or an adaptation of policy initiatives developed previously in Canada, Ireland and Wales which were centred on the civic promotion of minority-language visibility, specified service delivery and on the extension of the individual rights agenda to minority-language concerns. Given the current societal marginality of Gaelic, it is timely to consider the limitations of the derivative thinking which is encapsulated in the 2005 Gaelic Language (Scotland) Act. This act borrowed heavily from language-act legislation in Canada (1988),

Wales (1993) and Ireland (2003). The Scottish Gaelic variant of these language rights discourses contributed to the policy process which abstracted the policy out of its own social context and communal challenges through deference to established thinking in other minority-language contexts.

Additionally, a reassessment of the current approach is required because of its failure to establish a cogent diagnosis of the societal condition it failed to address. The state-backed policy intervention in support of Gaelic progressed from a non-policy situation up to the 1980s to a policy configuration of civic promotion aimed chiefly at symbolic visibility and status building initiatives, in tandem with developing a Gaelic-medium education, mostly as subject options or class streams within schools with pre-existing English-medium provision. It is noteworthy that learner discourses have come to the fore in language-policy debates in Scotland in recent years. Such top-down prioritisation via education policy is a common fault in language revitalisations (Fishman 1991). It is a well-established dynamic in Ireland that the heritage requirements of providing for the second-language learning of Irish have dominated language-policy concerns since the inception of the Irish state (Ó Giollagáin 2014a,b; Ó Giollagáin and Ó Curnáin 2016). It is not surprising, given the rapid contraction of the minority speaker groups, that this vacuum would be filled by language identity ideologies centred on the wider political contexts (cp. correlations of Gaelic practice and ability with teenager identity as a Gael (4.8.1.2; 4.9.2), and the contrast in Gaelic attitudes between the teenager Gaelic-medium focus groups and the teenager English-medium focus groups (Gaelic 4.10.1.2; English 4.10.2.2)). This focus is similar to the language policies in Wales and Ireland where public policy on language is more orientated towards the requirements of minority-language learners rather than the concerns of the vernacular group (cf. Ó Giollagáin and Ó Curnáin 2016; Brooks and Roberts 2013).

The evidence from the demolinguistic, the preschool and Teenager Survey in Chapters 2, 3 and 4 respectively, indicates that the current situation of vernacular Gaelic in the Western Isles is continuing to deteriorate and is progressing towards a primary focus on Gaelic as a heritage language. If this Gaelic-as-heritage approach replaces vernacular practice, Gaelic may perhaps be performed or taught or researched by relatively few, but may be spoken to a high degree of fluency by even fewer. On the current trajectory in the Western Isles, the demise of the remaining cohort of Gaelic native speakers ironically presents, so to speak, a 'window of opportunity' for secondary bilinguals of Gaelic to outnumber the native speakers (as currently in Ireland), i.e. postvernacularism. Whilst Gaelic language educational outputs can superficially be maintained through current policy instruments, the prospects for any real linkage to the cultural richness and linguistic wellspring of Gaelic will erode over time. A set of recommendations is presented in Chapter 9 to address the current trajectory towards loss of vernacular Gaelic.

8 CONTEMPORARY SOCIOLINGUISTIC PROFILE OF GAELIC IN LANGUAGE PLANNING
AND POLICY CONTEXT: RELEVANCE OF MANAGEMENT MODELS

397

8.4.3 TENSIONS IN INDIVIDUALIST IDEOLOGIES AND COMMUNAL MINORITY-LANGUAGE VISION

Given the current neo-liberal zeitgeist, the challenges of refocusing minority-language policy on a non-normative culture (such as Gaelic) are considerable, or even insurmountable unless there is a change of paradigm. Some of the limitations of the existing policy provision stem from its neutral view of establishing compelling diagnostics and prognostics of the societal fragility in the existing speaker community. By dint of hopeful assertions, the individualistic view displays itself as being in a discursive dialogue with an envisioned future and the potential of growing the number of speakers, and this display is dependent on supports from policy agencies. It endeavours to talk its way, mostly in the majority language as medium, to a permanently future language revitalisation. It is reliant on a civic ideology which is comfortable with an individualistic view of non-normative minority culture. On the other hand, a collective approach is clearly necessary in realistic RLS. The collective approach is both spatial in focus and group-oriented in its philosophy. Its starting point seeks to address the process of societal disempowerment which has led to the current demographic contraction and the lack of social viability in the remaining social networks in which the minority language is spoken. Table 8.2 contrasts how an individualistic and a collective perspective on minority sociolinguistics articulate with the challenges of addressing minority-language public policy concerns.

	Individualistic Perspective	Collective or Communal Perspective
1	Focuses on the **civic status** of the minority language vis-à-vis the polity's political culture	Focuses on endangerment issues stemming from the minority group's societal decline as a **differentiated culture**
2	Aspirationally assumes growth of the minority group by **institutional means** of language-policy innovation centred on **minority-language schooling**	**Socio-politically**, it realises that envisioning a collective approach to the future is challenging and contentious, as a result of the well-established demographic contraction of the autochthonous group and its **non-optimal** experience of **power relations**, it requires collective agency
3	Adopts a **neutral** perspective on the process of language **acquisition** with overreliance on education and unreal aspirations for formal intervention	Its focus is on the **collective transmission** of the cultural assets of the linguistic minority and seeks to integrate the support of those who have acquired a minority-language competence in other social or institutional contexts
4	Promotes minority-language adherence as an assumed additive bilingualised competence and as **complementary** to normative majority-language competence	Seeks to **redress** issues associated with the reduced acquisition of the minority language in the context of the erosion of the social salience and collective practice of the threatened language and its culture

	Individualistic Perspective	Collective or Communal Perspective
5	Policy initiatives reflect a preference for sectoral and **institutional planning**	Emphasises **small language planning initiatives** aimed at capacity building within the speaker group through linkages with broader institutional supports
6	Ideologically, it adopts a **utopian** view of future possibilities rooted in appeals to minority-language tolerance in discourses focused on postmodernist diversity	Ideologically, it is concerned with the historical threat of loss, and with the **collective revitalisation** efforts to prevent the assimilation and the de-ethnicisation of the group into the competing linguistic culture(s)
7	Develops a sense of empowerment through aligning itself with middle class aspirations, and it establishes a **discursive leadership**	Identifies the need for **socio-economic capacity-building** measures aimed at group reinforcement
8	Feigns a resilient demeanour as an optional, occasional culture **additional to normative majority** culture, by an expansive definition of what constitutes participation in non-normative minority networks.	Seeks to engage proactively with the societal process of the minority's disfavoured status. It realises that those possessing the devalued cultural resources of the minority are in a **competitive dynamic** with the socio-cultural status of the dominant group's assets.

Table 8.2 Comparative discursive features between the individualistic and collective focus of minority-language concerns

8.4.4 LINGUISTIC IMPLICATIONS OF THE DECLINE OF PRIMARY GAELIC SOCIALISATION

In Chapter 2, we identified a social transition from the context of primary Gaelic socialisation to some efforts at secondary acquisition and practice. The bilingual contact dynamic between the dominant majority language and the minority subordinated language has clear detrimental functional implications for the acquisition of vernacular Gaelic. The timeline of this three-step transition is depicted in Table 8.3, which depicts a typical three-generation language shift scenario.

8 CONTEMPORARY SOCIOLINGUISTIC PROFILE OF GAELIC IN LANGUAGE PLANNING AND POLICY CONTEXT: RELEVANCE OF MANAGEMENT MODELS

399

Period	Socio-economic	Language of socialisation	Linguistic normativity
→ 1960s	Traditional	Primary socialisation in Gaelic-speaking social densities	Gaelic as communally normative
(1970s) → 1980s	Modernising	Competing socialisation of English with weakening transmission of Gaelic and the growth of networked function of English in cohorts critical to language socialisation (young families, youth networks)	Waning Gaelic normativity with an English-language transitional *lingua franca* function
1990s →	(Post-)Modern with residual traditional minority socio-cultural assets	Dominant capacity of socialisation through English with general confinement of Gaelic to efforts at secondary acquisition	Normative English

Table 8.3 *Transition from the primary socialisation of Gaelic to secondary acquisition in the Western Isles*

The progressive erosion of the basis of primary socialisation of Gaelic has resulted in the reduced acquisition of Gaelic among the young in the remaining bilingual networks of the islands. The contraction of the primary socialisation in Gaelic in this unidirectional bilingual dynamic has precipitated the societal context for an imbalanced bilingualism, from the joint perspective of competence and practice of Gaelic among the young minority bilinguals. Minority imbalanced bilingualism refers to the disadvantage in linguistic function of the minority language as compared with higher linguistic competences in the majority language, among bilingual speakers of minority languages who acquire their dual competence in a societal context where majority-language acquisition is prevalent or dominant during the critical phase for minority-language acquisition (e.g. Montrul 2008; Gathercole and Thomas 2009; Benmamoun *et al.* 2013; Péterváry *et al.* 2014; Lenoach 2012; 2014; Ó Curnáin 2007; 2009; 2012; 2016). This imbalance in linguistic function is mirrored also in the less-than-favourable socio-cultural status of the minority-language group vis-à-vis the societal power of the majority language, and also in social praxis, which boosts the dominance of the majority language in youth socialisation processes (Ó Giollagáin *et al.* 2007b: Part 4). The contact between bilinguals and monolinguals resulting from the socio-economic modernisation of the vernacular Gaelic communities has brought about the higher linguistic function in English among the younger generations of the residual Gaelic speaker group, as evidenced in the IGRP. In a parallel process, the social context for the elaboration of a linguistic competence in Gaelic becomes less favoured and competitively disadvantaged by the growing functions and domains of English practice.

In this modernising minority-language context, the requirements felt by parents and caregivers for children to adhere to norms of high linguistic function in the majority language necessitate and encourage the practice of English in the Gaelic communities; and can discourage minority-language maintenance. These understandable parental concerns for full majority-language acquisition and competence are very common drivers of loss of full intergenerational transmission of perceived minority or threatened languages and their cultures (Batibo 2005). This in turn means that English competes with Gaelic in the realms of primary socialisation to the detriment of the former normative capacities of the minority-language, Gaelic. Both the weakening of the saliency of the familial transmission of Gaelic and the related erosion of the social density of speakers has led to the current situation of the limited functionality in Gaelic or weak or no Gaelic acquisition as the norm when compared to the high levels of functionality in English among the bilinguals and their peers (Chapters 2–6). Various aspects of non-optimal Gaelic acquisition are discussed in Dorian (e.g. 1978, 1981); Nance (2013); Smith-Christmas and Smakman (2009) and Michelle Macleod *et al.* (2014). Regarding Irish, Péterváry *et al.* (2014) is the most in-depth examination of the incomplete acquisition of native Gaeltacht Irish.

In setting out to establish a baseline diagnosis of the current prevalence of Gaelic in this recessive trajectory in the islands, the IGRP sought also to trace the societal transition from normative Gaelic to normative English. We propose a three-generational classification of this social dynamic from the diachronic perspective of the formative socialisation processes. Table 8.4 describes five key sociolinguistic categories (A–E) as they were manifested in the preceding early-life phase of the minority cohorts of (1) the elderly and (2) middle-aged. The categories for (3) the youngest cohort describe the contemporary and synchronic depiction of this normative transformation of the Gaelic group, i.e. its current sociolinguistic condition.

8 CONTEMPORARY SOCIOLINGUISTIC PROFILE OF GAELIC IN LANGUAGE PLANNING
AND POLICY CONTEXT: RELEVANCE OF MANAGEMENT MODELS

401

Generational comparison of the Gaelic group	A. Geography of minority	B. Socialisation of minority	C. Normative culture of minority	D. Mode of minority acquisition	E. Linguistic function of minority
(1) Elderly minority bilinguals	*In situ* high speaker densities	Primary socialisation	Communal	Early monolingual	Elaborated vernacular function
(2) Middle-aged minority bilinguals	Contracting density of speakers in expansion of the monolingual majority group	Contracting networked socialisation	Diminished	Dual bilingual acquisition in contracting Gaelic and expanding English networks	Dual networked and social-ly-compartmen-talised bilingual function often with consider-able codemixing
(3) Young minority bilinguals	Dispersed low or marginal speaker densities	Mainly restricted to secondary, institutional inputs	Eroded, communally insignificant	Bilingualised restricted minority input and uptake	Reduced minority function in asymmetrical disadvantage with majority full competence

Table 8.4 Generational comparison of the current sociolinguistic condition of the Gaelic group

Projecting forward to the next phase of this social trajectory under present circumstances, the corresponding categories could develop as shown in Table 8.5.

Future generation	A. Geography of minority	B. Socialisation of minority	C. Normative culture of minority	D. Mode of minority acquisition	E. Linguistic function of minority
Second-generation non-normative secondary bilinguals	Post-spatial	Post-communal	Post-societal	Post-familial and non-intergen-erational	Post-collective and post-functional

Table 8.5 Possible trajectory of the sociolinguistic condition of the Gaelic group

These categories of possible future bilingual contexts in Table 8.5 are explained further in Table 8.6.

Sociolinguistic categorisation	Emergent second-generation of non-normative minority bilinguals
Future bilinguals A new generation of post-communal minority bilinguals could possibly emerge in what would be the second generation of non-normative minority bilingualism, but at a further remove from the remnants of Gaelic vernacular practice. This possibility is conditional on continuing institutional support and language-policy developments to protect the position of Gaelic in Scotland's civic apparatus.	
A. **Geography of minority**	**Post-spatial**: Under current conditions, Gaelic vernacular geography will most likely be erased.
B. **Socialisation of minority**	**Post-communal**: The future possible non-primary socialisation of Gaelic among secondary bilinguals will be contingent on the heritage appeal of eroded culture in subordinated identity formation processes in minority-language institutional provision. This process in turn will be dependent on the degree of institutional support and influence of secondary bilinguals leading these institutions.
C. **Normative culture of minority**	**Post-societal**: Given the current non-normativity of Gaelic practice, it is possible that the young will encounter difficulties in transcending a passive or a reactive relationship with the authenticity, authority and institutional roles of secondary bilingual speakers in Gaelic-oriented support agencies and schools. Productive minority-language identity formation will prove very challenging in the absence of (young) minority peer-group authority and social status to reinforce group identity in the emerging generation.
D. **Mode of minority acquisition**	**Post-familial and non-intergenerational**: With the demise of the vernacular community, the optional institutional/school-based acquisition of Gaelic will become the predominant possibility for learning or acquiring Gaelic, to the exclusion of almost every other sociolinguistic practice. It will be difficult for the acquisition process to achieve sociolinguistic outcomes above a complementary cultural addition to high-functioning majority-language attainment. It is also likely that the minority-language acquisition process will be primarily embedded in the socio-cultural assets and status system of the dominant linguistic group.
E. **Linguistic function of minority**	**Post-collective and post-functional**: The acquisition of Gaelic will be incomplete and serve symbolic functions. More precisely, it is likely that linguistic competence in Gaelic in the future will be practiced in institutional and other formal contexts. Secondary Gaelic then becomes the focus of individualistic and institutional relativism. In the absence of a normative target for acquisition, various degrees of minority-language competences will probably emerge in this putative scenario.

Table 8.6 *Possible sociolinguistic categorisation of future non-normative minority bilinguals*

8 CONTEMPORARY SOCIOLINGUISTIC PROFILE OF GAELIC IN LANGUAGE PLANNING
AND POLICY CONTEXT: RELEVANCE OF MANAGEMENT MODELS

403

We also wish to examine the linguistic geography of the shift from Gaelic vernacular function in the islands to English vernacular dominance among the residual bilingual Gaelic speakers, whereby Gaelic has been relegated to marginal networks (Table 8.4). In this context, any credible policy interventions will have to contend with the series of challenges outlined in Table 8.7.

Sphere	Problem	Challenge
1. **Social density of minority**	The social group possessing the most significant cultural and linguistic resources of Gaelic ethnolinguistic identity has lost its remaining social density of speakers. Its age profile is biased toward the older generations.	How does language policy aim: • to protect the remaining densities of Gaelic speakers? • to integrate vernacular supports with efforts to increase the number of Gaelic learners? • to assist Gaelic speakers and learners to gain community salience and productivity?
2. **Weak collective transmission of the language and its cultural resources**	The remaining group lacks the support of an active collective group to reinforce and support the emerging cohort of speakers. Gaelic acquisition is now an isolated familial and communal activity.	What social interventions would be feasible and acceptable to assist the continued collective practice of Gaelic and the socio-cultural resilience of the speaker group?
3. **Imbalanced bilingualised context of Gaelic acquisition**	The limited levels of Gaelic acquisition are dependent on the relationship with the functional linguistic culture of English which is omnipresent during the critical phase for language acquisition (up to 8 years of age).	How can language policy, community policy and educational supports articulate with each other in a manner which enhances the linguistic function and educational attainment in Gaelic, particularly in the critical early phase for language acquisition? What collective and institutional efforts would be feasible and acceptable to protect and encourage Gaelic social and educational inputs without detriment to anxieties regarding functionality in English?

Sphere	Problem	Challenge
4. Marginal Gaelic-language socialisation	Youth peer-group socialisation processed through the medium of Gaelic is now very weak. There are very few or no substantial institutional or communal initiatives which tackle this glaring sociolinguistic deficit.	What interventions would be practicable to achieve policy coherence between familial transmission, school acquisition, educational development and the natural inclusion of Gaelic in youth socialisation processes?
5. Limited institutional coherence	Besides the circumscribed provision for GME, there is a lack of a coordinated institutional approach to the social challenges of supporting Gaelic as a living *in situ* linguistic identity.	What agencies and institutions will give leadership and confidence to speakers and learners that the current socio-cultural condition of Gaelic is going to be addressed in a strategic multi-dimensional approach?
6. Non-focused ideological prerogatives in education and language development aims	Educational policy for Gaelic in the islands is more focused on meeting the ideological requirements of developing and expanding GME provision. This has resulted in the construction of an ideological artifice which assumes or attempts to imply that exposure to limited institutional provision in support of Gaelic can compensate for weaknesses in familial and communal transmission and acquisition.	Can minority-language education policy redress the societal reality of linguistic and cultural erasure?
7. Under-developed civic culture in support of Gaelic	Apart from GME and apart from the civic promotion of Gaelic and high-status cultural and aesthetic performance, the existing leadership mechanisms have failed to galvanise group support for strategies aimed at supporting the speech community.	How can the remaining speaker group be empowered in their current predicament and be given a sense of ownership of the mechanisms and processes which might be devised to address their situation?

Table 8.7 Spheres for policy interventions among the residual bilingual Gaelic group

8 CONTEMPORARY SOCIOLINGUISTIC PROFILE OF GAELIC IN LANGUAGE PLANNING
AND POLICY CONTEXT: RELEVANCE OF MANAGEMENT MODELS

405

8.5 DEVELOPMENT OF DISCOURSES ON GAELIC

In this section, we will outline developments of discourses regarding the Gaelic language, and provide some commentary and critique. Much recent academic research on the situation of Gaelic in Scotland, and recommendations on how to ameliorate its position, have focused on the national development of Gaelic in line with the Gaelic Language (Scotland) Act of 2005.[82] This Act recognises Gaelic as belonging to Scotland as a whole rather than to a specific linguistic geography, such as the Highlands or the Western Isles. It therefore justifies a set of nation-wide policy initiatives, with an emphasis on revitalisation efforts being focused on increasing the numbers of speakers through educational provision, primarily implemented in schools. This approach is currently the main way that Gaelic policy is actually put into practice by Gaelic development bodies and the Scottish Government.

The national approach has its advantages from a number of perspectives: the extension of Gaelic-medium education, the creation of Gaelic language plans by public sector bodies, increasing the general visibility and civic symbolic usage of Gaelic through the use of bilingual signage and through aspects of official corporate identity. This approach, however, has its limitations in how it intends to sustain and revitalise the remaining highly threatened Gaelic communities.

In the various discourses on Gaelic revitalisation, we can trace the shifting focus from, on the one hand, an engagement with Gaelic as a vernacular of rural speaker groups, to, on the other hand, an emphasis on Gaelic as a post-spatial, aspirational, innovative, non-vernacular language. The change of focus occurred around the turn of the millennium. This discursive shift evolved in parallel with the official approach to language revitalisation following the passing of the Act, and represents a shift in academic thinking from the relative importance in language maintenance of the speaker group to the significance of the individual 'player', asserting their symbolic role in minority-language discourses and politics. The following discussion demonstrates:

a. The shifting focus away from policy requirements of the vernacular community (8.5.1–2)
b. The re-alignment of the policy focus to facilitate educational innovation and to enhance the civic presence of Gaelic in Scottish national culture (8.5.3–4)
c. The emergence of a guiding language ideology regarding Gaelic in which academics are dominant (8.5.4–5).

The following sections include referenced quotes from participants in these debates in order (a) to allow the participants to speak for themselves and (b) to trace how

---

82 Henceforth in this chapter, the Gaelic Language (Scotland) Act 2005 will be referred to as the Act.

emphasis and opinions have shifted over time. Although, these various contributions could be subjected to analytical critique, we have purposefully avoided extensive commentary on them to present an overview of the evolution of the discourse.

8.5.1 RECOGNITION OF THE VERNACULAR COLLECTIVE

In publications prior to the 2005 Act, it was common to recognise the central importance of the surviving Gaelic communities. For instance, three years before the Act's implementation, McLeod (2002a) refers to what he describes as unprecedented investment in Gaelic across a range of initiatives, distributed unevenly, and that this investment had failed to deliver any palpable change in Gaelic usage at community or familial level: 'Instead of grappling with the fundamental challenge of halting or reversing language shift, there has been a disturbing tendency to rely upon — and perhaps even to believe — the rhetoric of the glossy brochure and the press release' (McLeod 2002a: 279). In this work, the Western Isles were specifically referenced as the heartland of the language, with over 75% of the region's (non-urban) population returned as Gaelic speakers in the 1991 Census, with the suggestion that no concrete initiative had aided 'the preservation, or spread, of Gaelic as a spoken community language' (McLeod 2002a: 280).

In previous work, McLeod (1998) differentiated the Gael from the mainstream Scot and others by virtue of the Gaelic language, as a conduit for a distinct way of life and culture:

> The claim of Gaelic speakers to recognition as an ethnic group is also strengthened by the fact that a very high proportion of Gaelic speakers, relative to the UK's other autochthonous language communities, are native speakers born and brought up in Gaelic-speaking communities in the Hebrides and West Highlands. It would be safe to say that at least 90% of Gaelic speakers come from such backgrounds ... In the case of Gaelic, then, there is a very significant link between the ability to speak the language and a distinct culture and way of life, and the language is the badge of a community that has long been outside the societal mainstream. (McLeod 1998: 7)

This view clearly espouses the notion of a Gaelic community, and acknowledges the geographic context and 'ethnic' background from which a significant majority of competent Gaelic speakers come. McLeod (2002b) contrasts the higher speaker densities in the islands with the very low urban densities:

> it is in areas of highest density that the most important steps towards integrating Gaelic into economic life can be taken, although there may also be significant opportunities to provide goods and services to the

8 CONTEMPORARY SOCIOLINGUISTIC PROFILE OF GAELIC IN LANGUAGE PLANNING
AND POLICY CONTEXT: RELEVANCE OF MANAGEMENT MODELS

407

numerically large communities of Gaelic speakers in the Scottish cities, even though the density of such speakers in the overall population is very low. (McLeod 2002b: 53)

8.5.2 SOCIAL DENSITIES AND GAELIC SPEAKER GEOGRAPHIES

The issue of speaker geography, and its implications for language-policy priorities, is addressed by Dunbar (2010a). Based on 2001 Census data, he states that:

almost half [of Gaelic speakers] lived outside of the traditional 'Highlands' … However, in all these areas, they form a tiny percentage of the local population … In this context, the opportunities for regular social use of Gaelic — something that is of obvious and critical importance in minority-language maintenance … are extremely limited, to the point of being almost non-existent for most Gaelic speakers. (Dunbar 2010a: 86)

Dunbar (2010a: 85) also acknowledges: 'the heartlands are likely to have made a much larger contribution to overall numbers of speakers, and this may remain the case for some time to come', and that 'most Gaelic speakers in Scotland acquired their Gaelic in the home … it is also likely that most of them were raised in so-called "heartland" areas'. He further cautions that: 'A failure to address the state of the language in those areas could be fatal in terms of the survival of Gaelic as a spoken language' (Dunbar 2010a: 87).

Dunbar also touches on the difficulties facing Gaelic in its traditional locus (2010a: 86): 'there is growing evidence that intergenerational transmission of Gaelic in the "heartlands" is extremely fragile, and that we may be nearing or at a linguistic tipping point' and portrays Gaelic's position as a community language as resting on a 'knife-edge': 'given the massive barriers to the establishment of Gaelic as a community language elsewhere, and given the centrality of language use in the home-community nexus in any language maintenance effort, failure to act with urgency would be highly irresponsible' (Dunbar 2010a: 89–90).

However, alongside the depiction of Gaelic sociolinguistic fragility, he warns of the risks involved in area-specific planning which deals with a 'heartland', as a 'heartland' focus could potentially impact negatively on a vision or strategy with a national focus:

a language policy which focuses on a 'heartland' or group of 'heartlands' may run the risk of ignoring or devaluing activity in other areas, including urban areas, where there are many signs of linguistic vitality and where many speakers and learners of the language live … there is a perceived danger that the needs and aspirations of such speakers may be overlooked by an excessive focus on the 'heartlands' … the special recognition of a linguistic 'heartland' might be perceived by some to carry with it the risk of an essentialising agenda, in which certain types of speakers living in certain places — namely, native speakers supposedly living in more traditional social and cultural contexts in the 'heartlands' — are idealised and prioritised on the basis that they are somehow more 'legitimate'. (Dunbar 2010a: 84–85)

Dunbar's preferred option is to position Gaelic language policy within a national civic agenda: 'Welsh, Irish and Gaelic are all recognised to varying extents as "national" languages, part of the common heritage of the entire population of the three nations, and not the sole preserve of any residual "heartland"' (Dunbar 2010a: 85). Similarly McLeod (1998: 8) emphasises the national dimension and 'the importance of Gaelic for Scotland as a whole, and to relocate Gaelic to the centre of Scottish life'. More recently, however, writing on Gaelic as 'an ambiguous national language', McLeod (2014: 5) suggests that the significance of Gaelic's place in Scottish national life and identity is 'tenuous' and 'contested'. This form of binary thinking leads Dunbar to conclude that any move to ground language policy within geographic or spatial parameters would be potentially 'illiberal':

to the extent that the formal recognition of a linguistic heartland is a precursor to highly intrusive language policies — and it has to be said that no such policies have yet been implemented, or even articulated, in any of the three jurisdictions — there is a concern about the possibly illiberal nature of the language policy that may result from any such recognition. All of these concerns are legitimate. In particular, I shall not be advocating that language planning efforts on behalf of Gaelic should be limited to the 'heartlands', nor that any policy for the 'heartlands' should take precedence over local planning in other areas or at a national level. (Dunbar 2010a: 85)

However, as a counterbalance to a national focus, Dunbar (2010a: 85) acknowledges that differing requirements in specific areas should be considered: 'more localised language planning needs to take place in order to address the particular and quite different challenges faced by Gaelic speakers in different parts of the country'. In the circumstances where such plans have emerged, it is debatable whether these plans mainly represent an articulation with the administrative framework and elements of service provision envisaged in the Act, or offer a significant strategic engagement with different challenges faced by Gaelic speakers.

8 CONTEMPORARY SOCIOLINGUISTIC PROFILE OF GAELIC IN LANGUAGE PLANNING
AND POLICY CONTEXT: RELEVANCE OF MANAGEMENT MODELS

409

8.5.3 GAELIC 'HEARTLAND' AND LEARNERS IN SCOTTISH NATIONAL CULTURE

Following the publication, in 2000, of the findings of the report of the Taskforce on Public Funding of Gaelic, *Revitalising Gaelic: A National Asset / Ag Ath-Bheothachadh Gàidhlig: Neamhnuid Nàiseanta* (often termed *The MacPherson Report*), Alasdair MacCaluim and Wilson McLeod (2001: 4) suggested that: 'the decreasing numbers of native Gaelic speakers and low levels of intergenerational transmission mean that increasing numbers of Gaelic learners must be attracted and brought to fluency if there is to be a realistic prospect of reversing language shift'. This suggested approach emphasises policies to facilitate the emergence of a cohort of Gaelic learners as a compensation for vernacular decline. They further argued that:

> Gaelic has ceased to be a community language on the Highland mainland and could only be said to be a community language in a limited number of areas in the Western Isles, Tiree and parts of Skye. Even in these communities, the position of Gaelic is rapidly weakening, with less than one-third of primary school children in the Western Isles undergoing education through the medium of Gaelic ... there is no prospect that the number of Gaelic speakers will increase, or even remain stable, unless action is taken to promote Gaelic elsewhere. (MacCaluim and McLeod 2001: 15)

MacCaluim and McLeod's (2001) criticism of the *MacPherson Report* focused on its perceived 'vagueness':

> Also ambiguous is the statement that the Gaelic development agency should 'concentrate the management of Gaelic activities in locations in the Gaelic heartlands, with appropriate distribution to accommodate the "energy centres" and the language's national disposition' (MacPherson 2000: 17). This sentence not only fails to define the 'Gaelic heartland' or 'energy centres' but also seems to be internally inconsistent. (MacCaluim and McLeod 2001: 9)

In essence, their criticism of the *MacPherson Report* rested on fears that the urban, lowland learners and speakers of Gaelic would be sidelined from Gaelic development efforts (MacCaluim and McLeod 2001: 2, 19), which is in keeping with one of their opening criticisms concerning 'the choice of appointments' to the taskforce: 'Every member of the Macpherson committee was a native speaker of Gaelic who has been brought up in the Hebrides' (MacCaluim and McLeod 2001: 4).

Dunbar (2016) returns to this issue of territoriality and how speaker geographies intersect with issues of language-policy priorities and a national focus on Gaelic:

Given that Gaelic has traditionally been associated with the Scottish Highlands … one would think that the concept of a 'heartland' such as the Irish Gaeltacht would similarly be central to legislation and policy in Scotland, but … this is generally not the case… It may, however, be due to the fact that … a large number of Gaelic-speakers now live outside of those 'heartlands', and there has been a significant amount of activity in support of the language in places like Glasgow and Edinburgh. As a result, many of the present generation of Gaelic activists — the ones who have been involved in the development over the last 30 years or so of the current legislative and policy context — have sought to resist any attempt to limit the development of policy to the traditional 'heartlands'. Ironically, because Gaelic is generally not conceived of by most Scots as being 'the' national language, and has arguably only recently been accepted as contributing in a significant way to Scotland's national identity … . (Dunbar 2016: 474–75)

He notes the lack of recognition in the Act of traditional Gaelic-speaking communities: 'the Gaelic Language (Scotland) Act 2005 … eschewed the idea of a 'Gàidhealtachd' or a 'heartland' altogether (2016: 479). With respect to the Act's planning and implementation framework, he states that:

the Bòrd has now produced two such plans … both national plans make no reference to the 'heartlands' or the 'Gàidhealtachd'. In the first national plan, targets … were set at a national level only … the Bòrd claimed that '[t]he most valuable resource we have is the communities where Gaelic is spoken and is still used in a range of everyday situations'; however, even here, while recognising the importance of Gaelic in such 'heartland' communities — a term the Bòrd did not use — they committed to promoting the increased use of, and confidence in, Gaelic 'in *all* communities' … the strategy with respect to Gaelic usage and status planning was conceived of without reference to particular areas of the country, and in national terms. (Dunbar 2016: 482)

This general 'heartland' debate revolving around the territorial dimension of Gaelic policy in communities is questionable on several levels. It is often conducted as a competitive demand for focus and resources, and envisaged as a beggar-my-neighbour dynamic in Gaelic's contrasting social geographies. The associated debate is fuelled by an assumed opposition between an implied static rural peripherality and a supposedly nascent urban dynamism. Additionally, the use of the term 'heartland' suggests the existence of a core mutually-reinforcing community of speakers in a specific geographic area. In relation to minority sociolinguistics, the complacent application of the term 'heartland' to the minoritised bilingual condition

8 CONTEMPORARY SOCIOLINGUISTIC PROFILE OF GAELIC IN LANGUAGE PLANNING
AND POLICY CONTEXT: RELEVANCE OF MANAGEMENT MODELS

411

of the remaining fragile Gaelic rural communities contradicts their experience of demographic contraction. Both the use of the term, and the underlying tension associated with the debate, actually may serve to deflect attention from legitimate concerns about the sustainability of existing Gaelic communities, without being of any benefit to rationales in support of purported emerging Gaelic networks in non-traditional locations or contexts.

The Gaelic-policy public bodies generally avoid the term 'heartland'. In addition to issues of terminological laxity, it is quite clear that the dominant concerns of 'many of the present generation of Gaelic activists' (Dunbar 2016: 474–75) have succeeded in eroding the strategic rationale, and thus, the public policy traction to address Gaelic's territoriality. The Gaelic 'heartlands', or more accurately, the remaining socio-geographic densities of Gaelic have largely been written out of language-policy discourses. In this discursive erasure, it is hard to see their place in an assumed binary opposition between Highlands/Islands and Lowland Gaelic priorities. The present misdirected policy debate asserts post-spatial credentials and yet is founded upon an unbalanced binary juxtaposition of Gaelic geographies, which continues to disproportionately occupy the attention of activists and academics. This unproductive debate will most likely continue unless those participating in Gaelic urban revitalisation attempt to redress the loss of Gaelic communities.

8.5.4 PROSPECTS FOR POST-VERNACULAR USE OF GAELIC

In response to the crisis in vernacular viability, McLeod (2015: 101) observes that:

Activists have shifted their terms of reference and debate accordingly, so that questions such as whether a language community can meaningfully exist in the absence of intergenerational transmission have come to the fore, or how 'post-vernacular' language use might meaningfully function. As in past centuries, the dominant position of English is unquestionable, but varying strategies seem possible, some more polarising or puristic than others. In this sense there is continuity through the long centuries of language minoritisation.

MacCaluim (2006: 185–97) calls for adult learners to be placed at the centre of efforts to reverse language shift and advocates a national strategy to increase their numbers, in order to offset the net loss of 750 Gaelic speakers per annum. He makes this recommendation in spite of his own acknowledgement that: 'it is unlikely that the total number of individuals who have learned Gaelic to fluency as adults is as high as 750' (MacCaluim 2006: 197) and that many adult learners are relatively advanced in years and are, therefore, highly unlikely to have any impact on intergenerational transmission.

McLeod's (2005b) work on Gaelic in Edinburgh illustrates the difficulties such an approach as MacCaluim's would entail, given the low speaker density and its scattered distribution, the lack of inter-group social interaction existing in the city at the time, and the fact that the 3,085 Gaelic speakers enumerated in the 2001 Census for the city (2005b: iv), represented just 0.69% of Edinburgh's population. It is highly likely that the highest proportion of those Gaelic speakers were native speakers originally from the communities of the Highlands and Islands who had acquired Gaelic at home (Dunbar 2010a). In spite of the relatively high absolute number of Gaelic speakers, McLeod (2005b: iv) found that there was: 'Little reason for optimism: the rate of language transmission from generation to generation is very low, few people use Gaelic as their main home language, and hardly any families in the city use Gaelic consistently'. McLeod summarises the urban promotion of Gaelic as: 'To a very considerable extent, Gaelic appears to be a private, almost hidden language in Edinburgh' (2005b: 13) and emphasises 'the scale of the challenges involved in efforts to promote Gaelic in Edinburgh, and in similar urban environments where the proportion of Gaelic speakers is minimal. Gaelic language use is extremely low: in the home, in social settings, in the workplace. Clearly, very few people in Edinburgh live their lives through Gaelic' (2005b: 26).

8.5.5 ACADEMIC-LED GAELIC LANGUAGE IDEOLOGIES

The preceding discussion of academic approaches to the societal use of Gaelic in Scotland, and the related area of policy making and application, indicates that the sociolinguistic discourse on Gaelic is preoccupied with an unnecessary binary tension. Indeed, McLeod (2009: 16) has suggested that studies in the field of Gaelic sociolinguistics are potentially more politically-charged than in other language communities, because discussions often orbit around the issue of language death (see also McEwan-Fujita 2006: 292). The thinking associated with this binary opposition assumes a false conflict between addressing spatially specific vernacular fragility, on the one hand, and engaging in a broader national civic effort to increase the numbers of speakers or learners, on the other. In relation to this binary debate, the issue of vernacular retreat has been eclipsed by a growing academic focus on purported ideological concerns of learners, or 'new speakers' to use the more 'fashionable' term. This new-speaker discourse has a post-structural, postmodernist focus and rejects established notions of linear language shift or revitalisation trajectories. McLeod and O'Rourke (2015: 153) argue that:

> the traditional ideological model of language 'shift' or decline in minority-language research came to be seen as a rupture of essential connections between language, place and identity (in Fishmanian terms). This model presupposes linear linguistic trajectories and is therefore ill-equipped

8 CONTEMPORARY SOCIOLINGUISTIC PROFILE OF GAELIC IN LANGUAGE PLANNING
AND POLICY CONTEXT: RELEVANCE OF MANAGEMENT MODELS

413

to interpret more complex situations in which people learn and 'use' minority languages outside of the home domain and thereby become new speakers.

Hence, in the view of McLeod and O'Rourke, urban communities will be increasingly important in the future development of Gaelic speakers. However, they discuss the growth of an urban or Lowland population of Gaelic speakers in the context of census data collection methods which make it impossible to calculate how many recorded Gaelic speakers are 'new speakers' (2015: 154). By implication, it is also impossible to calculate how many of this population are 'non-new speakers', i.e. native speakers of Gaelic. McLeod and O'Rourke (2015: 156) offer a further expansion on this point:

> In the absence of sociolinguistic surveys concerning the demographics of Gaelic speaking in Edinburgh and Glasgow, it is not possible to know the size and characteristics of the 'new speaker' community in the two cities and the extent to which the research sample reflects the group as a whole. It is very unlikely, however, that the total number of new speakers (as defined above in terms of linguistic ability in Gaelic and regular use of Gaelic) in the two cities exceeds a few hundred.

Hence, the clear counter-argument against the discourse regarding a concept of a 'new speaker' community, given the very small numbers involved and their geographic dispersal.

McLeod and O'Rourke (2015: 169–70) suggest that contemporary society is characterised by social mobility, which leads to hybridity, multiplicity, fluidity and, hence, diversity, and engenders questions about which language forms are 'authentic' and 'legitimate' if adopted by 'new speakers' in new spaces. They posit that: 'The spread of Gaelic outside of traditional Gaelic-speaking strongholds and into spaces previously dominated by English unsettles the traditional ideology of sociolinguistic authenticity. The data in our study suggest that a rootedness in place continues to shape new speaker identities'. In response to such rhetoric, one can note that (a) it has become abundantly clear since at least 2011 (Munro *et al.* 2011) that the threatened Gaelic communities are no longer 'strongholds'; (b) spaces 'previously dominated by English' remain overwhelmingly English-speaking communities and localities; and (c) the irony of appropriating salience to a small number of 'new speakers' while problematising the vernacular autochthony.

McLeod and O'Rourke's (2015) ideological explorations of Gaelic language politics are in keeping with the 'new-speaker' tropes, i.e. contesting of minority-language authenticity, agency and validity, which has been explored in other sociolinguistic contexts (e.g. Myhill (2003); Woolard (2008); Jaffe (2015); and, in terms of Celtic minority languages: Armstrong (2013); Hornsby (2015a,b); O'Rourke (2011), O'Rourke and Ramallo (2011; 2013); O'Rourke and Pujolar (2013); O'Rourke, Pujolar and Ramallo (2015); O'Rourke and Walsh (2015); Nic Fhlannchadha and Hickey (2016); Smith-Christmas *et al.* (2018)). Much of the new-speakerist discourse about Scottish Gaelic represents a particularly chronic example of a socially dissociated academicism (dissociated from the main speaker group and often based on small samples of informants).

The on-going problematising of the concept of 'nativeness' in minority-language culture is a common theme in new-speaker discourses. Such 'problematization of the native speaker concept' (O'Rourke and Pujolar 2013: 47) has tended to be explored from a sociolinguistic or identity perspective of minority-language learners and, thus aligns itself with the binary opposition of prioritising non-traditional speaker contexts at the expense of a vernacular focus. The debate is framed by McLeod, O'Rourke and Dunmore (2014: 1) as follows:

> In the past, the 'new speaker' category has been examined using other terms and concepts, some of them more familiar, including 'non-native speaker', 'second-language speaker', 'L2 speaker', 'learner' and so on. The use of the term 'new speaker' can be understood as an attempt to move away from some of the older labels and concepts which have been shown to be problematic, including 'native' speaker and 'nativeness'.

In fact, the problematising of the native speaker concept is not restricted to minoritised language contexts, but is also a pre-occupation of some discourses concerning globalising English and its millions of speakers (Davies 2003; Mufwene 2010). It is, however, arguable that, positing a 'new speaker' category in order to 'move away' from use of the term 'native speaker' actually serves to cloud the issues. Coining a new term does not avoid the need for critical classification and analysis, which is at the heart of sociology and linguistics. In short, if there is such a new category as 'new speaker', what might a category of 'old speaker' or 'non-new speaker' represent (if not some concept similar to native speaker)?

Leaving aside the 'them and us' dynamic which this academic discourse has engendered by this sociolinguistic set-aside, those interested in language policy in Scotland are still faced with the difficult question as to what policy interventions are feasible to address the vernacular decline of Gaelic. In light of the knowledge and experience which has been gained since the passing of the 2005 Gaelic Language Act, a process of legislative review is now opportune. Given the stark reality of the Gaelic-speaking group, such a review would require a 'fit for purpose' examination of the legal and administrative context, the scope of provision and the effectiveness of specific societal applications which have emerged from the Act. From a sociolinguistic perspective, the public face of Gaelic development is deficient in relation to community focus and engagement with strategic goals. This results in a distancing of these communities from Gaelic officialdom and academic discourses (see 4.10 and

8 CONTEMPORARY SOCIOLINGUISTIC PROFILE OF GAELIC IN LANGUAGE PLANNING
AND POLICY CONTEXT: RELEVANCE OF MANAGEMENT MODELS

415

5.7), and a pursuit by most Gaelic bodies of secondary linguistic goals and activities rather than focusing on first-order priorities in relation to strengthening the social use of the language within communities. This is yet again an instance of the mistaken prioritising of high status issues, as pointed out by Fishman in his discussions of GIDS (see 1.3).

Gaelic policies and academic debates, which have developed in parallel with the rollout of the 2005 Act, have concentrated on education and the perceived concerns of Gaelic learners, which have latterly been styled as the 'new-speaker discourse'. This asymmetrical focus on Gaelic learners following the ratification of the Act poses a challenge to its ongoing legislative credibility and sustainability, if its intent continues to be undermined by an ineffectual engagement with issues of concern to the vernacular Gaelic community. Unless the 'lost voices' of vernacular Gaelic are included, the development of Gaelic language plans will only become official instruments for avoiding pressing issues and priorities. This would be a perverse policy outcome from what was initially well-intentioned language legislation.

8.6 CONCLUSION

The over-arching language policy for Gaelic is being implemented in a way that is dissociated from the severity of the challenge experienced by the speech community. It is the equivalent of standing by while witnessing the dissolution of the culture and the group, and yet claiming future aspirations for their cultural capital. The underlying philosophy informing the National Gaelic Language Plans, emanating from the Gaelic Language (Scotland) Act 2005, has been deficient in engagement with the communal requirements of supporting a threatened minority vernacular. The elaboration of the strategic intent behind the National Gaelic Language Plan 2018–2023 will indicate in due course if this third national plan represents a new departure for Gaelic's communal and vernacular challenges:

> In implementing our priorities and commitments, we need to recognise that not all Gaelic users are the same, and that Gaelic is used as the language of choice by many people in different communities across Scotland, in island and rural areas, as well as in towns and cities across the country. There are also Gaelic speaking communities in other countries and technology has created another type of community, via radio, TV and online, which links individuals worldwide. Increasing usage in and across these communities requires a variety of solutions but also offers huge opportunities for the different types of community to support each other. (Bòrd na Gàidhlig 2018a: 35)

New stark evidence often requires a re-appraisal of existing theories and practices. In this instance, current policy provisions for Gaelic are not succeeding in promoting the maintenance and revival of Gaelic speech communities. The task of re-appraisal compels us to ascertain whether policies can be changed to address the implications of the new research findings. Alternatively, if modification is not a feasible option, current approaches should be discarded for a new policy dispensation.

Language promotion and revival are extremely challenging enterprises, especially in very recent post-shift contexts. A case in point is the common aversion to language promotion initiatives in areas of the officially-designated Irish Gaeltacht which have or had recently undergone language shift (except for the acceptance of developmental grants and resources; cf. Ó Giollagáin 2006). Appeals by RLS agencies to post-shift communities often risk falling on deaf ears because the memories of cultural loss are still vivid in those communities.

Engaging with the communities in the islands currently requires three fundamental prerequisites:

a. Placing the Gaelic-speaking group at the centre of policy concerns
b. Providing an honest narrative and description of their situation
c. Developing an agenda of productive and coherent plans capable of encouraging participation in cooperative activity to improve these circumstances.

This agenda will require a strategy which draws on collective strengths, ambitious vision and targeted leadership, as well as tenacious individual engagement.

Gaelic policy bodies and groups have developed an inflated sense of discursive importance which has at times camouflaged or deflected from the process of vernacular decline. In one sense, Gaelic now 'lives' as much or even more so in discourse than it actually exists in society. While island communities are undergoing rapid language loss, the failure of public policy to engage with the processes driving decline has exacerbated matters, some of which include:

• A naturalised or fatalistic acceptance of a trajectory of decline
• Under-utilisation of the existing linguistic resources, especially in relation to the social transmission of Gaelic
• Non-optimal deployment of institutional support and collective resources
• The maintenance of an illusion of adequacy vis-à-vis Gaelic policy in the face of language loss.

The current language policy may rest on an undeclared assumption that the demographic and spatial limitations of the existing group of speakers is not extensive enough or politically significant enough to justify policy attention and, thus, expenditure on troubling and complicated societal issues.

8 CONTEMPORARY SOCIOLINGUISTIC PROFILE OF GAELIC IN LANGUAGE PLANNING
AND POLICY CONTEXT: RELEVANCE OF MANAGEMENT MODELS

417

A recent series of policy commitments articulated by the Scottish Government and Bòrd na Gàidhlig appear to signal a new and focused set of initiatives to engage more productively with the current reality.[83] Of importance in the context of the IGRP research and the proposed approach set out in Chapter 9 is the collaborative commitment between the Scottish Government, Bòrd na Gàidhlig and Comhairle nan Eilean Siar to 'work together to deliver a community offer in the Western Isles'. The extent and format of such a 'community offer' have yet to be articulated, but for these suggested commitments to have productive traction in reversing the decline of Gaelic in the islands, it would be advisable to put community agency at the centre of any future efforts.

The current crisis demands clarity of vision and sincere engagement from the language-policy practitioners in academia and in public bodies. In this regard, it would be more productive for the policy makers to either re-evaluate current policies or to indicate openly if it is their opinion that the situation of the vernacular is now too perilous and intractable to ameliorate; so that, at least, the remaining speakers would know that they would be left to their own efforts, and whatever resources they can muster, rather than being led astray to dissipate their energy on less relevant or even irrelevant initiatives.

Community members, policymakers and academics have been, and are, aware of the problems faced by the few areas where Gaelic has its remaining vernacular presence (cf. Lewin 2018 and Misneachd 2018). The main future import of the current policy trajectory can only provide a context for a form of 'resource extraction' from the dwindling vernacular group, mainly to serve the requirements of those participating in the metropolitan aspirations of a Gaelic postmodernity on behalf of those who do not possess this vernacular resource. This is a common situation in language revitalisation scenarios. The alternative to this public policy conundrum lies in a concerted effort to rebalance priorities and resources in favour of the Gaelic vernacular group. Any continued reluctance to support societal engagement risks culminating in the death of vernacular Gaelic among the remaining speaker group.

---

83 http://www.gaidhlig.scot/gaelic-set-for-big-boost-as-public-bodies-reveal-range-of-new-key-commitments/.

9 TOWARDS A NEW MODEL FOR THE REVIVAL OF THE GAELIC COMMUNITY

In this chapter, we set out a new model for the revival of the Gaelic community. In section 9.1, we explore the need and present the basis for credible Gaelic policies and community interventions. In section 9.2, we discuss language planning and policy in a community development framework with reference to some of the international literature. In section 9.3, we present our proposal for a new Participatory Minority Language Cooperative to be operationalised as Urras na Gàidhlig (the Gaelic Community Trust). An overview of the new model is presented in section 9.4 and section 9.5 contains a summary description of the operational strands comprising the model. Section 9.6 contrasts the societal and the institutional approaches to language policy and planning. Sections 9.7 and 9.8 provide detailed exposition of the four main strategic priorities within the model. In suggesting a new model for Gaelic policy it is important not to underestimate the challenges involved in taking a new course of action. Adopting a more positive and relevant approach necessarily entails counteracting the effects of inertia and of the many years of linguicidal initiatives against Gaelic; contending with those who benefit from the *status quo* and, more pointedly from a communal perspective, Gaelic revitalisation will also have to address the sociolinguistic reality of two generations of general English-language dominance in the islands.

9.1 INTRODUCTION

Based on our analysis, the various modules of this research project set out the evidence and rationale for a process of policy re-alignment (cf. Figure 9.1 below). The unsustainability of the *status quo* (from the autochthonous perspective) and the ongoing loss of vernacular Gaelic communities is the chief rationale for proposing an alternative strategy. In addressing problems affecting groups or societies, it is widely acknowledged that there are four interlinked steps in effecting purposeful change:

1. Identify the problem or the challenge
2. Agree collectively to address the challenge systematically
3. Set out feasible and credible solutions or interventions for relevant stakeholders (individuals, communities and formal bodies)
4. Encourage stakeholders to participate in developing an agreed strategy to engage creatively and pro-actively with the problem.

The depiction in this study of the fragility of the Gaelic-speaking collective of the Western Isles indicates the need for a new paradigm which is focused on the societal and linguistic reality of the existing speaker group, rather than an approach too narrowly mediated through and dominated by institutional aspirations. Credible language development policies in this challenging environment will initially depend on identifying cooperative mechanisms in the Gaelic community to address their societal condition. Agreement on alternative pathways for development will be required before better language outcomes can be made. The alternative path we propose is based on the framework of a Participatory Minority Language Cooperative.

Given the severity of the crisis facing the Gaelic-speaking group in the islands, engaging positively with this condition is an enormous individual, communal and institutional challenge. When we consider that the dominant culture had previously the capacity to bilingualise the dominated culture and to naturalise or depoliticise the process of language shift in the minority, the ethnopolitical and organisational challenges are immense. These challenges are even greater given the unsuitability of current provision, and the weakness of civic engagement and indifferent or only mildly-supportive public attitudes towards the role of Gaelic in Scottish society. The extent of the challenges in the current condition suggests three main options:

1. Do nothing positive for the Gaelic-speaking group, or adopt a *laissez-faire* attitude and await the societal demise of Gaelic
2. Use the mechanisms of the 2005 Gaelic Language Act to require of the Scottish Government and Bòrd na Gàidhlig to address the vernacular crisis
3. Address the crisis through a radical new departure of encouraging, supporting and resourcing a community-development approach among those best placed to address the issue — the remaining vernacular group.

Each of the three options entail various obstacles and difficulties, which we discuss separately here.

Option 1 — the *laissez-faire* approach — poses a political and public policy conundrum for Scottish political life, especially in the context of devolution. The post-devolution settlement has encouraged the promotion of Gaelic in Scotland as a public good, and has sought to enhance the civic presence and status of Gaelic in Scottish public and cultural life. The imminent social erosion of Gaelic will force political and public bodies in Scotland to contend with the language-policy irony that they are promoting policy aspirations for a language which has very few vernacular speaker-groups or a recognisable communal presence in society. Promoting a language with no *in* *situ* community exposes public policy to potential criticism, i.e. that public bodies are promoting the institutional life of a language despite their failure to promote the language in society. Institutionally-promoted languages, organised independently of socio-cultural context, run the risk of becoming pseudo-cultures. An obvious difficulty with this option is the political embarrassment or possible accusation of pretence in spending public resources and energy on a secondary version of a culture, while ignoring the destruction and loss of the primary habitat of that culture (see various authors on the importance of protecting the social habitat of threatened languages: Fishman's (1991: 58) 'potential oases', Ó Sé's (2000) 'crannóga' [safeguarded dwelling], Ó Curnáin's (2009) 'tearmann teanga' [language sanctuary], and safeguarding the higher social densities of Irish speakers in the Category A Gaeltacht districts as discussed in Ó Giollagáin *et al.* 2007a,b and Ó Giollagáin and Charlton 2015).

Option 2 — the extension of existing mechanisms to address the crisis — also entails significant problems. Using existing public policy mechanisms would necessitate giving Bòrd na Gàidhlig primary responsibility for addressing language-community regeneration. Requiring of Bòrd na Gàidhlig to address the contraction of the Gaelic group in the islands would involve a significant change in corporate and institutional culture and in their operational remit. This option would entail a significant rebalance in the Bòrd's remit and priorities away from its current emphasis on formal provision, mainly in the educational sphere, but also from its effort to promote the largely symbolic civic status of Gaelic. For Option 2 to be meaningful, the Bòrd would need to invest considerable effort and resources in developing socially-relevant initiatives to promote Gaelic in communities.

Option 3 — the new departure — would be very difficult and challenging on various fronts: individually, socially, politically and ethnolinguistically. Resisting, let alone reversing the societal process of language shift, requires an enormous collective effort by the language community. This level of communal resolve in turn would have to be backed by informed and sympathetic political and institutional goodwill, and supported by the strategic competence of capacity-building agencies.

However, Gaels still exist, and the public consultation aspect of this research indicated a desire among some of them to engage with their reality in a way which is meaningful to their sense of community. A clear benefit of our proposed model is that it extends resources and responsibility for a new approach to those who live with the Gaelic societal reality and who seek to revive Gaelic. The third option set out above is admittedly the most difficult to put into practice for both the community and public agencies, but it represents the least bleak option of the three and the most equitable option for extending agency to the Gaels. Arriving at the stage where the new approach becomes an acceptable and feasible option first requires a decision to forge a new path to revitalise this valuable cultural inheritance for future generations.

9.2 COMMUNITY DEVELOPMENT CONCEPTS FOR SMALL COMMUNITY LANGUAGE PLANNING

Cooper (1989: 183) points out that: 'language planning cannot be understood apart from its social context or the history that produced the context'. The interface between processes of language revitalisation and where power lies is also important, and as Bernard Spolsky (2004: 40) points out, this relationship between language policy and power is a two-way process of exchange. The development and direction of policy should not be wholly confined to public authorities directing resources and suggesting directives from the top down to the community. Socially-relevant policy should instead encourage and influence grass-roots actions both at the local level from groups already embedded in the community, and networked initiatives across communities as a mechanism to share knowledge and experience. This type of policy focus allows for local initiatives, state input and cooperation among communities in varying sociolinguistic contexts.

The revised approach to Gaelic should allow for local democratic responsibility, and for cooperation among those who experience different forms of Gaelic social networks. It should also take account of key aspects of a number of other language-planning and policy approaches which inform minority-language sustainability: the pathway-to-impacts model of Grin (2003b); the Jeroen Darquennes (2007) revitalisation methodology; the cultural autonomy model and institutional completeness models of Bourhis and Landry (2008) and Bourgeois and Bourgeois (2012); and the vernacular-in-crisis interventionist approach suggested by Ó Giollagáin and Ó Curnáin (2016) for the Irish Gaeltacht. The common feature of these various frameworks is that they emphasise the interdependency between:

a. The societal condition of the *in situ* language group
b. The salience of language use in the target community
c. The acquisition of language competence
d. The strategic relevance of developmental supports and resource allocation to the language minority
e. Factors of power relations in determining control over language development mechanisms.

In suggesting a new course of action for Gaelic in its last remaining vernacular communities, we are mindful of Kaplan and Baldauf's (1997) caution that language policy and planning do not necessarily yield results within short time periods and according to political cycles where rapid tangible results are expected. Language policy for threatened linguistic minorities is time-consuming, and requires on-going long-term strategic and resource commitments.

Tonkin (2015) emphasises the importance of the collective in language planning. Reflecting the work of Cooper (1989) and others (as discussed in Chapter 8), Tonkin (2015: 194) suggests that perspectives have shifted from viewing language planning as a state or institutional function: 'to seeing planning and policy as occurring at all levels, from the most formal to the most informal'. He also cautions that long-term language planning trajectories and outcomes are not amenable to individual and institutional aspirations alone: 'Change may come about through conscious desire, but that desire tends to be that of the collective, or a politicized part of that collective, rather than the deliberate efforts of individuals or even institutions'. Addressing the requirements of the threatened Gaelic collective will entail the radical transfer of a significant element of power, control and responsibility away from state-level institutional and official structures towards more localised collective initiatives of the speaker community.

Effective policy interventions clearly require dynamic interactions between the state and community organisations, especially in the context of devising an agenda to tackle the sociolinguistic crisis of a declining language minority. To revive Gaelic across the Western Isles, locally-situated institutions under the direct control of the speaker community, along with voluntary organisations, have to become pivotal actors in language planning and policy implementation, and need to play a critical role in any successful initiation and implementation of language revitalisation strategies. For the National Gaelic Language Plans to have practical community meaning beyond their civic assertions, it is important that responsibility for and control of language-policy aims lie in the hands of the Gaelic community.

9.2.1 COMMUNITY CAPACITY DEVELOPMENT OF THE GAELIC GROUP

Successful engagement and intervention in community structures are dependent upon an informed awareness of local dynamics. Alison Gilchrist (2009) and Margaret Ledwith (2016) explore the dynamics of community development in relation to networks and examine how power interacts with community development at every level, from grassroots projects to movements for change. Earlier models on community intervention can be found in the work of Jack Rothman (1974) and Jerry D. Stockdale (1976). The Rothman typology considered three mechanisms of intervention: locality development, social action and social planning. Stockdale suggested that the social planning model should differentiate contrasting motivations to reflect differing aspects of more centralised and community-wide planning, and community or interest-based advocacy planning.

Rothman (2007: 12) elaborated further on his original concept of community intervention to propose three distinct forms as follows:

- **Data-driven Planning and Policy** which relies on conveying social realities as revealed in empirical facts, as a precursor to proposing and enacting particular solutions to social challenges
- **Community Capacity Development** assumes that change is best accomplished when the people affected by problems are empowered with the knowledge and skills needed to understand their circumstances, and then work cooperatively together to overcome them; this approach to community development places a premium on consensus as a tactic and on social solidarity as a medium and outcome
- **Social Advocacy** focuses on promoting equity or social justice for the target community, and the application of socio-political pressure on the people or institutions that may have induced the problem, or that obstruct measures aimed at its amelioration.

The 'Community Capacity Development' strand in this interventionist thinking relates to the civil-society dimension of Bourhis and Landry (2008: 193): 'the degree of control a language community has within cultural and social institutions related to its language and cultural vitality'. Extending this thinking into the wider economic and community infrastructure, Éamonn Ó Neachtain (2016) has considered the tensions associated with the failure to fully integrate policies related to regional economic development and language planning within the Irish Gaeltacht, and the subsequent impact of these policy interventions on the Irish-speaking community of the officially-designated Gaeltacht. A key conclusion from Ó Neachtain's (2016: 539) doctoral research was that socio-economic and sociolinguistic planning need to be closely integrated and:

> that there is a fundamental and defensible need for a differentiated form of development model required to support Threatened Minority Language (TML)-communities *in situ*. For it to be more effective and resilient and to possess the capacity to introduce and sustain structural change, the postulates of such an institutional model of planning should be based on an explicit approach to development which commits to integrated, spatial development across all policy domains and socio-economic sectors within the TML-territory. An exclusive policy prioritising employment-led development, while critical in terms of objective development outcomes, is not sufficient to address the totality of the TML challenge.

Our new proposal of the Participatory Minority Language Cooperative links these planning dimensions primarily to **Level 3** of Figure 8.1 above. This new framework for the development of Gaelic is expressed at the level of community and society.

9.2.2 STRENGTHENING LINGUISTIC RESILIENCE IN THE GAELIC-SPEAKING COMMUNITY

In the context of localised language planning and development, it is useful to explore the central concept of 'community resilience' (Norris *et al.* 2008). Community resilience represents the collective capacity of communities to adapt positively to societal challenges. In the context of threat and societal risk, enhancing social resilience is a prerequisite to developing a feasible integrated agenda of sustainability, be that socio-economic, environmental or cultural. This conceptual framework can help community members to assess how best the remnants of the Gaelic-speaking community can realise their own potential in order to effectively revive a functioning Gaelic collective. Raising the levels of social capital (Putnam 2000) within the vernacular Gaelic community should form a key aspect of any interventionist process.

9.3 NEW ORGANISATIONAL STRUCTURE URRAS NA GÀIDHLIG

The proposed Participatory Minority Language Cooperative framework will establish, over time, a societal approach to Gaelic development in the islands through which local socio-economic and cultural initiatives, organised as networked cooperation, will aim to increase the familial and social presence of Gaelic. Within the proposed framework of the Participatory Minority Language Cooperative, the central new structure suggested is Urras na Gàidhlig (the Gaelic Community Trust). Urras na Gàidhlig is a proposed community development trust for the Gaelic collective. This community organisation will be based in the islands and under the direct control of a representative cohort of community members. The Participatory Minority Language Cooperative framework will require Bòrd na Gàidhlig to rethink and re-evaluate their current direct role in Gaelic-focused development in the Western Isles and channel responsibilities and resources to this new community-focused organisation Urras na Gàidhlig. We use the working title of Urras na Gàidhlig to refer to this new organisational structure that would assume the role of a Gaelic community development trust. Similarly, community-related elements in the Gaelic language plans of public bodies based in the Western Isles should also be transferred to Urras na Gàidhlig. The main geographic focus of Urras na Gàidhlig will be the Western

Isles but other locations, for example in the Highlands and Argyll, wishing to adopt this agenda will also be encouraged to partake in the revival.

Urras na Gàidhlig will establish mechanisms to suggest, design, initiate and elaborate social and entrepreneurial activity in close cooperation with and proximity to local communities. The Urras language development model is envisaged as a participatory minority-language cooperative which offers mutual support and practical benefits to its participants. In combining community development measures with Gaelic policy concerns, the Urras brings decision-making and instigating initiatives as close as organisationally possible to the target community.

In the broader civic context, Bòrd na Gàidhlig will have an advisory and strategic function to:

    a. Coordinate the strategy of the Urras with national Gaelic policy

    b. Provide advice and expertise to the Urras

    c. Link the Urras with complementary initiatives and projects in which cooperation between familial, communal and institutional Gaelic networks could be enhanced both in the context of the islands, the Scottish and British polities and the diaspora

    d. Facilitate educational opportunities to acquire Gaelic.

9.4 OVERVIEW OF A NEW ORGANISATIONAL MODEL

As stated above, the framework in which this language development model is based is that of a Participatory Minority Language Cooperative, with Urras na Gàidhlig as its principal operational mechanism. The chief aims of the model are:

    a. To develop a resource-backed strategic facility for the Gaelic community in order to enable them to improve their societal condition in a cooperative way

    b. To protect the social presence of Gaelic in the islands from sociolinguistic habitat loss

    c. To enhance the social viability of Gaelic as a core component of island life and identity.

The successful development of this model of cross-community support networks depends upon local actors who are prepared to take responsibility for the design and implementation of plans for local engagement, and for the creation of participatory networks. It assumes a culture of democracy and participation, including a positive attitude to productive change within the community. The initial phase of the strategy will include measures to clarify the need for a new departure. Establishing the model will also require the explicit support of public bodies, principally the Scottish

Government, Bòrd na Gàidhlig, Highlands and Islands Enterprise and relevant local authorities, and in particular Comhairle nan Eilean Siar.

The main framework of the proposed new community model is based on the following four principles: 1) stakeholder collaboration; 2) local communities partnership; 3) small community management; and 4) national collaboration. These principles entail:

1. **The proposed model framework would be developed in collaboration and partnership with all relevant stakeholders. The proposed framework should:**
   - Be based on a transfer of responsibility and requisite funding support to a new locally-based organisation
   - Enable Gaelic maintenance and revitalisation efforts to come under the direct operational control of communities across the Western Isles
   - Create a new partnership between official bodies and the Gaelic community in the islands.

2. **Partnership, participation and innovation drive the proposed organisational model, in order to identify new locally-based solutions:**
   - A community-focused approach is expected to lead to the involvement of local actors at all levels, enable the creation of new partnerships and generate a spirit of positivity for engagement with the social reality of Gaelic.

3. **The participating communities will be based on appropriate geographic units:**
   - Over time, these areas should form a network of localities across the Western Isles and be self-reinforcing in cooperative activities and mutual support.

4. **The new organisation will develop a community-led language action framework which addresses the current reality of Gaelic across the Western Isles:**
   - The action framework of the Urras should be based on a 20-year horizon with assessment of progress conducted every five years. The Urras strategy should be linked to the strategic aims of the National Plan for Gaelic, but configured for the local situation.
   - In line with the ethos of local autonomy, the new community organisation will have control of finance, management and representation.
   - This framework is to be organised in a manner which allows for strategic inputs from the educational sector in the islands and for broader linkages with educational networks throughout Scotland.

There are six over-arching components to the Participatory Minority Language Cooperative framework. Figure 9.1 gives an outline indication of these components required for the establishment of the Urras.

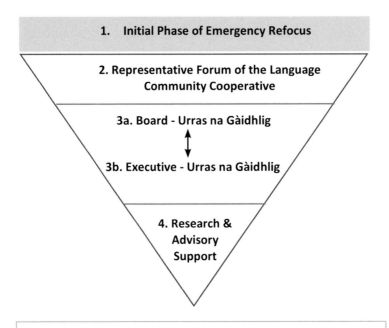

Figure 9.1 *Participatory Minority Language Cooperative: Component Levels 1–6*

A central aim of this proposed model is to enhance the collective agency of the vernacular speaker group. In Level 1 of the *Initial Phase of Emergency Refocus* (Figure 9.1), moving from the current policy dispensation to the community-based approach will require the initial acknowledgement of the severity of the sociolinguistic crisis and the need for concrete measures to draw relevant community and official stakeholders into an agreed process of community action to set about establishing Urras na Gàidhlig.

Level 2 in Figure 9.1 indicates the democratic dimension of the Language Community Cooperative, exercised through the *Representative Forum*, which will function as a form of Gaelic assembly. This forum will be membership-based and will act as the representative voice of the community cooperative. It will also provide the mechanism for electing the requisite leadership to give direction and foster cooperation across the communities and their various partnerships. The forum's role will be to appoint a relevant number of directors of Urras na Gàidhlig (Level 3a in Figure 9.1) from within the membership group, to ensure governance and management oversight of the community cooperative and of the operational executive of Urras na Gàidhlig (Level 3b). The Urras directors will also ensure that an effective strategic interface exists between community members, executive and operational activities and with other supportive agencies.

The *Research and Advisory* function (Level 4 in Figure 9.1) will provide research, advisory and strategic support. This function also provides for technical advice in respect of minority community language planning and management across the two dimensions of inputs and outputs:

- Strategic planning and sociolinguistic advice affecting the design, management and implementation of community language projects
- Monitoring of sociolinguistic outcomes.

Once fully implemented, it is expected that the new community development approach will yield a number of *Socio-economic returns on investment* (Level 5, Figure 9.1) and *Sociolinguistic returns on participation* (Level 6). These returns on investment are envisaged to generate new Gaelic language-based enterprises and other employment opportunities; the introduction of family support and incentive schemes; mechanisms of support to parents and carers to raise their children as fluent Gaelic speakers; and youth participation at various levels of Gaelic language renewal. The overall outcome is envisaged to generate returns of socio-economic and linguistic capital for the revitalisation of Urras-supported communities.

9.5 A BRIEF DESCRIPTION OF THE KEY STRANDS OF THE MODEL

A generalised schema of the whole model is shown in Figure 9.2.

The schema indicates the interaction of three complementary developmental strands:
- Strand A: National Gaelic Policies
- Strand B: Community Nexus for cooperation and participation
- Strand C: Leadership, Governance and Capacity Building and Implementation.

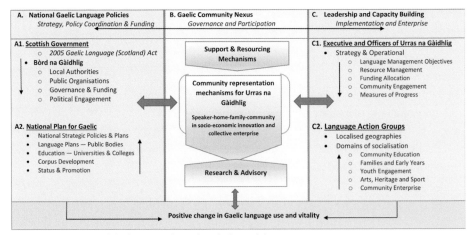

A. National Gaelic Language Policies	B. Gaelic Community Nexus	C. Leadership and Capacity Building
Strategy, Policy Coordination & Funding	*Governance and Participation*	*Implementation and Enterprise*

A1. Scottish Government
- o 2005 Gaelic Language (Scotland) Act
- Bòrd na Gàidhlig
  - o Local Authorities
  - o Public Organisations
  - o Governance & Funding
  - o Political Engagement

A2. National Plan for Gaelic
- National Strategic Policies & Plans
- Language Plans — Public Bodies
- Education — Universities & Colleges
- Corpus Development
- Status & Promotion

Support & Resourcing Mechanisms

Community representation mechanisms for Urras na Gàidhlig

Speaker-home-family-community in socio-economic innovation and collective enterprise

Research & Advisory

C1. Executive and Officers of Urras na Gàidhlig
- Strategy & Operational
  - o Language Management Objectives
  - o Resource Management
  - o Funding Allocation
  - o Community Engagement
  - o Measures of Progress

C2. Language Action Groups
- Localised geographies
- Domains of socialisation
  - o Community Education
  - o Families and Early Years
  - o Youth Engagement
  - o Arts, Heritage and Sport
  - o Community Enterprise

Positive change in Gaelic language use and vitality

Figure 9.2 *Schema of the key strands in the whole model*

The schema sets out the three strands which comprise a proposed new organisational model for community engagement in the revitalisation processes. The proposed systems model is an adapted version of the policy-to-outcome framework suggested by Grin (2003b: 47). The model takes into consideration:

    a. The weakness of existing policy initiatives (e.g. National Plan for Gaelic and Language Plans of public bodies)

    b. The crisis in the vernacular communities; and, given both of these problems,

    c. The strategic urgency in reframing Gaelic policy within a community-focused model.

The model comprises three interdependent strands.

1.   **Column A** comprises the strategic and institutional strand of the model which is under the direct control of the Scottish Government and Bòrd na Gàidhlig. It entails the civic-national dimension of Gaelic policy, mainly through the development of language plans aimed at the sectoral promotion of Gaelic provision, administrative initiatives and language projects.

2.   **Column B** is the community strand under the direct management and control of the proposed new organisational mechanism, Urras na Gàidhlig, which aims to drive discrete revitalisation efforts to stimulate intergenerational transmission and the use of Gaelic in the community. This strand entails the civic-communal dimension of local language development through membership participation and defined governance structures. Column B is shown at the centre of the model as it forms the community nexus between the national supports in Column A

and the capacity-building initiatives, led by Gaelic Language Action Groups in conjunction with the staff of Urras na Gàidhlig, as envisaged in Column C. This element of the model provides for the strategic and operational linkage between state bodies and the community. It also allows the community to continue to benefit from the relevant aspects of the language-policy *status quo*, while opening up a new dynamic to address local priorities. In this respect, it envisages a progressive strategic reform of language policy in favour of community engagement.

3. **Column C** comprises the executive dimension of the model. It entails the professional support that the officers of Urras na Gàidhlig will offer to local communities to address developmental priorities, as identified by Gaelic Language Action Groups formed by local members and supporters of Urras na Gàidhlig. This strand allows for:
   a. Local initiatives and community members to benefit from professional supports of the Urras staff and governance structures
   b. Participants to coordinate local activity with national policy Gaelic initiatives, particularly in the educational sector
   c. Local participants to identify developmental priorities and to set the language policy and planning agenda for the local community.

The Participatory Minority Language Cooperative model gives authority and responsibility back to the Gaelic communities of the Western Isles to engage with their own circumstances. The model is focused on key domains, and is built on a resource prioritisation system. It assists communities to address the primary issue of language shift from Gaelic. The envisaged support mechanisms and cooperative dynamic, backed by ongoing strategic advice, will strengthen the skills, abilities, and confidence of individuals, families and groups to take effective action and leading roles in the development of Gaelic within their respective communities. The forum or assembly mechanisms for the Urras na Gàidhlig participants act as the voice of the wider community, and provide the local and collective authority to the Urras directors and executive to operate on behalf of the members.

9.6 STRENGTHENING COMMUNITY SOCIAL CAPITAL AND LINGUISTIC RESILIENCE

If a minority language can be considered a public good (Grin 2003b), it can also be considered as a resource which can be subject to planning approaches and developmental frameworks. Björn Jernudd and Jyotirindra Das Gupta (1971: 187) indicated that 'the logic of language planning is dictated by the recognition of language as a societal resource'. However, the prestige given by the community to this resource is dependent on the value they attach to the language in relation to communicative and socio-cultural parameters. For Scottish Gaelic, the language has a relatively high degree of status as symbolic value (the Gaelic Language Act) and cultural performance (MG ALBA [Gaelic-medium television] and music and cultural industries), but relatively low in communicative value, as evidenced by the teenager cohort responses in Chapter 4 and by the low level of practice in younger generations. The most common reasons for the teenagers who reported being supportive of Gaelic were associated with utilitarian reasons of the advantages of being bilingual and of Gaelic boosting employment opportunities (section 4.7.2, Figure 4.38), a response corresponding more with the instrumental and individual dimension of the civic promotion of Gaelic in Scottish culture than its communal function.

In Table 9.1, we present a contrastive summary of the current institutional approach (Column II) and our proposed societal approach (Column I) to language policy and planning, although clearly a complementary and integrated combination of both approaches is necessary. Our contention is that current approaches to Gaelic language planning and policy implementation follow an 'institutionally sanctioned' pathway illustrated in Column II in Table 9.1. This is a formalised construct controlled by public policy and with Gaelic development actions implemented primarily through public-sector organisations. Whilst this is one pathway to implement public policy in relation to revitalisation of the language, it should not be viewed as the only way to boost the number of functions and domains for Gaelic use in the community. We propose a complementary pathway, which we have termed a 'societal approach', as outlined in Column I in Table 9.1. This approach views the societal continuity of Gaelic as a public good in Scotland. This pathway puts communal initiative and the agency of the local community at the centre of the revitalisation process and signals that they, as individuals, as families and as a collective, have ownership of actions to improve the state of Gaelic in their communities.

Dimension	I. Societal Approach	II. Institutionally-Sanctioned Approach
View of Social Structure	Socially generated and collectively sustained: • Requires local networked leaderships	Authorised by formal institutions: • Dependent on formal direction
Form of Participation	Bottom-up Communal Networks: • Organic • Continuity from existing social resource (backed by formal interventions to counteract established forces of minoritisation)	Top-down Agency Networks: • Institutionally conceived • Facilitated by formal intervention (backed by the social capital of the majority culture)
Perspective on Language Function	Realised through communal/societal interaction: • Pragmatic exchange across social/institutional domains	Dependent on institutional ambition: • Circumscribed by formal resources and by level of engagement/interest
Geography	*In situ* and open to links with initiatives in other areas outside traditional Gaelic locations: • Local to autochthonous group and locally networked, with potential to integrate other adherents	Diverse/networked with neutral locus: • Distant and sparsely linked to social networks • Post-spatial
Self-Ascription / Identity	Primarily from the extant in-group: • Synchronic and diachronic • Communal and individual	Fluid/relativist/situational: • Synchronic and multi-spatial • Individual, aspirationally networked
Nature of Social Engagement	Oriented towards the communal participatory function of language: • Focused on participating in and protecting existing resource and building resilience of those contributing to its collective sustainability in various language geographies • Cultural and communicative	Performance orientated: • Concentrated on the elaboration of institutional aims • Occupied by non-linear concerns • Centred on key formal domains: school, activism/pastime and entertainment/media

Table 9.1 Contrasts in policy focus between societal and institutional approaches

The two types of policy focus are contrasted here in opposition to each other, reflecting the current circumstances in which the institutionally-sanctioned approach dominates Gaelic language planning and policy concerns, due to an imbalance in the attention afforded to formalised administrative structures over social initiatives and engagements. The current approach needs to be rebalanced towards societal engagement. The new approach suggested here envisions the 'institutional' and the 'societal' approach as a complementary set of policy pathways to develop language group resilience and vitality in a range of key dimensions central to Gaelic continuity.

The chief aim of the social approach (Column I), therefore, is to bolster the *in situ* and networked practice of Gaelic in the minority-language geographies, with particular emphasis on a core group of speakers wishing to contribute to the transmission, socialisation and comprehensiveness of Gaelic in the various social and formal domains.

Language planning cannot be solely regarded as being in the sphere of Government sponsored agencies. Other groups and power elites, in universities, in the educational sector in general, cultural bodies and the media, also play an important role in creating the strategic and policy context, including the justification for the promotion of particular pathways to support the revitalisation of a minority language like Scottish Gaelic. Given the marginal social presence of Gaelic in the islands, and in Scotland in general, it is important that the ongoing public policy debate avoids a sectoral mentality of prioritising the concerns specific to institutional sectors and disregarding the societal crisis. Such sectoralism would prolong Gaelic language planning and policy provision beyond the loss of vernacular Gaelic from society. In this vulnerable policy context of Gaelic planning outliving the Gaelic community, it will be only a matter of time before the institutional emperor is found to be wearing no societal clothes.

9.6.1 THE PRINCIPLE OF SUBSIDIARITY AND DECENTRALISATION

The model suggested here is based on the principle of subsidiarity and decentralisation. We suggest prioritising a bottom-up approach which would be bolstered by top-down inputs from key state agencies. From this perspective, the role of the Scottish Government, in conjunction with relevant public authorities, would concentrate on facilitating community initiatives backed by formal supports in key sectors, rather than the public authorities themselves adopting administrative responsibility to implement an agenda of change in community development policies for the Gaels. This principle of subsidiarity assumes a complementarity between a bottom-up (local) and a top-down (public authorities) partnership in which community actions and outcomes are prioritised (see the Scottish Government's emphasis on encouraging a process of decentralisation in the Programme for Government 2017–18, and Community Empowerment (Scotland) Act 2015). Reorienting the policy to this focus would see the central authority having a subsidiary function in revitalisation efforts and performing only those tasks which cannot be undertaken at a more local level. This approach rests on identifying correctly the tasks for which the community has the capacity and willingness to take responsibility. In the context of the crisis now facing Gaelic in Scotland, the central rationale for subsidiarity pivots on the need to decentralise policy and activity. The Gaels, who are the guardians of the language, are the most important community to maintain the language and the culture by knowing, understanding and appreciating the subtleties and intricacies associated with their language and culture in society. This approach will facilitate a more productive, professional and community-focused engagement with Gaelic's societal reality.

9.7 RECOMMENDED STRATEGIC PRIORITIES AND ACTIONS

We do not set out an exhaustive list of strategic priorities and actions as a ready-made template for this proposed policy reform and community engagement agenda. Our intention is to suggest a number of key priorities and actions to create a productive environment to discuss and agree the most feasible and acceptable way forward, not least because the drafting and development of a new successful model requires the participation of those for whom the policy reform is intended. The main objective of the framework, as set out in Figure 9.2, is to support and empower the Gaelic community of the Western Isles to raise their children as fluent Gaelic speakers with pride in their language and culture and for the language to be a vital component of family and community life.

In order to engage meaningfully with the new language planning and development strategy, as proposed in Figure 9.2, a number of key stakeholder groupings will initially be central to creating a collegiate and productive public debate. These include:
   a. Local individuals who hold positions of influence and leadership within their communities
   b. Individuals with responsibility to enact change from within the formal policy structures of Scottish Government, Bòrd na Gàidhlig and local public bodies
   c. Research bodies with knowledge and expertise on the societal condition of the Gaelic-speaking group.

9.8 STRATEGIC PRIORITIES FOR INTERVENTION

We set out in this section the strategic priorities based on the four main elements of the interventionist framework illustrated in Figure 9.2: Strategic Priority 1 sets up the support and leadership for Urras na Gàidhlig; Strategic Priority 2 sets up support for the transmission of Gaelic to children; Strategic Priority 3 links national policy with the community engagement of Urras na Gàidhlig; and finally, Strategic Priority 4 adjusts language planning bodies to support Urras na Gàidhlig. These Strategic

Priorities and associated Priority Actions are by no means exhaustive, but provide a basis for the new progressive strategy.

9.8.1 STRATEGIC PRIORITY 1: URRAS EXECUTIVE AND PROFESSIONAL SUPPORT

The development of the planning model will entail the establishment of an executive to implement the aims of Urras na Gàidhlig. The role of the staff of Urras na Gàidhlig is to provide advice and support to families and community groups in developing initiatives and cooperative projects, which will lead to productive outcomes for the current and future generations of Gaelic speakers in the Western Isles.

Context

This executive and professional aspect of the model recognises that Gaelic-speaking families will need cogent and informed advice and support to engage with the new process, and for the remaining vernacular Gaelic networks to benefit from its initiatives. Urras na Gàidhlig's staff and executive will have responsibility for the delivery of support and advice among families and communities to ensure successful community and language regeneration processes. The main aim of this strategic priority is to protect and increase the demolinguistic vitality or density of the Gaelic group and at the same time to re-establish Gaelic autochthony. The Urras will aim to initially stabilise, and where feasible increase, the number of active speakers of Gaelic by realistic proportions for the various districts.

Actions

Priority Action 1a: Develop a fully-functioning and resourced Gaelic-language executive to administer the responsibilities of Urras na Gàidhlig in order to provide a range of services to Urras na Gàidhlig's membership:

i. To increase awareness within the vernacular Gaelic community of the importance of family and community for the intergenerational transmission of Gaelic, and for the future social sustainability of the Gaelic group.

ii. To establish a fund to support a network of Gaelic-speaking families in the islands. The fund will provide for practical assistance and bespoke advice regarding raising children through the medium of Gaelic, and to promote Gaelic-language socialisation among the young in general. This mechanism can be compared to Scéim Labhairt na Gaeilge (Irish-speaking Family Support Scheme), which was operated in the Irish Gaeltacht for decades.

iii. To support the development of a network of Gaelic-language community development advisors. The staff of Urras na Gàidhlig and local leaders will cooperate in acquiring the relevant competencies and language planning knowledge for organising, leading and managing sociolinguistic change within their own localities. Leaders will need to engage each registered or shareholder household, at various levels of participation with the Urras. The Urras will need to have each area agreed and designated to various advisors.

iv. To share research and policy expertise and know-how with local groups, public agencies and community organisations in relation to improving the status, acquisition and use of Gaelic amongst all age groups within the community.

v. To provide advice and support in acquiring collective resources to facilitate community members' involvement in activities that enhance and prioritise the use of Gaelic, particularly in social domains relevant to the youth.

vi. To utilise technological and social media mechanisms to promote and elevate the status and importance of Gaelic heritage and culture. To strengthen current social networks, and create new networks and communities of interest amongst the younger age cohort of speakers and learners of Gaelic.

vii. To develop and implement bespoke programmes of academic and strategic professional training in language policy and community development management.

viii. To establish mechanisms to negotiate and liaise with, as well as recruit, existing community bodies and organisations to participate in Urras-supported revitalisation.

Priority Action 1b: The Scottish Government, Bòrd na Gàidhlig and local authorities relevant to Urras na Gàidhlig will investigate the feasibility of introducing financial incentives to support Gaelic-speaking families in raising the next generation of Gaelic speakers.

9.8.2 STRATEGIC PRIORITY 2: YOUTH

In order to optimise the family-support mechanisms of Urras na Gàidhlig, it is essential that relevant aspects of the educational system in the Western Isles become capable of developing and delivering Gaelic-medium education of the highest standard to Gaelic speakers. In this regard, adopting a proactive and positive approach to ensure that children in all island primary schools have the option of acquiring fluency in Gaelic is advisable. Additionally, policy and education professionals will be encouraged to consider initiatives within the school environment, to enable Gaelic-medium socialisation to take hold and be sustained outside the formal classroom setting. Coordinating the familial and social support initiatives envisaged in Strategic Priority 1 with the associated priorities for the youth will be beneficial to the overall efficacy of the model. Clearly, the effective communal revival of Gaelic will need differentiated educational provision for young Gaels where they can speak Gaelic together. The combined aim of these actions is to protect and promote the spaces and contexts in which the monolingual use of threatened Gaelic is prioritised, as discussed in section 1.3 regarding bilingual acquisitional dynamics and minoritised disadvantage.

Context

There have been substantial gains and progress made in aspects of Gaelic-medium education across the Western Isles in recent years. Urras na Gàidhlig will need to support an increasing number of Gaelic-speaking households, to encourage youth socialisation in Gàidhlig, to increase Gaelic competence among the speakers, and in particular to increase support for the younger cohorts, who are favourably disposed, but lack the Gaelic competence to raise their children as Gaelic speakers. Early-years education provision will need to differentiate and support two demolinguistic groups: young Gaelic-speaking children and primarily monolingual English-speaking children. Consulting on educational policy in other minority-language jurisdictions, such as Ireland (and examining the Irish Government Policy on Gaeltacht Education 2017–2022), could facilitate this reassessment. Devising an education model aimed at achieving the highest levels of Gaelic fluency and literacy amongst school-children across the Western Isles is a major component of social, cultural and linguistic renewal in the islands.

Actions

Priority Action 2a: Comhairle nan Eilean Siar, along with relevant childcare and educational partners, will enable a more strategic approach to developing and implementing an adequately-resourced Gaelic Early Years Workforce Development Plan, which takes account of appropriate training in immersion education methodologies, and places a high value on staff skills and experience. Provision will target and support the two main demolinguistic groups in their acquisition needs.

Priority Action 2b: At primary and secondary level education, Comhairle nan Eilean Siar will reassess how pedagogical policies and school practices could better support educational attainment in order to sustain Gaelic.

Priority Action 2c: The learning support systems for children and parents outwith the formal school curriculum will be linked to initiatives undertaken as part of *Strategy Priority 1*. Such out-of-school initiatives and efforts will benefit from materials developed and provided by existing public bodies, such as Stòrlann Nàiseanta na Gàidhlig (Gaelic-education publisher).

Priority Action 2d: The Urras will encourage and support proactive Gaelic parenting and childcare, for instance elaborated language use with children, proactive reading of Gaelic and literacy activity in Gaelic with children. Such elaborated language use and literacy activity have been shown to be beneficial in (minority) language acquisition.

Priority Action 2e: The Urras will establish Gaelic-medium youth groups and activities to cultivate and develop Gaelic socialisation.

9.8.3 STRATEGIC PRIORITY 3: NATIONAL CONTEXT

Scottish public bodies are required and resourced by government to implement existing Gaelic policy. Amending the current policy framework to address newly-highlighted challenges, therefore, is predicated on political and institutional will to devise and implement policies and strategies to engage with issues which have been neglected or evaded in the existing approach.

Context
The evidence indicates that the Gaelic-speaking community is no longer sustainable under current circumstances and policy provision. Current national interventions are not engaging sufficiently with the social and sociolinguistic crisis of the vernacular Gaelic community. The aim of this strategic priority is to put the Gaelic vernacular crisis at the centre of national policy and planning.

Actions
Priority Action 3a: The Scottish Government and its agencies will recognise the vernacular autochthonous crisis and will demonstrate resolve to engage proactively with the challenges involved.

Priority Action 3b: The Scottish Government will commission a review of the Gaelic Language (Scotland) Act 2005, to assess whether the Act, as the primary statutory mechanism for Gaelic development, comprises the necessary range of instruments and 'rights' which are capable of addressing the challenges associated with maintaining and revitalising Gaelic within all discrete communal, spatial and networked domains for Gaelic.

Priority Action 3c: The Scottish Government, through relevant agencies, will commission a scoping exercise to identify the strength of social capital linkages in Gaelic development measures. For instance, to analyse how the undertakings of Bòrd na Gàidhlig, the main instrument of official policy (stemming from the 2005 Act), impact and promote Gaelic revival among the vernacular group. This scoping study will provide an understanding of the levels of current engagement among existing communal and emerging networks, and the extent of their productive relationships with formal support mechanisms.

Priority Action 3d: Bòrd na Gàidhlig alongside community partners will develop an effective monitoring and evaluation framework to assess the impact of the Gaelic language plans of public bodies on the vitality and use of the language across the distinct Gaelic communities identified in the 2018–2023 National Gaelic Language Plan.

Priority Action 3e: The Scottish Government will establish a high-powered committee to address the current emergency phase in initial language policy reform and to support the establishment and development of Urras na Gàidhlig.

Priority Action 3f: The Scottish Government will encourage all relevant government agencies to buy into the new model, in particular those bodies who are more comfortable with the *status quo* of English dominance in the current policy dispensation.

Priority Action 3g: The Scottish Government will set up an emergency fund and establish a budget to fund the initial phase of the establishment of Urras na Gàidhlig and the new policies.

Priority Action 3h: The Scottish Government in conjunction with Urras na Gàidhlig will set up a working group to establish the funding parameters of the ongoing activities of the Urras. This will be considered from two perspectives: a) the establishment of new funding streams, and b) the partial redirection of existing funding from other language policy budgets.

9.8.4 STRATEGIC PRIORITY 4: NATIONAL ENGAGEMENT IN THE ISLANDS

The Scottish Government and Bòrd na Gàidhlig will establish a working forum to formalise consultation mechanisms, which will elaborate and agree the adoption of a new model of engagement with the reality of the vernacular Gaelic community.

Context

Our proposed model for intervention indicates a reorientation of Gaelic language planning towards a community planning framework. In Strategic Priority 4, the different dynamics between the island communities are recognised and local agency is put at the heart of governance and language development structures. Additionally, it sets the approach within wider socio-cultural and socio-economic development strategies.

Actions

Priority Action 4a: The Scottish Government, in conjunction with Bòrd na Gàidhlig, will support and resource the implementation of the intervention model. This priority will require the decentralisation of policy implementation and control to the Gaelic speaking collective. This will be realised through a realistic mechanism of resource allocation to Urras na Gàidhlig.

Priority Action 4b: Establish a founding committee or group to set up Urras na Gàidhlig.

Priority Action 4c: Provision and implementation of adequate funding structures for Urras na Gàidhlig and their activities. Funding structures will include links with financial and other support from outside the islands, for instance philanthropy from the Scottish diaspora.

Priority Action 4d: Establish mechanisms of representation and power sharing in Urras na Gàidhlig.

Priority Action 4e: Develop mechanisms to empower a local leadership and to encourage community capacity building with Urras na Gàidhlig.

Priority Action 4f: Implement an ethos of inclusivity to include in the new model the various agencies and groups in the community who are more comfortable with the *status quo* of English dominance.

Priority Action 4g: Build foundations for socio-economic renewal around Gaelic and other local resources in cooperation with Urras na Gàidhlig.

Priority Action 4h: Encourage and recruit community cooperatives and other local agencies to become Gaelic development hubs.

9.9 CONCLUDING OBSERVATIONS

This study has produced challenging findings on the current sociolinguistic situation of the remaining Gaelic vernacular communities in Scotland, primarily in the Western Isles. Given the extent of the evidence in this publication concerning the extreme fragility of vernacular Gaelic, we can conclude that the remaining vernacular networks will not survive anywhere to any appreciable extent, under current circumstances, beyond this decade.

This trajectory means that Gaelic will soon cease to exist as a community language in any part of Scotland. In light of the critical challenge, it is clear that clinging to the current *status quo* in language planning and policy is not a credible option. Indeed, there is no sense in continuing to rely on vague under-informed aspirations on which much of the existing Gaelic policy framework is based. The analysis in this book of existing language planning and policy approaches to the Gaelic group has been critical, as have many participants in the community consultations, because of the lack of positive, real engagement of these policies with the severe level of threat facing the autochthonous group. Indeed, it is remarkable how both the tenor and the themes of the contributions by the community members to the public consultations on the social reality of Gaelic in the islands mainly contradict much of the official national narrative of Gaelic revival, revitalisation and vibrancy. In the contact and communication the members of the IGRP team had with many members of the island communities, no direct mention or talk was heard, for obvious reasons, of a 'Gaelic revival'.

The extent to which current policies and discourses are widely perceived as being distant from the concerns of the vernacular group gives a suitable starting point for a new departure. In facing such unambiguous evidence, individuals, communities and agencies face critical choices in what course of action to take. However, moving beyond the current mainly aspirational or symbolic phase in Gaelic policy would be a prerequisite to addressing the real-world concerns of a highly threatened minority-speaker group, as highlighted here. Indeed, adopting a new approach may be, perhaps, the only way to establish public trust in minority-language policy in Scotland and give credibility to collective efforts to support the Gaelic group. It has to be acknowledged, however, that the remaining Gaelic group faces daunting challenges in their efforts to arrest the trajectory of decline, even if backed by relevant, dynamic policy supports and related resources.

In contrast to the current ineffectual approach, the hope that we can take from this book is that it offers an evidence-based diagnosis of the problems and outlines a strategic approach to attempt to address the situation from a realistic perspective. In suggesting an alternative approach, a key aim of this book is to focus attention on the Gaelic crisis and on addressing the underlying causes of the demise of Gaelic as a functioning community language. Sincere efforts to tackle this crisis will have the dual effect of encouraging the Gaelic community that their concerns will be taken seriously by public bodies, on the one hand, and of enhancing the dynamism and integrity of public bodies who engage with this task, on the other. Official assertions about the desirability of protecting cultural plurality and diversity can have real social meaning and be worthy of public support if they are backed by positive and constructive initiatives. The timely adoption of coordinated initiatives to mitigate the Gaelic vernacular crisis, as the defining feature of Gaelic policy, would demonstrate that minority-language policy in Scotland is capable of adapting to new evidence and of dynamic engagement with critical concerns. Addressing a crisis is difficult, but it offers a greater prospect of giving hope to people than the alternative. The sociolinguistic crisis depicted in this book is emblematic of the fragility of many of the world's minority languages. Unlike the Scottish Gaelic situation, most minority-language groups are not afforded any official recognition or public support. In the context of the pervasive sociocultural threat to much of the world's ethnolinguistic diversity, there is a local duty of care on the Scottish public bodies to engage sincerely with their minority-language commitments, but there is also a global responsibility to demonstrate that they are capable of giving leadership, in their own context, on this critical global and local issue.

This study has set out an evidence-based diagnosis and prognosis of the Gaelic group's prevailing sociolinguistic situation, along with a positive, and potentially productive, prescription for addressing the challenge. Realising an ameliorative response can be envisaged in the following positive and rational sequence of events: (a) an admission by the community and public bodies that the situation is critical; (b) an acceptance among public bodies that the current policy interventions for the vernacular group are not fit for purpose; (c) an acknowledgment that an alternative approach is required if the loss of vernacular Gaelic is to be averted; (d) multilateral indications of a collective willingness to bolster the societal vitality of the Gaelic-speaking group; and (e) a reasonably swift re-orientation of LPP efforts (away from formal symbolic institutional provision) to re-balance power, financial provision and strategic resources in favour of embedded community groups and Gaelic familial and social networks, possessing the capabilities and the desire to initiate a process of change aimed at language-in-society revitalisation.

References

Abrams, D. and Strogatz, S. (2003) Modelling the dynamics of language death. *Nature* 424, 900. Available at: https://www.nature.com/articles/424900a.

Anderson, R. (2013) The history of Scottish education, pre-1980. In T. Bryce, W. Humes, D. Gillies and A. Kennedy (eds) *Scottish Education: Referendum* (4th edn). (pp. 241–250). Edinburgh: Edinburgh University Press.

Armstrong, T. (2013) 'Why won't you speak to me in Gaelic?' Authenticity, integration and the heritage language learning project. *Journal of Language, Identity, and Education* 12 (5), 340–356.

Barth, F. (ed.) (1969) *Ethnic Groups and Boundaries: The social organization of culture difference.* London: Allen and Unwin.

Batibo, H. (2005) *Language Decline and Death in Africa: Causes, consequences and challenges.* Clevedon: Multilingual Matters.

Beck, U. and Beck-Gernsheim, E. (2010 [2002]) *Individualization: Institutionalized individualism and its social and political consequences.* London: SAGE Publications.

Benmamoun, E., Montrul, S. and Polinsky, M. (2013) Heritage languages and their speakers: opportunities and challenges for linguistics. *Theoretical Linguistics* 39 (3–4), 129–181.

Bernstein, B. (1971) *Class, Codes and Control: Theoretical studies towards a sociology of language.* London: Routledge and Kegan Paul.

Bird, B. (1993) Attitudes to Gaelic: young adults in the Western Isles. In K. MacKinnon (ed.) *FASNAG II: Proceedings of the Second Conference on Research and Studies on the Maintenance of Gaelic* (pp. 1–7). Forfhais agus Sgrùdaidhean air Gnàthachadh na Gàidhlig. Ostaig: Isle of Skye.

Birnie, I. (2016) Gaelic language use: policy vs de facto linguistic practices (a case study). Soillse / Federation of Endangered Languages Conference. Conference presentation, *Small Language Planning: Communities in Crisis.* 7 June 2016, Glasgow.

Bòrd na Gàidhlig (No date) *Foghlam Bun-sgoile.* Inverness: Bòrd na Gàidhlig. Available at: http://www.gaidhlig.scot/bord/education/primary-education/.

Bòrd na Gàidhlig (No date) *Foglam Ro-sgoile*. Inverness: Bòrd na Gàidhlig. [Accessed 14 June 2016]. Available at: http://www.gaidhlig. org.uk/bord/ar-n-obair/foghlam-gaidhlig/foghlam-ro-sgoile or http://www.gaidhlig.scot/ga/bord/education/pre-school/.

Bòrd na Gàidhlig (2007a) *Plana Nàiseanta na Gàidhlig 2007–2012 / National Gaelic Language Plan 2007–2012*. Inverness: Bòrd na Gàidhlig.

Bòrd na Gàidhlig (2007b) *An Stiùireadh air Planaichean Gàidhlig / Guidance on the Development of Gaelic Language Plans*. Inverness: Bòrd na Gàidhlig. Available at: https://gaeliclanguageplansscotland.org.uk/files/development/Stiuireadh%20Phlanaichean%202007%20Beurla.pdf.

Bòrd na Gàidhlig (2012) *Am Plana Cànain Nàiseanta Gàidhlig 2012–2017 / National Gaelic Language Plan 2012–17*. Inverness: Bòrd na Gàidhlig. [Accessed 14 June 2016]. Available at: http://www.gaidhlig.org.uk/bord/am-bord/bord-na-gaidhlig/plana-naiseanta-canain-gaidhlig.

Bòrd na Gàidhlig (2017a) *Dàta Foghlaim Ghàidhlig 2016–17 / Gaelic Education Data 2016–17*. Inverness: Bòrd na Gàidhlig. [Accessed 28 August 2017]. Available at: http://www.gaidhlig.scot/wp-content/uploads/2016/12/Dàta-Foghlaim-AM-FOLLAIS-2016-17-egn-1-PUBLIC-Education-Data.pdf.

Bòrd na Gàidhlig (2017b) *Statutory Guidance on Gaelic Education*. Available at: https://www.gaidhlig.scot/bord/education/statutory-guidance/.

Bòrd na Gàidhlig (2018a) *Am Plana Cànain Nàiseanta Gàidhlig 2018–2023 / National Gaelic Language Plan 2018–23*. Inverness: Bòrd na Gàidhlig. Available at: http://www.gaidhlig.scot/bord/the-national-gaelic-language-plan/.

Bòrd na Gàidhlig (2018b) *Dàta Foghlaim Ghàidhlig 2017–18 / Gaelic Education Data 2017–18*. Inverness: Bòrd na Gàidhlig. [Accessed 14 August 2018]. Available at: http://www.gaidhlig.scot/wp-content/uploads/2018/04/Da%CC%80ta-Foghlaim-AM-FOLLAIS-2017-18-egn-1-PUBLIC-Education-Data.pdf.

Borgstrøm, C. (1940) *The Dialects of the Outer Hebrides. A Linguistic Survey of the Gaelic Dialects of Scotland*. Vol. 1. Oslo: Norwegian Universities Press.

Bourdieu, P. (1991) *Language and Symbolic Power*. Cambridge: Polity Press.

Bourgeois, D. and Bourgeois, Y. (2012) Minority sub-state institutional completeness. *International Review of Sociology* 22 (2), 293–304.

Bourhis, R. Y., El-Geledi, S. and Sachdev, I. (2007) Language, ethnicity and intergroup relations. In A. Weatherall, B. Watson and C. Gallois (eds) *Language, Discourse and Social Psychology* (pp. 15–50). New York: Palgrave Macmillan.

Bourhis, R. Y. and Landry, R. (2008) Group vitality, cultural autonomy and the wellness of language minorities. In R. Y. Bourhis (ed.) *The Vitality of the English-Speaking Communities of Quebec: From community decline to revival* (pp. 185–212). Montréal, Quebec: CEETUM, Université de Montréal.

Bourhis, R. Y., Moise, L. C., Perreault, S. and Senecal, S. (1997) Towards an interactive acculturation model: a social psychological approach. *International Journal of Psychology* 32 (6), 369–386.

Bourhis, R. Y., Montaruli, E., El-Geledi, S., Harvey, S-P. and Barrette, G. (2010) Acculturation in multiple host community settings. *Journal of Social Issues*, 66 (4), 780–802.

Boyd, S. (1998) North Americans in the Nordic region: elite bilinguals. *International Journal of the Sociology of Language* 133 (1), 31–50.

Breton, R. (1964) Institutional completeness of ethnic communities and the personal relations of immigrants. *American Journal of Sociology* 70 (2), 193–205.

Brooks, S. and Roberts, R. G. (eds) (2013) *Pa Beth Yr Aethoch Allan i'w Achub?* Llanrwst: Gwasg Carreg Gwalch.

Burmeister, M. (2008) Television as saviour for endangered languages? A survey among Scottish-Gaelic teenagers. In S. Sahel and R. Vogel (eds) *9. Norddeutsches Linguistisches Kolloquium* (pp. 1–26). Bielefeld: Universität Bielefeld.

Byers-Heinlein, K. (2013) Parental language mixing: its measurement and the relation of mixed input to young bilingual children's vocabulary size. *Bilingualism: Language and Cognition* 16 (1), 32–48.

Campbell, D. and MacLean, R. A. (1974) *Beyond the Atlantic Roar: A study of the Nova Scotia Scots.* Toronto: McLelland and Stewart.

Campbell, J. L. (1950) *Gaelic in Scottish Education and Life: Past, present and future.* (2nd edn). Edinburgh: W. and A. K. Johnston.

Coleman, J. (1976) *Language Shift in a Bilingual Hebridean Crofting Community.* Unpublished PhD thesis. Boston: University of Massachusetts. Available at: https://search.proquest.com/hnpscotsman/docview/302756741.

Comhairle nan Eilean Siar (2013) *Gaelic Language Plan 2013–2017.* Stornoway: Comhairle nan Eilean Siar. [Accessed 14 June 2016]. Available at: http://www.cne-siar.gov.uk/sgioba/documents/languageplan/plan_e.pdf.

Comhairle nan Eilean Siar (2016a) *Population and Migration.* Stornoway: Comhairle nan Eilean Siar.

Comhairle nan Eilean Siar (2016b) *Population Projections.* Stornoway: Comhairle nan Eilean Siar. Available at: https://www.cne-siar.gov.uk/strategy-performance-and-research/outer-hebrides-factfile/population/population-projections/.

Comhairle nan Eilean Siar (2017a) *Outer Hebrides Factfile: Population overview*. Stornoway: Comhairle nan Eilean Siar. Available at: https://www.cne-siar.gov.uk/strategy-performance-and-research/outer-hebrides-factfile/population/overview/.

Comhairle nan Eilean Siar (2017b) *Draft Gaelic Language Plan 2018–2022*. Stornoway: Comhairle nan Eilean Siar. [Accessed 14 January 2018]. Available at: https://www.cne-siar.gov.uk:8000/media/9762/pc18-22-1.pdf.

Comhairle nan Eilean Siar (2018) *Outer Hebrides Factfile: Population overview*. Stornoway: Comhairle nan Eilean Siar. Available at: https://www.cne-siar.gov.uk/strategy-performance-and-research/outer-hebrides-factfile/population/island-populations/.

Comhairle nan Eilean Siar (2019) *Outer Hebrides Factfile: Population: Island populations*. Stornoway: Comhairle nan Eilean Siar. Available at: https://www.cne-siar.gov.uk/strategy-performance-and-research/outer-hebrides-factfile/population/island-populations/.

Comunn na Gàidhlig (1997) *Secure Status for Gaelic*. Inverness: Comunn na Gàidhlig.

Comunn na Gàidhlig (1999) *Draft Brief for a Gaelic Language Act*. Inverness: Comunn na Gàidhlig.

Cooper, R. (1989) *Language Planning and Social Change*. Cambridge: Cambridge University Press.

Costa, J. (2015) New speakers, new language: on being a legitimate speaker of a minority language in Provence. *International Journal of the Sociology of Language* 231 (1), 127–145.

Coupland, N. (ed.) (2016) *Sociolinguistics: Theoretical debates*. Cambridge: Cambridge University Press.

Crystal, D. (2000) *Language Death*. Cambridge: Cambridge University Press.

Darquennes, J. (2007) Paths to language revitalization. In J. Darquennes (ed.) *Contact Linguistics and Language Minorities / Kontaktlinguistik und Sprachminderheiten / Linguistique de Contact et Minorités Linguistiques* (pp. 61–76). St. Augustin: Asgard.

Davies, A. (2001) Native speaker. In R. Mesthrie (ed.) (2001a) *Concise Encyclopedia of Sociolinguistics* (pp. 512–519). Amsterdam: Elsevier.

Davies, A. (2003) *The Native Speaker: Myth and reality*. Bristol: Multilingual Matters.

Davies, A. (2013) Is the native speaker dead? *Histoire Épistémologie Langage* 35 (2), 17–28.

De Leeuw, E., Schmid, M. S. and Mennen, I. (2010) The effects of contact on native language pronunciation in an L2 migrant setting. *Bilingualism: Language and Cognition* 13 (1), 33–40.

De Swaan, A. (2010) Language systems. In N. Coupland (ed.) *The Handbook of Language and Globalization* (pp. 56–76). Chichester: Wiley-Blackwell.

Denis, D., Gardner, M. H., Brook, M., Tagliamonte, S. A. (2019) Peaks and arrowheads of vernacular reorganization. *Language Variation and Change* 31 (1), 43–67.

Doerr, N. (2009) Investigating 'native-speaker effects': towards a new model of analysing 'native speaker' ideologies. In N. Doerr (ed.) *The Native Speaker Concept: Ethnographic investigations of native speaker effects* (pp. 15–46). Berlin: de Gruyter.

Doerr, N. (ed.) (2009) *The Native Speaker Concept: Ethnographic investigations of native speaker effects.* Berlin: de Gruyter.

Dorian, N. (1978) The fate of morphological complexity in language death: evidence from East Sutherland Gaelic. *Language* 54 (3), 590–609.

Dorian, N. (1980) Language shift in community and individual: the phenomenon of the laggard semi-speaker. *International Journal of the Sociology of Language* 25, 85–94.

Dorian, N. (1981) *Language Death: The life cycle of a Scottish Gaelic dialect.* Philadelphia: University of Pennsylvania Press.

Dorian, N. (1986) Abrupt transmission failure in obsolescing languages: how sudden the 'tip' to the dominant language in communities and families? In V. Nikiforidou, M. VanClay, M. Niepokuj and D. Feder (eds) *Proceedings of the Twelfth Annual Meeting of the Berkeley Linguistics Society* (pp. 72–83). Berkeley, CA: Berkeley Linguistics Society.

Dorian, N. (2014) *Small-language Fates and Prospects: Lessons of persistence and change from endangered languages: collected essays.* Leiden: Brill.

Duchêne, A. and Heller, M. (eds) (2012) *Language in Late Capitalism: Pride and profit.* London: Routledge.

Dunbar, R. (2000) Legal and institutional aspects of Gaelic development. In G. McCoy and M. Scott (eds) *Aithne na nGael – Gaelic Identities* (pp. 67–87). Belfast: The Institute of Irish Studies.

Dunbar, R. (2006) Gaelic in Scotland: the legal and institutional framework. In W. McLeod (ed.) (2006) *Revitalising Gaelic in Scotland: Policy, planning and public discourse* (pp. 1–23). Edinburgh: Dunedin Academic Press.

Dunbar, R. (2010a) Does Scottish Gaelic need a 'Gaidhealtachd' policy? In H. Lewis and N. Ostler (eds) *Reversing Language Shift: How to re-awaken a language tradition. Proceedings of the Fourteenth FEL Conference, Carmarthen, Wales, 13–15 September 2010* (pp. 84–91). Bath: Foundation for Endangered Languages.

Dunbar, R. (2010b) A research strategy to support Gaelic in Scotland. In G. Munro and I. Mac an Tàilleir (eds) *Coimhearsnachd na Gàidhlig an-Diugh: Gaelic communities today* (pp. 139–159). Edinburgh: Dunedin Academic Press.

Dunbar, R. (2011) An tèid aig an lagh cleachdadh mion-chànain a bhrosnachadh? Achd na Gàidhlig agus achdan chànan eile fon phrosbaig. In R. Cox and T. Armstrong (eds) *A' Cleachdadh na Gàidhlig: Slatan-tomhais ann an dìon cànain sa choimhearsnachd* (pp. 51–72). Ostaig: Clò Ostaig.

Dunbar, R. (2016) Language legislation and policy in the UK and Ireland: different aspects of territoriality in a 'Celtic' context. *International Journal on Minority and Group Rights* 23 (4), 454–484.

Dunmore, S. (2015) *Bilingual Life after School? Language use, ideologies and attitudes among Gaelic-medium educated adults.* Unpublished PhD thesis. Edinburgh: University of Edinburgh. Available at: https://era.ed.ac.uk/handle/1842/10636.

Dunmore, S. (2016) Immersion education outcomes and the Gaelic community: identities and language ideologies among Gaelic medium-educated adults in Scotland. *Journal of Multilingual and Multicultural Development* 38 (8), 726–741.

Dunmore, S. (2019) *Language Revitalisation in Gaelic Scotland: Linguistic practice and ideology.* Edinburgh: Edinburgh University Press.

Durkacz, V. (1982) *The Decline of the Celtic Languages: A study of linguistic and cultural conflict in Scotland, Wales and Ireland from the Reformation to the Twentieth Century.* Edinburgh: John Donald.

Duwe, K. (2003–2012) *Gàidhlig (Scottish Gaelic) Local Studies,* vols. 1–27. Hamburg. [Accessed 22 July 2016]. Available at: http://www.linguae-celticae.org/GLS_english.htm.

Eagleton, T. (1996) *The Illusions of Postmodernism.* Oxford: Blackwell.

Eberhard, D., Simons, G. and Fennig, C. (eds) (2019) *Ethnologue: Languages of the world* (22nd edn). Dallas, TX: SIL International. Available at: www.ethnologue.com/statistics/size.

Eckert, P. (2012) Three waves of variation study: the emergence of meaning in the study of sociolinguistic variation. *Annual Review of Anthropology* 41, 87–100.

Education Scotland (2017) *Quality and Improvement in Scottish Education 2012–16: Gaelic Medium Education.* Available at: https://education.gov.scot/Documents/QuISEGaelic%20Medium%20Education.pdf.

Edwards, J. (2012) *Multilingualism: Understanding linguistic diversity.* London: Continuum.

Edwards, J. (2017) Celtic languages and sociolinguistics: a very brief overview of pertinent issues. *Language, Culture and Curriculum* 30 (1), 13–31.

Ennew, J. (1978) *The Impact of Oil-Related Industry on the Outer Hebrides, with particular reference to Stornoway, Isle of Lewis.* Unpublished PhD thesis. Cambridge: Cambridge University.

Ennew, J. (1980) *The Western Isles Today.* Cambridge: Cambridge University Press.

Ferguson, C. (1983) Language planning and language change. In H. Cobarrubias and J. Fishman (eds) *Progress in Language Planning: International perspectives* (pp. 29–40). Berlin: Mouton.

Fishman, J. (1989) *Language and Ethnicity in Minority Sociolinguistic Perspective.* Clevedon: Multilingual Matters.

Fishman, J. (1991) *Reversing Language Shift: Theoretical and empirical foundations of assistance to threatened languages.* Clevedon: Multilingual Matters.

Fishman, J. (ed.) (2001a) *Can Threatened Languages Be Saved? Reversing Language Shift Revisited: A 21st century perspective.* Clevedon: Multilingual Matters.

Fishman, J. (2001b) Reversing language shift. In R. Mesthrie (ed.) (2001a) *Concise Encyclopedia of Sociolinguistics* (pp. 673–679). Amsterdam: Elsevier.

Fitzgerald, G. (1984) Estimates for baronies of minimum level of Irish-speaking amongst successive decennial cohorts: 1771–1781 to 1861–1871. *Proceedings of the Royal Irish Academy: Archaeology, Culture, History, Literature* 84C, 117–155. Dublin: Royal Irish Academy.

Frekko, S. (2009) Social class, linguistic normativity and the authority of the 'native Catalan speaker' in Barcelona. In N. Doerr (ed.) *The Native Speaker Concept: Ethnographic investigations of native speaker effects* (pp. 616–658). Berlin: de Gruyter.

Gathercole, V. M. and Thomas, E. M. (2009) Bilingual first-language development: dominant language takeover, threatened minority language take-up. *Bilingualism: Language and Cognition* 12 (2), 213–237.

General Register Office for Scotland (1994) *1991 Census. Topic monitor for Gaelic language Scotland.* Edinburgh: Government Statistical Service.

General Register Office for Scotland (2005) *Scotland's Census 2001: Gaelic report.* Edinburgh: General Register Office for Scotland. [Accessed 11 May 2016]. Available at: http://www.gro-scotland.gov.uk/files1/stats/gaelic-rep-english-commentary.pdf/.

Genesee, F., Holobow, N. E., Lambert, W. E. and Chartrand, L. (1989) Three elementary school alternatives for learning through a second language. *The Modern Language Journal* 73 (3), 250–263.

Gessner, S., Herbert, T., Parker, A., Thorburn, B. and Wadsworth, A. (eds) (2014) *Report on the Status of B.C. First Nations Languages 2014* (2nd edn). Brentwood Bay, Canada: First Peoples' Cultural Council.

Giddens, A. (1990) *The Consequences of Modernity.* Stanford: Stanford University Press.

Giddens, A. (1991) *Modernity and Self-identity: Self and society in the late modern age.* Stanford: Stanford University Press.

Gilchrist, A. (2009) *The Well-connected Community: A Networking approach to community development.* Bristol: The Policy Press.

Glaser, K. (2007) *Minority Languages and Cultural Diversity in Europe: Gaelic and Sorbian perspectives.* Clevedon: Multilingual Matters.

Goalabré, F. (2011) *Parental Choice of Minority Language Education in Language Shift Situations in Brittany and Scotland.* Unpublished PhD thesis. Milton Keynes: Open University. Available at: http://oro.open.ac.uk/54519/1/580660.pdf.

Goldenberg, S. and Haines, V. (1992) Social networks and institutional completeness: from territory to ties. *Canadian Journal of Sociology* 17 (3), 301–312.

Government of Canada (1988) *Official Languages Act* (based on first Official Languages Act, 1969). Ottawa. Available at: http://www.officiallanguages.gc.ca/en/language_rights/act.

Government of Ireland (2003) *Official Languages Act.* Dublin. Available at: https://www.chg.gov.ie/gaeltacht/the-irish-language/official-languages-act-2003/.

Government of Ireland, Department of Education and Skills / An Roinn Oideachais agus Scileanna (2016) *Policy on Gaeltacht Education 2017–2022.* Dublin. Available at: https://www.education.ie/en/Publications/Policy-Reports/Policy-on-Gaeltacht-Education-2017-2022.pdf.

Graffman, K., Smith-Christmas, C., Birnie, I., MacNeil, C. and MacKenzie, G. (2014) *Media Behaviour among Young Gaelic Speakers — A comparative study in Scotland, Sweden and Finland. Report for BBC ALBA.* Isle of Skye: Inculture and Soillse.

Grenoble, L. and Whaley, L. (eds) (1998) *Endangered Languages: Current issues and future prospects.* Cambridge: Cambridge University Press.

Grin, F. (1990). The economic approach to minority languages. *Journal of Multilingual and Multicultural Development* 11 (1–2), 153–173.

Grin, F. (2003a) Economics and language planning. *Current Issues in Language Planning* 4 (1), 1–66.

Grin, F. (2003b) *Language Policy Evaluation and the European Charter for Regional or Minority Languages.* Basingstoke: Palgrave Macmillan.

Grin F. (2016) Challenges of minority languages. In V. Ginsburgh and S. Weber (eds) *The Palgrave Handbook of Economics and Language* (pp. 616–658). London: Palgrave Macmillan.

Grin, F. (2018) On some fashionable terms in multilingualism research: critical assessment and implications for language policy. In P. Kraus and F. Grin (eds) *The Politics of Multilingualism:*

Europeanisation, globalisation and linguistic governance (pp. 247–274). Amsterdam: John Benjamins.

Grin, F. and Vaillancourt, F. (1999) *The Cost-effectiveness Evaluation of Minority Language Policies: Case studies on Wales, Ireland and the Basque Country.* Monograph series no. 2. Flensburg: European Centre for Minority Issues.

Hagège, C. (2009) *On the Death and Life of Languages.* Yale: Yale University Press.

Hall Aitken and Ionad Nàiseanta na h-Imrich (2007) *Outer Hebrides Migration Study: Final report.* Report for Comhairle nan Eilean Siar, Western Isles Enterprise and Communities Scotland. Glasgow: Hall Aitken.

Harrison, K. D. (2007) *When Languages Die: The extinction of the world's languages and the erosion of human knowledge.* Oxford: Oxford University Press.

Harrison, K. D. (2010) *The Last Speakers: The quest to save the world's most endangered languages.* Washington D.C.: National Geographic.

Haugen, E. (1959) Planning for a standard language in modern Norway. *Anthropological Linguistics* 1 (3), 8–21.

Hechter, M. (1975) *Internal Colonialism: The Celtic fringe in British national development 1536–1966.* London: Routledge and Kegan Paul.

Heller, M. and Dûchene, A. (2012) Pride and profit: changing discourses of language capital and nation-state. In A. Dûchene and M. Heller (eds) *Language in Late Capitalism: Pride and profit* (pp. 1–21). London: Routledge.

Her Majesty's Inspectorate of Education (1994) *The Provision for Gaelic Education in Scotland.* Livingston: HM Inspectorate of Education.

Her Majesty's Inspectorate of Education (2011) *Gaelic Education: Building on the successes, addressing the barriers.* Livingston: HM Inspectorate of Education.

Hewitt, S. (2017) Neo-speakers of endangered languages: theorizing failure to learn the language properly as creative post-vernacularity. *Journal of Celtic Linguistics* 18 (1), 127–154.

Hickey, T. (1997) *An Luath-Thumadh in Éirinn: Na naíonraí* [Early-immersion in Ireland: Preschools]. Dublin: Institiúid Teangeolaíochta Éireann.

Hickey, T. (1999) *Luathoideachas trí Ghaeilge sa Ghaeltacht* [Early-years Education through Irish in the Gaeltacht]. Galway: Údarás na Gaeltachta and Institiúid Teangeolaíochta Éireann.

Hickey, T. (2001) Mixing beginners and native speakers in minority language immersion: who is immersing whom? *The Canadian Modern Language Review* 57 (3), 443–474.

Hindley, R. (1990) *The Death of the Irish Language: A qualified obituary.* London: Routledge.

Hornberger, N. H. (2006) Frameworks and models in language policy and planning. In T. Ricento (ed.) *An Introduction to Language Policy: Theory and method* (pp. 24–41). Oxford: Blackwell.

Hornsby, M. (2015a) The "new" and "traditional" speaker dichotomy: bridging the gap. *International Journal of the Sociology of Language* 231 (1), 107–125.

Hornsby, M. (2015b) *Revitalizing Minority Languages: New speakers of Breton, Yiddish and Lemko.* Basingstoke: Palgrave Macmillan.

Hulstijn, J. H. (2017) *Language Proficiency in Native and Non-native Speakers: Theory and research.* Amsterdam: John Benjamins.

Jackson, K. (1958) The situation of the Scottish Gaelic language, and the work of the Linguistic Survey of Scotland. *Lochlann* 1, 228–234.

Jaffe, A. (2015) Defining the new speaker: theoretical perspectives and learner trajectories. *International Journal of the Sociology of Language* 231 (1), 21–44.

Jenkins, R. (2008) *Social Identity.* London: Routledge.

Jernudd, B. H. and Das Gupta, J. (1971) Towards a theory of language planning. In J. Rubin and B. H. Jernudd (eds) *Can Language be Planned? Sociolinguistic theory and practice for developing nations* (pp. 185–204). Honolulu: The University Press of Hawaii.

Jones, H. (2012) *A Statistical Overview of the Welsh Language.* Cardiff: Welsh Language Board. Available at: http://www.comisiynyddygymraeg. cymru/English/Publications%20 List/A%20statistical%20 overview%20of%20the%20 Welsh%20language.pdf.

Jones, K., Williams, C., Dunmore, S., McLeod, W. and Dunbar, R. (2016) *Assessment of the Impact of the National Gaelic Language Plan 2012–17: Final report for Bòrd na Gàidhlig.* Inverness: Bòrd na Gàidhlig.

Jones, M. C. (2005) Transfer and changing linguistic norms in Jersey Norman French. *Bilingualism: Language and Cognition* 8 (2), 159–175.

Kaplan, R. and Baldauf, R. (eds) (1997) *Language Planning from Practice to Theory.* Clevedon: Multilingual Matters.

Kaufmann, E. (2004) *Rethinking Ethnicity: Majority groups and dominant minorities.* London: Routledge.

Kristiansen, T. and Grondelaers, S. (2013) *Experimental Studies of Changing Language Standards in Contemporary Europe.* Oslo: Novus.

Krauss, M. (1992) The world's languages in crisis. *Language* 68 (1), 4–10.

Kulick, D. (1992) *Language Shift and Cultural Reproduction: Socialization, self and syncretism in a Papua New Guinean village.* Cambridge: Cambridge University Press.

Kyd, J. (ed.) (1952) *Scottish Population Statistics.* Edinburgh: Scottish History Society.

Laitin, D. (1993) The game theory of language regimes. *International Political Science Review* 14 (3), 227–239.

Lamb, W. (2008) *Scottish Gaelic Speech and Writing: Register variation in an endangered language*. Belfast: Cló Ollscoil na Banríona.

Latomaa, S. (1998) English in contact with "the most difficult language in the world": the linguistic situation of Americans living in Finland. *International Journal of the Sociology of Language* 133 (1), 51–71.

Learning and Teaching Scotland (2010) *Literacy and Gàidhlig: Principles and practice*. Dundee: Learning and Teaching Scotland.

Ledwith, M. (2016) *Community Development in Action: Putting Freire into practice*. Bristol: Policy Press.

Lenoach, C. (2012) An Ghaeilge iarthraidisiúnta agus a dioscúrsa [Post-traditional Irish and its discourse]. In C. Lenoach, C. Ó Giollagáin and B. Ó Curnáin (eds) (2012) *An Chonair Chaoch: An mionteangachas sa dátheangachas* (pp. 19–109) [The Blind Alley: The minority language condition in bilingualism]. Indreabhán, Co. Galway: Leabhar Breac.

Lenoach, C., Ó Giollagáin, C. and Ó Curnáin, B. (eds) (2012) *An Chonair Chaoch: An mionteangachas sa dátheangachas* (pp. 19–109) [The Blind Alley: The minority language condition in bilingualism]. Indreabhán, Co. Galway: Leabhar Breac.

Lenoach, C. (2014) *Sealbhú Neamhiomlán na Gaeilge mar Chéad Teanga sa Dátheangachas Dealaitheach* [Incomplete acquisition of Irish as a first language in subtractive bilingualism]. PhD thesis. National University of Ireland, Galway. Dublin: An Chomhairle um Oideachas Gaeltachta agus Gaelscolaíochta [Council for Gaeltacht and Irish-Medium Education]. Available at: http://www.cogg.ie/wp-content/uploads/phd-ciaran-lenoach.pdf.

Lewin, C. (2018) Radical action is needed to save Gaelic. In *The Herald*, 25 April 2018. Available at: http://www.heraldscotland.com/opinion/16181992.Agenda__Radical_action_is_needed_to_save_Gaelic/.

Lewis, H., Royles, E. and McLeod, W. (2019) *Promoting Regional or Minority Languages in a Global Age*. Revitalise: Aberystwyth University. Available at: http://revitalise.aber.ac.uk/en/resources/workshop-material/.

Lewis, M. P. and Simons, G. (2010) Assessing endangerment: expanding Fishman's GIDS. *Revue Roumaine de Linguistique* LV (2), 103–120.

Lewis, M. P. and Simons, G. (2016) *Sustaining Language Use: Perspectives on community-based language development*. Dallas, TX: SIL International. Available at: http://leanpub.com/sustaininglanguageuse.

Lewis, M. P. and Simons, G. (2017)
*Ecological Perspectives on Language
Endangerment: Applying the
sustainable use model for language
development.* Dallas, TX: SIL
International. Available at: http://
leanpub.com/ecologicalperspectives.

Lyon, J. (1996) *Becoming Bilingual:
Language acquisition in a bilingual
community.* Clevedon: Multilingual
Matters.

Mac an Tàilleir, I. (2006) A' Ghàidhlig
air a' Ghàidhealtachd 's anns na
h-Eileanan 1901–2001. Paper
presented at *Rannsachadh na
Gàidhlig* 4, 18–21 July 2006. Sabhal
Mòr Ostaig.

Mac an Tàilleir, I. (2010) A' Ghàidhlig
anns a' chunntas-sluaigh. In G.
Munro and I. Mac an Tàilleir (eds)
*Coimhearsnachd na Gàidhlig an-
Diugh: Gaelic communities today*
(pp. 19–34). Edinburgh: Dunedin
Academic Press.

Mac an Tàilleir, I. (2015) Cunntas-
sluaigh na h-Alba 2011: clàran
Gàidhlig. Research presentation on 7
July 2015, Sabhal Mòr Ostaig.

Mac a' Phearsain, S. A. (2011) *Steall à
Iomadh Lòn.* Inverness: CLÀR.

MacAulay, D. (1982) Borrow, calque,
and switch: the law of the English
frontier. In J. Anderson (ed.)
*Linguistic Form and Linguistic
Variation (Amsterdam Studies in
the Theory and History of Linguistic
Science, IV)* (pp. 203–337).
Amsterdam: John Benjamins.

MacAulay, D. (1986) New Gaelic.
Scottish Language 5, 120–125.

MacAulay, D. (1992) *The Celtic
Languages.* Cambridge: Cambridge
University Press.

MacCaluim, A. (2006) Air iomall
an iomaill? Luchd-ionnschaidh
na Gàidhlig ann an ath-thilleadh
gluasad cànain. In W. McLeod (ed.)
*Revitalising Gaelic in Scotland: Policy,
planning and public discourse* (pp.
185–197). Edinburgh: Dunedin
Academic Press.

MacCaluim, A. and McLeod, W. (2001)
*Revitalising Gaelic? A critical analysis
of the report of the taskforce on
public funding of Gaelic.* Edinburgh:
Department of Celtic and Scottish
Studies, University of Edinburgh.

MacDonald, F. (ed.) (2005)
Colloquium: Susan Parman's Scottish
Crofters: a historical ethnography
of a Celtic village. *Journal of Scottish
Historical Studies* 24 (2), 159–181.

MacDonald, M. (principal author)
(1982) *Cor na Gàidhlig: Language,
community and development.*
Inverness: Highlands and Islands
Development Board.

Macdonald, S. (1997) *Reimagining
Culture: Histories, identities, and the
Gaelic renaissance.* Oxford: Berg.

Macdonald, S. (1999) The Gaelic
renaissance and Scotland's identities.
Scottish Affairs 26 (1), 100–118.

Mac Donnacha, S., Ní Chualáin, F., Ní
Shéaghdha A. and Ní Mhainnín, T.
(2005) *Staid Reatha na Scoileanna
Gaeltachta 2004* [Study of Gaeltacht
Schools]. Dublin: An Chomhairle
um Oideachas Gaeltachta agus
Gaelscolaíochta [Council for

Gaeltacht and Irish-Medium Education].

MacKay, D. (1996) *We Did It Ourselves / Sinn Fhèin a Rinn e: An Account of the Western Isles Community Education Project / Pròiseact Muinntir nan Eilean, 1977–1992.* The Hague: Bernard Van Leer Foundation.

MacKinnon, K. (1972a) Education and social control. *Scottish Education Studies* (1872 Education Act centenary number) 4 (2), 125–138.

MacKinnon, K. (1972b) The school in Gaelic Scotland. *Transactions of the Gaelic Society of Inverness* XLVII, 374–391.

MacKinnon, K. (1977) *Language, Education and Social Processes in a Gaelic Community.* London: Routledge and Kegan Paul.

MacKinnon, K. (1978) *Gaelic in Scotland 1971: Some sociological and demographic considerations of the 1971 Census report for Gaelic.* Hatfield: Hertis Publications.

MacKinnon, K. (1981) *Scottish Opinion on Gaelic: A report on a national attitude survey for An Comunn Gaidhealach undertaken in 1981.* Hatfield: Hatfield Polytechnic.

MacKinnon, K. (1983) *Cape Breton Gaeldom in Cross-Cultural Context: The transmission of ethnic language and culture.* Hatfield: Hatfield Polytechnic.

MacKinnon, K. (1985) *Gaelic in Highland Region: The 1981 Census.* Report to An Comunn Gaidhealach. Inverness: An Comunn Gaidhealach.

MacKinnon, K. (1986) *Gaelic language regeneration amongst young people in Scotland 1971–1981 from census data.* Science Reports Series No. 15. Hatfield: Hatfield Polytechnic Social.

MacKinnon, K. (1987) Language-maintenance and viability in contemporary Gaelic-speaking communities: Skye and the Western Isles today (from survey and census data). *Scottish Gaelic Studies* XVI (1), 149–180.

MacKinnon, K. (1991) *Gaelic: A past and future prospect.* Edinburgh: Saltire Society.

MacKinnon, K. (1994a) *1991 Census: Gaelic Speakers – Monitors and Local Base Statistics: Regions, islands areas and districts.* Report to Highlands and Islands Enterprise and Comunn na Gàidhlig, Inverness, 21 Jan 1994. Inverness: Highlands and Islands Enterprise.

MacKinnon, K. (1994b) *Gaelic in 1994: Report to E.U. Euromosaic Project.* Bangor: University of Wales.

MacKinnon, K. (1994c) Gaelic language-use in the Western Isles. In A. Fenton and D. MacDonald (eds) *Studies in Scots and Gaelic: Proceedings of the third international conference on the languages of Scotland* (pp. 123–137). Edinburgh: Canongate.

MacKinnon, K. (1998) Gaelic in family, work and community domains: Euromosaic Project 1994/95. *Scottish Language* 17, 55–69.

MacKinnon, K. (1999) Can the heartlands hold? Prospects of postmodern speech-communities in the Celtic homelands. Paper to the *11ᵗʰ International Congress of Celtic Studies*, University College Cork, 25ᵗʰ–31ˢᵗ July 1999.

MacKinnon, K. (2000) Neighbours in Persistence: Prospects for Gaelic maintenance in a globalising English world. In G. McCoy and M. Scott (eds) *Aithne na nGael / Gaelic Identities* (pp. 144–155). Belfast: The Institute of Irish Studies.

MacKinnon, K. (2006a) The Western Isles Language Plan: Gaelic to English language shift 1972–2001. In W. McLeod (ed.) *Revitalising Gaelic in Scotland: Policy, planning and public discourse* (pp. 49–71). Edinburgh: Dunedin Academic Press.

MacKinnon, K. (2006b) *Euromosaic National Gaelic Use Survey 1994/5 Western Isles Sample: Family and community – the Euromosaic Survey*. Ferintosh: SGRÙD. Accessed 11 May 2016 at: http://www.sgrud.org.uk/.

MacKinnon, K. (2010a) The Gaelic language group: demography, language-usage, transmission, and shift. In M. Watson and M. Macleod (eds) *The Edinburgh Companion to the Gaelic Language* (pp. 128–145). Edinburgh: Edinburgh University Press.

MacKinnon, K. (2010b) Growing a new generation of Gaelic speakers: an action plan in response to a ministerial initiative. In H. Lewis and N. Ostler (eds) *Reversing Language Shift: How to re-awaken a language tradition. Proceedings of the Fourteenth FEL Conference*, Carmarthen, Wales, 13–15 September 2010 (pp. 63–67). Bath: Foundation for Endangered Languages.

MacKinnon, K. (2011a) A language on the move: geographical mobility of Gaelic speakers in contemporary Scotland. Paper presented at the *Economic and Social History Society of Scotland: Spring Conference*, 6–7ᵗʰ May 2011, Glasgow (see MacKinnon 2014).

MacKinnon, K. (2011b) Growing a new generation of Gaelic speakers: an action plan in response to a ministerial initiative. In J. Kirk and D. Ó Baoill (eds) *Strategies for Minority Languages: Northern Ireland, the Republic of Ireland, and Scotland* (pp. 212–222). Belfast Studies in Language, Culture and Politics. Belfast: Cló Ollscoil na Banríona.

MacKinnon, K. (2011c) Runaway language shift: Gaelic usage in home, community and media in the Isle of Skye and Western Isles, 1986/8, 1994/5, and 2004/5 – any prospects for reversal? In R. Cox and T. Armstrong (eds) *A' Cleachdadh na Gàidhlig: Slatan-tomhais ann an dìon cànain sa choimhearsnachd* (pp. 201–226). Ostaig: Clò Ostaig.

MacKinnon, K. (2012) *Gaelic media, community, and runaway language shift: Report to Bòrd na Gàidhlig*. Ferintosh: SGRÙD. Accessed 27 April 2016 at: http://www.sgrud.org.

uk/anfy/report_to_b%C3%B2rd_ na_g%C3%A0idhlig/gaelic-media-community-runaway-language-shift. htm.

MacKinnon, K. (2014) A language on the move: geographical mobility of Gaelic speakers in contemporary Scotland. *Journal of Celtic Linguistics* 15 (1), 53–68.

MacKinnon. K. and MacDonald, M. (1980) *Ethnic Communities: The transmission of language and culture in Harris and Barra*. Report to Social Science Research Council. Hatfield Polytechnic Social Sciences Reports Series No. SSR 12. Hatfield: Hertis Publications.

MacLeod, K. M. (2017) *Gaelic in Families with Young Children: Education and, language choice*. Unpublished PhD thesis. Edinburgh: University of Edinburgh. Available at: https://blogs.glowscotland.org. uk/gc/public/glasgowlangs/uploads/ sites/9909/2019/09/ThesisKMacL. pdf.

MacLeod, M. (1963) Gaelic in Highland education. *Transactions of the Gaelic Society of Inverness* XLIII, 305–334.

MacLeod, M., Macleod, M. C., Coyle, D. and Thirkell, A. M. (2014) *Young Speakers' Use of Gaelic in the Primary Classroom: A multi-perspectival pilot study*. Isle of Skye: Soillse. Available at: http://www.soillse.ac.uk/wp-content/uploads/YoungSpeakers_ Final.pdf.

MacLeod, M. and Smith-Christmas, C. (eds) (2018) *Gaelic in Contemporary Scotland: The revitalisation of an endangered language*. Edinburgh: Edinburgh University Press.

MacLeod, M. K. (1981) *The Interaction of Scottish Educational Developments and Socio-Economic Factors on Gaelic Education in Gaelic-speaking Areas, with Particular Reference to the Period 1872– 1918*. Unpublished PhD thesis. Edinburgh: University of Edinburgh. Available at: https://era.ed.ac.uk/ handle/1842/18393?show=full.

MacNeil, C. A. (1995) *Gaelic Television: The picture from children and teenagers*. Sleat, Isle of Skye: Lèirsinn Research Centre, Sabhal Mòr Ostaig.

MacNeil, M. and Stradling, B. (2001) Strategies for sustaining the Gaelic communities in Scotland: an exploration of community-based and educational services on issues of language and culture. In S. Skålnes (ed.) *Sustaining and Supporting the Lesser Used Languages* (pp. 12–52). Oslo: Norwegian Institute for Urban and Regional Research. Accessed 11 May 2016 at: http://www.nibr.no/ static/pdf/notater/sigrids-rapport. pdf.

MacPherson, J. A. (2000) *Ag Ath-Bheothachadh Gàidhlig: Neamhnuid nàiseanta / Revitalising Gaelic: A national asset*. Taskforce on Public Funding of Gaelic. Edinburgh: Scottish Executive.

Matras, Y. (2009) *Language Contact*. Cambridge: Cambridge University Press.

McEwan-Fujita, E. (2006) Gaelic doomed as speakers die out? The public discourse of Gaelic language death in Scotland. In W. McLeod (ed.) *Revitalising Gaelic in Scotland: Policy, planning and public discourse* (pp. 279–293). Edinburgh: Dunedin Academic Press.

McEwan-Fujita, E. (2010) Sociolinguistic ethnography of Gaelic communities. In M. Watson and M. MacLeod (eds) *The Edinburgh Companion to the Gaelic Language* (pp. 172–217). Edinburgh: Edinburgh University Press.

McLeod W. (1998) Autochthonous language communities and the Race Relations Act. *Web Journal of Current Legal Issues* 1. Available at: http://miris.eurac.edu/mugs2/do/blob.

McLeod, W. (2001) Gaelic in the new Scotland: politics, rhetoric, and public discourse. *Journal on Ethnopolitics and Minority Issues in Europe* 2, 1–33.

McLeod, W. (2002a) Gaelic in Scotland: a renaissance without planning. In Hizkuntza Biziberritzeko *Saoiak / Experiencias de Inversión del Cambio Lingüístico / Récupération de la Perte Linguistique / Reversing Language Shift* (pp. 279–295). Vitoria-Gasteiz: Eusko Jaurlaritzaren Argitalpen Zerbitzu Nagusia/Servicio Central de Publicaciones del Gobierno Vasco.

McLeod, W. (2002b) Language planning as regional development? The growth of the Gaelic economy. *Scottish Affairs* 38 (1), 51–72.

McLeod, W. (2005a) Gaelic in Scotland: the impact of the Highland Clearances. In N. Crawhall and N. Ostler (eds) *Creating Outsiders: Endangered languages, migration and marginalisation. Foundation for Endangered Languages: Proceedings of the Ninth Conference*, Stellenbosch, South Africa, 18–20 November 2005 (pp. 176–183). Bath: The Foundation for Endangered Languages.

McLeod, W. (2005b) *Gaelic in Edinburgh: Usage and attitudes.* Research report. Edinburgh: Department of Celtic and Scottish Studies, University of Edinburgh. [Accessed 11 May 2016]. Available at: https://www.poileasaidh.celtscot.ed.ac.uk/aithisggaidhligdeURB.pdf.

McLeod, W. (ed) (2006) *Revitalising Gaelic in Scotland: Policy, planning and public discourse* (pp. 139–154). Edinburgh: Dunedin Academic Press.

McLeod, W. (2008) Linguistic Pan-Gaelicism: A dog that wouldn't hunt. *Journal of Celtic Linguistics* 12 (1), 87–120.

McLeod, W. (2009) Gaelic in Scotland: 'existential' and 'internal' sociolinguistic issues in a changing policy environment. In B. Ó Catháin (ed.) *Sochtheangeolaíocht na Gaeilge: Léachtaí Cholm Cille XXXIX* (pp. 16–61). Maigh Nuad: An Sagart.

McLeod, W. (2011) Planaichean reachdail Gàidhlig: cothroman is cnapan-starra. In R. Cox and T. Armstrong (eds) *A' Cleachdadh na Gàidhlig: Slatan-tomhais ann an dìon cànain sa choimhearsnachd* (pp. 227–248). Ostaig: Clò Ostaig.

McLeod, W. (2013) Gaelic, Scots and other languages. Article published online in *Bella Caledonia,* 3 October 2013. Available at: http:// bellacaledonia.org.uk/2013/10/03/ gaelic-scots-and-other-languages/.

McLeod, W. (2014) Gaelic in contemporary Scotland: contradictions, challenges and strategies. *Europa Ethnica* 71 (1–2), 3–12.

McLeod, W. (2015) The introduction of English in Gaelic Scotland, Ireland and Wales: the dynamics of imposition, acquiescence and assertion. *Revista Canaria de Estudios Ingleses* 71, 91–102.

McLeod, W. (2019) The nature of minority languages: insights from Scotland. *Multilingua* 38 (3), 1–14.

McLeod, W., O'Rourke, B. and Dunmore, S. (2014) 'New Speakers' of Gaelic in Edinburgh and Glasgow. Isle of Skye: Soillse. Available at: http://www.soillse.ac.uk/wp-content/ uploads/New-Speakers%E2%80%99- of-Gaelic-in-Edinburgh-and- Glasgow.pdf.

McLeod, W. and O'Rourke, B. (2015) 'New speakers' of Gaelic: perceptions of linguistic authenticity and appropriateness. *Applied Linguistics Review* 6 (2), 151–172.

McPake, J. and Stephen, C. (2016) New technologies, old dilemmas: theoretical and practical challenges in preschool immersion playrooms. *Language and Education* 30 (2), 106–125.

Mesthrie, R. (ed.) (2001a) *Concise Encyclopedia of Sociolinguistics.* Amsterdam: Elsevier.

Mesthrie, R. (2001b) Language maintenance, shift and death. In R. Mesthrie (2001a) *Concise Encyclopedia of Sociolinguistics* (pp. 493–498). Amsterdam: Elsevier.

Mewett, P. (1982) Exiles, nicknames, social identities and the production of local consciousness in a Lewis crofting community. In A. P. Cohen (ed.) *Belonging: Identity and social organisation in British rural cultures* (pp. 222–246). Manchester: Manchester University Press.

Miller, B. G. (2003) *Invisible Indigenes: The politics of nonrecognition.* Lincoln: University of Nebraska Press.

Ministerial Advisory Group on Gaelic (2002) *A Fresh Start for Gaelic*: *Report by the Ministerial Advisory Group on Gaelic / Cothrom ùr don Ghàidhlig: Aithisg le Buidheann Comhairleachaidh an Riaghaltais air Gàidhlig.* Edinburgh: Scottish Executive.

Misneachd (2018) *Plana Radaigeach airson na Gàidhlig / A Radical Plan for Gaelic.* No place of publication. Available at: https://issuu.com/ misneachd/docs/misneachd-plana_ radaigeach_airson_n.

Montrul, S. (2008) *Incomplete Acquisition in Bilingualism: Re-examining the age factor.* Amsterdam: John Benjamins.

Morrison, M. (2006) A' chiad ghinealach – the first generation: a survey of Gaelic medium-education in the Western Isles. In W. McLeod (ed.) *Revitalising Gaelic in Scotland: Policy, planning and public discourse* (pp. 139–154). Edinburgh: Dunedin Academic Press.

Moseley, C. (ed.) (2010) *Atlas of the World's Languages in Danger.* (3rd edn). Paris: UNESCO. Available at: http://www.unesco.org/culture/en/endangeredlanguages/atlas.

Mufwene, S. (2010) Globalization, global English, world English(es). In N. Coupland (ed.) *The Handbook of Language and Globalization* (pp. 31–55). Chichester: Wiley-Blackwell.

Müller, M. (2003) Sprachkontakt und Sprachwandel auf der Insel Skye (Schottland). *Studies in Eurolinguistics* 3. Berlin: Logos Verlag Berlin (Sprachkontakt und Sprachzerfall auf der Insel Skye (Schottland), PhD thesis).

Müller, M. (2006) Language use, language attitudes and Gaelic writing ability among secondary pupils in the Isle of Skye. In W. McLeod (ed.) *Revitalising Gaelic in Scotland: Policy, planning and public discourse* (pp. 119–138). Edinburgh: Dunedin Academic Press.

Munro, G., Taylor, I. and Armstrong, T. (2011) *The State of Gaelic in Shawbost: Language abilities and attitudes in Shawbost.* Sleat: Sabhal Mòr Ostaig. [Accessed 12 September 2017]. Available at: https://www.academia.edu/5549349/Cor_na_G%C3%A0idhlig_ann_an_Siabost_The_State_of_Gaelic_in_Shawbost.

Murray, J. (1873) *The Dialect of the Southern Counties of Scotland: Its pronunciation, grammar and historical relations, with an appendix on the present limits of the Gaelic and Lowland Scotch and the dialectal divisions of the Lowland tongue, and a linguistical map of Scotland.* London: Asher and Co., for the Philological Society.

Murray, J. and Morrison, C. (1985) *Bilingual Primary Education in the Western Isles, Scotland, 1975–81.* Stornoway: Acair.

Myhill, J. (2003) The native speaker, identity, and the authenticity hierarchy. *Language Sciences* 25 (1), 77–97.

Nance, C. (2013) *Phonetic Variation, Sound Change and Identity in Scottish Gaelic.* PhD thesis. Glasgow: University of Glasgow. Available at: http://theses.gla.ac.uk/4603/1/2013nancephd.pdf.

National Assembly for Wales (2012) *Official Languages Act.* Cardiff. Available at: http://www.legislation.gov.uk/anaw/2012/1/introduction/enacted.

Nettle, D. and Romaine, S. (2000) *Vanishing Voices: The extinction of the world's languages.* Oxford: Oxford University Press.

NicAoidh, M. (2010) Plana Cànain nan Eilean Siar – ag amas air neartachadh. In G. Munro and I. Mac an Tàilleir (eds) *Coimhearsnachd na Gàidhlig an-Diugh: Gaelic communities today* (pp. 49–59). Edinburgh: Dunedin Academic Press.

Nic Fhlannchadha, S. and Hickey, T. (2016) Minority language ownership and authority: perspectives of native speakers and new speakers. *International Journal of Bilingual Education and Bilingualism* 21 (1), 1–16.

NicLeòid, S. (2015) *A' Ghàidhlig agus Beachdan nan Sgoilearan: Cothroman leasachaidh ann am foghlam tro mheadhan na Gàidhlig.* Isle of Skye: Clò Ostaig.

NicLeòid, S. L. and Dunmore, S. (2018) Sòisealachadh cànain agus leantainneachd dà-chànanach am measg cloinne agus inbhich a rinn FMG. *Scottish Gaelic Studies* 31, 74–94.

Norris, M. J. (2004) From generation to generation: survival and maintenance of Canada's aboriginal languages, within families, communities and cities. *TESL Canada Journal*, 21 (2), 1–16.

Norris, F. H., Stevens, S. P., Pfefferbaum, B., Wyche, K. F. and Pfefferbaum, R. L. (2008) Community resilience as a metaphor, theory, set of capacities, and strategy for disaster readiness. *American Journal of Community Psychology* 41 (1–2), 127–150.

Ó Curnáin, B. (2007) *The Irish of Iorras Aithneach, County Galway*, vols I–IV. Dublin: Dublin Institute for Advanced Studies.

Ó Curnáin, B. (2009) Mionteangú na Gaeilge [Minoritizing Irish]. In B. Ó Catháin (ed.) *Sochtheangeolaíocht na Gaeilge: Léachtaí Cholm Cille 39* (pp. 90–153) [The Sociolinguistics of Irish, Colmcille Lectures XXXIX]. Maynooth: An Sagart.

Ó Curnáin, B. (2012) An Ghaeilge iarthraidisiúnta agus an phragmataic chódmheascta thiar agus theas [Post-traditional Irish and the pragmatics of code-mixing in Western and Southern Irish]. In C. Lenoach, C. Ó Giollagáin and B. Ó Curnáin (eds) *An Chonair Chaoch: An mionteangachas sa dátheangachas* (pp. 284–364) [The Blind Alley: The minority language condition in bilingualism]. Indreabhán, Co. Galway: Leabhar Breac.

Ó Curnáin, B. (2016) Cróineolaíocht na Gaeilge iarthraidisiúnta i gConamara, 1950–2004 [The Chronology of post-traditional Irish in Connemara, 1950–2004]. *Éigse* 39, 1–43.

Ó Curnáin, B. (forthcoming) Demolinguistic analysis of language shift in Ireland and elsewhere.

Ó Duibhir, P. (2018) *Immersion Education: Lessons from a minority language context.* Bristol: Multilingual Matters.

Ó Giollagáin, C. (2002) Scagadh ar rannú cainteoirí comhaimseartha Gaeltachta: gnéithe d'antraipeolaíocht teangeolaíochta phobal Ráth Chairn. *The Irish Journal of Anthropology* 6, 25–56.

Ó Giollagáin, C. (2004a) A contrastive view of Irish language dynamics. *Collegium Antropologicum* 28 (1) (supplement), 73–81.

Ó Giollagáin, C. (2004b) Ár scéal inár dteanga féin: Dinimicí teanga Ghaeltacht ár linne. In B. Ó Conaire (ed.) *Aistí ag iompar scéil: In ómós do Shéamas P. Ó Mórdha* (pp. 153–170). Dublin: An Clóchomhar.

Ó Giollagáin, C. (2005) Gnéithe d'antraipeolaíocht theangeolaíoch Phobal Ros Muc, Co. na Gaillimhe. In J. Kirk and D. Ó Baoill (eds) *Legislation, Literature and Sociolinguistics: Northern Ireland, the Republic of Ireland, and Scotland.* Belfast Studies in Language, Culture and Politics 13 (pp. 138–162). Belfast: Cló Ollscoil na Banríona.

Ó Giollagáin, C. (2006) Gnéithe de stair theorainn na Gaeltachta. In A. Doyle and S. Ní Laoire (eds) *Aistí ar an Nua-Ghaeilge: In ómós do Bhreandán Ó Buachalla* (pp. 95–116). Dublin: Cois Life Teoranta.

Ó Giollagáin, C. (2011) Speaker diversity in the majority-minority linguistic context. *Annales, Series Historia et Sociologia* 21 (1), 101–112.

Ó Giollagáin, C. (2014a) Unfirm ground: a re-assessment of language policy in Ireland since independence. *Language Problems and Language Planning* 38 (1), 19–41.

Ó Giollagáin, C. (2014b) From revivalist to undertaker: new developments in official policies and attitudes to Ireland's 'First Language'. *Language Problems and Language Planning* 38 (2), 101–127.

Ó Giollagáin, C., Mac Donnacha, S., Ní Chualáin, F., Ní Sheaghdha, A. and O'Brien, M. (2007a) *Comprehensive Linguistic Study of the Use of Irish in the Gaeltacht: Principal findings and recommendations.* Dublin: The Stationery Office.

Ó Giollagáin C., Mac Donnacha, S., Ní Shéaghdha, A., Ní Chualáin, F. and O'Brien, M. (2007b) *Staidéar Cuimsitheach Teangeolaíoch ar Úsáid na Gaeilge sa Ghaeltacht: Tuarascáil chríochnaitheach* [CLS: Comprehensive Linguistic Study of the Use of Irish in the Gaeltacht: Final report]. Dublin: The Stationery Office.

Ó Giollagáin, C., Lenoach, C. and Ó Curnáin, B. (2012) An Réamhrá [Introduction]. In C. Lenoach, C. Ó Giollagáin and B. Ó Curnáin (eds) *An Chonair Chaoch: An mionteangachas sa dátheangachas* (pp. 3–17) [The Blind Alley: The minority language condition in bilingualism]. Indreabhán, Co. Galway: Leabhar Breac.

Ó Giollagáin, C. and Charlton, M. (2015) *Nuashonrú ar an Staidéar Cuimsitheach Teangeolaíoch ar Úsáid na Gaeilge sa Ghaeltacht* [UCLS: Update of the Comprehensive Linguistic Study of the Use of Irish in the Gaeltacht: 2006–2011]. Na Forbacha: Údaras na Gaeltacha.

Ó Giollagáin, C. and Ó Curnáin, B. (2016) *Beartas Úr na nGael: Dálaí na Gaeilge san iar-nua-aoiseachas* [A New Deal for Irish: The condition of Irish in postmodernity]. Indreabhán, Co. Galway: Leabhar Breac.

Ó Giollagáin, C. and Ó Curnáin, B. (forthcoming) Minority language promotion and protection. In *The Routledge Handbook of Language Policy and Planning*.

Ó Giollagáin, C., Péterváry, T., Ó Curnáin, B., Charlton, M. and Uí Ghiollagáin, Á. (forthcoming) *Demolinguistics in the context of minority language groups: the case of Irish in Ireland.*

O'Hanlon, F. (2012) *Lost in Transition? Celtic Language Revitalization in Scotland and Wales: The primary to secondary school stage.* Unpublished PhD thesis. Edinburgh: University of Edinburgh. Available at: https://era.ed.ac.uk/handle/1842/7548.

O'Hanlon, F., Paterson, L. and McLeod, W. (2012) *Language Models in Gaelic-medium Pre-school, Primary and Secondary Education.* Isle of Skye: Soillse. Available at: http://www.soillse.ac.uk/wp-content/uploads/Modailean-C%C3%A0nain-ann-am-Foghlam-Ro-sgoile-Bun-sgoile-agus-%C3%80rd-sgoile-Meadhain-Gh%C3%A0idhlig_6.pdf.

O'Hanlon, F. and Paterson, L. (2015a) *Scotland's Census 2011: Gaelic report (part 1).* Edinburgh: National Records of Scotland. [Accessed 9 November 2015]. Available at: https://www.scotlandscensus.gov.uk/documents/analytical_reports/Report_part_1.pdf.

O'Hanlon, F. and Paterson, L. (2015b) *Scotland's Census 2011: Gaelic report (part 2).* Edinburgh: National Records of Scotland. [Accessed 9 November 2015]. Available at: http://www.scotlandscensus.gov.uk/documents/analytical_reports/Report_part_2.pdf.

O'Hanlon, F. and Paterson, L. (2015c) Gaelic medium education since 1872. In M. Freeman, R. Anderson and L. Paterson (eds) *The Edinburgh History of Education in Scotland* (pp. 304–325). Edinburgh: Edinburgh University Press.

Ó hIfearnáin, T. (2018) The ideological construction of boundaries between speakers, and their varieties. In C. Smith-Christmas, N. P. Ó Murchadha, M. Hornsby and M. Moriarty (eds) *New Speakers of Minority Languages: Linguistic ideologies and practices* (pp. 151–164). London: Palgrave Macmillan.

Ó Laoire, M. (2008) The language situation in Ireland: an update. In R. Kaplan and R. Baldauf (eds) *Language Planning and Policy: Europe, vol. 3 The Baltic states, Ireland and Italy* (pp. 256–261). Clevedon: Multilingual Matters.

Oliver, J. (2005) Scottish Gaelic identities: contexts and contingencies. *Scottish Affairs* 51 (1), 1–24.

Olthuis, M-L., Kivelä, S. and Skutnabb-Kangas, T. (2013) *Revitalising Indigenous Languages: How to recreate a lost generation*. Clevedon: Multilingual Matters.

Ó Murchadha, N. (2012) Caighdeáin, caighdeánú agus torthaí ar chaighdeánú na Gaeilge. In F. Farr and M. Moriarty (eds) *Language, Learning and Teaching: Irish research perspectives* (pp. 167–194). Berlin: Peter Lang.

Ó Murchadha, N. P. (2013) Authenticity, authority and prestige: Teenagers' perceptions of variation in spoken Irish. In T. Kristiansen and S. Grondelaers (eds) *Experimental Studies of Changing Language Standards in Contemporary Europe* (pp. 71–96). Oslo: Novus.

Ó Murchadha, N. P. (2018) *An Ghaeilge sa Nua-Aoiseacht Dhéanach*: *An meon i leith éagsúlacht teanga sa Ghaeilge*. An Spidéal: Cló Iar-Chonnacht.

Ó Murchadha, N. P. and Migge, B. (2017) Aspects of the sociolinguistics of the Celtic languages. *Language Culture and Curriculum* 30 (1), 1–12.

Ó Murchadha, N. P., Hornsby, M., Smith-Christmas, C. and Moriarty, M. (2018) New speakers, familiar concepts? In C. Smith-Christmas, N. P. Ó Murchadha, M. Hornsby and M. Moriarty (eds) *New Speakers of Minority Languages: Linguistic ideologies and practices* (pp. 1–22). London: Palgrave Macmillan.

Ó Neachtain, É. (2016) *Regional Development in Minority Language Territories: State policies, structures and interventions in the Irish Gaeltacht*. Unpublished PhD thesis. Galway: National University of Ireland, Galway. Available at: https://aran.library.nuigalway.ie/handle/10379/6012.

Ó Riagáin, P. (1997) *Language Policy and Social Reproduction: Ireland 1893–1993*. Oxford: Clarendon Press.

O'Rourke, B. (2011) Whose language is It? struggles for language ownership in an Irish language classroom. *Journal of Language, Identity and Education* 10 (5), 327–345.

O'Rourke, B. and Ramallo, F. (2011) The native-non-native dichotomy in minority language contexts: comparisons between Irish and Galician. *Language Problems and Language Planning* 35 (2), 139–159.

O'Rourke, B. and Pujolar, J. (2013) From native speakers to "new speakers" – problematizing nativeness in language revitalization contexts. *Histoire Épistémologie Language* 35 (2), 47–67.

O'Rourke, B. and Ramallo, F. (2013) Competing ideologies of linguistic authority amongst "new speakers" in contemporary Galicia. *Language in Society* 42 (3), 287–305.

O'Rourke, B., Pujolar, J. and Ramallo, F. (2015) New speakers of minority languages: the challenging opportunity. Foreword, *International Journal of the Sociology of Language* 231 (1), 1–20.

O'Rourke, B. and Walsh, J. (2015) New speakers of Irish: shifting boundaries across time and space. *International Journal of the Sociology of Language* 231 (1), 63–83.

Ó Sé, L. (2000) *Crannóga: An epidemiological approach to the Gaeltacht*. Dublin: Johnswood Press.

O'Toole, C. and Hickey, T. M. (2017) Bilingual language acquisition in a minority context: using the Irish–English communicative development inventory to track acquisition of an endangered language. *International Journal of Bilingual Education and Bilingualism* 20 (2), 146–162.

Outer Hebrides Community Planning Partnership / Compàirteachas Plana Coimhearsnachd Innse Gall (2018). Available at: http://www.ohcpp.org.uk/.

Parman, S. (2005 [1990]) *Scottish Crofters: A historical ethnography of a Celtic village*. London: Thomson/Wadsworth.

Paterson, L., O'Hanlon, F., Ormston, R. and Reid, S. (2014) Public attitudes to Gaelic and the debate about Scottish autonomy. *Regional and Federal Studies* 24 (4), 429–450.

Pavlenko, A. (2018) Superdiversity and why it isn't: reflections on terminological innovation and academic branding. In B. Schmenk, S. Breidbach and L. Küster (eds) *Sloganization in Language Education Discourse: Conceptual thinking in the age of academic marketization* (pp. 142–168). Clevedon: Multilingual Matters. Available at: https://www.researchgate.net/publication/292157452_Superdiversity_and_why_it_isn't_Reflections_on_terminological_innovations_and_academic_branding.

Péterváry, T., Ó Curnáin, B., Ó Giollagáin, C. and Sheahan, J. (2014) *Iniúchadh ar an gCumas Dátheangach: An sealbhú teanga i measc ghlúin óg na Gaeltachta – Analysis of Bilingual Competence: Language acquisition among young people in the Gaeltacht*. Dublin: An Chomhairle um Oideachas Gaeltachta agus Gaelscolaíochta [Council for Gaeltacht and Irish-Medium Education].

Pietikäinen, S., Kelly-Holmes, H., Jaffe, A. and Coupland, N. (2016) *Sociolinguistics from the Periphery: Small languages in new circumstances*. Cambridge: Cambridge University Press.

Polinsky, M. (2011) Heritage languages (pp. 1–26). [On-line research guide accessed 15 August 2016]. Available at: http://scholar.harvard.edu/files/mpolinsky/files/obo.2-1.pdf?m=1360041229.

Pollock, I. (2007) *The Acquisition of Literacy in Gaelic-medium Primary Classrooms in Scotland*. Unpublished PhD thesis. Edinburgh: University of Edinburgh. Available at: https://pdfs.semanticscholar.org/0331/

Pollock, I. (2010) Learning from learners: teachers in immersion classrooms. In G. Munro and I. Mac an Tàilleir (eds) *Coimhearsnachd na Gàidhlig an-Diugh: Gaelic communities today* (pp. 117–125). Edinburgh: Dunedin Academic Press.

Prattis, J. I. (1990) Industrialisation and minority-language loyalty: the example of Lewis. In E. Haugen,

D. McLure and D. Thomson (eds) *Minority Languages Today* (pp. 21–31). Edinburgh: Edinburgh University Press.

Putnam, R. D. (2000) *Bowling Alone: The collapse and revival of American community.* New York: Simon and Schuster.

Ravenstein, E. G. (1879) On the Celtic languages in the British Isles: a statistical survey. *Journal of the Royal Statistical Society* 42 (3), 579–643.

Ricento, T. (2000) Historical and theoretical perspectives in language policy and planning. *Journal of Sociolinguistics* 4 (2), 196–213.

Ricento, T. (ed.) (2006) *An Introduction to Language Policy: Theory and method.* Oxford: Blackwell.

Roberts, A. (1991) Parental attitudes to Gaelic-medium education in the Western Isles of Scotland. *Journal of Multilingual and Multicultural Development* 12 (4), 253–269.

Roche, G. (forthcoming) Does ideological clarification help language maintenance? Exploring the revitalisation paradox through the case of Manegacha, a minority language of China's Tibetan regions. *Multingua: Journal of Cross-Cultural and Interlanguage Communication.*

Romaine, S. (2007) Preserving endangered languages. *Language and Linguistic Compass* 1 (1–2), 115–132.

Rothach, G., Mac an Tàilleir, I. and Dòmhnallach, B. (2016) *Comas is Cleachdadh Cànain sa Choimhearsnachd, agus an Cunntas-sluaigh 2011.* Aithisg airson Bòrd na Gàidhlig. Inverness: Bòrd an Gàidhlig.

Rothman, J. (1974) Three models of community organization practice. In F. Cox, J. Ehrlich, J. Rothman and J. Tropman (eds) *Strategies of Community Organization* (pp. 25–45). Itasca, IL: Peacock.

Rothman, J. (2007) Multi modes of intervention at the macro level. *Journal of Community Practice* 15 (4), 11–40.

Rubin, J. (1986) City planning and language planning. In E. Annamalai, B. H. Jernudd and J. Rubin (eds) *Language Planning. Proceedings of an institute* (pp. 105–122). Honolulu: Central Institute of Indian Languages, East–West Center.

Sayers, D. (2012) Standardising Cornish: the politics of a new minority language. *Language Problems and Language Planning* 36 (2), 99–119.

Schmidt, A. (1985) *Young People's Dyirbal: An example of language death from Australia.* Cambridge: Cambridge University Press.

Scotland's Census 2001. Available at: http://www.scotlandscensus.gov.uk/documents/additional_tables/AT_001_2001_to_AT_012_2001.xlsx.

Scotland's Census 2011. Available at: http://www.scotlandscensus.gov.uk/ods-web/data-warehouse.html#additionaltab.

Scottish Government (2003) *Partnership for Government.* Accessed at: http://www.gov.scot/Publications/2003/05/17150/21952.

Scottish Government (2005) *Gaelic Language (Scotland) Act*. Edinburgh: Scottish Parliament. Available at: https://www.legislation.gov.uk/asp/2005/7/contents/enacted.

Scottish Government (2017) *Programme for Government 2017–18*. Edinburgh: Scottish Government. Available at: https://beta.gov.scot/publications/local-governance-review-letter-22-june-2018/.

Scottish Qualifications Authority (2011a) *Curriculum for Excellence Gaelic Working Group – Group's Report, February 2011*. Edinburgh: Scottish Government. Available at: https://www2.gov.scot/resource/doc/91982/0114490.pdf.

Scottish Qualifications Authority (2011b) *Summary Statistics for Schools in Scotland*. Edinburgh: Scottish Government. Available at: https://www.webarchive.org.uk/wayback/archive/20170401113547/http://www.gov.scot/Publications/2011/12/06114834/0.

Scottish Qualifications Authority (2017) *Gaelic Language Plan 2015–20*. Glasgow: Scottish Qualifications Authority.

Selkirk, 5th Earl (1806) *Observations on the Present State of the Highlands of Scotland, with a View of the Causes and Probable Consequences of Emigration*. Edinburgh: A. Constable and Co.

Sheng, L. Ying, L. and Gollan, T. H. (2014) Assessing language dominance in Mandarin-English bilinguals: convergence and divergence between subjective and objective measures. *Bilingualism: Language and Cognition* 17 (2), 364–383.

Simons, G. F. and Fennig, C. D. (eds) (2018) *Ethnologue: Languages of the World*. (21st edn). Dallas, TX: SIL International. Available at: http://www.ethnologue.com.

Simpson, A. (2007) *Language and National Identity in Asia*. Oxford: Oxford University Press.

Simpson, A. (2008) *Language and National Identity in Africa*. Oxford: Oxford University Press.

Smith-Christmas, C. (2012) *I've lost it here dè a bh' agam: Language shift, maintenance, and code-switching in a bilingual family*. Unpublished PhD thesis. Glasgow: University of Glasgow. [Accessed 1 June 2016]. Available at: http://theses.gla.ac.uk/3798/.

Smith-Christmas, C. (2016) *Family Language Policy: Maintaining an endangered language in the home*. Basingstoke: Palgrave Macmillan.

Smith-Christmas, C. and Smakman, D. (2009) Gaelic on the Isle of Skye: older speakers' identity in a language-shift situation. *International Journal of the Sociology of Language* 200, 27–47.

Smith-Christmas, C., Ó Murchadha, N. P., Hornsby, M. and Moriarty, M. (eds) (2018) *New Speakers of Minority Languages: Linguistic ideologies and practices*. London: Palgrave Macmillan.

Spolsky, B. (2004) *Language Policy*. Cambridge: Cambridge University Press.

Stephen, C., McPake, J., McLeod, W., Pollock, I. and Carroll, T. (2010) *Review of Gaelic-medium Early Education and Childcare / Breithneachadh air Foghlam Tràth agus Cùram Cloinne Meadhan-Ghàidhlig*. Dùn Èideann: Rannsachadh Sòisealta, Riaghaltas na h-Alba. [Accessed 11 May 2016]. Available at: http://www.gov.scot/Publications/2010/06/24102055/0.

Stephen, C., McPake, J., McLeod, W. and Pollock, I. (2011) *Young Children Learning in Gaelic: Investigating children's learning experiences in Gaelic-medium pre-school. Research Briefing, 6E*. Stirling: University of Stirling.

Stephen, C., McPake, J. and McLeod, W. (2012) Playing and learning in another language: ensuring good quality early years education in a language revitalisation programme. *European Early Childhood Education Research Journal* 20 (1), 21–33.

Stephen, C., McPake, J. and McLeod, W. (2013) *Ensuring High Quality Learning Opportunities in Gaelic-medium Preschool: Challenges and opportunities*. Stirling: University of Stirling. [Accessed 11 May 2016]. Available at: https://www.britishirishcouncil.org/sites/default/files/file%20attachments/Ensuring%20high%20quality%20learning%20opportunities%20in%20%20Gaelic-medium%20preschool.pdf.

Stephen. C., McPake, J., Pollock, I., and McLeod, W. (2016) Early years immersion: learning from children's playroom experiences. *Journal of Immersion and Content-Based Language Education* 4 (10), 59–85.

Stiùbhart, M. (2011) Cainnt nan deugairean. In R. Cox and T. Armstrong (eds) *A' Cleachdadh na Gàidhlig: Slatan-tomhais ann an dìon cànain sa choimhearsnachd* (pp. 275–282). Ostaig: Clò Ostaig.

Stockdale, J. D. (1976) Community organization practice: an elaboration of Rothman's typology. *Sociology and Social Welfare* 3 (5), 541–551.

Strubell, M. (1996) How to preserve and strengthen minority languages. Paper presented at the *International Ivar Aasen Conference* 15 November 1996, Generalitat de Catalunya, Barcelona.

Strubell, M. (1998) Can sociolinguistic change be planned? *Proceedings of 1st European Conference, Private Foreign Language Education in Europe: Its contribution to the multilingual and multicultural aspect of the European Union*. Thessaloniki, November 1997 (pp. 23–31). Thessaloniki: Palso.

Strubell, M. (1999) From language planning to language policies and language politics. In P. J. Weber (ed.) *Contact and Conflict: Language planning and minorities* (pp. 237–248). Plurilingua XXI. Bonn: Dümmler.

Strubell, M. (2001a) Catalan a decade later. In J. Fishman (ed.) (2001a) *Can Threatened Languages Be Saved?*

Reversing Language Shift Revisited: A 21st century perspective (pp. 260–283). Clevedon: Multilingual Matters.

Strubell, M. (2001b) Some aspects of a sociolinguistic perspective to language planning. In K. De Bot, S. Kroon, P. Nelde and H. van de Velde (eds) *Institutional Status and Use of National Languages in Europe* (pp. 91–106). Plurilingua XXIII. Sankt Augustin: Asgard Verlag.

Tanner, M. (2004) *The Last of the Celts.* New Haven: Yale University Press.

Thomas, E. M. and Roberts, D. B. (2011) Exploring bilinguals' social use of language inside and out of the minority language classroom. *Language and Education* 25 (2), 89–108.

Thomson, D. S. (ed.) (1994) *The Companion to Gaelic Scotland.* Glasgow: Gairm.

Tollefson, J. (1991) *Planning Language, Planning Inequality: Language policy in the community.* London: Longman.

Tonkin, H. (2015) Language planning and planned languages: how can planned languages inform language planning? *Interdisciplinary Description of Complex Systems* 13 (2), 193–199.

Toribio, J. A. (2004) Convergence as an optimization strategy in bilingual speech: evidence from code-switching. *Bilingualism: Language and Cognition* 7 (2), 165–173.

UK Government (1993) *Welsh Language Act.* London. Available at: https://www.legislation.gov.uk/ukpga/1993/38/contents.

UNESCO (2003) *Language Vitality and Endangerment: Ad hoc expert group on endangered languages.* Document submitted to the International Expert Meeting on UNESCO Programme Safeguarding of Endangered Languages, Paris, 10–12 March 2003.

Vallee, F. (1954) *Social Structure and Organisation in a Hebridean Community: A study of social change.* Unpublished PhD thesis. London: London School of Economics.

Varro, G. (1998) Does bilingualism survive the second generation? Three generations of French–American families in France. *International Journal of the Sociology of Language* 133 (1), 105–128.

Walker, J. (1808) *An Economical History of the Hebrides and Highlands of Scotland.* Edinburgh: no publisher indicated.

Walsh, J. and McLeod, W. (2008) An overcoat wrapped around an invisible man? Language legislation and language revitalisation in Ireland and Scotland. *Language Policy* 7, 21–46.

West, C. and Graham, A. (2011) *Attitudes Towards the Gaelic Language.* Edinburgh: Scottish Government Social Research. Available at: https://www.gaidhlig.scot/wp-content/uploads/2016/12/

West-Graham-2011-Beachd-a-phobail-CR11-01-Public-attitudes.pdf.

Will, V. (2012) *Why Kenny Can't Can: The language socialization experiences of Gaelic-medium educated children in Scotland.* Unpublished PhD thesis. Ann Arbor: University of Michigan. Available at: http://hdl.handle.net/2027.42/96018.

Williams, G. (1992) *Sociolinguistics: A sociological critique.* London: Routledge.

Williams, G. (2010) *The Knowledge Economy, Language and Culture.* Clevedon: Multilingual Matters.

Withers, C. (1981) The geographical extent of Gaelic in Scotland, 1698–1806. *Scottish Geographical Magazine* 97 (3), 130–139.

Withers, C. (1982) Gaelic-speaking in a Highland parish: Port of Menteith 1724–1725. *Scottish Geographical Magazine* 98 (1), 16–23.

Withers, C. (1984a) *Gaelic in Scotland 1698–1981: The geographical history of a language.* Edinburgh: John Donald.

Withers, C. (1984b) 'The shifting frontier': the Gaelic-English boundary in the Black Isle, 1698–1881. *Northern Scotland* 6 (1), 133–155.

Withers, C. (1986) 'Moral statistics': a note on language and literacy in the Scottish Highlands in 1822. *Local Population Studies* 36, 36–46.

Withers, C. (1988a) *Gaelic Scotland: The transformation of a culture region.* London: Routledge.

Withers, C. (1988b) *Urban Highlanders: Highland-Lowland migration and urban Gaelic culture, 1700–1900.* East Linton: Tuckwell Press.

Woolard, K. (2008) Language and identity choice in Catalonia: the interplay of contrasting ideologies of linguistic authority. In K. Süselbeck, U. Mühlschlegel and P. Masson (eds) *Lengua, Nación e Identidad. La Regulación del Plurilingüismo en España y América Latina* (pp. 303–323). Frankfurt am Main: Vervuert / Madrid: Iberoamericana.

Zell, E. and Krizan, Z. (2014) Do people have insight into their abilities? A metasynthesis. *Perspectives on Psychological Science* 9 (2), 111–125.

Index

S

Sayers, Dave, 307

Scalpay (Harris), 2, 14, 27, 54, 239–41, 246, 248–52, 254, 257, 268, 273, 275, 277–79, 287, 301–04, 312, 314, 337–38, 340–41, 346–47

Schmidt, Annette, 306

Scotland,
  Central Belt of, 28, 133
  Highlands and Islands of, 23, 132, 135–36, 235, 244, 363, 393, 406–08, 411–13, 426
  Lowlands of, 22, 244, 363

Scots, 20

Scottish Office, 375

Secure Status for Gaelic (report), 375

Sgoil Bhàgh a' Chaisteil / Castlebay Community School (Barra), 123, 223

Sgoil Ghàidhlig Ghlaschu (Glasgow), 128–29

Sgoil Lìonacleit (Benbecula), 123, 131, 223

Sgoil MhicNeacail / Nicolson Institute (Lewis), 123, 131, 223

Sgoil Sir E. Scott (Harris), 123, 223

Shader (Lewis), 27

Shawbost / Siabost (Lewis), 239, 242, 286, 340, 379

Simons, Gary F., 7, 8–9, 365

Skye and Lochalsh, 244

Sleat (Isle of Skye), 90

Smith-Christmas, Cassie, 11–12, 90, 296n56, 390

South Point (Lewis), 67, 70, 76

South Uist, 18, 26–27, 36, 39, 42–44, 51, 55–56, 58, 65–66, 72, 76–78, 88, 112, 121, 229, 239, 242, 273, 275–77, 280, 301n59, 337, 359

SQA (Scottish Qualifications Authority), 124n33, 126, 128

Staffin (Skye), 1–2, 13–14, 39, 41–42, 44, 46n16, 49n17, 67, 70, 72, 76–77, 87, 96–98, 123, 273, 278–79, 285, 349, 360n70, 362

Stephen, Christine, 92–95, 102, 118–19

Stiùbhart, Mòrag, 136

Stockdale, Jerry D., 423–24

Stoneybridge (South Uist), 18

Stornoway (and district) (Lewis), 1, 14, 31, 33, 37, 42–44, 51–52, 55–56, 58, 65, 67, 76–78, 88, 95, 129, 135, 215, 229–30, 237, 243, 273, 276, 278, 280–282, 285, 363

Stradling, Bob, 132–33, 235

Strogatz, Stephen H., 54

Strubell, Miquel, 370–71, 377–78

T

Taskforce on Public Funding of Gaelic (MacPherson Task Force), 375, 410

Thomas, Enlli Môn, 119

Thomson, Derick S., 22

Tiree, 1–2, 13–14, 36, 39, 41–42, 49n17, 55–56, 65, 72, 76–77, 87–88, 96, 97n26, 98, 123, 129, 273, 276, 279, 285, 349, 362, 410

TML (Threatened Minority Language), 424

Tolsta (Lewis), 46, 351n69

Tonkin, Humphrey, 423

U

UHI (University of the Highlands and Islands), 137

Uig District (Lewis), 66, 68, 70, 76, 88, 273, 275, 278, 281

UNESCO (United Nations Educational, Scientific and Cultural Organization), 7–8, 366–67

Urras na Gàidhlig [Gaelic Community Trust], 419, 425–31, 435–41